Remedies

BY **JOHN A. BAUMAN**
U.C.L.A.

KENNETH H. YORK
Pepperdine University

JOHN H. BAUMAN
South Texas College of Law

Eleventh Edition

THE **barbri** GROUP
A THOMSON COMPANY

EDITORIAL OFFICES: 111 W. Jackson Blvd., 7th Floor, Chicago, IL 60604
REGIONAL OFFICES: Chicago, Dallas, Los Angeles, New York, Washington, D.C.

PROJECT EDITOR
Steven J. Levin, B.A., J.D.
Attorney At Law

QUALITY CONTROL EDITOR
Sanetta M. Hister

Summary of Contents

Text Correlation Chart

Gilbert Law Summary REMEDIES	Laycock *Modern American Remedies* 2002 (3rd ed.)	Leavell, Love, Nelson, Kovacic-Fleischer *Equitable Remedies, Restitution and Damages* 2000 (6th ed.)	Re, Re *Remedies* 2000 (5th ed.)	Shoben, Tabb, Janutis *Remedies* 2002 (3rd ed.)	Thompson, Sebert, Gross, Robertson *Remedies: Damages, Equity and Restitution* 2002 (3rd ed.)	Rendleman *Remedies* 1999 (6th ed.)
I. INTRODUCTION						
A. Introduction	Page 1-2, 8-10	Page 1-2	Page 2-4	Page	Page	Page 1-2
B. Types of Remedies	2-8	1-14	4-8	2-6, 13-43	9-14	2-13
II. DAMAGES						
A. Tort vs. Contract Damages	11-19, 53-74, 115-129	259-285	728-749	334-555, 680-703	53-78	64-86, 542-547
B. Limitations on Damages	74-146	265-269, 285-305, 320-322	786-805	596-659	75-121	19-64, 86-101, 532, 613-616
C. Other Damages Issues	83-92, 103-110, 216-228, 719-770, 905-950	308-320, 322-352	818-823, 876-891, 957-1013	398-416, 556-595, 646-659, 704-793	120-182, 190-198, 607-621	97-140, 567-572, 600-606
III. EQUITABLE REMEDIES						
A. Nature of Equitable Remedies	7-8, 233, 367-370, 1111-1113	2-14, 1176-1217	5-7, 22-68	5-6, 908-941	243-248, 305-315	8-13, 156-158, 211-244
B. Requirements for Equitable Remedies	233-476, 959-1032	97-115, 715-788	5-19, 174-248, 253, 326-330, 347, 352, 501-520, 1048-1060	46-69, 126-166, 265-278, 322-331, 1004-1043	258-272, 279-292, 299-305, 386-403, 438-447	158-202, 244-258, 299-304
C. Enforcement and Effect of Equitable Decrees	775-855	162-258	71-140, 152-169	209-254	315-347, 400-404, 413-426	258-299
D. Ancillary Equitable Remedies	440-509, 511-554	10-11, 15-75, 470-495, 787-788	254-280, 311-351	167-208	350-385, 436-438	184, 202-211
IV. RESTITUTION						
A. Nature of Restitution	565-577	364-366	7, 650	796-828	463-508	3, 313-326
B. Legal and Equitable Remedies	577-712	366-417, 1115-1132	650-726	798-805, 843-868	461-463, 531-536, 544-565	326-354
V. INJURIES TO TANGIBLE PROPERTY INTERESTS						
A. Misappropriation of Money	592-596, 686-700		724-725	869-880	544-565	358-361
B. Injuries to Personal Property	712-716	496-554	4, 495-500, 677-680, 720-726, 830-838	435-467, 828-859	355-357, 735-742, 745-770	364-410
C. Injuries to Real Property	19-37, 716-718	555-714	445-495, 692-699, 824-830, 838-851	49-52, 416-434, 468-491, 838-839	767, 773-780, 788-824	410-479
VI. INJURIES TO BUSINESS AND COMMERCIAL INTERESTS						
A. Remedies for Business Torts—In General			728, 787-800			

Gilbert Law Summary REMEDIES	Laycock *Modern American Remedies* 2002 (3rd ed.)	Leavell, Love, Nelson, Kovacic-Fleischer *Equitable Remedies, Restitution and Damages* 2000 (6th ed.)	Re, Re *Remedies* 2000 (5th ed.)	Shoben, Tabb, Janutis *Remedies* 2002 (3rd ed.)	Thompson, Sebert, Gross, Robertson *Remedies: Damages, Equity and Restitution* 2002 (3rd ed.)	Rendleman *Remedies* 1999 (6th ed.)
B. Remedies for Inducing Breach of Contract	68-74		352, 356, 728			
C. Remedies for Interference with Plaintiff's Mere "Expectancy"	44-56		704-713		56-58	
D. Remedies for Diversion of Benefits		465-469, 1057-1061		853-854	909-920	
E. Remedies for Patent Infringement	517-526, 583-585, 605-606, 834-835, 965, 967-968					
F. Remedies for Copyright Infringement	463-464, 573-574, 584, 603-621					
G. Remedies for Destruction or Misappropriation of Trade Secrets	271-276, 284-285, 585, 602	393-397, 553-554				
H. Remedies for Misappropriation of Creative Works and Ideas	572-577					
I. Remedies for Trademark and Trade Name Infringement	573, 579-585, 596, 608, 846-847, 965-966, 995-1000, 1010, 1109					
J. Remedies for Unfair Competition	572					
K. Performers' Remedies for Misappropriation of Right of Publicity		836-845				
L. Remedies for Product Disparagement—Trade Defamation		831-836			709-710	
VII. INJURIES TO PERSONAL DIGNITY AND RELATED INTERESTS						
A. Defamation	196-197, 201, 421-433	788-832	1108-1130	289-293, 838-839	692-713	
B. Privacy	62-63, 186-188	832-845	1131-1149	64-69	716-733	199
C. Familial Relations		845-854	1149-1188	525-526		
D. Associational Relations		854-861	1204-1235		256	
E. Academic Status		860-861				
F. Religious Status						
G. Civil and Political Rights	198-200, 260-264, 269-270	741-751, 751-788, 1113-1115, 1187-1191	905-911	16-17, 266-269, 1011-1013	268, 390, 441-443, 684-692	177-178
VIII. PERSONAL INJURY AND DEATH						
A. Personal Injuries	146-162, 162-181, 598-600	878-899	851-913	491-526	104-121, 581-594, 605-646	21-27, 31-64, 72-77, 86-101

Gilbert Law Summary REMEDIES	Laycock *Modern American Remedies* 2002 (3rd ed.)	Leavell, Love, Nelson, Kovacic-Fleischer *Equitable Remedies, Restitution and Damages* 2000 (6th ed.)	Re, Re *Remedies* 2000 (5th ed.)	Shoben, Tabb, Janutis *Remedies* 2002 (3rd ed.)	Thompson, Sebert, Gross, Robertson *Remedies: Damages, Equity and Restitution* 2002 (3rd ed.)	Rendleman *Remedies* 1999 (6th ed.)
B. Survival of Personal Injury Actions		906-914		526		
C. Wrongful Death Actions	153-162, 175-181, 201-213	906-914	931-946	526-541	647-654	32-45
D. Injuries to Others	102-103	899-905	946-956	525, 535-538	648-663	32-45
IX. FRAUD						
A. Election of Remedies	637-639	964-973		155-166	841-848	648-659
B. Affirmance of the Contract —Damages Remedy	53-55	924-949	536-544		859-895	490-500
C. Rescission of the Contract	621-623, 623-629, 659-661	949-973	536-562	433-434, 810-814	825-858, 866-870, 895-908	659-664, 668-672
D. Statutory Remedies— Consumer Protection	741-755, 915-920					
X. DURESS, UNDUE INFLUENCE, AND UNCONSCIONABLE CONDUCT						
A. Duress	627, 662-664	1070		893-894		677-681
B. Undue Influence		1070		893-894		672-677
C. Unconscionability	76-77, 80, 86, 90-92, 959-960, 969-978	986-988	583-587	140-141, 150-155		681-687
XI. MISTAKE						
A. General Considerations				810	921-937	
B. Mistake in Bargaining Transactions	52-53, 626-628	445-448, 688-704, 956, 975-977	563-583	811-828	937-970	702-717
C. Defenses		445-448		880-881, 893	937	
D. Mistake in Integration— Reformation as Remedy	556-560	979-983	563, 572-581		970-985	714-717
E. Mistake in Gratuitous Transactions	566-567, 708-709			894-902		
XII. REMEDIES FOR BREACH OF CONTRACT						
A. Special Conditions Applicable to Specific Performance		929-936	352-444	86-87, 105		480-490
B. Land Sale Contracts	263-268, 364-365, 397-400, 658-661	1044-1095	352-396, 762-773	92-95, 112, 119, 121, 416-434	987-1004	500-503, 510-518, 547-567, 572-578
C. Contracts for the Sale of Chattels	37-41, 47-53, 68, 74-82, 88-98, 383-392	989-1044	352-362, 752-762	114-125, 350-398	1014-1039	504-510, 518-542
D. Construction Contracts	92-98, 756-766	1115-1120	397-399, 778-786	335-340	273-278, 1005-1014	513-518

| Gilbert Law Summary

REMEDIES	Laycock *Modern American Remedies* 2002 (3rd ed.)	Leavell, Love, Nelson, Kovacic-Fleischer *Equitable Remedies, Restitution and Damages* 2000 (6th ed.)	Re, Re *Remedies* 2000 (5th ed.)	Shoben, Tabb, Janutis *Remedies* 2002 (3rd ed.)	Thompson, Sebert, Gross, Robertson *Remedies: Damages, Equity and Restitution* 2002 (3rd ed.)	Rendleman *Remedies* 1999 (6th ed.)
E. Service Contracts	435-440, 585-592	1095-1166	403-405, 773-778	589-590, 597-603, 816	1040-1061	585-647
XIII. REMEDIES IN CONNECTION WITH UNENFORCEABLE CONTRACTS						
A. Contracts Unenforceable Because Not in Writing	629-637		600-627		297, 981-985	688-691
B. Contracts Unenforceable Because of Impossibility or Frustration of Purpose				99-101		
C. Contracts Unenforceable Because of Lack of Capacity to Contract						691-695
D. Agreements Unenforceable Because of Illegality						717-730

Capsule Summary

I. INTRODUCTION

A. INTRODUCTION   §1

The law of remedies encompasses the **form and type** of relief granted by courts. Remedies may be categorized according to function.

B. TYPES OF REMEDIES

1. Function of Remedies

a. Damages

(1) Compensatory damages   §3
This remedy provides an award of money to compensate for loss or injury. The function of **tort** awards is to **make the plaintiff whole**; **contract** damages compensate for loss and also operate as a **protection of plaintiff's expectation interest**.

(2) Nominal damages   §4
Nominal damages is an award of money granted when the plaintiff's right has been violated, but **no loss** is sustained, or the extent of **injury cannot be measured.**

(3) Punitive damages   §5
Punitive damages provide an award of money in addition to compensatory damages to **punish** the defendant for **willful, wanton, or malicious** conduct and to deter such conduct.

b. Restitution   §6
Restitution restores to the plaintiff any benefit that the defendant may have gained from his misconduct (*i.e.,* **unjust enrichment**).

(1) Note   §7
Restitution is usually **substitutionary,** providing monetary recovery measured by unjust gain (*e.g.,* quasi-contract, constructive trust, equitable lien, or subrogation), although it may also be **specific,** providing **recovery of a precise thing** (*e.g.,* replevin, ejectment).

c. Specific relief   §9
Specific relief provides the **performance** promised, rather than its money equivalent.

4. **Consequential Damages Limitation—Rule of Hadley v. Baxendale** §23
   The rule of **Hadley v. Baxendale** limits special damages in breach of contract cases to those *arising naturally* from the breach or within the *reasonable contemplation* of the parties at the *time the contract was made.* The rule serves to reduce the risk of commercial enterprise, and is adopted in principle by the Uniform Commercial Code ("U.C.C."). Generally, a person *cannot* recover consequential damages for mental anguish, although for *serious emotional distress* based on contracts with common carriers, innkeepers, or funeral homes, such damages may be allowed.

5. **Proximate Cause Limitation in Torts Cases** §27
   Under the proximate cause doctrine, a defendant is liable for injuries *reasonably foreseeable as a natural consequence of the defendant's wrongful act*. Proximate cause relates only to the issue of *liability; i.e.,* it does not act as a limit on damages. The *thin skull doctrine* imposes liability even if the harm is increased by a particular plaintiff's condition.

   a. **Qualifications** §30
      Absent privity of contract or injury, a plaintiff may *not* recover for *economic loss* in a *negligence* case, even if the economic loss was proximately caused by the defendant's negligence. Similarly, recovery for economic loss in *product liability* cases is generally denied whether the case is based on negligence or strict liability.

B. **LIMITATIONS ON DAMAGES**

1. **Certainty as to Existence of Damages** §32
   There must be proof sufficient to establish a *probability of loss,* although it is usually not necessary to prove the amount of damages with mathematical certainty. The certainty requirement is most often in controversy in loss of profits cases. A claim for *future damages* requires proof that there is a better than 50-50 chance that such damages will occur (*"all or nothing"* approach).

2. **"Special" Damages Must Be Pleaded** §40
   Special (as opposed to general) damages must be pleaded to be recoverable.

   a. **General damages** §41
      General damages are damages that so naturally result from the wrong that the defendant is on notice that they will be claimed. General damages need *not* be specially pleaded.

   b. **Special damages** §42
      Special damages are losses that cannot be presumed or estimated simply because a wrong has occurred; they are unique or "special" to the plaintiff and must be specially pleaded so as to give the defendant *adequate notice*.

3. **Causation Requirement** §45
   A defendant is liable only for injuries caused by her wrongful act or omission. Causation questions are usually resolved by the *"but for"* test (*i.e.,* but for the defendant's act, the loss would not have occurred).

no matter how willful the conduct, unless an independent tort is also present.

(3) Other damage must be proved §62

Punitive damages are parasitic; a cause of action for damages must be proven before punitive damages are awarded.

(4) No fixed standard of measure §63

Subject to some judicial review, the jury may award an amount it considers "suitable." However, most courts require a **reasonable relationship** measure—*i.e.,* damages sufficient to punish the defendant but not bankrupt him.

(5) Insurance §65

Until recently, it was against public policy to insure against punitive damages. However, with the expansion of the bases for liability (*e.g.,* vicarious liability), some courts permit such coverage.

(6) Multiple plaintiff cases §66

Numerous cases have upheld punitive damage awards in multiple tort situations. Opinions differ as to whether repetitive awards (often resulting in a defendant's bankruptcy) violate due process, an issue on which the Supreme Court has yet to rule.

b. Prejudgment interest §68

A court may sometimes award interest from the time the **cause of action arose** to the date of judgment. The amount is generally governed by statute.

c. Counsel fees §72

In the absence of **statutory authorization** or an **enforceable contract,** attorneys' fees are generally not recoverable.

(1) Exceptions §73

Fees may be recovered where a **"common fund"** is created by one litigant for the benefit of others, and in certain insurance claims.

3. "Collateral Sources" Rule—No Mitigation §75

There is no mitigation of the damages the defendant must pay because of compensation paid to the plaintiff from collateral sources—*i.e.,* sources not purporting to act on the defendant's behalf, such as the plaintiff's insurance benefits or welfare payments. (However, some courts allow mitigation if the collateral source is proceeds from an insurance policy that the defendant paid for.) This rule may result in double compensation, although most insurance policies contain subrogation clauses that allow the insurer to recover from the defendant in the plaintiff's stead.

a. Statutory changes §81

Some no-fault statutes effectively abrogate the collateral sources rule by barring a plaintiff from recovering damages from the defendant for injuries compensated by the plaintiff's insurance. Other statutes modify the rule in certain cases.

b. **No injunctions against criminal prosecutions** §141

Generally, prosecution under a **valid** statute is **not enjoinable.** However, injunctions may be granted for **prosecution under an unconstitutional or inapplicable statute** if irreparable harm is threatened. *Note:* Declaratory judgments **may be used to test the validity or applicability of a criminal statute**.

(1) **Limitations on federal injunctions** §145

Federal courts are prohibited from enjoining state court proceedings with certain exceptions listed in the Anti-Injunction Act (*e.g.*, cases arising under the Civil Rights Act). Further, federal intervention in **state criminal prosecutions** is permitted only where there is **both** a present and **immediate threat to a federal right** and **no opportunity** to protect it in state court.

c. **Police acts** §152

No injunction will lie prohibiting law enforcement officers from performing assigned duties, but **harassment** not in the line of duty may be enjoined. Also, prisoners have some right to injunctive relief to protect constitutional rights, and damages may be awarded to victims of illegal or oppressive official action (*Bivens* case).

4. **Special Equitable Defenses—Unclean Hands and Laches**

a. **"Unclean hands"** §157

The "unclean hands" defense is usually confined to the plaintiff's inequitable (unethical, immoral) conduct **directly related** to the subject of the litigation. The court refuses to aid **either** party. Unrelated inequitable conduct does not bar suit unless such conduct constitutes a "public fraud." *Note:* Unclean hands does not bar recovery **at law**, although there is some contrary dicta. Application of the "unclean hands" doctrine is discretionary.

b. **Laches** §164

Laches is an **unreasonable delay** in bringing an equity action, during which time the defendant's situation has **changed** to the extent that an additional and unnecessary detriment would result if suit were allowed. Even if there is a statute of limitations, laches may bar suit **before** expiration of the statutory period. Laches does **not** bar a legal claim.

C. **ENFORCEMENT AND EFFECT OF EQUITABLE DECREES**

1. **Enforcement of Equitable Decrees**

a. **Contempt proceedings** §168

Due process requires that equity decrees be sufficiently **specific** so as to adequately inform the enjoined party of the requirements of the order.

(1) **Civil contempt** §170

Violation of a decree **ordering the defendant to take action** (affirmative decree) or **prohibiting her from committing certain acts** (negative decree) may result in civil contempt—confining the defendant until she complies with the terms of the decree. *Note:* A defendant may not be imprisoned for nonpayment of debts.

(2) Compare—criminal contempt
Criminal contempt is **punitive,** *i.e.,* punishing past acts of disobedience of the court's order (imprisonment for fixed term), while **civil** contempt is **remedial** (imprisonment until performance occurs). Punishment for criminal contempt must be in compliance with general requirements for criminal proceedings (*e.g.,* right to counsel applies, etc.).

(3) Void and erroneous orders
Violation of erroneous but **jurisdictionally valid** orders may result in criminal contempt. Note that the **collateral bar rule** prohibits a collateral attack on the erroneous grant of an injunction. However, when an order is **void** due to lack of subject matter jurisdiction, it cannot generally be enforced by civil or criminal contempt, although violators of void orders **involving First Amendment rights** may be subject to criminal contempt unless the order is transparently invalid.

(4) Parties bound
Only parties (and their privies) with knowledge of the court decree are bound. Nonparties acting independently are free to ignore the injunction.

b. Writs of assistance
If the defendant has been ordered to deliver possession of property to the plaintiff, a writ of assistance may be issued to place the plaintiff in possession.

c. Writs of sequestration
Writs of sequestration may be issued to deprive the defendant of income and rents from property by holding the property until he complies with the decree.

2. Legal Effect of Equitable Decrees

a. Specific performance of contract for sale of land within state
If the court has jurisdiction over the property (res) and the defendant, it may order specific performance of the contract. Lacking personal jurisdiction, statutes allow the plaintiff to proceed **quasi in rem**.

b. Decrees affecting land in another state
Even though the court has no jurisdiction over the res, the court may enforce its decree in personam **if** it has **personal** jurisdiction over the defendant.

(1) Other decrees
The same principles apply if the court orders the defendant to **perform acts outside of the state.**

not a consolidation of actions but a separate suit in equity—may lie. A bill of peace is commonly applied where *repeated actions* between the same parties are too costly for the plaintiff to pursue, or where a party is subject to repeated vexatious legal actions. Also, if a person has been sued by *multiple parties,* all claimants may be joined in a single bill of peace, providing the various claims involve *common issues of law and fact* (and in a minority of jurisdictions, common right or title).

(1) Virtual demise of multiple party bill of peace §223
Because of the jury trial requirement for damages issues, and the availability of *class actions*, multiple party bills of peace may be eliminated as a practical matter.

b. Interpleader §224
When a stakeholder is subjected to multiple conflicting claims regarding the "stake," she may tender the stake into court and interplead the claimants. The rights of the various claimants are then litigated. Modern interpleader is governed by statute and requires that the claims be *mutually exclusive* and that the court have *in personam jurisdiction* over all claimants.

c. Bills quia timet §227
A bill quia timet is issued to prevent *future litigation.* Such bills include: injunctions against future torts (where injury is certain to result), bills to cancel documents, bills to remove clouds on title, quiet title suits, and declaratory judgment suits (statutory extension of equitable bill quia timet).

IV. RESTITUTION

A. NATURE OF RESTITUTION

1. Substantive Basis §233
The substantive basis of restitution is *unjust enrichment.* The defendant must have a *benefit* that is *unjust* for him to retain.

a. No recovery for benefits voluntarily conferred upon another §237
Restitutionary remedies are generally not available to "officious intermeddlers" who voluntarily confer benefits, except where emergency situations involving risk to another's life or property occur.

2. Purpose of Restitution §239
The purpose of restitution is to return to the status quo ante by compelling the defendant to *return specific property* or by awarding the injured party a *sum of money* equivalent to the value of the defendant's benefit.

B. LEGAL AND EQUITABLE REMEDIES

1. Restitution at Law—Quasi-Contract §240
The legal remedy of restitution in money arose from the common law action of assumpsit. The assumpsit action was a proper remedy for implied-in-fact contracts (agreements created by parties' *conduct*), as well as

implied-in-law contracts (quasi-contracts) that are not contracts at all (as there are no promises or agreements), but rather instances of unjust enrichment where the law imposes an obligation to pay.

2. Restitution in Equity

a. Constructive trust   §249
A constructive trust imposes a duty on the defendant to *transfer property to the plaintiff*. It is imposed by law without regard to intentions of the parties, unlike an express trust.

(1) Requirements for imposition   §252
For a constructive trust:

(a) The *defendant has legal title* to the property;

(b) *Retention would result in unjust enrichment;* and

(c) The *remedy at law is inadequate.*

(2) Effect of sale to bona fide purchaser   §253
Transfer of property to a bona fide purchaser ("BFP") cuts off the plaintiff's right to a constructive trust over the property, but does *not* cut off her rights to proceeds arising from transfer.

b. Equitable lien   §254
An equitable lien is a charge on property to *secure a debt* or other obligation, and gives the holder of the lien the right to sell the property to satisfy the debt.

(1) Requirement   §255
An equitable lien may be imposed where there is an *unjust benefit* traceable to property owned by the defendant.

(2) Distinguish—constructive trust   §256
A plaintiff often has the option of a constructive trust or equitable lien remedy. However, where money is misappropriated to improve land *already owned* by the defendant, an equitable lien is the *only* available remedy.

(3) Lien enforcement   §257
A lien is enforced by *foreclosure and sale,* but is *cut off* by prior sale to a BFP.

c. Subrogation   §259
Subrogation applies when one person nonofficiously *discharges an obligation* for which *another* is primarily liable and which the latter ought to pay. As a result, the party who paid is subrogated to the position of the creditor and is entitled to any security interest or priority the creditor may have had.

d. Accounting for gains   §264
Equitable restitution is based on the *disgorgement of ill-gotten gains* and thus may result in an accounting for profits that the plaintiff, in good conscience, should have received.

V. INJURIES TO TANGIBLE PROPERTY INTERESTS

A. MISAPPROPRIATION OF MONEY

1. Legal Remedies

a. Conversion   §266
Where money has been wrongfully misappropriated, the injured party may seek damages in a conversion action. However, conversion requires *identification* of the *specific money* taken.

b. Quasi-contract   §268
The alternative remedy—quasi-contract—"waives the tort" of conversion. The plaintiff need show only that the wrongdoer is *unjustly enriched* by the misappropriation in order to recover the misappropriated money. Note that the *tort* count of conversion will support recovery of *punitive damages.*

2. Equitable Remedies

a. Constructive trust   §272
A constructive trust for the benefit of the injured party may be imposed—which allows the plaintiff to *trace* misappropriated money to its product—under the theory that ownership of property is not lost by a change in form.

(1) Note   §278
Constructive trust is usually not available against any other assets of the defendant because title was not acquired by use of the *specifically identified* stolen money.

b. Equitable lien   §279
If misappropriated funds are traced to property the defendant already owns, an equitable lien may be imposed to avoid unjust enrichment. *Subrogation* also is an available remedy.

c. Commingled funds   §282
Certain presumptions are available to assist in tracing misappropriated monies that have been commingled with funds belonging to the wrongdoer, *e.g.*, "first in, first out" rule. However, modern decisions reject the presumptions, and instead give an equitable lien to the claimant for the *full amount* of her claim on all funds in the account and *any property purchased* with funds traced from the account.

(1) Note   §291
Where the funds of several claimants are commingled, each has a *pro rata* interest in the fund.

B. INJURIES TO PERSONAL PROPERTY

1. Tortious Destruction of Chattel   §292
The measure of damages for tortious destruction of chattels is the *value* of the property at the time of the destruction, *less salvage* value, *plus interest.* The plaintiff may *not* recover for loss of use unless the chattel cannot be replaced. The value of the chattel may be *market value, reproduction*

cost less deterioration, or (in cases where market value is clearly inadequate compensation) *value to the owner.*

2. **Tortious Damage to Chattels** §305

The measure of damages for tortious damage to chattels is either the *difference in the value* of the chattel before and after the harm, or the *reasonable cost of repair plus loss of use.* Loss of use is measured by the rental value of a substitute chattel.

3. **Tortious Taking and Retention of Chattels** §312

The *specific restitutionary* remedies include self-help, replevin, and the mandatory injunction. Alternatively, the plaintiff may seek a *monetary* award as *substitutionary* relief (*e.g.,* conversion, quasi-contract), and the equitable remedy of constructive trust.

a. **Specific restitution**

(1) **Self-help** §313

Reasonable force may be used to recapture the chattel.

(2) **Replevin** §315

Replevin is a legal remedy granting a judgment to return the chattel *plus* detention damages. The right to replevy may be *lost* by the defendant's acquisition of title by *adverse possession*, which requires visible, notorious, hostile, adverse possession.

(a) **Constitutionality** §320

Generally, prejudgment seizure of the defendant's property without a hearing is invalid. After a series of Supreme Court decisions, state statutes were amended to provide for prejudgment replevin in limited circumstances, *e.g.,* where there is a threat to remove disputed property from the state.

(b) **Measure of detention damages** §323

Detention damages may be measured by either loss of *market value* (if the goods are held for sale) or the value of *lost use* (if the goods were not held for sale); lost use is measured by *either* the rental value or by lost profits. Rental value is *offset* by upkeep costs and depreciation. Note that detention damages are not limited to the chattel's value.

(c) **Judgment for conversion** §331

The defendant may *alternatively* obtain the chattel's value by a conversion action, recovering its value at the time of seizure plus interest. Conversion is the remedy if the defendant is *not in possession* of the chattel at the time a replevin action is filed.

(d) **Judgment for defendant** §335

If replevin is wrongful, the defendant is entitled to *return* of the chattel or its value, plus *detention damages*.

usually the *difference between the value* of the land before and after the injury or the *restoration cost.*

a.	**Damage to buildings**	§359

If an improvement (such as a building) is *destroyed,* the value of the improvement itself measures the loss. The most common measure is *reproduction cost less physical depreciation,* but other formulas are also used. If the improvement is *damaged,* measure of damages is usually *cost of repair* plus *compensation for loss of use.*

b.	**Crop damage**	§363

The measure of damages for tortiously destroyed or injured crops is the *diminution in value* test. If immature crops are damaged, the *probable yield* is taken into consideration.

c.	**Tree damage**	§364

Trees may be valued apart from the land, *or* the injured party may measure damages by the diminution in the value of the land.

d.	**Mental suffering**	§365

Mental suffering is usually *not* compensable here unless there is aggravated misconduct.

2. Waste

a.	**Voluntary waste**	§366

Voluntary waste consists of *deliberate destructive acts* by one rightfully in possession (*e.g.,* a tenant). The common law remedy was *treble damages* plus forfeiture of the tenancy. Equitable relief (a prohibitory injunction) is available along with damages for past injuries.

b.	**Permissive waste**	§371

Permissive waste involves acts of *omission or neglect* by a tenant that damage the freehold. The measure of damages is the *cost of repairs;* equitable relief is *seldom* available.

c.	**Ameliorating waste**	§374

Ameliorating waste consists of acts by a tenant that *alter* the freehold but result in an *increase of the value* of the property. Damages are usually *not* available as there is no diminution in value. Equitable relief (injunction) may be available in the case of a short-term lease.

d.	**Equitable waste**	§377

If a person not normally chargeable with waste (hence, no remedy at law) makes changes to property, equitable relief may be available. An example would be a mortgagor or buyer in possession who damages property sufficiently to impair the security interest of the mortgagee or seller.

3. Trespass with Ouster

a.	**Ejectment**	§385

A person wrongfully excluded from possession of realty may bring a common law action of ejectment if she can show a *right to possession* and *wrongful withholding* by the defendant.

(1) Mesne damages §386
The plaintiff may sue for mesne damages (mesne profits) to compensate for *loss of use;* the measure of damages is *rental value* or *actual benefit* to the wrongdoer.

(2) Good faith improvements §387
Improvements made in good faith by a trespasser could be taken by the plaintiff without compensation at common law, unless she also sought mesne damages, in which case a *setoff* equal to the improvement's value would be allowed.

(a) Equitable relief §389
If the plaintiff sought equitable relief (*e.g.,* quiet title action) she was required to "do equity" by compensating the improver as a condition of receiving the relief sought. In many states, "betterment statutes" variously provide for removal of the improvement, or give the landowner the option of paying for the improvement or selling.

b. Unlawful detainer §392
Detainer, along with forcible entry and detainer, involves a statutory proceeding that enables the plaintiff to regain possession quickly and inexpensively. The plaintiff is entitled to recover possession, plus rental value of lost use and consequential damages.

c. Equitable relief and restitution §397
Neither equitable relief nor restitution is available to recover possession during an ouster.

4. Encroachment §398
Damages are available based on the rental value or market value of the property, depending on whether the jurisdiction views encroachment as a *continuing trespass* or a *permanent invasion.* A *mandatory injunction* ordering removal of the encroachment is available, but the *balance of hardships* defense is available to the defendant if the encroachment was inadvertent and the hardship to the defendant greatly outweighs the hardship to the plaintiff.

5. Trespass to Land—Severance

a. Timber §408
The plaintiff has several actions available when a trespasser severs timber: trespass to land (diminution in land value damages), conversion, quasi-contract, and replevin. The measure of the recovery in conversion depends on whether the severance of the timber was willful or inadvertent.

b. Minerals §413
In cases of trespassory severance of minerals, the rules are the same as those for the wrongful cutting of timber. *Innocent trespassers* are liable for a royalty to the landowner who is *unable to exploit* the minerals. If the landowner *could extract* the minerals, damages are the value of the mined product, *less the reasonable cost of mining it*. If

the trespass was *willful*, damages are measured by the value of the minerals with no costs deduction.

    c.   **Injunctive relief**   **§416**

An injunction is available against a trespasser who wrongfully misappropriates and removes a part of the realty. Courts generally consider legal remedies inadequate because of the *continuous* nature of the trespass and the unique value of realty.

6.   Trespass to Land Not Involving Severance

    a.   **Debris dumped on plaintiff's land**   **§419**

This is compensable by *damages* (the measure of which is either the rental value of the property affected or the cost of removal) or a *mandatory injunction* requiring removal of the debris.

    b.   **Oil well drilling on plaintiff's land**   **§427**

The plaintiff may recover for injury to the land and for *loss of speculative value* if the trespasser's test well is dry, or for the *value of exploration rights* if the trespasser strikes oil.

7.   Simple Acts of Trespass   **§429**

Acts of trespass causing no injury to realty are compensable by at least *nominal* damages; consequential damages may also be available. An *injunction* is also available, and some courts also grant *restitution* of the value of the use. *Punitive damages* may be awarded if a simple trespass occurs in the face of a landowner's protest.

8.   Interference with Easements

    a.   **Damages**   **§439**

If an easement is *destroyed,* the plaintiff is entitled to the amount equal to the diminution in the value of the property. If there is an *interference,* damages are the cost of the removal of the obstruction.

    b.   **Injunctions**   **§442**

If a defendant interferes with a legally recognized easement, the plaintiff may be entitled to injunctive relief, but the defendant may be able to plead hardship. The same considerations apply to enforcement of restrictive covenants in deeds.

9.   Nuisances

    a.   **Private nuisance**   **§446**

A private nuisance is an *unreasonable* interference with the plaintiff's use and enjoyment of the land. In determining what activity constitutes nuisance, a court must *balance* the competing landowners' interests.

       (1)   **Damages**   **§447**

Damages are measured by the value of the *lost use and enjoyment* of the property. At common law, the plaintiff could *not* recover for *future* injury, but most states have adopted the *permanent nuisance doctrine* which allows recovery for permanent diminution in the value of the land as well as the value of past interferences. Courts are split on whether the plaintiff must take reasonable steps to mitigate damages (***avoidable consequences*** rule).

(2) Injunctive relief §453

A negative injunction is available in this situation. Some courts will balance the hardships or grant relief conditionally. A few jurisdictions will not issue an injunction and limit the plaintiff to damages.

(3) "Coming to the nuisance" §461

Although the plaintiff's moving to the nuisance is ordinarily ***not*** a defense, it may be ***important in determining damages***. Many states have adopted ***right-to-farm statutes*** to protect agricultural activities from nuisance actions brought by landowners moving onto adjacent land.

(4) Effect of zoning ordinances §465

If a landowner's use complies with zoning ordinances, some courts consider the ordinance as an absolute bar to enjoining the nuisance.

b. Public nuisance §466

The doctrine of public nuisance originally dealt with encroachments on public land, but the doctrine now includes use of property in such a way as to endanger public health, safety, and welfare, and in some states, anything affecting numerous people that is injurious to health, offensive to the senses, or that obstructs free use of property, *e.g.*, usurious small loans business, unlicensed medical practice, environmental harm.

(1) Injunctive relief §472

An injunction is available if criminal prosecution is an inadequate remedy.

(2) Private suits to enjoin §473

Although public nuisances are usually abated by the state (through the attorney general), a private individual may maintain a suit where the nuisance causes her ***special and individual damage***.

(a) RICO violations §474

Private causes of action for treble damages are permitted for ***injury to property*** caused by RICO violations, *e.g.*, apartment ***owners*** affected by drug dealers may recover, but tenants may not (no tangible injury to property).

VI. INJURIES TO BUSINESS AND COMMERCIAL INTERESTS

A. REMEDIES FOR BUSINESS TORTS—IN GENERAL

1. Damages

a. **Total destruction of established business** §475

If an established business is totally destroyed, the owners may be entitled to damages based on a projection of *profits* over the *probable lifetime* of the business destroyed. The *avoidable consequences rule* is applicable and the court may award recovery of *lost profits prior to the ultimate destruction*. Alternatively, the owners may recover the *market value* of the business destroyed.

b. **Partial destruction of established business** §486

If an ongoing business is partially destroyed, the business entity itself may sue for diminution of market value, loss of profits, or a share of the market sales the business could have been expected to attain without the injury. *Punitive damages* are available if malice is shown.

c. **Injury to new business** §493

If a new business (with no record of profits) is destroyed, it is difficult to prove what future profits would have been. Thus, recovery for lost future profits is rarely allowed.

2. **Equitable Remedies** §495

Provable damages for interference with a business are usually speculative, and harm is potentially irreparable. Thus, *injunctive relief is available*.

3. **Restitutionary Remedies** §496

Legal or equitable remedies may be available when profits or income have been *diverted* from the plaintiff and acquired by tortious activities of the defendant.

B. **REMEDIES FOR INDUCING BREACH OF CONTRACT**

1. **Damages** §497

Damages may be available against a tortfeasor who wrongfully induces a person to breach a contract with another. Proof of actual damages is required.

a. **Measure of damages** §498

In a *majority* of jurisdictions, the tortfeasor is liable for all *damages proximately caused* (which may include mental suffering, damage to reputation, etc.). A minority of states hold the defendant liable only for such damages as the plaintiff could have recovered *against the contract-breacher*. In any case, the plaintiff has the burden of proving that the contract would have been profitable.

(1) **Unenforceable contracts** §501

The plaintiff may sue for interference with an unenforceable contract (*e.g.,* an oral land sale contract), but there is little authority as to the proper measure of damages.

(2) **Contracts terminable at will** §502

Recovery for a contract terminable at will is allowed in the majority of states, with damages reflecting the probability of nontermination.

Restitutionary remedies such as a constructive trust or equitable accounting are available.

by *tortious means*, e.g., customer list cases. Injunctions are also granted to prevent a defendant from breaching an *agreement not to disclose* secrets. Although some courts permanently enjoin a wrongdoer, the majority limit the injunction to a period of *"lead time,"* i.e., the time the defendant saved in starting competitive production because of early access to the secret.

b. Accounting §574
In addition to an injunction, the plaintiff may obtain an accounting as to the infringer's *profits*.

H. REMEDIES FOR MISAPPROPRIATION OF CREATIVE WORKS AND IDEAS

1. Common Law Copyright—Federal Preemption §575
State copyright law has been preempted by the federal copyright statute, but there are still a few areas remaining where the state protection is available (*e.g., unpublished* works not in tangible form, violations of rights not equivalent to those given federal protection, e.g., breaches of contract or trust, invasion of privacy, deceptive trade practices).

2. Remedies Available §577
Once the plaintiff proves the "copying" occurred *outside* the copyright statute, he may obtain damages, restitution, or an injunction.

3. Disclosures Made in Confidence §582
If a writer or inventor discloses ideas in confidence and under circumstances manifesting an expectation of payment, contractual, quasi-contractual, and equitable (*i.e.*, injunction and/or accounting for profits) remedies are available.

4. Private Letters and Correspondence §587
At common law, the *receiver* of correspondence is deemed to own the paper or material upon which the letter is written, but the *sender* retains an interest in the verbal expressions. Federal copyright law largely preempts this area.

I. REMEDIES FOR TRADEMARK AND TRADE NAME INFRINGEMENT

1. General Theories §590
Different jurisdictions provide dissimilar remedies to protect trademarks, depending on the jurisdiction's general theory of the basis for protection. General theories include: *"palming off"* (protection of goodwill); *confusion of source* (likelihood of public confusion); *misappropriation* (trade name is property right); and *dilution* (the defendant's unauthorized use dilutes advertising impact).

2. Lanham Act and Remedies §605
The Lanham Act provides for the registration of trademarks; it does *not* preempt state laws and remedies. The remedies under the Lanham Act are: recovery of the defendant's *profits,* any *damages* sustained by the plaintiff, and *costs of the action.* The plaintiff, in cases of *willful* infringement, may receive *treble damages* or injunctive relief. Laches and unclean hands are equitable defenses.

proof of the loss of particular customers. Consequential damages may also be recovered.

2. **Equitable Remedies—Injunctions** §646

Injunctive relief was traditionally unavailable in cases of product disparagement, but courts moved to enjoin product disparagement where it was part of an overall enjoinable tort (*e.g.,* unfair competition). The modern trend is to grant injunctive relief where the encroachment upon free speech is **outweighed** by the harm caused by the denial of an injunction. Trade defamation also includes defamations by **omission**. Injunctive relief has also been granted for **false advertising** that impinges on products of others.

VII. INJURIES TO PERSONAL DIGNITY AND RELATED INTERESTS

A. DEFAMATION

1. **Substantive Elements** §652

At common law, **all libel is actionable per se**, *i.e.,* pecuniary loss need not be proved. **Slander**, however, requires proof of **special damages**, unless it imputes a serious crime or loathsome disease, or discredits a person in her trade or profession. A **minority** of states require proof of special damages if a written statement, **innocent on its face**, has a defamatory implication when connected with **extrinsic factors**. Additionally, several Supreme Court cases require **proof of fault** for a defamatory publication (below).

a. **Constitutional limitations** §655

Public officials and public figures must show **"actual malice"** on the part of the defamer (*i.e.,* **knowledge** of falsity or **reckless disregard** for the truth). A **private citizen** defamed by statements involving **matters of public concern** must establish that the media was **at least negligent**.

2. **General Damages** §658

At common law, where the defamation is actionable per se, damages are **presumed.** The factors considered in establishing damages include **plaintiff's reputation** and his standing in the community, the **extent and permanence** of the defamatory statement, and the statement's **effect on people**. Mitigation may be based on the plaintiff's prior bad reputation, and also on proof of the defendant's **good faith and retraction.**

a. **Constitutional limitations in actions against news media** §661

Because of First Amendment considerations, certain limitations have been imposed by the Supreme Court. No action lies for defamation of a **public official** absent proof of malice (*supra*). **Private citizens** must prove at least negligence in actions involving matters of **public concern** against the media; damages are limited to **actual injury**. However, private citizens may also recover **punitive damages** in cases not involving matters of public concern.

3. **Injunctions** §673

Injunctive relief is **not** available against a **personal** defamation as "equity will not enjoin a libel." Furthermore, there is a strong **public policy against** *prior restraints on speech.* Sometimes an injunction will lie if there is a **strong and clear showing of harm** that outweighs public policy, if the defamable statement is **part of other enjoinable conduct** (*e.g.* intimidation, conspiracy), or, in conjunction with declaratory relief, to **prevent repetition** of the statement.

4. Mitigation §681

In many states, the defendant may mitigate damages by publishing a retraction, but requiring a newspaper to publish a reply to attacks or criticisms violates the guarantee of a free press.

5. Restitution §683

Claims for restitution based on unjust enrichment seldom arise because the defendant derives no economic gain or benefit. However, in the few cases where the defendant has derived some benefit, courts have **denied** any restitutionary relief.

B. PRIVACY

1. Substantive Elements §684

The right of privacy protects against unreasonable interference with a person's solitude or seclusion, public disclosure of private facts, and the commercial exploitation of another's personality. The right to be free from publication of embarrassing details on one's private life must be reconciled with First Amendment rights. Public records are publishable, but lower courts recognize liability for truthful publication of **private matters not** of public interest.

a. False light cases §691

If publicity places the plaintiff in a false light, she must show that the defendant **knew** the matter was false or offensive or that it was published in **reckless disregard** thereof.

b. No survival of action §692

A claim based on public disclosure of embarrassing private facts does not survive the injured party's death.

2. Remedies §693

Damages for mental anguish (including **punitive** damages in cases of **ill will or reckless disregard** of the plaintiff's rights) and **injunctive relief** for continuing invasion of privacy are available. Restitutionary remedies are not proper unless the right of publicity (*supra*) is involved.

C. FAMILIAL RELATIONS §702

The common law provided actions for alienation of affections, criminal conversation (adultery), and seduction. In jurisdictions where such actions still exist, **damages** are the proper remedy.

1. Children §713

In divorce cases, the decree often provides that parents are prohibited from making disparaging remarks about each other, but is difficult to supervise or enforce. Also, injunctive relief may be sought in disputes regarding a child's surname.

suffering and disfigurement) and *special damages* (for loss of past and future earnings and past and future medical expenses).

a. Amount of damages   §738

Damages are in the discretion of the jury, although some states have tried to limit damages, particularly in medical malpractice cases. The common law and the Federal Tort Claims Act provide for a single *lump sum payment* to the plaintiff, although the parties can agree among themselves for a settlement on the basis of installment payments.

2. Economic Losses   §740

As part of any compensatory damages award, the plaintiff is entitled to recover all economic losses *proximately caused* by the injury, *i.e.*, special damages (above).

a. Future medical expenses   §741

The plaintiff must establish a *probability* that future medical treatment will be necessary and the approximate cost. However, because there is *uncertainty* in ascertaining future expenses in *toxic exposure torts* cases (*e.g.*, asbestos, AIDS), defendants are increasingly being required to pay the *costs of medical monitoring* (subject to strict requirements, *e.g.*, significantly increased risk of disease). Note that the *fear of acquiring a disease* is *not* compensable, although resulting emotional distress is.

b. Future earnings   §751

Future earnings are determined on *probabilities* over the plaintiff's expected working life, even for a plaintiff with no earnings history. Earnings are computed without regard to any reduction in life expectancy caused by the injury. Damages awards are rendered in a lump sum.

3. Noneconomic Losses   §764

The plaintiff is entitled to recover for past and future noneconomic losses (general damages). These include: physical pain, emotional anguish, loss of enjoyment of life (in some jurisdictions), and sometimes for market services (*e.g.,* costs of hiring someone else to mow the lawn). Courts may set aside a jury verdict if it appears that the issue of amount of damages was presented to the jury on the basis of legally improper instructions or legally improper arguments from counsel (*e.g., "golden rule"* argument), or the court may invoke the remedies of additur or remittitur.

a. No-fault insurance   §784

Jurisdictions with no-fault insurance plans may limit or eliminate recovery for noneconomic losses.

4. Rules Affecting Amount of Damages Recoverable

a. Rule of avoidable consequences   §785

The plaintiff must take all reasonable steps to avoid aggravating the injuries, *e.g.,* seek medical care, retrain for new career (if necessary).

the contract. Affirmance may be manifested by accepting the benefits *after discovering* the fraud, delay in disaffirming, or commencing suit for damages.

3. Rescission of Contract §859
Commencement of an action for rescission is *not an irrevocable election* of remedies. The election of remedies doctrine is based on an estoppel principle and thus requires a showing of *detrimental reliance.* If the injured party gives notice of rescission and tenders back the consideration, and the wrongdoer *accepts*, the contract is rescinded and the plaintiff may not seek damages.

4. Suing in the Alternative §863
Suing in the alternative is allowed, but there must be an election of remedies prior to judgment. Note that the U.C.C. rejects the election of remedies doctrine.

B. AFFIRMANCE OF THE CONTRACT—DAMAGES REMEDY

1. Substantive Elements §866
If the injured party elects to affirm the contract, the remedy is an action at law for damages. The essential elements to plead and prove the cause of action are:

a. *Misrepresentation of a fact;*

b. *Scienter;*

c. *Intent* of defendant to induce reliance;

d. *Materiality* (justifiable reliance);

e. *Actual reliance* by the plaintiff; and

f. *Damages* to the plaintiff.

2. Measure of Compensatory Damages §878
Courts are split on the measure of damages in cases involving the sale of property. Some apply an *out-of-pocket* rule (awarding the difference between what the plaintiff paid and the actual value of what was received). Others apply a *benefit-of-bargain* rule (awarding the difference between the actual value of what is received and the value it would have had as represented). *Actual value* means market value.

3. Other Damages Recoverable §882
The plaintiff may recover *consequential* damages and, where fraud is *intentional and malicious,* punitive damages. In U.C.C. cases, *incidental* as well as consequential damages are recoverable. Where the misrepresentation is collateral to the purchase, the defendant is liable for losses proximately caused by his misrepresentation. Similarly, in cases where the seller sues the fraudulent buyer or cases where the sale of property is not involved, the measure of damages is the loss proximately caused by the wrongdoer's fraud.

C. RESCISSION OF THE CONTRACT

1. Substantive Elements §888
The essential elements for rescission are:

(i) *Misrepresentation* of fact (or *mistake*);

(ii) *Materiality* (not necessary if misrepresentation is intentional);

(iii) *Reliance;* and

(iv) *Injury* (but *pecuniary* loss need not be shown).

Note that scienter is *not* required.

2. Mechanics of Rescission §896
The same basic procedures apply whether rescission is "at law" or "in equity." An alternative to rescission is the statutory declaratory judgment procedure, which serves the same function.

a. Rescission at law §897
The plaintiff may sue at law to recover property (or its value) she has conferred upon the defendant under a contract voidable for fraud, duress, or mistake. This is predicated upon the theory that *the plaintiff has already disaffirmed* and invokes the court's aid to obtain recovery of property or its value. A normal cause of action is *quasi-contract,* but replevin or conversion may also lie.

(1) Notice and offer to restore §898
To recover at law, *before* commencing the action, the plaintiff must have given the defendant *prompt* notice of disaffirmance and restored or offered to restore (tendered) anything of value she received from the defendant under the contract.

(2) Exceptions §900
Tender back is not required if: (i) the benefit is worthless; (ii) money would be tendered in hope of return of money (set-off is allowed); or (iii) the plaintiff disposed of the property received *before* fraud was discovered.

b. Rescission in equity §904
The party seeking rescission files a bill offering "to do equity" and seeking a *decree* rescinding the contract and ordering an accounting and restitution of benefits. As in rescission at law, the plaintiff must give notice and, in some jurisdictions, tender back is necessary.

(1) Procedure §906
Whether rescission is legal or equitable may affect the *right to a jury trial*; a few states have a unitary procedure.

3. Legal Remedies After Rescission of Fraudulent Contract §907
Replevin (for the chattel itself), conversion ("forced sale at the chattel's real value"), and quasi-contract ("for goods sold and delivered" to recover value of the chattel) are the applicable legal remedies.

4. Equitable Remedies for Fraud §912

If equitable jurisdiction is established, *restitution* in equity is available (the defendant must *account* to the plaintiff for the value of the benefits fraudulently obtained).

a. Rescission of land sale contract §914

Upon a *seller's fraud*, the buyer will recover the *consideration* paid, *expenditures to maintain* the property (less depreciation) and for *improvements, insurance, and taxes*, and *incidental expenses*. The *seller* will recover, as an *offset*, possession of the land and the value of its use. Upon a *buyer's fraud*, the seller recovers the land and the value of its use. In this case, the *buyer's offset* includes the *consideration paid* plus interest, taxes paid, and expenditures for *necessary improvements only.*

b. Rescission for sale of business §918

In a case involving rescission of the sale of a business, the buyer recovers the consideration paid with interest, but compensates the seller for use of the property, measured either by rental value or the profits, whichever is *less*.

5. Special Damages §919

Special damages are not inconsistent with a restitutionary proceeding. However, where rescission is based on a *material breach* of contract, the **Hadley v. Baxendale** limitation applies. Consequential damages are not allowed in *mutual mistake* cases.

6. Punitive Damages §922

Punitive damages are available after rescission if fraud and the requisite malice are shown.

7. Uniform Commercial Code §923

The U.C.C. permits "revocation of acceptance" and recapture of goods, plus incidental damages.

D. STATUTORY REMEDIES—CONSUMER PROTECTION §924

Many states have consumer protection statutes that provide recovery for deceptive practices of sellers. Remedies include compensatory and punitive damages as well as injunctive relief. These statutes often provide for class actions.

X. DURESS, UNDUE INFLUENCE, AND UNCONSCIONABLE CONDUCT

A. DURESS

1. Basic Remedy §925

Duress is *not* an actionable tort per se. Therefore, the basic remedy is *restitution* for unjust enrichment.

2. Defined §927

Duress is conduct that overcomes the free will of another and thus renders *involuntary whatever transaction* is involved. The test is *subjective,* and it must appear that, under the circumstances, the injured party had no other lawful way out. The coercion must be from the person receiving the benefit.

3. Remedy Depends on Nature of Duress

a. Void transaction §932

If the duress consists of *physically forced acts* or acts *under hypnosis or involuntary intoxication,* the transaction is void; *i.e.,* the plaintiff made no *intentional act*.

b. Voidable transaction §934

More frequently, a duressed person's acts are *intentional, but not volitional* because no free choice was involved. Such transactions are voidable.

c. Criminal proceedings or threat thereof §946

Courts are split on whether restitution is the proper remedy where criminal prosecution is threatened or instituted. *Bad faith* must be shown, and, if the duressed person is innocent of crime, he can sue for damages for malicious prosecution.

d. Civil proceedings or threat thereof §950

Generally, restitution is *not* available for duress from threat of civil proceedings unless the plaintiff was threatened with such irreparable loss that he had no alternative but to submit to the coercion.

e. Oppressive refusal to perform public duty without payment §953

In cases involving an oppressive refusal to perform a public duty without payment (*e.g.,* a building inspector who would not issue a permit, despite the owner's compliance with all laws, absent payment of a "bribe"), restitution is generally allowed.

f. Business compulsion—"economic coercion" §954

The common law notion of "duress to property" gave rise to the concept of business compulsion. The *"inequitable exercise of legal rights"* includes (i) threats to exercise a reserved right to terminate a contract, (ii) threats to breach a contract, and (iii) refusals to deal at all or only on exorbitant terms.

(1) Note §955

None of the above may constitute duress by itself, but in combination may be sufficient to constitute economic duress. The duress must result from the defendant's conduct and not just from the victim's financial embarrassment or necessity.

(2) Remedy §957

Restitution is the remedy, but if the coercion results in a restraint of trade, *antitrust laws* may *supersede* the right to recover under state restitution laws.

B. UNDUE INFLUENCE

1. Definition and Substantive Nature §958

"Undue influence" is the equitable equivalent of common law duress, and is derived from equitable jurisdiction over fiduciary and confidential relationships. It occurs when *one party is under the domination of another*, and the dominant party exercises *unfair persuasion*.

B. MISTAKE IN BARGAINING TRANSACTIONS

1. Overperformance of Contract §981

Overperformance of contract refers to the situation in which parties are free from error in entering into a contract, but a mistake is made in the performance (*e.g.,* incorrect land surveys, payments based on faulty calculations). Restitution does not depend on whether the mistake was mutual or unilateral.

a. Overpayment of money §982

The remedy for overpayment of money is in ***quasi-contract***.

b. Land contracts §984

If money is overpaid and there is a ***shortage of acreage***, restitution is possible if payment was "per acre," but not if the price was for the entire unit. If ***too much land is conveyed***, the usual remedy is reconveyance by reforming the deed. ***Alternative remedies*** include rescission or paying extra compensation at the contract rate.

c. Overperformance of services §987

There is ***no*** remedy for overperformance of services unless the recipient was aware of the extra work performed.

d. Insurance policy endorsements §988

Reformation is the appropriate remedy where an insurance endorsement reflects higher coverage than was agreed.

2. Mistaken Performance in Reliance on Nonexistent Contract §989

This refers to the situation where the parties are mistaken as to the existence of the subject matter of the "contract." ***Restitution*** of any payments made or value given is the normal remedy.

3. Mistake in Basic Assumptions §995

If one or both parties executed a contract under a mistake as to a basic fact or circumstance affecting the value of the contract, the normal remedy is rescission. The mistake must go to the very ***basis of the bargain***; mere materiality is not enough.

a. Sale of goods §998

In cases of mistake in contracts involving the sale of goods, the mistake must go to the ***nature*** or ***identity*** of the subject matter.

b. Conveyances of land interests §1002

In cases involving the conveyance of land, if the transaction is ***executory***, a ***material*** mistake may be a defense to specific performance.

(1) Quantitative mistake §1003

If the mistake is quantitative and the sale is per acre, restitution of the overpayment is awarded. If the sale is in gross, there is no remedy unless what remains is an essentially different piece of land.

(2) Qualitative mistake §1004

No remedy exists for a qualitative mistake ***unless*** a condition is stated in the contract, or the intended use of the land turns out to be impracticable for reasons unknown to the parties at the time of contracting. Restitution is not available in a case of mistake if the risk has been *allocated, e.g.,* by an "as is" clause. Rescission is rare in conveyance of *title* cases, but more common for *leases*.

c. Settlement of claims §1010
Ordinarily, compromises *cannot* be rescinded for mistake. However, if the errors concern the "basic" facts of the compromise, rescission is possible.

4. Unilateral Mistake §1014
There is *no* rescission for a purely unilateral mistake, but if the mistake is "basic" and *unconscionable hardship* would ensue, a remedy has been granted, subject to the defendant's right to recover reliance damages resulting from the rescission. Relief in *mistaken bid cases* is usually limited to cases of *clerical error,* rather than poor judgment.

C. DEFENSES

1. In General §1020
Because the defendant is equally mistaken, and therefore innocent, defenses are recognized when the enrichment was not the result of the defendant's tort or breach.

2. Change of Position §1021
Where the defendant has *disposed* of the benefit received by mistake, and restitution in money would be harsh, restitution is denied. However, this defense *does not apply* if the defendant has used the benefit to pay normal bills and living expenses or if it was used in the business to produce other income.

3. Discharge for Value §1024
If the defendant has *paid* for the benefit mistakenly conferred or accepted in satisfaction of a debt owed her by another, this is a valid defense.

4. Compromise and Settlement §1029
Compromise and settlement is a defense because it is, in effect, an assertion that no mistake was made.

5. Mistake of Law §1030
Traditionally no restitution was granted for a mistake of law, but numerous exceptions to the rule were recognized (*e.g.,* fiduciary relationship, superior knowledge by one party), and today many jurisdictions reject any distinction between mistakes of fact and mistakes of law.

6. Negligence of Plaintiff §1031
Plaintiff's negligence (*e.g.,* failure to read documents) is often asserted as a defense. Negligence per se is not a defense, but it is a factor that may decide close cases when other defenses are present.

D. MISTAKE IN INTEGRATION—REFORMATION AS REMEDY

belief that the other intended donees had predeceased donor) are usually remedied by restitution. In the case of mistake as to size of gift, most courts allow restitution.

b. Remedies of donee §1054
If a donee claims that a donor failed to make an intended gift or that the amount given was less than intended, and the donor is living, the donee is ***denied relief*** (although recovery under a promissory estoppel theory may be had if the donee detrimentally relied on the promise of gift). If the donor is deceased and the donative intent is clear, many courts allow "quasi-specific performance."

2. Inter Vivos Trusts §1057
Relief is available to a beneficiary for mistake occurring in a ***revocable*** trust; however, a mistake in an ***irrevocable*** trust must be ***"basic"*** for relief to be allowed.

3. Wills §1058
Reformation has, in limited situations, been used as a method of implementing a testator's "probable intent" in cases of mistake in will provisions (*e.g.,* tax law changes ***after*** the decedent's death). A constructive trust may be used to remedy a mistake in the revocation of a will.

XII. REMEDIES FOR BREACH OF CONTRACT

A. SPECIAL CONDITIONS APPLICABLE TO SPECIFIC PERFORMANCE

1. Introduction §1060
General conditions that must be satisfied for the remedy of specific performance to be applicable, regardless of the type of contract involved, are: (i) ***inadequate remedy*** at law; (ii) contract is ***definite and certain;*** (iii) all ***conditions precedent*** are met; (iv) enforcement ***operates equitably;*** and (v) enforcement is ***feasible.***

2. Mutuality of Remedy §1061
Mutuality of remedy was once required for specific performance to be available. The modern view requires ***only*** mutuality of performance.

3. Contractual Modification of Remedies §1064
The U.C.C. permits modification of remedies in sale of goods cases. Modification has also been permitted in land sale contracts with a clause setting forth the parties' agreement to exclude the remedy of specific performance.

B. LAND SALE CONTRACTS

1. Introductory Note §1065
In analyzing possible remedies for breach of land sale contracts, it is necessary to determine whether the breach occurred ***before or after*** execution and delivery of the deed by the seller. Whether the contract is a simple buy-sell agreement or provides for installment payments also has a major effect on the remedies available to the aggrieved party.

a. **Equitable conversion**   §1066
Executory land sale agreements create an immediate equitable interest in the land. The **buyer** is regarded as the equitable owner **from
the time the contracts are signed**.

(1) **Seller's interests**   §1067
The seller retains legal title subject to the duty to convey. His
contractual right to payment is secured by a **vendor's lien**. The
seller's interest passes upon his death **as personalty** to his next
of kin or legatee.

(2) **Buyer's interests**   §1075
The buyer's contract right to conveyance, based on the duty to
pay the contract price, creates an **equitable interest** based on
the buyer's ability to specifically enforce the contract. If the
buyer has made a partial payment, a **vendee's lien** attaches to
the property to secure restitution if the seller breaches. The
buyer's right to specific performance is cut off by sale to a bona
fide purchaser.

(a) **Risk of loss**   §1078
Risk of loss has traditionally been on the **buyer** (strict
construction of equitable conversion doctrine), but risk may
be shifted by the contract itself, or the buyer may be held
equitably entitled to the seller's insurance (if any). The
traditional rule has been changed in a number of jurisdictions, either by judicial decisions or by statute (*i.e.*, the
Uniform Vendor and Purchaser Risk Act) so that the risk
is on the buyer only if she has taken **possession** or **legal
title has actually been transferred** to her.

(b) **Other interests**
Note that the buyer's equitable interests may be transferred or mortgaged. The buyer's interest passes to her
heirs as realty upon the buyer's death. Generally, assign-
ees of a buyer's interest assume the benefits and burdens
of the buyer's equitable interest and thus, the vendor may
sue the assignee to enforce the contract.

2. **Buyer's Remedies for Seller's Breach of Executory Land Sale Contract**

a. **Damages**   §1087
When the seller **refuses to convey**, some jurisdictions apply an **out-
of-pocket loss** rule, while others have adopted the **benefit-of-bargain**
rule. A few jurisdictions have awarded consequential damages as well.
If the seller transfers title but delays conveyance beyond the date agreed
upon, damages for delay are available if the damages were within the
contemplation of the parties (rule of **Hadley v. Baxendale**).

b. **Specific performance**   §1092
Specific performance is available as an alternative to damages. The
remedy at law is deemed inadequate because of the unique aspects

of the real estate. *Note: **Liquidated damages*** provisions in the contract do **not** nullify the buyer's right to specific performance. Also, the buyer may be entitled to ancillary equitable relief to compensate for losses resulting from the **delay** in performance.

c. **Specific performance with abatement** §1097

If the seller is unable to perform as promised because of some **defect** in title, the buyer may nevertheless insist upon specific performance with an abatement of the purchase price to reflect the value of the defect. A **limitation** exists requiring the decree to **operate equitably**.

d. **Specific performance—in lieu of damages** §1104

Traditionally, equity allowed a buyer to receive damages (instead of specific performance) when the buyer did not learn of the seller's inability to convey until after the trial had begun. Some courts preclude this remedy.

e. **Restitution** §1105

Instead of seeking damages or specific performance, the buyer may **rescind** after the seller's material breach and seek restitution of benefits conferred upon the seller.

3. **Buyer's Remedies for Seller's Breach After Conveyance** §1108

The buyer may sue for damages resulting from the seller's breach of covenant (*e.g.,* cloud on title). However, if the buyer accepted a **quitclaim deed** from the seller, **no** such remedy is available.

a. **Overpayment** §1110

If the seller has conveyed, but as a result of a mistake transfers less land than the parties believe, **restitution** may be available for overpayment.

b. **Warranty of habitability** §1111

Many jurisdictions imply a warranty of habitability in the sale of **new** homes. Damages are measured by the diminution in value.

4. **Remedy of a Seller in Default** §1112

A seller in default will be awarded specific performance with abatement only if his breach of the contract is **immaterial**. Such relief is not available for a material breach.

5. **Seller's Remedies for Buyer's Breach of Executory Land Sale Contract** §1115

The seller's remedies may depend on the classification of the contract as a buy-sell agreement or an installment land sale contract.

a. **Buy-sell or marketing contract** §1116

Buy-sell or marketing contracts call for payment of the price and delivery of the deed on a given date. The buyer breaches the contract by refusing to tender payment.

(1) **Damages** §1117

The seller's damages are the difference between the market value of the land and the contract price on the date set for performance, **plus** consequential damages. The seller has a **duty to mitigate** by attempting a prompt resale.

the policy against forfeitures and allows the **buyer to recover** all payments **in excess of the seller's harm.**

    b.   **Specific performance**   §1155

        Specific performance is generally **not** available to a buyer in default. A minority of jurisdictions allow specific performance if the buyer is not guilty of laches and she pays the full balance owed to the seller.

C. **CONTRACTS FOR THE SALE OF CHATTELS**

  1. **Caveat**   §1159

      In 2001, a revision of Article 2 (Sales) of the U.C.C. was proposed. If approved and adopted by the states, certain changes, some of which are substantive, will modify some of the sections below (*e.g.*, addition of consequential damages to the seller's remedies in sections 2-706 through 2-710).

  2. **Buyer's Remedies Against Seller for Nondelivery**

    a.   **Damages**   §1160

        If the seller fails to make delivery or repudiates a contract, the buyer may recover damages measured by:

        (1)   The **difference between market price** at the time the buyer learned of the breach and the **contract price**;

        (2)   Together with **incidental and consequential** (*e.g., **lost profits***) damages; and

        (3)   **Less expenses** saved by the breach.

    b.   **Cover**   §1163

        As an alternative to ordinary damages, the buyer may "cover" by making a **substitute purchase** of goods due from the seller, provided this is reasonable and without undue delay. The buyer may then recover the difference between the cost of cover and the contract price, plus incidental or consequential damages.

    c.   **Replevin**   §1166

        Replevin is available for goods "identified to the contract" if cover cannot be effected.

    d.   **Specific performance**   §1167

        Courts allow specific performance if the goods are **unique** or in other proper circumstances (if **damages are difficult to measure**; e.g., long-term output contracts).

    e.   **Rescission**   §1170

        Rescission is a meaningless remedy in the case of a wholly executory contract.

  3. **Buyer's Remedies Against Seller Following Delivery or Acceptance**

    a.   **Delay in delivery**   §1171

        If there is a material delay in delivery, the buyer may reject the goods when tendered. If the delay constitutes an immaterial breach, the buyer must accept the goods, but may recover damages for the delay.

b. Nonconforming goods §1173

When the seller sends nonconforming goods, the buyer may accept the goods and sue for **breach of warranty** under the U.C.C. The measure of damages is the difference at the time and place of the acceptance between the goods accepted and the value they would have had *if they had been as warranted. Incidental and consequential* damages may be awarded as well.

(1) Revocation of acceptance §1183

Alternatively, the buyer may revoke her acceptance and recover as much of the contract price as she has paid, plus damages for nondelivery, and maintain a security interest in the rejected goods in her possession.

4. Remedies of Buyer in Default §1186

Under the U.C.C., a buyer in default is entitled to restitution of any amount by which the sum of her payments *exceeds* reasonable liquidated damages.

5. Seller's Remedy for Buyer's Nonacceptance of Goods

a. Damages §1188

The measure of damages when the buyer wrongfully rejects goods is the difference between the **market price** (at the time and place of tender) and the **unpaid contract price,** together with incidental damages. The **avoidable consequences rule** applies, and the seller must minimize the loss.

b. Alternative measure of damages §1192

Where the seller has an **unlimited supply** of a commodity and the **demand** is limited, the seller may recover the profit he would have made from the full performance of the buyer.

c. Resale §1193

The seller may also choose to resell the goods and recover the difference between the resale and contract prices, plus incidental damages.

d. Rescission §1194

The seller may "cancel" the contract.

e. Specific performance §1195

Specific performance is rarely available where a buyer has refused to accept goods because legal remedies are usually adequate.

f. Action for the full price §1196

An action for the full price is available **only** when the seller is unable after reasonable effort to resell the goods at a reasonable price.

6. Seller's Remedies After Delivery and Acceptance of Goods §1197

If a buyer accepts goods and refuses to pay, the seller's remedies are an *action for full price, reclaiming goods* if the buyer becomes insolvent, and *restitution* if the buyer *repudiates after part performance* by the seller.

7.   Remedy of Seller in Default   §1205

At common law and under the Uniform Sales Act, the seller who partially performed and then repudiated was entitled to recover reasonable value of goods less damages to the buyer. *Note:* The *U.C.C.* lacks any such provision, and no cases have granted the seller such a remedy under the U.C.C.

D.   CONSTRUCTION CONTRACTS

1.   Builder's Remedy of Damages Against Owner

a.   Before performance by builder   §1207

If an owner breaches a construction contract before the builder begins to build, damages are the builder's *lost profit*.

b.   After full performance   §1208

If an owner breaches a construction contract after full performance by the builder, the builder's remedy is an action for the *price*.

c.   After part performance   §1209

If an owner breaches a construction contract after the builder partially performs, there are several formulas for measuring damages. The builder also has a *mechanic's lien* against the property.

2.   Builder's Restitutionary Remedy Against Defaulting Owner   §1213

If an owner repudiates after partial performance, the builder may *rescind* and sue in quasi-contract for the value of the benefit conferred. The measure of recovery is usually the value of services, but the minority position limits the builder to a proportionate share of the contract price.

3.   Restitutionary Remedy for Builder in Default   §1216

A contractor who has committed a *material* breach of a construction contract may not enforce the contract and has no damages remedy at law. While there is a general agreement that a builder is entitled to restitution for the value of work performed, courts are widely split over conditions under which recovery may be had. If the breach is *immaterial* and the builder has *substantially completed* the job, he may sue for the *contract price less damages* resulting from his breach.

4.   Owner's Remedy of Damages for Builder's Breach

a.   After substantial performance by a builder   §1221

If a builder breaches, but has substantially performed, the owner is entitled to the *cost of repair or replacement* to bring the building up to contract standards *or* (if the repair is not economically feasible) to the *difference in the value* in the building as built and the value it would have had if it had been constructed in accordance with the contract.

b.   Abandonment after part performance (material breach)   §1222

If a builder abandons a project after part performance, damages are measured by what the owner must pay to complete construction, less anything still owing to the builder, plus *special damages*.

6. Injunctive Relief §1251

Specific performance is *not* available to either party. However, *breach of a negative covenant* may be enjoined, at least where services contracted for are unique and extraordinary. Reinstatement may be ordered by statute in employment discrimination cases.

7. Covenants Not to Compete §1259

Equity will enforce covenants not to compete, provided the restriction is *reasonable as to time and place* and *no broader than necessary* to protect the employer. Injunctive relief is granted only if the legal remedy is inadequate (*e.g.*, unique services, employee carrying away trade secrets or goodwill).

a. Blue pencil rule §1265

If a restrictive covenant is overbroad, some courts hold it void and unenforceable. Others will enforce it to a reasonable extent if the reasonable and unreasonable restraints are severable. A court may deny injunctive relief if continuous and protracted court supervision is required.

8. Contracts to Lend Money §1267

The traditional measure of damages for breach of a contract to lend money (*i.e.*, the additional interest required for a replacement loan) has been expanded to allow recovery for resulting injuries within the contemplation of the parties when the contract was made.

XIII. REMEDIES IN CONNECTION WITH UNENFORCEABLE CONTRACTS

A. CONTRACTS UNENFORCEABLE BECAUSE NOT IN WRITING

1. In General §1268

Under certain circumstances, the bar to enforcement under the Statute of Frauds (or Statute of Wills) may be removed by invoking the equitable doctrines of part performance or estoppel. Otherwise, the sole remedy is restitution.

2. Types of Statutes—Remedial Effect §1269

Statutes vary among the jurisdictions. If the Statute makes the contract *"unenforceable,"* restitution may be had *only* against the party who has *repudiated* the oral contract. If the contract is deemed *"void,"* the plaintiff may repudiate and seek restitution. Certain statutes are aimed at *oral real estate brokerage contracts,* and *no* remedies are allowed.

3. Restitutionary Remedies—Common Problems §1273

If the problem involves valuation, most courts will permit the introduction of evidence of a "contract" rate or price. The majority also permit recovery above the level of "contract" price if unjust enrichment is proved. Reliance damages are not allowed when the plaintiff seeks restitution.

4. Part Performance Doctrine—Remedy of Specific Performance §1281

Because restitution often fails to compensate the plaintiff for her part performance in reliance on the "contract," the harshness of the Statute of Frauds is mitigated by the "part performance doctrine" when applicable to *land sale contracts.* Sufficient part performance is generally *payment plus possession,* or *improvement* to property by the buyer.

    a. Sale of goods   §1290

Under the U.C.C., oral contracts for the sale of goods for $500 or more are enforceable only if *payment* for goods has been made and accepted or for goods that have been *received* and accepted.

5. Estoppel to Assert Statute of Frauds as a Defense   §1291

A number of states allow enforcement of oral contracts by invoking estoppel. Evidence of acts by the plaintiff in reliance on the defendant's promise is admissible even though not "referable" to the contract. The plaintiff may collect damages as well as sue for specific performance.

6. Oral Agreements to Devise Realty in Exchange for Services   §1293

The remedies available where there is an oral agreement to devise realty in exchange for services (*e.g.,* "take care of me for the rest of my life and I will leave you everything in my will") are *quasi-contract, specific performance* (where the services are unusual), or *damages* (if the doctrine of estoppel to assert the Statute of Frauds is recognized).

B. CONTRACTS UNENFORCEABLE BECAUSE OF IMPOSSIBILITY OR FRUSTRATION OF PURPOSE

1. Effect of Impossibility or Frustration   §1297

If full performance by one party is a condition precedent for recovery on a contract or one party *assumes* the risk of loss, supervening impossibility results in breach of contract, with the usual remedies. Otherwise, impossibility excuses both parties, and restitution is the *sole remedy*.

2. General Guidelines for Restitution   §1298

The English rule tended to let the loss remain where it fell. The American rule is that *each party must pay for what he has received*.

3. Application of Guidelines After Part Performance

    a. Employment cases   §1301

If an employee fails fully to perform because of death or disability, courts will allow quantum meruit recovery for services up to the time of disability.

    b. Remodeling and repair contracts   §1304

Where an owner employs a contractor to remodel or repair and the house is destroyed after remodeling is partly finished, restitution is generally allowed, contrary to ordinary construction contracts.

4. Failure of Consideration Cases   §1307

Where the plaintiff has fully performed, but counterperformance is prevented by supervening impossibility, the remedy is specific restitution or, alternatively, the *value of the performance rendered*.

5. Where Impossibility Occurs After Breach   §1311

The right to a judicial remedy occurs at the *time* of a breach. If the breaching party has no excuse at that time, subsequent developments do not affect his liability. The rule is contra where the breach is merely ***anticipatory repudiation.***

C. CONTRACTS UNENFORCEABLE BECAUSE OF LACK OF CAPACITY TO CONTRACT

1. **Minors' Contracts** §1313

   Contracts entered into by a person under the age of majority are generally unenforceable (with statutory exceptions). Most statutes provide that a minor may ***disaffirm*** any such contract, but are in disagreement as to whether a minor must restore the benefits received.

   a. **Estoppel to disaffirm** §1318

      If a minor has falsified his age, he is usually held to be estopped from disaffirming.

   b. **Bona fide purchaser** §1319

      In most jurisdictions, a BFP of property sold by a minor takes it subject to the minor's power of disaffirmance.

   c. **Exculpatory contracts** §1320

      A minor may avoid an otherwise valid release from liability for injuries to the minor.

   d. **Necessities of life** §1321

      A minor is liable in ***quasi-contract*** for the reasonable value of food, clothing, shelter, etc., provided during his minority.

2. **Mental Incapacity** §1323

   Mental incompetents have the same liability as minors for ***necessities.*** Furthermore, most courts require full restitution of any benefits obtained (or the value thereof) as long as the party furnishing the goods was ***unaware*** of the incapacity. However, because mental incompetents cannot form the requisite intent to deceive, ***no estoppel to disaffirm*** can be created by their representations.

3. **"Ultra Vires" Corporate Contracts** §1326

   Contracts made by a corporation that are beyond the powers of the corporate entity are ultra vires.

   a. **Private corporations** §1327

      Although the common law allowed ultra vires as a defense in some circumstances, the ***modern law abolishes ultra vires as a defense***. Acts in excess of corporate power are remediable by the ***state*** in ***quo warranto*** proceedings, ***or*** by a ***shareholders' suit*** to enjoin the ultra vires activity. Shareholders' derivative suits against officers or directors can require them to pay damages to the corporation for ultra vires acts that resulted in corporate loss.

   b. **Municipal and public corporations** §1332

      Municipal corporations have only such powers as are conferred by the state. ***Restitution*** is generally allowed where there has been a ***violation of administrative regulations*** and the governmental entity has benefited.

   (1) Statutes prohibiting collusion   **§1334**
     Where the violation is of a statute designed to prevent collusion between contractors and government officials, the contractor is usually denied quasi-contractual recovery. Where there is collusion by a contractor, a municipal corporation may recover any money paid.

4. Contracts by Unlicensed Contractors   **§1337**
  Many statutes prohibit unlicensed contractors from suing on construction contracts, and contractor's rights to quasi-contractual relief or mechanic's lien are usually denied as well. However, if an owner asserts a right under the contract, the unlicensed contractor may assert his claim by way of ***set-off***.

D. AGREEMENTS UNENFORCEABLE BECAUSE OF ILLEGALITY

1. In General   **§1340**
  An "illegal" contract is one that is criminal, tortious, or otherwise against public policy. The "general rule" is that there is ***no remedy***. However, some courts will enforce lawful provisions if they can be severed from illegal provisions. The doctrine of ***unclean hands*** militates against relief in equity.

2. Cases Where Defense of Illegality Is Not Applied   **§1346**
  The defense of illegality applies only if the public interest would be directly offended by the enforcement of the contract. If the claimed illegality is not directly involved with the performance or enforcement, the defense will be rejected and remedies (damages, specific performance, etc.) will be granted. Such circumstances include failure of the intended illegal purpose and cases where the illegality is collateral or remote. Third parties may not invoke the defense.

3. Exceptions to Defense of Illegality   **§1350**
  Restitution may be allowed where the public policy against the illegality is ***outweighed*** by the interest in preventing unjust enrichment.

  a. Plaintiff not "in pari delicto"   **§1351**
    If one party is not equally at fault with the other and ***no serious crime*** is involved, the relatively innocent party may be entitled to relief (*e.g.*, the plaintiff's status as a member of a statutorily protected class; the plaintiff's justifiable ignorance or mistake, coercion, fraud).

  b. "Locus poenitentiae"   **§1357**
    Even though the parties are in pari delicto, restitution will be permitted if the plaintiff backs out of the bargain ***before*** its illegal aspect has been accomplished. However, this rule is not applied if a serious crime is contemplated.

  c. Public policy exception   **§1359**
    An illegal bargain may be rescinded by either party if a condition contrary to public policy would otherwise ***continue*** to exist.

4. Restitution of Illegal Gain as Among Participants

a. **Among partners in an illegal enterprise**   §1360

The general rule is that a court will **not** "divide the spoils" between the parties to an illegal joint venture. However, where there is a *regular business partnership* and the illegality is only incidental (*e.g.*, lack of license), or in cases where no gains have been derived from innocent third parties, courts may fashion remedies to reach equitable results.

b. **Principals and agents**   §1363

An agent may not assert a principal's illegal act as a defense to her duty to account. However, if the agent is *actively involved* in the illegal venture (not merely receiving proceeds), the agent and principal are treated as *co-participants,* and the principal may not compel the agent to account.

Approach to Exams

The law of remedies deals with the *nature* and *extent* of relief a court may award for the infringement of a legal right.

Role of History: The doctrines and concepts that make up the law of remedies have evolved piecemeal, rather than in any systematized fashion. In many instances, the doctrines are based on historical precedents or archaic doctrines that have little current relevancy. Most importantly, the historic division between law and equity has had, and continues to have, a pervasive and profound effect on remedial choices. In any event, an awareness and understanding of the historical development of these doctrines is essential to your understanding of modern day remedial problems.

Role of Statutes: In many areas, the common law doctrines have been modified (and in some cases expanded) by statute. It follows that the choice of remedies in such areas must be based on the content and interpretation of such statutes. You should especially realize that some of these statutes are of such widespread enactment (*e.g.*, the Uniform Commercial Code) that the common law remedies have been virtually supplanted.

Role of Substantive Law: The initial step in your analysis of remedial problems is to identify the substantive law area underlying the claim for relief—whether tort, contract, or unjust enrichment. Once you have identified the area of law, you can begin your analysis of remedial rights. In each case, the availability of damages, restitution, and injunctive or other equitable relief should be separately considered. Use the following questions to help you focus on the issues.

1. **Is There a Damages Remedy Available?**

    a. Has *causation* of the plaintiff's injury by the defendant's act or omission been shown?

    b. What is the *measure* of compensatory damages?

        (1) If a "diminution in value" standard is used, *how* and *when* is "value" determined?

        (2) Has the standard of *certainty* been met?

    c. In *contract* cases, are any additional items recoverable as *consequential* damages under the rule of **Hadley v. Baxendale**?

    d. In *tort* cases, is the defendant's conduct sufficiently willful or malicious so that *punitive* damages should be awarded?

e. Are there any *limitations* on damages?

   (1) Does the *avoidable consequences rule* apply?

   (2) Has the plaintiff taken steps to *mitigate damages* suffered?

2. Is a Restitutionary Remedy Available?

a. Does the defendant have a *"benefit"* which is *"unjust"* for him to retain?

b. How should the "benefit" be *measured*—its actual value to the defendant, its cost to the plaintiff, what it would have cost the defendant to buy elsewhere, etc.?

c. Is the plaintiff *limited* to a quasi-contract action, or may she obtain restitution in equity, by way of a constructive trust, equitable lien, accounting, or subrogation?

d. Are there any *defenses* to restitutionary relief—*e.g.*, change of position, discharge for value (bona fide purchaser), or possibly the equitable defenses below?

3. Is Equitable Relief Available?

a. Is the remedy at law *inadequate*?

b. Would equitable relief be *feasible* and *fair*?

c. Are *special equitable doctrines* applicable—laches, unclean hands, unconscionability, duress, mistake, estoppel, etc.?

Chapter One: Introduction

Outline

CONTENTS

Chapter Approach

This chapter introduces you to basic classifications and terminology concerning remedies. Although the information contained in this chapter is mainly background material, it is not unimportant—quite the contrary; for almost any remedies question, you need to understand the following basic concepts.

A. Introduction

1. Scope of Subject [§1]

The law of remedies is concerned with the principles and rules governing the *form and type of relief* awarded by courts to protect and vindicate rights recognized by the substantive law.

2. Classification of Remedies [§2]

Judicial remedies may be conveniently classified according to function and by historical origin.

B. Types of Remedies

1. Function of Remedy

a. Damages

(1) Compensatory damages [§3]

Compensatory damages provide an award of money to the aggrieved party to compensate for any loss or injury. It is a substitutionary remedy—*i.e.,* money for harm. In *tort* cases, the objective of damages is *to make the plaintiff whole* by awarding sufficient money to indemnify the plaintiff for the loss. In *contract* cases, the objective of damages is not only to compensate for loss, but also *to protect the plaintiff's expectation interest* by awarding a sum of money equivalent to what the plaintiff would have received if the contract had been performed.

(2) Nominal damages [§4]

Nominal damages are awarded in situations where the plaintiff's right has been violated, but *no loss is sustained* or the *extent of the injury cannot be measured*. Such an award is in effect a declaration of the plaintiff's right and a determination that the defendant has wrongfully infringed upon it. [**Kincaid Enterprises v. Porter**, 753 S.W.2d 503 (Mo. 1988)—breach of contract gives rise to nominal damages and submissible case regardless of amount of actual loss]

(3) Punitive damages [§5]

A sum of money may be awarded in addition to compensatory damages to *punish* the defendant for *willful, wanton, or malicious conduct* and to *deter* such conduct by the defendant and others.

b. Restitution [§6]

The remedy of restitution restores to the plaintiff any benefit the wrongdoer may have gained from misconduct. The objective of the remedy is to compel the wrongdoer to disgorge any *unjust gain or enrichment*.

(1) Substitutionary remedies [§7]

Restitutionary remedies are usually substitutionary—*i.e.,* they provide the plaintiff with a *monetary* recovery measured by the unjust gain, rather than with the precise thing wrongfully obtained by the defendant. Examples of substitutionary restitutionary remedies include quasi-contract actions at law, and constructive trust, equitable lien, and subrogation in equity.

(2) Specific remedies in restitution [§8]

Specific restitutionary remedies provide *recovery of the precise thing* wrongfully obtained by the defendant from the plaintiff. In this sense, replevin of chattels and ejectment are restitutionary. A mandatory equity decree ordering the return of real or personal property is another example.

c. Specific relief [§9]

The remedy of specific relief gives to the injured party the precise *performance* promised rather than its equivalent in money. Specific performance of contracts, in which the defendant is ordered to perform his promise, illustrates this type of relief.

d. Preventive relief [§10]

Preventive relief affords protection of the plaintiff's rights by a decree prohibiting (enjoining) the defendant from doing certain acts or engaging in particular activities infringing on the plaintiff's interests.

e. Declaratory relief [§11]

A declaratory judgment *conclusively determines the rights of parties* involved in a contested issue, thereby settling the controversy without awarding any additional relief, such as damages, restitution, or a coercive decree.

2. Historical Origins of Remedies [§12]

Historically, remedies have been classified as either legal or equitable.

a. Legal remedies [§13]

Legal remedies, developed through the common law forms of action, are largely substitutionary and result in *judgments for money* to compensate for loss or injury. This is the origin of the remedy called *damages*. These judgments are enforced by various forms of execution in which property of the defendant is sold to realize the amount owed to the plaintiff.

(1) But note

Legal remedies may also be restitutionary, as, for example, actions in *quasi-contract* (explained *infra*), judgments of *ejectment* (to recover possession of realty), and *replevin* (to recover chattels). Even in these cases, the judgments are enforced by *writs* executed by the sheriff or marshal.

b. Equitable remedies [§14]

Equitable remedies, developed in the Court of Chancery, are generally specific and impose personal obligations or duties on the defendant. Whether these decrees are prohibitory in form (*i.e.*, ordering the defendant to desist from certain acts) or affirmative (*i.e.*, requiring action to be taken), the decree is ordinarily enforced by *coercing* appropriate conduct from the defendant—ordinarily by contempt proceedings.

c. Limitation [§15]

An injured party is not entirely free to select the remedy he considers most desirable. The choice of remedies is subject to the basic limitation (which grew out of the historical division between law and equity) that *equitable remedies are appropriate only where legal remedies are not adequate or are nonexistent.*

LEGAL VS. EQUITABLE REMEDIES—IN GENERAL		gilbert
	LEGAL REMEDIES	**EQUITABLE REMEDIES**
ORIGIN	Common law	Court of Chancery
FORM OF REMEDY	*Substitutionary* (*i.e.*, judgments for money) or *restitutionary* (*e.g.*, judgments of replevin)	Coercion of appropriate conduct from defendant
WHEN AVAILABLE	When money or restitution is adequate compensation for the injury	When the legal remedy is inadequate or unavailable
EXAMPLES	Compensatory damages, punitive damages, recovery in quasi-contract	Injunction, specific performance

---

EXAM TIP   **gilbert**

It is very important to remember that equitable relief generally will **not be granted if the remedy at law will suffice**. Thus, if damages can adequately compensate a plaintiff, as in most cases involving a breach of contract for the sale of goods, an equitable remedy, such as specific performance, will not be available.

---

3. **Imprecise Classification—The Consequences [§16]**

The classifications of remedies above are usually observed in legal analysis, but the word "damages" is diluted in usage. For instance, reference may be made to equity decrees for payment of money as "equitable damages" and restitutionary judgments for money are, as often as not, called "restitutionary damages" or "the restitutionary measure of damages." Moreover, the classifications are not likely to be observed in common parlance. This is of little practical consequence except when the unqualified word "damages" appears in statutes or documents.

a. **Interpretation of statutes [§17]**

In the case of statutes, the term "damages" is usually given the traditional definition—*i.e.,* "an award of money recoverable in an action at law."

---

e.g. **Example:** Internal Revenue Code section 104(a)(2) states that "gross income does not include . . . the amount of any damages received . . . on account of personal injuries." Sparrow, a taxpayer, sought to exclude from income money received as "back pay" in settlement of a sex discrimination claim under Title VII of the Civil Rights Act of 1964. *Held:* Back pay is an equitable remedy akin to restitution and therefore the money is not excludable. [**Sparrow v. Commission of Internal Revenue,** 949 F.2d 434 (D.C. Cir. 1991); **United States v. Burke,** 504 U.S. 229 1867 (1992); *and see infra,* §735]

---

cf. **Compare:** A typical consumer protection statute denounces unfair or deceptive commercial practices, and provides that "if damages are assessed in such case" judgment shall be for treble the amount fixed. Purchaser, a buyer of real property, sought to rescind the contract—based on fraud and deceptive trade practices—and recover the amount paid. The trial court trebled the award based on the consumer protection statute. The appellate court reversed, stating "[r]escission is inconsistent with damages." If an automobile purchaser aggrieved by a defective steering mechanism which can be replaced for $250 (damages, which if trebled would be $750) were able to elect to rescind and recover the purchase price of $15,000, the trebled award would be $45,000. If the purchase price were $50,000, the award would be $150,000. Therefore, the award here is not "damages" and is not subject to trebling under the statute. [**Winant v. Bostic,** 5 F.3d 767 (4th Cir. 1993); **Smith v. Bennett Ford,** 864 S.W.2d 817 (Ark. 1993)—Federal Odometer Fraud Act]

---

b. Interpretation of insurance contract—environmental litigation [§18]

On the other hand, classifying damages as a remedy to compensate for loss has become of enormous significance in environmental litigation. Polluters who have been ordered to remedy, prevent, or remove hazardous waste sites have looked to their insurance carriers for indemnification for these expenses, which are estimated to total $125 billion. The insurance policies in question cover "damages to persons or property, for which the insured is legally liable," or some similar variation. Insurers assert that they are required by contract to indemnify only for legal (*i.e.,* compensatory) damages assessed against their insureds; that expenses to comply with orders to take preventative measures are equitable; that costs incurred in obeying clean-up orders are equitable and restitutionary, as they are designed to restore the status quo ante rather than to compensate for losses. Most debatable are costs of clean-up of toxic waste dumps mandated by governmental agencies, *e.g.,* under the Comprehensive Environmental Response, Compensation and Liability Act of 1980 ("CERCLA"), where there has as yet been no property or personal injury *off* the premises. There is no disagreement that these are not traditional legal damages, but the hundreds of decisions are divided on the issue of whether the policy language provides coverage to the polluters. The apparent majority holds that it does. [*See, e.g.,* **Boeing Co. v. Aetna Casualty & Surety Co.**, 784 P.2d 507 (Wash. 1990); *and see* **AIU Insurance Co. v. Superior Court**, 51 Cal. 3d 807 (1990)—response costs (but not costs of preventive measures taken before the pollution occurred) are covered] But formidable authority holds that there is no coverage, leaving the polluters to pay the costs if they can afford them. [*See* **Maryland Casualty v. ARMCO**, 822 F.2d 1348 (4th Cir. 1987), *cert. denied*, 484 U.S. 1008 (1988); *and see* **Continental Insurance v. Northeastern Pharmaceutical & Chemical Co.**, 842 F.2d 977 (8th Cir. 1988)]

(1) Comment

Since the classification of remedies has been thoroughly argued in all such cases, the departure from standard classifications is likely due less to misapprehension than to the canons of insurance policy interpretation and the practice of giving nontechnical construction to the language.

(2) Note

Do not expect to see the above language regarding coverage in new liability policies.

Chapter Two: Damages

CONTENTS

Chapter Approach

Chapter Approach

This chapter explains and describes doctrines and principles generally applicable to the law of damages. For exam purposes, it is particularly important for you to be aware of the distinct limitations governing the recovery of tort and contract damages (*e.g.*, recovery in tort is limited by *proximate cause*, while contract recovery may be limited by the requirement that *consequential damages* be foreseeable), as well as the *general limitations* that apply to both types of damages (*e.g.*, certainty requirement).

A. Tort vs. Contract Damages

1. In General [§19]

The law of damages attempts to establish *standards for measuring* the monetary award needed to compensate the aggrieved party for losses and injuries.

2. Tort Damages [§20]

If a party has sustained harm because of a tort, the objective of the remedy of compensatory damages is to place the injured party in substantially as good a position as she occupied *prior to the wrong*.

3. Contract Damages [§21]

If a party is injured by breach of a contract, the objective of compensatory damages is to place the injured party in substantially as good a position as she would have had *if the contract had been performed*. *Rationale*: This measure of damages protects the plaintiff's *expectation interest* by awarding any profits that might have been realized from full performance of the contract.

EXAM TIP   **gilbert**

If you forget a particular measure of damages, remembering the difference in the objectives of tort damages versus contract damages may help you out. Tort damages are intended to **restore** the plaintiff's past condition, whereas contract damages are intended to put the plaintiff into an **expected** (*i.e.*, future) condition.

---

a. Distinguish—reliance damages [§22]

As an alternative, in cases where profits are difficult or impossible to prove, the injured party may recover expenditures made in reliance on the contract. Ordinarily, this involves expenses incurred in preparing to perform or in part performance prior to breach of the contract.

Example: Wartzman, a lawyer, was employed to incorporate an entity, Hightower Productions, Ltd. ("Hightower"), in furtherance of a promotional scheme. Because of Wartzman's failure to file certain disclosures required by the state's security laws, Hightower was not allowed to sell stock to the public. As a result, the project failed. Hightower was able to recover from Wartzman as reliance damages losses incurred in preparing to go forward with the promotion. [**Wartzman v. Hightower Productions, Ltd.**, 456 A.2d 82 (Md. 1983)]

(1) But note

Reliance damages will be offset by any loss that defendant can prove plaintiff would have suffered had the contract been fully performed. Otherwise the reliance measure of recovery would put the injured party in a *better* position than if the contract had been completed. If plaintiff's losses on full performance exceed reliance damages, there is no damage remedy at all (but other remedies may be available). [**Bausch & Lomb, Inc. v. Dressler**, 977 F.2d 720 (2d Cir. 1992)]

4. Consequential Damages Limitation in Contract Cases—Rule of Hadley v. Baxendale [§23]

The landmark case of **Hadley v. Baxendale**, 156 Eng. Rep. 145 (1854), states a rule limiting damages for breach of contract that is still followed. The rule is that "special damages for breach of contract are not recoverable unless they can fairly and reasonably be considered as arising *naturally* from the breach *or as being within the contemplation of the parties, at the time the contract was made*, as the probable result of the breach."

a. Basic effect [§24]

This rule has the effect of restricting liability and thus *reducing the risk of commercial enterprises*. To hold the defendant contract-breaker liable, the plaintiff must show that the loss was one that would naturally result from the breach, or that at the time the contract was made the parties knew of the particular facts that would make the loss expectable. [*Compare* **Hector Martinez & Co. v. Southern Pacific Transportation Co.**, 606 F.2d 106 (5th Cir. 1979)— lost use of a dragline (*i.e.*, an excavating machine) from delay in shipment foreseeable; *with* **T.M. Long Co. v. Jarrett**, 397 A.2d 735 (N.J. 1979)—loss of use of capital equipment due to delay in shipping steel plates not recoverable when defendant did not have notice that the plates were specially manufactured and not easily replaceable]

Example: In *Hadley*, the court ruled that delay in delivering machinery by a carrier did not subject the carrier to liability for lost profits. The carrier had no reason to suspect that the plaintiff's mill would close down because of the delay.

> **cf.** **Compare:** In **Krauss v. Greenbarg**, 137 F.2d 569 (3d Cir. 1943), the court found that the defendant *knew* that its failure to deliver on schedule would subject the plaintiff to the provisions of a penalty clause. Hence, the defendant was held liable for such losses.

EXAM TIP | **gilbert**

In an exam situation, you should determine whether a party in a contract action can recover consequential damages flowing from the other party's breach (*e.g.,* lost profits from work stoppage caused by other party's breach). However, be sure to remember that these damages must be *foreseeable*; *i.e.,* they must arise naturally from the breach or be within the contemplation of the parties at the time the contract was made.

---

b. Uniform Commercial Code [§25]

The U.C.C. adopts the principle of *Hadley* by limiting the buyer's consequential damages to losses resulting from requirements or needs "which the seller at the time of contracting had reason to know . . . ." [U.C.C. §2-715(2)(a)]

c. Mental anguish [§26]

The general rule is that damages for mental anguish may *not* be recovered in an action for breach of contract. [*See* **Erlich v. Menzes**, 21 Cal. 4th 543 (1999)—denying recovery for emotional distress caused by negligent performance of a contract to build a house; *and see* **Dean v. Dean**, 821 F.2d 279 (5th Cir. 1987)] An exception to this rule allows recovery for mental suffering when the contract is one where *serious emotional distress* is a *particularly likely result* of a breach. Typical examples are contracts of carriers, innkeepers, and funeral homes. [*See, e.g.,* **Ross v. Forest Lawn Memorial Park**, 153 Cal. App. 3d 988 (1984)—mother was entitled to damages for emotional distress when cemetery negligently breached its promise to exclude "punk rockers," including a "punk rocker" wearing a dress adorned with live rats, from her teenage daughter's funeral]

5. Proximate Cause Limitations in Torts Cases [§27]

Tort damages are limited by the doctrine of proximate cause. Under the doctrine, a defendant is liable for injuries that are *reasonably foreseeable as a natural consequence of the defendant's wrongful act*. Foreseeability in tort relates only to the issue of *liability*. It does not impose a limit on the recovery of *damages*, as in contract cases.

a. Unforeseeable extent of injury—"thin skull" doctrine [§28]

A negligent defendant is liable for the resulting harm even though the harm is increased by the particular plaintiff's condition at the time of the negligent conduct. [**Schafer v. Hoffman**, 831 P.2d 897 (Colo. 1992)—degeneration in plaintiff's knee aggravated by the accident]

b. Possible alternative view [§29]

At least one court has applied the rule of **Hadley v. Baxendale,** *supra,* §23—focusing on foreseeability of damages rather than on foreseeability of liability—in a negligence action in order to limit the defendant's liability in a *contract-like commercial setting*. [**Evra Corp. v. Swiss Bank Corp.,** 673 F.2d 951 (7th Cir. 1982)] In *Evra Corp.,* a bank not in privity of contract with the plaintiff failed to make a prompt transfer of funds ($27,000) requested by the plaintiff's bank, which resulted in the plaintiff defaulting on and losing a long-term ship charter contract that was at a very favorable rate. The plaintiff sued the bank to recover its lost profits (over $2 million). The court reasoned that the plaintiff's recovery in this commercial setting should not be any more expansive than it would be if the parties were in privity of contract and held that the defendant was not liable—because the defendant did not know the terms of the plaintiff's shipping contract, the plaintiff's damages were not foreseeable.

c. Qualification—purely economic losses [§30]

It is the accepted common law rule that absent privity of contract or an injury to person or property, a plaintiff may not recover for economic loss in a *negligence* case even though proximately caused.

Example: Plaintiffs alleged that defendants negligently designed a hotel and that this negligence contributed to its destruction by fire. Plaintiffs, employees of the hotel, sought to recover lost wages for the period of unemployment resulting from the fire. *Held:* No recovery. [**Local Joint Executive Board v. Stern,** 651 P.2d 637 (Nev. 1982)]

Example: A public bridge was closed because of defective steel furnished by the prime contractor, Pittsburgh-Des Moines Corp. Establishments whose customers used the bridge sustained a loss of business due to the closure. *Held:* The establishments could not recover in tort for their purely economic loss. [**Nebraska Innkeepers, Inc. v. Pittsburgh-Des Moines Corp.,** 345 N.W.2d 124 (Iowa 1984)]

Example: Tusch Enterprises, the buyer of a duplex, sought to recover on a negligence theory for certain structural defects causing loss of rental income and property damage. *Held:* These economic losses cannot be recovered in a negligence action, but only in an action for breach of a warranty of habitability. [**Tusch Enterprises v. Coffin,** 740 P.2d 1022 (Idaho 1987); *and see* **Jim Walter Homes v. Reed,** 711 S.W.2d 617 (Tex. 1986)]

Example: Daanen & Janssen, Inc. purchased from a distributor of Cedarapids, Inc. a replacement part for a crushing machine manufactured by Cedarapids, Inc. The part was defective, causing loss of income and repair costs. *Held:* The economic loss doctrine precluded recovery of these losses in a tort action. [*See* **Daanen & Janssen, Inc. v. Cedarapids, Inc.,** 573 N.W.2d 842 (Wis. 1988)]

Example: A train derailment allegedly caused by B&O Railroad's negligence resulted in a loss of wages for employees of a plant damaged in the derailment. *Held*: The employees could not recover for economic loss in an action based on B&O Railroad's negligence. [*See* **Aikens v. Baltimore & Ohio Railroad,** 501 A.2d 277 (Pa. 1985)]

Compare: Gregory entered into a contract with the county to renovate heating and air conditioning equipment in a county building. Because of Gregory's lack of diligence in completing the work, J'Aire Corp., a tenant of the county operating a restaurant on the premises, lost business. *Held:* The loss was foreseeable and closely connected with Gregory's conduct. Hence the complaint should not have been dismissed. [**J'Aire Corp. v. Gregory,** 24 Cal. 3d 799 (1979)]

d. Qualification—products liability cases [§31]

Recovery for purely economic loss in products liability cases is generally denied whether the theory of the complaint is negligence or strict liability. The injured party must look to the contract for relief. This has the effect of restricting the remedy to breach of warranty as provided by the Uniform Commercial Code.

Example: National Tank Co. manufactured a tank that ruptured but caused no damage to person or property. It did cause losses to Moorman Manufacturing Co.'s business operations. The court denied recovery for these purely economic losses. [**Moorman Manufacturing Co. v. National Tank Co.,** 435 N.E.2d 443 (Ill. 1982); *and see* **Florida Power & Light v. Westinghouse Electric Corp.,** 510 So. 2d 899 (Fla. 1987); *but see* **Board of Education v. A, C and S, Inc.,** 525 N.E.2d 950 (Ill. 1988)—finding that asbestos-containing products created a health hazard rather than mere economic loss]

(1) Rationale

This restrictive approach to the recovery of economic loss appears to be due to a fear of imposing unlimited liability of unknown dimensions.

B. Limitations on Damages

1. Certainty as to Existence of Damages [§32]

Damages may be an essential element in stating a valid claim against a defendant (*e.g.*, in negligence claims). In these cases, damages must be proved with certainty and not be left to speculation and conjecture. This means that there must be *proof sufficient to establish a probability of loss* in the minds of reasonable persons. [**United States Trust Co. v. O'Brien**, 143 N.Y. 284 (1894); **Highland Construction Co. v. Union Pacific Railroad**, 263 P.2d 1042 (Utah 1984)]

a. **Certainty as to extent of damages [§33]**

The "certainty" requirement does not mean that damages have to be proved with mathematical precision in every case. In many instances, if the *existence* of damages is *certain* (*i.e.*, there is sufficient proof that plaintiff has sustained some damage), recovery will be permitted even though the *extent or amount* of damages is *uncertain*. The fact of damages having been proved, the court may infer the amount necessary to compensate the plaintiff. [**Texaco, Inc. v. Pennzoil Co.**, 729 S.W.2d 768 (Tex. 1987); **Buell, Winter, Mousel v. Olmstead & Perry**, 420 N.W.2d 280 (Neb. 1988)]

---

e.g. **Example:** Subcontractor sued to recover the balance due on a construction contract, and General Contractor filed a cross-complaint seeking damages for breach by Subcontractor of a subcontract. The evidence clearly showed that Subcontractor *had* breached the subcontract, but General Contractor had kept no separate cost record to establish the amount of loss. *Held:* General Contractor may recover damages for Subcontractor's breach. The *fact* of damages being established, *uncertainty as to amount is not fatal* to the cause of action, and the claimant as the prevailing party may recover costs, although the award itself may be nominal. [**Wenzler & Ward Plumbing & Heating Co. v. Sellen**, 330 P.2d 1068 (Wash. 1959)]

---

b. **"Certainty" as limitation in loss of profits case [§34]**

The application of the certainty doctrine is most frequently found in the attempt to estimate the loss of commercial profits. If the plaintiff is a business with an *established* record of profitability, the certainty standard can be met. With new businesses, however, recovery of lost profits is frequently denied on the ground that they are speculative and uncertain. [**Kenford Co. v. County of Erie**, 67 N.Y.2d 257 (1986)—prospective profits from operation of a proposed domed stadium; **Lowder v. Missouri Baptist College**, 752 S.W.2d 425 (Mo. 1988)—prospective profits from operation of a proposed health club] More recent cases have tended to be less rigid, permitting recovery if plaintiff can establish a reasonably certain factual basis for the computation. [**MacLean & Associates v. American Guaranty Life Insurance Co.**, 736 P.2d 586 (Or. 1987)—wrongful termination of a proposed cable TV system, expert testimony found sufficient; **Hiller v. Manufacturers Product Research Group of North America, Inc.**, 59 F.3d 1514 (5th Cir. 1995)—evidence of canceled specific contracts of sale held sufficient; *and see infra*, §493]

EXAM TIP **gilbert**

If faced with an exam question involving lost profits of a *new business*, do *not* simply assume that these damages must be denied as uncertain. Look for facts that might allow for a more certain calculation, as in the last two cases, above.

c. Certainty as to future damages

(1) "All or nothing" approach [§35]

All future damages are inherently uncertain both as to their existence and extent. To prove their existence there must be a showing that they will more likely than not happen or that there is a reasonable probability that they will occur. In short, there must be better than a 50-50 chance of future damages; otherwise, the claim will be dismissed. However, if future damages are more likely than not to occur, they will be assessed by taking evidence as to the amount of harm expected to be proximately caused. This approach is commonly referred to as *"all or nothing."*

Examples: A personal injury plaintiff is an outstanding under-graduate student who has been accepted for law school. Since the chances of her becoming an attorney are better than 50%, the calculation of future earnings will be based on those of a lawyer rather than a student or simply a college graduate.

Compare: John has been exposed to a toxic substance. His statistical probability of developing cancer is 43%. He has no present cause of action. [**Pollock v. Johns-Manville Sales Corp.,** 686 F. Supp. 489 (D.N.J. 1988)] Had the risk been 51%, John presumably would have been allowed to claim damages for the enhanced risk of injury.

(a) Qualifications [§36]

Where defendant's actions result in fear of an increased risk of contracting a disease (*e.g.,* cancer), some courts have permitted recovery. [**Sterling v. Velsicol Chemical Corp.,** 855 F.2d 1188 (6th Cir. 1988)] Other courts have permitted recovery of medical monitoring costs where evidence clearly establishes the toxic exposure. [**Potter v. Firestone Tire & Rubber Co.,** 6 Cal. 4th 965 (1993); *see infra*, §743]

(2) Alternative approach [§37]

The alternative to the "all or nothing" approach would be to estimate the maximum amount as well as the probability of future damages. The award would be fixed at the maximum damages possible multiplied by the determined probability percentage. This approach finds support from academicians but very little from the judiciary.

(a) Qualification—value of lost chance of prize cases [§38]

In a limited group of cases, the injury consists of the loss of a chance to win a prize. One way of valuing the chance is to simply divide the prize by the number of entrants. This notion dates back to the well-known case of **Champlin v. Hicks,** [1911] 2 K.B. 786, where the plaintiff, one of 50 contestants for 12 prizes in a beauty contest, lost any chance of winning when she was not notified of the time to appear until too late.

(b) Qualification—value of lost chance in medical malpractice cases [§39]

A patient suffering from disease or injury and rated as having only a 20% chance of survival undergoes emergency treatment during which medical malpractice occurs. The patient dies. Since there is less than a 50-50 probability that the doctor's misconduct caused the death, the standard "all or nothing" approach requires dismissal of the action. [**Kramer v. Lewisville Memorial Hospital**, 858 S.W.2d 397 (Tex. 1993)—three judges dissenting] However, a sizable number of recent cases have recognized some form of the lost chance doctrine and allowed proportional compensation (here, 20%). [**Perez v. Las Vegas Medical Center**, 805 P.2d 589 (Nev. 1991)—three to two decision]

DETERMINING FUTURE DAMAGES—"ALL OR NOTHING" APPROACH VS. ALTERNATIVE APPROACH — gilbert

	"ALL OR NOTHING" APPROACH	ALTERNATIVE APPROACH
WHEN WILL FUTURE DAMAGES BE AWARDED	When there is more than a 50% chance that future damages will occur.	When any future damages are possible.
METHOD OF COMPUTATION OF AWARD	Evaluate evidence as to amount of harm expected to be proximately caused.	Multiply maximum future damages possible by the probability percentage that they will occur.
EXAMPLE	Jennifer has a 49% chance of developing a heart condition after receiving an electric shock. She will not recover for these future damages under the "all or nothing" approach.	Jennifer has a 49% chance of developing a heart condition after receiving an electric shock. If she develops a heart condition, she will be damaged in the amount of $1 million. She will be awarded 49% of $1 million (i.e., $490,000) under the alternative approach.

2. "Special" Damages Must Be Pleaded [§40]

Another basic damages rule is that "special" damages (as opposed to "general" damages) must be pleaded to be recoverable.

a. General damages [§41]

General damages are those that so naturally result from the wrong (*e.g.*, pain from physical injury) that the defendant is in effect *on notice* that these will be claimed from the mere fact that a lawsuit is filed complaining of the wrong. Hence, such damages need not be specially pleaded to be recoverable.

b. **Special damages [§42]**

On the other hand, special damages are the losses that cannot be presumed or estimated simply because the wrong has occurred (*e.g.*, wage losses from physical injury). They are losses or expenses unique or "special" to the plaintiff; as such, they must be specially pleaded if they are to be claimed in order to give defendant *adequate notice* of the nature and extent of the claim against him.

(1) **Classification of lost profits [§43]**

Lost profits are considered to be general damages in a breach of contract case, while in a tort case, they are considered to be special damages. [*See* **Moore v. Boating Industry Associations**, 754 F.2d 698 (7th Cir. 1985)]

(2) **Special damages as element of claim [§44]**

Moreover, there are certain actions that lie only if special damages have been sustained (*e.g.*, fraud). In such cases, the requirement that special damages be pleaded is *essential* to *state a cause of action*.

3. **Causation Requirement [§45]**

A defendant is liable only for those injuries that in fact were caused by her wrongful act or omission. Questions of causation are ordinarily resolved by the "but for" test—*i.e.*, *but for* defendant's act, the loss would not have occurred.

a. **Contract vs. tort [§46]**

Note that in *both* tort and contract cases, the causation test must be met. In contract cases, however, losses caused by the defendant's breach are also limited by *Hadley* (*see supra*, §23). In tort cases, *liability is limited only by the doctrine of proximate cause.*

4. **Rule of Avoidable Consequences [§47]**

The rule of avoidable consequences states that a party may not recover for losses that could have been avoided by the use of reasonable means. [**Anderson v. Bauer**, 681 P.2d 1316 (Wyo. 1984)] The burden of proof is on the defendant to establish that damages could have been lessened. [*See* **Jones v. Consolidated Rail Corp.**, 800 F.2d 590 (6th Cir. 1986)]

a. **Rationale**

The purpose of the rule is to avoid economic loss. This purpose is achieved by denying recovery to the injured party for any item of loss that could have been reasonably avoided, thus encouraging the injured party to mitigate losses. Numerous illustrations of this doctrine will be found in the chapters that follow (*see, e.g., infra*, §785). It is to be distinguished from steps taken by the *defendant* to lessen liability, also often referred to as mitigation of damages.

b. Effect of inflation [§48]

The plaintiff is *not required* to take action to prevent an increase in costs due to inflation. *Rationale*: The increase is not a real increase in cost to the defendant, who will be paying an award with money which has also decreased in value. Including a rise in costs due solely to inflation within the duty to minimize damages simply means that the claimant rather than the wrongdoer must bear the risk of inflation. [**Anchorage Asphalt Paving Co. v. Lewis**, 629 P.2d 65 (Alaska 1982)]

c. Distinguish—contributory or comparative negligence [§49]

The avoidable consequences doctrine is to be distinguished from the contributory and comparative negligence doctrines. The contributory and comparative negligence doctrines refer to conduct of the plaintiff that occurs *before* and is a *cause* of the original injury, while the avoidable consequences doctrine usually refers to the failure of the plaintiff to limit the injurious effects of the injury *after* it has occurred.

C. Other Damages Issues

1. Agreed (or Liquidated) Damages [§50]

If damages are difficult or impossible to ascertain, contractual provisions providing for payment of a stipulated sum of money upon breach of the agreement are upheld if the amount to be paid bears a *reasonable relationship to the anticipated loss*. [**United Air Lines v. Austin Travel Corp.**, 867 F.2d 737 (2d Cir. 1989); **Coldwell Banker v. Meide & Son**, 422 N.W.2d 375 (N.D. 1988); **Walter Implement v. Focht**, 730 P.2d 1340 (Wash. 1987); *and see infra*, §1095] The burden of proof of unreasonableness is on the challenging party. [**Shallow Brook Associates v. Dube**, 599 A.2d 132 (N.H. 1991)—22% of total contract price not unreasonable]

a. Effect of valid liquidated damages clause [§51]

If a liquidated damage clause is enforceable, it is controlling and actual damages need *not be proved*. [**Young Electric Sign v. United Standard West**, 755 P.2d 162 (Utah 1988)] The nonbreaching party has no duty to mitigate the damages (*i.e.*, avoid the consequences). [**Lake Ridge Academy v. Carney**, 613 N.E.2d 183 (Ohio 1993)]

b. Distinguish—penalty [§52]

If the damages clause is *designed* to assure payment of more than actual damages, it is considered a "penalty" and is *unenforceable*. [**Lake River Corp. v. Carborundum Co.**, 769 F.2d 1284 (7th Cir. 1985)]

c. Distinguish—alternative remedies [§53]

A liquidated damage clause that allows the nonbreaching party to seek *either* actual damages *or* the liquidated amount is *unenforceable*. [**Grossinger Motorcorp v. American National Bank & Trust**, 607 N.E.2d 1337 (Ill. 1992); **Catholic Charities of Archdiocese of Chicago v. Thorpe**, 741 N.E.2d 651 (Ill. 2000); *and see infra*, §1095]

2. Maximizing the Award

a. Punitive damages

(1) Torts cases [§54]

An award of punitive damages serves the twin purposes of punishment and deterrence. [*See* **Tuttle v. Raymond III**, 494 A.2d 1353 (Me. 1985)] Punitive damages are awarded in tort cases where the defendant has been guilty of *willful misconduct* motivated by actual malice toward the plaintiff. A majority of jurisdictions and the United States Supreme Court in **Smith v. Wade**, 461 U.S. 30 (1983), have gradually *extended liability* for punitive damages to include "reckless or callous disregard of or indifference to the rights and safety of others." California recently expanded liability still further by adding "despicable conduct" to the list. Punitive damages are thus available in a wide range of tort cases including products liability claims. [*See* **G.D. Searle & Co. v. Superior Court**, 49 Cal. App. 3d 22 (1975)]

(a) Constitutional challenges

1) Excessive fine challenge [§55]

Not all jurisdictions agree that punitive damages are proper in civil litigation, and a sustained attack on their constitutionality has been launched by the business community. The Supreme Court, in **Browning-Ferris Industries v. Kelco Disposal**, 492 U.S. 257 (1989), upheld an award of punitive damages in a civil action between private parties against an assertion that the award violated the Excessive Fine Clause of the Eighth Amendment.

2) Due process challenges [§56]

Subsequently, the Court upheld an award of punitive damages against a due process attack. In rejecting the argument that the award was the "product of unbridled jury discretion," the Court noted that the jury was properly instructed and the award was reviewed by both the trial and appellate courts. [**Pacific Mutual Life Insurance Co. v. Haslip**, 111 499 U.S. 1 (1991)] The rationale of *Haslip* provided the basis for upholding a $10 million punitive damage award in **TXO Production Corp.**

v. Alliance Resources Corp., 509 U.S. 443 (1993). The Court refused to state a constitutional test to determine whether an award is excessive, and ruled instead that "general concerns of reasonableness" determine whether the award is "grossly excessive."

a)   Procedural safeguard required [§57]

In **Honda Motor Co. v. Oberg,** 512 U.S. 415 (1994), a $5 million punitive damage award was attacked on the ground that Oregon law did not provide a procedure for reducing or setting aside such an award solely on the basis of the amount of the award. The Court reversed the award, holding that the failure to provide a procedural safeguard against an arbitrary deprivation of property violated the Due Process Clause. The Court went on to note that the Constitution does impose a substantive limit on the size of punitive damage awards, but stated that the formulation of a standard to identify an unconstitutionally excessive award was not at issue in the *Honda* case.

b)   Test for determining when punitive damages are excessive [§58]

The Court created a test for determining when a fine is "grossly excessive" in violation of the Due Process Clause in **B.M.W. v. Gore,** 517 U.S. 559 (1996). Ignoring earlier comments, the Court laid down three guideposts for the determination of the excessiveness of an award in violation of the Due Process Clause: (i) the *reprehensibility* of the conduct; (ii) the *ratio of the award to the actual compensatory damages* assessed; and (iii) the *difference between this award and sanctions imposed by statute* for comparable compensable *criminal* misconduct.

1/   De novo standard of review [§59]

The standard of review on appeal is a *de novo* review of whether the standards enunciated by *Gore* have been properly applied. [**Cooper Industries v. Leatherman Tool Group,** 532 U.S. 424 (2001)]

(b)   Vicarious liability [§60]

There has been a division of authority on the issue of vicarious liability for punitive damages. Some courts hold principals (including corporations) vicariously liable for conduct of their agents resulting in punitive damages. [**Thiry v. Armstrong World Industries,** 661 P.2d 515 (Okla. 1983)] Most jurisdictions, however, have restricted vicarious liability to misconduct by employees at a managerial level, or to situations where the employer has specifically directed or ratified the employee's act. [**Loughry v. Lincoln First Bank,** 67 N.Y.2d 369 (1986); **Gould v. Taco Bell,** 772 P.2d 511 (Kan. 1986)]

(2) Contracts cases [§61]

Punitive damages are *not* awarded in breach of contract cases no matter how willful the breach unless the defendant's conduct can be described as amounting to an independent tort. [*But see* **Davis v. Gage,** 682 P.2d 1282 (Idaho 1984)]

(3) Must other damage be proved? [§62]

Punitive damages are parasitic and cannot be awarded until a *cause of action* for damages is first established. Moreover, if *"special" damages* must be proved to establish a cause of action (as in fraud cases), proof of such loss is a prerequisite to recovery of punitive damages. If *no special damages* are required, then punitive damages are recoverable in tort cases even where only nominal general damages are awarded (*e.g.,* a malicious battery may result in general damages of one dollar, plus punitive damages). [**Island Creek Coal Co. v. Lake Shore, Inc.,** 692 F. Supp. 629 (W.D. Va. 1988)—compensatory damages indispensable predicate for award of punitive damages; **James v. Public Finance Corp.,** 47 Cal. App. 3d 995 (1975)—award of punitive damages upheld in abuse of process case where actual injury was shown but compensatory damages were not included in verdict]

(4) Measure of punitive damages [§63]

No fixed standard for measuring punitive damages exists in most jurisdictions. Subject to the usual judicial review for passion and prejudice, the jury has discretion to award an amount it considers a "suitable punishment."

(a) Limitation [§64]

In some jurisdictions, the *costs of litigation* may be used as a measure. Most courts, however, follow a rule that the amount of punitive damages should be sufficient to *punish without financially annihilating* the defendant. [**Ace Truck & Equipment Rentals v. Kahn,** 746 P.2d 132 (Nev. 1987)—award of 30-40% of net worth of defendants found to be excessive] These courts insist that the amount of punitive damages bear some *reasonable relationship* both to the amount of compensatory damages otherwise recoverable by the plaintiff *and* to the net assets of the defendant. [**Little v. Stuyvesant Life Insurance Co.,** 67 Cal. App. 3d 451 (1977)—$2.5 million punitive damages held grossly disproportionate to the net assets of the company ($16,860,000) and the compensatory damages ($172,325);

thus award reduced to $250,000 or new trial ordered] There is, however, a wide disparity of views as to what is reasonable. [**Goshgarion v. George**, 161 Cal. App. 3d 1214 (1984)—10.7% of defendant's net assets held reasonable; **Contractor Utility Sales Co. v. Certain-Teed Corp.**, 748 F.2d 1151 (7th Cir. 1984)—four to one ratio upheld; **Devlin v. Kearney Mesa**, 155 Cal. App. 3d 1214 (1984)—27 times compensatory and 17.5% of net worth not excessive; *but see* **Arab Termite & Pest Control v. Jenkins**, 409 So. 2d 1039 (Fla. 1982)—since punitive damages serve a function different than do compensatory damages, there need be no reasonable relationship between them; **Lane County v. Wood**, 691 P.2d 473 (Or. 1984)—punitive damages are not to compensate but to give bad actors a legal spanking; **Thiry v. Armstrong World Industries**, *supra*, §60—wealth of defendant may be shown since punishment is achieved only "if defendant is stung by the award"]

(5) Punitive damages and insurance [§65]

Until recently, the majority of decisions took a strong public policy stand against the coverage of punitive damages by insurance. However, with the gradual relaxation of the requirement of actual malice and the increasing imposition of punitive awards of a vicarious nature, the situation has been reversed. [*See* 72 A.B.A. Journal 68 (1986)—lists applicable rules in various states] Of course, the mere holding that punitive damages are insurable does not mean that insurers will enthusiastically cover such liability.

(6) Punitive damages in multiple plaintiff cases [§66]

The economic effect of multiple punitive damage awards on a defendant faced with numerous claims arising from the same wrongful act has caused concern. One solution is the so-called one bite/first comer proposal, which would limit recovery of punitive damages to the first litigant. However, this was specifically rejected as an inappropriate remedy in **State *ex rel.* Young v. Crookham**, 618 P.2d 1268 (Or. 1980). Arguing that more appropriate solutions can be found, the court suggested as possible ways to deal with the problem either class actions or the introduction of evidence by defendant of prior awards of individual punitive damages or of criminal sanctions. [*See* **Owens-Corning Fiberglass Corp. v. Malone**, 972 S.W.2d 35 (Tex. 1998)—court limited proof of prior awards to the actual amount paid (not the amount stated in the verdict)] Numerous cases have upheld punitive damage awards in multiple tort situations. [*See* **Jackson v. Johns-Manville Products Corp.**, 781 F.2d 394 (5th Cir. 1986)] Whether repetitive awards violate due process is the subject of a difference of opinion. [*See* **McDermott v. Kansas Public Service Co.**, 712 P.2d 1199 (Kan. 1986)—found constitutional; **Dunn v. HOVIC**, 1 F.3d 1371 (3rd Cir. 1993)—court suggested that the problem should be resolved by Congress or legislatively] The Supreme Court has not as yet ruled on the constitutionality of multiple awards that frequently result in defendant's bankruptcy.

(a) Class action as solution [§67]

The class action solution to the multiple plaintiff problem faces formidable obstacles both (i) procedurally by way of due process arguments [*see* **Amchen Products v. Windsor,** 521 U.S. 591 (1997); **Ortiz v. Fibreboard Corp.,** 527 U.S. 815 (1999)], and (ii) in the methodology for computing the award made to each individual member of the class [*see* **Southwestern Refining Co. v. Bernal,** 22 S.W.3d 425 (Tex. 2000); *In re* **Exxon Valdez,** 246 F.3d 673 (9th Cir. 2000)].

TORT DAMAGES VS. CONTRACT DAMAGES — gilbert

	TORT	CONTRACT
GOAL OF COMPENSATORY DAMAGES	To place injured party in substantially as good a position as she occupied *prior to the wrong*	To place injured party in substantially as good a position as she would have had *if the contract had been performed*
DOES FORESEEABILITY LIMIT RECOVERY OF DAMAGES?	No	Yes
CERTAINTY REQUIRED?	Yes	Yes
CAUSATION REQUIRED?	Yes	Yes
MENTAL ANGUISH DAMAGES RECOVERABLE?	Yes	No
PUNITIVE DAMAGES RECOVERABLE?	Yes	No

b. Prejudgment interest [§68]

In certain situations, interest may be awarded on the amount found to be due *from the time the cause of action arose* to the date of the judgment as compensation for withholding the money.

(1) Case law [§69]

Earlier case law tended to restrict the award of such interest to cases of liquidated claims—*i.e.*, claims for a fixed sum such as the balance due under a promissory note.

(a) Note

There is some authority allowing prejudgment interest even on unliquidated claims. For example, Restatement (Second) of Torts section 913 states a rule permitting such interest to be awarded for torts to *property or pecuniary interests* "if the payment of interest prior to trial is required to avoid an injustice."

(b) And note

Prejudgment interest is not intended to punish defendant but merely to compensate plaintiff for being denied the opportunity to invest and earn interest on the amount of damages. [**Mathews v. DeSoto**, 721 S.W.2d 286 (Tex. 1986)] Thus, prejudgment interest is *not* awarded on punitive damages. [**Matanuska Electric Association v. Weissler**, 723 P.2d 600 (Alaska 1986)]

(2) Statutes [§70]

In most states today, the rules governing the award of prejudgment interest are statutory. For example, California Civil Code section 3287 authorizes recovery from the time the debt is due if the right to recover is "certain or capable of being made certain by calculation"—meaning the debt is liquidated or can be made so by reference to objective data. Thus, in **Levy-Zentner Co. v. Southern Pacific Transportation Co.**, 74 Cal. App. 3d 762 (1977), the plaintiff's loss was caused by a negligently set fire. Prejudgment interest was allowed from the date that the amount of loss was established by the plaintiff's experts and not disputed by the defendant.

(a) Rate [§71]

The interest rate is generally prescribed by the applicable state law. Where federal law applies, and there is no governing statute, courts have used the rate applicable to short-term risk-free obligations. [**Southern Pacific Transportation Co. v. San Antonio**, 748 F.2d 266 (5th Cir. 1984); **McCramm v. United States Lines**, 803 F.2d 771 (2d Cir. 1986)—average interest rate paid on six-month U.S. Treasury Bills]

c. Counsel fees [§72]

Unlike in England, attorneys' fees and litigation costs are *not* recoverable in the United States in the absence of *statutory* authorization (*e.g.*, in divorce or separation suits and particularly civil rights cases) or an *enforceable contract*. [**Walker v. Columbia Broadcasting System, Inc.**, 443 F.2d 33 (7th Cir. 1971)] (To be distinguished, of course, are attorneys' fees *incurred as damages* because the tort of another has required a person to bring or defend *other actions* to protect her interests. [**Collins v. First Financial Services**, 818 P.2d 411 (Ariz. 1991)])

(1) Exceptions [§73]

There are exceptions to this general rule of nonrecovery—principally receivership or bankruptcy suits and shareholders' derivative suits where a *"common fund"* is created by one litigant for the benefit of others, and certain claims for payment of life or fire insurance. In such cases, the court may award counsel fees to the prevailing party even without any contractual or statutory authority. [*See* **Walker v. Columbia Broadcasting System, Inc.,** *supra*] But note that fees paid from the fund are really paid by the plaintiffs rather than by the defendants. The fees paid may be calculated either on a percentage of recovery basis, or on an hourly fee basis for the time actually spent in preparing the case. [*See* **Sala v. National Railroad Passenger Corp.,** 721 F. Supp. 80 (E.D. Pa. 1989)]

(2) Unilateral provisions [§74]

One-sided contract provisions for attorneys' fees are *valid* in many states (*e.g.*, "Tenant agrees to pay any attorneys' fees incurred by Landlord in any action to enforce this lease"). Under such a provision, if Tenant wins the action, she *cannot* recover her attorneys' fees from Landlord because the contract does not so provide.

(a) But note

Some states now allow uncontracted-for recovery by statute. [*See, e.g.*, Cal. Civ. Code §1717—construes contract providing for attorneys' fees to one of the parties as authorizing award to the *"prevailing" party* in any action to enforce contract]

3. "Collateral Sources" Rule—No Mitigation of Damages Because of Benefits from "Collateral Sources" [§75]

A tortfeasor-defendant is not entitled to have his liability reduced on account of compensation paid to the plaintiff from "collateral" sources—*i.e.*, sources not purporting to act on behalf of the defendant. *Rationale:* The rationale for the collateral sources rule is that a wrongdoer's liability cannot be mitigated by the fact that the plaintiff was prudent enough to provide for such protection in advance against losses of this type, or that the plaintiff's employer or the state was willing to pick up the bill.

Examples: Payments from collateral sources include those received by an injured plaintiff under sickness or medical *insurance paid for by plaintiff or plaintiff's employer*; sick leave benefits paid by plaintiff's employer; state disability insurance benefits; or Social Security benefits or other pension benefits. [*See* **Johnson v. Baker,** 719 P.2d 752 (Kan. 1986)—grants and scholarships awarded to plaintiff cannot be used to mitigate damages; **Perry v. Larson,** 794 F.2d 279 (7th Cir. 1986)—same with unemployment compensation; **Phillips v. Western Co.,** 953 F.2d 923 (5th Cir. 1992)—same with disability payment from insurance paid for by employer (payment ruled deferred compensation and hence a collateral source)]

a. **Exception [§76]**

Some jurisdictions make an exception to the rule if the insurance has been paid for by the *defendant*. [*See* **Poltrock v. Chicago & North Western Transportation Co.,** 502 N.E.2d 1200 (Ill. 1986)]

b. **"Welfare" benefits [§77]**

Most courts follow the collateral sources rule even if the benefits received by plaintiff were rendered gratuitously by the state or public charity.

---

e.g. **Example:** Phil was injured in a car accident by Dave. Phil, laid off work due to his injury, was forced to seek medical care at a charity hospital and to apply for public welfare to support himself and his family. The payments and support rendered to Phil *cannot* be shown to reduce the damages recoverable against Dave in most courts. [*See* **Hudson v. Lazarus,** 217 F.2d 344 (D.C. Cir. 1954); *and see* Restatement (Second) Torts ("Rest. 2d Torts") §920A]

---

(1) **Note**

Home health care services gratuitously furnished by a family member also generally do not reduce the damages recoverable against the defendant. [**Bandel v. Friedrich,** 584 A.2d 800 (N.J. 1991)]

c. **Contract cases [§78]**

Courts have been reluctant to apply the collateral sources rule to contract cases. This is generally explained by reference to the rule governing the award of contract damages: No one shall profit more by a breach of an obligation than from its full performance. [**Hurd v. Nelson,** 714 P.2d 767 (Wyo. 1986)] The "credit for benefit" rule can be applied, however. (*See infra,* §82.)

d. **Criticism [§79]**

Application of the collateral sources rule often results in double compensation to the plaintiff for the same loss.

(1) **Subrogation [§80]**

A partial answer to this criticism is that there is no "double compensation" if the benefits are paid under plaintiff's own medical insurance, or insurance provided by plaintiff's employer, because most insurance policies contain *subrogation* provisions, which operate to assign to the insurance company plaintiff's claim against the tortfeasor to the extent of the payments received.

(2) **But note**

There is no subrogation in many cases—*e.g.*, where the plaintiff continues to receive wages from the employer, or takes sick leave, or retires on an early pension.

e. **Statutory changes [§81]**

Some "no fault" statutes, in effect, abrogate the collateral sources rule by specifically providing that an injured party is precluded from recovering damages from the tortfeasor for injuries that are compensated directly by the injured party's insurance carrier. [*See* **Ramirez v. Veeley**, 757 P.2d 160 (Colo. 1988)—loss of a year's earnings paid by plaintiff's insurance carrier not recoverable] Other statutes modify the collateral sources rule in certain cases by, *e.g.*, limiting the application of the rule in cases involving life insurance or workers' compensation benefits [**Kiss v. Jacob**, 633 A.2d 544 (N.J. 1993)], or by authorizing reduction of the judgment by 50% of the collateral source payments [**DeCastris v. Gutta**, 604 N.E.2d 359 (Ill. 1992)].

4. Credit for Benefit Rule [§82]

When the defendant's tortious conduct results in an injury to the plaintiff or her property, but that conduct also *directly benefits the plaintiff*, the value of the benefit may be considered in mitigation of damages. Similarly, where the defendant's breach of contract enables the plaintiff to enter a more advantageous contract, that factor must be taken into account in computing damages for the breach. [**Macon-Bibb County Water & Sewer Authority v. Tuttle/White Constructors**, 530 F. Supp. 1048 (D. Ga. 1981); **Kramer v. Board of Education**, 635 N.W.2d 857 (Wis. 2001)—no recovery for teacher whose employment contract was breached, but who was subsequently employed at a salary that was more than the total of his earnings under the repudiated contract plus consequential damages; *and see infra*, §424]

5. Computing the Award—Present Value of Future Losses [§83]

As will be discussed later (*see infra*, §739), courts have no power to render modifiable installment judgments payable as future losses are sustained. Rather, a court may award only a single lump-sum judgment, which must constitute the present valuation of all damages the plaintiff may suffer—past, present, and future.

a. Future economic losses must be discounted to present value [§84]

To determine the "present value" of the future economic losses that the plaintiff may suffer, the jury must be instructed to compute the total amount of such losses, and then to discount same to its *present value*. In other words, plaintiff is entitled to a judgment for a *lump sum which, if presently invested*, would produce the amount of the economic losses plaintiff is expected to sustain in the future.

(1) Distinguish—pain and suffering [§85]

Note that only future *pecuniary* losses (*e.g.*, medical expenses, loss of earnings) are discounted to their present value. Awards for future pain and suffering and other noneconomic losses are *not* discounted by most courts. [**Bychinsky v. Sentry Insurance**, 423 N.W.2d 178 (Wis. 1988); *In re* **Air Crash Near New Orleans**, 789 F.2d 1092 (5th Cir. 1986); *but see* **Oliveri v. Delta Steamship Lines**, 849 F.2d 742 (2d Cir. 1988); *and* **De Chico v. Metro-North Commuter Railroad**, 758 F.2d 856 (2d Cir. 1985)—contra; *and see infra*, §776]

b. **Method by which future economic losses are discounted [§86]**

Suppose the plaintiff is totally disabled, and the jury determines that her life and work expectancy is 30 years, and that her loss of earnings and medical expenses over this period of time will be $200,000. How is the present value of plaintiff's future economic losses determined?

(1) *The simplest method* is to calculate what dollar amount, invested at compound interest at current rates, would produce the total amount of damages at the end of the period. Thus, under the above facts, $40,120 invested at 5.5% interest would produce $200,000 at the end of 30 years. *But note:* While some courts approve the above method, it is *not* a fair measure because it assumes no withdrawals during the 30-year period. Hence the method is inappropriate in personal injury cases, because it must be assumed that the plaintiff will need to withdraw sums annually to cover medical expenses and lost earnings.

(2) *The more appropriate method* is to anticipate annual withdrawals of both principal and interest. (Annuity tables are commonly used for this purpose.) Under this method, the $200,000 future economic losses discussed above would have a present value of $96,980, and this is the amount that most courts would award. [**Rambaum v. Swisher,** 423 N.W.2d 68 (Minn. 1988)—using annuity method in discounting to present value]

c. **Rate of interest [§87]**

The above discounting is based on an investment at an *assumed* rate of interest. The rate is of paramount importance because the lower the assumed rate, the higher the plaintiff's recovery.

(1) **Statutory interest rate [§88]**

Some courts discount future losses based on a statutory interest rate (the interest rate on unpaid judgments—typically 7%).

(2) **Ad hoc basis [§89]**

Other courts (particularly federal courts) figure the interest rate on an ad hoc basis—whatever rate of interest a person with reasonable skill would obtain by investing the sum of money in question. Under this approach, the larger the sum available for investment, the higher the interest rate assumed. [**Madore v. Ingram Tank Ships,** 732 F.2d 475 (5th Cir. 1984)—current market rate should be used]

(3) **Bank interest rates [§90]**

Still other courts choose bank interest rates—on the rationale that the injured party should not bear the burden of searching out investments that will pay more than those readily obtainable at local banks.

d. **Inflation as allowable factor [§91]**

Increasingly, of course, it is evident that the "future dollars" with which the plaintiff is to be compensated will really not be worth as much as their present dollar counterparts—*i.e.*, that inflation in the cost of living will increase the amount that the plaintiff will have to spend for medical care, and increase the amount of lost earnings as well.

(1) Traditional view [§92]

Traditionally, the courts have held that awards for future losses will *not* be adjusted for inflationary trends, because of lack of evidence that inflation will continue. [12 A.L.R.2d 611] This means that the lump sum award will be discounted to present value at current interest rates.

(2) Offset rule [§93]

Some courts allow for an inflationary trend by assuming that the inflation factor is offset by higher interest rates and that they cancel each other out. [**Beaulieu v. Elliott,** 434 P.2d 665 (Alaska 1967)—sometimes called the "Alaska rule"; *and see* **Kaczkowski v. Bolubasz,** 421 A.2d 1027 (Pa. 1980)] Under this rule, there is no discount of the lump sum to present value.

(3) Current trends [§94]

The Supreme Court has approved of taking future inflation into account in calculating future losses. Once the losses have been determined (increased by anticipated inflation), the sum will be discounted to present value at what economists call the "real rate" of interest. Essentially the "real rate" of interest is estimated by examining current rates and recognizing that lenders are taking into consideration that their loans will be repaid with cheaper dollars. Hence, the current rates are jacked up to include anticipated inflation. By "squeezing" this factor out, the real rate is determinable. Estimates of the real rate vary widely, but generally have been coming out at from 1½ to 3%. [**Jones & Laughlin Steel Co. v. Pfeiffer,** 462 U.S. 523 (1983); *and see* **Sosa v. M/V Lago Izabel,** 736 F.2d 1028 (5th Cir. 1984)]

EXAM TIP   **gilbert**

The amount of damages recoverable may depend upon whether the plaintiff chooses to sue on a contract theory or in tort. A typical opportunity for choosing between tort and breach of contract theories exists where there has been a negligent performance of a contract, such as malpractice by professionals—doctors, architects, lawyers, and the like. [See 65 A.L.R.3d 249] The choice may have a number of effects other than escaping the restrictive rule of **Hadley v. Baxendale** (see *supra*, §23) for the more advantageous tort measure of damages. Some of the significant effects include: (i) the possibility of punitive damages; (ii) the recovery of prejudgment interest; (iii) damages for mental suffering; (iv) differing statutes of limitation; (v) applicability of the Statute of Frauds; and (vi) the assignability and survival of the cause of action.

---

6. Breach of Implied Covenant of Good Faith and Fair Dealing as a Tort

a. Insurance cases [§95]

The breach of an implied covenant of good faith and fair dealing is sometimes treated like a tort. The most dramatic area in which this principle operates is in third party liability insurance cases where the insurer fails to accept an offer to settle a claim against its insured within policy limits, thereby exposing the insured to an uncovered judgment above policy limits. [**Crisci v. Security Insurance Co.**, 66 Cal. 2d 425 (1967)] In this case, the insurer is liable for the excess *plus* damages for mental suffering caused by the failure to settle. [*See also* **Rova Farms Resort Inc. v. Investors Insurance Co.**, 323 A.2d 495 (N.J. 1974)]

(1) Note

A majority of jurisdictions also regard the denial of a first party insurance claim (*e.g.*, a fire insurance claim) without a reasonable basis as a tortious breach of the covenant of good faith and fair dealing. [**State Farm Fire & Casualty Co. v. Simmons**, 963 S.W.2d 42 (Tex. 1998); **Gruenberg v. Aetna Insurance Co.**, 9 Cal. 3d 566 (1973)]

b. Wrongful discharge of employees under at will contracts [§96]

A few courts have recognized a tort cause of action in employment termination cases [*see* **K Mart v. Ponsock**, 732 P.2d 1364 (Nev. 1987)], but the California Supreme Court, in **Foley v. Interactive Data Corp.**, 47 Cal. 3d 654 (1988), decided that tort remedies are not available for breach of an employment contract where employees allege they have been discharged in violation of the implied covenant of good faith and fair dealing. (*See infra*, §1238.)

c. Other cases [§97]

So far tort actions for breach of the covenant of good faith have been limited to contracts involving a *special relationship* between the parties. [*See* **Seaman's Direct Buying Service v. Standard Oil Co.**, 36 Cal. 3d 752 (1984); **Multiplex Insurance Agency v. Cal Life Insurance**, 189 Cal. App. 3d 925 (1987)] Pressures to extend the doctrine to ordinary commercial transactions have generally been unsuccessful. [*See* **Martin v. U-Haul Co. of Fresno**, 204 Cal. App. 3d 396 (1988)—termination of dealership; **Premier Wine & Spirits v. E. & J. Gallo Winery**, 846 F.2d 537 (9th Cir. 1988)—termination of distributorship; **Harris v. Atlantic Richfield Co.**, 14 Cal. App. 4th 70 (1993)—refusal to recognize new tort of breach of a commercial contract in violation of public policy; *but see* **Dunfee v. Baskin-Robbins**, 720 P.2d 1148 (Mont. 1986)—tort action allowed for breach of covenant of good faith in franchising agreement]

Chapter Three: Equitable Remedies

CONTENTS

Chapter Approach

Chapter Approach

This chapter describes the distinctive characteristics and requirements of equitable remedies. As you analyze exam questions involving equitable remedies, keep in mind the following:

1. Equitable relief is granted only in cases where the *remedy at law* (damages) *is inadequate or nonexistent.* Therefore, you must discuss the inadequacy of the legal remedy.

2. Equitable relief is *specific and personal* ("equity acts in personam"). The court directs a person to do or refrain from doing some act. However, keep in mind the *modifications* of this traditional view, particularly in cases involving title to land.

3. Equitable relief is *discretionary*. You must always consider such matters as hardship, unclean hands, undue delay, and the practicality of the remedy sought.

A. Nature of Equitable Remedies

1. In General [§98]

The bulk of equitable remedies comprise decrees for *specific performance* of contracts (*see infra,* Chapter XII.); *injunctions* against wrongful acts (*see infra,* Chapters V., VI., and VII.); and *accountings* from fiduciaries and the like. Equitable *restitutionary* remedies are covered *infra,* §§249 *et seq.*

2. Distinctive Characteristics [§99]

As compared to the legal remedy of damages, the following are the distinctive characteristics of equitable relief:

a. Specific and direct [§100]

Whereas legal remedies tend to be substitutionary (*i.e.,* money damages are substituted for the harm), equitable remedies are specific and direct orders to the defendant *personally to perform* the contract *or to remedy* the harm.

b. Preventive [§101]

A strong preventive element pervades equitable remedies, particularly injunctions. Legal remedies exist only after the wrong, and their deterrent effect is purely collateral.

c. **Discretionary [§102]**

Whereas legal remedies are a matter of right, equitable remedies are usually said to be discretionary.

d. **Flexible and fair (or just) [§103]**

The equity decree is adaptable to the particular case and is directed to a fairly balanced result rather than one framed in accord with rigid legalistic rules. [*See* **Curtin v. Department of Motor Vehicles,** 122 Cal. App. 3d 423 (1981)]

e. **Enforcement in personam [§104]**

The enforcement of equity decrees is accomplished primarily by coercive measures *directed against the person*, as compared to the method of collecting money damage claims out of the judgment debtor's property.

LEGAL VS. EQUITABLE REMEDIES—DISTINCTIVE CHARACTERISTICS — gilbert

	LEGAL	EQUITABLE
TYPE OF RELIEF	Usually substitutionary (*i.e.*, money damages)	Order for defendant personally to perform or to remedy the harm
DOES THE COURT HAVE DISCRETION WHEN DECIDING WHETHER TO GRANT RELIEF?	No	Yes
METHOD OF ENFORCEMENT	Usually collection of money damages out of judgment debtor's property	Coercive measures directed at the person (*e.g.*, contempt proceedings)

3. **Historical Background—Reasons for Distinctive Characteristics**

a. **Petitions to King referred to Chancellor [§105]**

During the medieval and Renaissance periods in England, an important administrative adjunct of the monarchy was the Chancery, presided over by the Chancellor. Petitions for redress of grievances, particularly when there was no hope of recourse to the law courts, were frequently directed to the King. Such petitions were couched in humble pleadings (bills) in no particular form, and might or might not be granted at the King's pleasure. As a matter of administrative convenience, such petitions came to be referred to the obvious official, the Chancellor, who eventually formalized the procedures in the Court of Chancery or Equity.

b. **Ground on which Chancellor would act [§106]**

The cases would be accepted only if they presented a situation incapable of redress in the law courts (hence the *requirement of no legal remedy*). Furthermore, whether *any* relief would be granted was a matter of *discretion* with the Chancellor, and the form of relief was *flexible* in the sense that defendant would be ordered to do whatever seemed just or equitable under the circumstances.

c. **Chancellor as "King's conscience" [§107]**

The Chancellors were, at the time, usually high ecclesiastical figures (bishops and even cardinals) and had a claim to operate on the "conscience" of the parties. A failure to obey was contemptuous of the authority of the Crown and its agents. Moreover, being trained in canon law, some notions of the Roman "aequitas" (or "equity") may have influenced the Chancellor's decision-making process.

d. **Friction with law courts [§108]**

Friction developed between the common law courts and Chancery. A tribunal purporting to rest on principles of equity and good conscience had a superficial appeal, but a court directly under the control of the Crown (and a companion court to Star Chamber, at that), disposing of cases without regard to the rules or procedures or remedies of law, and at the whim of Chancellors' "consciences" (as variable as the length of their feet), was not acceptable to the common law tradition embodied in such judges as Lord Coke.

e. **Resolution—equity can act "in personam, but not in rem" [§109]**

Among other issues, the practice of issuing injunctions against the enforcement of common law judgments obtained (at least in the opinion of the Chancellor) by inequitable means brought matters to a head in the famous dispute between Lord Coke and Chancellor Ellesmere in the early 17th century. A commission was appointed, headed by Lord Bacon, resolving the issue more or less in favor of equity, the principle being recognized that the equity decree does not affect the legal judgment, but operates only upon the person who holds it (*infra*, §§189 *et seq.*). It follows in theory that equity decrees do not affect legal rights, titles, or property interests as such, although they may bring about alteration of such rights and titles by coercing the defendant into executing the necessary legal papers to do so. It is in this fashion that equity is said "to act in personam rather than in rem."

4. **Procedural Merger of Law and Equity [§110]**

Dating from the Judicature Acts in the 1870s in England, the trend there and in the United States has been to combine legal and equitable procedures. In practically all states today, any civil court is authorized to award either legal or equitable relief. There are, however, still a few procedural distinctions between an action "at law" and a suit "in equity." (*See* further discussion in Civil Procedure Summary.)

a. Jury trials [§111]

There was no jury trial in equity cases; therefore, the constitutional *right* to a jury trial exists only with respect to actions "at law." However, an *advisory* jury may be convened in equity suits. [**Ruiz v. Ruiz,** 104 Cal. App. 3d 374 (1980)]

(1) "Equitable clean-up" doctrine [§112]

The application of this rule is complicated by the "equitable clean-up" doctrine, which historically meant that once equitable jurisdiction attached, the court determined not only equitable issues but also any legal issues incident to the entire case. [*See* **Hinville v. Wilson,** 628 S.W.2d 422 (Mo. 1982); **Washington University Medical Center Redevelopment Corp. v. Wolfgren,** 730 S.W.2d 289 (Mo. 1987)] Furthermore, the court may award any appropriate remedy, including "damages," without a jury trial.

Example: Buyer filed suit for specific performance of a contract to purchase two aircraft. Seller thereafter sold the aircraft to a third party, thus preventing specific performance. The court decreed payment akin to damages and denied any right to a jury trial. [**King Aircraft Sales Inc. v. Lane,** 846 P.2d 550 (Wash. 1993)]

(2) State courts [§113]

In state courts, the determination of the right to jury trial is generally made by applying a historical test. Another test is whether the "right" asserted is one arising from equitable principles; *e.g.,* promissory estoppel gives rise to an equitable right; therefore, there is no right to jury trial even though only money damages are given as the remedy. [**Nimrod Marketing (Overseas) v. Texas Energy Investment Corp.,** 769 F.2d 1076 (5th Cir. 1985)—court applied Texas law and determined that there was no right to jury trial in equitable promissory estoppel claim; **Wyle v. Alioto,** 191 Cal. App. 3d 1128 (1987)—corporate alter ego doctrine is equitable; hence there is no right to jury trial; **Williams v. Tritt,** 415 S.E.2d 285 (Ga. 1992)—claim for accounting is equitable and there is no right to a jury trial]

(a) Note

Where legal and equitable issues are joined, the parties are entitled to jury trial on the legal issues. [**Selby Constructors v. McCarthy,** 91 Cal. App. 3d 517 (1979)] In these cases, whether the legal or equitable issues are tried first is crucial because of the collateral estoppel effect of the judgment. Generally, state courts try the equitable issues first [*see* **Wyle v. Alioto,** *supra*], but some state courts and the federal courts hold that the legal issue should be tried first to the jury [*see* **Smith v. University of Detroit,** 378 N.W.2d 511 (Mich. 1985); *and see infra,* §114].

> **EXAM TIP** **gilbert**
>
> Remember that although today legal and equitable issues can be decided together in the same case, rather than in separate courts of law and equity, generally there still is *no right to a jury trial on an equitable claim*. Therefore, if a party in state court asserts her right to a jury trial concerning the legal issue, often the *legal and equitable claims will have to be divided*, with a jury deciding the legal claims and a judge deciding the equitable claims.

(3) Federal courts [§114]

In federal courts, the Supreme Court has extended the right to trial by jury to money claims where traditionally it would not have been granted. [*See* **Dairy Queen, Inc. v. Wood**, 369 U.S. 469 (1962)—suit for an accounting and injunction against trademark infringement; **Ross v. Bernhard**, 396 U.S. 531 (1970)—shareholder derivative suits] But claims for unintentional employment discrimination under Title VII of the 1964 Civil Rights Act in which the complainant is allowed to seek only back pay and reinstatement are equitable in nature and must be tried to the court. [**Journigan v. Eastover Bank for Savings**, 805 F. Supp. 415 (S.D. Miss. 1992)] In general, the federal approach to whether the case is legal or equitable for jury purposes is to look at the "remedies" sought, rather than the "right" asserted.

b. Appellate procedures [§115]

Historically, equity cases were tried on written interrogation rather than by examination and cross-examination of live witnesses. Any appellate review was a *de novo* case as to the facts. This is still the rule in some states.

c. Subject matter jurisdiction [§116]

In many states, lowest-level trial courts (*e.g.,* justice, township, or municipal courts) are not granted general equity powers. Their jurisdiction is generally limited to damage actions at law, subject to specified maximum monetary jurisdiction. A few states confer *limited* equity powers on such courts. [*See* Cal. Civ. Proc. Code §86] The United States Claims Court has no jurisdiction to grant specific equitable relief. [*See* **Pauley Petroleum, Inc. v. United States**, 591 F.2d 1308 (Ct. Cl. 1979)]

B. Requirements for Equitable Remedies

1. Equitable Jurisdiction—Distinguished from Power [§117]

The procedural merger of law and equity does not affect the question of whether equitable *remedies* are the appropriate ones in a given case. This question depends on the existence of what was traditionally referred to as "equitable jurisdiction."

a. Primary jurisdiction [§118]

Primary jurisdiction refers to the *power* of a court—*i.e.,* whether the court may handle a particular case.

(1) Actions in personam [§119]

For actions in personam, there must be jurisdiction over the *subject matter and* over the *person* (defendant). Because of the nature of equity cases, *most* of them fall into this category—but, for that matter, so do all legal actions for damages.

(a) Note

"Subject matter" jurisdiction refers to the *type* of case over which the court is empowered by statute or constitution to preside—*i.e.,* appellate courts hear appellate cases; criminal courts try criminal cases; probate courts try probate cases, etc.

(2) Actions in rem [§120]

For actions in rem (or quasi in rem) there must be jurisdiction over the *subject matter and the res* (property) in dispute; personal jurisdiction over the defendant is not essential.

b. "Equitable jurisdiction" [§121]

Assuming a civil court has primary jurisdiction, it may grant equitable remedies *based on the principles developed by the Chancery courts.*

(1) Requirement—no adequate remedy at law [§122]

Here the impact of history remains; *i.e.,* before granting equitable remedies, the court must find that legal remedies are *nonexistent or inadequate* and thus that a denial of equitable relief will result in *irreparable injury.* "Irreparable injury" means harm that cannot be rectified or compensated for by damages or any other legal remedy. [**Wisconsin Gas Co. v. Federal Energy Regulatory Commission,** 758 F.2d 669 (D.C. Cir. 1985)] To establish irreparability, it is enough to show that legal remedies are *seriously deficient* as a mode of redress for the harm suffered. [*See* **Roland Machinery Co. v. Dresser Industries,** 749 F.2d 380 (7th Cir. 1984)]

(a) Note

Contemporary writers have challenged this conventional "hierarchy" of remedies, urging that in the special context of judicial engineering of social change through "structural injunctions" (*i.e.,* injunctions to structure educational systems, prisons, etc.), primacy should be given to the equitable remedy. The injunction is a superior device for defining social goals and regulating the method for reaching them. [*See* Fiss & Rendleman, *Injunctions* (2nd ed.)] However, this may be merely another instance of the inadequacy of the legal remedies.

EXAM TIP   **gilbert**

Do not confuse "irreparable harm" or "irreparable injury" with "inadequate remedy at law," and do not use the terms synonymously. Whereas inadequate legal remedy is required for *all* equitable remedies, irreparable injury is a *separate prerequisite* to the granting of the equitable remedy of a *preliminary* injunction. Typical irreparable injury situations involve continuing wrongs where the loss is difficult to calculate. If a single act results in a completed tort, however, equitable relief is denied; there must be a threat of continuing harm before the irreparability requirement can be satisfied.

---

(2) Caveat [§123]

Where injunctions are authorized by statute, many courts hold that traditional equity requirements need not be met. The injured party *need only show violation of the statutory requirements.* [**People v. Staunton Landfill**, 614 N.E.2d 1286 (Ill. 1993); *but see* **Weinburger v. Romero-Barcelo**, 458 U.S. 305 (1982)—statutory scheme contemplated the exercise of discretion and the balancing of equities; **Amoco Production Co. v. Village of Gambell**, 480 U.S. 531 (1987)—traditional equitable discretion applied to enforcement of Alaska Land Conservation Act]

(3) Effect on jurisdiction [§124]

If a modern court grants equitable remedies where a basis for equitable relief does not exist, there may be an abuse of discretion (subject to reversal on appeal), but the court's judgment or decree is *not* void for lack of jurisdiction. [**Titan Oil & Gas v. Shipley**, 517 S.W.2d 210 (Ark. 1974)]

2. Conditions of Equitable Relief [§125]

As previously stated, equitable relief is discretionary. Thus, in addition to the requirement that there be no adequate remedy at law, an equitable remedy will not be granted unless a court is satisfied that certain other conditions of general application are satisfied.

a. Tort cases

(1) Balancing the equities [§126]

Before a court will grant relief by way of a prohibitory or mandatory injunction, the court must be assured that it will not impose an *undue hardship* on the defendant. This is sometimes called "balancing the equities," and is particularly important in encroachment and nuisance cases (*see infra*, §§398-407, 446-474).

(2) Feasibility of relief [§127]

The equitable remedy sought must be *effective and enforceable*. Unless a court can be assured that the injunction will accomplish some useful purpose, it will be denied. The feasibility of effective injunctive relief is particularly significant in cases involving status.

b. Contract cases [§128]

Conditions that must be met when the equitable remedy of specific performance is sought include:

(1) Contract definite and certain [§129]

Specific performance is granted only where the terms of the contract being enforced are *sufficiently certain* so that the court can determine what it must order each party to do to carry out the agreement. [**Genest v. John Glenn Corp.**, 696 P.2d 1058 (Or. 1985)] Although a contract may be too uncertain to be specifically enforced, it may be sufficiently certain to award the legal remedy of *damages*. [*But see* **Homart Development Co. v. Sigman**, 868 F.2d 1556 (11th Cir. 1989)—"Georgia case law holds that a contract whose terms are too indefinite to state a cause of action for specific performance cannot support an alternative cause of action for damages"]

Example: Seller agrees to sell a home to Buyer for $100,000, on "terms to be agreed upon." Unless Buyer agrees to pay cash, specific performance cannot be granted, since the court cannot supply for the parties the missing terms governing payment. [*See* **Reed v. Alvey**, 610 P.2d 1374 (Utah 1980)—specific performance permissible by requiring full payment at time of tender of conveyance]

Example: Buyer agreed to buy land, the contract providing for the payment of the deferred balance in 15 annual installments with interest at 6%. This was held to be too uncertain for specific performance because the contract had no provisions as to when and how interest was to be paid. [**Bryant v. Clark**, 358 S.W.2d 614 (Tex. 1962); *but see* **Wiggins v. Shewmake**, 374 N.W.2d 111 (S.D. 1985)—specific performance of "residential real estate purchase does not require an expansive recitation of mortgage financing details"]

Compare: Sometimes missing terms can be *inferred from custom or business usage,* and in such cases, specific performance may be granted. [**Larwin-Southern California v. JGB Investment Co.**, 101 Cal. App. 3d 626 (1979); **Okun v. Morton**, 203 Cal. App. 3d 805 (1988)]

---

(2) Conditions precedent—time of the essence clauses [§130]

Specific performance will be granted only if the *plaintiff has complied with all conditions precedent* to the defendant's obligation to perform. Failure to comply with a "time of the essence" clause in a land sale contract is a familiar application of this principle.

Example: Land sale contracts frequently include a provision that the buyer's timely tender of the purchase money is a condition precedent to the seller's duty to convey. [*See* **Wilson v. Klein**, 715 S.W.2d 814 (Tex. 1986)—failure of buyer to tender purchase price defeated specific performance and relieved seller of obligation to convey]

(a) Construction of clauses [§131]

Such "time of the essence" clauses are not necessarily strictly construed against the buyer. Courts instead examine the *surrounding circumstances* to determine the intent of the parties to the agreement. [**Nash v. Superior Court**, 86 Cal. App. 3d 690 (1978); **Kaiman Realty Inc. v. Carmichael**, 655 P.2d 872 (Haw. 1982)—court refused to enforce the clause where forfeiture would be harsh and unreasonable; **Curley v. Mobil Oil Corp.**, 860 F.2d 1129 (1st Cir. 1988)—to make time of the essence, notice must be given that agreement will terminate if there is no timely performance] *Partial performance* by the buyer is a particularly significant factor (*see infra*, §§1149-1154).

(b) Waiver [§132]

Repeated acceptance of late payments may result in a waiver of the clause, but this too is dependent on the circumstances. A *nonwaiver clause* may be sufficient to keep the time of the essence provision effective [**Sanson v. Gonzales**, 688 P.2d 676 (Ariz. 1984)], or the *clause may be reinstated* by notice that payments must be promptly made [**Gordon v. Schumacher**, 733 P.2d 35 (Or. 1987)].

(3) Enforcement must operate equitably [§133]

Specific performance is denied if enforcement will cause *great hardship*, or if the contract resulted from *misrepresentation, mistake, sharp practice, or other unfair acts.*

(a) Unilateral mistakes or "sharp" practices [§134]

Specific performance may be denied if enforcement is inequitable even though the contract itself cannot be rescinded, as, for example, in cases of unilateral mistake or sharp practice.

Example: Seller owns a tract of land that he wishes to sell as one parcel. Buyer wishes to buy only a small portion of the tract. At Seller's insistence, a contract of sale is executed for the entire tract. Subsequently, Buyer asks Seller to divide the tract into two parcels, allegedly for Buyer's tax advantage. After the division is accomplished and two contracts are drawn up, Buyer seeks to enforce only the contract for the small tract he originally sought. Specific performance will be denied. [**Brooks v. Towson Realty Inc.,** 162 A.2d 431 (Md. 1960)]

Compare: Seller failed to realize that by selling the property, payment of a second mortgage was accelerated. Seller demonstrated no additional hardship. *Held:* The mistake was insufficient either to bar Buyer's suit for specific performance or to be the basis of an action for rescission. [**DaSilva v. Musso,** 53 N.Y.2d 543 (1981)]

(b) Inadequate consideration [§135]

In the absence of fraud, accident, or mistake, equity will *not* abrogate a contract simply because it is unprofitable, improvident, or causes hardship. [**Dunkin' Donuts of America v. Middletown Donut,** 495 A.2d 66 (N.J. 1985)] Thus, while inadequate consideration *by itself* is generally held *not* a sufficient reason for denying specific performance, when combined with other factors such as unfairness or sharp practice, specific performance will be denied.

1) Note

In some jurisdictions (*e.g.,* California), adequacy of consideration *must be pleaded and proved* by the plaintiff as a *prerequisite* for specific performance. [100 A.L.R.2d 551]

2) Distinguish

In other jurisdictions, inadequacy of consideration may be a *defense* to specific performance by showing that the contract is harsh and inequitable.

Example: Gates, a prospector, agreed to transfer to Marks a one-fifth interest in "whatever *property* Gates might thereafter acquire in Alaska" in exchange for $1,000 and the cancellation of an $11,000 debt. Gates discovered gold worth $750,000. Specific performance was *denied* on the ground that the contract was unconscionable. [**Marks v. Gates,** 154 F. 481 (9th Cir. 1907)]

Compare: Jones agrees to give Smith $10,000 to seek mining leases in Alaska in exchange for a 25% interest in *any minerals found* (a "grubstake" contract). Such aleatory contracts are not considered harsh or unreasonable in the light of the *high risk of loss* involved.

---

a) Caution

Unfairness and sharp practice are defenses to a suit for

specific performance but *do not invalidate the contract.* The damages remedy is still available to the nonbreaching party. [**Yackey v. Pacifica Development Co.,** 99 Cal. App. 3d 776 (1979)]

(4) Enforcement must be feasible [§136]

Specific performance is not granted if enforcement of the decree is *unreasonably difficult* or if judicial supervision will be extended over a long period of time. [**Abrams v. Rapoport,** 516 N.E.2d 943 (Ill. 1987); **CBL & Associates v. McCrory Corp.,** 761 F. Supp. 807 (M.D. Ga. 1991)—no preliminary injunction to force shopping mall tenant to continue to operate under lease]

(a) Note

In **Okun v. Morton,** *supra,* §129, the California appellate court in granting specific performance referred to the rule as "archaic" and generally restricted to construction and employment contracts. Enforcement problems in these types of contracts are discussed *infra,* §§1207-1267.

EXAM TIP   **gilbert**

The equitable remedies of injunction in tort cases and specific performance in contract cases *both require enforcement to be feasible*. Always remember that courts generally do not wish to police their remedies over long periods of time, so if an injunction or specific performance request will require *ongoing action* by the defendant that will need to be supervised by the court, the court likely will *not* grant the request due to infeasibility of enforcement.

CONDITIONS TO GRANTING EQUITABLE RELIEF— A SUMMARY   **gilbert**

TORT (INJUNCTION) ACTIONS:

☑ No adequate remedy at law

☑ "Balancing of the equities" (*i.e.,* no undue hardship on defendant as result of injunction)

☑ Enforcement is feasible

CONTRACT (SPECIFIC PERFORMANCE) ACTIONS:

☑ No adequate remedy at law

☑ Contract terms are definite and certain

☑ Plaintiff has complied with all conditions precedent

☑ No great hardship will be imposed and there is no misrepresentation, mistake, sharp practice, or other unfair acts on the part of the plaintiff

☑ Enforcement is feasible

3. **Subject Matter of Equitable Relief [§137]**

The early requirement that property interests and not personal interests be at stake is no longer a dominant factor for equitable jurisdiction. In certain types of cases, however, equity continues to deny relief, although now generally on grounds that other remedies are adequate or for reasons of policy.

a. **No injunctions against crimes [§138]**

Injunctions against acts that are themselves crimes are refused for the reason that the equitable remedy deprives the defendant of the *right to jury trial* and the *procedural safeguards* of the criminal law (such as proof beyond a reasonable doubt). Moreover, disobedience of the injunction may subject the defendant to double punishment—once for contempt, and a second time for violation of the criminal law. [**City of Chicago v. Festival Theatre Corp.**, 438 N.E.2d 159 (Ill. 1982); **United States v. Bay Mills Indian Community**, 692 F. Supp. 777 (W.D. Mich. 1988)—injunction prohibiting defendant from operating casino on tribal land denied; **United States v. Menominee Indian Tribe**, 694 F. Supp. 1373 (E.D. Wis. 1988)—injunction prohibiting gambling denied]

(1) **Exception—public nuisance [§139]**

However, an injunction may be granted prohibiting a public nuisance even though the activity also constitutes a crime (*see infra*, §§466-474).

(2) **Exception—tort causing irreparable injury [§140]**

Injured persons have also been granted injunctive relief against tortious activity causing irreparable injury to property even though that activity is in violation of the criminal law. [**Airlines Reporting Corp. v. Barry**, 825 F.2d 1220 (8th Cir. 1987); **Fargo Women's Health Organization v. Lambs of Christ**, 488 N.W.2d 401 (N.D. 1992)—disruptive actions of abortion clinic protestors enjoined]

b. **No injunction against criminal prosecution under valid statute [§141]**

The general rule is that no injunction will be issued prohibiting the enforcement of a valid criminal statute simply because of the alleged innocence of the plaintiff. An adequate remedy at law is available to the plaintiff by pleading not guilty to the charge. [**Sullivan v. San Francisco Gas & Electric Co.**, 148 Cal. 368 (1905); **Garono v. State**, 524 N.E.2d 496 (Ohio 1988)]

(1) **Injunction may be granted if statute unconstitutional [§142]**

A prohibitory injunction may be granted if the statute being enforced is found to be unconstitutional and its enforcement will cause *irreparable injury* to *the plaintiff's property rights*. [**Air Curtain Destructor Corp. v. City of Austin**, 675 S.W.2d 615 (Tex. 1984)]

 Example: The usual case involves a regulatory statute that the plaintiff must either obey and sustain a loss of business, or disobey and run the risk of severe penalties. Thus, where a city enacted an ordinance requiring the plaintiff to remove all of its billboards, injunction was granted because the statute was held unconstitutional, and denying relief would cause irreparable injury to the plaintiff's business, as well as a multiplicity of suits. [**Stoner McCray System v. Des Moines,** 78 N.W.2d 843 (Iowa 1956)]

(a) Note

Personal rights have also been protected against irreparable injury under unconstitutional statutes. [*See* **Kenyon v. City of Chicopee,** 70 N.E.2d 241 (Mass. 1946)—injunction granted prohibiting enforcement of unconstitutional ordinance forbidding distribution of handbills; remedy at law was inadequate since it would require defending against numerous invalid prosecutions]

(2) Injunction may be granted if statute does not apply [§143]

In some situations enforcement of *valid* statutes may be enjoined if irreparable injury is threatened and the plaintiff claims the terms of the statute do not apply to him.

Example: State X threatened to prosecute Huntworth's teacher placement service under a statute making it criminal for an employment agency to charge a fee. Injunctive relief was granted against state enforcement as to Huntworth on the ground that Huntworth's activities are "not within the terms of the statute and he should not be forced to violate it in order to test its validity" [**Huntworth v. Tanner,** 152 P. 523 (Wash. 1915)]

(a) Distinguish—declaratory relief [§144]

Alternatively, the declaratory judgment procedure (*see infra,* §232) may be used to test the validity or the application of a criminal statute. Such a determination protects the plaintiff without interfering with the enforcement of the criminal law. Usually, the declaratory judgment procedure is limited to situations where the alleged criminal conduct is *malum prohibitum* (*e.g.,* business regulations) rather than malum in se (homicide, assaults). [**Bunis v. Conway,** 17 App. Div. 2d 207 (1962)—declaratory relief granted to determine whether sale of book was illegal because of alleged obscenity]

(3) Limitations on injunctive relief [§145]

Federal courts are prohibited from enjoining proceedings in state courts (including criminal prosecutions), with certain exceptions specified in the Anti-Injunction Act. [28 U.S.C. §2283]

(a) Statutory exceptions [§146]

The exceptions stated in the Anti-Injunction Act are situations in which the injunction is *specifically authorized* by an Act of Congress and is *necessary* to aid the jurisdiction of the federal court and to protect and effectuate its judgments. For example, injunctions are permitted in cases arising under the Civil Rights Acts, because they are one of the expressly authorized exceptions to the Anti-Injunction Act. [**Mitchum v. Foster**, 407 U.S. 225 (1972)]

(b) State criminal prosecutions [§147]

Although early decisions permitted injunctive relief against state criminal prosecutions if they were shown to have a "chilling effect" on First Amendment rights [**Dombrowski v. Pfister**, 380 U.S. 479 (1965)], the current rule is that "a federal court should not enjoin a state criminal prosecution begun prior to the institution of the federal suit except in *very unusual situations*, where necessary to prevent immediate irreparable injury." Thus, federal intervention depends upon proof that there is *both* a present and *immediate threat to a federal right* and *no opportunity* to protect it in the state court prosecution. [**Younger v. Harris**, 401 U.S. 37 (1971)]

1) Note

This is true even if related criminal proceedings are pending in the federal court before the state prosecution commences. As long as "no proceedings of substance on the merits have taken place in the federal court," the federal court must not enjoin or intervene in the state prosecution (absent extraordinary circumstances). [**Hicks v. Miranda**, 422 U.S. 332 (1975)]

2) And note

The possibility of a "chilling effect" on First Amendment rights does *not* by itself justify federal intervention. Moreover, there is not sufficient irreparable injury where the defense of a single state prosecution will protect the federal right.

3) Distinguish

If *no state proceedings have been instituted*, a claim for preliminary injunctive relief against the enforcement of an allegedly unconstitutional statute may be considered without regard to *Younger* type restrictions. [**Doran v. Salem Inn, Inc.**, 422 U.S. 922 (1975)—injunction granted upon a showing of irreparable harm to business; **Rushia v. Town of Ashburnham**, 701 F.2d 7 (1st Cir. 1983)—injunction denied for failure to show irreparable injury]

(c) **State civil proceedings [§148]**

The requirement of "extraordinary circumstances" to justify federal injunctive relief against state criminal proceedings also applies to state *nuisance proceedings*, which are civil in nature. [**Huffman v. Pursue Ltd.**, 420 U.S. 592 (1975)—federal court intervention to prevent closure of theatre for exhibiting allegedly obscene motion pictures held subject to *Younger* standards] *Younger* abstention was also held to apply where a federal injunction was sought to preclude enforcement of a *judicial order* by civil contempt [**Juidice v. Vail**, 430 U.S. 327 (1977)] and to test the constitutionality of the *Texas appeal bond statute* [**Pennzoil Co. v. Texaco, Inc.**, 481 U.S. 1 (1987)]. The protection extended to state court civil proceedings is *not* total, however. In **New Orleans Public Service v. City of New Orleans**, 491 U.S. 350 (1989), a federal injunction action against a city rate proceeding was upheld, the Court ruling that the city council proceedings were *not judicial* in nature. [*See also* **Johnson v. Kelly**, 583 F.2d 1242 (3d Cir. 1978)—state court quiet title action]

(4) Distinguish—declaratory relief [§149]

If enforcement of an allegedly unconstitutional state or local ordinance is *merely threatened*, declaratory relief is available in the federal court without establishing the circumstances necessary to justify injunctive relief. [**Steffel v. Thompson**, 415 U.S. 452 (1974)]

(a) **Requirement of case or controversy [§150]**

If declaratory relief is sought, however, it is necessary to establish that there is a *genuine case or controversy*. Thus, to qualify as plaintiff, a party must establish a *personal stake* in the outcome—*i.e.*, must show some direct injury if the statute were to be enforced. [**O'Shea v. Littleton**, 414 U.S. 488 (1974)—invalidating attempts to challenge bond, sentencing, and jury fee practices by plaintiffs not charged with a crime; **Rizzo v. Goode**, 423 U.S. 362 (1976)—applying "personal stake" requirement to deny sweeping equitable relief (including receivership of Philadelphia Police Department) sought under Civil Rights Act of 1871 (42 U.S.C. §1983)]

(5) State court injunctions against federal actions [§151]

State courts may *not* enjoin in personam actions in federal court, regardless of whether federal litigation is pending or prospective. [**General Atomic Co. v. Felter**, 434 U.S. 12 (1977)]

c. **No injunction against police acts [§152]**

An injunction prohibiting a law enforcement officer from performing assigned duties will not be granted. *Rationale:* Fear of undue harassment of officials and interference with the administration of the criminal law is generally stated as the basis for this rule.

(1) Distinguish—harassment not in line of duty [§153]

If the activities involved have no connection with official duties and result in harassment of the plaintiff, an injunction may be granted. [**Uptown Enterprises v. Strand,** 195 Cal. App. 2d 45 (1961)—harassment of owner of drive-in movie by sheriff; **Adams Apple Distributing Co. v. Zagel,** 501 N.E.2d 302 (Ill. 1986)]

(2) Prisoners [§154]

While prisoners have only limited rights, injunctive relief has been granted to protect such constitutional rights as the right to practice one's religion and the right against cruel and unusual punishment. [**Procunier v. Martinez,** 416 U.S. 396 (1974)—censorship of personal correspondence held unconstitutional where it did not further a legitimate and substantial government interest in security of the prisoners]

---

e.g. Example: Litigation, frequently in the form of class actions, has resulted in equitable decrees that extensively regulate the administration of prisons. For instance, in **Taylor v. Perini,** 455 F. Supp. 1241 (N.D. Ohio 1978), the court, among other things, ordered prison administrators to: (i) refrain from obstructing, censoring, or reading prisoners' correspondence with lawyers; (ii) make job assignments in prison shops reflective of the prison's racial composition; (iii) provide prisoners with paper, pens, and postage necessary for the preparation and mailing of legal material; and (iv) restrict periods of solitary confinement to a maximum of 15 consecutive days.

(a) Structural injunction [§155]

Injunctions such as the one issued in *Taylor, supra,* that restructure entire governmental bureaucracies have been labeled "structural injunctions." By means of these detailed and specific decrees courts have undertaken the management of prisons, schools, mental institutions, and other similar government-run institutions. Enforcement of such decrees obviously involves unique enforcement problems. [*See* **United States v. City of Yonkers,** 856 F.2d 444 (2d Cir. 1988); **Spallone v. United States,** 493 U.S. 265 (1990); *and see infra,* §§733-735] The Supreme Court has now cautiously approved steps taken to phase out court involvement in managing these institutions. [*See* **Freeman v. Pitts,** 503 U.S. 467 (1992)—desegregation plan; **Rufo v. Inmates of Suffolk County Jail,** 502 U.S. 367 (1992)—supervision of a jail]

(3) Damages [§156]

Courts have recognized that an injured party may have a cause of action for damages for illegal or oppressive official conduct that violates constitutionally protected rights. In **Bivens v. Six Unknown Named Agents,** 403 U.S. 388 (1971), the Court upheld the plaintiff's cause of action against federal officials who performed an unconstitutional search and seizure by implying a cause of action for damages directly from the Fourth Amendment. A similar right of action for violations of federal rights by state officials is provided by 42 U.S.C. section 1983. [**United States ex rel. Motley v. Rundle,** 340 F. Supp. 807 (E.D. Pa. 1972); *see infra,* §§733-735]

EXAM TIP — gilbert

If in an exam situation you determine that the requirements for an injunction have been met, remember that the following *cannot be enjoined*:

- *Crimes* (*unless* the activity is a public nuisance or a tort involving irreparable injury);

- A *criminal prosecution under a valid statute* (*unless* (i) the plaintiff claims that the statute does not apply to him and irreparable harm is threatened, or (ii) a federal court is enjoining a state court criminal proceeding pursuant to an exception to the federal Anti-Injunction Act where great and immediate irreparable injury will result); and

- A *law enforcement officer's performance of her duties*.

---

4. Special Equitable Defenses—Clean Hands and Laches

a. "One who comes into equity must come with clean hands"

(1) "Unclean hands" defined [§157]

"Unclean hands" is usually confined to inequitable (unethical, immoral) conduct by the plaintiff, *directly related to the subject of the litigation.* The maxim applies even though the plaintiff's misconduct has not injured anyone, and even though the defendant participated in the misconduct. The court refuses to aid *either party* to such a transaction. [**Green v. Higgins,** 535 P.2d 446 (Kan. 1975); **Isabell v. Brighton Area Schools,** 500 N.W.2d 748 (Mich. 1993)]

(a) No injury due to unclean hands required [§158]

In applying the maxim, most courts consider direct injury to the defendant because of plaintiff's misconduct irrelevant, since these courts assert that the purpose of the maxim is to protect their own integrity. [**Northeast Women's Center v. McMonagle,** 665 F. Supp. 1147 (E.D. Pa. 1987)] Some courts, however, require that plaintiff's misconduct has caused defendant injury. [**Bistricher v. Bistricher,** 659 F. Supp. 215 (E.D.N.Y. 1987)—"New York rule"; **Right to Life Advocates, Inc. v. Aaron Women's Clinic,** 737 S.W.2d 564 (Tex. 1987)]

(b) Prior unrelated inequitable conduct [§159]

Prior inequitable conduct unrelated to the issue or the parties does *not* bar the plaintiff's suit. Thus, if the plaintiff sues to enjoin a nuisance, the defendant cannot forestall injunction by asserting that plaintiff acquired title to the land by defrauding an aged widow. [**Proimos v. Fair Automotive Repair**, 808 F.2d 1273 (7th Cir. 1987)—franchisor may enforce franchise contract against franchisee although guilty of deceptive advertising; **Pratt v. Blunt**, 488 N.E.2d 1062 (Ill. 1986)—law firm allegedly guilty of unethical conduct with respect to clients granted injunctive relief against a former associate engaged in unethical solicitation of firm's clients]

1) Exception—"public frauds" [§160]

A departure from the foregoing is found where the plaintiff has been committing a *fraud on the public.*

---

e.g. Examples: A business developed and maintained by *misleading advertising* may be denied protection from "unfair" competition. [**American University v. Wood**, 128 N.E. 330 (Ill. 1920); **Alpo Petfoods v. Ralston Purina Co.**, 720 F. Supp. 194 (D.D.C. 1989)] Similarly, the Ku Klux Klan lost an equity suit to protect its name and insignia. [**Knights of the Ku Klux Klan v. Strayer**, 34 F.2d 432 (3d Cir. 1929)]

(c) Application of doctrine discretionary [§161]

The application of the "unclean hands" doctrine is discretionary. Whenever application of the doctrine will cause an inequitable result, the courts generally reject it. [**Health Maintenance Network v. Blue Cross**, 200 Cal. App. 3d 23 (1988)]

(2) Personal culpability by plaintiff required [§162]

Because the disqualification of the plaintiff derives from her personal conduct, a principal is *not* barred by reason of inequitable behavior of her agent—*unless* the principal is asserting a claim based on a benefit obtained by the agent's action. [**Washington Capitols Basketball Club, Inc. v. Barry**, 419 F.2d 472 (9th Cir. 1969)]

(3) "Unclean hands" generally no bar to recovery at law [§163]

The plaintiff's "unclean hands" preclude only relief in equity. Thus, if the plaintiff frames the claim for relief so that it is clearly an action *at law*, she is entitled to recover notwithstanding her own immoral or unethical (but not illegal) conduct in the transaction. Otherwise, plaintiff would be barred from any relief (legal or equitable) although she has not done anything illegal. [**Natcontainer Corp. v. Continental Can Co.**, 362 F. Supp. 1094 (S.D.N.Y. 1973)—"unclean hands" no defense to civil antitrust suit for damages; **Kay v. Vatterott**, 657 S.W.2d 80 (Mo. 1983)—unclean hands no defense to action for breach of construction contract]

(a) But note—some courts contra

Some courts *do allow* the "unclean hands" defense in suits at law. [*See* **F.E.L. Publications v. Catholic Archbishop of Chicago,** 506 F. Supp. 1127 (N.D. Ill. 1981)—in a copyright infringement action, court declared that doctrine of unclean hands was not limited to suits in equity but is "equally suited to damage actions"; **Byron v. Clay,** 867 F.2d 1049 (7th Cir. 1989)—Judge Posner suggests that with merger of law and equity "it is difficult to see why equitable defenses should be limited to equitable suits"] One explanation for some of these decisions is that the cases involve situations where the conduct *also involves recognized legal defenses.* [**McKinley v. Weidner,** 698 P.2d 983 (Or. 1985); **Blain v. The Doctor's Co.,** 222 Cal. App. 3d 1048 (1990)]

b. "Equity aids the vigilant"—laches

(1) "Laches" defined [§164]

Laches is an *unreasonable* delay in initiating or pursuing an equity cause, during which time the situation of the other party has *changed* to the extent that an additional and unnecessary *detriment* would be imposed if the suit were allowed (*e.g.,* evidence lost or destroyed as a result of the plaintiff's unreasonable delay in proceeding). [**Environmental Defense Fund Inc. v. Alexander,** 614 F.2d 474 (5th Cir. 1980)—expenditure of $176 to $286 million before the challenge was asserted; **EEOC v. Dresser Industries, Inc.,** 668 F.2d 1199 (11th Cir. 1982)—"classic elements" of undue prejudice caused by delay: unavailability of witnesses, changed personnel, and the loss of pertinent records; *but see* **University of Pittsburgh v. Champion Products, Inc.,** 686 F.2d 1040 (3d Cir. 1982)—long period of delay in asserting claim against manufacturer for infringement of university trademark did not preclude prospective injunctive relief]

(2) Laches and the statute of limitations [§165]

Even if there is a statute of limitations expressly applicable to equity suits, and that statute has not run, laches may still bar plaintiff's suit *before the expiration of the statutory period.*

(a) Distinguish—no statute of limitations [§166]

If there is no expressly applicable statute of limitations, the determination of whether plaintiff's delay is "unreasonable" is made by reference to the statute of limitations applicable to the analogous legal action—*e.g.,* the statute of limitations for recovery of damages to land may be used by analogy in an equity suit to enjoin a trespass. If the analogous statute *has not* run, the equity suit may still be barred by laches, but the *burden is on the defendant* to establish the defense. If the analogous statute *has* run, the *burden* is usually put *on the plaintiff* to show why laches should not be invoked as a bar. [**Shell v. Strong,** 151 F.2d 909 (10th Cir. 1945)]

(b) Laches no bar to legal action [§167]

Laches is an equitable defense and cannot be used to defeat a legal claim for money damages. [**Bauer v. P.A. Cutri Co.,** 253 A.2d 252 (Pa. 1969); **Phipps v. Robinson,** 858 F.2d 965 (4th Cir. 1988)—laches not a defense to ejectment action; **Estate of Younge v. Huysmans,** 506 A.2d 282 (N.H. 1985)—damages for breach of contract granted but specific performance denied because of laches]

1) But note

There are suggestions that an analogous defense, "equitable estoppel," may be available to defeat a legal claim. [*See* **Standard Oil Co. of California v. United States,** 685 F.2d 1322 (Ct. Cl. 1982); **Regent International Hotels v. Las Colinas Hotels,** 704 S.W.2d 101 (Tex. 1985)]

EXAM TIP   **gilbert**

If you feel a party may be entitled to equitable remedies on an exam, make sure the following equitable defenses do not apply:

- *Unclean hands* (*i.e.,* inequitable conduct by the plaintiff that is directly related to the subject of the litigation); and

- *Laches* (*i.e.,* unreasonable delay in initiating or pursuing an equitable claim, during which the defendant has changed his position and thus unnecessary detriment would be imposed if the suit were allowed to continue).

Remember, however, that these defenses generally *apply only in equity*, not in actions at law.

C. Enforcement and Effect of Equitable Decrees

1. Enforcement of Equitable Decrees

a. Contempt proceedings

(1) Specificity [§168]

To be enforceable, equity decrees must be formulated with sufficient specificity to apprise the enjoined party of the obligations imposed by the decree. This is a requirement of due process. [**H. K. Porter Co. v. National Friction Products,** 568 F.2d 24 (7th Cir. 1977); *Ex parte* **Blasingame,** 748 S.W.2d 444 (Tex. 1988)]

(2) Methods of enforcement [§169]

There are two types of contempt: civil and criminal. The objective of civil contempt is to *secure the benefits of the decree* for the complainant. The purpose of criminal contempt is to *vindicate the authority of the court* by punishing past acts of disobedience. [**Latrobe Steel Co. v. United Steelworkers of America**, 545 F.2d 1336 (3d Cir. 1976); **Fatemi v. Fatemi**, 537 A.2d 840 (Pa. 1988); *and see infra*, §174]

(a) Affirmative or mandatory decrees [§170]

Decrees requiring the defendant to take action (*e.g.*, to cancel a deed) can effectively be enforced by *civil contempt* proceedings resulting in confinement in prison until the decree is obeyed: Defendant "has the keys to the jail in his pocket."

1) Decrees ordering defendant to pay money [§171]

Although decrees ordering the payment of money are in effect mandatory decrees, they are *not enforceable by imprisonment for civil contempt*. This is due to the constitutional and statutory prohibitions against imprisonment for debt. [**McQuady v. McQuady**, 523 So. 2d 785 (Fla. 1988); **Combs v. Ryan's Coal Co.**, 785 F.2d 970 (11th Cir. 1986)]

a) Exceptions [§172]

Alimony and support decrees, and decrees ordering fiduciaries to pay over money, are not regarded as "debts" within the constitutional and statutory prohibitions referred to above; hence they *are* enforceable by imprisonment for contempt if the payments are not made. But even in these cases, civil contempt is regarded as remedial. Proof of the inability to comply with the order results in a release from incarceration. [**United States *ex rel.* Thom v. Jenkins**, 760 F.2d 736 (7th Cir. 1985); **Nab v. Nab**, 757 P.2d 1231 (Idaho 1988)—imprisonment for unrelated crime as basis for establishing inability to continue child support payments; *cf.* **Commodity Futures Trading Commission v. Wellington Precious Metals, Inc.**, 950 F.2d 1525 (11th Cir. 1992)—defendant failed to establish that his spending several months in jail was proof that he was unable to pay]

(b) Negative or prohibitory decrees [§173]

When the defendant is enjoined (prohibited) from committing certain acts, and he violates the injunction by committing the acts nonetheless, he may be ordered to pay money—either by way of compensation for the harm done, or on the theory of an in terrorem fine designed to coerce the defendant into *future* obedience. *Rationale:*

Imprisoning the defendant for contempt is obviously *not* going to achieve the purpose of the original injunction, because he has already committed the act that the injunction sought to prohibit. (The only exception might be where the injunction was against a *course of conduct*, in which event imprisonment for contempt for one violation may effectively deter him from future disobedience.) [*See* **Perfect Fit Industries v. Acme Quilting Co.**, 646 F.2d 800 (2d Cir. 1981)]

(3) Civil vs. criminal contempt [§174]

The distinction between civil and criminal contempt turns upon the purpose of the proceeding (*see supra*, §169). Thus, if the remedy provided in the contempt proceeding is *imprisonment*, it is *remedial* (*i.e.*, civil) **if** the defendant remains committed *until the affirmative act* required by the court's order is performed. It is *punitive* (*i.e.*, criminal) **if** the sentence is limited to imprisonment *for a fixed term*. [*See* **Hicks ex rel. Feiock v. Feiock**, 485 U.S. 624 (1988); **King v. Department of Social & Health Service**, 756 P.2d 1303 (Wash. 1988)—incarceration in dependency case may continue indefinitely until it is shown to have lost its coercive effects] If the relief provided in the contempt proceeding is a money *fine*, it is *remedial* (civil) when the fine is paid to the plaintiff, and *punitive* (criminal) when paid to the court. [**Hicks ex rel. Feiock v. Feiock**, *supra*]

Example: In **International Union, United Mine Workers v. Bagwell**, 512 U.S. 821 (1994), the trial court entered a complex decree setting out a code of conduct governing the defendant union's strike activities and announced that the union would be fined $20,000 to $100,000 for each violation of the decree. The union violated the decree more than 400 times and hence was fined more than $64 million in a civil proceeding before the trial court. The original complainants settled with the union, but the state insisted on collecting its part of the fine (some $52 million). The state contended that the fines were coercive; thus, the contempt proceeding was civil and no jury trial was required. The Supreme Court reversed, ruling that the fines were punitive and hence the contempt was criminal, requiring a jury trial. *Rationale*: The Court rejected the state's argument that the fines were coercive because they were announced in *advance* of violation. Hence the Court found that the fines were more closely analogous to fixed, retrospective criminal fines that the union had no opportunity to purge once imposed.

(a) Exception—fine payable to court may be remedial [§175]

A fine payable to the court may also be remedial when the fine is designed to coerce behavior. Thus a court may order that a fine be assessed unless the defendant either performs an affirmative act required by the decree [**City of Providence v. Kalian**, 524 A.2d 250 (R.I. 1988)] or refrains from doing acts prohibited by the decree.

(b) **Exception—fine for past violations may be remedial [§176]**

A civil contempt proceeding is possible against a defendant presently in compliance with an injunction to secure a monetary award to compensate for injuries incurred as the result of past violations. [**Cancer Research Institute v. Cancer Research Society,** 744 F. Supp. 526 (S.D.N.Y. 1990)]

(c) **Significance of distinction [§177]**

Most jurisdictions require that punishment for criminal contempt be in compliance with the requirements for criminal proceedings generally (*e.g.,* right to counsel, right to jury trial, right to confront and cross-examine witnesses, etc.). [**Mitchell v. Superior Court,** 43 Cal. 3d 107 (1987)] Thus, in *International Union, supra,* the failure to provide a jury trial in the *criminal* contempt proceeding invalidated the contempt citation. The safeguards of the criminal law are *not* required in *civil* contempt proceedings. [**Curlee v. Howle,** 287 S.E.2d 915 (S.C. 1982)—no right to jury trial in a civil contempt proceeding; **State *ex rel.* Department of Human Services v. Rael,** 642 P.2d 1099 (N.M. 1982)—no right to counsel in civil contempt proceeding] Since civil contempt is remedial, it is error to impose criminal contempt sanctions in a civil contempt proceeding. [*In re* **Silevin,** 361 N.W.2d 189 (Neb. 1985); **Land Use Regulation Commission v. Tuck,** 490 A.2d 649 (Me. 1985)]

1) **Statutory classification**

Oregon has tried to solve the problem of classification by statute. Under the legislation, a contempt order is either punitive or remedial, depending on the sanction. [**Douthit v. Swift,** 865 P.2d 479 (Or. 1993)]

CIVIL VS. CRIMINAL CONTEMPT — gilbert

	CIVIL CONTEMPT	CRIMINAL CONTEMPT
PURPOSE	To *secure the benefits* of the equity decree for the plaintiff	To vindicate the authority of the court by *punishing* past disobedience
NATURE OF IMPRISONMENT AS REMEDY FOR CONTEMPT	Defendant incarcerated until affirmative act required by the court order is *performed*	Defendant incarcerated for a *fixed term*
NATURE OF FINE AS REMEDY FOR CONTEMPT	Defendant generally pays fine to the *plaintiff*	Defendant generally pays fine to the *court*

(4) Void and erroneous orders [§178]

Enforcement by contempt of erroneous but jurisdictionally valid orders is treated differently from orders that are void because the court lacks subject matter jurisdiction.

(a) Valid orders [§179]

An erroneous but *jurisdictionally valid* order must be obeyed until reversed or set aside on appeal. Violation of these orders may be punished by *criminal* contempt. Civil contempt, however, is not available because a plaintiff is not entitled to the benefits of an order erroneously entered. [**United States v. United Mine Workers,** 330 U.S. 258 (1947); **Bachynsky v. State,** 747 S.W.2d 847 (Tex. 1988)]

1) Collateral bar rule [§180]

The erroneous granting of the injunction cannot be attacked in the contempt proceeding (*i.e.,* there can be no collateral attack on a decree rendered by a court having valid jurisdiction over the proceedings). The decree can only be attacked directly by *appeal.* [See **Ex parte Purvis,** 382 So. 2d 512 (Ala. 1980); *but see* **Pedini v. Bowles,** 940 F. Supp. 1020 (N.D. Tex 1996)—rejecting the collateral bar rule on the basis of Texas law and allowing the attack]

(b) Void orders [§181]

Injunctions entered by courts *lacking subject matter jurisdiction* are *void* and consequently are *not enforceable* by either civil or criminal contempt. [**Bachynsky v. State,** *supra;* **In re Berry,** 68 Cal. 2d 137 (1968)]

1) Exception [§182]

Some courts rule that a violator of an order made without subject matter jurisdiction is subject to criminal contempt if the claim of subject matter jurisdiction is not frivolous and insubstantial. Thus, a court may conduct appropriate proceedings to determine if it has jurisdiction and its orders entered in those proceedings are enforceable by criminal contempt. [**United States v. United Mine Workers,** *supra;* **In re Catholic Conference,** 824 F.2d 156 (2d Cir. 1987)]

(c) Void orders involving First Amendment rights [§183]

Injunctions violating First Amendment rights are void. Nevertheless, violation of these orders subjects the violator to *criminal contempt* unless the order is transparently invalid. [*Compare* **Walker v. City of Birmingham,** 388 U.S. 307 (1967)—contempt available; *with* **In re Providence Journal Co.,** 820 F.2d 1342 (1st Cir. 1986)—order patently unconstitutional, contempt not allowed; *modified,* **In** *re* **Providence Journal Co.,** 820 F.2d 1354 (1st Cir. 1987)—en banc decision required publisher subject to allegedly unconstitutional prior restraint to make "good faith effort" to seek emergency relief from appellate court before violating order]

1) Note

The California Supreme Court has permitted a collateral attack where an injunction was found to be void for vagueness under First Amendment standards. But compare **People *ex rel.* Gallo v. Acuna,** 14 Cal. 4th 1090 (1997), where the court ruled than an anti-street gang injunction was sufficiently specific to withstand a First Amendment attack for vagueness.

(5) Parties bound

(a) Party to the action [§184]

No formal service of the decree is required to hold a party to the action in civil contempt if he disobeys the injunction with knowledge that the court has issued it. [**Vuitton et Fils S.A. v. Carousel Handbags,** 592 F.2d 126 (2d Cir. 1979)]

(b) Nonparties [§185]

Only parties and privies are bound by an equitable decree. Nonparties acting independently in furtherance of their own objectives are free generally to ignore the injunction; *i.e.,* they cannot be held in contempt for disobeying it. [**Alemite Manufacturing Co. v. Staff,** 42 F.2d 832 (2d Cir. 1930); **Saga International v. John D. Brush & Co.,** 934 F. Supp. 1283 (D. Cal. 1997)—former president of company not a party nor a privy to a party and hence not bound]

---

e.g. Example: Decree prohibits Mary from continuing to trespass on Sal's land. Hunter independently goes hunting on the land even though he knows of the injunction. Hunter cannot be held in civil contempt. [*See* **Kean v. Hurley,** 179 F.2d 888 (8th Cir. 1950); **People v. Conrad,** 55 Cal. App. 896 (1997)]

---

1) But note

A person who is not named a party to the action *may* be held in contempt by proof either that the nonparty acted in concert or participated in the disobedient act of the party or that the nonparty was subject to the injunction because legally identified (as successor or assignee) with a party. [**G. & C. Merriam Co. v. Webster Dictionary Co.,** 639 F.2d 29 (1st Cir. 1980); **Waffenschmidt v. Mackay,** 763 F.2d 711 (5th Cir. 1985)— nonparties aiding and abetting enjoined party in security fraud held in contempt]

2) And note

The court is concerned only with the actuality of concert or participation and not the motives that prompt the participation. Independent motivation does not mean that a person is not acting in concert. This rule has been effectively applied against anti-abortion protestors. [**New York State National Organization for Women v. Terry,** 961 F.2d 390 (2d Cir. 1992)]

EXAM TIP   **gilbert**

Generally, nonparties are not bound by an equity decree—only parties and their privies are bound. However, watch out for the exception! A nonparty can be bound if he either (i) acts in *concert* with the defendant or *participates* in the disobedient behavior, or (ii) is *legally identified* with the defendant (*e.g.,* as successor or assignee).

---

b. Writs of assistance (writs of possession) [§186]

If the defendant has been ordered to deliver possession of property to the plaintiff (*e.g.,* after a foreclosure sale), a writ may be issued to the sheriff or other official to place the plaintiff in possession. [*See* **Hamilton v. Nakai,** 453 F.2d 152 (9th Cir. 1971)—suggesting a writ of assistance in favor of Hopi Indians in a dispute with Navahos over possession of reservation lands; *In re* **Lease Cancellation of Smith,** 719 P.2d 397 (Haw. 1986)—writ of assistance is a method of enforcing court judgment directing specific act]

c. Writs of sequestration [§187]

If contempt proves ineffectual in coercing performance of an equity decree, further pressure may be applied by *depriving the defendant of income* by sequestering his property and the rents and profits therefrom. The property is held by the court until the defendant complies. [*See* Fed. R. Civ. P. 70—authorizing this in specific performance cases; **Hirko v. Hirko,** 398 A.2d 1353 (N.J. 1979)—sequestration of insurance policies]

(1) Enforcement of money decrees [§188]

In the past, the writ was used *to enforce money decrees* by *selling* the sequestered property and applying the proceeds to the money claim—a case of equity acting *in rem.* In *modern* practice, under a merged procedure, authorization for the use of the *writ of execution* to enforce money decrees has largely replaced this practice. [**Hellwig v. Hellwig,** 426 N.E.2d 1087 (Ill. 1981)—sequestration of marital assets in proceeding to dissolve a marriage]

2. Legal Effect of Equitable Decrees

a. Specific performance of contract for sale of land within state [§189]

If the land is within the state, the court has jurisdiction over the res (land). If there is personal jurisdiction over the defendant (the vendor), she may be ordered to convey (and be imprisoned until she complies). If there is *no* personal jurisdiction, statutes uniformly permit the plaintiff to proceed *quasi in rem—i.e.,* the local land is attached and the nonresident defendant given notice of pending litigation. The court's decree of specific performance can be carried out by appointment of an officer of the court to execute a conveyance on behalf of the absent defendant; or, alternatively, the decree itself may be regarded as a valid conveyance of title. [**Garfein v. McInnis,** 248 N.Y. 261 (1928)]

(1) Note

Historically, equity decrees operated only in personam, and coercion of the defendant was essential to effect a conveyance. The in rem effect given to equity decrees mentioned above is generally the result of statutory changes and the adoption of code procedure.

(2) Application

The maxim that equity acts in personam still retains validity, however. Injunctions prohibiting certain acts by a defendant do not make those acts done in violation of the decree invalid. Thus, an injunction ordering a defendant not to change a beneficiary on an insurance policy does not render a change made in violation of the decree a nullity. The defendant may be in contempt, but the change of beneficiary is effective. [**Estate of Korzekwa v. Prudential Insurance Co.,** 669 S.W.2d 775 (Tex. 1984)]

b. Decrees affecting land in another state

(1) No power to order conveyance without personal jurisdiction over seller [§190]

A court has no primary jurisdiction directly to affect title to land in another state—*e.g.,* outside its geographical jurisdiction. Such a decree is in rem and there is no jurisdiction over the res.

(2) Court may act in personam as to land outside state [§191]

Even so, *if* the court has *personal* jurisdiction over the defendant-seller of the land, equity may act "in personam"; *i.e.,* the court may order the defendant to execute a conveyance of the title to the out-of-state land.

(a) Result of compliance [§192]

If the defendant complies, well and good (the fact that the conveyance was executed under the court's duress does *not* affect its validity as a conveyance).

(b) Result of noncompliance [§193]

But if the defendant-seller fails to execute the conveyance and departs the jurisdiction, the court's decree is *ineffective. Rationale:* The decree itself can have no direct effect on title in another state (*see* above), and contempt proceedings will not be available to coerce compliance because the defendant is beyond the court's reach.

(3) Similar rules apply if court orders acts outside state [§194]

The same principles apply if the plaintiff seeks an injunction directing the defendant either to perform, or to refrain from performing, some *act* outside the state (*e.g.,* suit to compel the defendant to repair property located in another state, to refrain from trespassing on land in another state, or to refrain from bringing a lawsuit in another state). Without personal jurisdiction over the defendant, a court can grant no relief whatsoever; with personal jurisdiction, it *can* grant the injunctive relief sought, but the enforcement of its decree by contempt may be impossible if the defendant refuses to comply and leaves the forum state.

Example: P claimed that the United States had wrongfully seized and occupied his cattle ranch in Honduras for use as a military base. In an action filed in the District of Columbia, the court held on appeal that the complaint stated a cause of action. The extraterritorial location of the property did not bar equitable relief. [**De Arellano v. Weinberger,** 745 F.2d 1500 (D.C. Cir. 1984); *and see* **Bashir v. Bache,** 581 So. 2d 613 (Fla. 1991)—the court ordered defendant over whom it had personal jurisdiction to join in his ex-wife's petition to a Pakistani court to allow their son to travel to the United States for a 30-day visit]

(4) Recognition of equity decrees by other states [§195]

Because of the residual effect of the notion that equity acts only in personam, the *propriety* of issuing orders such as those in the paragraphs above (§§191-194) depends upon the *likelihood* of their being recognized and enforced abroad. This involves considerations of *full faith and credit* and *comity*, which turn on the *type* of decree involved.

(a) Decrees for payment of money [§196]

Equity decrees ordering a defendant to pay money are *entitled to "full faith and credit,"* meaning that they are constitutionally entitled to recognition and enforcement in every other state. [**Dorey v. Dorey,** 609 F.2d 1128 (5th Cir. 1980)—support decree]

(b) Decrees affecting title to land in other state [§197]

With regard to the adjudication of equities in land located in other states, there is *no clear holding* that such decrees are entitled to "full faith and credit." [*See* **Fall v. Eastin,** 215 U.S. 1 (1909)]

1) But note

As a practical matter, decrees affecting title to land in other states *will* be given recognition and enforcement in the state where the land is located. Some states do so on the basis of *full faith and credit,* while others do so on the basis of *comity* (cooperation), and still others do so on the theory of *res judicata* (issues once litigated are binding). [*See* **Day v. Wiswall,** 464 P.2d 626 (Ariz. 1970); **McKay v. Palmer,** 427 N.W.2d 620 (Mich. 1988)—decree given full faith and credit]

(c) Decrees requiring acts in other state [§198]

With regard to other forms of equity decrees, there has been no ruling by the Supreme Court requiring that they be given full faith and credit. Enforceability will depend on comity.

---

e.g. Example: If a court in State X issues an injunction that the defendant cease or reduce the commission of a nuisance by closing down a factory in State Y, there may be good reasons for State Y to disregard the contention that the equities have been settled by the State X decree. Equitable relief is *discretionary*. The local courts are entitled to retain the prerogative to exercise discretion as to equity decrees affecting local interests that were not represented in the court where the decree was entered.

(d) Injunctions against foreign suits [§199]

In the absence of fraud, oppression, or gross impropriety, a court will *not* enjoin a party from *prosecution* of an action in a foreign state. [**Tabor & Co. v. McNall,** 333 N.E.2d 562 (Ill. 1975); **Pfaff v. Chrysler Corp.,** 610 N.E.2d 51 (Ill. 1992); **Gau Shan Co. v. Bankers Trust Co.,** 956 F.2d 1349 (6th Cir. 1992); *but see* **SpanEng Associates v. Weidner,** 771 F.2d 464 (10th Cir. 1985); **Laker Airways v. Sabena,** 731 F.2d 909 (D.C. Cir. 1984)—granting injunction to protect court's jurisdiction]

1) Note

Whether such injunctions when issued are entitled to full faith and credit has never been resolved by the Supreme Court. There is a division of authority on the point, with some courts holding that the injunction must be enforced. [*See* **Smith v. Walter E. Heller & Co.,** 82 Cal. App. 3d 259 (1978)] In **Baker v. General Motors,** 522 U.S. 222 (1998), the most recent Supreme Court decision raising the full faith and credit issue, the Court was asked to enforce a Michigan injunction in a subsequent lawsuit in Missouri. In that case, General Motors obtained an injunction prohibiting an employee from *testifying* in litigation brought against the company. The employee was subsequently subpoenaed to testify in a lawsuit brought against General Motors in Missouri. General Motors sought to prevent that testimony by arguing that the Michigan injunction should be accorded full faith and credit. In rejecting this argument, the Court ruled that a Missouri court was not required to apply Michigan enforcement procedures to a case filed in Missouri by a person not a party to the Michigan litigation. A decree by the Michigan court "cannot command obedience elsewhere on a matter the Michigan court lacks authority to resolve."

D. Ancillary Equitable Remedies

1. Introduction [§200]

Equity decrees and orders are frequently sought as ancillary relief to a pending lawsuit that may or may not otherwise involve equitable issues. They are sought as a means of *preserving rights or expediting* the pending lawsuit.

2. Maintaining Status Quo Pending Final Decree

a. Temporary restraining orders [§201]

The purpose of a temporary restraining order ("t.r.o.") is to maintain the status quo pending issuance of a preliminary injunction.

(1) Grounds for issuance [§202]

The *grounds* upon which such orders may be issued are usually *emergent* in nature; threats of *irreparable harm* from the delay are required (*see infra*, §208).

(2) *Ex parte* orders [§203]

A t.r.o. may be issued *ex parte—i.e.,* on affidavits of the complainant *without* affording the defendant notice or opportunity to be heard. But the plaintiff must make a strong showing as to why such notice and hearing should not be required. [*See* Fed. R. Civ. P. 65]

(a) Note

The issuance of an *ex parte* order without such a showing is subject to *constitutional* (due process) attack. [**Carroll v. President of Princess Anne**, 393 U.S. 175 (1968)]

(b) And note

Although a t.r.o. may issue without notice and opportunity to be heard, it does not become *binding* until the defendant has received at least informal notice of its existence and contents. [**Walker v. City of Birmingham**, 181 So. 2d 493 (Ala. 1966)]

(3) Duration [§204]

The duration of a t.r.o. is *limited* to from 5 to 15 days (normally 10), after which it automatically expires unless renewed.

(4) No appeal [§205]

Unlike a preliminary injunction, a t.r.o. is not appealable. [**Geneva Assurance Syndicate, Inc. v. Medical Emergency Services**, 964 F.2d 599 (7th Cir. 1992)]

b. Preliminary injunctions [§206]

Preliminary injunctions, also called temporary injunctions, interlocutory injunctions, or injunctions pendente lite, are to be distinguished from t.r.o.s.

(1) Procedure [§207]

Preliminary injunctions are issued only *after notice and an adversary hearing*—usually shortly after the action is commenced. Again, the purpose is to retain the status quo. Such an injunction remains in force *pending trial on the merits*, after which it will be dissolved or made permanent. An *injunction bond* is usually required (*see infra*, §213).

(2) Factors affecting granting of preliminary injunctions [§208]

Many of these factors are the usual ones taken into consideration when issuing permanent injunctions. But they are given greater emphasis at this point because the substantive issues have not been decided and the defendant deserves protection against potential injustice. *All the listed factors apply with even greater emphasis to t.r.o.s.*

(i) There must be potentially *irreparable harm* threatened to the plaintiff unless the injunction is issued;

(ii) The *balance of hardships* must weigh heavily in the plaintiff's favor;

(iii) The *likelihood of success on the merits* must favor the plaintiff;

(iv) The *interest of the general public* must be considered; and

(v) The *status quo* should be maintained.

[*See* **Estate of Presley v. Rossen**, 513 F. Supp. 1339 (D.N.J. 1981); **Michael-Curry v. Knutson Shareholders**, 423 N.W.2d 407 (Minn. 1988)]

(a) Note

The above factors are interrelated so that a very strong showing as to one factor may offset a weak showing as to another. However, some federal courts have stated that the first step should be to balance the likelihood of harm to plaintiff; and, if a decided imbalance of hardship appears in the plaintiff's favor, the "likelihood of success on the merits" factor can be displaced so that plaintiff need only have "raised questions going to the merits, so serious, substantial, difficult and doubtful as to make them fair ground for litigation." [**Blackwelder Furniture Co. v. Seilig Manufacturing Co.**, 550 F.2d 189 (4th Cir. 1977)]

(b) Distinguish

A slight variant of this rule is stated by the Second Circuit: "[T]here must be a showing of possible irreparable harm and either (i) probable success on the merits or (ii) sufficiently serious questions going to the merits to make them a fair ground for litigation *and* a balance of hardships tipping decidedly toward the party requesting the preliminary relief." [**Buffalo Courier-Express, Inc. v. Buffalo Evening News,** 601 F.2d 48 (2d Cir. 1979); *and see* **Los Angeles Memorial Coliseum Commission v. National Football League,** 634 F.2d 1197 (9th Cir. 1980)—adds "advancement of the public interest (in certain cases)"]

(c) Mathematical formula

Judge Posner provided a "simple formula" to solve the problem: Grant the preliminary injunction only if the harm to the plaintiff if the injunction is denied, multiplied by the probability that the denial would be an error (*i.e.,* that the plaintiff will win at trial), exceeds the harm to the defendant if the injunction is granted, multiplied by the probability that granting the injunction would be an error. [*See* **American Hospital Supply v. Hospital Products Ltd.,** 780 F.2d 589 (7th Cir. 1985)] However, the Seventh Circuit has since shifted to a more "subjective and intuitive" application of this approach. [**Abbott Laboratories v. Mead Johnson Co.,** 971 F.2d 6 (7th Cir. 1992)]

(d) Irreparable harm [§209]

The basic requirement of irreparable harm to the plaintiff has been variously defined. In one case, it meant "injury for which a monetary award cannot be adequate compensation." [**Loveridge v. Pendleton Woolen Mills,** 788 F.2d 914 (2d Cir. 1986)] In another case, however, it was said not to mean harm "beyond the possibility of repair or beyond compensation in damages" but to include "intangible harm not readily subject to measurement by any certain pecuniary standard." [**Prentice Medical Corp. v. Todd,** 495 N.E.2d 1044 (Ill. 1986)] Also, in **United Steelworkers v. Textron,** 836 F.2d 6 (1st Cir. 1987), emotional distress over possible loss of medical insurance was found to constitute irreparable injury.

EXAM TIP   **gilbert**

In an exam situation, be sure to differentiate whether a party is requesting a t.r.o. or a preliminary injunction. While both are intended to maintain the status quo, a t.r.o. is more of an *emergency* measure intended to maintain the status quo until a preliminary hearing can be held—the duration usually is limited to no more than *10 days*. Because of the t.r.o.'s emergency nature, it can be issued with little, or on strong showing of a reason, even no notice to the opposing party. However, a preliminary injunction is a more *long-term* measure to maintain the status quo until completion of a *trial on the merits* of the underlying case. As a result, a preliminary injunction only will be issued after the opponent receives both notice and an adversary hearing.

(3) Comment on "status quo" factor—mandatory vs. negative decrees at preliminary injunction stage

(a) Status quo defined [§210]

"Status quo" means things the way they were before the dispute arose—the "last uncontested status which preceded the pending controversy." [**Foundry Services v. Beneflux Corp.**, 206 F.2d 214 (2d Cir. 1953)]

(b) Mandatory injunctions disfavored at preliminary injunction stage [§211]

Since mandatory injunctions (in addition to being difficult to supervise) *change* the status quo, they generally are *not* granted at the preliminary stage unless there are *exceptional circumstances*. Otherwise, the effect would be to award everything the plaintiff asked for without a trial on the merits. [**Shodeen v. Chicago Title & Trust Co.**, 515 N.E.2d 1339 (Ill. 1987)]

1) But note

"Exceptional circumstances" will justify a mandatory injunction even at the preliminary injunction stage (*e.g.*, compelling a defendant to repair a dam on his property before it breaks and floods plaintiff's land, or compelling defendant to remove a pet Canadian black bear from his urban property [**Lakeshore Hills, Inc. v. Adcox**, 413 N.E.2d 548 (Ill. 1980)]; or removing an obstruction blocking a road [**Wheatly Grading Contractors Inc. v. DFT Investments**, 261 S.E.2d 614 (Ga. 1979)]; or creating a fund for medical treatment pending trial [**Friends for All Children v. Lockheed Aircraft**, 746 F.2d 816 (D.C. Cir. 1984)]; or ordering a school board to return a student diagnosed as having AIDS back to a normal classroom setting [**Robertson v. Granite City Community Unit School District**, 684 F. Supp. 1002 (S.D. Ill. 1988)]).

2) And note

If the defendant has *violated* a prohibitory injunction and thus altered the status quo, a mandatory injunction is proper to force him to undo that which he did. [**Keys v. Alligood**, 100 S.E. 113 (N.C. 1919)—defendant violated preliminary injunction prohibiting interference with roadway; mandatory injunction proper to compel him to restore road to its prior condition]

(c) Where the status quo is a "state of action" [§212]

The "mandatory negative" distinction is serviceable only when the status quo is a state of inaction. But suppose the status quo is the supply of water through pipes to the plaintiff, and the defendant shuts off the water. In this case a mandatory decree (in effect, if not in language) is required to *maintain* the status quo pending trial. The *proper test* of the propriety of a preliminary injunction is not whether it is mandatory or negative, but whether it maintains the *last uncontested status*. [**Courier Times, Inc. v. United Feature Syndicate, Inc.,** 445 A.2d 1288 (Pa. 1982)—order compelling defendant to continue supplying comic strips; **Crowe v. De Gioia,** 447 A.2d 173 (N.J. 1982)—order requiring defendant to continue to support unmarried cohabitant; **United States v. Price,** 688 F.2d 204 (3d Cir. 1982)—order requiring defendant to fund a diagnostic study; **Tustin v. Heckler,** 591 F. Supp. 1049 (D.N.J. 1984)—order restoring terminated Social Security disability payments]

(4) Injunction bonds [§213]

As additional protection against the possible improvident granting of a preliminary injunction, the plaintiff is required to post security, in an amount discretionary with the court, to cover such costs and damages as may be incurred by a wrongfully enjoined party. [Fed. R. Civ. P. 65(c); **Medafrica Line S.P.A. v. American West African Freight Conference,** 654 F. Supp. 155 (S.D.N.Y. 1987); **Hoxworth v. Blinder, Robinson & Co.,** 903 F.2d 186 (3d Cir. 1990)—"the requirement is almost mandatory"]

(a) Exceptions [§214]

Exceptions are made in suits brought by governmental entities, and, in a number of environmental cases brought by "public interest" groups, the size of the bond has been placed at a minimal amount. [*See* **Brown v. Artery Organization,** 691 F. Supp. 1459 (D.D.C. 1987)—only nominal bond required in litigation involving the Fair Housing Act; **Borough of Palmyra Board of Education v. F.C.,** 2 F. Supp. 2d 637 (D.N.J. 1998)—bond requirement waived for indigents seeking to assert rights under federal Rehabilitation Act]

(b) Limitation on recovery [§215]

Ordinarily, a party injured by an improvidently issued temporary injunction proceeds on the bond of the opposing party and any sureties and is limited to a recovery of the amount of the penalty of the injunction bond. [**Stevenson v. North Carolina Department of Insurance,** 262 S.E.2d 378 (N.C. 1980); **Jensen v. Torr,** 721 P.2d 992 (Wash. 1986)] The only remedy for compensation beyond the face amount of the bond is a motion to increase the bond during the pendency of the action, though this depends on local statutes and court rules. [**Venegas v. United Farm Workers,** 552 P.2d 210 (Wash. 1976); **Wallace v. Miller,** 140 Cal. App. 3d 636 (1983)—no recovery in the absence of a bond]

c. Civil arrest [§216]

An ancient writ "ne exeat" was used to detain the defendant within the jurisdiction so that an in personam decree could be enforced against him. Its use today is largely restricted to marital and custody disputes, though it is still on the statute books in many states. [**Mussallam v. Mussallam,** 364 S.E.2d 364 (N.C. 1988); **Roberts v. Fuhr,** 523 So. 2d 20 (Miss. 1987)]

d. Receivers [§217]

In any case in which a fund or property is in dispute, a court having equitable jurisdiction may appoint a receiver to protect and manage the property as an ancillary measure pending ultimate disposition of a case. This remedy is commonly invoked in partnership or corporate dissolution proceedings, proceedings to foreclose a mortgage, and even in domestic relations proceedings (where one spouse charges that the other is threatening to dissipate their commonly owned property). [**Omaha Indemnity Co. v. Wining,** 949 F.2d 235 (8th Cir. 1991); *cf.* **Reebok International v. Marinatech Enterprises,** 970 F.2d 552 (9th Cir. 1992)—court sequestered defendant's assets as part of its inherent equitable powers to issue provisional remedies]

3. Ancillary Remedies to Cut Down on Multiple Litigation

a. Bills of peace [§218]

Where a multiplicity of legal actions would otherwise exist, a bill in equity will lie. The effect is *not* a consolidation of legal actions, but a new separate equity suit—very likely with the parties reversed (*i.e.,* the defendant in the legal action may be the plaintiff in the bill of peace suit).

(1) Multiple actions at law between same parties

(a) Where repeated actions too costly [§219]

Typically, the plaintiff may have multiple legal actions against the defendant that are too expensive for the plaintiff to assert individually. In such cases, equitable jurisdiction exists to bring a single injunction suit solely on the ground of multiplicity.

Example: Dairy A repeatedly picks up and holds onto Dairy B's milk bottles. Repeated actions for replevin or damages would be too costly and inadequate. Dairy B may have a so-called bill of peace. [**Denver Milk Bottle Case & Can Exchange v. McKinzie,** 287 P. 868 (Colo. 1930)]

(b) Where actions vexatious [§220]

Similarly, where the plaintiff has been subjected to repeated vexatious legal actions filed by the defendant, which the plea of res judicata cannot stop (*e.g.,* repeated ejectment actions brought against plaintiff in the name of fictitious claimants), a bill of peace may lie to enjoin the defendant from filing any further action. [**Nuttelman v. Julch,** 424 N.W.2d 333 (Neb. 1988); *but see* **Hooker Chemicals v. Attorney General,** 298 N.W.2d 710 (Mich. 1980)—bill of peace not allowed when res judicata provides adequate protection against harassment]

1) **Note**

This equitable remedy is now codified by "vexatious litigant" statutes. [*See* **Ruderer v. United States,** 462 F.2d 897 (8th Cir. 1972)]

2) **Comment**

A modern example of this type of bill of peace is the *Younger* type of case (*supra,* §147), in which an injunction is sought against repeated bad faith, harassing criminal prosecutions or the threat thereof and the accused has no adequate legal remedy. (*See supra,* §154.)

(2) Actions involving multiple parties [§221]

Under early procedure, where numerous plaintiffs held similar claims at law against a single defendant, an obsolete form of bill of peace enabled them to file a single equity suit against the defendant. [**Sang Lung v. Jackson,** 85 F. 502 (N.D. Cal. 1898)—now obsolete because of joinder rules and class actions] Today, the bill of peace is used primarily where the *plaintiff has been sued* (perhaps in various courts) by *multiple* parties, in actions at law arising out of a single tort or breach of contract. For example, a manufacturer is sued by separate individuals claiming tort damages for nuisance; or an insurance company is sued by many policyholders because of blanket cancellation of policies. In such cases, plaintiff may *join all the claimants as defendants* in a single bill of peace in equity. (Note again that this has the effect of reversing parties.) [**American Lead Co. v. Davis,** 38 N.E.2d 281 (Ind. 1941)]

(a) Requirements [§222]

The various claims must involve *common issues of law and fact* (Pomeroy's rule; a minority rule holds that there must be a common right or title) [**Tribbette v. Illinois Central Railroad,** 12 So. 32 (Miss. 1892)], and there must be a *prospect* of actually *saving litigation.* This may be accomplished by enjoining all the pending legal actions save one and setting up a model trial before a jury on the liability issue. [**Hale v. Allinson,** 188 U.S. 56 (1903)]

(b) Virtual demise of this type of bill of peace [§223]

At present, the utility of this form of bill of peace in federal cases is jeopardized by the suggestion in **Dairy Queen, Inc. v. Wood,** *supra,*

§114, that a jury trial may be necessary on all damage issues that might be presented. If this is the case, no saving in litigation would be in prospect.

(c) Comment

In addition to the jury trial problem, the availability of *class actions* in modern law may eliminate the multiple-party, potentially vexatious legal actions that gave rise to this form of bill of peace. Also, the statutory declaratory judgment accomplishes the same purpose.

b. Interpleader [§224]

Interpleader is essentially a two-stage proceeding. In the first stage, a "stakeholder," who is being subjected to multiple and conflicting claims regarding the "stake" or res, tenders it into court and interpleads the claimants (names them all as parties to the suit). The rights of the multiple claimants are litigated during the second stage.

(1) Requirements [§225]

The original equitable bill required that:

(i) The *same thing or debt be claimed* by the various claimants;

(ii) The *adverse claims be derived from a common source*;

(iii) The *stakeholder have no claim or interest* in the subject matter; and

(iv) The *stakeholder have incurred no independent liability*.

[*See* **United States v. Olson,** 4 F.3d 562 (8th Cir. 1993)]

(2) Statutes [§226]

The equitable bill has largely been supplanted by statutory interpleader [*e.g.,* 28 U.S.C. §1335] or rule interpleader [*e.g.,* Fed. R. Civ. P. 22]. The modern form eliminates the above elements except for the requirement that the claims be *mutually exclusive.* [**Libby, McNeil & Libby v. City National Bank,** 592 F.2d 504 (9th Cir. 1978)]

(a) Caution

Modern interpleader still retains its equity characteristics to the extent that, to be effective, *in personam jurisdiction must be had* over all claimants. [**State Farm Fire & Casualty Co. v. Tashire,** 386 U.S. 523 (1967); **Lain v. John Hancock Mutual Life Insurance Co.,** 398 N.E.2d 278 (Ill. 1980)—liability insurer seeks to interplead all claimant victims of multi-party accident]

c. Bills quia timet [§227]

The term "quia timet" is roughly translated to mean "because he has reason to fear," and refers to a variety of ancillary equitable remedies *to prevent future litigation* at law that plaintiff has reason to fear may arise. [*See* **Escrow Agents' Fidelity v. Superior Court**, 4 Cal. App. 4th 491 (1992)] In a broad sense, it includes bills of peace and interpleader, above. Other varieties follow:

(1) Injunctions against future torts [§228]

Injunctive relief is granted only where injury is *certain* to result from the threatened action. [**Helix Land Co. v. City of San Diego**, 82 Cal. App. 3d 932 (1978)—injunction prohibiting flood control work denied because injury was not imminent and certain; **Nothaus v. City of Salem**, 585 S.W.2d 244 (Mo. 1979)—no injunction against a sanitary landfill because proof failed to show that injury was "practically certain" to result; *but see* **Freedman v. Briarcraft Property Owners**, 776 S.W.2d 212 (Tex. 1989)—construction of parking lot enjoined because injury was "reasonably certain" to occur]

(2) Bills to cancel documents [§229]

Bills to cancel documents are appropriate in some circumstances. For example, in a suit to cancel a promissory note executed by the plaintiff and delivered to the defendant by mistake (or without consideration), equitable relief is proper because the defendant might negotiate the instrument to a "holder in due course" (*see* Commercial Paper & Payment Law Summary) who would cut off any defense the plaintiff might have to the instrument, thus rendering any remedy at law inadequate.

(a) Limitation

There is a basic requirement that the instrument sought to be canceled *not* be void on its face. *Rationale:* The plaintiff would have no reason to fear legal action on such an instrument because no one can be a "holder in due course" of such an instrument.

(3) Bill to remove cloud on title [§230]

This is a special form of a bill to cancel. Traditionally:

(a) *Only* a cloud upon *real*, not personal, property may be canceled;

(b) *Only written*, not oral, claims may be canceled; and

(c) *Only legal titles* may be quieted—a holder of an equitable claim may not file against the holder of the legal title.

(4) Quiet title suits [§231]

Statutory actions, eliminating many of the defects of the original equitable bills, now prevail. However, the remedy may still be denied to an equitable claimant suing to quiet title against the legal owner. [*See* **Santoro v.**

Carbone, 22 Cal. App. 721 (1972)] Also, courts frequently hold that a suit to quiet title is restricted to a party in possession since ejectment is an adequate legal remedy for one out of possession. [**Fort Mojave Tribe v. La Follette,** 478 F.2d 1016 (9th Cir. 1973); **Bragg v. Marion,** 663 P.2d 505 (Wyo. 1983)]

(5) Declaratory judgment suits [§232]

This remedy is the statutory extension of the equitable bill quia timet, allowing declaration of rights *in advance* of legal actions (*e.g.,* a dispute between contracting parties as to interpretation of their contract obligations before any actual breach thereof). The principal characteristics are:

(a) *There must be a "case or controversy"* (few jurisdictions allow purely advisory opinions; *see supra,* §150).

(b) *The decision must have the effect of terminating the controversy.* [**Loy v. Bunderson,** 320 N.W.2d 175 (Wis. 1982); *and see* further discussions in Civil Procedure Summary]

Chapter Four:
Restitution

CONTENTS

Chapter Approach

Chapter Approach

In analyzing questions concerning restitution, you need to keep in mind two things:

1. The substantive basis of restitution is **unjust enrichment**. Therefore, you must consider whether a **benefit** has been conferred on the defendant that is **unjustly retained**.

2. There are **legal** restitutionary remedies (*e.g.*, quasi-contract) **and equitable** restitutionary remedies (*e.g.*, constructive trust, equitable liens, subrogation, and accounting). Consider the characteristics and requirements of each type before deciding on the most appropriate remedy.

A. Nature of Restitution

1. Substantive Basis [§233]

The substantive basis of restitution is unjust enrichment. The defendant must have a **benefit** that is **unjust for her to retain**. [Restatement of Restitution §1 (1937) ("Rest. Restitution"); Restatement (Third) of Restitution, Discussion Draft §1 (May 2000)]

a. Meaning of "benefit" [§234]

"Benefit" means some advantage and includes the receipt of tangible or intangible property or services, the satisfaction of obligations owed by defendant, or the saving of expense.

(1) Measurement of benefit [§235]

How to measure the restitutionary recovery is much debated and will be considered in detail in the chapters that follow. While economic value to the recipient is generally used as the standard [**Murdock-Bryant Construction v. Pearson**, 703 P.2d 1197 (Ariz. 1985)], restitution is allowed in cases where defendant's assets have not been increased nor her economic situation improved. Thus, restitution is available for recovering the value of services rendered in drilling a well even if the well is worthless because no water is found. Similarly, construction of a building that is useless and adds nothing to the market value of the land is nevertheless regarded as a "benefit" for the purpose of determining the availability of restitution. In these cases, restitution is measured by the reasonable value of the materials and services. [**Horseshoe Estates v. 2M Co.**, 713 P.2d 776 (Wyo. 1986)]

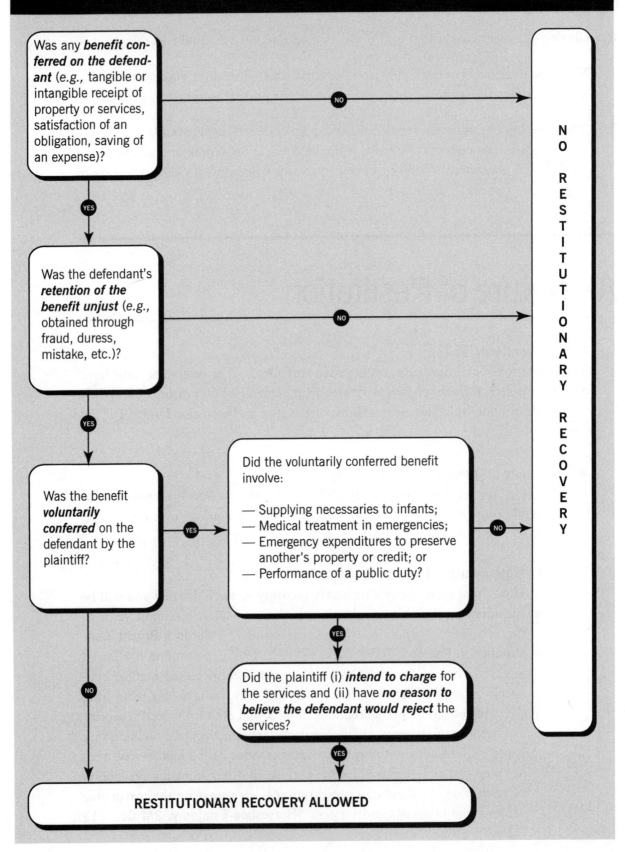

Was any **benefit conferred on the defendant** (e.g., tangible or intangible receipt of property or services, satisfaction of an obligation, saving of an expense)?

Was the defendant's **retention of the benefit unjust** (e.g., obtained through fraud, duress, mistake, etc.)?

Was the benefit **voluntarily conferred** on the defendant by the plaintiff?

Did the voluntarily conferred benefit involve:

— Supplying necessaries to infants;
— Medical treatment in emergencies;
— Emergency expenditures to preserve another's property or credit; or
— Performance of a public duty?

Did the plaintiff (i) **intend to charge** for the services and (ii) have **no reason to believe the defendant would reject** the services?

NO RESTITUTIONARY RECOVERY

RESTITUTIONARY RECOVERY ALLOWED

b. **"Unjust" retention [§236]**

Restitution is required only where the retention of the benefit is "unjust." Determination of when retention of a benefit is "unjust" is the principal subject matter of the law of restitution. Obvious examples are benefits obtained by fraud, duress, mistake, or tortious misconduct (but there are numerous other instances that will be examined in the sections that follow). On the other hand, the retention of benefits conferred on defendant as the result of legitimate contractual arrangements is not unjust and hence restitution is not awarded. [**Alaska Sales & Service v. Millet,** 735 P.2d 743 (Alaska 1987); *and see* **Farmers New World Life Insurance v. Jolley,** 747 S.W.2d 704 (Mo. 1988)—no unjust benefit in retaining attorney's fee although settlement award on which it was based had to be returned]

(1) **No recovery for benefits voluntarily conferred upon another [§237]**

An "officious intermeddler" has no right to restitution; any benefits *voluntarily* conferred by one person upon another may be retained. A voluntary payment is one made without mistake, fraud, or coercion on a demand that is not enforceable against the payor. [**Sturdevant v. Mills,** 580 P.2d 923 (Mont. 1978)]

Example: Norton *voluntarily* pays a mortgage note owed by the Haggetts to Northfield Savings Bank. Norton cannot recover the payment from the Haggetts. Although the Haggetts had a benefit, it was voluntarily conferred. [**Norton v. Haggett,** 85 A.2d 571 (Vt. 1952); *and see* **Bank of Nova Scotia v. Bloch,** 533 F. Supp. 1356 (D.V.I. 1982)]

Example: Where the ownership of a horse was in dispute between Sarah and Will, the owner of a stable, Charlie, expended services in caring for the horse, although Sarah had neither requested Charlie to do so nor promised to pay for those services. Charlie sought to recover the reasonable value of such services from Sarah. *Held:* Charlie had no right to recovery since there was *neither agreement nor acquiescence* by Sarah; Charlie was no more than a volunteer. [*See* **Bailey v. West,** 249 A.2d 414 (R.I. 1969)]

Example: A dam was repaired by adjoining lakeshore property owners. Other property owners, whose property was benefited by the repairs, refused to participate in the project. Restitution was denied. [**Knaus v. Dennler,** 525 N.E.2d 207 (Ill. 1988); *and see* **Board of Directors v. Western National Bank,** 487 N.E.2d 974 (Ill. 1985)]

Example: Cooper, an attorney, brought an action claiming compensation for furnishing senior White House officials with a memo that saved Salomon Brothers from criminal prosecution. Compensation was denied because the services were neither requested nor accepted. [**Cooper v. Salomon Brothers, Inc.,** 1 F.3d 82 (2d Cir. 1993)]

Example: Hazel lived in the same house with Nelson, cared for him, and bore his child. Upon Nelson's death, restitution for Hazel's services was denied because there was no evidence that Nelson knew Hazel expected compensation and accepted the services on that basis. [**Wade v. Brooks,** 413 S.E.2d 333 (S.C. 1992)]

Compare: Sandra paid her ex-husband's hospital bill. Restitution was granted to Sandra because the court ruled that this was not a gratuity but was intended to be a loan to tide him over a financial crisis. [**Cole v. Cole,** 517 N.E.2d 1248 (Ind. 1988)]

(2) Exceptions [§238]

Exceptions to the rule of nonrecovery by "volunteers" are made in situations where it is thought desirable policy to encourage intervention *to protect another's life or property.* [*See* Rest. Restitution §§112 *et seq.*] These exceptions include:

(i) *Supplying necessaries to infants*;

(ii) *Medical treatment in emergencies*;

(iii) *Emergency expenditures* to preserve another's *property or credit*; and

(iv) *Performance of a public duty*—*e.g.,* removal of road obstruction caused by defendant.

[*See* **Hebron Public School District v. United States Gypsum,** 690 F. Supp. 866 (D.N.D. 1988)—removal of asbestos from school building; **Hazelwood Water District v. First Union Management,** 715 P.2d 498 (Or. 1986)—installation of anti-flowback device to prevent water pollution; *but see* **Hiland Apartments v. City of Hillsboro,** 642 N.E.2d 421 (Ohio 1994)—restitution denied to party who repaired a city alley without the city's consent]

(a) **Note**

Even in these exceptional cases, there must be an *intent to charge*, and in emergency situations, there must be *no reason to believe that the services would be rejected*. [**Nassr v. Commonwealth**, 477 N.E.2d 987 (Mass. 1985)—no restitution for Commonwealth's services in abating a nuisance because Commonwealth failed to prove intent to charge]

Example: During the 1970 power blackout in New York, the United States provided electricity to Con Edison, a power company that had a duty to provide electricity. The United States took that duty upon itself, with intent to charge, and such services were necessary to satisfy the requirements of public decency, health, and safety. Thus, recovery was allowed under the doctrine of emergency assistance. [**United States v. Consolidated Edison of New York**, 452 F. Supp. 638 (S.D.N.Y. 1977)]

Example: If a vessel deviates from its course to rescue the crew of a burning ship at the request of the ship's owner, the costs of the deviation are recoverable in quasi-contract. [*In re* **Ta Chi Navigation Corp.**, 583 F. Supp. 1322 (S.D.N.Y. 1984)]

---

2. Purpose of Restitution [§239]

The objective of restitutionary remedies is to restore the status quo ante by compelling the defendant to return unjust benefits. This may be accomplished either by compelling the *restoration of specific property* wrongfully withheld (specific restitution—replevin, ejectment, or a mandatory injunction), or by *awarding* to the injured party a *sum of money* measured by the value of the benefit received by the defendant. These latter *substitutionary* methods of restitution are considered in the following sections.

a. Note

In most of the cases involving disrupted transactions considered in the sections that follow, a contract exists in the sense that an *agreement supported by consideration* has been made. For various reasons, the injured party may choose not to enforce that agreement but instead to claim restitution of benefits conferred. The restitutionary claim rests on the basic premise that benefits conferred in reliance on a contract breached by the defendant are unjustly retained.

(1) Distinguish

A somewhat similar situation results when a "contract" is contemplated but never reaches fruition. Services may be requested to further the ultimate goal of a contract that is *never reached*. If the services benefit the person requesting them, restitution for their reasonable value will be an appropriate remedy. (*See* above.) However, when the person requesting the services does *not* benefit from such services, there is a problem.

Example: Suppose work is done to fix up premises at the request of a putative tenant but no binding lease ever ensues. Without a contract, there are no contract remedies. One solution has been to find "promissory estoppel" under section 90 of the Restatement of Contracts, thereby allowing at least reliance damages. The other is to permit restitution (quantum meruit) measured by the market value of the services, abandoning the "unconscionable requirement of 'benefit' to the defendant." Both of the above approaches were combined in the case of **Earhart v. William Low Co.**, 25 Cal. 3d 503 (1979), where improvement work done at defendant's request was not on defendant's property.

B. Legal and Equitable Remedies

1. Restitution at Law—Quasi-Contract

a. Background [§240]

The legal remedy of restitution in money (as distinguished from the common law actions of replevin or ejectment where restitution is in specie) evolved from the common law action of *indebitatus assumpsit*. Originally an action to compensate for breach of an assumed duty or undertaking, assumpsit was later extended to provide a remedy for breach of simple contracts. In the landmark case of **Moses v. MacFerlan**, 97 Eng. Rep. 676 (1760), Lord Mansfield further expanded the action by holding that assumpsit would lie in a situation where there was no agreement at all but where the defendant had money that "in justice and fairness" ought to be paid back to the plaintiff. The obligation to repay was thus imposed by law as a matter of "natural justice." The action to enforce the obligation was said to be "quasi ex contractu" (as if a contract). This comment of Lord Mansfield is the basis for the common reference to legal restitution as "quasi-contract."

b. Contracts vs. quasi-contracts [§241]

Since the action of assumpsit was also proper for breach of an express contract or a contract implied in fact, considerable confusion in terminology and usage has resulted. It is, therefore, important to keep certain basic distinctions in mind.

(1) Implied-in-fact contracts [§242]

Implied-in-fact contracts are actual agreements, but whereas express contracts are established by language, implied-in-fact contracts are created by *conduct* of the parties (*e.g.*, raising one's hand to bid at an auction in response to the auctioneer's request for a bid at a specified price). [*See* **Heaton v. Imus**, 608 P.2d 631 (Wash. 1980); **Eaton v. Engelcke Manufacturing, Inc.**, 681 P.2d 1312 (Wash. 1984)]

(a) Means of recovery [§243]

At common law, the quantum counts in assumpsit were used to recover for breach of implied-in-fact contracts. For breach of an employment contract, *quantum meruit* (for so much as he deserves) was the proper count. For breach of a contract for the sale of goods, the proper count was *quantum valebant* (for so much as they are worth). When the technical refinements of the common law lost significance, it became the practice to use either common or quantum counts in these situations.

(b) Quantum meruit actions [§244]

Quantum meruit actions are inherently ambiguous. As indicated above, some are based on factual situations where a promise to pay may be implied from the conduct of the parties. But many actions labeled quantum meruit are brought in situations where there is no agreement and the promise is implied in law to avoid unjust enrichment of the defendant. These actions are restitutionary and are discussed below (*see infra,* §245). [**Weichert Co. Realtors v. Ryan**, 608 A.2d 280 (N.J. 1992)]

1) Distinguish

Where there is an *express written contract* breached by the defendant after partial performance, the plaintiff has an option of either enforcing the contract or seeking restitution of the value of the benefit conferred on the defendant. [**Harker Heights v. Sun Meadows Land**, 830 S.W.2d 313 (Tex. 1992); **J.A. Sullivan Corp. v. Commonwealth**, 494 N.E.2d 789 (Mass. 1986); *and see infra*, §§1213-1240]

2) Note

The ambiguity as to quantum meruit arises because the common count can be used in either the contract or the quasi-contract case. [*See* **Ramsey v. Ellis**, 484 N.W.2d 331 (Wis. 1992)]

(2) Implied-in-law contracts (quasi-contracts) [§245]

Implied-in-law or quasi-contracts are *not contracts at all*. There is no promise and no agreement. Rather, quasi-contract actions are restitutionary and, therefore, *lie only in situations of unjust enrichment* where the law imposes an obligation to repay. The only relation between quasi-contracts and actual contracts is that at common law, assumpsit was the proper action to recover in both situations. [**Board of Education v. Rettaliata,** 78 N.Y.2d 128 (1991)]

(a) Historical background [§246]

At common law, proper pleading in these cases was by the common counts in indebitatus assumpsit. These were simple pleading formulas, the most familiar of which stated that the defendant was indebted to the plaintiff *"for money had and received"*; or *"for goods sold and delivered"*; or *"for work and labor performed."*

1) Note

Originally, restitution was permitted only where the common count "for money had and received" could be pleaded, but subsequently the use of other counts was authorized. It is still common practice today to use what are, in effect, streamlined common counts in pleading these cases under modern codes and the Federal Rules. [*See* Form 8 of Fed. R. Civ. P. Appendix; *and see* **Belmont International v. American International Shoe,** 831 P.2d 15 (Or. 1992)]

2) Comment

Because restitution at law has this complicated historical background, it is still the practice to refer to the remedy as "quasi-contract" even though *it has nothing whatever to do with consensual agreements*. In the sections that follow, the various situations in which the law imposes an obligation to restore a benefit will be examined under the caption *"Restitution."*

(b) Advantages of quasi-contract [§247]

Election to sue in quasi-contract may offer important *procedural advantages*—*e.g.,* a longer statute of limitations, or the right to counterclaim, attach, or assign the claim. [**H. Russell Taylor's Fire Prevention Service, Inc. v. Coca-Cola Bottling,** 99 Cal. App. 711 (1929)— contract, not tort, statute of limitations applies to quasi-contract action] *Caution:* Under the Tucker Act, the United States is liable for claims based on implied-in-fact contracts but not on contracts implied-in-law. [**Hatzlachh Supply Co. v. United States,** 444 U.S. 460 (1980); *and see* **Mass Transit Administration v. Granite Construction Co.,** 471 A.2d 1121 (Md. 1984)—sovereign immunity not waived as to implied-in-law claims under state law]

(c) Disadvantages of quasi-contract [§248]

There may be disadvantages to choosing quasi-contract over an alternative tort remedy. For example, joint tortfeasors are jointly and severally liable; only the defendant who *gained* by a joint tort is liable in quasi-contract.

2. Restitution in Equity—Constructive Trust, Equitable Lien, Subrogation, Accounting

a. Constructive trust [§249]

A constructive trust has been referred to as a "fraud rectifying" trust since its purpose is to prevent unjust enrichment. Unlike the express trust, it is imposed by law *without regard to the intention of the parties.* The constructive trust is thus analogous to a quasi-contractual obligation in that both are imposed by law to compel the restoration of unjust gains. [Rest. Restitution §1; *and see* **American Family Care v. Irwin,** 571 So. 2d 1053 (Ala. 1990)]

(1) Nature of remedy [§250]

Restoration of any unjust enrichment is accomplished by imposing a duty on the defendant to *transfer property to the plaintiff.* This is the sole obligation of the defendant as constructive trustee, and this obligation is enforced by mandatory injunction. [*See* **Harmon v. Harmon,** 613 P.2d 1298 (Ariz. 1980)]

(2) Time of creation [§251]

A constructive trust comes into existence "on the date of the order or judgment of a court of competent jurisdiction declaring that a series of events has given rise to a constructive trust." [**Palmland Villas I Condominium Association v. Taylor,** 390 So. 2d 123 (Fla. 1980)]

EXAM TIP   **gilbert**

Remember that a constructive trust is a court ordered *remedy* for unjust enrichment, not an express trust created by an individual. The court makes the unjustly enriched party a trustee, but the trustee's *only duty is to transfer* the unjustly gained property to the proper party.

---

(3) Requirements [§252]

Requirements for the imposition of a constructive trust are:

(a) *The defendant has legal title* to property upon which the constructive trust can be imposed (if the defendant has no title to the property—mere possession is not enough—the remedy is unavailable, for there can be no trust without a trust res) [*see* **Burch & Cracchiolo v. Pugliani,** 697 P.2d 674 (Ariz. 1985)—prerequisite to imposition of constructive trust is identification of specific property belonging to claimant; **Raben-Pastal v. City of Coconut Creek,** 490 So. 2d 975 (Fla. 1986); *but see* **Rosebud Sioux Tribe v. Strain,** 432 N.W.2d 259 (S.D. 1988)—constructive trust in amount of $173,921 for funds misappropriated by attorney although res on which trust was to be imposed was dissipated down to $85];

(b) *The retention of the property* by defendant would result in *unjust enrichment*; and

(c) *The remedy at law is inadequate* (at least according to some authorities). *Insolvency of the defendant* satisfies this requirement— *i.e.*, a showing that any money judgment obtained against defendant would not be paid.

EXAM TIP   gilbert

If presented with the choice between a constructive trust and another remedy, be sure to keep in mind the following advantages of a constructive trust:

- It permits the plaintiff to claim *specific property* and thus may allow him to take *priority over other creditors* of the defendant;

- The plaintiff has the advantage of any *increase in value* of the property because the imposition of a constructive trust results in a transfer of legal ownership of the property from defendant to plaintiff; and

- The plaintiff may take advantage of the equitable doctrine of *tracing* (see *infra*, §274).

---

(4) Effect of sale to bona fide purchaser [§253]

A transfer of title to a bona fide purchaser ("BFP")—one who pays *value* and takes *without notice* of the facts giving rise to the constructive trust—cuts off plaintiff's right to a constructive trust against the item so transferred (but it does *not* cut off plaintiff's rights against the proceeds obtained in the transfer, which may constitute a substitute trust res).

(a) Distinguish

Transfer to a non-BFP (*e.g.*, a donee or a purchaser who *knows* of plaintiff's claim) does *not* cut off plaintiff's equity; a constructive trust can be imposed as to such transferee the same as against the transferor. [*See In re* **Marriage of Allen**, 724 P.2d 651 (Colo. 1986)—proceeds of embezzled funds transferred to wife in a marriage dissolution proceeding did not make wife a BFP]

b. Equitable lien [§254]

A lien is a charge on property *to secure debts or other obligations* and gives the holder the right to *sell* the property to satisfy the debt. Liens may be created either by agreement or by judicial proceedings. The equitable lien as a restitutionary remedy is one imposed by a court to avoid unjust enrichment. [Rest. Restitution §161]

(1) Requirement for lien [§255]

The requirement for the imposition of an equitable lien is an *unjust benefit* traceable to property owned by the defendant. [*See* **Bocker Co. v.**

Eagle Bank of Madison City, 525 N.E.2d 146 (Ill. 1988)—essential elements of equitable lien are "(1) a debt, duty or obligation owing by one person to another, and (2) an identifiable res to which that obligation fastens"]

(2) Distinguish—constructive trust [§256]

Sometimes the aggrieved party will have a *choice* of either the constructive trust or the equitable lien. For example, if Dan misappropriates money from Paula and uses the money to buy land, either remedy may be invoked. If Paula elects the constructive trust remedy, she recovers the land (and thus has the advantage of any increase in value). If Paula chooses the equitable lien alternative, a lien is imposed on the land for the full amount of the debt (but this is the maximum recovery allowed). Thus, the equitable lien may be advantageous where the land has *decreased* in value. Paula may seek a money judgment for the full amount of her claim and have the security of the lien to the extent of the value of the land. [**Provencher v. Berman,** 699 F.2d 568 (1st Cir. 1983)]

(a) Note

Where money is misappropriated and used to improve *property already owned* by the wrongdoer, *only* the equitable lien remedy is appropriate because a constructive trust may be used only on property that was *acquired* with misappropriated money. Because the wrongdoer is enriched to the extent of the improvement financed by plaintiff's money, an equitable lien may be imposed to prevent such unjust enrichment. [**Frambach v. Dunihue,** 419 So. 2d 1115 (Fla. 1982)]

(3) Effect of sale to bona fide purchaser [§257]

The equitable lien may be imposed only to the extent that plaintiff's property can be traced to the wrongdoer. Since the lien is equitable, it is *cut off* by transfer of the property to a *BFP*.

(4) Enforcement of lien [§258]

Enforcement of the equitable lien ordinarily is by court-ordered *foreclosure and sale* of the property. But in proper circumstances, the court may order the claim satisfied in other ways—*e.g.,* by executing a *formal encumbrance* in plaintiff's favor.

c. Subrogation [§259]

Subrogation is an equitable doctrine applied where one person *nonofficiously discharges an obligation for which another is primarily liable* and which the latter ought to pay. Thus, subrogation is a remedy for unjust enrichment resulting from the use of plaintiff's property to discharge a debt or lien, rather than to acquire property. [Rest. Restitution §162]

CONSTRUCTIVE TRUST vs. EQUITABLE LIEN

	CONSTRUCTIVE TRUST	EQUITABLE LIEN
DEFINITION	Remedy imposed by the court to avoid unjust enrichment in which the unjustly enriched party (the defendant) becomes *trustee* over the unjustly acquired property and must *transfer* it to the innocent party (the plaintiff).	Remedy imposed by the court to avoid unjust enrichment, in which the innocent party (the plaintiff) obtains a *lien* over the unjustly enriched party's (the defendant's) property, which can then be *sold* at a foreclosure sale pursuant to the lien.
REQUIREMENTS	• Defendant has legal title to the property; • Defendant's title was gained through use of the misappropriated property (*i.e.*, plaintiff's misappropriated property (usually money) must be traced to defendant's newly acquired property—key: trace and identify—*see infra*, §279); and • Retention of the property by the defendant would result in unjust enrichment.	• Defendant has legal title to the benefited property; and • The unjust benefit can be traced to the plaintiff's property.
IF THE PROPERTY IS WORTH *LESS* THAN THE CLAIM, CAN THE PLAINTIFF SUE THE DEFENDANT FOR THE REMAINDER OWED?	No	Yes
IF THE PROPERTY IS WORTH *MORE* THAN THE CLAIM, DOES THE PLAINTIFF HAVE TO RETURN THE SURPLUS VALUE TO THE DEFENDANT?	No	Yes, recovery is limited to the amount of the lien.
IS THE REMEDY CUT OFF BY A BONA FIDE PURCHASER OF THE PROPERTY?	Yes	Yes

(1) Unjust enrichment [§260]

Subrogation is allowed *only* in situations where an unjust or inequitable benefit is conferred on the defendant. Thus, in **Smart v. Tower Land & Investment Co.,** 597 S.W.2d 333 (Tex. 1980), subrogation was denied to a mortgagee who paid delinquent taxes after purchase of the property at the mortgage foreclosure sale. Since buyers at foreclosure sales would take delinquent taxes into account in bidding at the sale, the court ruled that "the equities of this suit" did not entitle the mortgagee to subrogation.

(2) Definition [§261]

Subrogation is accomplished by reviving in equity, for the benefit of the aggrieved party, an obligation similar to the one discharged. The plaintiff is said to be subrogated to the position of the creditor. Thus, the interests acquired by the plaintiff (subrogee) depend on the nature of the original claim. [**Northwest Farm Bureau Insurance Co. v. Althauser,** 750 P.2d 1166 (Or. 1988)]

(a) Secured creditor [§262]

If the creditor had a secured claim, the subrogee can reach the security; if the creditor had a preference, the subrogee is entitled to that priority if it is not personal to the creditor.

Example: Payor, by mistake, pays a secured debt owed by Debtor to Creditor. Payor is entitled to be subrogated to the position Creditor held prior to payment and thus both debt and security are revived for the benefit of Payor. [*See* **Banton v. Hackney,** 557 So. 2d 807 (Ala. 1989)]

(b) Unsecured creditor [§263]

If the creditor had neither security nor a preference, the only advantages provided by subrogation over a quasi-contract action are procedural, *e.g.,* a longer statute of limitations.

(3) Note

The remedies of subrogation, constructive trust, and equitable lien all require *tracing* of plaintiff's property to defendant to establish the unjust enrichment (*see infra,* §274), and all may be cut off by sale to a *bona fide purchaser* (*see* above).

d. Accounting for gains [§264]

The development of restitution in equity did not embrace the restrictive notion of early quasi-contract at law that the "benefit" should come directly from the plaintiff or even be accompanied by any detriment to the plaintiff. The focus in equitable restitution is upon the *disgorgement of ill-gotten gains.*

This approach is derived from and illustrated by the equitable requirement that a trustee cannot retain any gain from a violation of the trust even though the beneficiary sustained no loss. Hence, in many instances in the chapters that follow, there is discussion of equitable restitution in the form of accounting for profits—*i.e.,* profits that in good conscience should be disgorged to the beneficiary of the fictitious constructive trust.

(1) Note

Caution is necessary in referring to "equitable restitution" so that no misunderstanding results. For example, in **Securities and Exchange Commission v. Huffman,** 996 F.2d 800 (5th Cir. 1993), the court, in approving a disgorgement order to pay over to the S.E.C. funds received from illegal activities in violation of the securities law, noted that "disgorgement is not precisely restitution . . . . It is an equitable remedy [and] does not aim to compensate the victims of wrongful acts as restitution does. Thus a disgorgement order might be for an amount more or less than is the requirement to make victims whole."

Chapter Five:
Injuries to Tangible
Property Interests

CONTENTS

Chapter Approach

This chapter covers remedies for the invasion of proprietary interests in money, personalty, and realty. Although exam questions in these areas may concern many topics discussed in this chapter, the most likely areas for testing are those listed below.

1. **Misappropriation of Money**

   Be sure you understand the equitable doctrine of *tracing* and the problem of *commingled funds*. These are favorite topics for exam questions.

2. **Injuries to Personalty**

   Questions involving an invasion of someone's interest in personal property generally emphasize the tort of *conversion*. If so, you should:

   a. *Identify the tort* of conversion;

   b. *Discuss* the availability of the alternate remedies of (i) specific restitution by *replevin* or *mandatory injunction*, (ii) *compensatory damages*, and (iii) *quasi-contract* (waiver of tort and suit in assumpsit).

   c. *Explain how the award differs* depending on the remedy chosen.

3. **Injuries to Realty**

   These questions tend to focus on *trespass* (including *encroachments*) and nuisances. In either case, be sure to explain and apply the *"balancing of hardships"* doctrine.

A. Misappropriation of Money

1. **Legal Remedies [§265]**

   Two legal remedies are available to the injured party for the wrongful misappropriation of money: She may either sue for damages in a tort action for *conversion*, or, in the alternative, "waive the tort" and seek restitution in *quasi-contract*. [**Weiss v. Marcus,** 51 Cal. App. 3d 590 (1975)]

   a. **Conversion [§266]**

      At common law, to make out a prima facie case for conversion of money, it was not enough that the plaintiff showed that a wrongdoer exercised unlawful dominion over money; the plaintiff also had to *identify the specific money* taken. This often presents an insurmountable burden of proof. Thus, at common law, conversion was limited to simple situations where bags of coins, etc., were converted. [*See* **Mid-America Fire & Marine Insurance v. Middleton,** 468 N.E.2d 1335 (Ill. 1984)—money in coin or bills]

(1) Modern view [§267]

While courts no longer require plaintiffs to identify the specific money taken, they still require plaintiffs to show that a *specific identifiable fund* was taken. [**Eggert v. Weisz,** 839 F.2d 1261 (7th Cir. 1988)—conversion denied, no identifiable fund; *but see* **Intermarkets U.S.A. v. C-E Natco,** 749 S.W.2d 603 (Tex. 1988)—proceeds of letter of credit constitutes specific identifiable fund; **Hodnett v. Harmon,** 523 So. 2d 443 (Ala. 1988)—retention by dealer of manufacturer's rebate to buyer constituted conversion of funds]

b. Quasi-contract [§268]

The alternative legal remedy for misappropriation of money is quasi-contract—"waiving the tort" of conversion and suing on a common count for money had and received. Since the objective here is restitution, the injured party need establish only that the wrongdoer is *unjustly enriched* by the misappropriation of the plaintiff's money. [**Shahood v. Cavin,** 154 Cal. App. 2d 745 (1957); **Alarcon v. Dickerson,** 719 S.W.2d 458 (Mo. 1986)]

c. Measure of recovery [§269]

Since money has a constant value, the actual recovery in either conversion or quasi-contract is identical. However, the *tort* count for conversion will also support a recovery for *punitive damages*. [**Allen v. Allen,** 551 P.2d 459 (Or. 1976)]

EXAM TIP   **gilbert**

When determining whether a party should sue for misappropriation of money in a tort action for conversion, or "waive the tort" and sue in quasi-contract for money had and received, check to see whether the plaintiff can prove that a *specific identifiable fund* was taken. If not, quasi-contract is the preferred approach because it only requires unjust enrichment of the defendant, whereas conversion requires identification of the specific fund taken. If a specific identifiable fund was taken, you should next identify whether the facts lend themselves to recovery of *punitive damages* (generally, willful misconduct motivated by actual malice toward the plaintiff; *see supra,* §54). If the facts do support recovery of punitive damages, consider suing in conversion rather than quasi-contract, because punitive damages may be recoverable in conversion, but not quasi-contract.

---

d. No recovery against innocent purchaser [§270]

Because money is negotiable by simple delivery, title to money is effectively transferred when delivered to a bona fide purchaser for value. Thus, the victim (owner of funds) has no valid claim against the innocent purchaser of stolen money, since the courts apply the maxim that where the equities are equal, the law (*i.e.,* legal title) prevails.

Example: Bank Robber used funds he stole to pay his income taxes. The court treated the director of the IRS as a bona fide purchaser of the funds because Bank Robber's tax liability was a valid debt, and the money was received without notice that it was stolen. [**Transamerica Insurance Co. v. Long**, 318 F. Supp. 156 (W.D. Pa. 1970)]

(1) Distinguish—personal property

As discussed below, the rule is different where *tangible* personal property is stolen; in such case, title *cannot* be acquired from a thief (*see infra*, §357).

2. Equitable Remedies [§271]

Retention of misappropriated money constitutes *unjust enrichment*, and the equitable remedies of constructive trust, equitable lien, and subrogation may be imposed to provide *restitution* to the injured party against the wrongdoer.

a. Constructive trust [§272]

The constructive trust arises from a court decree declaring that the money is held for the benefit of the injured party and ordering its return. As previously explained, no constructive trust may be decreed unless there is a subject matter (a res) upon which it can be imposed (*see supra*, §252). Thus, it is essential to the imposition of a constructive trust that the stolen money be *specifically identified* and *traced* to the possession of the wrongdoer. [**Weiss v. Marcus,** *supra*, §265; **People *ex rel*. Hartigan v. Candy Club,** 501 N.E.2d 188 (Ill. 1986)—two essential elements of constructive trust are (i) existence of identifiable property to serve as the res and (ii) possession of that res or its product by person who is to be charged as constructive trustee]

(1) Adequacy of remedy at law [§273]

There is a difference of opinion as to whether the party seeking a constructive trust must establish the inadequacy of the remedy at law. Particularly where tracing is involved, most courts seem to ignore any such requirement.

(2) Tracing [§274]

One of the principal advantages to be gained by electing the constructive trust remedy is the ability to *trace the money to its product.* The rationale of the equitable doctrine of tracing is that the plaintiff has a property right in the misappropriated money and that *ownership of that property is not lost by a change in form.* Thus, where the plaintiff can trace and identify the product of the misappropriated money, a constructive trust is imposed and the plaintiff is allowed to reclaim that property as her own. [**Pena v. Toney,** 98 Cal. App. 3d 534 (1979); **Namow Corp. v. Egger,** 668 P.2d 265 (Nev. 1983); **Marcus v. Otis,** 168 F.2d 649 (2d Cir. 1948)]

(a) Useful when wrongdoer insolvent [§275]

A constructive trust is an obviously superior remedy when the wrongdoer is insolvent and there are numerous competing creditors with claims against the wrongdoer's assets. The constructive trust is a particularly potent weapon in bankruptcy situations because it gives the claimant priority over other creditors. [*See In re* **Haber Oil Co.**, 12 F.3d 426 (5th Cir. 1994)] However, not all courts agree with this theory, and there are conflicting decisions. [*See, e.g., In re* **Omegas Group, Inc.**, 16 F.3d 1443 (6th Cir. 1994)] Moreover, proposed revisions of the Bankruptcy Code may limit the use of common law doctrines that affect the disposition of the bankruptcy estate.

Example: Teller embezzled money from Bank. The money could be traced to a home that Teller purchased. A constructive trust was declared in favor of Bank for a one-half interest in the home (the court found Teller's innocent wife to be the owner of the other one-half interest). [*See* **Fidelity & Deposit Co. v. Stordahl**, 91 N.W.2d 533 (Mich. 1958); *and see In re* **Marriage of Allen** *supra*, §253—constructive trust imposed on marital property acquired with embezzled funds]

(b) Insurance proceeds [§276]

Generally, where embezzled money is traced to premiums paid on a life insurance policy, the injured party is also permitted to impose a constructive trust on a proportionate share of the proceeds, at least up to the total amount embezzled. [**General Motors Co. v. Thompson**, 567 P.2d 80 (Okla. 1977); Rest. Restitution §210] Some courts hold that the face amount of the policy should measure recovery if all the premiums have been paid with the stolen money.

(c) Cut off by sale to bona fide purchaser [§277]

Since the doctrine of tracing is equitable, the right of reclamation *terminates* when the property comes into the hands of a bona fide purchaser (who has a superior equity).

Example: Because of tax lien problems, Curry could not obtain a mortgage on his own. Instead, he caused legal title of property in which he held an equitable interest to be transferred to McDonough, who used the property as collateral to obtain a $35,000 loan from Union Savings & Loan ("Union"). McDonough was supposed to turn over the proceeds to Curry, so that Curry could pay off the tax liens. Instead, McDonough absconded with the funds to Las Vegas and Union foreclosed on the property. *Held:*

Union was a bona fide purchaser for value (the mortgage loan proceeds) whose rights cut off Curry's equitable interest in a constructive trust. [**Union Savings & Loan Association v. McDonough,** 655 N.E.2d 426 (Ohio 1995)]

Compare: The wife of a fiduciary who improperly purchased land for her with trust funds was a donee and not a bona fide purchaser of the funds, and, hence, was subject to imposition of a constructive trust. [**McMerty v. Herzog,** 702 F.2d 127 (8th Cir. 1983); *and see* **Cox v. Waudby,** 433 N.W.2d 716 (Iowa 1988)—homestead nature of property did not prevent tracing]

---

(3) No constructive trust against wrongdoer's other assets [§278]

The right to recover assets obtained by a wrongdoer through use of misappropriated funds is clear (*see* above). However, suppose the wrongdoer merely uses the misappropriated funds to pay off his personal debts or otherwise cover his living expenses. Can his victim obtain a constructive trust against the wrongdoer's remaining assets (*e.g.,* property already owned by the wrongdoer before the misappropriation), or is the victim relegated to the status of a general creditor, which means she must share such assets with the wrongdoer's other creditors?

(a) "Swollen assets" theory

Some courts, applying the "swollen assets" theory, find that the use of the plaintiff's money to pay debts avoids the necessity of using other funds of the wrongdoer and hence "swells" his estate. Thus, a constructive trust is accordingly imposed on the defendant's assets. [*See* **Slater v. Oriental Mills,** 27 A. 443 (R.I. 1893)]

(b) Better view

However, this theory is clearly fallacious, since the payment of a debt does not increase the defendant's assets, but merely substitutes one obligation for another. Hence, the better (and majority) view is that the plaintiff *cannot* obtain a constructive trust; she is no better off than any other general creditor.

b. Equitable lien [§279]

As just indicated, a constructive trust is inappropriate if the misappropriated funds are traced to property already owned by the wrongdoer (since title to that property was not acquired with the stolen money). However, an equitable lien may be imposed on property already owned by the wrongdoer in certain cases *to avoid unjust enrichment* of the wrongdoer.

Example: If Husband uses Wife's money to improve a house that Husband already owns, a constructive trust *cannot* be imposed (title was not acquired with the stolen money). However, an equitable lien is an appropriate remedy because otherwise Husband would be unjustly enriching himself at Wife's expense. [*See* **Fulp v. Fulp,** 140 S.E.2d 708 (N.C. 1965)]

---

c. Subrogation
See supra, §§259-263.

d. Commingled funds [§280]
What are the victim's rights if the wrongdoer commingles his own funds with the funds misappropriated from the victim?

(1) Early common law rule—no recovery [§281]
If the plaintiff's money is traced to a bank account and commingled with the defendant's personal funds, the original English common law rule was that there could be no tracing since "money has no earmark."

(2) Later common law—presumptions to identify funds [§282]
Subsequently, certain presumptions were developed as to the ***intent of the misappropriator*** in withdrawing funds from the commingled account. [*See* **United States v. Banco Cafetero Panama,** 797 F.2d 1154 (2d Cir. 1986)—discussion of presumptions in case where government attempted to trace proceeds of drug trafficking]

(a) Withdrew own funds first [§283]
One presumption holds that the wrongdoer acted honestly and first withdrew his own funds from the commingled account. Hence, those funds remaining belong to the claimant. [*Re* **Hallett's Estate,** 13 Ch. D. 696 (1880)—"rule of Jessel's bag"; *and see* **Sadacca v. Monhart,** 470 N.E.2d 589 (Ill. 1984)—modern application of this presumption]

(b) "First in, first out" [§284]
Another presumption is that the withdrawals are made in the same order as contributions to the account—*i.e.,* a first in, first out rule. [**Clayton's Case,** 43 Eng. Rep. 551 (1816)]

(c) Most beneficial to claimant [§285]
A third presumption is that the wrongdoer acted honestly and in a way most beneficial to the claimant. Thus, if the first funds withdrawn were profitably invested, the claimant could claim that investment. [*Re* **Oatway,** 2 Ch. D. 356 (1903)]

(3) Modern approach—equitable lien [§286]
These presumptions had nothing to do with the wrongdoer's actual

intention, and thus the Restatement and later judicial decisions reject the presumptions as unrealistic. Since it cannot be determined whose money is taken or whose remains, an *equitable lien* is given to the claimant for the *full amount* of her claim on both the funds remaining in the account and *any property purchased with funds traced* from the account. [Rest. Restitution §211]

(a) Constructive trust as alternative remedy [§287]

In cases of a *conscious wrongdoer*, the claimant is given the option of the *constructive trust* remedy (so that she can share in any *increased value, see supra*, §272). But the constructive trust is limited to the claimant's pro rata share of the fund. Thus, if the fund is $2,000, of which $1,000 belongs to the claimant and $1,000 belongs to the wrongdoer, the claimant is entitled to one-half of any property purchased with money from the account. [Rest. Restitution §211]

(b) Lien limited by withdrawals [§288]

If withdrawals from the fund cause the balance in the account to sink below the amount of the injured party's claim, the injured party may assert an equitable lien only to the extent of the *lowest intermediate balance* of the account even though there are later additions to the fund; *i.e.,* there are no presumptions that the later deposits are by way of restitution, in the absence of an express intention by the wrongdoer to restore the claimant's funds. [Rest. Restitution §212; *In re* **Columbia Gas Systems, Inc.**, 997 F.2d 1039 (3d Cir. 1993)—rule applied in Chapter 11 bankruptcy proceedings; *In re* **Mahen & Rowsey**, 817 F.2d 682 (10th Cir. 1987)]

1) "Lowest intermediate balance" [§289]

Calculation of the lowest intermediate balance may be difficult. As a matter of practical convenience in the case of bank deposits, the daily closing balance is used. [*See* **Republic Supply Co. v. Richfield Oil Co.**, 79 F.2d 375 (9th Cir. 1935)]

2) Presumption of restitution in fiduciary cases [§290]

If the commingled account is a fiduciary account to begin with (*e.g.,* an express trust), a subsequent redeposit by the trustee *is* considered to be made as restitution. [**Universal C.I.T. Credit Corp. v. Farmer's Bank of Portageville**, 358 F. Supp. 317 (E.D. Mo. 1973)]

(c) Commingled funds of several claimants [§291]

If the wrongdoer commingles money of several persons in one account, each claimant has a *pro rata* interest in the funds, which may be asserted as an equitable lien or constructive trust. [Rest. Restitution §213]

1) Note

Some courts in this situation apply the rule in **Clayton's Case**, *supra,* §284 (first in, first out), and hold that withdrawals are made in the same order as contributions, but this seems clearly wrong because no rational inference can be drawn that money first deposited is first withdrawn. [*In re* **Walter J. Schmidt Co.,** 298 F. 314 (S.D.N.Y. 1923)]

B. Injuries to Personal Property

1. Tortious Destruction of a Chattel [§292]

The measure of damages for the tortious destruction of a chattel is the *value* of the property at the time of destruction, *less salvage*, with *interest* computed from the time of valuation. [Restatement of Torts §927]

a. Loss of use generally not recoverable [§293]

Because it is assumed that the injured party will immediately replace the destroyed chattel, the general rule denies recovery for loss of use. Instead, interest is awarded from the time of valuation. [**Executive Jet Aviation v. United States,** 507 F.2d 508 (6th Cir. 1974)]

(1) Limitation [§294]

Recent cases support recovery of additional damages for loss of use of the chattel if the property is such that it *cannot be replaced* quickly in spite of reasonable efforts to obtain a replacement. In such cases, damages for loss of use are recoverable during the period of time needed for replacement. [*See* **Dennis v. Ford Motor Co.,** 471 F.2d 733 (3d Cir. 1973)—damages for loss of use based on the costs of truck plaintiff had to rent while awaiting delivery of new truck; *and see* **DTS Tank Service, Inc. v. Vanderveen,** 683 P.2d 1345 (Okla. 1984)] These damages may include *loss of profits.* [*See* **McPherson v. Schlemmer,** 749 P.2d 51 (Mont. 1988)—loss of profits resulting from destruction of exotic breeder cows; **Felice Fedder Oriental Art v. Scanlon,** 708 F. Supp. 551 (S.D.N.Y. 1989)—lost profits as a result of disruption of business by an accident]

(2) Cost of replacement [§295]

Additional losses proximately caused by the destruction, such as costs in procuring the replacement (*e.g.,* freight, taxes, and financing charges), are also recoverable in such cases.

DESTRUCTION OF CHATTEL—BASIC DAMAGES gilbert

THE BASIC MEASURE OF DAMAGES FOR THE TORTIOUS DESTRUCTION OF A CHATTEL IS CALCULATED AS FOLLOWS:

Value of Property at Time of Destruction

−   Salvage Value

+   Interest from the Time of Valuation

Damages*

*Some courts will also add in costs incurred to procure a replacement, and, if the chattel cannot immediately be replaced, damages for loss of use.

---

b.   Determining value of chattel destroyed [§296]

The value of the chattel may be computed in various ways:

(1)   Market value [§297]

Market value is the usual measure of value and represents the price the chattel would bring if offered for sale by a leisurely seller to a willing buyer. [Rest. Torts §911]

(a)   "Market" [§298]

A question may arise as to which "market" to look to in determining value. For the *ordinary* consumer, it is the *retail* market since that is the price she must pay for a replacement. For destruction of the stock of goods of a *retailer*, however, the *wholesale* price is determinative, since that is what the retailers pay to replace merchandise. In the case of a manufacturer, the selling price (of goods destroyed) is used, even though this obviously exceeds replacement cost. [Rest. Torts §911; *but see* **Acme Delivery Service v. Samsonite Corp.,** 663 P.2d 621 (Colo. 1983)—manufacturer who lost no sales may recover only cost of manufacturing plus prejudgment interest]

(b)   Time of valuation [§299]

Destroyed chattels are valued at the *time of destruction*, thus avoiding the problem of inflation in determining the cost of replacement. Prejudgment interest is presumed to insure full indemnification. [*See* **Felice Fedder Oriental Art v. Scanlon,** *supra*]

(c)   Other measures [§300]

In **Williams v. O'Neal Ford,** 668 S.W.2d 545 (Ark. 1984), the trade-in allowance of a converted car was used to establish value. In farm areas, catalog prices might be used. [**Rensch v. Riddles Diamonds,** 393 N.W.2d 269 (S.D. 1986)]

(2) Reproduction cost less deterioration [§301]

An alternative method of valuation is to compute the cost of reproduction less deterioration (to the extent that the destroyed chattel has been used).

(3) Value to the owner [§302]

Ordinarily, courts *exclude* evidence of special value of the chattel to the owner because this may introduce subjective elements that are difficult to assess accurately. However, in cases where *market value fails to compensate* for the loss adequately, courts *permit* such evidence to be introduced. Particularly in cases involving household furnishings, personal clothing, family keepsakes, pictures, etc., where market value is clearly inadequate (*e.g.,* second-hand clothing), the measurement of damages is allowed in terms of the value of the destroyed property to the owner. [**De Spirito v. Bristol County Water Co.,** 227 A.2d 782 (R.I. 1967); *but see* **Meisner v. Patton Electric Co.,** 781 F. Supp. 1432 (D. Neb. 1990)— second-hand items that became antiques revert to a market valuation]

(a) Factors considered in measuring value [§303]

Evidence is admitted to show the original cost of the chattel, the length of time the chattel was used, the condition of the chattel, and replacement cost. [**Van Bibber v. Norris,** 404 N.E.2d 1365 (Ind. 1980)]

(b) "Sentimental" value [§304]

Courts in these cases purport to *exclude sentimental value*; but where substantial compensation is awarded for the loss of, *e.g.,* family portraits, this factor must inevitably have been considered. [**Mieske v. Bartell Drug Co.,** 593 P.2d 1308 (Wash. 1979)—sentimental value excluded in valuing destroyed home movie film, but award of $7,500 affirmed; **Van Bibber v. Norris,** *supra*—$5,000 for conversion of Norris family tree; **Campins v. Capels,** 461 N.E.2d 712 (Ill. 1984)—award in excess of replacement cost of United States Auto Club rings justified because of special significance and owner's attachment to the property; **Jankowski v. Preiser Animal Hospital,** 510 N.E.2d 1084 (Ill. 1987)—in valuing pet dog, actual value to owner "may include some element of sentimental value"; **Ladeas v. Carter,** 845 S.W.2d 45 (Mo. 1992)—videotape of plaintiff's father's last words]

METHODS OF DETERMINING VALUE OF DESTROYED CHATTEL—A COMPARISON		gilbert	
	MARKET VALUE	REPLACEMENT VALUE	VALUE TO OWNER
METHOD OF COMPUTATION	Ordinary consumer—retail value Retailer—wholesale value	Cost of reproduction minus deterioration resulting from owner's use of property	Court considers original cost, length of time used, condition of property, and replacement cost
POSSIBLE REASONS FOR USING PARTICULAR METHOD OF VALUATION	There is a readily available market for the property (e.g., factory-produced furniture held for retail sale)	The market value is not easily determinable (e.g., custom-built furniture sold by craftsman)	Property has worth to owner beyond objective valuation (e.g., family photographs or a gold bracelet that is a family heirloom)

2. Tortious Damage to Chattels [§305]

If chattels are wrongfully *harmed* (rather than destroyed), the measure of damages is either the *difference in value* of the chattel before and after the harm, or the *reasonable cost of repair plus loss of use*. [Rest. Torts §928; **Costley v. Holman**, 608 P.2d 614 (Or. 1980)]

a. Diminution of value [§306]

The diminution test ordinarily defines value as *market value*, comparing market value before the damage to market value afterwards. Some courts applying this test use *cost of repairs* as the measure of the drop in value. [**Costley v. Holman**, *supra*]

b. Cost of repairs [§307]

If the loss is measured by the cost of repairs, allowance must be made for any difference between original value and value after repairs.

Example: Dave vandalizes Jake's new car. The car may be restored to its original working condition, but the mere fact of repair may still cause a drop in value for which Jake is entitled to compensation. [*See* **Julian v. Ralph**, 206 So. 2d 121 (La. 1968); **Rosenfield v. Choberka**, 140 Misc. 2d 9 (1988)]

(1) Note

If the cost of repairs *exceeds* the market value of the chattel, damages are usually limited to the market value, since it would be uneconomical to spend more on repairs than the chattel is worth. [*See* **Hewlett v. Barge Bertie**, 418 F.2d 654 (4th Cir. 1969)]

(2)   And note

In computing damages, a party performing its own repairs may also include properly calculated overhead expenses. [**Curt's Trucking Co. v. City of Anchorage,** 578 P.2d 975 (Alaska 1978)—repair of telephone cable; *but see* **Ohio Power Co. v. Huff,** 231 N.E.2d 897 (Ohio 1967)—repair of power pole]

c.   **Loss of use [§308]**

The value of the loss of use is measured by the *rental value* of the chattel. If a substitute is procured, the rental value of the substitute is recoverable. [**Julian v. Ralph,** *supra;* **American Telephone & Telegraph Co. v. Connecticut Light & Power,** 470 F. Supp. 105 (D. Conn. 1979)—loss of use may be measured by market rental value of damaged chattel adjusted for depreciation and overhead expense; Rest. 2d Torts §931] Some courts permit consideration of the *personal inconvenience* of the plaintiff as well as the rental cost of a substitute. [**Camaraza v. Bellavia Buick,** 523 A.2d 669 (N.J. 1987)]

(1)   Illustration—substitute for automobile [§309]

The most common situation involves repair to an automobile. The injured party may recover the value of the lost use measured by the *cost of renting* a substitute for a reasonable period of time to complete repairs. From the rental cost must be deducted the cost of *oil, gas, and depreciation* which the injured party would be required to pay if using her own automobile.

(a)   Note

As discussed *supra* (§294), in cases of total destruction, rental value of a substitute vehicle may be recovered for a reasonable period in which to procure a replacement vehicle. [**Brown v. Morgan,** 449 So. 2d 606 (La. 1984)]

(2)   Where no substitute procured [§310]

Loss of use is recoverable *even if no substitute is actually procured;* otherwise recovery would depend on the financial ability of plaintiff to rent a substitute. [**Koninklijke, Luchtvaart Maatschaapig, N.V. v. United Technologies Corp.,** 610 F.2d 1052 (2d Cir. 1979)—"it is not the actual use but the right to use that is compensable"]

Example: Valencia's truck was damaged by Shell Oil Co.'s negligence. Vallencia had the truck repaired within one month of the accident but was financially unable to pay the cost of the repairs and consequently could not obtain possession of the truck, and Shell initially refused to pay. After 17 months, Shell paid for the repairs. Valencia was held entitled to recover for loss of use during the entire period. While Valencia had a duty to take reasonable steps to minimize his loss, the evidence established that he was unable to pay for or procure a substitute vehicle. [**Valencia v. Shell Oil Co.,** 23 Cal. 2d 840 (1944); *and see* **Persinger v. Lucas,** 512 N.E.2d 865 (Ind. 1987)—storage costs recoverable where owner financially unable to pay towing charge]

(3) Loss of business use [§311]

If a vehicle is used in a business, loss of use while procuring a substitute may be measured by *lost profits*, subject however to the rule of avoidable consequences (*see supra*, §47). [**Sharp v. Great Southern Coaches Inc.,** 510 S.W.2d 266 (Ark. 1977)] But it has been held in commercial cases that no loss of use damages can be recovered in the absence of *actual financial loss*. [*See* **CTI International, Inc. v. Lloyds Underwriters,** 735 F.2d 679 (2d Cir. 1984)—denying recovery of rental income to be received from rental of damaged and destroyed containers where evidence showed availability of substitute containers; *but see* **K.L.M. v. United Technologies Corp.,** 610 F.2d 1052 (2d Cir. 1979)—loss of use damages measured by rent of leased chattel allowed even without proof of actual financial loss; **Kuwait Airways Corp. v. Ogden Allied Aviation Services,** 726 F. Supp. 1389 (E.D.N.Y. 1989)—damages for loss of use of vehicle recoverable even without showing that profitable vehicle trips were canceled or that substitute vehicle was rented]

EXAM TIP — **gilbert**

When considering damages due to loss of use of business chattels, be sure to determine whether the business *lost profits* as a result of the loss of use. Damages for loss of use generally are measured by the rental value of the chattel. However, lost profits due to inability to use the chattel may be much higher than the chattel's rental value. If a business loses profits as a result of the loss of use of the chattel, and the lost profits could not be avoided by reasonable means, courts will allow the value of the lost profits to be used instead of the rental value.

(a) Note

When plaintiff is unable to establish the value of lost use, it has been held that it may be measured by *interest* at the legal rate, based on the value of the chattel when taken, for the period of the wrongful detention. [**Foresight Enterprises v. Leisure Time Properties,** 466 So. 2d 283 (Fla. 1985)]

3. Tortious Taking and Retention of Chattels [§312]

Specific *restitutionary* remedies designed to restore possession of the chattel itself include self-help, replevin, and the mandatory injunction. Alternatively, the injured party may seek a *monetary* award as substitutionary relief. Available remedies are damages for conversion, quasi-contract (waiver of tort and suit in assumpsit), and the equitable remedy of the constructive trust.

a. Specific restitution

(1) Self-help [§313]

The common law recognizes the privilege of a possessor of chattels, in limited circumstances, to use *reasonable force to recapture* them from one who retains them without a claim of right. [Rest. Torts §§100-108] A similar privilege is accorded to the secured creditor by section 9-609 of the Uniform Commercial Code, which allows recapture if it can be accomplished without a breach of the peace.

(a) Improvement to chattel [§314]

The privilege of recapture is not lost if the chattel has been improved by the wrongdoer as long as the chattel can still be identified and title has not shifted by *accession* (*see infra*, §346). [Rest. Restitution §42(2)]

(2) Replevin [§315]

The legal remedy of replevin enables the plaintiff to obtain a judgment for the *return* of the chattel (writ directed to sheriff to take from the defendant and return to the plaintiff), *plus* detention damages. [**Steel Motor Service v. Zalke,** 212 F.2d 856 (6th Cir. 1954)]

(a) Background [§316]

The common law form of action known as replevin evolved as a remedy for unlawful distress of chattels. It had the peculiar characteristic of entitling the plaintiff to the restoration of the chattels *at the commencement of the action*, after which the propriety of the distraint was litigated. Hence, the word "replevin" may have different connotations: (i) the underlying action to recover possession, and (ii) prejudgment procedures to obtain possession. The second connotation is sometimes called "prejudgment replevin" and has evolved into the statutory provisional remedy named "claim and delivery," which includes cases where the chattel was *lawfully obtained but wrongfully detained* (*i.e.*, where only *detinue* would lie at common law). Prejudgment replevin is designed to aid plaintiffs, but a suit to recover a chattel may be prosecuted to judgment regardless of whether prejudgment possession of the chattel is obtained. [**Clifford Banking Co. v. Bankhead,** 738 S.W.2d 948 (Mo. 1987)]

(b) Acquisition of title by adverse possession [§317]

The right to regain possession of stolen chattels may be *lost* if the defendant has acquired title by adverse possession. However, mere possession by the defendant, even though long continued, is insufficient. To acquire title, the possession must be visible, notorious, hostile, and adverse.

1) "Visible and notorious" [§318]

Traditionally, the rule was that the statute of limitations did not run as to stolen chattels until the adverse possession was visible and notorious. However, in **O'Keefe v. Snyder,** 416 A.2d 862 (N.J. 1980), the court held that, absent fraud or concealment, the statute began to run at the time of the theft, *unless* the owner could show that commencement of the statute should be deferred. The adoption of this so-called discovery rule (applicable in medical and legal malpractice cases) shifted the burden of proof from the defendant-possessor (to prove the elements of adverse possession) to the plaintiff-claimant (to show that the facts giving rise to the cause of action could not have been discovered sooner by reasonable diligence). [*But see* **DeWeerth v. Baldinger,** 658 F. Supp. 688 (S.D.N.Y. 1987)— court ruled against good faith purchaser of stolen Monet painting because her possession of painting in her home was not sufficiently open and notorious to constitute adverse possession; **Autocephalous Greek Orthodox Church v. Goldberg & Fineman Fine Arts,** 917 F.2d 278 (7th Cir. 1990)—statute of limitations did not start to run until chattels discovered in defendant's possession; *compare* **Solomon Guggenheim Foundation v. Lubell,** 77 N.Y.2d 311 (1991)—statute of limitations does not run until the true owner demands return of the property and the holder refuses to deliver it]

(c) Procedure [§319]

Seizure of the chattel at the commencement of the action is at the option of the plaintiff. If the plaintiff wishes immediately to replevy the property, she is required to post a *bond* as security for the defendant in case an adverse judgment is rendered. Most jurisdictions also provide a "rebonding" procedure, which permits the defendant to retain the chattel until final judgment by posting security to indemnify the plaintiff if the plaintiff is successful in the lawsuit.

1) Constitutionality [§320]

The traditional method of prejudgment replevin resulted in a seizure of the property from the defendant without a hearing. This procedure was held unconstitutional in **Fuentes v. Shevin,** 407 U.S. 67 (1972), on the ground that procedural due process requires a *judicial hearing* to determine the plaintiff's right to possession *before* seizure of the defendant's property.

a) Note

The broad language in *Fuentes* was limited by the Court in a subsequent decision, **Mitchell v. W.T. Grant Co.,** 416

U.S. 600 (1974), which *upheld* a Louisiana statute authorizing sequestration of a debtor's assets without notice or hearing. The Louisiana statute was deemed valid because it permitted sequestration only in certain limited cases, and required that the writ be issued by a judge rather than a clerk (as in *Fuentes*), thus assuring judicial control of the seizure process from beginning to end.

b) Distinguish

However, in a subsequent case, **North Georgia Finishing v. Di-Chem Inc.**, 419 U.S. 601 (1975), the Supreme Court, in striking down a garnishment statute (another provisional remedy), indicated by way of dicta that the more stringent test of *Fuentes* may be resuscitated. Thus, state statutes governing replevin (claim and delivery), as well as other provisional remedies including preliminary injunctions, were amended to comply with these decisions. [*See, e.g.,* **First National Bank of Arizona v. Superior Court of Maricopa County,** 541 P.2d 392 (Ariz. 1975)]

c) Exception

A writ of replevin may still be issued ex parte in narrowly defined situations such as theft, the withholding of credit cards, or the threat to conceal the disputed property or remove it from the state. However, it is error to issue the writ unless these facts can be clearly established. [*See* **Sea Rail Truckloads v. Pullman, Inc.,** 131 Cal. App. 3d 511 (1982)]

(d) Judgment for plaintiff [§321]

If the plaintiff wins the replevin action, she is entitled to a *judgment for the return of the chattel* and, in addition, *damages for its detention* until it is returned to her.

1) Detention damages must be recovered in same action [§322]

Detention damages are part of the replevin claim, and hence must be recovered in the original action. Any subsequent separate suit for such damage would be barred by the rule against splitting a cause of action and by the res judicata effect of merger (all parts of a single cause of action are merged in a judgment on the claim, whether or not actually litigated). [**McFaddin v. H.S. Crocker Co.,** 219 Cal. App. 2d 585 (1963)]

2) Measure of detention damages

a) **Goods held for sale [§323]**

If goods are held for sale, the measure of detention damages is the market value of the goods at the time the defendant first takes possession, *less* market value at the time the action is brought. [**Gicinto v. Credithrift of America,** 549 P.2d 870 (Kan. 1976)]

b) **Goods not held for sale [§324]**

If goods are not held for sale, detention damages are the value of the lost use, which may be measured *either* by the *rental value* of the chattel or by *lost profits*. [*See* **Ben Lomond, Inc. v. Campbell,** 691 P.2d 1042 (Alaska 1984)—award of $13,000 for loss of use measured by rental value of generator plus punitive damages of $50,000; *but see* **Flickinger v. Mark IV Apartments,** 315 N.W.2d 794 (Iowa 1982)—no detention damages may be awarded where property was available to plaintiff whenever she wished to reclaim it]

1/ **Damages not limited to value of chattel [§325]**

Detention damages are not limited to the value of the chattel that was detained.

---

e.g. **Example:** The police wrongfully had plaintiff's car towed. The towing company refused to release plaintiff's car to him unless he was willing to pay the storage and towing fees that the police owed the towing company for towing the car. Plaintiff filed suit for the return of his car and for detention damages. The car was worth about $1,200 when it was towed and about $50-$60 at the time of trial. The court held that because the car had a rental value of about $10 per day, and the car was detained for 957 days, the proper detention damages were $9,750. [**Morfeld v. Bernstrauch,** 343 N.W.2d 880 (Neb. 1984)]

2/ **Plaintiff's burden [§326]**

To recover for lost use, the plaintiff may be required to show that the property would have been used or rented. [*See* **Korb v. Schroedel,** 286 N.W.2d 589 (Wis. 1980); *and see* **International Harvester Credit Corp. v. Hellend,** 503 N.E.2d 548 (Ill. 1986)]

EXAM TIP   **gilbert**

If an exam question involves replevin, don't forget to mention detention damages in your answer. It's not enough just to get the chattel back; the rightful possessor should be compensated for being deprived of the chattel. If the chattel was held for sale, seek the *difference in market price* between the time the defendant took the chattel and the time the action was brought. If the chattel was *not* held for sale, seek damages for loss of use based on the *rental value or profits* the plaintiff lost by having been deprived of the chattel.

3/   Offset for upkeep and depreciation [§327]

If detention damages are measured by the chattel's *rental value*, the amount awarded should take into account the chattel's *upkeep costs* and *depreciation* during the period of detention. [**Fran-Well Heater Co. v. Robinson**, 182 Cal. App. 2d 125 (1960)]

4/   Reduction for delay [§328]

It has been held that failure to mitigate damages by promptly filing suit to recover the chattel warrants a *reduction in damages* for lost use. [**Culligan Rock River Water Conditioning Co. v. Gearhart III**, 443 N.E.2d 1065 (Ill. 1982)]

3)   Alternative judgment for value of property if not returned [§329]

If the injured party seeks and recovers a judgment for possession, an alternative judgment is also rendered for the *value* of the chattel in case it cannot be seized and recaptured. In such cases, its value is determined *at the time of the trial* together with *detention damages* computed on a periodic basis (daily, weekly, etc.) and included in the judgment. [*See* **Roche v. Barbaro**, 378 So. 2d 1334 (Fla. 1980)]

a)   Rationale

The justification for awarding both the chattel value and detention damages is that the injured party is relying on *satisfaction* of the judgment for return of the chattel and consequently will not replace it in the market. Thus to be fully indemnified, the injured party must recover not only the value of the chattel at the time of trial, but also damages for loss of use. [**Steel Motor Service v. Zalke**, *supra*, §315]

b)   Alternative judgment for benefit of plaintiff [§330]

The alternative judgment for the value of the chattel

wrongfully taken is for the benefit of the injured party (owner). The defendant does *not* have the option of retaining the chattel by paying its value. [**S.T. Enterprises v. Brunswick Corp.**, 315 N.E.2d 1 (Ill. 1974)]

4) Judgment for conversion [§331]

If the injured party elects to take judgment for the *value* of the chattel (waiving any right to return of the chattel) the case is regarded as one for conversion—*i.e.*, a "forced sale" of the property from the plaintiff to the defendant. Value is generally determined at the time of seizure, and *interest* is awarded on this amount. However, *no detention damages* are recoverable in such cases. [**Steel Motor Service v. Zalke**, *supra*]

(e) Effect of defendant disposing of chattels prior to judgment [§332]

The plaintiff must allege in the complaint that the defendant is in *possession* of the chattels at the time the replevin action is commenced. (If the defendant is not in possession, the plaintiff's remedy is conversion.) What happens, however, if the defendant disposes of the chattels prior to the trial of the replevin action? A judgment for possession is obviously ineffective because the defendant no longer has the chattels. Two possibilities are open to the plaintiff:

1) Amend complaint [§333]

Plaintiff may seek to amend the complaint to state a cause of action for *conversion*. If she does this, she may obtain a judgment for the value of the chattels *at the time of seizure*, plus *interest* to date of judgment (*see* above).

2) Prove wrongful disposal of chattels [§334]

Alternatively, the plaintiff may attempt to prove that the defendant disposed of the chattels wrongfully, for the purpose of defeating the writ. Such evidence justifies a court retaining the action as replevin or detinue, thereby authorizing the court to enter an alternative judgment for the value of the property *at time of trial*, plus *detention damages*. If the value of chattels has increased, this obviously is a far better remedy for the plaintiff than conversion. [*See* **Fran-Well Heater Co. v. Robinson**, *supra*]

a) Application

The principle operates in bailment cases where the property cannot be returned. Rather than merely being liable for the value at the time of conversion plus interest, the bailee may in the alternative be liable for the value at the time of trial.

(f) Judgment for defendant [§335]

If the replevin is wrongful, the defendant is entitled to a judgment for the *return* of the chattel or its value, *plus detention damages.* [**First National Bank v. Southwest Yacht & Marine**, 684 P.2d 517 (N.M. 1984)—double damages awarded for loss of use under New Mexico's statute]

(3) Mandatory injunction [§336]

A mandatory injunction ordering the defendant to return a converted chattel will be granted if the remedy at law (replevin or damages) is not adequate. To establish the inadequacy of the remedy at law, the plaintiff must show that the chattel that was wrongfully taken is "*unique.*" [*See* Rest. Torts §946]

EXAM TIP gilbert

The requirement of "uniqueness" really sets injunction apart from the other restitutionary remedies available for tortiously taken and retained chattels. Suppose a fact pattern tells you that Henry borrows Charles's brand new, $60,000 Corvette and then refuses to return it. Can Charles sneak over to Henry's house at night, jump into the car while it is sitting in the driveway, and drive off? Sure, *self-help* is available. Can Charles ask the court to order the sheriff to go get his Corvette? You bet, *replevin* is available. Can Charles ask the court to order Henry to turn over the Corvette—seemingly the most straightforward remedy? No! The brand new Corvette is not unique. Charles can go to any Chevrolet dealer to get a replacement. Change the facts so that Henry borrowed Charles's unique painting "Blue Corvette on Black Velvet," by a noted artist, and suddenly an *injunction* is available.

(a) "Unique" chattels [§337]

While uniqueness is variously defined, the underlying principle is that the chattel *cannot be duplicated in the market.* [**Modern Dust Bag Co. v. Commercial Trust Co.**, 91 A.2d 469 (Del. 1952)] Included within this definition are articles that quite literally are one of a kind, *e.g.*, the Duke of Somerset's Etruscan altarpiece or classic paintings. [**Kunstsammlugen Zu Weimar v. Elicofon**, 536 F. Supp. 829 (E.D.N.Y.), *aff'd*, 678 F.2d 1150 (2d Cir. 1981)] The uniqueness test is also satisfied by proof of sentimental value (*e.g.*, family jewelry or keepsakes). [**Charles Simkin & Sons v. Massiah**, 289 F.2d 26 (3d Cir. 1961); **Schiller v. Miller**, 621 So. 2d 481 (Fla. 1993)—discussion of adequacy of damages where jewelry (including an engagement ring) was claimed by plaintiff]

(b) Money damages inadequate [§338]

The remedy at law of money damages is not adequate in these cases because the injured party cannot go into the market with money and replace the converted article.

(c) Replevin inadequate [§339]

Replevin is not deemed an adequate remedy in these cases because there is no assurance that the writ will ever be successfully executed by the sheriff or other appropriate officer (leaving the plaintiff with an alternative money judgment, which again would be inadequate). On the other hand, if a mandatory injunction is issued, the burden of producing the chattel is imposed on the defendant, who must either comply or face charges of contempt. The same result may be obtained by combining the provisional remedies of a preliminary injunction and claim and delivery.

SUMMARY OF RESTITUTIONARY REMEDIES FOR TORTIOUSLY TAKEN AND RETAINED CHATTELS	gilbert
SELF-HELP	The person entitled to possession, who acts promptly after dispossession, may use *reasonable force* to recapture the chattel from a person retaining it without a claim of right.
REPLEVIN	The person entitled to possession obtains a court order (writ) instructing the *sheriff to seize* the chattel and return it. The court may also award *detention damages*.
MANDATORY INJUNCTION	The person entitled to possession obtains a court order (injunction) instructing the *person in possession* of the chattel to return it. The chattel must be *unique*.

b. Substitutionary relief—damages and restitution

(1) Conversion [§340]

Conversion is the unlawful exercise of *dominion* over chattels of another. (*See* Torts Summary.)

(a) Measure of damages [§341]

The measure of damages for a conversion includes: (i) the *value* of the property at the time of the conversion; (ii) the *interest* on that amount from that date; (iii) *punitive damages* if the plaintiff proves malice or oppression; and (iv) in some jurisdictions, compensation for *consequential damages* such as expenditures incurred in seeking the recapture of the property. [Rest. 2d Torts §927]

1) Distinguish—trespass to chattels [§342]

Be sure to note the difference between the measure of damages used when there is an assertion of ownership (*i.e.*, conversion) versus no assertion of ownership (*i.e.*, tortious damage to chattels or "trespass to chattels"). When there is no assertion of ownership, damages are limited to the loss in value of the chattel or the cost of repair plus loss of use (*see supra*, §305), whereas the entire value of the chattel can be recovered in a conversion case. Thus, if the defendant has interfered with the plaintiff's use or possession of personal property, but the interference does not constitute an assertion of ownership justifying an action for conversion, trespass to chattels may be the more appropriate remedy. [*See, e.g.*, **Thrifty-Tel v. Bezenek**, 46 Cal App. 4th 1559 (1996)—a hacker's use of plaintiff's long distance telephone line was ruled compensable as a trespass although not as a conversion; *and see* **CompuServe Inc. v. Cyber Promotions, Inc.**, 962 F. Supp. 1015 (S.D. Ohio 1997)—unsolicited e-mail advertising using plaintiff's online computer communication system caused injury to plaintiff sufficient to sustain a cause of action for trespass to chattels but not for conversion]

(b) Value [§343]

"Value" ordinarily means market value *at the time of conversion*. [**Mohr v. State Bank of Stanley**, 734 P.2d 1071 (Kan. 1987)—commercial paper]

1) Chattels fluctuating in value [§344]

Where market value is fluctuating, as is the case with stocks and certain commodities, varying rules have been employed for determining the time at which value is to be computed:

(i) The time between the conversion and the trial at which the chattel reaches its *highest value* (it being presumed that plaintiff would have chosen to sell at this point) [**Kenney v. Koch**, 737 P.2d 491 (Mont. 1987)] (*Note*: This rule seems clearly wrong, since it assumes "superhuman sagacity" on the part of the plaintiff. It is now generally rejected in favor of the next two rules, which apply the avoidable consequence principle to limit the recovery. [*See* Rest. 2d Torts §927, comment (e)]);

(ii) The time at which the chattel reaches its *highest intermediate value* between the *date of the wrong* and a *reasonable time thereafter for replacement* in the market; and

(iii) The time at which the chattel reaches its *highest intermediate value* between the time the plaintiff *learned of the wrong* and a *reasonable time thereafter for replacement* in the market [**Rauser v. LTV Electrosystems, Inc.**, 437 F.2d 800 (7th Cir. 1971); **Wong v. Paine, Webber, Jackson & Curtis**, 208 Cal. App. 2d 17 (1962)].

a) Note

At least one court has given the plaintiff the choice between either the time of the conversion or the time described in (iii), above. [**Fawcett v. Heimbach**, 591 N.W.2d 516 (Minn. 1999)]

2) No market at place of conversion [§345]

If there is no market for the goods at the place of conversion, the measure of damages is the value of the property at the time of the conversion at the *nearest* market (with an appropriate adjustment for the cost of transportation). [**Peter Saltpeter Energy Co. v. Crystal Oil Co.**, 524 S.W.2d 383 (Tex. 1975)]

3) Effect of converter enhancing value—doctrine of accession [§346]

If a wrongdoer has improved the chattel, the plaintiff may recover the value of the chattel as improved only in situations where the conversion was *willful*. An *innocent* converter is *not* liable for the enhanced value.

Example: Don innocently purchases Penny's logs from a thief for $100 and saws them into lumber worth $200 at the time the action is commenced. Purchase of stolen goods is a conversion, but Don was acting innocently; hence, Penny may recover only $100 from Don. If Don's conversion had been willful (Don was the thief or knew that the logs were stolen), Penny could recover the full $200. [Rest. 2d Torts §927, comment (f)]

a) Distinguish—value greatly enhanced [§347]

If the improvements greatly enhance the value of the property so that the value of the original property is insignificant in comparison to the value of the new product, *title passes* to the person who in good faith improved the property. The original owner may then recover only for the *value of* the unimproved property originally taken.

Example: Bill's Corvette was stolen and stripped. After passing through several hands, Sartin purchased the shell of the Corvette in good faith and added an engine, tires, transmission, etc., and rebuilt the shell into a functioning automobile. Sartin sold the car, and it was subsequently resold several times. The car was once again stolen. When the police recovered the car, they traced it back to Bill through the serial number stamped on the Corvette's body. *Held:* Because Sartin acted in good faith and greatly improved the shell of the Corvette, he gained title to the car and was liable to Bill only for the value of the shell. [**Capital Chevrolet v. Earheart**, 627 S.W.2d 369 (Tenn. 1981); *but see* **Bancorp Leasing v. Stadeli Pump**, 724 P.2d 948 (Or. 1986)—Plaintiff's engine installed in truck acceded to the truck and thus was subject to claim of creditor of truck's owner]

4) Value affected by plaintiff's demand for return [§348]

If the converter refuses the owner's demand for return of the chattels, the plaintiff-owner may elect to set value at the *time of demand* (except as to improvements made by an innocent converter; *see* above), *or at the time of disposition*, if the chattels are subsequently disposed of. [Rest. 2d Torts §927, comments (g), (h)]

(c) Effect of successive conversions of same chattel [§349]

If a chattel is converted by a succession of people (*e.g.*, Alex steals the chattel and sells it to Becky, who sells it to Cindy, who sells it to Deanna, etc.), the plaintiff may seek and recover judgment against each successive converter but is, of course, entitled to only one satisfaction. Thus, if the original converter pays full value of the chattel to the owner, the payment *precludes* any further recovery from subsequent converters. [**Baram v. Farugia**, 606 F.2d 42 (3d Cir. 1979)]

1) Note

However, each successive converter is liable for the value of the chattel on the date of his acquisition, *except* to the extent of *improvements* made by a previous *innocent* converter.

Example: Alex willfully converts Phineas's chattel worth $100 and transports it to market where it is worth $150. There, Alex sells it for value to Becky, who is without notice (an innocent conversion). Becky improves the chattel so that it is valued at $200. Becky sells it to Chloe (another conversion) for $200. Phineas is entitled to judgment against Alex, Becky, and Chloe for $150. [*See* Rest. 2d Torts §927, comment (d); *and see* **Bay Springs Forest Products, Inc. v. Wade**, 435 So. 2d 690 (Miss. 1983)—market value of timber delivered at mill was appropriate measure of damages in suit by owner against innocent purchaser from willful trespasser]

(d) No duty on plaintiff to mitigate by accepting chattel back [§350]

The common law rule does *not* require the plaintiff to accept the return of the chattel by defendant in mitigation of damages. Rather, the plaintiff may insist on a "forced sale" of the chattel to the converter.

1) Note

If the plaintiff does accept the return of the chattel, damages are reduced to the extent of the value of the chattel at the time of the return, but the plaintiff may then also recover for loss of use. [*See* **Norris v. Bovina Feeders,** 492 F.2d 502 (5th Cir. 1974)]

2) Restatement view

Restatement of Torts section 922 has proposed a rule of mitigation in all cases of *innocent* conversion where there is a prompt offer to return and the chattel is substantially unharmed. As of now, however, there is little authority to support this sensible proposal. [*See* **Plymouth Fertilizer Co. v. Balmer,** 488 N.E.2d 1129 (Ind. 1968)—noting section 922 had not been adopted in state]

(2) Quasi-contract (waiver of tort and suit in assumpsit) [§351]

As an alternative to the tort action, the injured party may seek restitution of the benefit acquired by the wrongdoer as a consequence of the conversion. Traditionally, this is referred to as a waiver of tort and a suit in assumpsit on the implied obligation imposed by law to repay the benefit tortiously obtained.

(a) Common law—disposition required [§352]

The common law originally permitted the action only where the wrongdoer had disposed of the converted chattels for money. The plaintiff then sued on a common count for *money had and received.* [**Jones v. Hoar,** 5 Pick. (22 Mass.) 285 (1827); *and see* **Mattson v. Commercial Credit Business Loans,** 723 P.2d 996 (Or. 1986)—recent application of rule in conversion of lumber case]

(b) Modern rule [§353]

This requirement has been abandoned by most jurisdictions today. Thus, even if the chattels are still in the wrongdoer's possession, the plaintiff may sue on a common count for *goods sold and delivered* (conversion is "forced sale"), recovering the reasonable value of the property.

1) Effect of election [§354]

If the chattels *are* sold by the converter for money, some jurisdictions permit the plaintiff to elect *either* common count. But if the plaintiff chooses the count "for money had and received," recovery is limited to the proceeds of the sale. [*See* **Canepa v. Sun Pacific,** 126 Cal. App. 2d 706 (1954)]

(c) Measure of recovery [§355]

Having "waived the tort and sued in assumpsit," the measure of recovery is ex contractu (contractual) rather than ex delicto (tort), and the measure is therefore the *benefit to the defendant*, rather than the harm to the plaintiff.

Example: Deanna converted certain mining equipment belonging to Paul that had been stored at a remote mining site in Alaska. Paul waived the tort and sued on a common count for goods sold and delivered. In computing the recovery, the court held that the "benefit to Deanna" must be determined by finding the nearest market value and then *deducting freight charges* (since Paul would have had to incur these freight charges if he was going to sell at such a market). [**Felder v. Reeth**, 34 F.2d 744 (9th Cir. 1929)]

Compare: If the action had been in tort for conversion, the measure would be the *harm to Paul* (rather than merely the benefit to Deanna). In this event freight charges would have to be added, rather than subtracted, because Paul had acquired the property for use in his mining venture, and his loss would be the cost of acquisition *plus* transportation to the mining site.

(3) Restitution for value of use [§356]

An attractive option available to the injured party, particularly in cases where she has reacquired possession of the chattel, is to waive the tort of conversion and seek restitution for the value of its use. Recovery is measured either by the reasonable rental value of the chattel or by the actual benefits acquired from the use of the chattel by the wrongdoer.

Example: Darius used Paris's egg washing machine without permission and without Paris's knowledge one day per week for three years. Paris offered to sell the machine to Darius but Darius refused to purchase it. Paris then sued for the value of Darius's use. Paris was held entitled to recover for the unjust enrichment of Darius from his unauthorized use of Paris's machine. Such use resulted in a saving of labor costs of $10 per week, and this "negative" enrichment of Darius was recoverable—even though Paris sustained no actual loss. [**Olwell v. Nye & Nissen Co.**, 173 P.2d 652 (Wash. 1946)]

Example: At the time Dawn's employment in a video store was terminated, she had in her possession several tapes belonging to her employer. Upon discovering the tapes in her closet several months later, Dawn returned them. *Held*: Employer may recover the rental value of the tapes during the period of detention. [**Schlosser v. Welk**, 550 N.E.2d 241 (Ill. 1990)]

(4) Constructive trust [§357]

To impose a constructive trust, the injured party would have to show that the wrongdoer had acquired legal title to property (the trust res). However, neither the thief nor a purchaser from a thief acquires title to converted property. Therefore, the constructive trust remedy is ordinarily *not* available in these cases.

(a) Distinguish

On the other hand, if the thief *exchanges* the converted property for money (as to which he does obtain title), the injured party may, by tracing and identification, impose a constructive trust on the money or its product. [**Mattson v. Commercial Credit Business Loans,** *supra*, §352—Plaintiff may trace and impose constructive trust on funds from sale of converted lumber]

1) Inadequacy of legal remedy

In such a case, the inadequacy of the legal remedy may be shown by the defendant's insolvency or by the necessity for an *accounting*.

Example: Paul alleged that furs had been stolen from him, that Don had received the stolen furs knowing they were stolen, and that Don had disposed of them for a huge profit. This was a proper case for equitable relief (by constructive trust). The allegations were held to show that Don was a "trustee ex maleficio" with a *duty to account* for the funds realized on the sale of the stolen furs. [**Fur & Wool Trading Co. v. George I. Fox,** 245 N.Y. 215 (1927)]

SUMMARY OF SUBSTITUTIONARY REMEDIES FOR TORTIOUSLY TAKEN AND RETAINED CHATTELS — gilbert

CONVERSION	The plaintiff can recover the *value* of the property at the time of conversion, *interest* from the date of conversion, *punitive damages* if the defendant acted with malice or oppressively, and, in some jurisdictions, *consequential damages*, such as costs of seeking recapture.
QUASI-CONTRACT	The plaintiff gets restitution of any *benefit that the defendant received* as a result of the conversion.
RESTITUTION FOR VALUE OF USE	The plaintiff gets restitution of the chattel's *reasonable rental value* or of the *actual benefits acquired from use* by the wrongdoer.
CONSTRUCTIVE TRUST	A plaintiff generally cannot use a constructive trust to recover tortiously taken and retained chattels because a constructive trust may be imposed only on property to which the defendant has title (and neither a thief nor his transferees have title to tortiously taken chattels), but it may be imposed on *cash proceeds* from the disposition of the converted chattels.

C. Injuries to Real Property

1. Tortious Destruction of or Injury to Realty [§358]

The usual measure of damages in cases of destruction of or injury to realty is either (i) the difference between the *value of the land before* the injury and the *value after* the injury, or (ii) the *cost of restoration*. A flexible approach is used in determining the appropriate measure. [*See* **Weld County Board v. Slovek,** 723 P.2d 1309 (Colo. 1986); Rest. Torts §929]

a. Destruction of buildings [§359]

If an improvement such as a building is destroyed, the value of the building itself measures the loss. The value of the building is determined by various formulae:

(1) *Reproduction cost less physical depreciation* is the most common method and is used with all types of buildings. It is the only method that works in cases involving special purpose property when there is no active market for the type of property involved (*e.g.*, schools, hospitals, churches, etc.). [**Trinity Church v. John Hancock Mutual Life Insurance,** 502 N.E.2d 532 (Mass. 1987)]

(2) *Market value* may be used, but this requires a deduction for the value of the raw land.

(3) *Capitalization of income* produced by the building is another method of valuation.

(4) *The "broad evidence rule"* permits consideration of all of the above plus such other factors as obsolescence in the case of commercial property and original cost less depreciation. [**McAnarney v. Newark Fire Insurance Co.,** 247 N.Y. 176 (1928)]

b. Damage to buildings [§360]

If an improvement is damaged, the measure of damages ordinarily applied is the *cost of repair* plus *compensation for loss of use*. [**Raven's Cove Townhomes, Inc. v. Knuppe Development Co.,** 114 Cal. App. 3d 783 (1981)]

(1) Cost of repair [§361]

Only *reasonable* repair costs can be recovered, and in some jurisdictions such damages *may not exceed* the diminution in the value of the realty. An *exception* to this limitation is made if there is a personal reason to repair, as in situations where the injury is to a personal residence. [*See*

McKinney v. Christiana Community Builders, 229 Cal. App. 3d 611 (1991); **Orndorff v. Christiana Community Builders**, 217 Cal. App. 3d 683 (1990)]

(2) Increased value [§362]

If the repairs enhance the value and useful life of the injured property beyond its pre-tort condition, a *deduction* from the cost of repairs is made to prevent a windfall to the injured party. [*See* **Alton & Southern Railway v. Alton Transportation Co.**, 399 N.E.2d 173 (Ill. 1979); *and see* **Freeport Sulphur Co. v. S/S Hermosa**, 526 F.2d 300 (5th Cir. 1976)]

c. Crop damage [§363]

If immature crops are destroyed or damaged, the loss is measured by the *diminution in value* test. Since immature crops have no market value, however, the loss is computed by considering the *probable yield less cost of production and marketing*. Thus, if an immature field of wheat is destroyed, damages are measured by the value of the probable yield (*i.e.*, the number of bushels of wheat that probably would have been harvested) less the costs of cultivating, threshing, and marketing the wheat. Some courts also suggest a deduction (as a sort of insurance premium) for natural disasters such as floods, hail, fire, etc. [**Crow v. Davidson**, 96 P.2d 70 (Okla. 1939); **Kula v. Prososki**, 424 N.W.2d 117 (Neb. 1988)]

d. Damage to trees [§364]

For injury to or destruction of trees, the injured party *either* may value the trees separately and apart from the land or may measure damages by the diminution in value to the land. [**Brereton v. Dixon**, 433 P.2d 3 (Utah 1967); *see* Annot., 90 A.L.R.3d 800 (1979); 95 A.L.R.3d 508 (1979)] The difference between the measures of damages has particular relevance when statutes provide for trebling the award.

(1) Note

In many cases trees will have no value apart from the land (*e.g.*, shade trees or hedges), and consequently the *diminution in value* test must be employed. However, *replacement cost* may be considered as an alternative to the diminution in value test if it is reasonable and practical (*e.g.*, for an ornamental hedge). [**Kebschull v. Nott**, 714 P.2d 993 (Mont. 1986)—diminution in value standard proper for destruction of underbrush and noncommercial trees; **Bumgarner v. Bumgarner**, 862 P.2d 321 (Idaho 1993)—cost of restoration is proper measure of recovery for destruction of ornamental trees]

(2) But note

In other cases, as where mature timber is destroyed, the trees have a separate value apart from the land and this value can be used as the measure of loss. For example, if fruit trees are injured, damages may be measured by the loss of use or income during the period of restoration, plus the reasonable expense of restoration. [**Watkins v. FMC Corp.**, 531 P.2d 505 (Wash. 1975)]

e. Mental suffering [§365]

Ordinarily, mental suffering is *not* compensable in a trespass case, but in some cases of aggravated misconduct recovery has been allowed.

Example: Defendant developed land adjacent to plaintiff's land into residential lots. While developing the lots, defendant, among other things, pushed tons of dirt onto plaintiff's land, thus destroying part of plaintiff's fence, went onto plaintiff's land to access a sewer hook-up, built a coffer dam around the sewer and thereby caused flooding on plaintiff's land, and permanently blocked a watercourse that ran through plaintiff's land. In an action to recover damages for trespass, plaintiff testified that defendant's actions upset him and that he never knew what defendant would do next. The court held that a plaintiff could recover damages for mental distress that accompanies a trespass if it is the natural consequence and probable result of the defendant's trespass, and that, given the circumstances here, a jury award of damages for mental suffering was justified. [**Senn v. Bunick**, 594 P.2d 837 (Or. 1979)]

---

2. Waste

a. Voluntary waste [§366]

Voluntary waste consists of *deliberate destructive acts* done by a tenant (*i.e.,* by one rightfully in possession of realty).

(1) Common law remedy [§367]

The common law remedy for such acts of waste (authorized by ancient statutes) was treble damages plus forfeiture of the tenancy. This remedy is preserved today in many jurisdictions, although the forfeiture provision is sometimes omitted. [**Dorsey v. Speelman**, 459 P.2d 416 (Wash. 1969)]

(a) Treble damages [§368]

Although treble damages are authorized by these statutes, they are discretionary with the court and are granted only in cases of *willful and wanton* misconduct.

(b) Compensatory damages [§369]

Compensatory damages are measured either by the difference in value of the property before and after the injury or by the cost of repair or restoration. [**Helton v. City of St. Joseph**, 340 S.W.2d 198 (Mo. 1960); **Meyer v. Hansen**, 373 N.W.2d 392 (N.D. 1985)]

(2) Equitable remedy [§370]

Equitable relief is readily available against acts of voluntary waste because of the inadequacy of the remedy at law. Because, by definition, such waste results in permanent injury to the freehold estate, money damages cannot compensate for this loss. A *prohibitory injunction* ordering the defendant to desist from the destructive acts is granted. Damages for past injuries may be awarded as incidental relief. [**Chosar Corp. v. Owens,** 370 S.E.2d 305 (Va. 1988)]

b. Permissive waste [§371]

Permissive waste involves acts of *omission or neglect* by a tenant that cause damage to the freehold. Generally this consists of failure to keep the premises in proper repair ("wind and water tight"). [**Zauner v. Brewer,** 596 A.2d 388 (Conn. 1991)]

(1) Damages [§372]

Damages for permissive waste are generally measured by the *cost of repairs*. The cause of action arises as each act of waste is committed or suffered.

(2) Equitable remedy [§373]

Courts are very hesitant to grant equitable relief in cases of permissive waste. This is partly explained by the general reluctance of equity courts to enter mandatory injunctions compelling affirmative acts of restoration. Courts also emphasize a policy against undue interference with the enjoyment of the estate by the tenant. Some courts assert that the recovery of the cost of repairs provides an adequate remedy at law. [**City of Philadelphia v. Pierre Uniforms,** 535 A.2d 142 (Pa. 1987)—damages an adequate remedy]

c. Ameliorating waste [§374]

Ameliorating waste consists of acts done by a tenant that alter the freehold but that result in an *increase in the value* of the property. Typical examples are the conversion of a warehouse into a store, or terracing a pasture so that it can be used for cropland.

(1) Damages [§375]

In these cases, no damages can ordinarily be recovered because there is no diminution in the value of the property.

(2) Equitable remedy [§376]

Equity courts thus provided the only remedy. Whether injunctive relief will be granted depends on the circumstances.

 Example: Doherty held a reversion after the expiration of a 999-year lease. Allman, the lessor, wanted to change the warehouse that was on the leasehold estate into apartments. Doherty sought to enjoin the change. *Held:* Given the great length of time before Doherty's reversion became possessory, the proposed change would not cause any injury to Doherty. Thus, the injunction was denied. [**Doherty v. Allman**, (1878) L.R. 3 App. Cas. 709]

---

cf. **Compare:** On the other hand, a substantial change in the premises proposed by a tenant holding under a *lease for a short period of time* may be enjoined if contrary to the wishes of the landlord. The landlord has the right to have the property returned at the end of the lease without material alteration, even if that change enhances the value of the property. (Generally today the right to make such alterations is governed by the provisions of the lease.)

---

d. **Equitable waste [§377]**

If material changes in the premises are being made *by a person who is not legally chargeable* with waste, relief in equity by way of injunction may be granted. This is called "equitable waste" because there is no wrong or remedy provided at law. Typical examples are tenancies for life "without impeachment for waste" and acts done by persons who are in possession as buyers under land sale contracts or as mortgagors.

(1) **Tenant without impeachment for waste [§378]**

Tenancies "without impeachment for waste" were created to avoid the possibility of forfeitures (usually by life tenants) for changes made in the freehold. (*See* Property Summary.) Such provisions were given literal effect by the law courts, and no matter how destructive the tenant might be, no legal liability attached for his acts. Because of the nonexistence of a remedy at law, equity courts provided relief in situations where the tenant's acts were outrageous and ruinous to the freehold (*e.g.,* removal of windows or roofs from dwellings, or cutting and removal of all of the ornamental trees and shrubbery on the premises).

(2) **Mortgagor [§379]**

The mortgagor is considered the owner of the property and consequently is ordinarily *not* chargeable at law for acts of waste. Some courts, however, hold that the mortgagor is liable for voluntary but not permissive waste. [**Camden Trust Co. v. Handle**, 26 A.2d 865 (N.J. 1942)]

(a) **Illustration—voluntary waste [§380]**

A mortgagor has been held liable for acts of voluntary waste *committed in bad faith* that impair the mortgagee's security, even when the mortgagor would be protected from liability on the underlying debt by anti-deficiency legislation (*i.e.,* statutes that provide that the mortgagee's only remedy in event of default is to foreclose the mortgage, and that no action for any deficiency will lie against the mortgagor). [**Hickman v. Mulder,** 58 Cal. App. 3d 900 (1976); *and see* **Prudential Insurance v. Spencer's Kenosha Bowl,** 404 N.W.2d 109 (Wis. 1987)—grantee of mortgaged property who did not assume mortgage liable for both voluntary and permissive waste that jeopardized mortgagee's security]

1) Injunctive relief allowed for voluntary waste [§381]

Even where an action at law for voluntary waste is authorized, it is not an adequate remedy for the mortgagee, who is concerned only with the adequacy of the security for the debt. Hence, *injunctive relief may be granted* to prohibit destructive acts of waste, the governing principle being the preservation of a reasonable margin of security (*i.e.*, the difference between what the lending agency will lend and the full value of the property constituting the security). What constitutes "impairment of the security" depends on margin requirements in the vicinity for the type of property involved (raw land or buildings). [*See* **Jaffe-Spindler Co. v. Genesco, Inc.,** 747 F.2d 253 (4th Cir. 1984); **Payne v. Snyder,** 661 S.W.2d 134 (Tex. 1983)—if collateral is of sufficient value to secure the debt, there is no action for waste]

---

e.g. **Example:** A mortgage loan agreement included an exculpatory clause barring the lender from bringing an action for monetary damages from waste and limiting the remedy to foreclosure. The mortgagor willfully failed to pay taxes, an act held to be waste ("a tax lien on secured property is as costly as a leaky roof"). Since the legal remedy was barred by the exculpatory clause, equitable relief by way of an injunction was allowed (even though this required the payment of money). [*See* **Travelers Insurance Co. v. 633 Third Avenue Associates,** 973 F.2d 82 (2d Cir. 1991)]

(b) Distinguish—permissive waste [§382]

Injunctive relief is generally *not* granted for permissive waste (failure to repair). For this type of misconduct, the only protection must be found in the terms of the mortgage instrument (*e.g.*, provision may authorize foreclosure of mortgage for nonrepair).

(c) Receivership [§383]

Receivership is also an appropriate remedy to protect the lender from voluntary or involuntary waste by the mortgagor. [55 A.L.R.3d 1041]

COMPARISON OF REMEDIES FOR WASTE   gilbert

TYPE OF WASTE	CIRCUMSTANCES	REMEDY
VOLUNTARY WASTE	Tenant commits **deliberate destructive acts** on the realty (*e.g.,* life tenant leases farmland for use as a toxic waste dump).	Many states permit **treble damages**, although such damages generally are imposed only if the defendant acted wantonly or recklessly; **compensatory damages** generally are measured by the cost of repair or the difference in the realty's value before and after the waste. A **prohibitory injunction** might also be issued.
PERMISSIVE WASTE	Through omission or neglect, tenant **allows realty to fall into disrepair** (*e.g.,* life tenant fails to repair barn roof after a hail storm, leading to future water damage and decay).	Damages generally are measured by the **cost of repairs**. Injunctions generally are not available.
AMELIORATING WASTE	Tenant alters realty in a way that **increases its value** (life tenant converts an under-used warehouse into a thriving store).	Generally, damages are not available because there is no diminution in the value of the property. A court **might grant an injunction** if the lease is for a short period.
EQUITABLE WASTE	Tenant makes material changes to realty but is **not legally chargeable** with waste (*e.g.,* the buyer of a farm under an installment contract leases the land for use as a toxic waste dump).	A court may **grant an injunction** if the destructive acts impair the security of the seller or mortgagee.

(3) Buyer in possession [§384]

Once having taken possession under an executory land sale contract, the buyer is regarded as the equitable owner of the land, owing a balance on the purchase price. Thus, the same rules apply to the buyer in possession as apply to the mortgagor. The buyer may use the property in any way she chooses as long as she does not *impair the security* of the seller. Just as in the analogous case of the mortgagee, the seller is entitled to injunctive relief against the buyer's acts only to the extent necessary to preserve a reasonable margin of security for the debt. [**Miller v. Waddingham**, 91 Cal. 377 (1891); *and see* **Kruger v. Horton**, 725 P.2d 417 (Wash. 1986)—damages denied to seller on forfeited land sale contract where no diminution in value of property was shown to have resulted from alleged acts of waste]

3. Trespass with Ouster

a. Ejectment [§385]

A party who has been wrongfully excluded from possession of realty has available the common law remedy of ejectment. Essential elements of the cause of action are (i) proof of *right to possession* and (ii) *wrongful withholding* by the defendant. A successful plaintiff is entitled to judgment for recovery of the property and for mesne damages. [**Deakyne v. Lewes Anglers, Inc.**, 204 F. Supp. 415 (D. Del. 1962)]

(1) "Mesne damages" or "profits" [§386]

"Mesne damages," also referred to as "mesne profits," compensate for the *loss of use* of the land and are measured by the *rental value* of the property or the *actual benefit* gained by the wrongful occupant, whichever is greater. All other damages that have been sustained by reason of disturbance of the plaintiff's possession are also recoverable in the action. [**Dumas v. Ropp**, 588 P.2d 632 (Idaho 1977)]

(2) Good faith improvements by trespasser [§387]

If the defendant mistakenly enters into possession of the plaintiff's land and in *good faith* makes *valuable improvements* on the property, the common law rule allows the plaintiff to recover possession in ejectment without paying for these improvements. Thus, the plaintiff may keep scot-free whatever the defendant built on the land, even though the defendant acted in good faith thinking the land belonged to him.

(a) Setoff allowed [§388]

If besides ejectment, the plaintiff also seeks mesne damages, courts then permit the defendant to *set off* against these damages the value of the improvements. However, no affirmative judgment is allowed, and total defeat of the plaintiff's claim for mesne damages is the best that the defendant can achieve. [**Roesch v. Wachter**, 618 P.2d 448 (Or. 1980); **Oneida Indian Nation v. Oneida County**, 719 F.2d 525 (2d Cir. 1983); *compare* **Uhlhorn v. Keltner**, 723 S.W.2d 131 (Tenn. 1986)—setoff for permanent improvements disallowed because defendants did not hold property they improved under "color of title"]

(b) Equitable relief [§389]

An exception is recognized where *equitable relief* is sought by the landowner (*e.g.*, a suit to quiet title or cancel a deed). In such cases, the common law rule is that the landowner must "do equity" by paying for the improvements as a condition of being awarded the relief sought.

(c) Action by improver [§390]

A *few* jurisdictions give the good faith improver an independent claim in equity to prevent unjust enrichment.

e.g **Example:** A mistaken improver counterclaimed for equitable relief in the plaintiff's action for ejectment. The court held that equitable relief should be granted to avoid unjust enrichment, and decreed that the landowner should convey the portion of his land mistakenly utilized by the defendant upon payment of its value. [**Comer v. Roberts**, 448 P.2d 543 (Or. 1968); *and see* **Sommerville v. Jacobs**, 170 S.E.2d 805 (W. Va. 1969)—innocent encroacher may recover either the value of the improvement or the right to purchase the land at its value without the improvement]

(d) Statutes [§391]

The harsh common law rule has been changed by statute in many states. These enactments (called "betterment statutes") variously provide for removal of the improvement, or give the landowner the option of paying for the improvement or selling the land to the defendant. The California statute provides for an independent action by the good faith improver to recover compensation for improvements and may even warrant imposition of an equitable lien on the property. [*See* **Okuda v. Superior Court**, 144 Cal. App. 3d 135 (1983)]

b. Unlawful detainer [§392]

Unlawful detainer (as well as forcible entry and detainer) is another statutory provisional remedy to obtain possession of realty by one entitled to it.

[**McGlothlin v. Kilebert,** 672 S.W.2d 231 (Tex. 1984)] Compare this remedy with "replevin," which performs the same function with regard to personal property (*see supra*, §315).

(1) Issue is possession, not title [§393]

An unlawful detainer action is a summary proceeding; the only issue litigated is the plaintiff's right to possession. [**Union Oil Co. v. Chandler,** 4 Cal. 3d 716 (1970)]

(a) But note

Defenses that are directly related to the issue of possession (*e.g.*, breach of warranty of habitability, retaliatory eviction) and which, if established, would result in the tenant's retention of the premises, may be interposed. [**S.P. Growers Association v. Rodriguez,** 17 Cal. 3d 719 (1976); *but see* **Leve v. Delph,** 710 S.W.2d 389 (Mo. 1986)—retaliatory eviction defense not allowed]

(2) Plaintiff's recovery [§394]

The successful plaintiff in these actions is entitled to a judgment for recovery of possession, rental value of the lost use, and any consequential damages sustained. Treble damages are often authorized by statute if the defendant's ouster was willful.

(3) Criticism of remedy [§395]

Most statutes subject this remedy to so many procedural requirements, limitations, and equitable defenses that the objective of providing speedy return of the property is seldom realized.

c. Equitable relief [§396]

Injunctive relief is *not* available against a party wrongfully withholding possession of realty. The legal remedies of ejectment and forcible entry and detainer are considered adequate. [**Warlier v. Williams,** 73 N.W. 539 (Neb. 1897); **Pullem v. Evanston Y.M.C.A.,** 464 N.E.2d 785 (Ill. 1984)—injunctive relief denied to tenant evicted from room in the Y.M.C.A.]

d. Restitution [§397]

There is no separate action for restitution for the value of the use of land in possession of the wrongdoer during an ouster. The explanation for this rule is historical. The proper form of action was assumpsit, and at common law, title could not be tried in a transitory action (one maintainable other than at the site of the land). Moreover, the action of trespass for mesne damages following recovery of possession in ejectment provides adequate compensation for the deprivation of use.

SUMMARY OF REMEDIES AVAILABLE FOR OUSTER   **gilbert**

EJECTMENT	A party who can show a right to possession and wrongful withholding by the defendant may recover the land plus "mesne damages" (damages measured by the *rental value* of the property or the *actual benefit gained* by the wrongful occupant), plus all other damages reasonably related to the ouster.
UNLAWFUL DETAINER	A provisional remedy to obtain possession of property; the only issue is the plaintiff's right to possession. Besides *possession*, the plaintiff can be awarded damages for loss of use measured by *rental value* and *consequential damages*.
INJUNCTIVE RELIEF	*Generally not available* because the legal remedies (ejectment and unlawful detainer) are considered adequate.
RESTITUTION	*Generally there is no separate action for restitution* for use during ouster because of historical reasons.

4. Encroachment

a. Damages [§398]

Where, by mistake or inadvertence, a building or other structure is constructed in such a way as to encroach on plaintiff's property, a claim for *trespass* arises. In some jurisdictions, the encroachment is treated as a *continuing trespass* with damages measured by rental value of the property. In other jurisdictions, the trespass is regarded as a *permanent invasion* and damages are assessed as either diminution in value of the property encroached upon or the value of the strip of land on which the building sits. [**Kratze v. Independent Order of Oddfellows,** 500 N.W.2d 115 (Mich. 1993); *compare* the permanent nuisance doctrine, *infra,* §449]

(1) Effect of distinction on statute of limitations

The classification as a continuing trespass, as opposed to a permanent invasion, may have important consequences for *statute of limitations purposes.* For example, in **509 6th Avenue Corp. v. New York City Transportation Authority,** 15 N.Y.2d 48 (1964), Defendant constructed a subway in 1939, which encroached upon Plaintiff's property. Upon discovery of the encroachment in 1960, Plaintiff sought damages. Defendant pleaded a three-year statute of limitations. The court held that the trespass was a *continuing* one giving rise to successive actions; consequently, the claim was not barred at least until Defendant acquired a prescriptive right. [*But see* **Williams v. South & South Rentals,** 346 S.E.2d 665 (N.C. 1986)—denied right to bring successive actions for continuing trespass]

b. Ejectment [§399]

Because the encroachment constitutes an ouster, ejectment is a possible remedy. The difficulty, however, is in the enforcement of the judgment. Even though plaintiff receives a judgment for possession, there is no practical way for the sheriff or marshall to remove the encroachment and restore the plaintiff to possession. Consequently, ejectment is *not an adequate remedy* in encroachment cases.

c. Self-help [§400]

Self-help is an available remedy in encroachment cases, although it is not practicable in most instances. However, if the encroachment is a simple one (*e.g.*, tree branches hanging over plaintiff's property), self-help may be found to be an adequate remedy precluding injunctive relief. [*See* **Jones v. Wagner**, 624 A.2d 166 (Pa. 1993)]

d. Injunction

(1) Legal remedies inadequate [§401]

Because the encroachment deprives the plaintiff of the land (which is unique), money damages are deemed not adequate. And, as indicated above, ejectment is not a practical or effective remedy. Therefore, an encroachment is a proper case for equitable relief in the form of a *mandatory* injunction ordering the defendant to remove the encroachment. [**Williams v. South & South Rentals**, *supra*—defendant ordered to remove one-foot encroachment by apartment building on plaintiff's land]

(2) Balance of hardships defense [§402]

Because the cost of removal to the defendant may far exceed the value of the land restored to the plaintiff, courts "balance the hardships" in determining whether the injunction should issue. [Rest. Torts §941] The considerations guiding the court are (i) the avoidance of judicial approval of private eminent domain by the encroacher while at the same time (ii) preventing extortion by the encroachee. [**Kratze v. Independent Order of Oddfellows**, *supra*]

(a) No "balancing" if deliberate encroachment [§403]

Hardships will be balanced only in cases of *inadvertent* encroachment. If the defendant's conduct is deliberate and intentional, an injunction ordering removal will be granted regardless of the hardships on defendant. Otherwise, the defendant would be permitted a sort of private eminent domain. [*See* **Missouri Power & Light Co. v. Barnett**, 354 S.W.2d 873 (Mo. 1962)—house ordered removed from power company's easement; **Calhoon v. Communications Systems Construction, Inc.**, 489 N.E.2d 23 (Ill. 1986)—trespass by cable company over plaintiff's protest]

Was the defendant's encroachment **deliberate and intentional**?

YES → The court probably will **order the defendant to remove** the encroachment regardless of cost.

NO ↓

Will removal of the encroachment cause hardship to the defendant that would **greatly outweigh** the hardship the plaintiff would suffer if the encroachment is not removed?

YES → The court probably will **not order removal** of the encroachment and instead will **order the defendant to pay the plaintiff the value** of the property encroached upon.

NO ↓

The court probably will **order the defendant to remove** the encroachment.

(b) Inadvertent encroachment [§404]

If the encroachment is inadvertent, courts balance the hardship to the plaintiff of not getting an injunction (the loss of the land) against the hardship to the defendant if the injunction is granted (the cost of removal). The hardship on the defendant *must greatly outweigh* that on the plaintiff before an injunction is denied. [**Seid v. Ross,** 853 P.2d 308 (Or. 1993)]

Example: By a good faith mistake, defendant's home was constructed 15 feet over the boundary line of his land. The mistake was not discovered until *20 years* later when plaintiff purchased the property encroached upon and had the boundary line surveyed. Plaintiff sued and an injunction ordering removal of the building was *granted*. *Rationale:* Even though removal was costly, the invasion constituted 9% of plaintiff's property and increased the congestion on his lot. [**Peters v. Archambault,** 278 N.E. 729 (Mass. 1972); *and see* **Goulding v. Cook,** 661 N.E.2d 1322 (Mass. 1996)—removal of defendant's septic system from plaintiff's land ordered, the court emphasizing the significance of the concept of private property]

Compare: Defendant purchased two lots in 1948 and built a lodge on a foundation that already existed on the lots. In 1985, plaintiff entered into a contract to purchase lots adjacent to defendant's lots for $18,000. Plaintiff intended to build an apartment complex on the lots and had them surveyed for suitability. A survey showed that defendant's lodge encroached on plaintiff's lot by 1.2 feet, but defendant did not know of the encroachment. Plaintiff purchased the lots and brought suit against defendant seeking an order to force defendant to remove the encroachment. Removal of the encroachment would have caused defendant's building to collapse, and the encroachment did not prevent plaintiff from developing his land. Under these circumstances, an order for removal is not proper. [**Kratze v. Independent Order of Oddfellows,** *supra,* §402]

(c) Laches and public interest [§405]

Other factors considered include *laches* and the *public interest*, if any, that might be affected by the injunction. The plaintiff must also be prepared to do equity—*e.g.*, by permitting the defendant to trespass on the plaintiff's land for the purpose of removing the encroachment.

(d) Public instrumentality [§406]

If the defendant is a public instrumentality with eminent domain power, no injunction is granted since the property of the plaintiff could then be condemned, and equity does not do a useless thing. [*See* **Nueces County Drainage District v. Bevly,** 519 S.W.2d 938 (Tex. 1975)—denying injunctive relief against a public agency even in the absence of eminent domain powers]

(3) Denial of injunction [§407]

If the injunction is denied, the denial is *conditioned on the payment by the defendant of the value of the property* encroached upon.

5. Trespass to Land—Severance

a. Timber [§408]

Recovery for the wrongful severance of timber by a trespasser depends on the theory adopted by the landowner and whether the trespass is classified as willful or innocent.

(1) Trespass to land [§409]

If the plaintiff sues under a trespass theory, the usual measure of damages is the *diminution in the value of the land* because of the severance of the trees. Sometimes the loss is measured by "stumpage value," which is the price one would pay for the privilege of cutting the timber. [**Pearce v. G.R. Kirk Co.,** 602 P.2d 357 (Wash. 1979)]

(a) Note

In some jurisdictions, actual damages as thus computed may be doubled or trebled, depending on the defendant's conduct. Under these statutes, trebling generally requires proof of malice and willfulness. [**Crofoot Lumber Co. v. Ford,** 191 Cal. App. 2d 238 (1961); *and see* **Johnson v. Jensen,** 433 N.W.2d 472 (Minn. 1988)—both treble damages and punitive damages allowed for a willful trespass]

(2) Conversion [§410]

If the plaintiff sues under a conversion theory, damages are measured by the *value of the logs* after severance. If the trespass was innocent, some courts permit the costs of severance to be deducted. On the other hand, if the trespass was *willful*, the landowner may recover the value of the logs even if manufactured into lumber with no deduction for manufacturing costs (*see* doctrine of accession, *supra*, §346).

(3) Quasi-contract [§411]

The landowner may elect to waive the tort and seek restitution of the value of the benefit received by the trespasser. If the trespass was innocent, the trespasser is liable only for the value of the logs; if a conscious wrongdoer, then the trespasser is liable for the value of the property as improved (*e.g.,* as lumber) at the time of demand by the landowner.

(4) Replevin [§412]

If the landowner can locate and identify the timber, he may replevy it without payment for any improvements. (*See supra, §315.*)

b. Minerals [§413]

The rules applicable to the wrongful cutting of timber also apply to the wrongful misappropriation of minerals.

(1) Innocent trespasses [§414]

Innocent trespasses are divided into two cases:

(a) *If the landowner is unable to exploit the minerals himself,* recovery against an innocent trespasser is limited to a *royalty* payment, which is the price paid for the *right to mine* (similar to stumpage value in the timber case). [**Bowman v. Hibbard**, 257 S.W.2d 550 (Ky. 1953)]

(b) *If the landowner could extract the minerals,* the measure of damages is the value of the product after it is mined, *less the reasonable cost of mining it.* This measure awards to the landowner the *net* profit of the mining venture.

(2) Willful trespasses [§415]

If the trespass was deliberate and intentional, the landowner is awarded the value of the minerals as extracted with no deduction for the cost of mining. [*See* **Bowman v. Hibbard**, *supra*]

c. Injunctions [§416]

Injunctive relief is available against a trespasser who wrongfully misappropriates and removes part of the realty—whether timber, minerals, or the soil itself.

(1) Legal remedy inadequate [§417]

The remedy at law is not adequate in these cases for several reasons: First of all, there is the *continuous nature of the trespass,* which violates the landowner's right of absolute dominion over the property. In addition, there is the peculiar and unique value of land, and courts regard any injury to land as irreparable in the sense that money cannot replace whatever has been misappropriated. But once the timber or minerals have been severed, no injunction will be issued against their removal. These things are now ordinary chattels and not unique.

(2) Plaintiff's lack of title as defense [§418]

Traditionally, if the defendant asserted as a defense that the plaintiff lacked title to the realty, equity courts dismissed the bill until the issue was settled in the law courts. However, under modern codes that unify courts of law and equity, the title issue should merely be severed for trial by jury (assuming a proper demand for jury has been made). [*See* **St. Louis Smelting & Refining Co. v. Hoban,** 209 S.W.2d 119 (Mo. 1948)]

6. Trespass to Land Not Involving Severance

a. Debris dumped on plaintiff's land [§419]

If the trespass results from placing dirt, rocks, and other materials on the property of another, the following remedies are available.

(1) Damages for trespass [§420]

There are several methods for measuring damages in these cases:

(a) Rental value [§421]

Damages may be measured by the rental value of the property affected. This relief is available even though the land was not damaged and was not being used by the landowner. [**Don v. Trojan Construction Co.,** 178 Cal. App. 2d 135 (1960)]

1) Note

Successive damages actions may be necessary if the debris is not removed and the trespass is continuous. [**Wheelock v. Noonan,** 108 N.Y. 179 (1888)]

(b) Cost of removal [§422]

Alternatively, damages may be measured by the cost of removal of the debris or obstruction. [*See* **Dandoy v. Oswald,** 113 Cal. App. 570 (1931)—dirt placed on plaintiff's land; although the value of the land for farming had not depreciated, the cost of removal was recoverable]

1) Limitation [§423]

The total damages awarded for cost of removal and restoring the land to its original condition may not exceed the value of the property prior to the defendant's acts. [*See* **Green v. General Petroleum Corp.,** 205 Cal. 328 (1928); *and see* **Myers v. Arnold,** 403 N.E.2d 316 (Ill. 1980)—cost of restoration is the appropriate measure where it can be "accomplished without expending amounts wholly disproportionate to the value of the land"]

2) Credit for benefit [§424]

A trespass may actually benefit the property, and credit for that benefit will reduce the tortfeasor's damages.

 Example: A trespass that drains a marsh on the plaintiff's land may increase its value. [*See* Rest. 2d Torts §920]

> **cf.** **Compare:** Where defendant brought in an oil well on property adjoining plaintiff's, and the well cast mud and oil on plaintiff's house, plaintiff was entitled to recover the cost of restoring his house, even though the value of plaintiff's property was greatly enhanced (because of the discovery of oil on defendant's property). [**Green v. General Petroleum Corp.,** *supra*] (It is arguable that even though plaintiff's land was enhanced in value, there was a diminution in value of the property *as a residence.*)

(2) Injunction [§425]

Equitable relief in the form of a *mandatory* injunction *compelling removal* of the debris or obstruction may be available. [**Wheelock v. Noonan,** *supra*]

(a) Legal remedy inadequate [§426]

The remedy at law is not adequate because if rental value is the measure of damages, then a multiplicity of actions is necessary without terminating the occupation. Moreover, the burden of removing the debris and recovering expenses should not be borne by the landowner but instead should be placed on the trespasser. [*But see* **Belinsky v. Belinsky,** 497 A.2d 84 (Conn. 1985)—court denied an injunction, ruling that the damages remedy is adequate to recover the cost of removing thousands of tires from plaintiff's property]

1) Note

Self-help may be an adequate remedy if the obstruction is trivial (*e.g.,* one boulder), but in **Wheelock v. Noonan,** *supra,* huge rocks to the height of 18 feet were piled on the plaintiff's property. [*See* **Richmond v. General Engineering Enterprises,** 454 So. 2d 16 (Fla. 1984)—self-help ruled adequate remedy for overhanging branches of tree]

b. Oil well drilling on plaintiff's land [§427]

If the trespasser enters upon the property and drills a test well that proves to be dry, the landowner may recover damages for any physical injury to the land and, in addition, may recover compensation for the *loss of the speculative value of the land as an oil prospect.* [**Humble Oil & Refinery Co. v. Kishi,** 291 S.W. 538 (Tex. 1925)—Defendant drilled a test well on Plaintiff's property without the right to do so, but failed to find oil; Plaintiff could recover the diminution in market value even though there was no intrinsic damage to his property]

(1) If oil is found [§428]

The above rule is inappropriate if the wrongful acts of the trespasser reveal the *presence* of oil because the speculative value of the land is *increased.* Hence in such cases, courts allow the landowner to recover for the *value of the exploration rights* on the theory that the trespasser had acquired a benefit by the trespass and must pay for it. [**Shell Petroleum Corp. v. Scully,** 71 F.2d 772 (5th Cir. 1934)—without plaintiff's consent, defendant discharged dynamite blasts on plaintiff's land to determine the presence of oil, and the shots revealed favorable signs for oil in vicinity; plaintiff could recover for the reasonable value of the exploration rights on a quasi-contract theory]

7. Simple Acts of Trespass

a. Damages [§429]

For simple acts of trespass causing no injury to the realty (*e.g.,* walking across the property), the landowner nevertheless has a cause of action for at least *nominal* damages. [**Staples v. Hoefke,** 189 Cal. App. 3d 1397 (1987); **Hoaglin v. Decker,** 713 P.2d 674 (Or. 1986)—restricting common law rule of strict liability to cases of intentional trespass]

(1) Consequential damages [§430]

Consequential damages may be recoverable in a simple trespass case.

---

e.g. Example: Abortion protesters trespassed on plaintiff clinic's property, causing minimal property damage but a considerable loss of business. Rejecting defendant's argument that damage should be limited to the actual damage to plaintiff's equipment, the court affirmed a judgment of $42,974 for loss of business as a consequence of the trespass. [**Northeast Women's Center v. McMonagle,** 689 F. Supp. 465 (E.D. Pa. 1988)]

---

(2) Punitive damages [§431]

A simple act of trespass accomplished in the face of protest by the landowner supports an award of punitive damages.

---

e.g. Example: Steenberg sold a mobile home to Jacque's neighbor and asked Jacque for permission to move the home across Jacque's land because that route was easier than using the public road. Jacque, fearful of allowing others on his land because he lost an adverse possession action a few years before, refused to grant permission. Steenberg's assistant was heard to tell employees "I don't give a _ _ _ _ what [Mr. Jacque] said, just get the home in there any way you can." Ultimately, the delivery crew cut across Jacque's field to deliver the home, and Steenberg's assistant is said to have giggled and laughed when he heard what had occurred. Under these circumstances, the court ruled that it was proper to award $1 nominal damages and $100,000 punitive damages. [**Jacque v. Steenberg Homes,** 563 N.W.2d 154 (Wis. 1997)—who's laughing now?]

b.   Injunctions [§432]

Injunctive relief may also be available to prohibit the trespass. The remedy at law is not adequate because the recovery is nominal and would not prevent repetition of the trespass. As a result, there will be a multiplicity of actions without ever securing the landowner's exclusive rights of possession.

Example: Contrary to Pedro's wishes, Diego brought saddle horses onto Pedro's hotel grounds to rent to Pedro's customers; injunction was held to be the proper remedy, because otherwise Pedro would be compelled to file costly actions at law where recovery of damages would be only nominal. [**Champie v. Hot Springs Co.,** 233 P. 1107 (Ariz. 1925)]

Example: An injunction was properly granted to prohibit golf balls from being propelled onto plaintiff's property from neighboring golf course. [**Fenton v. Quaboag Country Club,** 333 N.E.2d 216 (Mass. 1967)]

Example: An injunction was properly granted in a boundary line dispute because threatened repeated trespasses made amounts recoverable at law "disproportionate to expense." [**Pliske v. Yuskis,** 403 N.E.2d 710 (Ill. 1980)]

(1)   Abortion protests [§433]

Injunctions are also the remedy employed against protesters interfering with access to clinics where abortions are performed. [*See* **Roe v. Operation Rescue,** 919 F.2d 857 (3d Cir. 1990); **Town of West Hartford v. Operation Rescue,** 726 F.2d 371 (D. Conn. 1990)]

(2)   Note—easement prevention [§434]

Some courts reason that an injunction is needed to prevent the creation of an easement. However, this is *not* a valid argument since each action of trespass would toll the prescriptive period.

c.   Restitution [§435]

Whether a restitutionary action will lie for the value of any benefit accruing to the trespasser from the use of another's land is a disputed question.

(1)   Quasi-contract [§436]

For historical reasons of an obscure nature (which need not be reviewed here), the common law did *not* permit assumpsit to lie in cases of trespass to land. (This restrictive view was accepted by the Restatement of Restitution. [Rest. Restitution §129(2)])

(a) Distinguish—modern view [§437]

A number of jurisdictions have repudiated the common law rule and will permit a landowner to sue on a common count for the value of the trespasser's use and occupation of the property—the measure of the "benefit" to the trespasser being the *value of the trespassory use*. (This position is now endorsed by section 46 of the proposed revision of the Restatement of Restitution. [*See* Tentative Draft No. 2, Rest. Restitution (1984)])

Example: Diego made excessive use of an easement across Peabody's property by transporting coal thereon. Peabody was held entitled to recover in quasi-contract for the value of Diego's unauthorized use of Peabody's land—measured by the *value of an easement permitting such use.* (The court found that the value of such an easement was 1¢ per ton of coal transported, and awarded restitution accordingly.) [**Raven Red Ash Coal Co. v. Ball,** 39 S.E.2d 231 (Va. 1946)]

Compare: Under facts similar to those in *Raven, supra,* a landowner sought damages on a trespass theory. The court ruled that the proper measure of damages for trespass is either the depreciation in the rental value of the land or the diminution in the value of the use of the land during the time of the trespass. [**Middle States Coal Co. v. Hicks,** 608 S.W.2d 56 (Ky. 1980)]

(2) Restitution in equity [§438]

Because of the courts' general reluctance to grant quasi-contractual relief in this area (*see* above), suits may be filed in equity to enjoin the unauthorized use or trespass. When equitable jurisdiction is properly invoked, equity courts *may* grant restitution as *ancillary* relief.

Example: Edwards exhibited a cave that extended under land owned owned by Lee, although the only entrance was on Edwards's land. While the trespass was a continuing one, there was no physical damage to Lee's land. Lee sued for an injunction against the trespass and an accounting for the profits made by Edwards's unauthorized use of Lee's land. The court held that Lee was entitled to the "benefit" gained by Edwards from the unauthorized use, measured by a *share* of the *net profits* derived from Edwards's operation. (*But note:* It may be better to think of this as a case of appropriation of a business opportunity rather than an application of historical notions about trespass.) [**Edwards v. Lee's Administrators,** 96 S.W.2d 1028 (Ky. 1936)]

SUMMARY OF REMEDIES AVAILABLE FOR ACTS OF SIMPLE TRESPASS	**gilbert**
DAMAGES	A plaintiff can recover for any damages caused by the trespass, or *nominal damages* if no substantial damage was caused. *Punitive damages* are available if the trespass was intentional and in the face of protests by the landowner.
INJUNCTIONS	A plaintiff may obtain an injunction to prohibit repeated simple acts of trespass, because *multiple suits for nominal damages* (the legal remedy) is not considered an adequate remedy.
QUASI-CONTRACT	Some courts will allow a landowner to bring a quasi-contract action against a trespasser for the *value of the trespassory use*, but others will not for historical reasons.
RESTITUTION IN EQUITY	If a plaintiff seeks an injunction, the equity court can in addition grant restitution of the *benefit gained by the trespassory use*.

8. Interference with Easements

a. Damages [§439]

For destruction or interference with easements (such as roadways, parking, access, etc.) the owner of the easement has a cause of action for damages to indemnify her for the loss.

(1) For destruction [§440]

If the easement is *destroyed*, the loss may be measured by the *diminution in the value of the plaintiff's property* to which the easement attached.

Example: Dante constructed a building on his land in such a way as to block the public view of Palmer's adjacent property (retail stores). *Held:* Dante had destroyed Palmer's easement for ingress and light and air (view); the injury is permanent and diminution in value of Palmer's property is the proper measure of damages. This could be shown by appraisers and also by the loss in rental value of Palmer's property. [**Kitzman v. Newman**, 230 Cal. App. 2d 715 (1964)]

Example: Dali constructed a building on a parking lot which Pablo had the right to use by the terms of a commercial lease. *Held:* The loss in value of Pablo's leasehold is measured by Pablo's lost profits. [**Lucky Auto Supply v. Turner**, 244 Cal. App. 2d 872 (1966)]

(2) For interference [§441]

If the easement is not destroyed, but instead is interfered with (*e.g.*, by placing a barrier across a road), damages may be measured by the *cost of removal* of the obstruction.

(a) Note

Additional items of damages may include the value of lost use, expenses incurred because of the interference and, where the interference is malicious, punitive damages.

b. Injunctions [§442]

If an easement is legally recognized, injunctive relief is granted because of the inadequacy of the remedy at law.

(1) Remedy at law inadequate [§443]

The damages remedy is not considered adequate in these cases because money cannot compensate for the loss of unique property rights. Although easements are intangible, they are recognized as interests in land and thus are included within the general equity doctrine that loss of dominion over land is irreparable at law. Additionally, if the interference is *continuing*, the resulting multiplicity of damage actions also makes the remedy at law inadequate.

(2) Easement must be recognized at law [§444]

Before relief can be granted in equity, there must be a *legally protected right*. Thus, for example, where easements of light and air are *not* recognized at law, no protection will be given in equity.

Example: Day constructed an addition to its hotel which blocked out the sun on the beach in front of Knight's hotel. Equity courts could not grant injunctive relief because easements for light and air were *not* recognized under appropriate local law. [**Fontainebleu Hotel Corp. v. Forty-Five Twenty-Five, Inc.,** 114 So. 2d 357 (Fla. 1959)] (Although with the trend toward use of solar energy, it is likely that some equity court will soon recognize a protectable interest in access to sunlight. [*See, e.g.,* **Prah v. Maretti,** 321 N.W.2d 182 (Wis. 1982)—recognizing right to unobstructed sunlight])

(3) Balance of hardships defense [§445]

Assuming an easement is recognized by the law or is created by deed restriction, the injunctive remedy is still discretionary. Hence, in proper cases, a balancing of hardships may result in a denial of relief. Thus, if defendant constructed a 40-story building which through inadvertence violates a "setback" ordinance, the cost of reconstruction might far outweigh any advantage to an adjacent property owner from the additional light and air. Similarly, radical change in the character of a neighborhood rendering an easement for light and air obsolete may result in a denial of injunctive relief and an award of money damages only. [**Blakely v. Gorin,** 313 N.E.2d 903 (Mass. 1973)]

(a) Note

Injunctive enforcement of *restrictive covenants in deeds* involve similar considerations. [*Compare* **Glover v. Santangelo,** 690 P.2d 1083 (Or. 1984)—violation of building restriction against obstructing a view; mandatory injunction ordered; *with* **Foxwood Homeowner's Association v. Ricles,** 673 S.W.2d 376 (Tex. 1984)—balance of equities favored defendant; injunction denied]

9. Nuisances

a. Private nuisance [§446]

A private nuisance is defined as an *unreasonable* interference with the plaintiff's reasonable use and enjoyment of her land. (*See* Torts Summary.) In determining whether the defendant's activity constitutes a nuisance, a court must *balance* the interests of the competing landowners. The benefit resulting from the defendant's activity is weighed against the harm to the plaintiff. Mere annoyance or inconvenience will not support an action for nuisance [**Armory Park Neighborhood Association v. Episcopal Community Services,** 712 P.2d 914 (Ariz. 1985); **Pasulka v. Koob,** 524 N.E.2d 1227 (Ill. 1988)]; nor will a recovery predicated on unfounded fears be allowed [**Adkins v. Thomas Solvent Co.,** 487 N.W.2d 716 (Mich. 1992)—groundless fears of pollution by toxic waste site]. Furthermore, certain activities may be protected by statutory enactments. [**Steffens v. Keeler,** 503 N.W.2d 675 (Mich. 1993)—operation of pig farm protected by the Right to Farm Act]

(1) Note

Balancing at this stage determines whether a tort exists. Compare this with the "balancing of the hardships" doctrine used to determine whether injunctive relief should be given once the tort has been established (*see infra*, §455).

(2) Damages [§447]

The problem of computing damages in nuisance cases is complicated by the continuing character of the wrongful conduct. Whether compensation may be recovered for possible future invasions is the subject of varying views.

(a) Common law [§448]

The common law rule *denies recovery for future injury* and restricts damages to compensation for past invasions. The rationale for this limitation on damages is the argument that the defendant may desist from his misconduct at any time. Consequently, an award of permanent damages could result in overcompensation. Under this view, the injured party *may recover* for:

(i) *The value of the loss of use and enjoyment* of the property up to the commencement of the action measured by loss of rental value or loss of income;

(ii) *The costs incurred* in trying to abate the nuisance; and

(iii) *The personal discomfort and annoyance* of the occupants of the premises (which may be recovered by the owner-occupant for all).

[**Bowers v. Westvaco Corp.**, 419 S.E.2d 661 (Va. 1992)]

1) Caveat

Because of the close similarity between the torts of nuisance and trespass, some of the remedies rules are applied interchangeably. (*See supra*, §398.)

(b) Permanent nuisance doctrine [§449]

Most jurisdictions have formulated the "permanent nuisance doctrine." If the nuisance is found to be permanent, the injured party may recover damages not only for past invasions, but also for the *permanent diminution in value* of her land. [**Spaulding v. Cameron**, 38 Cal. 2d 265 (1952)]

1) What constitutes a "permanent" nuisance [§450]

There are two views as to when this doctrine applies. Some jurisdictions require the nuisance to be "lawful" in the sense that it cannot be abated. This restricts the doctrine to situations where the offending party has condemnation powers (*e.g.*, a municipality). [**Town of Troy v. Cheshire Railroad**, 55 Am. Dec. 177 (N.H. 1851)] Other courts use a physical test of "permanence," and merely require proof that it appears *improbable* as a practical matter that the nuisance can be abated (*e.g.*, sewage plant emits smell). [**Kentland-Elkhorn Coal Co. v. Charles**, 514 S.W.2d 659 (Ky. 1974); *cf.* **May v. Bell**, 416 A.2d 289 (Md. 1980)—permanence depends not on "possibility of abatement, but rather its likelihood"]

a) Note

At least one court has found the distinction between temporary and permanent nuisances "nebulous." Thus, in a case involving chemical contamination of property, the court allowed a recovery for diminution of market value even though the nuisance was for an indefinite (*i.e.*, not necessarily permanent) period of time. [**Mel Foster Co. Properties v. American Oil Co.**, 427 N.W.2d 171 (Iowa 1988); *but see* **Miller v. Cudahy Co.**, 858 F.2d 1449 (10th Cir. 1988)—salt pollution of aquifer created condition that might last for 200 years; injury nevertheless classified as continuing (*i.e.,* temporary) nuisance]

2) Caution

The consequences of this classification are of the greatest significance to a litigant. If the nuisance is permanent, there is but one cause of action and the injured party must recover all her damages or be barred from further action by *res judicata*. Moreover, the statute of limitations runs from the date of the first invasion. [*See* **Spaulding v. Cameron**, *supra*]

(c) Election doctrine [§451]

To protect the injured party from the serious consequences of an erroneous classification of the nuisance, some jurisdictions give the injured party the right to elect whether or not to treat the nuisance as permanent.

Example: Kingsbury operated a cotton gin that emitted fumes and lint, interfering with Kornoff's enjoyment of adjacent land. Kingsbury's use of his property was lawful, and hence the nuisance could not be abated. The court held that Kornoff could elect to treat the nuisance as "permanent," and recover damages both for the past interference together with the diminution in value of Kornoff's home; *i.e.,* Kornoff should not be forced to bring successive actions to be indemnified for the loss. [**Kornoff v. Kingsbury Cotton Oil Co.**, 45 Cal. 2d 265 (1955)]

---

1) Note

Modern cases have limited the election doctrine to "close" cases. [**Spar v. Pacific Bell**, 235 Cal. App. 3d 1480 (1992)—power lines buried for 25 years were overwhelmingly permanent; *and see* **Beatty v. Washington Metro Area Transit Authority**, 860 F.2d 1117 (D.C. Cir. 1988)—nuisance may be classified as "permanent" for purposes of assessing damages and as "continuing" for statute of limitations purposes]

(d) Avoidable consequences [§452]

Some courts have declared that a plaintiff need not take steps to ward off a nuisance, on the principle that one is required to avoid or mitigate damage only after the tort has been committed. Others, viewing the threat as a tort, require that reasonable steps be taken to avoid the harm. [**S.C. Loveland v. East West Towing, Inc.,** 608 F.2d 160 (5th Cir. 1979); **Crest Chevrolet-Oldsmobile v. Willemsen,** 384 N.W.2d 692 (Wis. 1986)—plaintiff need not mitigate; McCormick, Damages §37 (1935)]

(3) Injunctive relief [§453]

The injured party may also seek an injunction against the continuance of the activities that interfere with the use and enjoyment of her property. Such injunctive relief is ordinarily in the form of a prohibitory (negative) injunction. Since the remedy is equitable, there is no right to jury trial even on the issue of whether a nuisance exists. [**Stell v. Jay Hales Development Co.,** 11 Cal. App. 4th 1214 (1992)]

(a) Legal remedy inadequate [§454]

Equitable relief is available in nuisance cases for two reasons: (i) to avoid multiplicity of suits since at law the injured party can recover damages only for past injuries (unless the permanent nuisance doctrine applies); and (ii) because in many cases there is irreparable injury to land (the nuisance has the effect of destroying trees, crops, and other vegetation).

(b) Relief discretionary—balance of hardships doctrine [§455]

Equitable relief is again discretionary and may be denied if it would operate inequitably. This is frequently the issue where a plaintiff-landowner seeks an injunction that, if granted, would result in shutting down a very valuable and costly enterprise operated by the defendant. Faced with this dilemma, the courts have adopted widely varying approaches:

1) No "balancing" [§456]

Some courts *refuse* to "balance the hardships," and therefore grant the injunction—even if it means shutting down a useful enterprise. [**Whalen v. Union Bag & Paper Co.,** 208 N.Y. 1 (1913)—decree resulted in the closing of a paper mill]

2) "Balancing" [§457]

Other courts will "balance the hardships" so that if the economic consequences to the defendant *greatly* outweigh any gain that the plaintiff may get from the decree, the injunction is denied and the plaintiff may obtain damages only. Frequently in these cases, the *injury to the public* (loss of jobs, loss of a useful product) is a primary factor in the balancing process (*see supra,* §405). [**Steele v. Queen City Broadcasting Co.,** 341 P.2d 499 (Wash. 1959); Rest. Torts §936; *but compare* **Scott v. Jordan,** 661 P.2d 59 (N.M. 1983)—injunction closing down defendant's feedlot after a balancing; *with* **Padilla**

v. Lawrence, 685 P.2d 964 (N.M. 1984)—refusing to enjoin operation of manure processing plant, apparently because of economic hardship on defendant]

3) Conditional grant of relief [§458]

An intermediate approach attempts to accommodate the interest of both parties to the litigation by *granting relief conditionally*. This is the technique ordinarily employed today, rather than a flat denial or granting of the decree. The most famous example of this process is the decision in **Georgia v. Tennessee Copper Co.,** 206 U.S. 230 (1915), wherein the denial of the injunction was conditioned on the adoption by the copper company of certain procedures for abating the nuisance (in this case, the emission of copper sulphide fumes). [*See also* **Harford Penn-Cann Service v. Zymblosky,** 549 A.2d 208 (Pa. 1988)—alternative methods for abating dust problem; **Klein v. Copeland,** 482 So. 2d 613 (Iowa 1986)—regulation of Christmas exhibition to reduce its size and extravagance]

4) No injunctive relief [§459]

Some courts, however, absolutely refuse to grant injunctive relief, and restrict the injured party to the remedy of damages.

Example: Court denied an injunction against the operation of Atlantic's cement factory, which emitted dust on Boomer's adjacent property, on grounds that: there are no scientific devices available to reduce the pollution (thus a conditional decree would be pointless); if a lawful business is to be shut down, it should be by government regulation and not as the result of private litigation; and the plaintiff can be fully compensated for the loss by the payment of permanent damages. [*See* **Boomer v. Atlantic Cement Co.,** 26 N.Y.2d 219 (1970)]

(c) Class actions [§460]

A class action may be available to abate a nuisance. [*See* **Biechele v. Norfolk & Western Railway,** 309 F. Supp. 354 (N.D. Ohio 1969)]

1) But note

A class action for damages for a nuisance in the federal courts (diversity jurisdiction) is affected by the requirement that the damage to *each member of the class* must exceed the jurisdictional amount. [**Zahn v. International Paper Co.,** 414 U.S. 291 (1974)]

(4) "Coming to the nuisance" as a defense [§461]

The fact that the plaintiff has moved to the nuisance is ordinarily *not* a defense to an equity suit for injunctive relief. [42 A.L.R.3d 344; **Weida v. Ferry**, 493 A.2d 824 (R.I. 1985); **Harmon Motors v. Farmers Union Grain Terminal**, 337 N.W.2d 427 (N.D. 1983)]

(a) May still affect relief [§462]

Although not a defense, coming to the nuisance may be an important factor in determining what relief should be granted to the landowner. [**Escobar v. Continental Baking Co.**, 596 N.E.2d 394 (Mass. 1992).

---

e.g. **Example:** Del Webb developed Sun City next to an existing cattle feed lot. Although the court granted Del Webb an injunction against the feed lot operator, the injunction was conditioned on payment of moving cost incurred by the defendant. [**Spur Industries v. Del Webb Construction Co.**, 494 P.2d 700 (Ariz. 1972)]

EXAM TIP	gilbert

Coming to the nuisance is a popular exam ploy. Watch out for a fact pattern with a sympathetic defendant, such as a farmer whose family has been raising pigs on the same plot of land for generations without complaint from neighboring farmers, but who has been receiving complaints over the past five years from rich urban lawyers who have moved into country estates built by developers who bought out all of the farmer's neighbors. If the lawyers file a nuisance action, although some courts will take into account the plaintiffs' coming to the nuisance, *in no court will that fact be determinative*—all other relevant factors will also be considered.

(b) "Right to farm" statutes [§463]

"Right to farm" statutes have been adopted in many states to protect agricultural activities from nuisance actions brought by landowners moving into adjacent property. These statutes have been variously interpreted and may not completely prohibit actions for private nuisance. [*See, e.g.,* **Herrin v. Opatut**, 281 S.E.2d 575 (Ga. 1981)]

(c) Damages [§464]

Coming to the nuisance is *irrelevant* to an action for *damages* where the diminution in value resulting from the nuisance is reflected in the price plaintiff originally paid for the property. [**Kellogg v. Village of Viola**, 227 N.W.2d 55 (Wis. 1975)]

(5) Effect of zoning ordinances [§465]

If the landowner's use of the property is in compliance with applicable zoning ordinances, some courts regard the ordinance as an absolute bar to an action to enjoin the activity as a nuisance. Other courts regard the ordinance as simply a factor to be taken into account in determining whether or not to grant injunctive relief. [*See* **Hobbs v. Smith**, 493 P.2d 1352 (Colo. 1972)]

b. Public nuisance [§466]

As indicated *supra*, §138, a long-established rule of equity courts was that they would not enjoin crimes. Since this rule was originally associated with the notion that equitable jurisdiction did not extend to protection of "personal" interests, an exception arose where an injunction was sought against a crime that also invaded a public property interest (*i.e.*, a public nuisance).

(1) Background [§467]

The earliest cases of public nuisances (called "purprestures") involved *encroachments* on public property such as highways and parks. Equitable jurisdiction was assumed in these cases because abatement by injunction was often the only adequate remedy for such unlawful activity. The remedy of a criminal prosecution resulting in a small fine was clearly inadequate to vindicate public property rights.

(2) "Public nuisance" defined—and redefined

(a) Objectionable use of property [§468]

The definition of "public nuisance" was later extended to include the *use* of property in such a way as to endanger the public health and welfare. Public nuisances as thus defined included unruly saloons, bawdy houses, and gambling houses. [**People v. Lim**, 18 Cal. 2d 872 (1941)]

(b) Injurious activities [§469]

The definition has become even more expansive in some states [*See, e.g.*, Cal. Civ. Code §§3479-80—defining public nuisance as "anything injurious to health, or indecent or offensive to the senses, or an obstruction to the free use of property . . . which affects any considerable number of persons at the same time"] In some jurisdictions, activities such as the unlicensed practice of medicine and a usurious small loan business have been classified as public nuisances. [**People v. Laman**, 277 N.Y. 368 (1938); **State *ex rel.* Goff v. O'Neil**, 286 N.W. 316 (Minn. 1939)] (Under such definitions, virtually any crime may potentially be defined as a public nuisance.)

1) Environmental laws [§470]

The public nuisance doctrine has also been invoked to enforce various statutory environmental regulations. [*See, e.g.*, **Village** of **Wilsonville v. SCA Services Inc.**, 426 N.E.2d 824 (Ill. 1981)—hazardous waste; **Illinois v. City of Milwaukee**, 406 U.S. 91 (1972)—waste pollution]

2) Objective—reformation [§471]
The primary objective of an abatement action is to "reform" the property and therefore the injunction is directed at the use being made of the property, not at the activity itself. [**People ex *rel*. Van De Kamp v. American Art Enterprises**, 33 Cal. 3d 328 (1983)]

(3) Remedy [§472]
Even if the activity is classified as a public nuisance, equitable relief is granted only when a criminal prosecution would constitute an inadequate remedy. Generally, this requires proof that an injunction is essential to implementing the legislative policy in enacting the law violated.

(a) Illustrations
If criminal prosecutions fail to prevent the unlicensed practice of medicine, an injunction may be the only method available to protect the citizenry. In usury cases, there may be no effective remedy at law because each borrower may be so impoverished as to be unable to take advantage of statutory remedies. In other cases, a criminal prosecution, even if successful, may result in so small a fine that it is no deterrent to a continuation of the wrongful activity. [*See, e.g.,* **Turner v. United Buckingham Freight Lines, Inc.**, 211 N.W.2d 288 (Iowa 1973)—where truckers violated traffic regulation 1,730 times in 15 months, injunctive relief granted; **Pizza v. Sunset Fireworks Co.**, 494 N.E.2d 1115 (Ohio 1986)—criminal sanctions ineffective in protecting residents from illegal sale of fireworks]

(b) Caveat
Frequently, injunctive relief is authorized by statute upon proof of facts establishing the existence of a public nuisance. In these situations, the statute controls as to both parties plaintiff and the remedy. [*See* **People ex *rel*. Gow v. Mitchell Brothers Santa Ana Theater**, 114 Cal. App. 3d 923 (1981); **Mitchell v. Superior Court**, *supra*, §177—Red Light Abatement Law]

(4) Private suits to enjoin [§473]
Public nuisances are ordinarily abated by the state acting through the attorney general, but a private individual may maintain a suit if the nuisance causes her some *special and individual damage*. [*See, e.g.,* **Mark v. State Department of Fish and Wildlife**, 974 P.2d 716 (Or. 1999)]

Example: The owner of property next to a bawdy house clearly sustains an injury to her individual property rights and thus has standing to sue.

Compare: On the other hand, professional associations have no standing to enjoin unlicensed practice of their profession because licensing statutes are designed to protect the public from incompetence, not members of the profession from competition. [**Massachusetts Society of Optometrists v. Waddick,** 165 N.E.2d 394 (Mass. 1959)]

EXAM TIP	gilbert

Be careful not to confuse the requirements for bringing a *private nuisance action* with those for a private individual to bring a *public nuisance action*. To claim a *private* nuisance, a person must show an unreasonable interference with the use and enjoyment of his property. For a private individual to have standing to sue against a *public* nuisance, that person need not own any affected land, but must show a special injury different from the public at large.

(a) Possible remedies under RICO [§474]

Private causes of action for treble damages are permitted for *injury to property* caused by violation of the federal statute intended to combat racketeer-influenced and corrupt organizations. [18 U.S.C. §1964(c)—"RICO"] For example, apartment *owners* affected by drug dealers may recover under RICO but diminution in *tenants'* enjoyment of the premises is not a tangible injury to property as required for a private RICO action. [**Oscar v. University Students Co-op Association,** 965 F.2d 783 (9th Cir. 1992)—11 to 3 decision; dissenters favoring a cause of action on traditional nuisance principles]

Chapter Six:
Injuries to Business and Commercial Interests

CONTENTS

Chapter Approach

The topics in this chapter are not always included in a Remedies course. If they have been discussed in your class or readings, watch for questions concerning the *misappropriation doctrine* and the *right of publicity*, as these are the most likely to appear on a Remedies exam.

If you see such a question, use the following two-step approach:

1. Determine whether plaintiff has a *legally protected interest*;

2. If such an interest is established, then discuss the *appropriate remedy*—either an injunction and accounting of profits *or* restitution.

A. Remedies for Business Torts—In General

1. Damages

a. For total destruction of established business [§475]

If an established business has been totally destroyed as the result of the defendant's tortious acts, the owners of the business entity are the proper persons to bring suit (the business entity having been forced out of business). Several alternative theories of damage to the owners' interests are available:

(1) Lost future profits [§476]

The owner may be entitled to damages based on a projection of profits over the *probable lifetime* of the business destroyed. [**Lightning Luke v. Witco Corp.**, 4 F.3d 1153 (3d Cir. 1993)—punitive damages awarded in addition]

(a) "Lifetime" of business [§477]

Usually, the lifetime of a business is speculative, and therefore the defendant will interpose the argument that damages are "too uncertain." However, courts uniformly reject such argument on the rationale that a party who *causes the uncertainty* of damages (by destroying a going business) cannot evade liability on the basis of such uncertainty.

1) **Arbitrary period [§478]**

To solve the dilemma, courts frequently adopt some arbitrary period (*e.g.,* 10 years) as being the "probable lifetime" of a going business.

2) **Period of lease [§479]**

Occasionally, the continuity of a business may depend on facts such as the length of a lease on business premises. In such event, of course, the probable lifetime of a business must take into consideration the length of the lease, possibility of renewal, etc. [**Lanfranconi v. Tidewater Oil**, 376 F.2d 91 (2d Cir. 1967)— gasoline service station damages limited to expiration date of its lease in view of evidence that lease would not have been renewed]

(b) **"Avoidable consequences" [§480]**

The rule of "avoidable consequences" (*supra,* §47) applies so that, to the extent that time and assets are released for the production of income, an offset should be made.

(c) **Present value [§481]**

The entire lump-sum recovery for future profits must be *discounted* to its *present value* (*see supra,* §86).

(d) **Additional award [§482]**

Courts using this measure of damages also permit recovery of *lost profits prior to the ultimate destruction* of the business. [**Jim's Hot Shot Service v. Continental West Insurance Co.**, 353 N.W.2d 279 (N.D. 1984)]

(2) **Loss of total market value of business [§483]**

An alternative measure of damages is to award to owners the market value of the business destroyed. [**Aetna Life & Casualty Co. v. Little**, 384 So. 2d 213 (Fla. 1980); **Mattingly, Inc. v. Beatrice Foods Co.**, 835 F.2d 1547 (10th Cir. 1987)]

(a) **Proof [§484]**

Market value may be established by:

1) *Loss of bona fide purchase offers*, less any salvage value of the physical assets;

2) *Capitalization of past earnings records*, again less salvage; or

3) *Estimating the flow of future earnings*, and discounting the earnings to their present value, which may be assumed to represent market value.

(b) "Avoidable consequences" rule inapplicable [§485]

The "avoidable consequences" rule to minimize damages does *not* apply under this approach.

b. Partial destruction of ongoing business [§486]

If the business entity has been damaged but not totally destroyed, the action must be brought by the business entity itself. There are several approaches to the damages measure:

(1) Permanent damage approach [§487]

The business is entitled to recover for any diminution of market value of the enterprise, on the assumption that the impairment of its business will be permanent. [**West Haven Sound Development v. City of West Haven**, 541 A.2d 858 (Conn. 1988)]

(2) Loss of profits to trial approach [§488]

This approach requires repeated actions within the statutory period of limitations on claims of continuing injury. Proof of loss may be made by either of the following:

(a) Before-after measure [§489]

Compare the previous five years' record of earnings (or other selected period) with that of similar period after injury; or

(b) Comparison measure [§490]

Compare the business's earnings record with that of *similar* businesses.

(3) Market share approach [§491]

Damages based on loss of market share are measured by the share of total market sales that the plaintiff could *reasonably have been expected* to have attained without the injury.

(a) Note

This approach is useful when the plaintiff has been *foreclosed from entering a new market*. It has been used primarily in antitrust cases, but it is logically appropriate for use in other business tort actions.

(4) Punitive damages [§492]

Punitive damages may be awarded on proper showing of "malice."

c. Injury to new business [§493]

If the injured business is a new venture with no history of profits, recovery for loss of anticipated future profits is generally not allowed. *Rationale:* Since the success of a new business depends on a variety of circumstances, there is usually no reasonably certain basis for computing probable future profits. [**Universal Commodities, Inc. v. Weed**, 449 S.W.2d 106 (Tex. 1969)]

(1) Exception if damages reasonably certain [§494]

If in a particular case the plaintiff is able to prove with reasonable certainty that profits would have been made (and the amount of the profits), the profits may be recovered. (*Compare* the analogous situation of breach of contract for sale of goods, in which U.C.C. section 2-708 provides that seller need not show history of earnings to recover lost profits.)

EXAM TIP   **gilbert**

Notice the difference in treatment between tortious destruction of an existing business and tortious destruction of a new business. In both cases, damages for lost profits are quite speculative. After all, we can't possibly know what the future would have held for the business in either case. Nevertheless, when a plaintiff proves that a defendant tortiously destroyed the plaintiff's *existing* business, most courts will grant damages for lost profits (*see supra*, §§476 *et seq.*), but if a plaintiff proves that a defendant tortiously destroyed the plaintiff's *new* business, most courts will deny damages for lost profits unless the plaintiff has a reasonably certain basis on which to assess damages.

---

2. Equitable Remedies—Injunctions [§495]

The provable damages for tortious interference with a business are usually speculative, and the harm is potentially irreparable. Hence, jurisdiction to grant injunctive relief may be almost automatically assumed. In certain cases, equitable jurisdiction is also grounded on the fiduciary or confidential relationships common in the business world (*see infra*, §§519-527, 530).

3. Restitutionary Remedies [§496]

Restitutionary remedies, legal or equitable, become available if profits or income have been *diverted* from the plaintiff and acquired by the tortious activities of the defendant. The key problems will appear to center around the following factors:

a. *A sufficient showing of probability* that the business benefit would in fact have accrued to the plaintiff;

b. *Whether some relationship of "privity"* is necessary between the plaintiff and the defendant; and

c. *Whether the "unjust enrichment"* of the defendant is more attributable to his own independent efforts than to his commission of the tort. (A possible application of this principle might be noted in the previous section; *see* **Edwards v. Lee's Administrators**, *supra*, §438.)

B. Remedies for Inducing Breach of Contract

1. Damages [§497]

A cause of action exists against a defendant who has induced a third party to breach a contract with the plaintiff. Proof of actual damages is an essential element; hence, the statute of limitations begins to run when the damages are incurred, rather than at the time the contract was breached. [**Kronos, Inc. v. AVX Corp.**, 81 N.Y.2d 90 (1993)]

a. Measure of damages—in general

(1) Minority view [§498]

The minority view holds that the tortfeasor is liable only for whatever damages the plaintiff could have recovered against the contract breacher.

(a) Criticism

The liability of the contracting parties is limited by the rule of **Hadley v. Baxendale** (*see supra,* §23), which is a contract doctrine; there is no logic for limiting tort recoveries by this rule. Moreover, the contract in question may have a valid *liquidated damages provision* that would limit the liability of the contracting parties; such a provision should be irrelevant to the liability of one who has tortiously interfered with the contract.

(2) Majority view [§499]

A majority of states hold that an intentional tortfeasor is liable under the usual rule for *all damages proximately caused*. These may include mental suffering, damages to reputation, expenses of training replacements for employees hired away, as well as punitive damages if "malice" is shown. [*See* **Ramona Manor Convalescent Hospital v. Care Enterprises**, 177 Cal. App. 3d 1120 (1986)—lost profits; **Dorsett Carpet Mills v. Whitt Tile & Marble**, 734 S.W.2d 322 (Tenn. 1987)—lost profits]

Example: Pennzoil entered into an agreement with Getty Oil to acquire Getty stock. Subsequently, Texaco acquired this interest for itself by offering a higher price for the stock. In an action against Texaco for tortious interference with a contract, the court held that Pennzoil was not limited to contract damages but that a tort measure applied. The loss to Pennzoil was properly measured by the replacement cost of the oil rights that would have been acquired from Getty. [**Texaco, Inc. v. Pennzoil Co.**, 729 S.W.2d 768 (Tex. 1987)] Ultimately, the case was resolved through a $3 billion settlement.

---

b. Measure of damages—special cases

(1) Unprofitable contracts [§500]

Regardless of which of the above rules is adopted, the plaintiff has the burden of showing that performance of the contract would have been *profitable*. If in fact it is shown that the plaintiff would have lost money if the contract had been performed, no recovery is permitted. [**Selby v. Pelletier,** 472 A.2d 1285 (Conn. 1984)]

(2) Unenforceable contracts [§501]

Suppose the contract interfered with was at all times unenforceable (*e.g.,* an oral contract for the sale of land unenforceable under the Statute of Frauds). Practically all courts recognize that tortious interference with such a contract is actionable, but there is little authority as to the proper measure of damages. [**Buckaloo v. Johnson,** 14 Cal. 3d 815 (1975)]

---

e.g. **Example:** Donald, a real estate broker, "jumps" another broker's (Ivanna's) oral listing. The oral listing is unenforceable under a statute requiring all listings to be in writing, signed by the property owner. If Ivanna sues Donald for interference with the unenforceable listing, what is the measure of damages?

- If the court follows the rule that Ivanna is entitled to recover against Donald only what could be recovered against the contract breacher (owner), Ivanna would recover nothing or only nominal damages because Ivanna has no enforceable claim against the owner.

- There is some authority that would allow Ivanna to recover against Donald the full commission to which Ivanna would have been entitled had the contract with the owner been carried out. [*See* **Horn v. Seth,** 95 A.2d 312 (Md. 1953)]

(a) Criticism

Allowing the plaintiff to recover in full overlooks the fact that the contract breacher (owner) had *no legal obligation* to perform. The only obligation was a moral one. Consequently, from a strictly logical perspective, damages should be limited to the loss of the *moral probability* of performance. Unfortunately, this is very speculative and uncertain.

(3) Contracts terminable at will

(a) Minority view—no recovery [§502]

Some courts deny recovery for interference with contracts terminable at will of either party, on the basis that there is no certainty that the contract would have continued regardless of the third party's interference, and hence damages would be too speculative and uncertain. [**Noah v. L. Daitch & Co.,** 22 Misc. 2d 649 (1959)]

(b) Majority view [§503]

However, the general view is *contra*: Recovery is allowed for interference with contracts terminable at will on the rationale that "but for" the interference, the contract relationship might have continued; *i.e.*, the terminability factor affects only the *measure*, not the fact of damages. [**Berry v. Donovan,** 74 N.E. 603 (Mass. 1905); **SHV Coal Inc. v. Continental Grain Co.,** 545 A.2d 917 (Pa. 1988)—award of lost profits diverted by employee to defendant competitor]

1) The measure of damages should reflect the *probability* of *nontermination* by the party induced to breach.

2) In certain cases the court may conclude that there was a likelihood of termination in any event so that the damages recoverable will be minimal. However, as long as *some* damages can be established, the cause of action exists so that the plaintiff may claim additional damages such as *mental anguish*. [**United States Fidelity & Guaranty Co. v. Millanes,** 89 So. 732 (Ala. 1921)]

2. Injunctions Against Inducing Breach [§504]

Injunctive relief is rarely granted against third-party interference with existing contracts, not because equity lacks power to enjoin such conduct, but rather because these cases usually arise *after* the breach, and there is nothing left for equity to enjoin. However, in appropriate cases, equity *will* act to enjoin interference with existing contracts *including those involving personal services*. (As to the remedial problems surrounding this type of contract, *see infra*, §§1251-1258.)

a. Injunctions against continuous course of conduct [§505]

The usual ground upon which equitable relief by injunction is justified is that the third-party interference is part of a course of conduct that is likely to continue unless enjoined.

Example: A professional football team enjoined a university from trying to hire away its coach. [*See* **New England Patriots Football Club v. University of Colorado,** 592 F.2d 1196 (1st Cir. 1979)]

Example: A new sports league was enjoined from inducing professional athletes already under contract with major league ballclubs to breach their contracts and come to work for the new league. [*See* **American League Baseball Club of New York v. Pasqual,** 187 Misc. 230 (1946)]

Example: Paulette contracts for the exclusive right to distribute and sell a certain beverage manufactured by K-Cola. Darwin, a competitor of Paulette, induces K-Cola to supply Darwin with the beverage in violation of Paulette's exclusive rights. Darwin may be enjoined from further interference. [**E.L. Husting Co. v. Coca-Cola,** 237 N.W. 85 (Wis. 1931); *and see* **Imperial Ice v. Rossiter,** 18 Cal. 2d 33 (1941)]

(1) Note

The defendant may also be *enjoined from exploiting* any breaches he has already induced—*e.g.,* by prohibitory injunction against his entering into substitute contractual relations with the contract breacher. [**American Law Book v. Thompson,** 41 Misc. 396 (1903)]

b. Adequacy of other remedies [§506]

Whether injunctive relief will be granted depends on the adequacy of other remedies *available against the third-party tortfeasor,* and is not affected by the adequacy of the contract remedies against the party induced to breach. Thus, injunctive relief may be available even though the plaintiff clearly has an action at law for breach against the other party to the contract.

(1) And note

Injunctive relief is available even though the contract otherwise was *not* specifically enforceable, either positively or negatively.

3. Restitutionary Remedies

a. Conceptual difficulty—"benefit to defendant" [§507]

The substantive basis of restitution is unjust enrichment of the defendant, usually measured by the "benefit" that the defendant has obtained (*see supra,* §234). If a third-party tortfeasor is sued for interference with a contract between other parties, there is a conceptual difficulty in establishing the "benefit" to the tortfeasor.

(1) No direct benefit to inducer [§508]

Unlike the direct misappropriation of tangibles, a person who tortiously induces a breach of contract does not directly receive a benefit by the misappropriation; he is enriched only if he *subsequently* makes a profitable contract with the contract breacher.

Example: Denver induces Olivia, a professional singer, to break a contract to sing for John. At this point, there is no "enrichment" of John. It is only later, when Denver employs Olivia and sets up a concert tour, from which Denver realizes a profit of $30,000, that Denver can be said to have derived any "benefit."

(2) Restatement [§509]

Faced with this difficulty, the Restatement of Restitution section 133 *caveats* whether restitution of the defendant's profit is recoverable by the plaintiff.

(3) Argument against restitution [§510]

The argument *against* restitution is that the plaintiff's cause of action accrues when the contract is broken, at which point the plaintiff has both contract and tort remedies. The tortfeasor's subsequent actions do not change the plaintiff's rights or remedies in any respect, and nothing is taken from the plaintiff to the tortfeasor's "enrichment." [**Developers Three v. Nationwide Insurance Co.**, 582 N.E.2d 1130 (Ohio 1990)]

b. Cases allowing restitution [§511]

Notwithstanding the conceptual difficulty noted above, several cases have allowed restitution against a tortfeasor who induced a breach of contract. [*See, e.g.*, **Caskie v. Philadelphia Rapid Transit Co.**, 184 A. 17 (Pa. 1936)— allowing *equitable* restitution by way of an *accounting* for profits realized by the tortfeasor]

---

e.g. **Example:** Doyle induced a breach of contract for the sale of sugar by Prinze to the Norwegian government; the contract price was $6.60 per cwt. Later, Doyle entered into a contract to sell sugar to Norway at $11.00 per cwt. The court held that a quasi-contract action for "money had and received" would lie, and by dicta indicated that *the difference in price* was the proper measure of recovery. [**Federal Sugar Refining Co. v. United States Equalization Board**, 268 F. 575 (S.D.N.Y. 1920)] The case is noteworthy as expressly authorizing a recovery of the tortfeasor's profits in a *legal* action on the common counts. [*See also* **Sandare Chemical Co. v. Wako International**, 820 S.W.2d 21 (Tex. 1991)—recovery of profits made by tortfeasor from willful interference with contracted relationships involving the use of a medical diagnostic test]

SUMMARY OF REMEDIES FOR INDUCING BREACH OF CONTRACT	**gilbert**
DAMAGES	Most courts will award the plaintiff all damages *proximately caused* by the tortfeasor's act. Some courts limit damages to those that the plaintiff could have recovered from the breaching party.
INJUNCTIVE RELIEF	This *generally is not available* because the cases usually arise after breach (it's too late to enjoin anything). But where the tortfeasor's conduct is *continuing*, a court may issue an injunction.
RESTITUTION	It is *questionable whether restitution is available* because restitution is measured by the benefit to the defendant, and a person who tortiously induces a breach of contract does not directly receive a benefit; rather he benefits when he makes a subsequent contract with the breacher. But some courts will allow such an action.

C. Remedies for Interference with Plaintiff's Mere "Expectancy"

1. In General [§512]

In certain cases—some commercial and some noncommercial—the defendant may have tortiously interfered with a relationship between the plaintiff and another so as to deprive the plaintiff of a gain or advantage that she otherwise *might* have obtained, but as to which she had *no enforceable right* (*e.g.*, the unenforceable contract example, *see supra*, §501). The plaintiff has been deprived of a "hope" or "expectancy," but not of any actual property or right to obtain property.

a. Question as to appropriate remedy [§513]

In these cases, there is a basic question of what cause of action, if any, is available to the plaintiff to compensate for the loss resulting from the defendant's interference (as to which, *see* Torts Summary). But, assuming a tort action lies for the interference, the issue then is what is the proper remedy?

(1) Damages [§514]

If damages are sought, there is a basic problem as to *certainty of damages*. The plaintiff's loss is, strictly speaking, the *value of the probability* that the benefit would have reached her, and this is obviously difficult to establish.

(2) Restitution [§515]

The alternative remedy is *restitution*. Although the plaintiff's pecuniary loss from a remote expectancy may be dubious, in a great many of these cases the defendant's tortious conduct has brought him some tangible "benefit" that he otherwise would not have obtained. In such cases, restitution lies to compel the defendant to disgorge the benefit.

2. Interference with Testamentary Disposition [§516]

Interference with a testamentary disposition may be actionable where the defendant has tortiously (*e.g.*, by fraud or duress) induced a testator *to make* a testamentary disposition he otherwise would not have made; or where the testator has been *prevented* from making a will he otherwise would have made. The normal remedy is to impose a *constructive trust* in favor of the *intended* beneficiary. [*See* **Chambers v. Kane**, 424 A.2d 311 (Del. 1980)]

Example: Penelope is named as beneficiary under Tyler's will. Deanna fraudulently induces Tyler to change beneficiaries (*e.g.*, by falsely stating that Penelope is dead) and name Deanna instead. On Tyler's death, Deanna receives the property, but must hold the same as constructive trustee for Penelope. [11 A.L.R.2d 818]

Example: Dianna is named beneficiary under Thor's will. Thor has indicated an intent to *revoke* the will. By fraud or other tortious means, Dianna prevents revocation. Again, the court may impose a constructive trust in favor of Thor's intended beneficiary (if this can be clearly shown) or otherwise in favor of Thor's intestate heirs. *Rationale:* Dianna has benefited herself at someone else's expense. [**Latham v. Father Divine,** 299 N.Y. 22 (1949)]

Compare: Dante is neither a beneficiary under Thoreau's will nor an intestate heir. Nonetheless, he tortiously interferes with Thoreau's intended testamentary disposition, which would have benefited Paine (*e.g.,* by preventing Thoreau from executing a codicil to the will naming Paine as sole beneficiary). Under these facts, Dante has obtained no "benefit"; hence, constructive trust is *not* the proper remedy. Paine's only possible remedy is a *damages* action against Dante for the interference, and the courts are split on whether such action will lie. [11 A.L.R.2d 819; **Lowe v. Foundation Northern Trust Co.,** 96 N.E.2d 831 (Ill. 1951); **King v. Acker,** 725 S.W.2d 750 (Tex. 1987)—compensatory and punitive damages recoverable in tort action for interference with inheritance rights]

3. Benefits Obtained by Murder

a. Murder of testator [§517]

One who commits murder is not permitted to take as a beneficiary under the victim's will. *Rationale:* A wrongdoer should not be permitted to profit from his own wrong—*i.e.,* having deprived the testator of the right to *change* his will, it is in effect *presumed* that the testator would have changed his will, so that the murderer cannot retain any benefit under the will. [36 A.L.R.2d 963]

(1) Constructive trust as remedy [§518]

The murderer is usually held to be a *constructive trustee* of whatever gift is provided for him under the decedent's will. The question is for whom? If the murderer is the *sole* beneficiary under the will, he will be held constructive trustee for the victim's intestate heirs or next of kin. If there are other beneficiaries named in the will, the murderer holds as constructive trustee for the *residuary* beneficiary. [36 A.L.R.2d 967]

(a) Note

Some states have *statutes* that provide that the murderer holds on behalf of the person "who otherwise would have had the property." [*See, e.g.,* Cal. Civ. Code §2224] However, such person is not always certain in that the decedent's choice of recipient, had he foreseen his untimely death at the hands of his designated beneficiary, is unknown.

D. Remedies for Diversion of Benefits

1. Diversion of Benefits by Fiduciaries

a. Benefits obtained by breach of fiduciary duty [§519]

The remedies against fiduciaries for breach of duty are: (i) any loss or depreciation (*damages*); (ii) any profit made (*equitable restitution*); (iii) any profit that would have accrued if there were no breach (*lost profit damages*). [Rest. 2d Trusts §205; **St. James Armenian Church v. Kurkjian,** 47 Cal. App. 3d 547 (1975)]

(1) Express trust vs. constructive trust [§520]

In the case of an *express* trustee charged with making the trust res productive, the trustee may be held liable for the amount of income that a "prudent" investment would have yielded. However, this liability for failure to make the trust yield a normal rate of return is not carried over to the *constructive* trustee, whose only obligation is to turn over whatever property is being held.

b. Benefits obtained without breach of fiduciary duty [§521]

In addition to the above remedies for breach of fiduciary duty, an express trustee may be liable for benefits gained out of the fiduciary position itself—even where the benefit does *not* result from a technical breach of trust, and no loss is occasioned to the person to whom the obligation is owed. [Rest. 2d Trusts §203] The principle just stated is applied to afford equitable restitution (accounting for profits) in a variety of situations where there is no actual misuse of trust property, but rather *unjust enrichment* from *diverting* a benefit that might otherwise have accrued to the beneficiary. It is a variety of the "tortious interference with an expectancy" (*see supra*), and again, the probability that the benefit would ever have reached the plaintiff varies from strong to exceedingly tenuous. *Examples:*

(1) Diversion of corporate opportunities by directors or officers [§522]

A corporate director or officer who has acquired property or a profitable business opportunity that would have been of *advantage* to the corporation holds the opportunity or advantage in constructive trust for the corporation. Of course, corporate officers are not barred from acquiring *all* business opportunities—only those that could be a "*corporate opportunity.*"

(a) What constitutes "corporate opportunity" [§523]

Reflecting concern with the question of *probability* that the corporation would have received the benefit, two views have been followed:

1) The corporation must be shown to have had a *"tangible interest or expectancy"* in the opportunity. [**Abbott Redmont Thinlite Corp. v. Redmont**, 475 F.2d 85 (2d Cir. 1973)]

2) The corporation need merely show that the opportunity was in its *"line of business"*—regardless of whether it previously had interested itself, or likely ever would, in the matter. [*See* **Lincoln Stores v. Grant**, 34 N.E.2d 704 (Mass. 1941)] Obviously this rule is more stringent and places severe limitations on undisclosed or unapproved outside activities by directors of conglomerates, where every opportunity might be in the "line of business." (*See* further discussion in Corporations Summary.)

(2) Bribes, kickbacks, "side benefits" received by agents or fiduciaries [§524]
Everything of value obtained by a fiduciary *by virtue of the fiduciary relationship* belongs to the person to whom the fiduciary duty was owed (*e.g.,* employer, principal, etc.). Thus, any sort of "payola" received by an employee or agent, etc., may be recovered by the employer or principal through restitutionary remedies—a constructive trust if needed, or equitable accounting. [**County of Cook v. Barrett**, 344 N.E.2d 540 (Ill. 1975)—former county clerk; *but see* **United States v. Goodrich**, 687 F. Supp. 567 (M.D. Fla. 1988)—imposition of constructive trust in these cases is "to prevent the constructive trustee from retaining his ill-gotten profit, *not* to enrich the constructive beneficiary"; **Anderson v. Sharp County**, 749 S.W.2d 306 (Ark. 1988)—replevin is not available to recover jewelry given to judge as bribe]

(a) Nature of payment [§525]
It is *not* necessary that the fiduciary has acted "secretly" or against the best interests of the plaintiff. And it is immaterial that the benefit is at the *direct* expense of (*i.e.,* paid by) a third party, rather than the plaintiff. Likewise, it is immaterial that the principal (in the case of bribery, for instance) was in no position legally to have laid claim to the benefit in the first place.

Example: Xavier got a jury verdict for $130,000 against the city of Boston, but the judge entered a judgment n.o.v. Xavier prepared an appeal. In discussing settlement, the mayor of Boston wanted to know "what was in it for him." He received $30,000. Settlement with Xavier for $85,000 followed. Recovery by the city against the mayor was allowed, although it was expressly found that the $85,000 settlement was not improvident. [**Boston v. Santosuosso**, 30 N.E.2d 278 (Mass. 1940)]

Example: Defendant, a British Army sergeant, was paid $20,000 by smugglers. His sole action was to put on his uniform and ride on trucks carrying contraband that were then waved through checkpoints. His Majesty's Government took the $20,000 and was held not liable to return it. The benefit was obtained by the sergeant *by virtue of the post itself*; the actions were outside of his duty. "Any official position which enables the holder to earn money by its use gives his master a right to receive the money so earned even though earned by a criminal act." [**Reading v. Attorney General,** [1951] A.C. 507]

Example: A former C.I.A. agent breached his fiduciary obligations by failing to submit material for prepublication review. Profits the former agent earned from publishing the book may be impressed with a constructive trust. [**Snepp v. United States,** 444 U.S. 507 (1980)]

(b) Trebling award [§526]

The Robinson-Patman Act allows trebling of a company's recovery from its officers who profit from *commercial* bribery.

(3) Benefits obtained by use of "inside information" [§527]

Some cases go beyond diversion of any benefit or expectancy, and allow recovery of profits obtained by the wrongdoer even though the profit *might not have been obtained* by the person to whom the fiduciary duty was owed. These cases are concentrated, for the time being, in the area of *federal securities regulations* in corporation law.

Example: While taking notes in a director's meeting, Martha, a corporate secretary, learns of a plan to buy up treasury stock. Martha goes out on the open market and buys the corporation's stock, which then increases in value. Recovery of Martha's "secret profit" will be decreed. [**Brophy v. Cities Service,** 70 A.2d 5 (Del. 1949)] This type of case is simply a *diversion* of the corporation's opportunity to buy stock and actually is an act in competition with the principal.

Compare: Officers of a corporation, having access to unfavorable inside information, sold their stock on the open market, thereby avoiding the loss of several hundred thousand dollars. *Held:* The officers are liable *to the corporation* for the amount thus "saved." [**Diamond v. Oreamuno,** 24 N.Y.2d 494 (1949); *but see* **Schein v. Chasen,** 313 So. 2d 739 (Fla. 1975)—expressly rejecting *Diamond* rationale]

(a) Comment

The result in *Diamond* is inexplicable in terms of restitution and unjust enrichment because the officers were not in competition with the corporation and there was no "diversion" of benefits from the corporation. The corporate office was not abused. Moreover, *the gain was at the expense of the purchasers of the stock,* to whom the defendants were also clearly liable (for fraud and under S.E.C. Rule 10b-5), thus raising the question of multiple liabilities. [*See* **Frankel v. Slotkin,** 795 F. Supp. 76 (E.D.N.Y. 1992)—relief denied based on risk of double liability resulting from changes in security regulatory legislation]

2. Diversion of Benefits by Nonfiduciaries [§528]

Business opportunities are normally "up for grabs," and there is nothing unlawful in aggressive individuals acquiring for themselves benefits or opportunities being sought by others. There are limits, however, imposed by the substantive doctrine of unjust enrichment and the equitable restitutionary remedies of constructive trusts, accounting, etc. [**Empire Fire & Marine Insurance Co. v. Fremont Indemnity Co.,** 750 P.2d 1178 (Or. 1988)]

a. Imposter cases [§529]

One situation in which restitutionary remedies are appropriate is where the defendant has obtained through imposture a benefit intended for the plaintiff.

Example: Xian, having acquired a number of tax titles, offers them for sale to the former owners at substantial discounts below market value. Dion falsely represents to Xian that he is a former owner, and thereby obtains title cheaply to land formerly owned by Paco. A *constructive trust* may be imposed forcing Dion to transfer to Paco the title he obtained through imposture (upon Paco tendering the funds paid by Dion for the title). [**Bell v. Smith,** 32 So. 2d 829 (Fla. 1947)] *Rationale:* Xian never intended to deal with Dion; he intended to deal only with the former owner of the property (Paco). Consequently, there was *no volitional dealing* with Dion. It is immaterial that the gain or advantage came from a third party (Xian) who is not a party to the litigation. Lack of privity between Paco and Dion is also immaterial.

---

b. Broker cases [§530]

Restitutionary remedies may also be imposed in cases involving deception by real estate brokers—not because of any fiduciary duties owed by them to their clients, but because of their taking personal advantage of a transaction in which they appear to be disinterested.

(1) Illustration

Seller Sue employs real estate broker Deanna to sell certain property. Deanna thereby becomes an agent of the seller—*Deanna does not represent any buyer* with whom she negotiates. Buyer Bob tells broker Deanna that he will pay $10,000 for the property. Deanna tells seller Sue of the offer (without identifying the offeror), and Sue indicates her willingness to accept. Broker Deanna then goes back to the buyer and falsely states that the seller wants more money, and thereby extracts from Bob an offer to pay $15,000, which Deanna "accepts" on behalf of the seller. Bob then pays Deanna the $15,000, of which Deanna keeps $5,000 plus her commission, and turns the balance over to Sue. Both Bob and Sue are satisfied. Later, however, the truth comes out. Sue remains satisfied, saying she got the price she wanted. However, *Bob* sues Deanna for the $5,000. What result?

(2) Rule

The cases hold that the *buyer* is *entitled to restitution* from the broker of whatever "secret profit" (either money or land) the broker obtained. [**Harper v. Adametz,** 113 A.2d 136 (Conn. 1955)] In addition, the fraud on the buyer may be held to justify an award of *punitive damages* against the broker. [**Ward v. Taggart,** 57 Cal. 2d 736 (1959)] *Rationale:* The fraud here was on the buyer, but no tort action for damages lies because the essential element of pecuniary damage is missing; *i.e.,* the property was worth what the buyer paid for it (or at least, it may be very hard for the buyer to prove that it was not). Consequently, recovery is based on *unjust enrichment* of the broker.

(3) Criticism

The broker was the agent of the *seller,* not the buyer, and the "diversion of benefit" was from the seller, to whom a fiduciary duty was owed, and therefore the remedy for unjust enrichment belongs to the seller, not the buyer. The buyer should have no such remedy because he willingly paid the price demanded.

(4) Response

The courts have attempted to answer the above criticism by asserting that real estate brokers are licensed by the state and thus have duties of fair dealing *to all persons* with whom they negotiate. Having breached that duty (by falsely telling the buyer that the seller had rejected the lower offer), they are unjustly enriched.

E. Remedies for Patent Infringement

1. Regulated Exclusively by Federal Law [§531]

The regulation and control of patents is controlled exclusively by federal law. The national interest in uniform regulation of this subject matter *preempts* any state law or judicial action that would affect patent rights.

a. Exclusive jurisdiction in federal courts [§532]

Furthermore, the federal courts have sole and exclusive jurisdiction in patent infringement cases (there is *no* concurrent jurisdiction in state courts).

2. Federal Statutory Remedies [§533]

The remedies provided by the Patent Act in infringement actions are as follows:

a. Injunctions [§534]

The federal courts are empowered to grant injunctions "in accordance with the principles of equity" to protect patent rights. [35 U.S.C. §282; **Atlas Powder Co. v. Ireco Chemicals,** 773 F.2d 1230 (Fed. Cir. 1985)]

b. Damages [§535]

The plaintiff is entitled to recover "damages *adequate to compensate* for the infringement, but in *no event less than a reasonable royalty* for the use made by the infringer." [35 U.S.C. §284]

(1) Defendant's profits as evidence of damages [§536]

Formerly, the patent laws provided that the plaintiff was entitled to an *accounting* for profits made by the defendant through patent infringement (the logical measure of diversion of trade). This provision has now been deleted, but the defendant's profits may still be shown as *evidence of plaintiff's compensatory damages.* [*See* **Zegers v. Zegers, Inc.,** 458 F.2d 726 (7th Cir. 1972)]

(a) Note

An award of *lost profits* is proper if it can be demonstrated that "but for" the infringement, the patent holder would have made the sales. Evidence showing a reasonable probability that the patent holder would have made the sales actually made by the infringer will suffice. [**Standard Havens Products v. Gencor Industries,** 953 F.2d 1360 (Fed. Cir. 1992)]

(b) Limitation

There may be cases in which the patent holder (patentee) has not been exploiting the patent, and hence no trade was diverted. For example, the patent holder may have been intentionally withholding any use of the invention to protect a heavy investment in an early model or otherwise obsolete method of manufacture. In such cases, the defendant's profits from infringement of the plaintiff's patent should be held irrelevant. [*See* **Zegers v. Zegers, Inc.,** *supra*]

(2) Statutory minimum—reasonable royalty [§537]

If no other damages are provable, the plaintiff (patentee) is entitled to recover as a minimum a "reasonable" royalty for the infringer's use of the invention, *together with interest and costs.* [*See* **Fromson v. Western Litho Plate & Supply Co.,** 853 F.2d 1568 (Fed. Cir. 1988)]

(a) Test [§538]

The test is the *pecuniary loss to the patentee,* not the enrichment of the infringer. [**Universal Athletic Sales Co. v. American Gym,** 480 F. Supp. 408 (W.D. Pa. 1979)]

(b) What constitutes "reasonable" royalty [§539]

A "reasonable" royalty is the sum that the parties would have agreed upon *had they bargained in good faith*. [**Radio Steel & Manufacturing Co. v. MTD Products, Inc.,** 788 F.2d 1554 (Fed. Cir. 1986)]

1) Note

If there is an established royalty rate being paid by other licensees, evidence of that rate is admissible, but it is not conclusive as to "reasonableness" because the price paid for earlier licenses granted by the patentee may have been less than the patentee would have charged the defendant (*i.e.,* the earlier licenses may have been granted before the full value of the patent right was recognized). [**Russell Box Co. v. Grant Paper Box Co.,** 203 F.2d 177 (1st Cir. 1953)]

2) Willfulness [§540]

If the infringement is willful, "the court may increase damages up to three times the amount found or assessed." [35 U.S.C. §284; **H.B. Fuller v. National Starch & Chemical Corp.,** 689 F. Supp. 923 (D. Minn. 1988)—50% increase assessed]

c. Attorneys' fees [§541]

In "*exceptional cases,*" the court is also authorized to award reasonable attorneys' fees to the *prevailing party* in a patent infringement action. [35 U.S.C. §285] This requires a showing of fraud or *bad faith* by the losing party in maintaining or defending the action.

CHECKLIST OF PLAINTIFF'S REMEDIES FOR PATENT VIOLATION — gilbert

THE FOLLOWING REMEDIES SHOULD BE CONSIDERED IN PATENT VIOLATION CASES WHEN THE PLAINTIFF/PATENTEE PREVAILS:

☑ An *injunction* against further infringement

AND

☑ Damages *adequate to compensate* the plaintiff for the infringement

- The *defendant's profits* from using the patent may be used as evidence of reasonable damages
- If no other damages are provable, a statutory *reasonable royalty* may be recovered measured by the pecuniary loss to the patentee based on a sum the parties would have bargained for in good faith

AND

☑ *Treble damages* if the infringement was willful

AND

☑ *Attorneys' fees* if the infringer acted in bad faith

F. Remedies for Copyright Infringement

1. Regulated Exclusively by Federal Law [§542]

Copyrights, like patents, are regulated and controlled exclusively under federal law. State statutes and judicial action are *preempted* in the interest of uniform national regulation of the subject matter.

a. Exclusive jurisdiction in federal courts [§543]

Again, like patents, federal courts have exclusive jurisdiction in copyright infringement actions (*i.e., no* concurrent jurisdiction in state courts).

2. Federal Statutory Remedies [§544]

The remedies available in copyright infringement actions are as follows:

a. Injunctions [§545]

The court may issue an injunction to protect the copyright. [17 U.S.C. §502]

b. Impounding and disposition of infringing articles [§546]

The infringing copies may be ordered impounded during the pendency of the action, and when the infringement is established, the court may order them destroyed along with plates or other means by which they were made. [17 U.S.C. §503; **RSO Records, Inc. v. Peri,** 596 F. Supp. 849 (S.D.N.Y. 1984)— pirated records and tapes ordered destroyed]

c. Damages and profits [§547]

The copyright holder may recover actual damages and any additional profits made by the defendant that are not taken into account in computing actual damages. [17 U.S.C. §504] (Note that this changes the rule as to the measure of recovery in copyright cases that existed until 1978—*i.e.,* which allowed recovery of *both* damages and defendant's profits even though duplicative.) [**Robert R. Jones Associates v. Nine Homes,** 858 F.2d 274 (6th Cir. 1988)— damages for infringement of architectural plans measured by profits the plaintiff would have made on lost sales; since all of the infringer's sales were counted as sales lost by the plaintiff, all of the infringer's profits were included in the calculation of damages, and therefore it was improper to include the infringer's profits in the final award as additional item of damages; *and see* **Johnson v. Jones,** 921 F. Supp. 1573 (E.D. Mich. 1996)—award of actual damages rejected, but profit made by defendant awarded]

(1) Proof of profits [§548]

In proving the infringer's profits (*i.e.,* the restitutionary measure of recovery), the copyright owner is required to prove only the infringer's gross revenue. The defendant must prove deductible expenses and other elements of profit attributable to factors other than the copyrighted work. [**Kamar International v. Russ Berrie & Co.,** 752 F.2d 1326 (9th Cir. 1984)—deduction for overhead allowed only when infringer can demonstrate it was of actual assistance in sale of product; *and see* **Softel, Inc. v. Dragon Medical,** 891 F. Supp. 935 (S.D.N.Y. 1995)—deduction of fixed-cost, overhead expenses associated with the production of the infringing product allowed]

(2) Computation of profits [§549]

The defendant's profits are to be calculated in a manner that will give the benefit of every doubt to the copyright holder.

Example: Defendant wrote a book on the law of eminent domain but copied the section on "Damages" from Plaintiff's copyrighted book. The part copied was only 35% of Defendant's book but Plaintiff was awarded 50% of the profits realized by Defendant. [**Orgel v. Clark Boardman,** 301 F.2d 119 (2d Cir. 1961)]

---

d. Statutory ("in lieu") damages [§550]

Instead of damages or profits, the copyright owner may elect to recover a statutory amount between $750 and $30,000, as the court considers just. [17 U.S.C. §504c; **Walt Disney Co. v. Powell,** 897 F.2d 565 (D.C. Cir. 1990)]

(1) Character of defendant's conduct [§551]

The act also provides that the maximum award can be raised to $150,000 for willful infringement or reduced to $200 for innocent infringement.

(2) Fair use qualification [§552]

In the special instances of infringers who supposed that their use of the copyrighted material was fair (*e.g.,* lecturers, librarians, or archivists in nonprofit institutions), the court may remit statutory damages in whole or part.

e. Sound recordings—compulsory licensing [§553]

There is a special provision applicable to records and tapes, which provides for *compulsory licensing* of copyrighted musical compositions. By notifying the copyright holder of an intention to record such work and keeping accurate count of the copies made, any person is authorized to record and sell the copyrighted work, and thereupon to pay a prescribed statutory royalty (2.75¢ each recording or 0.5¢ per minute of playing time, whichever is greater). [17 U.S.C. §115]

SUMMARY OF REMEDIES FOR COPYRIGHT INFRINGEMENT	**gilbert**
INJUNCTION	A court may *enjoin violations* of copyrights.
IMPOUNDMENT AND DESTRUCTION	Infringing copies may be ordered *impounded during the suit* and *destroyed after the suit*.
DAMAGES AND PROFITS	The copyright holder may recover any *actual damages* and *any additional profits* made by the defendant that are not taken into account in computing actual damages.
STATUTORY DAMAGES	*In lieu of damages or profits*, the copyright holder may elect to recover a *statutory amount* between $750 and $30,000 (or, if the infringement was willful, up to $150,000).

G. Remedies for Destruction or Misappropriation of Trade Secrets

1. No Federal Preemption [§554]

As long as state "trade secret" laws do not actually conflict with the federal patent or copyright laws, they are valid. There is no preemption of state laws in this field because there is no national interest demanding uniform treatment of the subject matter. [**Kewanee Oil Co. v. Bicron Corp.**, 416 U.S. 470 (1974)] (There is, however, a Uniform Trade Secrets Act, which some states have adopted.)

a. Note

This is true *whether or not the trade secret is patentable* under the patent laws. *Rationale:* The federal policy of encouraging invention is enhanced, not impeded, by allowing state protection of inventions not otherwise patentable. And even where the invention is patentable, there may be legitimate reasons for not wanting to patent it (*i.e.,* the patent process requires publication of a secret, which often serves only to "educate" competitors, and spawns infringement actions). [**Kewanee Oil Co. v. Bicron Corp.**, *supra*]

2. Damages as Remedy [§555]

Any tortious appropriation or disclosure of that which is in fact a trade "secret" operates to destroy such "property" as is inherent in a trade secret. Hence, the measure of compensatory damages is the *investment value* of the trade secret—the amount necessary to compensate the plaintiff for the *loss of exclusivity of use*. [**Precision Plating & Metals v. Martin-Marietta Corp.**, 435 F.2d 1252 (5th Cir. 1972)]

a. **Measure of compensatory damages [§556]**

The plaintiff is entitled to recover the profits lost as the result of the defendant's unlawful acts (the net profit that the plaintiff would have made had the secret not been disclosed), *but not less than the net profits that the defendant reaped thereby.* [**Clark v. Bunker,** 453 F.2d 1006 (9th Cir. 1972)—recovery for defendant's profits *plus* income on funds plaintiff would have received but for defendant's tortious act; *and see* **Curtiss-Wright Corp. v. Edel-Brown Tool & Die Co.,** 407 N.E.2d 319 (Mass. 1980)—damages may be measured by "defendant's profits realized from his tortious conduct, the plaintiff's lost profits, or a reasonable royalty"; **J & K Computer Systems v. Parrish,** 642 P.2d 732 (Utah 1982)—may recover lost profits and costs of development]

(1) **Lost profits of plaintiff [§557]**

It is proper to base compensatory damages on the amount by which the plaintiff's profits deteriorated following the defendant's interference. [**Sperry Rand Corp. v. A-T-O, Inc.,** 447 F.2d 1387 (4th Cir. 1971)—plaintiff may recover fixed overhead and material costs incurred in producing product, *plus* a sum for damages resulting from *loss of future sales on replacement parts* to supplement the original product sold]

(2) **Net profits of defendant [§558]**

The usual question in determining the defendant's "net profits" is what expenses are properly deductible in calculating the profits. [*See* **USM Corp. v. Marson Fastener Corp.,** 467 N.E.2d 1271 (Mass. 1984)]

(a) **Administrative expenses [§559]**

If the defendant has a going business, she *cannot* deduct the *general or administrative expenses* incurred in the business at the time of her tortious acts. *Rationale:* The defendant would have incurred these anyway.

(b) **Development of new product [§560]**

But the defendant's expenses in developing and marketing a new product incorporating the trade secret are properly deducted, and so are all production costs. [**Carboline v. Jarboe,** 165 U.S.P.Q. 521 (1970)]

(c) **Taxes [§561]**

Federal income taxes paid by the defendant on profits earned from the tortious infringement of another's trade secrets are also deductible. [**W.E. Bassett Co. v. Revlon, Inc.,** 435 F.2d 656 (2d Cir. 1970); *but see* **USM Corp. v. Marson Fastener Corp.,** *supra*—great weight of authority denies deduction of income tax paid if infringement is willful]

(d) **Alternative method [§562]**

An alternative method of computing the defendant's "net profits" is a comparison of costs in producing the product without the trade secret with the costs of producing it using the secret. [**International Industries, Inc. v. Warren Petroleum Corp.**, 248 F.2d 696 (3d Cir. 1957)]

(3) Overlapping avoided [§563]

Recovery of the plaintiff's lost profits or the defendant's net profits is usually mutually exclusive, and hence there is no duplication or overlapping of damages.

b. Consequential damages [§564]

In addition to an award for his own lost profits or the defendant's net profits, the plaintiff is entitled to any other damages proximately resulting from the defendant's infringement. For example, if the plaintiff is forced to lower his own prices to meet competition engendered by disclosure of the trade secret, the plaintiff may recover not only the profits earned by the defendant, but also for losses resulting from being forced to lower prices. [**Julius Hyman & Co. v. Velsicol Corp.**, 233 P.2d 977 (Colo. 1951)]

c. Punitive damages [§565]

In addition to compensatory damages, the plaintiff may be entitled to recover punitive damages if he can establish that the defendant acted with "malice" or intent to injure plaintiff. [*See* **Sperry Rand Corp. v. A-T-O, Inc.**, *supra*, §557; *and see* **Softel, Inc. v. Dragon Medical**, *supra*, §548]

d. Prejudgment interest and attorneys' fees [§566]

Most courts treat claims for damages for infringement of trade secrets as *unliquidated* and *deny* prejudgment interest on the amount ultimately awarded. Attorneys' fees are sometimes awarded in trade secret cases, but the rule borrowed from the patent cases (*supra*) limits them to "exceptional cases" (*i.e.*, bad faith).

3. Reasonable Royalty [§567]

By analogy to the patent laws (*see supra*, §537), a reasonable royalty has occasionally been awarded for misappropriation of a trade secret when damages (above) or accounting for profits (below) are not an adequate remedy. [*See, e.g.,* **Forest Laboratories, Inc. v. Pillsbury Co.**, 452 F.2d 621 (7th Cir. 1971); *and see* **University Computing Co. v. Lykes-Youngstown Corp.**, 504 F.2d 518 (5th Cir. 1974)—damages measured by "fair licensing price"]

4. Equitable Remedies—Injunctions and Accounting

a. Injunctions [§568]

Equitable jurisdiction is based on the inadequacy of damages (*i.e.*, a secret is "unique"). Moreover, many cases involve breach of confidential relationships (*e.g.*, secrets disclosed in confidence by an employer to an employee), and equitable jurisdiction may also be invoked on this ground. [*See* **Boeing Co. v. Sierracin Corp.**, 738 P.2d 665 (Wash. 1987)—proof of irreparable harm not required under Uniform Trade Secrets Act to support injunction against misappropriation of trade secret]

(1) Tortious interference [§569]

Equity will enjoin a defendant who has obtained another's trade secrets by tortious means (*e.g.*, by stealing them or bribing an employee). The wrongdoer may be enjoined from making any use of the secret or disclosing it to any other person.

(a) Customer list cases [§570]

A special type of problem involving these considerations is the "customer list" or "route" cases. Typically, the rival employer (*e.g.*, a dairy or laundry) does not steal the list, it simply hires away the driver or salesperson who developed the route and made the customer contacts. In such cases, injunctive relief is generally limited to a *prohibition against soliciting* former customers and does not prohibit *acceptance* of patronage from them. [**Aetna Building Maintenance Co. v. West**, 39 Cal. 2d 198 (1952)]

(2) Agreements not to disclose specifically enforced [§571]

Employers frequently require their employees to sign elaborate agreements not to make any unauthorized use of trade secrets to which they may be exposed in the course of their employment. Such contracts are valid and specifically enforceable.

Example: An employee who gains knowledge of her employer's trade secrets and then is hired away by a competitor may be enjoined from using the former employer's secrets in her new employment (although she may be free to work in other departments or on other projects).

(3) Feasibility problem [§572]

The major problems in attempting to "fence in" a secret by in personam equity decrees are the drafting of an intelligible decree and the feasibility of its enforcement. This is particularly so where many individuals share in various aspects of the knowledge, but few are privy to the whole. [*See* **Julius Hyman & Co. v. Velsicol Corp.**, *supra*, §564—the chlordane formula]

(a) Note

The drafting problem is so acute that some decrees have been held "void for vagueness." [**American Can Co. v. Mansukhani**, 742 F.2d 314 (7th Cir. 1984); *and see* **Henry Hope X-Ray Products v. Marron**

Carrel, Inc., 674 F.2d 1336 (9th Cir. 1982)—confidential appendix was attached to the injunction specifying the prohibited acts]

(4) "Lead time" injunctions [§573]

The misappropriation of a trade secret frequently results in its disclosure so that *anyone* henceforth may use it—including the wrongdoer. Some courts permanently enjoin the wrongdoer from taking advantage of her wrong, but the majority limit the injunction against competition to the period of "lead" time—*i.e.,* the time saved by the wrongdoer in getting into competitive production by reason of the early access to the secret. [**Syntex Ophthalmics v. Novicky,** 591 F. Supp. 28 (N.D. Ill. 1983)—20-year duration for injunction, time it took plaintiff to develop process]

(a) And note

The owner of the process may be considered adequately compensated for the taking of a trade secret if the competitor has voluntarily refrained from engaging in competition for a period equivalent to the lead time. [**Northern Petrochemical Co. v. Tomlinson,** 484 F.2d 1057 (7th Cir. 1973)]

b. Accounting [§574]

In addition to injunctive relief, the owner of the trade secret may seek an accounting from the infringer as to any *profits* derived from the improper use, on a theory of unjust enrichment. [**Tilghman v. Proctor,** 125 U.S. 136 (1886)] Under modern practice, the measure of recovery is usually the same as in an action at law for damages (*see* above). [**Hayes-Albion v. Kuberski,** 311 N.W.2d 122 (Mich. 1981)—lost profits and punitive damages]

SUMMARY OF REMEDIES FOR MISAPPROPRIATION OF TRADE SECRETS — gilbert

DAMAGES	A court may award the *profits* that the plaintiff lost as a result of the defendant's unlawful acts, or the defendant's *profits* if they are more, plus *consequential damages*. If the defendant acted with malice, *punitive damages* are also available.
REASONABLE ROYALTY	Some courts have *analogized to patent cases* and have awarded a reasonable royalty.
INJUNCTION	A court may issue an injunction *prohibiting use of the misappropriated trade secret*, either permanently or for the time it would have taken the misappropriator to develop the information comprising the trade secret (a "lead time" injunction).
ACCOUNTING	In addition to an injunction, the owner of the trade secret may seek an accounting *to recover profits* that the misappropriator derived from improper use of the trade secret.

H. Remedies for Misappropriation of Creative Works and Ideas

1. Common Law Copyright—Federal Preemption [§575]

The federal copyright act explicitly preempts the area of state protection of literary property and ideas that existed under the rubric of "common law copyright" and covered original creative expressions that were tangible in form and otherwise *unpublished* or not dedicated to the public. [17 U.S.C. §301a]

2. Limited Common Law or Equitable Protection [§576]

However, the federal statute leaves some areas of state protection of creative works and ideas unaffected by preemption. [17 U.S.C. §301(b)] Hence, in these areas, judicial remedies developed under the traditional theory of common law copyrights—or by application of other doctrines such as invasion of personal rights, breaches of trust and confidence, or misappropriation of "property" or "quasi-property" rights (*see infra*, §§598, 612)—will apparently continue to be available under state law. Specifically the unaffected areas are:

a. *Unpublished works not filed in tangible form* (*e.g.,* an extemporaneous speech, original works of authorship communicated solely through conversations or live broadcasts, choreography that has not been notated); and

b. *Activities violating rights that are not equivalent to those rights granted exclusive federal protection,* including breaches of contract, breaches of trust, invasion of privacy, and deceptive trade practices such as passing off and false representations. [**Gladstone v. Hillel,** 203 Cal. App. 3d 977 (1988)—federal copyright law does not preempt state cause of action alleging fraud or conversion in wrongful acquisition of jewelry designs]

EXAM TIP   **gilbert**

When assessing remedies on your exam, you might be asked to explain in which court the plaintiff can file his action. It is easy to remember that the federal courts have exclusive jurisdiction over patent and copyright cases. However, what constitutes a patent or copyright case may be a little confusing. A person may choose not to apply for a patent—even if his idea is patentable—and treat his idea as a *trade secret*. In such a case, the secret holder may file an action in state court to protect the secret. *There is no similar choice under the copyright laws*. If material is copyrightable and the originator chooses not to file for a copyright, the federal courts still have exclusive jurisdiction.

---

3. Remedies Available [§577]

Assuming the creator, author, inventor, etc., is able to establish a substantive theory of protection against the "copying" of his creation or idea *outside* the copyright statute, damages, restitution, or injunctive relief may be granted.

a. **Illustrative case [§578]**

Cliff employed persons to attend classes at a nearby university and take short-hand notes of the professors' lectures. Cliff then had these notes transcribed and published, and sold them to students. Prof, one of the professors, sued for an injunction and damages, claiming common law copyright of his lecture materials. [**Williams v. Weisser,** 273 Cal. App. 2d 726 (1969)]

(1) **Injunction [§579]**

The court readily granted injunctive relief, finding that the lectures in class were *not* an unlimited publication of the materials, but rather were a limited disclosure for the purposes of education and with the implied understanding that the recipient would make no improper use of them.

(2) **Damages [§580]**

The court had problems with the measure of damages, however. There was evidence that a publisher of educational materials would have offered an author a 15% royalty and an "advance" of between $3,000 and $5,000. The court chose to make an award of $1,000 as "compensatory" damages—which can be rationalized only as the amount of the plaintiff's loss up to the date of judgment.

(a) **Comment**

An appropriate remedy would have been *restitution* by way of an accounting for the defendant's profits, but the plaintiff did not seek this remedy.

(3) **California statute [§581]**

In California, the matter is now governed by statute, which provides that the "author of any original work of authorship that is not fixed in any tangible medium of expression has an exclusive ownership" in the expression. [Cal. Civ. Code §980]

4. **Disclosures Made in Confidence [§582]**

If a writer or inventor discloses an idea in confidence and under circumstances manifesting an expectation of payment if the idea is used, most courts today enforce *contractual* remedies if the person to whom the idea is disclosed subsequently uses it. Any of the following remedial theories may be invoked:

a. **Breach of express contract [§583]**

If the disclosure was made subject to an express agreement between the parties to pay for any use of the matter disclosed, regular contract damages are recoverable.

b. **Breach of implied-in-fact contract [§584]**

Even without any express agreement, a court may hold that the *conduct* of the parties implied an agreement (offer and acceptance) to pay a reasonable sum for the use of the matter disclosed, in which event the court will determine what is "reasonable" based on the expectancies of the parties at the time of their negotiations. The court may find an implied-in-fact promise to pay either for the mere disclosure (regardless of any use), or only for the use of the "idea" following the disclosure. [**Desny v. Wilder,** 46 Cal. 2d 715 (1956); **Klekas v. EMI Films,** 150 Cal. App. 3d 1102 (1984)]

(1) Note

Recovery on either an express or implied-in-fact *contract* theory is available even if the matter disclosed is *otherwise not protectable*.

c. Quasi-contract [§585]

As an alternative to claiming any actual contract to pay for the use, the plaintiff may seek to recover on a quasi-contract for the *reasonable value* of the matter disclosed. Here, it must be shown that the plaintiff had some protectable property right before the courts will find that the defendant was "unjustly enriched."

e.g. **Example:** Prema disclosed to Doyle (a shipping company) models for cargo unloading. Doyle thereafter used Prema's idea, achieving considerable savings in its cargo handling expense. Prema was held entitled to recover in quasi-contract the amount of Doyle's *savings* (negative unjust enrichment). Such savings were held relevant to the "value" of the misappropriated services. [**Matarese v. Moore-McCormack Lines, Inc.,** 158 F.2d 631 (2d Cir. 1946)]

cf. **Compare:** Pavel submitted a script to Dante, and Dante subsequently made a motion picture that Pavel claimed was based on his script. The court held that if it could be shown that the script was *protectable literary property* (at that time under common law copyright), Pavel could recover in quasi-contract. Since Pavel failed to prove use of the script by Dante, restitutionary relief was denied. [**Weitzenkorn v. Lesser,** 40 Cal. 2d 778 (1953)]

d. Equitable relief [§586]

As an alternative to the foregoing, the plaintiff may seek to *enjoin* the defendant's unauthorized use of the matter disclosed by the plaintiff, and to obtain an *accounting* for any profits derived by the defendant through such use.

5. Private Letters and Correspondence [§587]

The law recognizes a *bifurcated* ownership of private letters and correspondence. The recipient is deemed to own the paper or material upon which the correspondence is written. However, the sender (author) retains a proprietary interest in the verbal expressions. Therefore, the recipient does *not* have unqualified title and cannot lawfully publish the correspondence or letters received from another. The correspondence is regarded as having been a *limited* disclosure of the author's verbal expression, and hence protected by common law copyright. [**Baker v. Libbie,** 97 N.E. 109 (Mass. 1912)—recipient enjoined from publishing letters received from sender]

a. Federal preemption [§588]

Under the copyright act, protection of private letters falls under the statutory copyright provisions (*supra,* §575). [**Maheu v. C.B.S.,** 201 Cal. App. 3d 662 (1988)—letter written by Howard Hughes to plaintiff]

b. Distinguish—right of privacy [§589]

Unauthorized disclosure or publication of private correspondence may also be remediable as an invasion of privacy; *see infra,* §§684-701.

I. Remedies for Trademark and Trade Name Infringement

1. General Theories and Their Effect on Remedies [§590]

The substantive law basis for trademark and trade name protection has been much debated, and different theories have been followed over the years. The remedies available depend on the particular theory accepted in a given jurisdiction. A short summary:

a. "Palming off" theory [§591]

The "palming off" theory is based on the premise that the defendant is selling her goods under the mark or name of the plaintiff and attempting thereby to divert the plaintiff's trade. *Head-to-head market competition* must be shown and *protection of goodwill* is the basis for relief.

(1) Background [§592]

The "palming off" theory was the original basis upon which recovery was permitted at common law, and every jurisdiction still allows recovery where these elements are shown.

(2) Remedies [§593]

The remedies are directed to the elimination of and compensation for the *diversion of trade*:

(a) *Damages* are based on the plaintiff's lost profits.

(b) *Injunctions* are limited geographically to the areas where the plaintiff is operating.

    (c) *Accounting* for the defendant's profits is essentially equivalent to the plaintiff's damages.

    (d) *Special damages* may also be recoverable for possible injury to the plaintiff's *business* reputation, if the defendant's mislabeled product is inferior.

b. Confusion of source theory [§594]

The confusion of source theory is based on the premise that the defendant is marketing her goods in such a manner as to lead to a *likelihood of public confusion*—a reasonably large segment of the public is likely to believe that the goods being marketed by the defendant are produced by the plaintiff, which is in fact not true—*e.g.*, "Ford" bicycles.

(1) Basis of theory—consumer protection [§595]

This approach introduces the idea of "consumer protection." The plaintiff is acting on behalf of the public and thus equitable remedies may be designed with customers' interests in mind.

Example: In a case involving a related type of unfair competition—the use of titles—a California court held that the national distributor of the French film "The Story of O" could not compel defendant-producer of "The Journey of O" to change its title (*i.e.*, no mandatory injunction), but could require him to take steps to dispel the likelihood of confusion by including disclaimers. [**Allied Artists Pictures Corp. v. Friedman,** 68 Cal. App. 3d 127 (1977)]

Compare: Use of the name "California Western" by a university caused public confusion and irreparable harm to the law school with the same name. [**California Western School of Law v. California Western University,** 125 Cal. App. 3d 1002 (1981)]

(2) Extent of protection [§596]

Protectability here extends to instances where the competition is not direct. There need not necessarily be any diversion of trade. [**Conan Properties, Inc. v. Conan's Pizza,** 752 F.2d 145 (5th Cir. 1985)—use of name for restaurant and its food items enjoined outside the Austin, Texas area]

(a) Note

A state court may thus be issuing an equity decree having extraterritorial effect (*see supra,* §194). In *Allied Artists, supra,* the trial court concluded that it lacked authority to make its decree operative outside California, but the appellate court remanded for further consideration stating that the injunction could apply nationwide absent any showing that the decree would conflict with the law of any other United States jurisdiction.

(3) Business reputation [§597]

The plaintiff's business reputation may also be protected from the defendant's "inferior" products under this theory. Thus, in **Dallas Cowboys Cheerleaders, Inc. v. Pussycat Cinema Ltd.,** 604 F.2d 200 (2d Cir. 1979), a preliminary injunction was granted prohibiting the exhibition of a motion picture film featuring a uniform closely modeled after that worn by the plaintiff group. The film, depicting the sexual escapades of the performers, was found to impugn the nature of the plaintiff's services and injure the plaintiff's reputation.

(4) Comment

The "confusion of source" approach finds support in language of the Lanham Act (*see* below).

c. "Misappropriation" theory [§598]

The misappropriation theory is based on the concept that a trademark, trade name, etc. is "*property*" in itself, rather than merely a reflection of the goodwill of the business. Protectability therefore extends to situations where there is *no* market competition or diversion of trade.

(1) Damages [§599]

Under this theory, the plaintiff cannot recover loss of profits as damages unless she can prove diversion of trade.

(2) Injunctions [§600]

Injunctions under this rationale tend to be broad geographically, and extend to areas where the plaintiff is not yet operating and to products not yet produced by the plaintiff.

(3) Quasi-contract [§601]

Quasi-contractual measure of recovery is possible—*i.e.,* to recover the value of what was "misappropriated" by the defendant.

d. "Dilution" theory [§602]

The dilution theory is based on the premise that the defendant's unauthorized use of the plaintiff's trademark, etc., is wrongful because it "dilutes" the advertising impact that the plaintiff's mark will have both in its present market and in any other market in which the plaintiff may thereafter choose to use it. This rationale rests more on statutes (*e.g.,* New York's) than cases. *Note:* The Lanham Act is not an antidilution statute (*see infra,* §608). [See **Mead Data Central v. Toyota Motor Sales,** 875 F.2d 1026 (2d Cir. 1989)—no dilution of computer assisted research service trade name "Lexis" by use of trade name "Lexus" on a luxury automobile]

(1) Requirements [§603]

To establish a claim on this theory requires evidence establishing that the trademark is truly of a distinctive quality or has acquired a secondary meaning in the mind of the public. [**Miss Universe v. Patricelli,** 753 F.2d 235 (2d Cir. 1985)]

(2) Remedy [§604]

The remedies are usually limited to an injunction. [*See* Cal. Bus. & Prof. Code §14330] Such injunctions tend to be worded so as to emphasize the protection against unlawful exposure of the mark (rather than merely diversion of trade).

SUMMARY OF THEORIES FOR RECOVERING FOR TRADEMARK OR TRADE NAME INFRINGEMENT	gilbert
PALMING OFF	Based on the premise that the defendant is trying to pass off his goods as those of the plaintiff. The defendant and plaintiff must be in head-to-head competition. Damages are based on the *plaintiff's lost profits*.
CONFUSION OF SOURCE	Based on the premise that the defendant is marketing her goods in a manner that will trick the public into thinking that they are the plaintiff's goods. Head-to-head competition is *not* required. *Injunction* is a common remedy here.
MISAPPROPRIATION	Based on the premise that the defendant has misappropriated the plaintiff's property interest in the trademark or trade name. Head-to-head competition is *not* required. Damages based on *lost profits* are recoverable, and courts *may enjoin* use of the misappropriated item. *Quasi-contractual relief* might also be available.
DILUTION	Based on the premise that the defendant's unauthorized use of plaintiff's trademark or trade name dilutes the impact of the plaintiff's mark in present and future markets. The plaintiff must establish that her trademark or trade name is *truly distinctive*. *Injunction* is the usual remedy.

2. Lanham Act and Remedies

a. Does not preempt state protection [§605]

Unlike the patent and copyright laws, the federal statute providing for the registration of trademarks and trade names (the Lanham Act) does *not* preempt state laws for registration of trademarks and trade names or preclude state remedies for infringement.

b. Substantive provisions [§606]

The Lanham Act permits *registration* of the mark or name with prima facie protection and a five-year period of contestability.

c. **Jurisdiction [§607]**

Infringement actions under the Lanham Act must be brought in the federal courts, but claims under state law may be joined.

d. **Basis for protection [§608]**

The essential factor that must be established for protection under the Lanham Act is whether there is a *"likelihood of confusion"* or a cause for mistake or deception. [**Transamerica Corp. v. Trans America Abstract Service, Inc.,** 698 F. Supp. 1067 (E.D.N.Y. 1988); **Home Box Office v. Showtime/The Movie Channel,** 832 F.2d 1311 (2d Cir. 1987)]

(1) Note

In general, the grounds for opposing registering marks or defending infringement suits (*e.g.,* on such issues as whether the mark has acquired a "secondary meaning") parallel the common law cases.

e. **Remedies [§609]**

The remedies available in an infringement action under the Lanham Act are specified in 15 U.S.C. section 1117. "Subject to the principles of equity," the plaintiff may recover:

(1) defendant's *profits*, (2) any *damages* sustained by the plaintiff, and (3) the *costs of the action*. The court shall assess such profits and damages or cause the same to be assessed under its direction. In assessing profits the plaintiff shall be required to prove defendant's sales only; defendant must prove all elements of cost or deduction claimed. In assessing damages the court may enter judgment, according to the circumstances of the case, for any sum above the amount found as actual damages, not exceeding *three times* such amount. And if the court finds that the amount of recovery based on profits is either inadequate or excessive it may in its discretion enter judgment for such sum as it finds to be just, according to the circumstances of the case. Such sum, in either of the above circumstances shall constitute compensation and not a penalty . . . . In a case involving a counterfeit mark . . . the plaintiff may elect . . . an award of statutory damages . . . of not less than $500 or more than $100,000.

Damages may be trebled in cases of willful infringement [**Ford Motor Co. v. Kuan Tong Industrial Co.,** 697 F. Supp. 1108 (N.D. Cal. 1987)], but punitive damages are not authorized by the Lanham Act [**Getty Petroleum Corp. v. Bartco Petroleum Corp.,** 858 F.2d 103 (2d Cir. 1988)]. Injunctive relief is also available. [*See* **Chevron Chemical Co. v. Voluntary Purchasing Group,** 659 F.2d 695 (5th Cir. 1981)]

> **Example:** Defendant used plaintiff's "Acrilan" mark on manufactured bedding when no Acrilan was contained in defendant's product. Defendant was ordered to account to plaintiff for the profits made even though defendant did not divert any trade from plaintiff (plaintiff made only the basic material, Acrilan, and merely supplied it to others who put it in the finished products). The rationale was based partly on the protection of the public, and partly on the punishment of defendant for its conduct. [**Monsanto Chemical Co. v. Perfect Fit Manufacturing Co.**, 349 F.2d 389 (2d Cir. 1965)]

> **Example:** Maier marketed "Black and White" beer infringing Fleischmann's registered trademark "Black and White" on scotch whisky. The court ordered an injunction and an accounting not only against the brewery that produced the beer, but also against the grocery chain that distributed it—even though the defendants could not be said to have diverted any trade from Fleischmann's scotch whisky. [**Maier Brewing Co. v. Fleischmann Distilling Corp.**, 390 F.2d 117 (9th Cir. 1968)]

> **Example:** Defendants deliberately misappropriated the mark of a singing group known as "The Drifters." The court ordered an accounting not only to compel defendants to pay back profits by which they were unjustly enriched but also "to deter others in similar positions from infringing valid marks." [**Marshak v. Green,** 505 F. Supp. 1054 (S.D.N.Y. 1981); *and see* **Playboy Enterprises, Inc. v. Baccarat Clothing Co.**, 692 F.2d 1272 (9th Cir. 1982)—infringement of the Playboy bunny; **Playboy Enterprises, Inc. v. P.K. Sorren Export Co.**, 546 F. Supp. 987 (S.D. Fla. 1982)—injunction, damages, and profits doubled]

f. **Equitable defenses [§610]**

The equitable defenses of laches and unclean hands are available to defend against actions brought to enforce trademarks registered under the Lanham Act. Thus, material false statements about the property to be protected will defeat the claim for equitable relief. [*See* **Fuddruckers, Inc. v. Doc's B. R. Others, Inc.**, 826 F.2d 837 (9th Cir. 1987)] Laches is available even in cases where the trademark is itself incontestable. [**Pyrodyne Corp. v. Pryotronics Corp.**, 847 F.2d 1398 (9th Cir. 1988)]

J. Remedies for Unfair Competition

1. **Original Basis—Protection of Goodwill [§611]**

Traditionally, the basis for the tort of unfair competition has been the protection of the goodwill of a business. Under this rationale, equitable remedies and damages are narrowly confined to the "passing off" cases—the copying by one competitor of the name, mark, ornamental features, or design of a product manufactured by another. Direct competition between the plaintiff and defendant is essential under this approach (*see* preceding section).

2. "Misappropriation" Approach [§612]

Some cases have now gone beyond mere protection of goodwill. They proceed on the rationale that each businessperson is entitled to protection against misappropriation of whatever "property" rights are created in the operation of her business. (This is the same rationale that runs through the patent, copyright, trade secret, common law copyright, and to some extent, the trademark decisions; *see supra*.)

a. Impact on remedies [§613]

This "misappropriation" rationale has been used to expand equitable jurisdiction to afford remedies against product simulation (copying of product appearance), and to the so-called free ride cases (where the defendant takes without compensation plaintiff's research and development work). Under this approach, a showing of direct competition between plaintiff and defendant is *not* required.

Example: The International News Service ("I.N.S.") copied news items published by the Associated Press ("A.P.") in New York and sold the items to its own subscribers on the West Coast. The time differential enabled newspapers subscribing to I.N.S. to meet the same deadlines as those subscribing to A.P. Thus, while A.P. did the work (it alone had the reporters abroad who were sending the news), I.N.S. was getting a "free ride." The Supreme Court held that an injunction would lie. *Rationale:* Although no one owns the "news" per se, *as between competitors* in the news-gathering business, a "quasi-property" right inheres in favor of the one that produced the news *so long as it still has commercial value.* [**International News Service v. Associated Press**, 248 U.S. 215 (1918)]

Example: The Metropolitan Opera ("the Met") had a profitable contract with C.B.S. whereby the Met received royalties from recordings made by C.B.S. of performances at the Met. At the same time, the Met broadcast its own performances for public enjoyment. Defendants recorded these radio broadcasts and sold them in competition with those made by C.B.S. under the contract. An injunction was granted, on the basis that the Met had "quasi-property" in the right to make commercial recordings of its live performances. [**Metropolitan Opera Association v. Wagner-Nichols Recorder Corp.**, 199 Misc. 786 (1950)]

Example: A baseball club was held to be entitled to enjoin radio broadcast of play-by-play description of baseball games from a vantage point outside the stadium; a "quasi-property" right was recognized in the right to broadcast the games. [**Pittsburgh Athletic Co. v. KQV Broadcasting Co.**, 24 F. Supp. 490 (W.D. Pa. 1938)]

Example: Plaintiff, creator of "Mutt and Jeff" comic strip, was held to be entitled to an injunction against a publisher who used "Mutt and Jeff" characters in cartoons not drawn by plaintiff; *i.e.*, a "quasi-property" right in the comic strip characters was recognized. [**Fisher v. Star Co.**, 231 N.Y. 414 (1921)]

3. Cases Rejecting "Misappropriation" Approach [§614]

While there is much support for the "misappropriation" rationale, there is also much resistance to it.

a. Criticisms of "misappropriation" approach [§615]

There are two major objections:

(i) Realistically, there may be *no "property" involved* in these cases (*e.g.*, publicly communicated material, as in *International News Service,* above). Without a "property" interest, or any claimed breach of trust or confidence, the traditional basis for equitable jurisdiction is lacking.

(ii) What the courts are really doing is *regulating the method* of competition. This is more appropriately a matter of federal regulation under the antitrust, patent, and copyright laws.

Example: Phonograph records made by plaintiff's orchestra were labeled "sold for home use only . . . not licensed for radio broadcast." Defendant broadcast them anyhow. Plaintiff sued for an injunction on an unfair competition theory, also claiming an equitable servitude on the phonograph records arising from the label notice. Injunction was *denied.* [**RCA Manufacturing Co. v. Whiteman**, 114 F.2d 86 (2d Cir. 1940); *but see* **Waring v. WDAS Broadcasting Station, Inc.**, 194 A. 631 (Pa. 1937)—contra]

Example: A community antenna company relayed to its customers television broadcasts picked up from regular stations. A television station sued to enjoin; relief was *denied.* [**Cable Vision, Inc. v. KUTV, Inc.**, 335 F.2d 348 (9th Cir. 1964)]

Example: Even in New York, where the misappropriation theory is frequently applied, the line was drawn in **Dior v. Milton,** 9 Misc. 2d 425 (1956). The court there refused to enjoin Milton's publication of Dior's designs for women's clothes (the "Dior look" and the "new look"). *Rationale:* To enjoin such designs would give monopoly protection to a "mere idea." However, the court pointed out that if persons attending preshowings of fashion expressly or impliedly *agree* to keep the designs confidential, equity may act to enjoin disclosure of the designs. In such cases, equitable jurisdiction is based on the *breach of trust and confidence*, rather than on any "misappropriation" of a property right.

4. **Constitutional Limitations on "Misappropriation" Approach—the *Sears-Compco* Decisions [§616]**

    Where the "misappropriation" consists solely of *copying nonpatentable* designs or characteristics of a competitor's product, no relief can be granted under state unfair competition laws. *Rationale:* To enjoin such copying would **conflict with the purpose of the patent laws**—which is to provide a legally protected monopoly only where the design or characteristic meets certain requirements of novelty, etc. Thus, if the plaintiff's design or product is not patentable under federal law, it is not protectable under state unfair competition laws unless deliberate "passing off" is shown. [**Sears, Roebuck & Co. v. Stiffel Co.**, 376 U.S. 225 (1964); **Compco Corp. v. Day Brite Lighting Inc.**, 376 U.S. 234 (1964)] This rule applies with equal force to products covered by an expired patent. [**Ives Laboratories, Inc. v. Darby Drug Co.**, 601 F.2d 631 (2d Cir. 1979)]

    ---

    e.g.　**Example:** Stiffel manufactured lighting fixtures. Sears sold lamps that duplicated the ornamental features found on Stiffel's lamps. There was *no "passing off"* (*see* below), as the fixtures carried Sears's mark. The Supreme Court held that even if Sears had deliberately copied ("appropriated") Stiffel's design, there was no relief available. *"A design not entitled to federal statutory protection can be copied at will."* [**Sears, Roebuck & Co. v. Stiffel Co.**, *supra; and see* **Bonito Boats v. Thundercraft Boats**, 489 U.S. 141 (1989)—Florida law protecting an unpatented boat design preempted by federal patent law]

    ---

    e.g.　**Example:** Mash claimed that C.B.S.'s television series about John Dillinger infringed on his copyrighted story and also constituted a common law misappropriation. The misappropriation claim was rejected by the court on the grounds of federal preemption by the Federal Copyright Act. [**Mash v. C.B.S., Inc.**, 704 F. Supp. 823 (N.D. Ill. 1989), *aff'd*, 899 F.2d 1537 (7th Cir. 1990)]

    ---

    a. **Distinguish—trade secrets [§617]**

        State *trade secret* laws have been upheld, however, because their purpose is **not** in conflict with the federal patent laws. Their purpose is to remedy breaches of confidence or trust, not to protect unpatentable designs generally. [*See* **Kewanee Oil Co. v. Bicron Corp.**, *supra*, §554]

    b. **Distinguish—"passing off" cases [§618]**

        As *Sears* and *Compco* both made clear, state unfair competition laws are not preempted where "palming off" or "passing off" is shown (marketing the product so as to make it appear that the defendant's product is the plaintiff's). This is not a matter of protecting unpatentable designs, but rather is a legitimate exercise of the state's police power to prevent confusion in the marketplace. [**Ives Laboratories, Inc. v. Darby Drug Co.**, *supra*]

    c. **Distinguish—"misappropriation of the product itself" [§619]**

        Furthermore, state unfair competition laws may be properly invoked to protect "misappropriation" of the product itself, as distinguished from a mere copying of its nonpatentable design characteristics.

---

e.g. **Example:** A television station telecast local news by reading verbatim from columns of a local newspaper. The court treated this as "piracy" of a "property" right. *Sears* and *Compco* were not applicable because they were concerned with *copying* an unpatentable product; whereas here the defendant has *misappropriated* the *product* itself. [**Pottstown Daily News Publishing Co. v. Pottstown Broadcasting Co.**, 247 F. Supp. 578 (E.D. Pa. 1965)—court relied on **International News Service v. Associated Press**, *supra*, §613]

---

cf. **Compare:** Motorola developed pagers that would provide customers real-time information about professional basketball games. The National Basketball Association ("NBA") brought suit against Motorola claiming, among other things, misappropriation under the New York privacy statute. The court held that much of New York's misappropriation law has been preempted by amendments to the Copyright Act. While it held that claims for misappropriation of "hot news" are not preempted, such claims are limited to cases in which the plaintiff can show: (i) the plaintiff generated or gathered information at a cost; (ii) the information is time-sensitive; (iii) the defendant's use of the information constitutes free riding on the plaintiff's efforts; (iv) the defendant is in direct competition with a product or service offered by the plaintiffs; and (v) the ability of other parties to free-ride on the efforts of the plaintiff or others would so reduce the incentive to produce the product or service that its existence or quality would be substantially threatened. The court concluded that the NBA did not meet the test here. [**National Basketball Association v. Motorola, Inc.**, 105 F.3d 841 (2d Cir. 1997)]

K. Performers' Remedies for Misappropriation of Right of Publicity

1. Nature of Right [§620]

Modern law recognizes a "property" right in a celebrity's name or likeness; *i.e.*, there is a commercial value surrounding the celebrity's image which is her stock in trade, and which the celebrity alone is entitled to exploit. Therefore, if a person uses a celebrity's name or likeness without the celebrity's consent, appropriate legal and equitable remedies are usually granted. But there are some cases to the contrary. [*See* **Carson v. National Bank of Commerce Trust & Savings**, 501 F.2d 1082 (8th Cir. 1974)—denying damages to Johnny Carson for the use of his name and picture since "misappropriation" theory was not recognized in Nebraska] A celebrity may also have a remedy under the Lanham Act (and possibly the New York

Civil Rights Act) if there is a "likelihood of consumer confusion." [**Allen v. National Video, Inc.,** 610 F. Supp. 612 (S.D.N.Y. 1985)—Defendant, a look-alike, portrayed Woody Allen in an advertisement]

a. "Right of privacy" [§621]

Frequently, this is called a "right of privacy," but it is distinct from that variety of the right of privacy discussed *infra,* §§684-701, which deals with the *right to be let alone* and which belongs to celebrity and noncelebrity alike.

(1) Noncelebrities [§622]

If the name or likeness of a noncelebrity is used, the interest involved is personal privacy and the preferred remedy is for *damages* for the invasion of the right to be let alone (mental suffering; *see infra,* §§693-695), plus an *injunction* against future invasions.

(2) Celebrities [§623]

If the name or likeness of a celebrity is used, the interest involved is in the nature of *diversion of income.* The celebrity wishes to prevent the defendant from cashing in on her saleable image. The preferred remedy would be an accounting for profits, or the reasonable value of the "property" interest misappropriated—*i.e.,* a quasi-contractual recovery in the nature of a royalty. The celebrity is not really desirous of stopping the publicity, but rather is interested in preventing anyone else from cashing in on it. (The closest analogy to such a claim is in the nature of patent or copyright infringement.)

2. Statutory Rights and Remedies [§624]

In several states, the right of publicity is protected by statute. [*See, e.g.,* N.Y. Civ. Rights Law §50 (captioned "Right of Privacy")—prohibits anyone from using the name or picture of a *living person* (celebrity or noncelebrity) for *advertising or trade purposes,* without that person's permission]

a. "Advertising or trade purposes" [§625]

Practically any commercial exploitation of the plaintiff's name or likeness may suffice. For example, the statute has been held to apply to the publication of a flattering but unauthorized (and inaccurate) biography of a baseball player. [**Spahn v. Julian Messner, Inc.,** 21 N.Y.2d 124 (1967)]

---

e.g. **Example:** Plaintiff made a television commercial advertising defendant's product. Following the expiration of the contract, defendant continued to use the commercial. An award of $1,000 compensatory and $15,000 punitive damages was affirmed. [**Welch v. Mr. Christmas Inc.,** 57 N.Y.2d 143 (1982)]

---

cf. **Compare:** Woody Allen brought an action against a clothing store for using a celebrity look-alike in its advertising. The court refused to grant relief under the state statute [N.Y. Civ. Rights Law §§50-51] because Allen's picture was not actually used. However, the court did find sufficient consumer confusion to grant injunctive relief under the provisions of the Lanham Act. [**Allen v. Men's World Outlet,** 679 F. Supp. 360 (S.D.N.Y. 1988)]

---

cf. **Compare:** The use by "Sports Illustrated" magazine of a picture of Joe Namath in connection with advertisements for increased circulation did not come within the protection of the New York statute, because such use was deemed only incidental advertising of the news media itself. [**Namath v. Sports Illustrated,** 80 Misc. 2d 531 (1975)]

---

b. **Criminal sanctions [§626]**

Violation of a statute protecting the right of publicity is a *misdemeanor.*

c. **Civil remedies [§627]**

In addition to the criminal sanctions that may be imposed, the injured party may seek any of the following remedies for violation of the statute [N.Y. Civ. Rights Law §51]:

(1) **Injunction [§628]**

"An equitable action" will lie (*i.e.,* an injunction).

(2) **Damages [§629]**

The plaintiff may also recover "damages sustained by reason of" the unauthorized use of her name and likeness.

(a) *Where a noncelebrity is involved,* this would authorize damages measured by *injury to feelings* (right to be let alone); *see infra,* §§693-695.

(b) *But where a celebrity is involved,* this authorizes recovery of "compensatory damages" measured by the interference with the celebrity's right to exploit his own image—*i.e.,* a genuine *diversion of trade.* [*See* **Spahn v. Julian Messner, Inc.,** *supra*—Plaintiff was entitled to $10,000 to reflect lost income from Plaintiff's planned autobiography; *and see* **Gautier v. Pro-Football, Inc.,** 278 App. Div. 431 (1951)]

(3) **Exemplary damages [§630]**

Exemplary damages are also authorized if the statutory violation is found to have been "knowing." [*See* **Rosenberg v. Lee's Carpet & Furniture Warehouse Outlet, Inc.,** 80 Misc. 2d 479 (1974)—exemplary damages may be awarded not only by a jury, but also by a judge in a non-jury trial]

(4) Analysis [§631]

The remedies provided under the New York statute do *not* include a quasi-contract action or restitutionary recovery for the *benefits derived* by the defendant which, under some circumstances, might be the most desirable remedy for the plaintiff (*see* below).

3. Nonstatutory Protection of Right of Publicity [§632]

Even where no statutory action is authorized, courts may be willing to grant relief against interference with a celebrity's right of publicity. These cases proceed on the *"misappropriation of a property right"* theory, recognizing the celebrity's right of publicity as sufficient "property" for legal and equitable relief. [*See, e.g.*, **Michaels v. Internet Entertainment Group**, 5 F. Supp. 2d 823 (D. Cal. 1998)—the Pamela Anderson videotape]

Example: Major league baseball players formed an Association to represent them in connection with commercial use of their names and baseball statistics. The Association charged a set price (minimum $2,500) for such commercial use. Without paying the license fee demanded by the Association, defendant marketed a table game using the names and statistics of major league players. Injunctive relief was granted. [**Uhlaender v. Henricksen,** 316 F. Supp. 1277 (D. Minn. 1970)—celebrity has a "legitimate, proprietary interest in his public personality"]

Example: Shaklee Corp. used the name and likeness of Heloise Bowles, author of the column "Hints from Heloise," in an advertising campaign. For this misappropriation, the court awarded $75,000 damages as the value of the endorsement and use of Heloise's name. The court in addition awarded $75,000 for invasion of privacy and $35,000 for exemplary damages. [**National Bank of Commerce v. Shaklee Corp.,** 503 F. Supp. 533 (W.D. Tex. 1980)]

Example: Defendant used the name "Here's Johnny" on its portable toilets. This was held to be an invasion of Johnny Carson's right of publicity, and $31,661 in damages were awarded. A prohibitory injunction was also granted. [**Carson v. Here's Johnny Portable Toilets, Inc.,** 698 F.2d 831 (6th Cir. 1983), 810 F.2d 104 (6th Cir. 1987)]

a. Protection not limited by public disclosure [§633]

Although the facts and figures regarding a celebrity may be readily available and fully disclosed to the public (*e.g.,* sports statistics), this does *not* justify a defendant making commercial use of the facts without the celebrity's consent. Again, it is the *misappropriation* of the celebrity's right of publicity that is actionable. [**Uhlaender v. Henricksen,** *supra*]

b. Protection not limited by fact that celebrity is not exploiting public image [§634]

Nor is the right to relief affected by the fact that the celebrity is not presently capitalizing on her own name or image. This is no justification for the defendant's doing so. The celebrity may desire to fill the void later on. [**Palmer v. Schornhorn Enterprises, Inc.,** 232 A.2d 458 (N.J. 1967)]

c. **Does protection of right of publicity survive death of celebrity? [§635]**
It is presently unclear whether the "property" concept underlying the right of publicity is such that the *heirs or descendants* of the celebrity can enforce the right which the celebrity could have enforced had she lived.

Example—Bela Lugosi: The decedent had starred in a series of "Count Dracula" movies and had thereby established a public image of himself as "Dracula." After his death, the defendant (which had the distribution rights on the movies, but nothing else) licensed various manufacturers to use the name "Dracula" on shirts, cards, games, Halloween masks, etc. Lugosi's widow and children brought suit. The trial court held that the decedent's right in his image as "Count Dracula" was a "property" right that *descended under his will* to the legatees of his estate, and that it was protectable by remedies of an *accounting* for profits and an *injunction* against any additional exploitation of the "Dracula" name without the permission of the decedent's heirs. [**Lugosi v. Universal Pictures,** 172 U.S.P.Q. 541 (1972)] However, the trial court's decision in the *Lugosi* case was overturned by an intermediate appellate court [70 Cal. 3d 552 (1977)], and that reversal was sustained by the California Supreme Court, which held that the right to exploit a name or likeness is personal and must be exercised in an artist's lifetime [**Lugosi v. Universal Pictures,** 25 Cal. 3d 813 (1979)].

Example—Al Capone: In a case raising similar issues, the court held that no cause of action existed in favor of the heirs of gangster Al Capone for the unauthorized use of his name, likeness, and personality in the television series "The Untouchables." The court held that under state law (Illinois), the right of action was "personal" to the celebrity and did *not* survive his death. [**Maritote v. Desilu Productions,** 230 F. Supp. 721 (N.D. Ill. 1964)]

Compare—Elvis Presley: Several cases involved attempts commercially to exploit deceased singer Elvis Presley's likeness through the sale of souvenir merchandise bearing that likeness. One case held that Elvis Presley's right of publicity *survived* his death because it had been exploited contractually during his life. [**Factors, etc. Inc. v. Pro Arts, Inc.,** 579 F.2d 215 (2d Cir. 1978), *cert. denied,* 440 U.S. 908 (1979); *and see* **Estate of Presley v. Russen,** 513 F. Supp. 1339 (D.N.J. 1981)—right of publicity survived and became part of Presley's estate] The distinction between Capone and Presley is that Presley created in his lifetime a commercially exploitable characterization as an entertainer. Capone's career was of a somewhat different order. However, **Memphis Development Foundation v. Factors, etc. Inc.,** 616 F.2d 956 (6th Cir. 1980) ruled to the contrary, holding that "right of publicity should not be given the status of a devisable right, even where, as here, a person exploits the right by contract during life." Note, however, that in a later case filed in Tennessee, the court held that under Tennessee state law, the right of publicity did descend. [**State** *ex rel.* **Elvis Presley International Memorial Foundation v. Crowell**, 733 S.W.2d 89 (Tenn. App. 1987)]

EXAM TIP   **gilbert**

If an exam fact pattern includes facts showing that a person is making money by exploiting a *deceased celebrity's public image*, be sure to note that *cases are split*. Few courts would likely find any kind of protectable right in a notorious criminal image. But even where a celebrity expended efforts to create a legitimate and exploitable public image during his life, the courts are split—some courts hold that the right ends with the celebrity's life, and some courts hold that it continues on to the celebrity's estate and heirs.

---

d. **No federal preemption of state laws [§636]**

It now appears that state laws protecting a celebrity's right of publicity are *not* preempted by federal law under the rationale of the *Sears* and *Compco* cases (*see supra*, §§616-619). A defendant's unauthorized exploitation of a celebrity's name or likeness is in effect a "misappropriation of the product itself." [*See* **Bi-Rite Enterprises v. Button Master**, 555 F. Supp. 1188 (S.D.N.Y. 1983)]

(1) **Caveat**

A player's performance in a baseball game is within the scope of the player's employment. Thus, the club's copyright of the broadcast of the game does, in this respect, preempt the player's right of publicity. [**Baltimore Orioles v. Major League Baseball Players**, 805 F.2d 663 (7th Cir. 1986)]

e. **Distinguish—mimicry and imitation [§637]**

A number of cases have refused to apply the rules against commercial exploitation of a celebrity's name or likeness to instances of mimicry of the celebrity's performance. [*See, e.g.,* **Sinatra v. Goodyear Tire & Rubber Co.**, 435 F.2d 711 (9th Cir. 1970)—singer on commercial imitated voice of Nancy Sinatra and sang song identified with her; **Shaw v. Time-Life Records**, 38 N.Y.2d 201 (1975)—copying musical arrangements of Artie Shaw] Many of these cases have relied on *Sears* and *Compco* as well as the lack of a protectable property interest. However, recent decisions show a *trend toward recognizing a cause of action*. [*See* **Allen v. National Video, Inc.**, *supra*, §620; **Midler v. Ford Motor Co.** 849 F.2d 460 (9th Cir. 1988)]

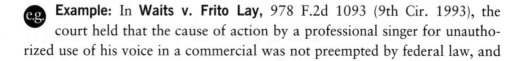 **Example:** In **Waits v. Frito Lay**, 978 F.2d 1093 (9th Cir. 1993), the court held that the cause of action by a professional singer for unauthorized use of his voice in a commercial was not preempted by federal law, and

allowed damages for misappropriation under state law in the amount of $375,000, including fair market value of services, injury to feelings, and injury to professional standing. The court also awarded $1.5 million in punitive damages against the ad agency, and $500,000 against the agency's client. However, overlapping damages under the Lanham Act were denied.

(1) Note

To the extent that an imitation is unflattering or derogatory, a defamation action is possible, but the plaintiff must meet the stringent standards mandated by *Gertz* and *Greenmoss*, *infra*, §§663-669. [*See* **Dworkin v. Hustler Magazine**, 867 F.2d 1188 (9th Cir. 1989)]

4. No Right of Publicity in Works of Art [§638]

Under United States law (contrary to European law), a painter or sculptor who sells the physical embodiment of her talent—painting, sculpture, etc.—thereafter has no protectable rights in the commercial exploitation of the "performance." Absent agreement (*see* below), any further right of publicity belongs to the person who purchased the work in question.

a. Artists' reservation of rights [§639]

However, artists can protect their right of publicity by *agreement* with the purchaser, specifically reserving the right to commercial exploitation of the work sold (*e.g.*, the right to make copies, photographs, etc.). Such contracts are valid and are sometimes held to create "*equitable servitudes*" or restrictive covenants on the artistic work in question, so as to be enforceable not only against the original purchaser, but against subsequent owners who acquire the work *with knowledge* of the artist's reservation of rights.

b. Statutory royalties [§640]

Although not literally a protection of artists' rights in items they have sold, statutes may afford artists a share in the increased value of their works. Thus, California Code section 986 gives an artist a *royalty* of 5% of the resale price at which her work is sold. Sales of less than $1,000 and those made after the death of the artist are exempt.

L. Remedies for Product Disparagement—Trade Defamation

1. Damages

a. Special damages required as element of substantive cause of action [§641]

Pecuniary damages must be pleaded and proved as an element of the cause of action for product disparagement. (This is unlike personal defamation, in which general damages for loss of reputation may be recoverable; *see infra*, §§652 *et seq.*)

(1) But note

Occasionally, the difficulty is overcome by pleading that the alleged defamation of the product also reflects on the *personal character* of the manufacturer. For example, Dagmar says, "Pia's hamburgers are advertised as beef but are made with horse meat." This implies that Pia is a liar and may be actionable as *defamation* without proof of special damage.

b. What constitutes recoverable damages [§642]

The special damages must consist of *loss of trade*, and the traditional rule requires pleading and proof of loss of *particular customers*.

(1) Effect [§643]

Under modern business circumstances, proving loss of trade is difficult at best, and absolutely impossible in a new business.

(2) Liberalized pleading [§644]

Recognizing this difficulty, many courts have liberalized the *pleading* requirements to permit a general allegation of loss of business, supported by facts indicating loss of sales as the natural and probable consequence of the wrong, together with facts showing why the plaintiff cannot name specific customers. [**Erick Bowman Remedy Co. v. Jensen-Salsberg Laboratories**, 17 F. 255 (8th Cir. 1926); *but see* **El Greco Leather Products Co. v. Shoe World**, 623 F. Supp. 1038 (E.D.N.Y. 1985)—"special damages must be alleged with sufficient particularity to identify actual losses"] However, even where the pleading requirement is liberalized, most courts still require *proof at trial* of loss of *particular* customers.

(a) Criticism

This proof requirement is often difficult to satisfy. Evidence of loss of specific customers is not easily obtainable in practice, or, if obtainable, hardly likely to be asked for as a matter of customer relations. [*See* **Continental Nut Co. v. Robert L. Berner Co.**, 315 F.2d 283 (7th Cir. 1968); *but see* **Advance Training Systems v. Caswell Equipment Co.**, 352 N.W.2d 1 (Minn. 1984)—if plaintiff cannot show loss of specific sales, a general decline in business resulting from disparagement is sufficient]

(3) Consequential damages [§645]

If the cause of action can be established by proof of special damages, the injured party may also recover for other consequential damages caused by the defamatory statement.

2. Equitable Remedies—Injunction

a. Early view—no injunctive relief [§646]

Although the remedy of damages for product disparagement is markedly inadequate, the earlier equity cases were concerned with censorship and "free speech" and therefore denied jurisdiction to enjoin *any* defamation, trade as well as personal. [**Hicks Corp. v. National Training Association**, 19 F.2d 963 (7th Cir. 1927)]

b. Exception where separate enjoinable tort proved [§647]

The majority of reported cases accept a modification of the rule against injunctive relief where the trade defamation is part of an *overall enjoinable tort*—typically, unfair competition. In such cases, the trade defamation may be enjoined as *part* of the overall conduct that is otherwise held to be a basis for equitable relief.

c. Modern trend [§648]

Under recent decisions, the blanket rule denying injunctive relief is being rejected, as is the requirement that the trade libel be shown to be part of some other enjoinable tort. Rather, the trend today is that injunctive relief may be granted against a trade libel as such, where the remedy at law is clearly inadequate, and the *encroachment on "free speech" is outweighed by the harm* that might be done if injunctive relief is denied. [**Martin v. Reynolds Metals Co.**, 224 F. Supp. 978 (D. Or. 1963)—Defendant posted signs on his property, adjacent to public highway, falsely claiming that air pollution "from Reynolds Metal Co. killed 831 of my cattle . . . endangers human health"; injunction granted requiring removal of signs]

(1) Trade defamations by customers of product [§649]

In former years, courts refrained from granting injunctive relief for trade defamations by customers of a product (*e.g.*, Dana paints on the side of her car, "I purchased this lemon from Page"), partly out of concern for "free speech," and partly because there was no competition between the plaintiff and defendant, and hence no separately enjoinable tort. While the cases are still divided, more and more courts recognize that the trade disparagement may be enjoinable by itself, particularly where a damages action would be inadequate and no legitimate interest would be served by allowing the libel to continue. [*See, e.g.*, **Schmoldt v. Oakley**, 390 P.2d 882 (Okla. 1964); *but see* **Hajek v. Bill Mowbray Motors**, 647 S.W.2d 253 (Tex. 1983); **Degroen v. Mark Toyota-Volvo**, 811 P.2d 443 (Colo. 1991)—injunctions refused on free speech grounds]

(2) Trade defamations by omission [§650]

Relief has been granted both for affirmative defamations and "*defamations by omission*." For example, Desi publishes a list of "all the good eating places in San Jose," and excludes Pancho's restaurant from the list, thereby disparaging Pancho's business. Or, Radio Co. broadcasts the "top 10 tunes of the week," omitting Prema's tune which is in fact one of the top 10 sellers. [**Advance Music Corp. v. American Tobacco Co.**, 268 App. Div. 707 (1945)—omission is actionable as a "prima facie tort," under New York tort law]

(a) Nature of injunctive relief

1) Where the omission reflects merely a *matter of judgment* (*i.e.,* whether the plaintiff's restaurant *is* one of the "good eating places in San Jose"), the sole relief granted would probably be to require a disclaimer on the published list—*e.g.,* to the effect that the list does not purport to be exhaustive.

2) But where the omission reflects a *factual disparagement* (*i.e.,* that the plaintiff's tune was not among the "top 10" in sales), a *mandatory* injunction to *include* the plaintiff's product may be appropriate, particularly if it can be shown that the omission could not be rectified in damages or by a prohibitory injunction against future publications continuing the same omission.

(3) False advertising [§651]

Injunctive relief has also been granted when false advertising impinges on the products of others.

Example: In **American Brands, Inc. v. R.J. Reynolds Tobacco Co.**, 413 F. Supp. 1352 (S.D.N.Y. 1976), plaintiff alleged that defendant falsely advertised its cigarettes as lowest in tar when, in fact, plaintiff's cigarettes had a lower tar content. The court held that a claim was stated for injunctive relief under the Lanham Act and entered a decree ordering defendant to "paint out" all such representations on billboards and to withdraw any material which included such words.

Example: In **U-Haul International Inc. v. Jartran, Inc.**, 793 F.2d 1034 (9th Cir. 1986), the court invoked the extraordinary remedy section of the Lanham Act for false comparative advertising to issue an injunction plus damages of $6 million for the cost of defendant's advertising, plus $13.6 million for plaintiff's corrective advertising costs, which, when doubled, amounted to almost $40 million.

Chapter Seven: Injuries To Personal Dignity and Related Interests

---

CONTENTS

Chapter Approach

This chapter discusses the various injuries to a person's dignity. For most exam questions concerning these topics, the principal problem is whether plaintiff has a *legally protected interest*. If you can establish such an interest, the normal remedy is a mandatory or prohibitory *injunction*. (The remedy at law is inadequate because damages are necessarily speculative and conjectural.)

Note: There is one special case where injunction is *not* the appropriate remedy. In the case of *defamation*, the sole remedy is generally *damages*; the injunction is usually precluded by free speech considerations. If you are faced with a defamation examination question, you should:

1.   Classify the utterance as libel or slander;

2.   Determine whether there are sufficient facts to establish an actionable claim for relief; and

3.   Consider the elements making up the damages.

A. Defamation

1. Substantive Elements [§652]
Defamation protects the interest in one's personal reputation. It consists of the twin torts of slander and libel, slander being oral and libel being written defamation.

EXAM TIP	gilbert

Language is important to lawyers, and probably to your professor as well, so you don't want to use the wrong terminology in an essay answer dealing with defamation. To keep libel and slander straight, just remember the "S" mnemonic: **S**lander is **S**poken.

a. Defamations "actionable per se" [§653]
At common law, *all libel is actionable per se*, which means that general damages may be recovered without proof of pecuniary loss. *Slander*, on the other hand, is not actionable without proof of *"special damages,"* which means that pecuniary loss must be shown. *Exceptions* are made where the slanderous statement (i) imputes a serious crime, (ii) imputes a loathsome disease, or (iii) discredits a person in his trade or profession. Some jurisdictions add a

fourth category, the imputation of unchastity to a woman. Slanderous statements that fall within these four categories are actionable per se (*i.e.*, without proof of special damages). [**Hoagburg v. Harrah's Marina Hotel,** 585 F. Supp. 1167 (D.N.J. 1984)—accusation that Plaintiff was a "card counter" not slanderous per se]

Example: Dahlia interrupted the filming of a television commercial, calling Pavel, a used car dealer, a "son of a bitch." *Held:* Special damages need *not* be pleaded or proved. The defamatory imputation of the words "son of a bitch" was established by extrinsic facts, and since those words affect Pavel in his business of selling cars, special damages need not be proved. [**White v. Valenta,** 234 Cal. App. 2d 243 (1965)]

CHECKLIST OF CATEGORIES OF SLANDER PER SE   **gilbert**

SLANDER ACTIONS REQUIRE PROOF OF DAMAGES UNLESS THE SLANDER FALLS WITHIN ONE OF THE FOLLOWING CATEGORIES:

- ☑ Imputation of a *serious crime*;
- ☑ Imputation of a *loathsome disease*;
- ☑ Discreditation of a person in his *trade or profession*;
- ☑ *Unchastity* of a woman (in some jurisdictions).

(1) Confusion of "actionable per se" with "defamatory per se" [§654]

The doctrine allowing recovery for defamations without proof of special damages ("actionable per se") has been modified in a *minority* of states to require proof of special damages if a *written* statement is not "defamatory per se" (*i.e.*, defamatory on its face). This latter rule stipulates that if a written statement was *innocent on its face*, and its defamatory implication became apparent only by connection with *extrinsic* factors ("libel per quod"), special damages had to be shown.

Example: Dante writes a letter to Kant falsely stating that Marx has given birth to a child; this is innocent on its face, but becomes defamatory if it appears that Marx is an unmarried woman and Kant knows this. [*See* **White v. Valenta,** *supra*; **Rannels v. S.E. Nichols, Inc.,** 591 F.2d 242 (3d Cir. 1979)]

(a) Rationale

Proponents of this minority rule argue that it prevents liability without fault. Statements not defamatory on their face might be published in good faith by a defendant who is entirely without fault. In such cases, there should be no liability without proof of special harm.

(b) Comment

The justification for this minority rule appears to have largely disappeared as a result of several Supreme Court decisions (discussed below) which require *proof of fault* before a defendant can be held liable for a defamatory publication. [*See* Rest. 2d Torts §569]

b. Constitutional limitations [§655]

"Free speech" considerations have been invoked to restrict defamation actions in several important regards:

(1) Defamation of public official and public figure—"malice" requirement [§656]

No action may be maintained on account of a defamation of a "public official" or "public figure," unless it is shown that the falsehood was published with "malice"—which here means *knowledge* of its falsity or with *reckless disregard* for whether or not it was true. [**New York Times Co. v. Sullivan,** 376 U.S. 254 (1964); **Hunt v. Liberty Lobby,** 720 F.2d 631 (11th Cir. 1983)]

(2) Defamation of private citizens [§657]

In **Gertz v. Robert Welch, Inc.,** 418 U.S. 323 (1974), the United States Supreme Court held that a defamation action brought by a private citizen against a magazine could not be maintained unless the defendant was *at least negligent* with regard to the falsity of the statement (*i.e.,* no strict liability for such defamations).

(a) Note

While *Gertz* involved defamation by the communications media, it was thought that the fault requirement would also be carried over to defamation actions brought against private individuals (*i.e.,* nonmedia defendants). [*See* Rest. 2d Torts §580B, comment c]

(b) But note

More recently, the Supreme Court declared that the distinguishing feature of *Gertz* was not that the defendant was part of the communications media, but rather that the alleged defamatory statements involved matters of *public concern.* [**Dun & Bradstreet, Inc. v. Greenmoss Builders, Inc.,** 472 U.S. 749 (1985); *see infra,* §§667 et seq.] In fact, Justice White, in a concurring opinion in *Dun & Bradstreet,* concluded that the decision implies that the fault requirement of *Gertz* is inapplicable in cases like *Dun & Bradstreet,* where the defamation involves only private matters.

2. **General Damages [§658]**

At common law, where the defamation is *actionable per se*, general damages are *presumed*; *i.e.*, the defamed party is *presumed* to have suffered injury to reputation, humiliation, and mental suffering as a proximate result of the defamation. As a result, substantial damages may be awarded at the discretion of the jury *even in the absence of any proof of actual pecuniary loss.*

a. **Relevant factors [§659]**

Factors considered in establishing general damages include the *extent of the circulation* of the defamatory statement and its *permanence*; the *reputation* and standing of the plaintiff; the *effect on people* who learned about the statement; and the *defendant's own reputation* in the community. [**Hogan v. New York Times Co.**, 211 F. Supp. 99 (D. Conn. 1962)]

(1) **Mitigation [§660]**

The defendant may offer in mitigation evidence establishing that the plaintiff's reputation for the trait involved was already a bad one. Also, proof of *good faith and retraction mitigates* compensatory damages and refutes any basis for punitive damages (below). Statutes in some states provide that prompt retraction by the defendant limits the plaintiff's recovery to actual pecuniary loss (*i.e.*, special damages).

b. **Constitutional limitations in actions against news media [§661]**

There are often vital First Amendment considerations (free speech and press) affected by awards of damages in defamation cases. The concern is that unrestricted damages could be used to punish unpopular expressions. Accordingly, the Supreme Court has imposed the following limitations:

(1) **Public officials [§662]**

As previously mentioned, no action lies for defamation of a public official or public figure unless the *plaintiff shows knowledge or reckless disregard* (malice).

(2) **Private citizen actions—Gertz v. Robert Welch [§663]**

As noted above, *Gertz* held that a private citizen in an action against the media cannot recover without proof of fault (at least negligence). The Court further limited any award of damages in these cases to *actual injury*.

(a) **"Actual injury" [§664]**

"Actual injury" is not limited to pecuniary loss. Recovery for reputational harm and personal humiliation is proper, but any such award must be supported by "competent evidence"; *i.e., there can be no presumed damages.*

(b) **Proof of malice [§665]**

If the plaintiff successfully establishes that the defendant acted with knowledge of the falsity or with reckless disregard of its truth, *Gertz* implied that presumed damages and punitive *are* recoverable.

(c) Effect of *Gertz* [§666]

Because *Gertz* involved defamation by a magazine, there was disagreement as to whether the limitation on presumed damages would be restricted to cases involving the news media.

(3) Private citizen actions—Dun & Bradstreet v. Greenmoss Builders [§667]

In **Dun & Bradstreet, Inc. v. Greenmoss Builders, Inc.** (*supra,* §657), a construction contractor sought damages for injuries to its reputation resulting from the publication of a false credit report by Dun & Bradstreet. The Supreme Court, by a plurality vote, ruled that the plaintiff could recover both *presumed and punitive* damages *without* proof of malice. [*See also* **Crump v. P & C Food Markets, Inc.,** 576 A.2d 441 (Vt. 1990)—presumed and punitive damages recoverable where defamation concerns private issue; **Snead v. Redland Aggregates,** 998 F.2d 1325 (5th Cir. 1993)—under Texas law presumed damages support punitive damage award but nominal damages do not]

(a) Limitation on *Gertz* [§668]

The plurality in *Dun & Bradstreet* ruled that *Gertz* applies only to situations where the alleged defamatory statement involves matters of *general public importance and concern.* Since the plaintiff in *Dun & Bradstreet,* unlike the plaintiff in *Gertz,* complained only about a matter of private concern (a false credit report), no special First Amendment protection was needed.

(b) Media vs. nonmedia defendants—distinction relevant? [§669]

In resolving the scope of First Amendment protection in *Dun & Bradstreet,* Justice Powell's majority opinion drew no distinction between media and nonmedia defendants. Both Justice White in his concurring opinion and Justice Brennan in his dissent explicitly rejected the suggestion that the First Amendment gives greater protection to the media than it does to others in exercising rights of free speech. However, in a later case [**Philadelphia Newspapers, Inc. v. Hepps,** 475 U.S. 767 (1986)—holding that when the allegedly libelous matter was of public interest, the plaintiff bears the burden of proof on falsity], the Court specifically declined to state whether the rule developed there would apply to nonmedia defendants. This case leaves uncertain the relevance of the distinction between media and nonmedia defendants.

(c) And note

In *Dun & Bradstreet* Justice White also suggested that the fault

FAULT AND DAMAGES RULES IN CONSTITUTIONAL DEFAMATION ACTIONS

gilbert

TYPE OF PLAINTIFF/ DEFAMATION	FAULT REQUIRED	DAMAGES RECOVERABLE
PUBLIC OFFICIAL OR PUBLIC FIGURE	*Actual malice* (knowledge of falsity or reckless disregard as to truth or falsity)	Presumed damages under common law rules and punitive damages where appropriate if other state law damage requirements are met (but some courts will not award punitive damages for fear of chilling First Amendment rights)
PRIVATE PERSON/ MATTER OF PUBLIC CONCERN	*At least negligence* as to statement's truth or falsity	Where plaintiff proves only negligence, damages are allowed only for proved "actual injury." Where plaintiff proves actual malice, presumed and punitive damages may be available if other state law damage requirements are met (but some courts will not award punitive damages for fear of chilling First Amendment rights)
PRIVATE PERSON/ MATTER OF PRIVATE CONCERN	*No fault* as to truth or falsity need be proved (suggested in concurring opinion of Justice White)	Presumed damages under common law rules and punitive damages where appropriate if other state law damage requirements are met (but some courts will not award punitive damages for fear of chilling First Amendment rights)

requirement of *Gertz* is inapplicable to cases where no issues of public concern are involved.

(4) Implication of *Dun & Bradstreet* [§670]

The opinions of the plurality in *Dun & Bradstreet* disclose dissatisfaction with the rationale of *Gertz* and a desire to curb the constitutionalizing of the common law of defamation. The extent of the erosion of the *Gertz* decision remains to be seen. (For a more extensive examination of the constitutional issues, *see* the Constitutional Law Summary.)

c. Constitutionality of punitive damages [§671]

There has been considerable uncertainty about the constitutionality of punitive damages in defamation actions, with conflicting decisions on the issue by federal district courts. The *Dun & Bradstreet* case, *supra*, resolves at least part of that uncertainty. In cases where a private citizen is suing for defamation not involving matters of public concern, an award of punitive damages does not violate the First Amendment.

(1) Free speech considerations [§672]

A number of lower courts have held that the freedom of speech guaranteed by the First Amendment is impermissibly "chilled" by the threat of large punitive damages awards which are *discretionary* with the jury and that may bear no direct relationship to any actual injury to the plaintiff. [*See, e.g.*, **Maheu v. Hughes Tool Co.**, 384 F. Supp. 166 (C.D. Cal. 1974); **Stone v. Essex County Newspapers, Inc.**, 330 N.E.2d 161 (Mass. 1975)—rejecting punitive damages in *any* defamation action whether based on negligence or reckless or willful conduct] Other lower court decisions are contra. [*See, e.g.*, **Davis v. Schuchat**, 510 F.2d 731 (D.C. Cir. 1975)—upholding punitive damages upon a finding of malice as long as the award "does not exceed the limits of propriety"; **DiSalle v. P.G. Publishing Co.**, 544 A.2d 1345 (Pa. 1988)—award of $2 million not excessive; persons who act in disregard of truth must accept risks of such conduct in the "free marketplace of ideas"]

3. Injunctions [§673]

It is well settled that injunctive relief is not available against *personal* defamation. In denying relief, the maxim "equity will not enjoin a libel" is frequently cited, but the reason for the rule is not always clearly articulated.

a. Rationales

(1) Damages are adequate [§674]

Some courts give the "adequacy" of the damages remedy as the reason for denying injunctive relief, but this is inaccurate; the payment of money is an inept remedy for the loss of reputation.

(2) Reputation is not "property" [§675]

Other courts rely on the outdated rule that "equity only protects property rights," and assert that a person's reputation is not "property." However, this rationale is also unconvincing. As shown earlier in this summary, equity frequently protects many intangible rights that hardly rise to the status of "property" (*e.g.,* intellectual property and ideas). Moreover, even where the defamation *does* affect "property" rights (as where a business or professional person is defamed—*e.g.,* calling a doctor a "quack"), injunctive relief is still refused. [**Gariepy v. Springer,** 48 N.E.2d 572 (Ill. 1943)—suit to enjoin defendant from calling lawyer plaintiff a "shyster"; injunction denied on the ground that "equity does not enjoin a libel"]

(3) Constitutional argument [§676]

It is submitted that the real basis for the general refusal to grant injunctive relief is the strong *public policy against prior restraints on speech—i.e.,* the rejection of any form of pre-publication censorship. [**Willing v. Mazzocone,** 393 A.2d 1155 (Pa. 1978)—injunction prohibiting defendant from carrying placard calling plaintiff law firm "thieves" reversed as an unconstitutional prior restraint; **Wilson v. Superior Court,** 13 Cal. 3d 652 (1975)—injunction prohibiting publication of election leaflets held to violate constitutional right of freedom of expression; *but see* **Bingham v. Struve,** 184 A.D.2d 85 (1992)—injunction granted against oral and written publication of accusation of rape]

(a) Limitation—strong and clear showing of harm [§677]

Public policy *may* be outweighed in appropriate cases, but it requires a strong and clear showing that the harm sought to be avoided by the injunction is of such major dimension as to justify the censorship.

Example: The United States sought to enjoin the publication of the "Pentagon Papers" by the defendant newspapers. The Court indicated that an injunction prohibiting such publication might be granted in the interest of national security, but held that the government had failed to establish by clear and convincing evidence that such interest was actually at stake. [**New York Times Co. v. United States,** 403 U.S. 713 (1972)]

(b) Limitation—part of other enjoinable conduct [§678]

Similarly, courts have recognized that where the defamatory expression is merely part of *other enjoinable conduct* (*e.g.,* intimidation, conspiracy, or unfair business competition), the injunction may be granted against slander or libel as *part* of the remedy for the other enjoinable act. (This is analogous to the rule in the trade disparagement cases, *supra*, §647.) [*See* **Murphy v. Daytona Beach Humane Society,** 176 So. 2d 922 (Fla. 1965)—denying injunction against defendant's claims that plaintiff had misused tax funds on grounds that "equity does not enjoin slander or libel in the absence of some independent basis of equity jurisdiction"]

(c) Limitation—prevention of repetition [§679]

Injunctive relief may also be granted to prevent future repetition of statements previously found to have been defamatory by the trial court. [**O'Brien v. University Community Tenants Union Inc.,** 327 N.E.2d 753 (Ohio 1975); *and see concurring opinion in* **Lothschuetz v. Carpenter,** 898 F.2d 1200 (6th Cir. 1990)]

EXAM TIP   **gilbert**

Be wary of a fact pattern raising the issue of enjoining defamatory speech. Your answer should point out that because of constitutional free speech concerns, courts generally will not grant such an injunction unless the plaintiff can make a *strong and clear showing* that the injunction is needed to avoid *great harm*, the defamatory expression is *part of some other enjoinable act*, or the injunction prohibits *repetition of speech* already found by a court to be defamatory.

---

b. Combined with declaratory relief [§680]

The Restatement (Second) of Torts suggests that injunctive relief may be appropriate *in conjunction with declaratory relief* to prevent repetition of a defamatory statement. The development of declaratory relief may prove to be the best remedy for protecting a person's reputation. [Rest. 2d Torts ch. 27—Special Note]

4. Mitigation [§681]

In many states, the defendant may mitigate damages by publishing a retraction of the defamatory statement. The Supreme Court has held, however, that a statute requiring a newspaper to publish a reply to criticisms or attacks is void as a violation of the First Amendment guarantee of a free press. [**Miami Herald Publishing Co. v. Tornillo,** 418 U.S. 241 (1974)]

5. Restitution [§682]

Most defamations result in detriment to the plaintiff (damage to reputation) with no corresponding gain or benefit to the defendant; hence, claims for restitution based on unjust enrichment of the defendant rarely arise.

a. No action for benefits to defendant [§683]

If the defendant *has* derived some economic gain or benefit from defaming the plaintiff, it would seem that the injured party should be permitted to "waive the tort" and sue in quasi-contract for restitution of such benefits. However, the few cases on point have *denied* any right to restitutionary relief.

Example: Page brought an action for money had and received seeking to recover the profits made by Delfina in publishing a libelous book about Page. The court denied recovery, asserting that the only remedy for libel is compensatory damages to Page's reputation. The court was concerned that the injured plaintiff might sit back while the publisher went to great efforts to produce profits, and then sue to compel the money to be paid over; this would be "too severe" a remedy. [**Hart v. E.P. Dutton & Co.**, 197 Misc. 274 (1949)]

B. Privacy

1. Substantive Elements [§684]

The right of privacy protects against unreasonable interference with a person's solitude or seclusion, the public disclosure of private facts, and the commercial exploitation of another's personality.

a. Application [§685]

The right of privacy can be invaded in various ways. Common illustrations include harassment by persistent suitors, private detectives, bill collectors, or photographers; electronic eavesdropping; the publication of private letters; and the public disclosure of facts about another's private life or affairs, such as illnesses, deformities, or a sordid past.

b. Distinguish—defamation [§686]

The tort of defamation protects a person's *reputation*. Privacy protects a person's "right to be let alone." In both types of cases, however, the injured party seeks recovery for humiliation and mental suffering.

c. Distinguish—right of publicity [§687]

The commercial exploitation of another's personality, the "right of publicity," is discussed *supra*, §§620 *et seq*.

d. Constitutional limitation [§688]

The right to be free from the publication of embarrassing details of one's private life must be reconciled with First Amendment rights.

(1) Public disclosure of private facts [§689]

The Supreme Court has held that no cause of action was stated against a television station for publishing on a news broadcast the true contents of a *public* record (in this case, the name of a rape victim). [**Cox Broadcasting Co. v. Cohn**, 420 U.S. 469 (1975)]

(a) Distinguish—private matters [§690]

Whether the truthful publication of private matters *not* of public interest or unrelated to public affairs may be constitutionally proscribed was left unanswered, and lower courts continue to recognize liability for this form of invasion of privacy. [*See, e.g.,* **Hendricksen v. California Newspapers Inc.**, 48 Cal. App. 3d 59 (1975)]

(2) "False light" cases [§691]

If the publicity places the injured party in a false light before the public, the plaintiff must show that the defendant *knew* that the matter published was false or offensive or it was published *in reckless disregard* thereof. [**Time, Inc. v. Hill,** 385 U.S. 374 (1967)—Broadway play based on a fictionalized account of plaintiff's experiences as a hostage of criminals]

Example: A newspaper feature story discussed the impact on a family resulting from the death of the father in a bridge collapse. The Court upheld a verdict for the plaintiff on the ground that the defendant had published the story knowing that the statements in it were false or made with reckless disregard of the truth. [**Cantrell v. Forest City Publishing Co.**, 419 U.S. 245 (1974)]

(a) But note

Concurring in the opinion in the *Cox Broadcasting Co.* case, *supra,* Justice Powell questioned whether the requirement of knowledge or reckless disregard of falsity enunciated in **Time, Inc. v. Hill** was constitutionally mandated following the decision in *Gertz* (*see supra,* §657), which permitted recovery for the negligent publication of a defamatory statement. Later cases indicate that the "malice" requirement will be retained, at least if the publication involves a public figure or a matter of public concern. [**Douglass v. Hustler Magazine,** 769 F.2d 1128 (7th Cir. 1985)]

(b) Restatement view

The Restatement (Second) of Torts section 652E takes no position as to whether recovery in false light cases might now be based on mere negligence.

(c) And note

When the false light invasion of privacy is based on language, the defamatory meaning of which does not appear on its face, special damages must be pleaded and proved. [**Fellows v. National Enquirer,** 42 Cal. 3d 234 (1986)]

e. No survival of action [§692]

It is clear that a claim for invasion of privacy based on public disclosure of embarrassing private facts does *not survive* the death of the injured party. [**Hendricksen v. California Newspapers**, *supra*; *and see supra*, §635—discussion of survival of claim based on invasion of right of publicity]

2. Damages [§693]

If a tortious invasion of the right of privacy is shown, the injured party may recover substantial damages for *mental anguish*, even without proof of any specific or pecuniary loss. [**Kinsey v. Macur**, 107 Cal. App. 3d 265 (1980)]

a. Measure of damages [§694]

No precise measure of damages exists for injuries of this sort. Assessment of the amount of compensation for the mental anguish is within the discretion of the trier of fact—just as in cases of defamation, intentional infliction of mental suffering, and malicious prosecution. [**Birnbaum v. United States**, 436 F. Supp. 967 (E.D.N.Y. 1977), *aff'd*, 588 F.2d 319 (2d Cir. 1978)]

b. Punitive damages [§695]

If proof supports a finding of malice in the sense of personal *ill will or reckless disregard of plaintiff's rights*, punitive damages may be assessed. [**Cantrell v. Forest City Publishing Co.**, *supra*; **Donnel v. Lara**, 703 S.W.2d 257 (Tex. 1985)—telephone harassment case in which award of $2 compensatory and $4,500 punitive damages was held proper and not excessive]

3. Injunction [§696]

If the invasion is a continuing one, injunctive relief is the most practical and effective remedy.

a. Protection of purely personal right [§697]

Earlier decisions declined to grant injunctive relief in privacy cases, supposedly on the basis that equity protects only "property" rights. Today, however, such reasoning is rejected outright by most courts. [**Hawks v. Yancy**, 265 S.W. 233 (Tex. 1924)—injunction to prevent rejected suitor from continuing to harass plaintiff; equity will protect purely personal rights because they "are infinitely more sacred and by every test are of more value than things that can be measured in dollars and cents"; **Kramer v. Downey**, 680 S.W.2d 524 (Tex. 1984)]

(1) Distinguish—First Amendment cases [§698]

If the invasion of privacy involves residential picketing or verbal harassment, the First Amendment rights of the defendant are involved. Thus, a court finding that a right of privacy has been invaded must nevertheless limit the injunction so as not to infringe on the defendant's right of free speech. [*See* **Valenzuela v. Aquino**, 763 S.W.2d 43 (Tex. 1988)—residential picketing; **Bachowski v. Salamone,** 407 N.W.2d 533 (Wis. 1987)—neighborhood squabble]

b. Adequacy of remedy at law [§699]
The availability of equitable relief now turns on the adequacy of legal damages. Except in cases of completed invasions, courts usually find money damages inadequate—because of the difficulty of assessing damages and because an award of money will not necessarily prevent repetition of the wrong.

Example: Galella, a freelance photographer, kept Jackie Onassis and her family under constant surveillance, following them everywhere they went and snapping photos in their faces. Injunctive relief was granted to prevent the continuing invasions of their privacy; Galella was ordered to approach no closer than 25 feet from Onassis and 30 feet from her children, and to desist "shadowing" them. [**Galella v. Onassis,** 487 F.2d 986 (2d Cir. 1973); **Galella v. Onassis,** 533 F. Supp. 1076 (S.D.N.Y. 1982)—contempt proceedings against Galella for violating injunction]

c. Statutory remedy [§700]
A California statute authorizes injunctive relief to prohibit various types of harassment. Harassment is defined as conduct that "seriously alarms, annoys or harasses," serves "no legitimate purpose," and causes "substantial emotional distress." [Cal. Civ. Proc. Code §527.6; *and see* **Bachowski v. Salamone,** *supra*—upholding constitutionality of similar harassment injunction statute]

4. Restitution [§701]
Restitution is not available in the cases here considered because the defendant's wrongful conduct usually results in injury to the plaintiff without enrichment of the wrongdoer. However, if the right of publicity aspect of privacy is involved, an injunction and an accounting of profits resulting from the commercial exploitation of the plaintiff's personality is possible (*see supra,* §§621, 627-631).

C. Familial Relations

1. Substantive Elements [§702]
Protection of familial relations is provided by actions for alienation of affections, criminal conversation (adultery), and seduction. At common law, these actions could be maintained only by a husband, but this has generally been changed by Married Women's Acts. In some states, however, statutes have been enacted abolishing some or all of these actions—usually because of the potentiality of their misuse for purposes of blackmail or extortion. [*See* **Hunt v. Hunt,** 309 N.W.2d 818 (S.D. 1981)—summarizes state of the law and abolishes these actions by judicial

decision; **O'Neil v. Shuckardt,** 733 P.2d 693 (Idaho 1986)—abolishing action in Idaho]

2. **Damages [§703]**

Where such actions are still permitted, the injured party may recover damages as indicated below.

a. **Alienation of affections [§704]**

In an action for alienation of affection, damages are recoverable for loss of affections and emotional distress. If a separation results, damages may also be awarded for loss of services and companionship. If the plaintiff is a stay-at-home spouse, loss of support is included. [**Wyman v. Wallace,** 588 P.2d 1133 (Wash. 1979)]

(1) **Mitigation [§705]**

Damages are reduced by showing prior disaffection, separation, or prior infidelity. [**Gorder v. Sims,** 237 N.W.2d 67 (Minn. 1975)]

(2) **Punitive damages [§706]**

Punitive damages may be awarded in proper cases.

b. **Criminal conversation [§707]**

In an action for criminal conversation, damages are awarded for emotional distress and humiliation, medical expenses, and loss of services. Punitive damages are also recoverable.

(1) **Mitigation [§708]**

Damages may be reduced by showing prior infidelity, consent, or unhappy family relations.

(2) **Joinder of actions [§709]**

A cause of action for criminal conversation may be joined with one for alienation of affections, and damages may be recovered for each. The damages are not duplicative; thus, the injured party may recover for mental anguish arising from each wrong. [**Lankford v. Tombari,** 213 P.2d 627 (Wash. 1950)]

c. **Seduction of a daughter [§710]**

Damages for seduction of a daughter include medical expenses, loss of society, and mental anguish and suffering. Punitive damages may also be recovered. In some jurisdictions, the seduced woman herself is given a cause of action, recovering damages for both mental anguish and humiliation, as well as the physical pain of pregnancy, if involved.

d. **Wrongful taking and concealment of children [§711]**

Compensatory damages for mental suffering and punitive damages may be awarded for the wrongful removal of children from the legal custody of their parent. [**Fenslage v. Dawkins,** 629 F.2d 1107 (5th Cir. 1980)]

3. Injunctive Relief

a. No injunctions against extramarital conduct [§712]

The injured spouse is usually denied equitable relief against alienation of affections, criminal conversation, or seduction. The reasons for the refusal are solely practical. As the court stated in **Lyon v. Izen,** 268 N.E.2d 436 (Ill. 1971): "The difficulty, if not impossibility of enforcement, and the very doubtful beneficial results to be obtained thereby, warrant the denial of such a decree." In sum, most courts believe that the problem of such extramarital conduct cannot be resolved by use of injunctions.

(1) And note

Courts have also refused to enter injunctions prohibiting the use of the married name by "the other woman," since ordinarily no "property" or other interest worthy of protection is found.

b. Relationship with children [§713]

In an attempt to maintain a parental relationship with children in divorce cases, a decree of dissolution of the marriage frequently prohibits the estranged couple from making disparaging remarks about each other. [*See* **Schultz v. Schultz,** 581 So. 2d 1290 (Fla. 1991)] These decrees are difficult to supervise or enforce and raise serious questions as to practicability. [*See* **Lynch v. Uhlenkopp,** 78 N.W.2d 491 (Iowa 1956); **Carrico v. Blevins,** 402 S.E.2d 235 (Va. 1991)—religious training]

(1) And note

In divorce cases, injunctive relief is also sought when there is a dispute as to the child's surname. The governing principle invoked in resolving these cases is whatever appears to be in the child's best interest. [*In re* **Grimes,** 609 A.2d 158 (Pa. 1992)]

D. Associational Relations

1. Exclusion from Membership

a. Social clubs [§714]

There is *no remedy* for being excluded from membership in a purely social or voluntary club, no matter how arbitrary. The reason for this rule is the reluctance of courts to interfere with the internal affairs of membership associations and the inability of a court to render an effective decree ordering people to associate with each other. [**Blatt v. University of Southern California,** 5 Cal. App. 3d 935 (1970); **Trautwein v. Harbourt,** 123 A.2d 30 (N.J. 1956)] However, admission practices of private associations may be attacked as an impermissible violation of civil rights (*see infra,* §§733-735) or of state laws prohibiting discriminatory practices [*but see* **Dale v. Boy Scouts of America,** 530 U.S. 640 (2000)—New Jersey public accommodation law does not apply to the Boy Scouts].

b. Professional organizations [§715]

Equitable relief is therefore restricted to situations where membership has *economic consequences*, such as professional societies. Even in such cases, relief is limited to a determination of whether the exclusion is *arbitrary or unreasonable*. [**Falcone v. Middlesex County Medical Society**, 170 A.2d 791 (N.J. 1961); **Pinsker v. Pacific Coast Society of Orthodontists**, 12 Cal. 3d 541 (1974)]

2. Expulsion from Membership [§716]

Early cases refused relief in cases of wrongful expulsion from an association because of the absence of a "property" right. However, courts now recognize that the real question is simply whether the injury to the plaintiff's interests is sufficiently serious to warrant judicial interference with the internal affairs of a social organization. [**Berrien v. Pollitzer**, 165 F.2d 21 (D.C. Cir. 1947)]

a. Requirement for relief [§717]

Today, limited relief is given for wrongful expulsion from even voluntary associations. However, expulsion will be enjoined only if there was a failure to provide a fair hearing in *good faith compliance* with the bylaws of the association, and the injured party has first *exhausted any internal remedies* that may be available to him. [**Moran v. Vincent**, 588 S.W.2d 867 (Tenn. 1979)—relief denied where expulsion from the order of the Eastern Star followed fair procedures and there was no showing of arbitrary or illegal action; **Hackethal v. California Medical Association**, 138 Cal. App. 3d 435 (1982)—reinstatement ordered because of absence of fair procedure]

b. Damages [§718]

While the usual remedy for wrongful expulsion is reinstatement, an invalid suspension of membership may result in an award of compensatory damages. Claims for such damages must be supported by probative evidence from which a reasonable estimate of the loss may be based. [*See* **Terrell v. Palomino Horse Breeders of America**, 414 N.E.2d 332 (Ind. 1980)—plaintiff's evidence was speculative and conjectural]

E. Academic Status

1. Student Admissions [§719]

Unless there is a failure to apply statutory standards or unconstitutional discrimination, courts are unwilling to review the administration of admission practices based on scholastic or academic standards.

a. "Affirmative action" programs [§720]

An admissions policy that considers race as a factor in admissions decisions is constitutional as long as: (i) target quotas are not established for the number of students of any particular minority; and (ii) each applicant is treated individually. [**Regents of the University of California v. Bakke,** 438 U.S. 265 (1978)]; *but compare* **Hopwood v. State of Texas,** 78 F.3d 932 (5th Cir. 1996)—where illegal discrimination was found]

2. Dismissal

a. For academic reasons [§721]

Courts generally refuse to review dismissal of students for academic reasons. [*See* **Susan M. v. New York Law School,** 76 N.Y.2d 241 (1990)—no judicial review of grading dispute; **Paulsen v. Golden Gate University,** 25 Cal. 3d 803 (1979)—declaratory judgment that student academically disqualified should be granted a law degree reversed] A student fully informed of the faculty dissatisfaction with her academic progress is accorded as much due process as required by the Fourteenth Amendment. [**Board of Curators of the University of Missouri v. Horowitz,** 435 U.S. 78 (1978)]

b. For disciplinary reasons [§722]

If a student is dismissed for disciplinary reasons, courts insist upon procedural due process. [**Goss v. Lopez,** 419 U.S. 565 (1975); **University of Texas Medical School v. Than,** 834 S.W.2d 425 (Tex. 1992)] Moreover, the rules governing student conduct must not infringe upon rights guaranteed by the First Amendment. [**Papish v. Board of Curators of the University of Missouri,** 410 U.S. 667 (1973)]

---

e.g. **Example:** A student was suspended from a private college because of irrational and disruptive conduct. The college guidelines provided that a student suspended for other than academic reasons is entitled to be heard by a student-faculty hearing board and to a review of its findings by the president. For failure to comply with the guidelines, the college was ordered to reinstate the student or provide a hearing as required by the guidelines. [**Tedeschi v. Wagner College,** 49 N.Y.2d 652 (1980)]

---

(1) Remedy [§723]

The remedy sought in these cases for the allegedly wrongful conduct is ordinarily equitable (reinstatement) because school officials have been considered immune from claims for damages, and there was thus no remedy at law. However, the Supreme Court has ruled that such officials are not absolutely immune from claims for damages for malicious expulsion brought pursuant to 42 U.S.C. section 1983 (for deprivations of federally protected rights by persons acting under color of state law). [**Wood v. Strickland,** 420 U.S. 308 (1975)] Damages in these cases are limited to compensation for actual injury, which includes any monetary loss as well as emotional distress caused by the violation of rights. (*See infra*, §735.)

3. Instructors [§724]

Teachers with "tenure" have obvious remedies based on breach of the employment contract. On the other hand, a *nontenured* teacher is not regarded as having any legitimate expectation of continued employment, and hence has no right to a hearing on the question of why her contract was not renewed at the end of the term.

a. Exception [§725]

If the state makes some charge against the nontenured teacher (involving loyalty, reputation, or conduct protected by the Constitution), then even a nontenured teacher is entitled to a hearing and the opportunity to rebut the charges made. In addition, a teacher may have a legitimate expectation in reemployment without explicit contractual tenure if tenure could be implied from the administration's words or conduct. [**Perry v. Sindermann**, 408 U.S. 593 (1972)]

b. Discrimination [§726]

If tenure is denied because of unlawful employment discrimination, relief may be granted under the Civil Rights Act. Thus, in **Kunda v. Muhlenberg College**, 463 F. Supp. 294 (E.D. Pa. 1978), a plaintiff claiming sex discrimination was reinstated with back pay and granted tenure conditioned on the successful completion of a master's degree within two years of the rendition of the decree.

F. Religious Status

1. Doctrinal Disputes [§727]

Courts have no jurisdiction over purely doctrinal ecclesiastical disputes, and thus provide no remedy for exclusions from church membership or the resolution of organizational disputes. [**Pfeifer v. Christian Science Committee**, 334 N.E.2d 876 (Ill. 1975); **Parish of the Advent v. Protestant Episcopal Diocese**, 688 N.E.2d 923 (Mass. 1997)]

2. Property Disputes [§728]

However, courts will assume jurisdiction where the controversy involves property rights, provided this can be done without resolving underlying controversies over religious doctrine. [**Presbyterian Church v. Mary Elizabeth Blue Hull Presbyterian Church**, 393 U.S. 440 (1969)—litigation over church property can be resolved where it involved only "neutral" principles of law, such as those governing the interpretation of deeds and corporate charters; **Scotts African Union Protestant Methodist Church v. Conference of African Union First Colored Protestant Methodist Church**, 98 F.3d 78 (3d Cir. 1996), *cert. denied*, 519 U.S. 1058 (1997); *and see* 52 A.L.R.3d 324]

G. Civil and Political Rights

1. **Political Rights [§729]**

   Political rights include the right to vote, to run for and hold a public office, and to participate in the activities of political parties.

   a. **Former law [§730]**

      Traditionally, such rights were not protected by injunction. Equity courts refused relief because (i) the remedy at law provided by the prerogative writs (quo warranto, mandamus, prohibition) was deemed adequate; (ii) the proper forum for resolution of such disputes was said to be with the executive or legislative branches of government under the separation of powers doctrine; and (iii) practical problems involved in speedily resolving the controversy and in supervising and enforcing the decree after it was rendered made injunctive relief inappropriate.

   b. **Modern law [§731]**

      The rule that equity will not protect political rights is now seriously eroded. Injunctive relief and damages are now available for denial of both the right to vote and the right to seek and hold public office. And, if necessary, courts will intervene to reapportion state legislatures and draw the boundaries of election districts. [**Baker v. Carr,** 369 U.S. 186 (1962)]

      (1) **Limitation**

          In **O'Brien v. Brown,** 409 U.S. 1 (1972), the Supreme Court refused to resolve an issue involving the *credentials of delegates* to the Democratic National Convention. The Court ruled that the issue could be resolved by the Convention without judicial intervention, especially when the time pressures involved were considered. [*And see* **Cousins v. Wigoda,** 419 U.S. 477 (1975)—overturning a state court injunction seeking to regulate participation of delegates in party conventions and caucuses; **Porter County Democratic Precinct Review Committee v. Spinks,** 551 N.E.2d 457 (Ind. 1990)—courts of equity have no jurisdiction with respect to matters of a political nature unless civil property rights are involved]

2. **"Matters of National Policy" [§732]**

   The foreign policy of the United States is not justiciable. A similar rule applies to such matters of national policy as atomic testing. Numerous attempts to adjudicate the validity of the Vietnam War failed either because of a lack of *standing* to sue or because the issue was held to be nonjusticiable. [*See* **Velvel v. Nixon,** 415 F.2d 236 (10th Cir. 1969); *compare* **Dellums v. Bush,** 752 F. Supp. 1141 (D.D.C. 1990)—injunction against military action against Iraq denied based on the "ripeness" doctrine]

3. Civil Rights [§733]

Statutes designed to recognize and protect civil rights sometimes prescribe remedies.

a. State statutes [§734]

Under state civil rights statutes, some courts have held that the statutory remedies are exclusive—thus precluding relief by injunction. [**Fletcher v. Coney Island,** 134 N.E.2d 371 (Ohio 1956); *but see* **Orloff v. Los Angeles Turf Club Inc.,** 30 Cal. 2d 110 (1947)—plaintiff entitled to injunctive relief for exclusion from public premises because statutory remedy ($100) was inadequate]

b. Federal act [§735]

The Federal Civil Rights Act [42 U.S.C. §1983] authorizes both legal and equitable remedies for violations of federally protected rights by persons acting under color of state law. Courts have had little hesitation in granting injunctive relief to protect constitutional rights of free speech, due process, or religious liberty. Damages, however, are not presumed. It has been held that damages are compensatory and are awarded only for actual injuries. [**Carey v. Piphus,** 435 U.S. 247 (1978)] Damages based on the abstract value or importance of constitutional rights are not a permissible element of compensatory damages in section 1983 cases. [**Memphis Community School District v. Stachura,** 477 U.S. 299 (1986); *but see* **Nolley v. County of Erie,** 802 F. Supp. 898 (W.D.N.Y. 1992)—allowing recovery of presumed damages for violation of plaintiff's right of privacy under §1983 (plaintiff segregated because of her HIV infection; recovery allowed for "injury likely to have occurred but difficult to establish")] Where the civil rights claim is based on discriminatory practices proscribed by Title VII or the Age Discrimination in Employment Act, the injured party is awarded back pay, front pay, and, in appropriate cases, reinstatement and punitive damages. [**Turner v. Barr,** 806 F. Supp. 1025 (D.D.C. 1992)]

Chapter Eight: Personal Injury and Death

CONTENTS

Chapter Approach

For all practical purposes, questions about personal injury or death involve only the remedy of *compensatory damages*. Therefore, your analysis of these questions should be as follows:

1. **Classify the Action**
    Is the plaintiff the *injured party* or is this action filed under a *survival or wrongful death* statute?

2. **Determine the Elements of Loss**
    According to your classification of the action, what are the *compensable* elements of loss?

    a. *If the personal injury action is brought by the injured party,* then medical expenses, loss of earnings, loss of future earnings, pain and suffering, and loss of enjoyment must all be considered.

    b. *If the action is under a survival or wrongful death statute,* the elements of loss under each statute must be isolated and the interaction between the two statutes is crucial.

3. **Determine the Extent of Compensable Loss**
    Consider the effect of the *collateral sources rule* and the *rule of avoidable consequences* in determining the extent of the loss for which plaintiff is entitled to compensation.

A. Personal Injuries

1. **Damages as Remedy—In General [§736]**
    The only effective remedy for tortiously caused personal injuries is an award of compensatory damages to the plaintiff. Usually, such injuries result in no economic benefit to the defendant, and hence there is no basis for any claim of unjust enrichment or restitutionary relief. Furthermore, injunctive relief is rarely sought because the invasion has already taken place, and usually there is no threat of repetition (although if a continuing course of conduct is involved, an injunction would clearly lie).

    a. **Elements of compensatory damages for personal injury [§737]**
        Damages for personal injury include *general damages* for pain and suffering

and disfigurement, as well as *special damages* for loss of past and future earnings and for past and future medical expenses.

b. **Amount of compensatory damage is within discretion of jury [§738]**
There is no objective formula for evaluating pain or disfigurement. The amount to be awarded is uniquely within the discretion of the trier of fact (jury), subject only to judicial review for excessive (or inadequate) awards resulting from passion and prejudice.

(1) **Note**
Some states have attempted to impose a *statutory cap* on the amount of damages that can be awarded in medical malpractice cases. [*See, e.g.,* **Jordan v. Long Beach Community Hospital,** 201 Cal. App. 3d 1402 (1988)—$250,000 cap on noneconomic damages constitutional; *but see* **Wheat v. United States,** 860 F.2d 1256 (5th Cir. 1988)—Texas statute void because it violated the Texas Constitution]

c. **Lump sum vs. installment damages [§739]**
The common law provides only for a single, lump sum award of damages that must compensate the plaintiff for all harm—past, present, and future—suffered as the result of the personal injury; *i.e.,* a court has *no power* (absent a statute) to render a judgment ordering the payment of damages in installments payable over a period of years, and variable in the light of future developments.

(1) **Comment**
Actually, such variable installment payments might be a far more accurate way of compensating for an injury, because the extent of recuperation or debilitation could be more accurately determined. However, our jurisprudence has made little provision for such a remedy. The principal objections are that it would defer ultimate payment too long, and would require too much court supervision (*e.g.,* the court would have to make sure that defendant established and maintained adequate reserves, etc.). [**Frankel v. United States,** 321 F. Supp. 1331 (E.D. Pa. 1970)]

(2) **But note**
The holdings in cases brought under the Federal Tort Claims Act have uniformly stated that only lump sum judgments could be entered. [**Frankel v. Heym,** 466 F.2d 1226 (3d Cir. 1972)] However, in **Hull v. United States,** 971 F.2d 1499 (10th Cir. 1992), the court approved the structuring of a damage award to a disabled child by placing the money in a reversionary trust in the event of the child's premature death. The court reasoned that the trust was consistent with *Frankel* in that the United States *did* pay a lump sum and the administration by a trustee relieved the judiciary of the burden of supervision.

(3) And note

Of course, the parties can always *agree* between themselves for a settlement on the basis of installment payments through a trust, annuity, or other device. Such an agreement would probably be enforced by a court even if it provided for contingencies based on future developments (*e.g.,* increase in payments if the plaintiff's doctor certified that the plaintiff was unable to return to work by the specified date).

(4) Statutory change

California has provided for periodic payment of future damages in medical malpractice actions. [Cal. Civ. Proc. Code §667.7]

2. Economic Losses [§740]

As part of any award of compensatory damages, the injured party is entitled to recover all *economic* losses *proximately caused* by the injury.

a. Medical expenses

(1) Proximate causation [§741]

As long as the chain of causation is proved, any sort of hospital, medical, or other therapeutic care is recoverable—including psychiatric care in appropriate cases (*e.g.,* plaintiff becomes so depressed as result of injury-caused disfigurement that she attempts to kill herself).

(a) But note

If the plaintiff has a preexisting physical condition that would inevitably have worsened, the plaintiff's damages must be reduced to take this fact into account. [**Maurer v. United States**, 668 F.2d 98 (2d Cir. 1981)]

(2) Past vs. future [§742]

The medical bills incurred up to the time of judgment in the personal injury case are easily proved. The plaintiff is also entitled to recover for *future* medical bills, limited only by the rule that damages not be speculative or uncertain. Hence, the plaintiff must produce evidence (usually through the plaintiff's doctor) establishing a *probability* that future medical treatment will be required, and the approximate cost of the treatment. [*See* Annot., 88 A.L.R.3d 117; *and see* **Simmons v. City of Bluefield**, 225 S.E.2d 202 (W. Va. 1976)] (*Note:* Future medical expenses must be discounted to their present value; *see supra,* §84.)

EXAM TIP **gilbert**

In evaluating economic losses from personal injury, be sure to distinguish between past and future losses. *Past losses* must be proved with precision and are recoverable in full. *Future losses* must be based on estimates and projections, and then reduced to present value.

(a) Uncertainty of future medical expenses in toxic exposure torts cases [§743]

Damages cannot be recovered for mere exposure to toxic substances, *e.g.*, asbestos, pesticides, and other carcinogens. There is *uncertainty as to the fact* of damage. (*See supra,* §32.) A calculation based on the possibilities of physical injury and the resulting amount of medical expenses is manifestly impracticable.

1) Fear of acquiring disease [§744]

The fear of acquiring a disease as the result of exposure, without more, is generally not compensable. On the other hand, if the fear takes the form of emotional distress with provable physical manifestations, or perhaps mental illness, there may be a recovery because these damages are present and quantifiable. [*See* **Hansen v. Mountain Fuel Supply Co.**, 858 P.2d 970 (Utah 1993)]

---

e.g. **Example:** One court allowed recovery where the fear (of contracting AIDS from being stuck by a possibly contaminated needle) was objectively reasonable given current, accurate information on AIDS transmission. However, continued fear after repeated tests showed no infection was not reasonable and not compensable. [**Williamson v. Waldman,** 696 A.2d 14 (N.J. 1997); *compare* **Metro-North Commuter Railroad v. Buckley,** 521 U.S. 424 (1997)—employee could not recover under Federal Employers' Liability Act ("FELA") for negligently inflicted emotional distress unless, and until, he had manifested symptoms of disease]

---

2) Cost of medical monitoring [§745]

Over strong objections that they are being made to pay for damages that have not occurred and may never actually occur, toxic tort defendants are increasingly being required to bear the cost of medical monitoring of the physical conditions of persons who have been exposed to the toxins but as yet show no symptoms of illness. The rationales for such decisions range from the obligations created by the "avoidable consequences" doctrine to the holding that the necessity of paying for diagnostic exams is a "detriment" for which the defendant is presently liable. However, the requirements for imposing these costs are strict: (i) significant exposure; (ii) significantly increased risk of disease; and (iii) existence of procedures for early detection. [**Hansen v. Mountain Fuel Supply Co.,** *supra;* **Abrian v. General Electric Co.,** 3 F.3d 329 (9th Cir. 1993); *but see* **Ball v. Joy Technologies,** 958 F.2d 36 (4th Cir. 1992)—contra]

a) Lump sum awards [§746]

Some courts have expressed concern about awarding a lump sum for medical monitoring, because there is no assurance that the money would actually be spent on monitoring. These courts have suggested that the defendant establish a type of trust fund dedicated solely to the payment of monitoring costs. [*See* **Hansen v. Mountain Fuel Supply Co.,** *supra*; *cf.* **Metro-North Commuter Railroad v. Buckley,** *supra*—under FELA, no separate tort cause of action existed to allow employee to recover lump sum medical monitoring costs]

b. Loss of earnings to date of trial [§747]

A plaintiff is also entitled to recover the difference between what she did earn and what she probably would have earned "but for" the injury up to the time of judgment. This covers *both* loss of actual *wages* and loss of earning *capacity*.

(1) Loss of actual earnings [§748]

A plaintiff is entitled to recover for the actual earnings (either in form of salary, commissions, or business profits) she lost by being off work due to the injury.

(a) Receipt of sick pay irrelevant [§749]

Under the "collateral sources rule" (*see supra,* §75), a tortfeasor's liability is *not* mitigated by the fact that the victim receives sick leave or other disability compensation from the victim's own employer or insurance company. Thus, even though the plaintiff may have been reimbursed in full for time off work, the defendant must pay as if the plaintiff had received nothing.

(2) Loss of earning capacity [§750]

Even if the plaintiff was unemployed or otherwise had no actual earnings accruing during her incapacity, she can recover if she establishes that she was deprived of earnings *opportunities* as the result of the injury. [Rest. 2d Torts §924, comment c]

(a) Type of proof

It is usually sufficient if the plaintiff shows that due to the injury she was *prevented from seeking* employment, and that positions were available for persons of her background and ability.

EXAM TIP   **gilbert**

Don't be fooled on your exam. Remember that a plaintiff who is injured after he is laid off can still recover for loss of earning capacity; he need only show that he was deprived of an *opportunity to work*.

---

(3) Loss must be proximate result of injury [§751]

There can be no recovery for loss of earnings or earning capacity unless the loss was *attributable to the injury*.

(a) Investment income [§752]

Obviously, if the plaintiff's sole income is derived from *investments*, she cannot recover for loss of income, because the injury does not affect her income-producing ability.

(b) Own business [§753]

If the plaintiff is *in business for herself*, she is entitled to recover for *loss of profits* (in lieu of salary) if it can be shown that this was *attributable to the loss of her services*, rather than extrinsic factors. [**Commercial Union Insurance Co. v. Rivera**, 358 F.2d 480 (1st Cir. 1966)]

1) Application

This loss-of-profits measure has been applied to merchants, farmers, furniture brokers, building contractors, wholesale dealers, etc. In each instance, their business is dependent in substantial part on the *services* of the owner. [**Smith v. Corsat**, 131 S.E.2d 894 (N.C. 1963)]

2) Note

The cost of hiring a *substitute* to do the work normally performed by the plaintiff is a proper item of deduction in computing the business loss. [**Powell v. Kansas Yellow Cab**, 131 P.2d 686 (Kan. 1942)]

3) But note

Business losses that would have occurred *regardless* of the plaintiff's presence or services are not recoverable (*e.g.*, retail sales drop off or a depreciation in inventory values).

c. Loss of future earnings [§754]

In addition to any loss of actual earnings up to the date of the trial, the plaintiff is entitled to recover for any impairment of her earnings or earning capacity in the future. Again, courts are required to render a lump sum damages award, and thus to make a *present valuation* of the probable future consequences of the injury. (As to computation of such present valuation, *see supra,* §86.)

(1) Based on work expectancy [§755]

If the plaintiff's disability is expected to continue for only a limited period of time, her loss of earnings will be computed accordingly. If, however, the disability is *permanent*, her loss of earnings will be based on her probable work expectancy—the number of years until *probable retirement*. (This may, of course, be less than her life expectancy.)

(a) **Work expectancy [§756]**

The plaintiff's probable work expectancy may be proved by actuarial tables of persons of her age, health, background, training, etc., at the time of the injury. Evidence as to the plaintiff's physical health prior to the accident is admissible to reflect on whether the plaintiff's actual work expectancy was greater (or lesser) than "normal." [**Earl v. Bouchard Transportation Co.,** 735 F. Supp. 1167 (E.D.N.Y. 1990); Rest. 2d Torts §924, comment e]

(2) Lost productivity [§757]

Expert evidence is admissible as to the victim's future employment prospects, including prospects for advancement and salary increases. On the basis of this evidence, the jury may estimate lost earning capacity. [**Kaczkowski v. Bolubasz,** 421 A.2d 1027 (Pa. 1980); **Masinter v. Tenneco Oil Co.,** 867 F.2d 892 (5th Cir. 1989)—permitting evidence that future salary would be reduced because of depression in oil and gas industry]

(3) Effect of no earnings history [§758]

If the injured person does not work outside the home, is a *minor* child, or otherwise had no prior earnings, the loss of future earning capacity must be computed on the basis of *probabilities*. [*See* **Waldorf v. Shuta,** 896 F.2d 723 (3d Cir. 1990)—unemployed paralegal not permitted to recover loss of future earnings based on assertion that he would have become an attorney]

(a) **Relevant factors [§759]**

The injured party's age, aptitude, progress in education, family background, health, marriage prospects, etc., are all relevant. [**Martin v. United States,** 471 F. Supp. 6 (D. Ariz. 1979)] Mere ambition is not. [**Carlson v. City Construction Co.,** 606 N.E.2d 400 (Ill. 1992)]

(b) **Actuarial tables [§760]**

Based on the foregoing factors, courts may rely on properly qualified actuarial tables to establish the injured party's probable earning *capacity*—even without any prior work history. Such actuarial tables usually consist of statistical averages showing earnings for various groups based on age, educational accomplishments (*e.g.,* high school dropout or university grad), geographic location (urban or rural); etc. [**Wilson v. B.F. Goodrich Co.,** 627 P.2d 1280 (Or. 1980)]

(4) Effect of shortened life expectancy [§761]

Evidence that the injury has shortened the plaintiff's life expectancy (and hence her work expectancy) does *not* reduce the damages. The defendant's liability is measured by what the plaintiff's services would have been worth "but for" the injury and thus is computed *without regard* to any reduction in her life expectancy caused by the injury. [*See* **Beeman v. Manville Corp.**, 496 N.W.2d 247 (Iowa 1993)—noting that Iowa follows the minority practice of calculating loss of earning capacity based on post-injury life expectancy]

(a) But note

The plaintiff's shortened life expectancy is *not* a separately compensable element of damages. The English rule is contrary. [*See* **Beeman v. Manville Corp.**, *supra*] However, courts are increasingly willing to allow the plaintiff to recover for an increased risk of future harm or the loss of chance of a recovery. [**Alexander v. Scheid**, 726 N.E.2d 272 (Ind. 2000)—summarizing case law]

EXAM TIP gilbert

Watch out for a defendant with the chutzpah to argue that the plaintiff's damages for loss of future earnings should be reduced because the injury that the defendant caused will shorten the plaintiff's life. Although the plaintiff cannot recover for the shortened life expectancy in most states, neither can the defendant use the shortened life expectancy as a basis for *reducing damages*.

---

(5) Effect of full physical recovery [§762]

Normally, of course, the fact that the plaintiff has recovered fully from the injury prior to trial precludes any award for loss of future earnings.

(a) Exceptions [§763]

But there may be exceptional cases where it is shown that the injury (although fully healed) *interfered with the plaintiff's career* in a way that will deprive the plaintiff of future earnings otherwise probably received.

---

e.g. **Example:** A quarterback on the University of Missouri football team suffered injuries that kept him from playing during his senior year. Although he completely recovered from the injuries, the fact that he was unable to play during his senior year at college probably caused a loss of the earnings he otherwise could have obtained in embarking on his athletic coaching career after college. [**Gooch v. Lake**, 327 S.W.2d 132 (Mo. 1959)]

---

3. Noneconomic Losses [§764]

In addition to economic losses, past and future, the injured person is entitled to be compensated for noneconomic losses, past and future. These are items of "general" damages, whereas the economic losses are often referred to as "special" damages.

a. **Physical pain [§765]**

The plaintiff is entitled to be compensated for the past, present, and future pain and discomfort caused by the injury.

(1) Jury question [§766]

The amount to be awarded as compensation is uniquely within the province of the trier of fact (jury). There are no guidelines or measure of damages here. Rather, it is a question of what the jury finds to be "adequate" compensation.

(a) Trial court correction [§767]

Amounts awarded by the jury are subject to correction by the trial court (usually in a motion for new trial or hearing). The trial judge may order a new trial if she finds the verdict resulted from passion or prejudice, or may do so *conditionally*—by invoking remedies of additur or remittitur (*e.g.,* granting a new trial unless the plaintiff agrees to accept less than the jury verdict). (*See* Civil Procedure Summary.)

(b) Appellate review [§768]

Jury verdicts are also subject to appellate review, but here the verdict will not be set aside as "excessive" or "inadequate" unless it "shocks the conscience" of the appellate court. A mere feeling that the verdict was too high or too low will generally *not* cause a reversal. [*But see* **Stratis v. Eastern Airlines,** 682 F.2d 406 (2d Cir. 1982)—appellate court reversed $1.2 million award for pain and suffering where plaintiff was unable to feel pain after the first four days because of quadriplegia]

(2) Permissible methods of presenting issue to jury [§769]

Courts are far more likely to set aside a jury verdict if it appears that the issue as to the amount of damages was presented to the jury on the basis of legally improper instructions from the trial judge or legally improper arguments from counsel.

(a) "Golden rule" argument [§770]

The "golden rule" argument is made when the plaintiff's counsel asks the jury to award the plaintiff whatever amount they (the jurors) would expect for suffering the injuries suffered by the plaintiff. "Do unto others as you would have them do unto you."

1) Note

This argument is *not permitted* and is ground for reversal of the verdict in the majority of jurisdictions. *Rationale:* The jurors are required to render a verdict *objectively* (as detached, reasonable persons)—not subjectively (what they as individuals might demand). [**Shroyer v. Kaufmann,** 426 F.2d 1032 (7th

Cir. 1970); 70 A.L.R.2d 935; *and see* **Lopez v. Langer,** 761 P.2d 1225 (Idaho 1988)]

(b) "Per diem" argument [§771]

The "per diem" argument is made when the plaintiff's counsel asks the jury to arrive at a dollar amount that they would regard as fair compensation to the plaintiff for *each day* (or conceivably each *hour* or *minute*) of pain and then multiply this figure for the period that the plaintiff has suffered—past, present, and future.

1) Comment

This argument is generally *permitted*, or at least held not erroneous per se. [60 A.L.R.2d 1347] The strongest objection to the argument is that there is no evidence to support it, and there is often no way of proving whether the suffering is constant, so that a constant multiplier is inaccurate. [*Compare* **Waldorf v. Shuta,** *supra*, §758—federal court held that it was reversible error to assert in closing argument that minimum dollar amount should be awarded for pain and suffering]

(c) Instruction that award must be based on pain and suffering "capable of proof" [§772]

Such an instruction may be erroneous, because in certain cases pain and suffering may be inherently *incapable of proof.* For example, the victim may be a child of very tender years (*e.g.,* a three-month-old baby) or a person whose sensory perception is impaired by age or illness. Nonetheless, such persons are entitled to damages for "pain and suffering," even though their suffering is incapable of proof. [**Capelouto v. Kaiser Foundation Hospital,** 7 Cal. 3d 889 (1972)]

(d) Cautionary instructions [§773]

The judge may properly instruct the jury to consider the following as limitations on any award of "pain and suffering" damages:

1) Must be based on remaining life expectancy [§774]

Pain and suffering damages can be allowed only through the plaintiff's remaining life expectancy—even if the plaintiff's life expectancy has been shortened as the result of the injury itself. (Note again that shortened life expectancy is *not* a separately compensable element of damages; *see supra,* §761.)

2) Subject to rule of avoidable consequences [§775]

An award of pain and suffering damages may be subject to the rule of avoidable consequences (*see supra,* §47, *and see infra,* §§785-788).

3) Present value of future damages [§776]

There is a split of authority as to whether the jury should be instructed to limit the award of damages for future pain and suffering by discounting the amount of the award to reflect its present monetary value. (*See* computation of awards for future losses, *supra*, §86.)

a) The *majority rule* is that such an instruction is improper (*i.e.*, there should be *no discounting* of damages for future pain to present value). *Rationale:* Such damages are not mathematically computed in the first place; moreover, the jury is presumed to arrive at its verdict by taking into account that the dollars they now award are intended to compensate for the pain and suffering that will occur in the future.

b) But there is also respectable authority *contra.* [*See, e.g.,* **Chiarello v. Domenico Bus Service, Inc.**, 542 F.2d 883 (2d Cir. 1976)**—upholding jury verdict in which pain and suffering of $230,000 was discounted to $137,048] The *Restatement* position is in between—*i.e.*, future pain and suffering damages "need not" be discounted. [Rest. 2d Torts §913A]

b. Emotional anguish [§777]

In addition to physical pain and discomfort, the plaintiff is entitled to be compensated for the mental and emotional anguish resulting from *disability or disfigurement*. For example, the scar across the face of a young girl may result in no pain or permanent disability but may cause grave emotional anguish.

(1) Causation requirement [§778]

As long as the anguish can be shown to be proximately caused, it is recoverable. The tortfeasor "takes his victim as he finds him," and the fact that the plaintiff is an abnormally sensitive or nervous person does not affect the plaintiff's right to recover for the anguish. Thus, if the plaintiff can convince the jury that she lives in constant terror of death from her injuries, she is entitled to be compensated therefor—even if a reasonable person would not react in this manner. [Rest. Torts §905]

c. "Loss of enjoyment of life"—hedonic damages [§779]

There are a number of cases in which the basic harm done is an interference with the enjoyment of life rather than physical pain or emotional anguish per se. (For example, an injury to an *amateur* violinist's hand which prevents her from playing the violin, which she has always enjoyed; an injury requiring the plaintiff to wear an artificial leg, which prevents him from playing tennis, his favorite sport and recreation.) The expression "hedonic damages" is used to cover this type of harm.

(1) Split of authority [§780]

Some cases have held that such interference is *not* a separately compensable element of damage. *Rationale:* It is too vague, speculative, and uncertain, and overlaps other allowable elements such as pain and suffering. [**McDougald v. Garber,** 73 N.Y.2d 246 (1989); **Poyzer v. McGraw,** 360 N.W.2d 748 (Iowa 1985)] Others hold that although such loss of enjoyment is not separately compensable, it *can* be argued to the jury as a factor in determining the "adequacy" of the amount to be awarded for pain and suffering. [**Huff v. Tracy,** 57 Cal. App. 3d 939 (1976); **Canfield v. Sandock,** 563 N.E.2d 1279 (Ind. 1990)]

(2) Modern trend [§781]

The trend today apparently is to allow such loss of enjoyment as a *separate* element of damages, in addition to whatever other pain and suffering damages are proved. [*See* **McAlister v. Carl,** 197 A.2d 140 (Md. 1964)—recognizing this rule, but particular claim (for inability to engage in swimming and horseback riding by a girl hoping to make a career in physical education) had not been adequately proved; **Bennett v. Lembo,** 761 A.2d 494 (N.H. 2000)—allowing loss of enjoyment damages as part of the compensation for permanent impairment]

(a) Comatose plaintiffs [§782]

Only a few jurisdictions allow recovery for loss of enjoyment of life by a comatose plaintiff who is not aware of the loss. [**Eyoma v. Falco,** 589 A.2d 653 (N.J. 1991); **Ocasio v. Amtrak,** 690 A.2d 682 (N.J. 1997)] Furthermore, since a permanently comatose plaintiff cannot personally benefit from an award for loss of enjoyment of life, it has been argued that such damages are "punitive" and not allowable against the United States when sued under the Federal Tort Claims Act ("FTCA"). The Supreme Court, in **Molzof v. United States,** 502 U.S. 301 (1992), resolved a conflict between the circuits by holding that only damages that are punitive in the common law sense are not recoverable from the United States. Hence, the federal liability under the FTCA for hedonic damages depends on state law.

d. Nonmarket services [§783]

Compensation may also be awarded for the value of such nonmarket services as mowing the lawn, shovelling snow, washing dishes, or shopping. The award is not duplicative of damages for loss of enjoyment of life. [**Dura Corp. v. Harned,** 703 P.2d 396 (Alaska 1985)]

e. Limitations—"no fault" insurance [§784]

Noneconomic losses as the result of personal injury may be restricted or eliminated in jurisdictions adopting "no fault" insurance plans. For example, under the Massachusetts "no fault" system, pain and suffering type damages are not recoverable in a tort action except in cases involving over $500 in medical expenses, or resulting in death or injury involving loss of some bodily member, permanent disfigurement, loss of sight or hearing, or fracture.

SUMMARY OF BASES FOR DAMAGES IN PERSONAL INJURY CASES	**gilbert**
GENERAL DAMAGES	**SPECIAL DAMAGES**
• Pain • Disfigurement • Emotional anguish • Loss of enjoyment of life ("hedonic damages") • Loss of nonmarket services (who'll mow the lawn?)	• Medical expenses (past, present, and future) • Lost earnings up to trial • Lost future earnings

4. Rules Affecting Amount of Damages Recoverable

a. Rule of avoidable consequences [§785]

All courts agree that the plaintiff must take "reasonable" steps to avoid aggravating the injuries. In the usual case, this means that the plaintiff must seek proper medical treatment (or perhaps even psychiatric treatment in the case of mental suffering) to "avoid" any increased damages from not obtaining such treatment.

Example: If Placido fails to obtain prompt medical care for a leg wound, and as a result the wound becomes gangrenous, ultimately resulting in amputation of the leg, Dulcea's liability is limited to the expenses and pain and suffering attributable to the original wound. Dulcea is *not* liable for the loss of the leg, or the expenses and suffering attributable to the loss of the leg.

(1) Treatment and surgery [§786]

This duty to "avoid" any aggravation of the damages may require the plaintiff to submit to painful treatment or even surgery, if a reasonable person in plaintiff's position would submit to the procedure. [**Sette v. Dakis**, 48 A.2d 271 (Conn. 1946)—plaintiff refused recommended surgery on his knee; damages limited to expenses and disability plaintiff would have sustained had he undergone the surgery; *but see* **Cannon v. New Jersey Bell Telephone**, 530 A.2d 345 (N.J. 1987)—no duty to mitigate where reasonable person would decline risky surgery; **Morris v. Sanchez**, 746 P.2d 184 (Okla. 1987)—in medical malpractice action for negligent sterilization, there is no duty to mitigate by resort to abortion]

(a) Refusal based on religious scruples [§787]

Whether persons with religious scruples are subject to the above rule can only be determined in the individual case in light of the "reasonableness" requirement. [**Lange v. Hoyt,** 159 A. 575 (Conn. 1932)] One recent case suggested that allowing the jury to consider the reasonableness of the plaintiff's religious scruples violated the Establishment Clause of the First Amendment. [**Williams v. Bright,** 230 A.D.2d 548 (1997); *compare* **Corlett v. Caserta,** 562 N.E.2d 257 (Ill. 1990)—patient's estate must bear proportionate share of tort liability for patient's wrongful death, to extent that patient's death was proximately caused by patient's refusal of reasonable life-saving treatment based on religious scruples]

EXAM TIP   **gilbert**

Be sure to remember that under the rule of avoidable consequences, a plaintiff generally *must seek treatment* to avoid aggravating the injuries. A plaintiff who fails to seek treatment usually cannot recover for *damages that could have been avoided* if treatment had been sought—even if the treatment is painful, as long as a reasonable person would submit to the treatment. (A paraphrase of an old saying is appropriate here: The courts help those who help themselves.) But watch out for plaintiffs *whose religion prohibits them from seeking the treatment* sought (*e.g.,* some religions prohibit their members from obtaining blood transfusions). The courts sometimes will take the plaintiff's religious scruples into account when weighing the reasonableness of a refusal of treatment.

---

(2) Loss of earnings [§788]

The rule of avoidable consequences may also apply to *loss of earnings* or impaired earning capacity. For example, if the plaintiff's hand is cut off so that she is no longer able to follow her career as a concert pianist, the plaintiff may be required to *retrain* for a new job (the costs of such retraining to be deducted from her probable earnings in the new career). If she fails to do so, damages may be limited to the *difference* between what she might have earned as a concert pianist and that which she might have earned had she retrained for a new career.

b. Mitigation by provocation [§789]

Provocation, of course, is irrelevant in a negligence action. Where an intentional tort is involved (*e.g.,* a battery), *some* courts—a minority—permit evidence that the plaintiff provoked the incident that resulted in the injury in order to mitigate the amount of damages recoverable. *Most courts,* however, hold that if the provocation does not amount to a defense to the intentional tort (as consent), it does *not mitigate* the damages recoverable. [**Earl v. Times-Mirror Co.,** 185 Cal. 165 (1921)]

(1) But note

Evidence of provocation is usually admissible in determining the allowance and amount of any *punitive* damages. [Rest. 2d Torts §921]

c. **Mitigation by compensation paid on behalf of defendant [§790]**

If the injured party has already received partial compensation for the injury from the defendant or any person *acting on the defendant's behalf*—*e.g.,* the defendant's insurance carrier—the jury must deduct the amount paid from the damages otherwise assessed against the defendant.

(1) Relief from joint tortfeasor [§791]

The same rule applies where the injured person has received payments from a *joint tortfeasor*. Even though such payments are not technically "on behalf of the defendant," they are treated as if they were.

(2) Relief from federal government [§792]

Where the injured person sues the United States Government as defendant-tortfeasor under the Federal Tort Claims Act, the Government *cannot* offset against the damages for which it is liable any hospitalization or other benefits (such as Social Security) furnished to the injured person. Such benefits are really not paid on behalf of the defendant (the government), but rather are from funds (*e.g.,* Social Security) to which the injured person presumably contributed, and hence fall under the *"collateral sources" rule*, below. [**United States v. Price,** 288 F.2d 448 (4th Cir. 1961)]

d. **"Collateral sources" rule [§793]**

A tortfeasor-defendant is not entitled to have his liability reduced on account of compensation paid to the plaintiff from "collateral" sources—*i.e.,* sources not purporting to act on behalf of the defendant. (*See supra,* §75.)

(1) Minority view—limits rule [§794]

A few jurisdictions limit the collateral sources rule to benefits for which the plaintiff *actually paid*. These courts hold that where the plaintiff has received benefits *gratuitously*, the plaintiff really has not been damaged and therefore the tortfeasor cannot be held liable.

> **e.g.** **Example:** Where the plaintiff received free medical treatment (as a professional courtesy), this minority view holds that the value of the treatment is *not* a proper element of damages against the defendant. [**Coyne v. Campbell,** 11 N.Y.2d 372 (1962)] Likewise, where the plaintiff's employer gratuitously continued plaintiff's salary, this minority view holds that the defendant is not liable for any damages based on "loss of earnings." [**Widdon v. Malone,** 124 So. 516 (Ala. 1929)]

(a) Distinguish—plaintiff's own insurance [§795]

Even under this view, benefits received under the plaintiff's own medical expense insurance (bought and paid for by the plaintiff) do *not* reduce the defendant's liability.

(b) Relief from federal government—Medicare [§796]

In an action against the United States Government under the Federal Tort Claims Act, *Medicare* benefits received by the plaintiff were held properly deducted from an award of special damages. The collateral sources rule did not preclude this deduction because the payment of Medicare benefits did not come from a source wholly independent of the party liable, but rather from general federal revenues, and there was no showing that the plaintiff had contributed to the Medicare fund. [**Overton v. United States**, 619 F.2d 1299 (8th Cir. 1980); *but see* **Silverson v. United States**, 710 F.2d 557 (9th Cir. 1983)—*Overton* distinguished on the basis of the plaintiff's contribution to Social Security; **Manko v. United States**, 636 F. Supp. 1419 (W.D. Mo. 1986)—collateral sources rule applies to payment received by plaintiff from Medicare A and B and Social Security payments, since these are benefits for which plaintiff had paid; *but see* **Bennett v. Haley**, 208 S.E.2d 302 (Ga. 1974)—although Medicaid is a form of public assistance for indigents, it is subject to the collateral sources rule]

(2) "No fault" insurance plans eliminate rule [§797]

There is no room for the collateral sources rule under "no fault" insurance systems—because under such systems the burden of compensation is cast on the injured person's *own* insurance company. Tort actions against the person causing the injuries are restricted (*see supra*, §784), and even where permitted, the damages recoverable may *exclude* benefits already received from the injured person's own insurance carrier.

e. Discounting to present value [§798]

A damages award that includes future pecuniary losses must be reduced to present value, but recovery for pain and suffering and other noneconomic losses is generally not discounted. [*See* **Friedman v. C & S Car Service**, 527 A.2d 871 (N.J. 1987)—citing conflicting views on the issue; *and see supra*, §§83-86, for an explanation of the discounting process]

f. Taxes as allowable factor [§799]

In general, the amount of damages received on account of personal injuries is *not* subject to federal or state income tax. [26 U.S.C. §104; *and see* Income Tax I Summary] (Punitive damages are taxable, however, as is any interest on the unpaid judgment.)

(1) Taxes on earnings loss disregarded [§800]

In most cases, the plaintiff is allowed to recover for loss of future earnings without regard to the fact that taxes would have to have been paid on those earnings had they been received. At least with respect to plaintiffs at the "lower or middle reaches of the income scale," the majority rule is that *income taxes are to be disregarded* in calculating the injured party's economic loss. [**United States Steel Corp. v. Lamp**, 436 F.2d 1256 (6th Cir. 1970); *but see* **Curtis v. Finneran**, 417 A.2d 15 (N.J. 1980)—contra]

(a) Note

Some authorities question whether the same rule should apply where the injured person is a high-bracket taxpayer, suggesting that, perhaps the earnings loss should be diminished to its after-tax value in such cases. [Rest. 2d Torts §914A; *and see* **Felder v. United States**, 543 F.2d 657 (9th Cir. 1976)—in wrongful death action, failure to deduct income taxes in computing lost earnings of decedent who was in very high tax bracket would in effect amount to impermissible punitive damages]

(2) Should jury be instructed? [§801]

The fact that personal injury or wrongful death damages are not subject to the income tax is certainly not universally known or understood by juries. Even so, most state courts today have *not* allowed the jury to be instructed on this point. [**Scanlon v. Hooper**, 293 S.E.2d 843 (N.C. 1982)— error to instruct that damages are exempt from income tax; **Robichaud v. Theis**, 858 F.2d 392 (8th Cir. 1988)]

(a) Federal courts [§802]

The United States Supreme Court in **Norfolk & Western Railway v. Liepelt**, 444 U.S. 490, *reh'g denied*, 445 U.S. 972 (1980), ruled that in a Federal Employers' Liability Act case, it is error to refuse to instruct that any award granted is not taxable income. In a diversity case it has been held that the federal rule will apply unless the state has a substantive reason for not instructing as to taxes. [*See* **In re Air Crash Disaster Near Chicago**, 803 F.2d 304 (7th Cir. 1986); *and see* **Bussel v. DeWalt Products Corp.**, 519 A.2d 1379 (N.J. 1987)— if requested, instruction must be given]

B. Survival of Personal Injury Actions

1. Common Law [§803]

Personal injury actions did not survive at early common law (so that it was cheaper to kill the victim than to wound him).

2. Modern Law [§804]

Survival statutes, in effect in practically every jurisdiction today, have reversed the common law rule and allow the decedent's estate to maintain whatever cause of action the decedent himself could have maintained had he survived.

a. **Scope of action [§805]**

Under these statutes, the decedent's estate is permitted to sue for whatever personal injury damages had accrued to the injured person *up to the time of death*. (Damages accruing *after* his death are compensated in *wrongful death actions*, below.)

b. **Damages recoverable [§806]**

Most jurisdictions permit the decedent's estate to recover for her medical expenses and loss of earnings during lifetime, together with an allowance for pain and suffering up until the time of death (although some jurisdictions eliminate any recovery for pain and suffering if the victim had died). [*See, e.g.,* Cal. Prob. Code §573]

(1) **Punitive damages [§807]**

Whether *punitive* damages can be recovered by survivors depends on the language of the statute—*e.g.,* California has switched from nonsurvival to survival of certain kinds of punitive damages under Probate Code section 573. [*See* **Dunwoody v. Trapnell,** 47 Cal. App. 3d 367 (1975)] In **Hofer v. Lavendar,** 679 S.W.2d 470 (Tex. 1984), the court held that there is a right to collect punitive damages from the estate of the deceased tortfeasor. But in **Tucker v. Marcus,** 418 N.W.2d 818 (Wis. 1988), the court ruled that punitive damages are improper where compensatory damages were not awarded because the plaintiff's negligence was found to contribute 70% to the accident.

3. **Interaction with Wrongful Death Actions [§808]**

As indicated, the decedent's estate generally maintains a claim for the decedent's personal injury damages prior to her death, while damages claims accruing after death are made in a wrongful death action. However, there is some interaction between the two.

a. **Condition precedent [§809]**

Wrongful death statutes are interpreted by some states to require as a condition precedent to the right of action that the decedent have the capability of maintaining an action for her injuries at the time immediately preceding her death. Thus, if the decedent was barred by the statute of limitations from suing for personal injuries, the wrongful death plaintiff is also barred. [**Adams v. Armstrong World Industries,** 596 F. Supp. 1407 (D. Idaho 1984)]

b. **Release [§810]**

Most courts hold that release by the injured person during her lifetime *precludes both* the personal injury action by her estate and the wrongful death action by her heirs.

c. **Recovery [§811]**

Moreover, most courts hold that if the victim brings an action for her injuries during her lifetime, any judgment obtained bars not only the survival action by her estate, but also the wrongful death action of her heirs. [*See* Rest. 2d Torts §925, comment i]

(1) Criticism

This makes sense as to the survival action, but is illogical as to the wrongful death action, because it means that the decedent's action during her lifetime eliminated a cause of action that was not hers (it belongs to her heirs and only arose upon her death; *see* below).

(2) Modern trend contra?

Recognizing this criticism, there is authority for allowing the wrongful death action to proceed even where the decedent sued and recovered for her injuries during her life.

Example: A wrongful death action under the Maritime Act was upheld even though the injured seaman had sued and recovered for his injuries before he died. The Court held that his recovery *did not bar* his heirs' wrongful death action for loss of support, services, and society. However, to avoid duplication of damages, the amount of his inter vivos recovery attributable to his *loss of future earnings* was deemed received by him as a trustee to *support* his dependents, and this amount was *offset* against the heirs' loss-of-support damages in the wrongful death action. [**Sea-Land Services, Inc. v. Gaudet,** 414 U.S. 573 (1974); *and see* **Alfone v. Sarno,** 432 A.2d 857 (N.J. 1981)]

C. Wrongful Death Actions

1. Background [§812]

There was *no action for wrongful death* at common law. The right of action was first established in England by Lord Campbell's Act (1846), and this statute became the prototype of most American wrongful death statutes (the "loss-to-survivors" type, *see infra*, §819).

2. Statutory Action [§813]

It is essential to keep in mind that the action for wrongful death is basically a statutory action. Although every jurisdiction today has some kind of wrongful death statute in effect, the wording and coverage of such statutes frequently differ. Therefore, the first question in a wrongful death case always is *whether the statute authorizes the particular action brought*. Unless it does, the common law rule of no recovery remains.

a. Nonstatutory action [§814]

Nevertheless, some courts have in effect recognized a "nonstatutory" wrongful death action by filling in gaps under present statutes to allow the action. [*See* **Moragne v. States Marine Lines,** 398 U.S. 375 (1970)—filling gaps in maritime death actions; *and see* **Gaudette v. Webb,** 284 N.W.2d 222 (Mass. 1972)—invoking common law principles to toll a statute of limitations under the wrongful death statute]

3. Types of Statutes [§815]

There are two main types of wrongful death statutes:

a. Loss-to-estate type (minority) [§816]

Some statutes authorize a unitary action in which the recovery goes to the decedent-victim's estate. Some of these statutes reach this result through authorizing a hybrid action to include both the survival of the decedent's personal injury action (above), and damages for his death. Other statutes simply provide directly that any recovery goes to the decedent's estate. In either case, the action is maintained by the executor or administrator.

(1) Measure of recovery [§817]

Under such statutes, the measure of recovery is the loss to the decedent's *estate*. This is viewed as the amount that the deceased would have accumulated during his lifetime "but for" his wrongful death (*i.e.,* the amount that would have passed to his estate had he lived out his normal life expectancy). [*See* **Sullivan v. Carlisle,** 857 S.W.2d 510 (Mo. 1993)]

(a) Note

Usually, but not invariably, courts interpret this to mean a *net amount*—*i.e.,* earnings or other income, less cost of living, etc.

(b) And note

The net accumulations are then *discounted to their present value*. The method for discounting is to compute the dollar amount which, if invested at current interest rates compounded, would produce the total loss to the estate at the end of the decedent's normal life expectancy (*see supra,* §86).

(2) Distribution of damages [§818]

The damages flowing into the decedent's estate are distributed in accordance with the applicable rules of testate or intestate succession (*i.e.,* to the beneficiaries under the decedent's will or his heirs at law if he died intestate).

b. Loss-to-survivors type (majority) [§819]

The "loss-to-survivors" type statute is the "true" type of wrongful death statute, stemming from Lord Campbell's Act (*supra,* §812). Here, the measure of recovery is the combined claims of the decedent's survivors who have suffered provable losses because of his death. [*See generally* **McKee v. Colt Electronics Co.,** 849 F.2d 46 (2d Cir. 1988)]

	SURVIVAL ACTION	"LOSS TO SURVIVORS" WRONGFUL DEATH
SURVIVAL ACTIONS VS. "LOSS TO SURVIVORS" WRONGFUL DEATH ACTIONS—A COMPARISON gilbert		
"OWNERSHIP" OF ACTION	Action belongs to **decedent** and passes to her estate	Action belongs to **wrongful death beneficiaries** as defined by statute
WHO BRINGS ACTION?	**Administrator** of estate, on behalf of estate	**Wrongful death beneficiaries** on their own behalf
BASIS OF DAMAGES	**Decedent's own losses up to time of death**—lost income, medical expenses, and pain and suffering	**Losses suffered by the wrongful death beneficiaries** as a result of loss of monetary support and companionship of decedent

(1) Who are "survivors"? [§820]

Under some statutes, any heir at law can claim a loss by reason of decedent's death. Other statutes, however, limit the claims to those who are the decedent's spouse, issue, parents, or siblings. Others empower the court to determine who may share in the award. [*See, e.g.,* Cal. Civ. Proc. Code §377—meretricious spouses are not within class of persons who may bring wrongful death actions; *and see* **Matuz v. Gerardin Corp.**, 207 Cal. App. 3d 203 (1989)—denying recovery to a cohabitant]

(2) Computing loss to survivors [§821]

The loss to the decedent's survivors may consist of both economic and noneconomic factors.

(a) Economic losses

1) Loss of support [§822]

If the decedent-victim was a wage earner or other income-provider, the loss of support contributions will be a major element of the survivors' damages.

a) Level of support based on decedent personally [§823]

Evidence is admissible to show just *how good* (or poor) *an income provider* the decedent was—*i.e.,* survivors may prove that the decedent devoted a larger-than-normal share of earnings to their support.

b) Support of children—maturity and possibly beyond [§824]

If the survivors are the decedent's *children*, they will normally be able to claim a loss of support *until maturity*. If they can prove that the decedent would have supported them beyond the age of majority (*e.g.,* advanced educational training), additional support can be claimed.

c) Remarriage irrelevant [§825]

If the survivors include the decedent's *spouse*, she will be entitled to claim support for the *balance of her life*. The fact that the spouse may be able to remarry—or even that she has already remarried—is *not admissible* in most courts. (The surviving spouse is under no duty to mitigate the consequences of her loss by remarrying; the doctrine of avoidable consequences is *not* applied here.) [**Exxon Corp. v. Brecheen,** 519 S.W.2d 170 (Tex. 1975)]

2) Loss of services [§826]

Particularly where the decedent-victim was the wife or mother of the survivors, the survivors suffer an economic loss in being deprived of her services. The cost of hiring substitutes (housekeepers, etc.) therefore is a compensable element of damage to the survivors. [**Haddigan v. Harkins,** 441 F.2d 844 (3d Cir. 1970)]

3) Funeral expenses [§827]

Funeral expenses are another compensable economic loss to the decedent's survivors and are recoverable in most states. (Some states do not allow funeral expenses, on the theory that the survivors would have had to pay the funeral expenses at some point in time, and the only damage is that they are compelled to pay earlier.)

4) Loss of inheritance compensable [§828]

Some courts (a minority) permit the survivors to recover that amount that the decedent might have accumulated during his lifetime, above and beyond that which he would have expended on their support, and which he might have left them as beneficiaries of his estate. In effect, this approaches the "loss to the estate" concept. [**Kuwalik v. ERA Jet Alaska,** 820 P.2d 627 (Alaska 1991)] However, most courts *reject* this measure of damage, on the ground that the decedent's testamentary estate and disposition thereof, had he lived, are simply too speculative. [*See* **Moss v. Executive Beechcraft, Inc.,** 562 F. Supp. 873 (W.D. Mo. 1983)—allowing recovery where properly supported by evidence; 91 A.L.R.2d 477; **Yowell v. Piper Aircraft,** 703 S.W.2d 630 (Tex. 1986)]

(b) Noneconomic losses [§829]

In addition to the pecuniary damages discussed above, wrongful death recoveries may include the following noneconomic losses to the survivors.

1) **Loss of decedent's society, comfort, and protection [§830]**

The loss of the decedent's care, comfort, protection, parental guidance, and nurture are often the most significant elements of damage in wrongful death actions. Some decisions have extended this nonpecuniary element to siblings, but the cases are divided. [*See* **Estate of Finley,** 601 N.E.2d 699 (Ill. 1992)]

a) **Considered tangible [§831]**

Many wrongful death statutes are construed as authorizing only "pecuniary" losses; *i.e.,* no damages for "sentimental losses" are recoverable. Nevertheless, the deprivation of the decedent's society, comfort, and protection is regarded as so *tangible* a loss to the survivors as to have a "pecuniary" connotation, rather than being regarded as a "sentimental" loss. [**McKee v. Colt Electronics Co.,** *supra,* §819; **Rodriguez v. United States,** 823 F.2d 735 (3d Cir. 1987)]

b) **Determining loss [§832]**

Evidence as to the *nature of the relationship* between the decedent and the survivors (*i.e.,* how loving a parent, how devoted a spouse, etc.) is admissible in establishing the extent of the loss. [*See* **Estate of Davis v. Johnson,** 745 F.2d 1066 (7th Cir. 1984)—no recovery where decedent father in mental institution]

c) **Some courts contra [§833]**

Some courts are contra. For example, in **Liff v. Schildkrout,** 49 N.Y.2d 622 (1980), the court of appeals held that a claim for loss of consortium was *not* a pecuniary injury compensable in a wrongful death action in New York.

2) **Decedent's trauma [§834]**

Some courts have held that the preimpact terror of the decedent was compensable under the state's wrongful death act. [**Malacynski v. McDonnell Douglas Corp.,** 565 F. Supp. 105 (S.D.N.Y. 1983); *and see* **M & M Pipe & Pressure Vessel Fabricators, Inc. v. Roberts,** 531 So. 2d 615 (Miss. 1988)]

3) **Damages for death of children [§835]**

Where a minor child is the victim, the surviving parents can prove little in the way of economic loss—because the cost of rearing a child is usually greatly in excess of any contributions that might be expected from the child. Because of this, and also because of the rule disallowing "sentimental" losses (above), many courts severely limit the damages awardable to the parents for the death of a child. [**Wilson v. Wylie**, 518 P.2d 1213 (N.M. 1973); **Garland v. Hevrin**, 724 F.2d 16 (2d Cir. 1983)—parents' recovery limited to pecuniary injuries] However, several cases have openly abandoned any purely pecuniary evaluation for the child's death. [**Dawson v. Hill & Hill Truck Lines**, 671 P.2d 589 (Mont. 1983); *but see* **Gabriel v. Illinois Farmers Insurance Co.**, 525 N.E.2d 864 (Ill. 1988)—these damages are not awarded where proof shows estrangement of parent and child] These cases recognize that there are compensable *noneconomic* damages to the parent—*i.e.*, the child as a source of pride, enjoyment, etc. However, the costs of rearing the child have to be deducted from this "lost investment." [**Wycko v. Gnodtke**, 105 N.W.2d 118 (Mich. 1960)]

a) Siblings [§836]

Several cases have also allowed siblings to recover. [*See, e.g.*, **Crystal v. Hubbard**, 324 N.W.2d 869 (Mich. 1982)—recovery by sibling allowed; *but see* **Clark v. Jones**, 658 P.2d 1147 (Okla. 1983)—no recovery by sibling for loss of love and companionship]

b) Damages limited by parents' life expectancy [§837]

Where noneconomic damages are allowed, they are *limited* to the life expectancy of the surviving parent. [**Bowen v. Constructors Equipment Rental Co.**, 196 S.E.2d 789 (N.C. 1973)]

c) Unborn children [§838]

The cases are not uniform as to whether there is an action for the death of an *unborn* child. [*See, e.g.*, **Miller v. Highland Insurance Co.**, 336 So. 2d 636 (Fla. 1976)—yes, in allowing medical and funeral expenses and even pain and suffering of parents, but excluding loss of future support and services; **Riley v. Koneru**, 539 N.E.2d 788 (Ill. 1992)—yes, including damages for loss of society; *but see* **State ex rel. Hardin v. Sanders**, 538 S.W.2d 336 (Mo. 1976)—no recovery]

(c) Prejudgment interest [§839]

Whether prejudgment interest may be awarded in wrongful death cases depends on the interpretation given to the governing state statute. In the case of *In re* **Air Crash Disaster Near Chicago**, 644 F.2d 633 (7th Cir. 1981), the court ruled that prejudgment interest *per se* is not allowable as a separate element of a wrongful death damages award, but that the use of interest is implicit in the calculation of the present value of the plaintiff's pecuniary loss as of the date of trial.

(3) "Hedonic" damages [§840]

In the context of *wrongful death statutes* aimed at compensating surviving relatives for their loss, "hedonic" damages (*e.g.,* the loss of enjoyment of life or the value of the deceased's life to him) are generally not recognized. [*See* **Ortega v. Plaxco,** 793 F. Supp. 298 (D.N.M. 1991); **Simmons v. Hartford Insurance Co.,** 786 F. Supp. 574 (E.D. La. 1992)] On the other hand, in an action by a deceased's estate for death *arising out of violation of a civil rights statute* which has a distinguishable goal, a strong argument has been made for "hedonic" damages. [*See* **Sherrod v. Berry,** 629 F. Supp. 159 (N.D. Ill. 1985)—§1983 action is akin to a tort claim]

(4) Punitive damages [§841]

Although there are several exceptions, most courts do *not* allow punitive damages in an action by the survivors, even if the decedent's death was intentionally caused. The reason is that the tortfeasor may have intended to harm the decedent, but the wrongful death action belongs to the survivors, and the tortfeasor had no "malice" as to them. [*See* **Pease v. Beech Aircraft Corp.,** 38 Cal. App. 3d 450 (1974); *In re* **Air Crash Disaster Near Chicago,** *supra*]

RECOVERY UNDER "LOSS TO SURVIVORS" TYPE OF WRONGFUL DEATH ACTIONS	**gilbert**
WHO MAY SUE?	In some states, any heir at law; in other states, decedent's spouse, issue, parents, or siblings. Still other states allow the courts to decide.
WHAT MAY BE RECOVERED?	Damages for the *pecuniary loss the survivor has suffered* as a result of the decedent's death, such as the value of lost support and services and funeral expenses. Some courts also allow recovery for loss of decedent's society, comfort, protection, etc.
WHAT MAY NOT BE RECOVERED?	Damages for the *decedent's* lost wages, medical expenses, pain and suffering, etc.; *punitive damages*. These are recovered in the survival action.

4. Limitations on Amount [§842]

Most wrongful death statutes have no maximum limit on recovery. However, a number of states do have dollar limitations; *e.g.,* in Massachusetts, the maximum recovery cannot exceed $30,000; in Kansas, except for pecuniary losses, damages may not exceed $25,000 [**Allman v. Holleman,** 667 P.2d 296 (Kan. 1983)]; and in California, in medical malpractice cases, noneconomic damages may not exceed $250,000 [**Green v. Franklin,** 190 Cal. App. 3d 93 (1987)].

D. Injuries to Others

1. Injuries to Spouse—Damages for Loss of Consortium

a. Common law action [§843]

The early common law held that the *husband* had a proprietary right to the services of his wife, and consequently that he had a right of damages for the loss of such services that had a provable pecuniary value. In due course, the husband's claim was expanded to include the elements of companionship, felicity, and sexual intercourse (the "incidents" of the marital relationship that gained the description of "consortium") that had typical nonpecuniary characteristics whose value could be left only to jury determination.

(1) Limitation

The above remedy was available only with respect to *injuries* to the wife. If she was killed, the husband's remedy was a *wrongful death* action (*see supra*).

(2) Note

The early common law did *not* recognize a right to damages in favor of the wife when the husband was injured. There was no common law right to *his* services; and in addition it was felt that the wife's pecuniary losses would be recouped in the husband's personal injury recovery.

b. Modern law [§844]

Under modern law, most jurisdictions allow the wife a right to damages for loss of consortium. [**Hitaffer v. Argonne Co.**, 183 F.2d 811 (D.C. Cir. 1950); **Rodriguez v. Bethlehem Steel Corp.**, 12 Cal. 3d 382 (1974)]

(1) Note

Other jurisdictions (*e.g.,* Massachusetts, Utah) obtain equality between the sexes by denying the right to damages for loss of "consortium" to both spouses. [**Cruz v. Wright**, 765 P.2d 869 (Utah 1988)]

(2) And note

Recent cases have extended the right to recover for loss of consortium to a *cohabitant*, assuming that she could establish the elements of the loss. [**Bulloch v. United States**, 487 F. Supp. 1078 (D.N.J. 1980)—divorced woman living apart from the victim, her former husband; *but see* **Elden v. Sheldon**, 46 Cal. 3d 267 (1988)—cohabitant has no claim for loss of consortium]

c. Punitive damages [§845]

It has been held that punitive damages may *not* be awarded as part of the compensation for loss of consortium. [**Hammond v. North American Asbestos**

Corp., 435 N.E.2d 540 (Ill. 1982); *but see* **Sheats v. Bowen,** 318 F. Supp. 640 (D. Del. 1970)]

2. Injuries to Children [§846]

At common law, a parent (father) is entitled to the earnings of a minor child and hence may recover for *pecuniary* loss resulting from injury to the child. [*See* **McKee v. Neilson,** 444 P.2d 194 (Okla. 1968)] Recent decisions have extended this to allow recovery also for loss of aid, comfort, society, and companionship of the child. [**Shockley v. Prier,** 225 N.W.2d 495 (Wis. 1975); *but see* **Burgess v. Superior Court,** 2 Cal. 4th 1064 (1992)—parents cannot recover for loss of child's consortium, but a possible claim for negligent infliction of emotional distress is not ruled out]

a. Distinguish—right of children to recover for parent's injuries [§847]

On the other hand, the majority of jurisdictions hold that a child has *no right* to damage for injuries done to one parent, it being urged that the other parent's claim for injuries protects the child. However, the number of jurisdictions recognizing this claim continues to grow, and may now number 18. Some jurisdictions have overruled precedents to the contrary and recognized the claim. [*See* **Gallimore v. Children's Hospital Medical Center,** 617 N.E.2d 1052 (Ohio 1993)—*overruling* **High v. Howard,** 592 N.E.2d 818 (Ohio 1992)]

3. Injuries to Employees [§848]

The early common law recognized a cause of action in favor of a master (*i.e.*, employer) against one who tortiously injured a servant (*i.e.*, employee) for the lost value of the servant's services. The modern rule is that an employer can recover for *economic* loss by reason of injury to his employees only when the tort is *intentional*, not negligent. [**Snow v. West,** 440 P.2d 864 (Or. 1968)]

4. Restitutionary Remedies [§849]

If a person is tortiously injured, and members of the victim's family pay the medical expenses and perform nursing services, restitution may be an appropriate remedy, at least if it can be proved that such services would *not* have been rendered gratuitously to the victim in any event (*i.e.*, that they were rendered with expectation of compensation).

a. Victim's action

These same expenses could be claimed as special damages in an action by the victim against the tortfeasor (subject to the avoidable consequences rule).

5. Wrongful Conception, Wrongful Birth, and Wrongful Life Cases

a. Wrongful conception cases [§850]

Wrongful conception usually results from negligence, *e.g.*, the negligent performance of a sterilization operation or a negligently filled birth control prescription, after which a child is born. The action typically is based on a medical malpractice tort, but may also be for breach of contract damages (subject to the rule in **Hadley v. Baxendale,** *see supra,* §23). Damages include (i) medical expenses in connection with the birth, (ii) pain and suffering of the mother, and (iii) expenses of raising the child to majority (apparently a minority rule unless the child is deformed). There is a division of opinion as to whether there should be an *offset* for the benefit of having the enjoyment, affection, and possible future support of the child. [**Burke v. Rivo,** 551 N.E.2d 1 (Mass. 1990)—offset allowed; **Lovelace Medical Center v. Mendez,** 805 P.2d 603 (N.M. 1991)—offset denied] The avoidable consequences doctrine cannot be invoked despite the availability of abortion or the placing of the child out for adoption.

b. **Wrongful birth cases [§851]**

Parents of a child born with serious physical or mental defects may have a cause of action against a physician who fails to detect or fails to inform the parents of a known potential defect in the fetus, which information would allow the parents to decide whether to have an abortion. A decisive majority of recent decisions recognize the cause of action. [*See* **Keel v. Banach,** 624 So. 2d 1022 (Ala. 1993)] The measure of damages includes: (i) medical and hospital expenses necessary to treat the defect and additional medical and educational costs incurred until the child's majority, (ii) physical pain suffered by the mother, and (iii) loss of consortium. The courts are divided as to damages for the parents' mental and emotional distress. [*See* **Keel v. Banach,** *supra*— yes; **Smith v. Cote,** 513 A.2d 341 (N.H. 1986)—no]

c. **Wrongful life cases [§852]**

A cause of action for wrongful life, on the other hand, *arises in favor of the child* who is born with birth defects that were known or detectable before birth and in time for an abortion. The apparent majority of decisions *do not recognize the cause of action* [*see* **Smith v. Cote,** *supra*] because of the incongruity of recovering damages for being alive. Some recognize the cause of action, but with the limitations of recovery to *specific damages*—special training and education related to the defect. [**Turpin v. Sortini,** 31 Cal. 3d 220 (1981)]

Chapter Nine: Fraud

Chapter Approach

Often a Remedies exam question will set up a fact situation in which the plaintiff was induced by fraudulent misrepresentations to enter into a contract. The key to answering these questions is to distinguish the tort remedy of *damages based on the affirmance* of the contract from the *restitutionary remedy based on a disaffirmance* of the contract.

Your approach to these questions should be:

1. Analyze the factual situation to determine *whether the contract has been affirmed*. Remember that this can be by accepting benefits, suing for damages, etc. And keep in mind the possible problems of *election of remedies*.

2. If the contract has been *affirmed*, then you simply need to (i) establish the *elements of the tort* (misrepresentation of fact, scienter, intent to induce reliance, "justifiable reliance," actual reliance, and damages) and (ii) determine *the rule of damages* to be applied (benefit-of-the-bargain or out-of-pocket rule).

3. If there has been *no affirmance* of the contract, *restitution* is available. In this case, be sure to distinguish between *legal* and *equitable* rescission.

One final note: Always remember that these remedies (damages and restitution) are *alternative* remedies; the court can grant one or the other, but not both.

A. Election of Remedies

1. Damages vs. Restitution [§853]

A party who is induced to enter into a contract by fraudulent misrepresentations of another has *alternative* remedies: she may either affirm the contract and seek *damages or rescind* the contract and seek restitution. As will be seen, these remedies are alternative, *not cumulative*, and thus at some point in the controversy a choice must be made between them.

2. Affirmance of Contract [§854]

By his conduct, an injured party may manifest consent to be bound by the contract. If he does so, he is said to have made a choice of substantive rights and is thereby limited to remedies consistent with the existence of the contract. "Affirmance of the contract" may be established in several ways:

a. Accepting benefits [§855]

Affirmance of the contract may be shown by continuing to accept its benefits *after discovery* of the fraud.

Example: After learning of fraudulent misrepresentations in the sale of stock, Martha accepts and deposits dividends from the stock in her bank account.

 Example: Pancho continues to operate a business for his own benefit after learning that a fraudulent misrepresentation had been made inducing him to buy the property. [**Porras v. Bass,** 665 P.2d 1249 (Or. 1983)—continuing possession after discovery of fraud; **McGregor v. Mommer,** 714 P.2d 536 (Mont. 1986)—continuing to operate business after discovering the fraud]

(1) Distinguish—U.C.C. rule [§856]
Under the U.C.C., a buyer does *not* waive the right to revoke acceptance of goods by continuing to use it, as long as the use is reasonable. [**McCullough v. Bill Swad Chrysler-Plymouth,** 449 N.E.2d 1289 (Ohio 1983)—continued use of defective automobile for 18 months; **O'Shea v. Hatch,** 640 P.2d 515 (N.M. 1982)—continued possession of a horse]

b. Delay in disaffirming [§857]
Affirmance may also be shown by silence and delay in disaffirming after learning of the fraud. [**Griffin v. Axsom,** 525 N.E.2d 346 (Ind. 1988)—five year delay; **Knudsen v. Jensen,** 521 N.W.2d 415 (S.D. 1994)—2.5 year delay]

c. Suing for damages [§858]
It is the general rule that the *commencement of an action for damages for fraud* is an affirmance of the contract, *precluding* a later amendment to a rescission theory. [**Wedgwood Diner v. Good,** 534 A.2d 537 (Pa. 1987)—recovery of damages from agent precluded rescission suit against principal]

(1) Note
An election of remedies does *not* occur when a plaintiff mistakenly pursues a remedy that does not exist. [**Fina Supply v. Abilene National Bank,** 726 S.W.2d 537 (Tex. 1987)—plaintiff's action on nonexistent fraud claim not a bar to subsequent reformation action]

3. Rescission of Contract [§859]
If there has been no affirmance of the contract manifested by the injured party's conduct, the injured party may elect the alternative remedy of rescission.

a. Filing suit for rescission not an election [§860]
Unlike filing suit for damages, the commencement of an action to rescind a contract ordinarily is *not* held to be an irrevocable election of remedies (assuming the notice and offer to rescind were rejected by the wrongdoer). Thus,

the plaintiff may be permitted to amend from a rescission theory to a cause of action for damages as long as no prejudice can be shown by the defendant-wrongdoer. The election of remedies doctrine is said to be based on an estoppel principle and this requires a showing of *detrimental reliance.*

Example: Plaintiff commenced an action seeking rescission of a contract of sale. However, before the action was tried, plaintiff sold the property, and then commenced a new action for damages. *Held:* There was no irrevocable election precluding a shift to the alternative remedy of damages because *no prejudice* was shown and no choice of inconsistent substantive rights was made. [**Schlotthauer v. Krenzelok,** 79 N.W.2d 76 (Wis. 1956)]

Compare: Plaintiff purchased stock from defendant and later gave notice of rescission, claiming fraud. Subsequently, plaintiff commenced an action seeking damages. *Held:* There *was* an irrevocable election of remedies on filing the rescission suit, because to permit plaintiff to claim damages after giving notice of rescission would permit plaintiff to *speculate without risk* in a fluctuating market (thus showing prejudice to defendant). [**Estate Counseling Service v. Merrill Lynch, Pierce, Fenner & Smith, Inc.,** 303 F.2d 527 (10th Cir. 1962)]

(1) Note

Where the plaintiff levies a writ of attachment in conjunction with a complaint seeking rescission and restitution, an irrevocable election results because the plaintiff's positive action has deprived the defendant of the use of the property to his prejudice. [**Roam v. Koop,** 41 Cal. 3d 1035 (1974)—but in this case the court ruled that the election of remedies doctrine is an affirmative defense that is waived if not pleaded]

b. Effect of judgment [§861]

If the plaintiff pursues the rescission theory to an adverse judgment on the merits, a subsequent action for damages may be *barred* either by res judicata (issue or claim preclusion) or by a ruling that an irrevocable election has been made because of prejudicial reliance. [*See* **Petty v. Darin,** 675 S.W.2d 714 (Tenn. 1984)]

c. Election by offer and acceptance [§862]

If the injured party gives notice of rescission and tenders back the consideration to the wrongdoer, the wrongdoer may choose to accept the tender. In such cases, the initial election is conclusive and no shift to the damages remedy is thereafter allowed. [**Paularena v. Superior Court,** 231 Cal. App. 2d 906 (1965)]

4. Suing in the Alternative [§863]

The injured party may commence a lawsuit pleading in the alternative for *either rescission or damages*. No election is compelled when the suit is filed, but an election may be required prior to submission of the case to judge or jury. [**Walraven v. Martin,** 333 N.W.2d 569 (Mich. 1983); **Bancroft v. Woodward,** 183 Cal. 99 (1920)]

a. **Note—alternative remedies [§864]**

Stated differently, there must be an election of remedies prior to judgment because the remedies are alternative, not cumulative. Thus, the ultimate judgment must grant *either* damages or restitution. It cannot grant both.

b. **But note—U.C.C. rule [§865]**

In sale of goods cases, the U.C.C. governs the remedies available to the parties. The official comments to section 2-703 state specifically that the Code "rejects any doctrine of election of remedies as a fundamental policy." For example, if a buyer rightfully rejects or revokes acceptance of the goods involved in the sale, the U.C.C. authorizes recovery of both the price paid and damages. The nonalternative nature of the remedies does not, however, permit inconsistent or double recoveries. [**General Motors Acceptance Corp. v. Anaya,** 703 P.2d 169 (N.M. 1985)]

B. Affirmance of the Contract—Damages Remedy

1. **Substantive Elements [§866]**

If the injured party elects to affirm the contract, his remedy is an action at law for damages. At common law, this was classified as an action on the case for deceit. The essential elements to plead and prove a cause of action in tort for deceit are:

a. **Misrepresentation of fact [§867]**

The misrepresentation must be of a fact and not a matter of opinion (unless by an expert) or a mere prediction or promise.

(1) **Active concealment [§868]**

Ordinarily, the misrepresentation will take the form of an affirmative statement; but active concealment of the truth is regarded precisely the same as affirmative misstatements. [**Posner v. Davis,** 395 N.E.2d 133 (Ill. 1979)—concealment of defects in home]

(2) **Distinguish—nondisclosure [§869]**

Active concealment must be distinguished from nondisclosure. At common law, nondisclosure is *not* actionable except in situations where there are fiduciary relations between the parties or where the wrongdoer made a previous statement innocently and subsequently discovers it to be false.

(a) Note

Recent cases have extended liability for nondisclosure to situations where the defendant has some *special knowledge* affecting the *value* of the property sold which is *not readily available* to the plaintiff. [**Lingsch v. Savage,** 213 Cal. App. 2d 729 (1963)—real estate broker who knew and *failed to disclose* that property sold had been condemned as untenantable held liable to purchaser for fraud; having such special knowledge, he owed duty to disclose; **Ollerman v. O'Rourke Co.,** 288 N.W.2d 95 (Wis. 1980)—undisclosed underground well]

b. Scienter [§870]

At common law, it was necessary to establish the defendant's *actual knowledge* that the representation was false (or at least *reckless disregard* for whether or not it was true). Subsequently, courts ruled that *negligent* misrepresentations are also actionable. [*See* **Cunha v. Ward Foods,** 804 F.2d 1418 (9th Cir. 1986)—adopting Restat. 2d Torts §552B permitting recovery of out-of-pocket damages for negligent misrepresentations; **Wilson v. Great American Industries,** 855 F.2d 987 (2d Cir. 1988)—in accord]

(1) Minority view [§871]

Today there are some cases permitting recovery (particularly for misrepresentation in connection with the sale of chattels) even though the misrepresentation is *innocently* made—*i.e.,* holding the defendant strictly liable for the defendant's misrepresentation. [**Johnson v. Healy,** 405 A.2d 54 (Conn. 1978)—sale of a home]

---

e.g. Example: Defendant innocently made various misrepresentations about the capabilities of a data processing system. These representations were not incorporated in the contract and there was a disclaimer of implied warranties. *Held:* Even though no cause of action could be stated on a warranty theory, recovery may be upheld on a fraud theory, based on the innocent representations made by defendant. [**Clements Auto Co. v. Service Bureau Corp.,** 444 F.2d 169 (8th Cir. 1971)]

(a) Comment

This allows an action for innocent misrepresentation that is functionally indistinguishable from *breach of warranty* actions, where strict liability has always been the rule.

(b) Restatement view [§872]

In a sale, rental, or exchange transaction, Restatement (Second) of

Torts section 552C makes sellers liable for innocent misrepresentations. Damages are **limited**, however, to the difference between the value of what the other has parted with and the value of what was received. Benefit of the bargain and consequential damages are excluded. [*But see* **Johnson v. Healy**, *supra*—proper test is stated to be "the difference in value between the property had it been as represented and the property as it actually was"]

c. **Intent to induce reliance [§873]**

It must be shown that the defendant intended to induce the plaintiff to rely on the misrepresentation.

d. **Materiality (justifiable reliance) [§874]**

The requirement of *"justifiable reliance"* by the plaintiff means that the misrepresentation relied on must be of a **material** fact. In effect, what is required is a material misrepresentation of a material fact. The first part of the rule requires the misrepresentation to be a **major departure from truth**; the second part requires the fact to be one that is **likely to induce action** by a reasonable person. The test of materiality is thus an **objective** one.

Example: Kirsner made two representations to Clark in connection with a contract for the sale of land: (i) that he (Kirsner) was the owner, whereas in fact a wholly owned corporation held title to the property; and (ii) that the annual ground rent was $75, whereas in fact the rent was $78. *Held*: These misrepresentations were both **immaterial**. The misstatement as to ground rent was material in the sense that it would influence the actions of a reasonable person, but the departure from truth was trivial. On the other hand, the assertion of ownership was totally false, but the fact of ownership by Kirsner's wholly owned corporation, rather than by Kirsner individually, was immaterial in the sense that it would not influence the decision to buy the property. [**Clark v. Kirsner**, 74 A.2d 830 (Md. 1950)]

Compare: Seller misrepresented the offering price of a farm, claiming that he had never offered to sell it for less than $8,500, whereas in fact he had frequently offered it for $6,000. This was held to be **material**, because it was likely to influence reasonable persons in determining the value of the property. [**Stuart v. Lester**, 1 N.Y.S. 699 (1888)]

e. **Reliance [§875]**

The plaintiff must have actually relied on the misrepresentation in entering into the contract. This is the causal element, usually tested by the "but for" test; *i.e.,* but for the misrepresentation, the plaintiff would not have entered into the contract. If the plaintiff made an independent investigation, learned the facts, and relied on **her own** judgment, there can be no recovery.

f. Damages [§876]

The plaintiff must show that she has sustained pecuniary loss as a result of her reliance on the misrepresentation. Such loss is an *essential element* without which no cause of action for fraud can be stated.

g. Distinguish—securities fraud [§877]

If remedies are sought for fraud pursuant to federal or state securities regulations, particularly where class actions are involved, the substantive elements of scienter and reliance may be modified. (*See* detailed discussion in Corporations Summary.)

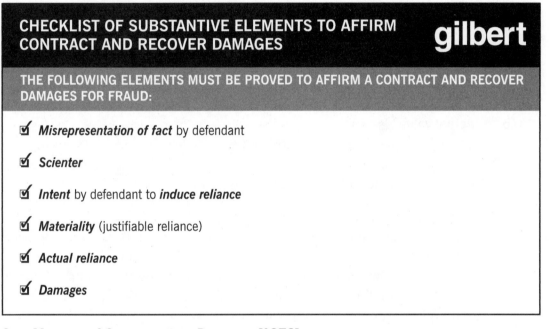

CHECKLIST OF SUBSTANTIVE ELEMENTS TO AFFIRM CONTRACT AND RECOVER DAMAGES — **gilbert**

THE FOLLOWING ELEMENTS MUST BE PROVED TO AFFIRM A CONTRACT AND RECOVER DAMAGES FOR FRAUD:

- ☑ *Misrepresentation of fact* by defendant
- ☑ *Scienter*
- ☑ *Intent* by defendant to *induce reliance*
- ☑ *Materiality* (justifiable reliance)
- ☑ *Actual reliance*
- ☑ *Damages*

2. Measure of Compensatory Damages [§878]

Courts are divided as to the proper measure of damages to be applied in fraud actions involving the sale of property. Some apply the so-called *out-of-pocket rule* of damages and award the difference between what the plaintiff paid and the actual value of what the plaintiff received. This is based on the premise that the action is one of tort and that the purpose of tort damages is to indemnify for loss. Other courts apply the *benefit-of-the-bargain rule* and measure damages by the difference between the actual value of what is received and the value it would have had if it had been as represented. This view favors the contract theory of damages which satisfies the plaintiff's expectation interest.

a. Illustration

Peter sought to recover damages for fraudulent misrepresentations made by Dianna in the sale of a farm. The land was represented as containing 4,000 cords of wood but in fact contained only 200 cords. Dianna contended that the land was nevertheless worth the purchase price. *Held:* Applying the benefit-of-the-bargain rule, Peter could recover (set off against the price) the value of the missing 3,800 cords of wood. *Rationale:* To apply the out-of-pocket rule would allow Dianna to misrepresent with impunity, because in this case the value of the land equaled the purchase price. [**Selman v. Shirley**, 91 P.2d 312 (Or. 1939)]

OUT-OF-POCKET VS. BENEFIT-OF-BARGAIN—A COMPARISON BASED ON SELMAN V. SHIRLEY	gilbert

OUT-OF-POCKET RULE		BENEFIT-OF-BARGAIN RULE	
Price paid	$2,000	Value as represented (land and value of timber)	$4,000
less		*less*	
Value received (fair market value of land)	$2,000	Value received (land and timber)	$2,100
Damages	$0	Damages	$1,900

b. **"Actual value" [§879]**

Both rules require a determination of "actual value" of what is received. Generally, actual value means *market value*, but in fraudulent stock sale cases, courts may look to the intrinsic or real value of the stock.

c. **"Value of property as represented" ("make-good" rule) [§880]**

To avoid the difficult task of proving the value of the property if it had been as represented, some jurisdictions apply a modification of the benefit-of-the-bargain rule known as the "make-good" rule. These courts permit the plaintiff to recover expenditures reasonably necessary to make the property conform to the seller's representations. [**Posner v. Davis,** *supra,* §868]

---

e.g. **Example:** Deft represented that the farm he was selling to Plant had a usable well. This was untrue, and Plant spent $800 to drill a new well. *Held:* Plant could recover the $800. This represented the difference between the actual value of the farm received and the value as represented. [*See* **Nunn v. Howard,** 288 S.W. 678 (Ky. 1926)]

---

d. **Flexible application [§881]**

Many jurisdictions are flexible as to which basic rule to apply in a particular case, and even a state otherwise committed to the *out-of-pocket* rule may measure the damages by the *benefit of the bargain* when the defendant who acquires the property is a *fiduciary*. [**Pepitone v. Russo,** 64 Cal. App. 3d 685 (1976); **Leyendecker & Associates v. Wechter,** 683 S.W.2d 369 (Tex. 1984)— "whichever rule gives the consumer the greatest recovery"]

3. **Other Damages Recoverable [§882]**

In addition to (or sometimes in lieu of) the basic measure of compensatory damages, the plaintiff may recover *consequential* damages proximately caused by the fraud. For example, the water well example, above, loss of crops because of lack of water would be recoverable. Damages for mental distress, however, are not ordinarily available in actions based on commercial fraud. [**Cornell v. Winschel**, 408 N.W.2d 369 (Iowa 1987); **Osbourne v. Captial City Mortgage Corp.**, 667 A.2d 1321 (D.C. 1995)—negligent misrepresentation]

a. Damages unrelated to value of property purchased [§883]

The out-of-pocket loss and benefit-of-the-bargain rules for measuring damages assume a situation in which a defrauded buyer seeks recovery against a seller for some deficiency or defect in the bargained-for subject matter. If the misrepresentation is *collateral to the purchase*, this method of measuring damages is at best awkward and frequently cannot be used at all. In such situations, some courts permit recovery of those losses *proximately caused* by the misrepresentation.

---

e.g. Example: Coleman purchased a new car from Dealer, who represented that Coleman's old car would be sold and that no further payments would be required. This was untrue, and Coleman was forced to pay a deficiency judgment. Coleman was held entitled to recover this amount from Dealer. [**Coleman v. Ladd Ford Co.**, 215 Cal. App. 2d 90 (1963)] *Note:* Neither the out-of-pocket nor the benefit-of-the-bargain rule applies here because the misrepresentation was extrinsic to the value of the new car, which was as represented. Presumably the limitations on recovery in such cases must be stated in terms of proximate cause.

---

e.g. Example: Ford induced Hanson to accept a franchise for an automobile dealership on the basis of misrepresentations as to the profits made by other dealers in neighboring towns. Hanson's business was a failure and Hanson was forced into bankruptcy, losing his investment. Hanson's losses were held proximately caused by Ford's misrepresentations and hence recoverable in a fraud action. [**Hanson v. Ford Motor Co.**, 278 F.2d 586 (8th Cir. 1960)] Note again that the ordinary rules for measuring damages are inapplicable because Hanson wishes to recover for business losses, not for defects in or deficiency in value of what he got from Ford.

---

b. Sale of goods cases [§884]

Some courts hold that the measure of damages in sale of goods cases is governed by the U.C.C. Thus, damages would be measured by the benefit-of-the-bargain rule and would *include incidental and consequential damages*. [**Continental Airlines v. McDonnell Douglas Corp.**, 264 Cal. App. 3d 779 (1989)]

c. Punitive damages [§885]

Punitive damages may be recovered if the fraud is *intentional and malicious* [**Esparza v. Specht**, 55 Cal. App. 3d 1 (1976); **Ostano Commerzanstalt v. Telewide Systems**, 880 F.2d 642 (2d Cir. 1989)], but some courts disallow this award in common law cases [**Computer Systems Engineering v. Quantel Corp.,** 740 F.2d 59 (1st Cir. 1984)].

d. Damages where buyer committed fraud [§886]

Where the seller is suing the buyer because of the buyer's fraud, the benefit-of-the-bargain rule is inapplicable. The reason is that in these cases the seller's claim is quite simply that she did not get sufficient compensation (not that the value of what she got was less than represented). Hence, recovery of damages is measured by out-of-pocket losses and any additional damage *proximately resulting* from the fraud. [**Channell v. Anthony,** 58 Cal. App. 3d 290 (1976); **Johnson Building Co. v. River Bluff Development,** 374 N.W.2d 187 (Minn. 1985)]

Example: Doc purchased drugs from Gov at 5% of value, fraudulently representing that the drugs were to be used in a nonprofit hospital. Doc resold the drugs at a profit. Gov (seller) was held entitled to recover the profit Doc made on the sale. Gov could have realized at least Doc's selling price, and hence Gov sustained at least that much of a loss. [**United States v. Bound Brook Hospital,** 251 F.2d 12 (3d Cir. 1958)]

Example: Peter sold shares of stock to Martha as the result of Martha's misrepresentation as to value. Martha subsequently sold the stock for a huge profit. Peter was entitled to recover Martha's profit which proximately resulted from the fraud. [**Janigan v. Taylor,** 344 F.2d 781 (1st Cir. 1965)]

e. Damages in fraud cases not involving sale of property [§887]

In fraud actions not involving the sale of property, neither the "benefit-of-the-bargain" nor the "out-of-pocket" rule is appropriate; resort is therefore made to the general tort principle of recovery of losses proximately caused.

Example: Pedro was fraudulently induced to leave his former employment and go to work for Diego. Pedro was discharged by Diego after four months. The measure of damages was held to be the difference between what Pedro *would have earned* in his former employment and what he *actually earned* during the period required for his retraining in another line of employment. [**Chapman v. Marketing Unlimited, Inc.,** 539 P.2d 107 (Wash. 1975); *and see* **Carnival Cruise Lines v. Goodin,** 535 So. 2d 98 (Ala. 1988)—cruise passenger awarded damages based on fraudulent representation that bathrooms were wheelchair accessible]

C. Rescission of the Contract

1. Substantive Elements [§888]

The cause of action for rescission based on a disaffirmance of the contract for fraud differs significantly from the cause of action for damages. The essential elements for rescission are:

a. Misrepresentation of fact [§889]

Both the rescission and the damages remedies require a misrepresentation of fact. In cases of nondisclosure, however, relief by way of rescission may be more freely given, because in such cases the injured party may also rely on *mistake*—which is itself a basis for rescission but not for damages (*see infra*).

b. No scienter required [§890]

The misrepresentation may be *innocent*; there is no requirement of scienter. The reason for this difference is that the injured party is only seeking restitution and it is unjust to retain a benefit resulting from a misrepresentation, even if innocently made.

c. Materiality [§891]

Whether materiality must be proved depends on whether the misrepresentation was innocently made or intentionally made.

(1) Innocent misrepresentation cases [§892]

If the misrepresentation is innocently made, "materiality" is an *essential element* of the cause of action for rescission—*i.e.,* if an injured party seeks to set aside a transaction because of an innocent misrepresentation, she must at least show that the misrepresentation was one *likely to induce action* by reasonable persons. [**Osterberger v. Hites Construction Co.**, 599 S.W.2d 221 (Mo. 1980)]

(2) Intentional misrepresentation cases [§893]

If the misrepresentation is intentional, the element of materiality *need not* be satisfied. *Rationale:* The wrongdoer is not permitted to retain a gain achieved by deliberately tricking a gullible or foolish person.

d. Reliance [§894]

The injured party must show that the misrepresentation caused her to enter into the transaction, just as in the case of a tort action for deceit seeking damages.

e. Injury [§895]

Unlike the tort action, *pecuniary loss need not be shown* as a necessary prerequisite to rescission. The party seeking relief must, of course, show some injury, but the governing principle for rescission is whether it is "unjust" for the wrongdoer to retain a benefit.

---

e.g. **Example:** Cindy refused to sell her home to Becky, and Alex was aware of this. Alex contracted to buy Cindy's home, asserting that he was buying the home for his own use, although in fact he was buying it for Becky.

Even though there was no pecuniary loss to Cindy, she was entitled to rescission of the contract. [**Archer v. Stone**, 78 Law T.R. (n.s.) 34]

 Example: Earl wished to buy a mink coat as a gift for his girlfriend, but sought a reduction in the price from $5,000 to $4,000. Saks pretended to agree, but in fact had reached a secret agreement with the girlfriend for the payment of the other $1,000. Upon discovery, Earl was entitled to rescission of the sale. Although there was no pecuniary loss, Earl was injured by not getting what he bargained for (the coat at a reduced price). [**Earl v. Saks & Co.**, 36 Cal. 2d 602 (1951)]

CHECKLIST OF SUBSTANTIVE ELEMENTS TO RESCIND CONTRACT

gilbert

THE FOLLOWING ELEMENTS MUST BE PROVED TO RESCIND A CONTRACT FOR FRAUD:

☑ *Misrepresentation* of fact

☑ *Materiality* if the misrepresentation was unintentional

☑ *Reliance*

☑ *Injury* (some injustice, but not necessarily pecuniary loss)

---

2. Mechanics of Rescission

a. Introductory note [§896]

Although the material on procedures for rescission is included at this point and will not be repeated, these same rules apply regardless of whether the substantive basis of rescission is mistake, duress, illegality, etc., as well as fraud. Moreover, the same procedures apply whether the rescission is "at law" or "in equity" (below).

(1) Note

The statutory declaratory judgment procedure is an alternative to rescission and serves the same function. It is particularly favored by insurance companies.

Example: Insured made a fraudulent misrepresentation on an application for life insurance. After his death, the insurance company seeks a declaratory judgment voiding the policy for fraud. Upon proof of the fraud, a judgment is entered voiding the policy on condition that the insurance company return the premiums. [**Monarch Life Insurance Co. v. Donahue**, 708 F. Supp. 674 (E.D. Pa. 1989)]

---

b. Rescission at law [§897]

A plaintiff may sue at law to recover property (or the value of property) she has conferred upon the defendant under a contract voidable for fraud, duress, or mistake. The action at law is predicated on the theory that the plaintiff *has already effected a disaffirmance of the contract* itself, and invokes the aid of the court solely to obtain recovery of the property or its value. The normal cause of action is *quasi-contract*, but replevin or conversion may also lie (*see infra*, §§907-910).

(1) Notice and offer to restore as conditions precedent [§898]

To establish the right to recover in an action at law, the plaintiff must plead and prove that, *prior to commencing the action*, she gave the defendant prompt *notice* of the contract disaffirmance, and restored or *offered to restore* (tendered) anything of value received from the defendant under the contract. [**Maumelle Co. v. Escola**, 865 S.W.2d 272 (Ark. 1993); **Guerrero v. Hagco Building Systems**, 733 S.W.2d 635 (Tex. 1987)]

(a) Rationale for requirement

The action at law is predicated on the theory that the contract has been disaffirmed so that the defendant's retention of property received from the plaintiff is *wrongful*. The common law judgment invariably follows a prescribed formula to the effect that the plaintiff "have and recover" from the defendant money or property wrongfully withheld. Therefore, to establish the "wrongfulness" of the defendant's retention, the plaintiff must give notice and tender *prior* to filing suit.

(2) Notice and offer must have been prompt after discovery of fraud [§899]

Prompt notice of disaffirmance is required as a matter of fairness to the defendant, who may otherwise rely on the performance of the contract. Since the requirement of promptness is based on a desire to protect the defendant-wrongdoer, courts usually will excuse delay in giving notice if no *prejudice* results to the defendant. [**Davenport v. Vlach**, 726 P.2d 941 (Or. 1986); **McGregor v. Mommer**, 714 P.2d 536 (Mont. 1986)]

(a) Note

Remember, however, that a long delay in giving notice may itself be regarded as an *affirmance* of the contract (*see supra*, §857).

Example: Plaintiff used a piano for two years after discovering that the seller had fraudulently represented it as new. Because of plaintiff's continued use, plaintiff was held to have *elected to affirm* the contract, and hence no rescission action (at law or equity) would lie. [**Bruton v. Bland**, 132 S.E.2d 910 (N.C. 1963)]

---

(3) Circumstances under which tender back may be excused [§900]

Courts have developed numerous exceptions to the requirement that the injured party must restore, or offer to restore, any benefit received from the defendant. Thus, for example, *no such tender back* need be made under the following circumstances:

(a) Benefit worthless [§901]

No tender back need be made where the property given is, or has become, worthless (*e.g.,* where the defendant sold shares of corporation in bankruptcy).

(b) Money [§902]

The plaintiff is *not* required to restore *money* in the hope that the defendant will do likewise. Any money received from the defendant can simply be set off against whatever the plaintiff still has coming from the defendant.

(c) Property disposed of [§903]

Where, *prior to discovery* of the fraud, the plaintiff has consumed or disposed of the property received from the defendant, tender back is impossible and hence is excused. [*See* **Robinson v. Katz,** 610 P.2d 201 (N.M. 1980)—termination of an underlying contract made return of the property impossible]

c. Rescission in equity [§904]

Because of the flexible nature of the equitable decree, rescission in equity can be accomplished judicially rather than by action of the injured party. The party seeking rescission files a bill offering "to do equity" and seeking a *decree* rescinding the contract and ordering an accounting and restitution of benefits. [**Commercial Communications v. State,** 613 P.2d 473 (Okla. 1980)]

(1) Requirements regarding notice and tender [§905]

In jurisdictions where the distinction between "legal" and "equitable" rescission is maintained, the requirements of notice and tender are applied differently in cases where the equitable remedy is sought. Restoration or tender is *not* a prerequisite to the equity suit because the court has capacity to protect the defendant by conditioning the decree (*e.g.,* on restoration by the plaintiff of any benefit received from the defendant). [**Kracl v. Loseke,** 461 N.W.2d 67 (Neb. 1990)] Prompt notice of rescission is still necessary, however, to avoid an affirmance of the contract, although the notice may be given in the pleadings. [*See* **Haumont v. Security State Bank,** 374 N.W.2d 2 (Neb. 1985)] (This practice is authorized in California by statute where there is no prejudice to the defendant. [Cal. Civ. Code §1691])

(a) Caution

Restoration of the status quo ante is still a prerequisite for rescission even though the suit is equitable. A plaintiff who is unable to restore the consideration is denied the remedy, absent some acceptable excuse. [*See* **Ledbetter v. Webb**, 711 P.2d 874 (N.M. 1985)]

EXAM TIP   **gilbert**

Be sure to keep in mind the above distinction between legal and equitable rescission. Both generally require restoring the defendant to the status quo ante; the difference is in timing. For legal rescission, the restoration (or tender) must be made *prior* to filing the action. For equitable rescission, the restoration can be made *simultaneously* with the actual rescission. In either case, the plaintiff must give prompt notice of his intent to seek rescission in order to avoid accepting (*i.e.,* affirming) the contract.

---

(2) Procedural distinctions [§906]

The distinction between legal and equitable rescission is important for determining the *right to jury trial*. It may also affect other procedural matters such as attachment, subject matter jurisdiction, and the statute of limitations.

---

e.g. **Example:** Becky seeks to rescind a contract for the purchase of worthless personal property for which she paid $1,000. Since the remedy sought is a money judgment, the rescission is deemed legal in nature, and there is a right to a jury trial.

---

cf. **Compare:** Becky seeks to rescind a contract for the sale of land requiring the cancellation of a deed. Equitable relief is required, and there would be no right to a jury trial. [**Hastings v. Matlock**, 217 Cal. App. 856 (1985)]

(a) Note

Some states (*e.g.,* California) have adopted a *unitary procedure* for both types of rescission, but the right to jury trial still depends on the nature of the relief sought, whether legal or equitable. Equitable relief is not available if the remedy at law is adequate, and generally this is the case if all the plaintiff seeks is a money judgment.

3. Legal Remedies Available After Rescission of Contract for Fraud [§907]

By giving notice of disaffirmance and making the required tender (*see supra*), the injured party places the wrongdoer in the position of retaining benefits unjustly; *i.e.,* the contract having been rescinded, whatever benefits the wrongdoer retains must be disgorged. The choice of the restitutionary remedy depends on the situation.

a. Replevin [§908]

If the defendant obtained a chattel from the plaintiff pursuant to a fraudulently induced contract of sale, the plaintiff may rescind the contract and *then* may sue in replevin for the chattel itself since the rescission of the contract for fraud destroys the defendant's right to retain the chattel.

Example: Plaintiff was induced to sell sugar to defendant by fraudulent misrepresentations of solvency. After having notified defendant of disaffirmance for fraud, plaintiff was held entitled to replevy the sugar itself. [**American Sugar Refining v. Fancher,** 145 N.Y. 552 (1895)]

---

(1) Caveat

In situations governed by the U.C.C., the sole remedy provided for a misrepresentation of solvency by a buyer is the "recapture" of the chattels by the seller. [*See* U.C.C. §2-702; *see infra,* §923]

b. Conversion [§909]

Retention of chattels after rescission of the contract is an unlawful exercise of dominion over them and permits the owner to sue in tort for damages—*i.e.,* a "forced sale" at the chattel's *real* value, rather than at any lower price specified in the fraudulently induced contract of sale.

c. Quasi-contract [§910]

Quasi-contract is by far the most common remedy for fraud. The injured party may "waive the tort" and sue on a common count (usually "for goods sold and delivered"), recovering the *value* of the chattels obtained by the defendant's fraudulent conduct.

Example: Defendant induced plaintiff to sell him bicycles by making fraudulent misrepresentations of credit. After notice of disaffirmance of the contract, plaintiff was held entitled to recover the reasonable value of the bicycles in an action on a common count "for goods sold and delivered." Although the express contract had been disaffirmed for fraud, plaintiff could sue on the *implied (in law) contract* arising from the retention of the bicycles by defendant. Plaintiff could thus recover their *real value*, regardless of any lesser figure as to which he may have been fraudulently induced under the express contract. [**Crown Cycle Co. v. Brown,** 64 P. 451 (Or. 1901)]

---

(1) Caveat

As noted (*supra,* §908), where the buyer misrepresents solvency as in this example, the U.C.C. limits the seller's remedy to recapture of the chattels. [U.C.C. §2-702]

d. Restitutionary damages—special case of securities fraud [§911]

The stock that a defrauded buyer has paid for may become worthless before the fraud is discovered. The simplest remedy is that of quasi-contract to recover the money paid. Section 12(a)(2) of the Securities Act of 1933 codifies this in part by saying that an investor harmed by fraud in a prospectus may sue "to recover the consideration paid with interest thereon, *less the amount of any income received thereon*, upon the tender of such security, or for damages if he no longer owns the security."

Example: Randall invests in a fraudulent tax shelter and receives tax benefits before the investment becomes worthless. Randall sues to recover his money and Loftsgaarden seeks to offset the tax benefits. The Supreme Court held that this is a suit for restitutionary "damages" and Loftsgaarden could not offset Randall's tax benefits because they were not income. [**Randall v. Loftsgaarden,** 478 U.S. 647 (1986)]

(1) Comment

The use of the word "damages" is confusing. If the action is for restitution, there should be no offset because the defendant received no benefit from the plaintiff's tax savings. If the action is for damages in the proper sense, the credit for benefit rule (*see supra*, §86) would seem to apply.

4. Equitable Remedies for Fraud

a. Equitable jurisdiction must first be established [§912]

As with every other case in which equitable remedies are sought, it must always be established that a proper basis for equitable jurisdiction exists. Usually, the ground is that the remedy at law (a judgment for damages) would be inadequate—and often the facts relied upon will be a showing that the wrongdoer is *insolvent*. In other cases, the "inadequacy" of the legal remedy will be made out by demonstrating that the relief sought cannot be granted by law courts—*e.g.*, where deeds must be canceled or executed.

b. Restitution in equity [§913]

If a proper basis for equitable jurisdiction is established, the plaintiff may be entitled to a decree ordering the defendant to *account* to the plaintiff for the value of the benefits fraudulently obtained—with the objective of "doing equity." [*See* **Roberts v. Sears, Roebuck & Co.,** 471 F. Supp. 372 (N.D. Ill. 1979)—inventor allowed to rescind assignment of patent on wrench and granted accounting of profits estimated to be more than $44 million]

c. Remedies upon rescission of land sale contract—fraud by seller [§914]

In a suit by a buyer against a seller for rescission of a land sale contract, the buyer will recover: (i) the *consideration* paid, with interest; (ii) expenditures for *improvements*, at cost if reasonable, but less depreciation; (iii) *expenditures to maintain* the property; (iv) *insurance and taxes*; and (v) *incidental expenses* (*e.g.*, costs of escrow and moving). [**Brunner v. La Casse,** 763 P.2d

662 (Mont. 1988); **Iota Management v. Boulevard Insurance Co.,** 731 S.W.2d 399 (Mo. 1987)]

(1) Vendee's lien [§915]

Upon rescission, the buyer's restitutionary claim is secured by a vendee's lien on the property. [**Utemark v. Samuel,** 118 Cal. App. 2d 313 (1953); **Iota Management v. Boulevard Insurance Co.,** *supra*]

(2) Note—seller's offset [§916]

To "do equity," the court's decree will provide that the seller recover from the buyer: (i) the *possession* of the land, and (ii) the *value of its use*—which may be computed at fair rental value or, in some jurisdictions, the actual benefit to the buyer if less. [*See* **Le Trace v. Elms,** 595 P.2d 1281 (Or. 1979)—buyer charged only with actual benefit derived from use of land; **Daugherty v. Young,** 615 P.2d 341 (Or. 1980)—buyer must pay reasonable value of use but is entitled to recover interest on difference between contract payments and reasonable rental value from date each payment was made]

d. Remedies upon rescission of land sale contract—fraud by buyer [§917]

In a suit by a seller against a buyer for fraudulently inducing a land sale contract, the seller will recover from the buyer: (i) the *possession* of the realty, and (ii) the *value of its use*—computed either at fair rental value or the buyer's profits, *at the seller's election.* [**Head & Seeman v. Greg,** 311 N.W.2d 667 (Wis. 1981)]

(1) Note—buyer's offset

To "do equity," the decree will provide that the buyer recovers from the seller: (i) the *consideration paid* plus interest; (ii) *taxes paid*; and (iii) expenditures for *necessary improvements only*, at cost.

e. Remedies upon rescission of the sale of a business [§918]

In a suit by a buyer against a seller for rescission of the sale of a business, the buyer recovers the consideration paid, with interest, but compensates the seller for the use of the premises by paying either reasonable rental value, or the profits, if any, *whichever is less.* [**McCoy v. West,** 70 Cal. App. 3d 295 (1977); **Widmer v. Leffelman,** 249 P.2d 476 (Or. 1952)]

5. Special Damages Awarded in Restitutionary Proceedings [§919]

The award of special damages is not inconsistent with or precluded by an election of the remedy of rescission and restitution. Where rescission is for the tort of fraud, the damages recovered are those proximately caused. However, where rescission is based on a *material breach of contract*, damages are controlled by the "contemplation of the parties" limitation of **Hadley v. Baxendale** (*supra,* §23). [**Runyon v. Pacific Air Industries,** 2 Cal. 3d 304 (1970)]

a. **Mutual mistake [§920]**

If the rescission is for a mutual mistake, consequential damages are not allowed. [**Carter v. Matthews,** 701 S.W.2d 374 (Ark. 1986); **Renner v. Kahl,** 722 P.2d 262 (Ariz. 1986)]

b. **Rescission precludes contract damages [§921]**

Election of the rescission remedy precludes the recovery of contract damages. Thus, where the contract is disaffirmed, lost profits may not be recovered. [**Wilkinson v. Smith,** 639 P.2d 768 (Wash. 1982); *and see* **Finke v. Woodward,** 462 N.E.2d 13 (Ill. 1984)—trial court erroneously awarded both rescission and benefit-of-the-bargain damages for breach of land sale contract]

(1) **Note**

Rescission of a contract containing a provision for attorneys' fees abrogates that provision and the prevailing party can no longer claim them. [**Golden Cone Concepts v. Villa Linda Mall,** 820 P.2d 1323 (N.M. 1991)]

6. **Punitive Damages [§922]**

According to recent decisions, punitive damages may be awarded following rescission, but such damages are permissible only if the rescission is based on fraud and the requisite malice can be shown. [**Michaels v. Morris,** 169 Cal. App. 3d 809 (1985); **Indiana & Michigan Electric Co. v. Harlan,** 504 N.E.2d 301 (Ind. 1987)]

7. **U.C.C. [§923]**

Remedies for misrepresentations as to solvency are now governed by U.C.C. section 2-702, which permits the *recapture of chattels* within certain time limitations. Section 2-608 also provides for *"revocation of acceptance"* within a reasonable time after discovering fraud. In addition to recovering the consideration paid, the buyer may also recover incidental damages, such as expenses incurred in the care and custody of goods. (*See* Sales Summary.)

D. Statutory Remedies—Consumer Protection

1. **Compensatory and Punitive Damages Available [§924]**

A number of jurisdictions now authorize statutory remedies for consumers who sustain damages as the result of false and deceptive practices by sellers. Frequently provision is made for class actions. Remedies provided include *compensatory and punitive damages* as well as injunctive decrees prohibiting continuance of the deceptive practice. [*See, e.g.,* Cal. Civ. Code §§1770-1784; Mass. Gen. Laws, ch. 93A; **Hernandez v. Atlantic Finance Co.,** 105 Cal. App. 3d 65 (1980); **Spies-Roberts, Inc. v. Opperman,** 741 S.W.2d 149 (Tex. 1987)—Texas Deceptive Trade

Practices Act; **Burdin v. Ogden Chrysler-Plymouth, Inc.,** 511 N.E.2d 1330 (Ill. 1987)—odometer tampering, Illinois Consumer Fraud Act]

Chapter Ten:
Duress, Undue Influence, and Unconscionable Conduct

CONTENTS

Chapter Approach

In the cases considered in this chapter, choice of remedy is no problem. *Restitution* or perhaps *rescission and restitution* are the sole remedies, because duress and undue influence are not torts and do not provide a basis for the remedy of compensatory damages. Examination questions thus necessarily focus on sorting out the degree of outrage necessary to induce a court to take action to restore to an aggrieved party whatever benefits have been extracted by the defendant's misconduct. This means that you must understand the various types of duress:

(i)   *Physical coercion*;

(ii) *Seizure of property*;

(iii) *Threat of legal proceedings*; and particularly

(iv) The newest concept of "*business coercion.*"

Keep in mind that even though the defendant's conduct does not constitute *duress*, it may still provide a basis for restitution if it meets the test of *undue influence*. Finally, if the question involves the sale of goods, be sure to consider the applicability of the U.C.C. *doctrine of unconscionability*.

A. Duress

1. Duress Not a Tort Per Se [§925]
Duress is a common law concept, but duress, per se, is *not* a common law tort. Certain forms of duress to the person may be actionable as intentional torts (*e.g.,* assault, battery, or false imprisonment), and in these forms may be redressed by compensatory damages. Also, some forms of duress, through civil or criminal proceedings, may give rise to separate claims for malicious prosecution or abuse of process. While there are recent decisions characterizing "business compulsion" as tortious (*see infra,* §§954-957), most forms of duress are *not* actionable torts per se.

2. Basic Remedy Is Restitution [§926]
Apart from the few cases above where the duress is actionable by itself, the only remedy for duress is *restitution for unjust enrichment*—including rescission of executed "bargains." The cause of action arises when the duress is removed, and the election to rescind an executed transaction must be pursued in accordance with the procedures outlined in the previous chapter—*i.e.,* a prompt notice of disaffirmance

and tender back of any benefits obtained (*see supra,* §§898, 905). Otherwise the plaintiff will be deemed to have affirmed by remaining silent or by accepting benefits. [**National Auto Brokers v. Aleeda Development Corp.,** 364 A.2d 470 (Pa. 1976)] (Note that because duress is not a tort per se, the plaintiff loses *all* remedies by affirming the transaction.)

3. What Constitutes "Duress"? [§927]

Duress basically refers to conduct by one person that *overcomes the free will of another* and therefore renders involuntary whatever transaction is involved.

a. Distinguish—fraud [§928]

Like fraud, duress is an *indirect* wrong, in that it is the *means* by which the plaintiff is induced to make a payment, or transfer property, or to yield some contractual advantage. However, unlike fraud, the duressed party is not misled; she knows what she is doing but has no choice, as her will is overcome.

b. Subjective test [§929]

Whether the plaintiff's will has been overcome is determined subjectively; *i.e.,* it is sufficient that the plaintiff's will was in fact overcome. It is irrelevant whether a "person of average firmness" would have yielded (the former, objective test, has been discarded).

EXAM TIP   **gilbert**

On your exam, remember that duress, like beauty, "is in the eye of the beholder"; *i.e.,* it is *subjective.* Be careful of facts emphasizing the timidity of the plaintiff. The fact that the plaintiff is afraid of his own shadow is *not* a defense to duress.

---

c. Sources of duress [§930]

The coercion must originate with and be applied by the person receiving the benefit. Others obtaining benefits as a result of the plaintiff's difficulties are *not* liable to make restitution. [**Joannin v. Ogilvie,** 52 N.W. 217 (Minn. 1892)—to obtain a loan, Alex was compelled by Becky to pay Becky's debt to Cindy; no restitution allowed against Cindy]

d. Submission as only alternative [§931]

A claim based on duress will not lie unless it appears that the plaintiff had no realistic alternative but to submit to the coercion; *i.e., it must appear that under the circumstances there was no other lawful way out.*

(1) Comment

This is usually the big obstacle to recovery on most claims of duress. Courts do not permit a party to "buy one's way out" of a transaction, and then turn around and sue for the money back, unless there simply was no other *lawful* way out of the transaction in the first place. If there was, the party is expected to exhaust any other remedies. Failing to do this, no judicial remedies will be granted. [*See* **Selmer Co. v. Blakeslee-Midway Co.**, 704 F.2d 924 (7th Cir. 1983)—settlement by subcontractor with prime contractor for extras because of "desperate financial straits" was held not to be duress; *compare* business duress, *infra*, §954]

4. **Remedy Depends on Nature of Duress**

a. **Duress that makes transaction void [§932]**
If the duress consists of physically forced acts or acts under hypnosis or involuntary intoxication, the transaction is entirely *void.* [*See* **Federal Deposit Insurance Corp. v. Meyer,** 755 F. Supp. 10 (D.D.C. 1991)] These are cases in which the plaintiff's will is not merely coerced; rather, there was *no intentional act* made by plaintiff.

Example: Pia is extremely ill and weak. Dora comes into Pia's sickroom, places a pen in Pia's hand, and *forces Pia's hand* into making a mark on a deed, which Dora then asserts is Pia's signature. The signature is void.

---

(1) **Remedial significance [§933]**
No rights can be obtained under a void deed, will, or contract. Hence, there is no effective transfer, there is nothing to rescind—and, *there can be no bona fide purchaser.*

b. **Duress that makes transaction voidable [§934]**
More frequently, the duressed person's act is intentional, but it was not volitional because she had no free choice in deciding whether to do it. In such cases, the act is not void, but merely *voidable* by the duressed person.

(1) **Physical duress [§935]**
This may consist of intimidation or force to the plaintiff that falls short of reducing her to an automaton. It may also consist of threats against persons in close kinship to the plaintiff—*e.g.,* forcing the plaintiff to sign a deed at gunpoint or by threats to kill her spouse.

(2) **"Duress to property" [§936]**
In certain cases, the wrongdoer applies coercion through claiming title or possession to property. (The name "duress to property" is really not accurate because the duress is to the owner, not the property.)

(a) **Chattels [§937]**
Duress to chattels occurs, for example, when the defendant wrongfully refuses to surrender chattels belonging to the plaintiff unless the plaintiff pays some improper charge. Remedies for such action include:

1) Replevin (usual remedy) [§938]

If chattels are wrongfully withheld, the legal remedy of replevin is usually an adequate remedy so that *submission* to the unlawful demand is *not* justified—hence, no restitution is needed.

2) Restitution (in special circumstances) [§939]

However, if there is some special compulsion requiring the plaintiff to obtain the chattels immediately (as where the goods were perishable, or were tools that the plaintiff needed immediately to earn a livelihood), restitution is available to recover the improper charge paid to the defendant to obtain the chattels. [**J. Abrams & Co. v. Clark,** 11 N.E.2d 449 (Mass. 1937)]

3) Civil proceedings [§940]

Duress to chattels may also be accomplished through civil proceedings in which the goods are seized or tied up (*see* below).

(b) Land [§941]

"Duress to land" occurs when the defendant wrongfully seizes the plaintiff's land, or wrongfully files a lien against plaintiff's title, and refuses to release the land or title unless plaintiff pays money or gives other consideration to which the defendant is not entitled.

1) Legal remedies [§942]

The legal remedies are usually adequate here (ejectment as to possession; quiet title as to wrongful liens). Consequently, if the plaintiff pays the money demanded or otherwise yields to the defendant's demands, restitutionary relief will be *denied*; again, restitution is available only where there was no other alternative.

2) Equitable remedies [§943]

If the defendant obtains a deed by coercion, a suit for rescission and cancellation is the appropriate remedy.

3) Restitution (certain circumstances) [§944]

Again, however, there may be special circumstances in which the plaintiff had no other choice but to submit—*e.g.,* as where clear title is needed for purposes of meeting a contract obligation, or obtaining financing without which the land or other valuable property will be lost. In such cases, if the plaintiff pays the improper charge demanded by the defendant, the plaintiff will be entitled to restitutionary relief to recover the payments. [**Leeper v. Beltrami,** 53 Cal. 2d 195 (1959)]

4) Civil proceedings [§945]

As with chattels, the duress may be effected through civil proceedings—*e.g.*, Dastardly files suit falsely claiming that he owns Pitstop's land, and records a lis pendens, tying up Pitstop's title; *see* below.

c. Duress through criminal proceedings or threat thereof [§946]

This type of duress occurs when the defendant makes a criminal charge against the plaintiff to the police (or threatens to do so) and refuses to withdraw the charge unless the plaintiff makes some payment or other consideration demanded by the defendant. A frequent variation occurs when the threat is made to prosecute a spouse or child unless the plaintiff signs a note or mortgage. [**Arians v. Larkin Bank,** 625 N.E.2d 1101 (Ill. 1993); **Osage Corp. v. Simon,** 613 N.E.2d 770 (Ill. 1993)—rescission granted in both cases]

(1) Bad faith essential [§947]

There is no basis for any remedy unless it can be shown that the defendant was acting in bad faith and for private gain. Claims made under mistake are not enough. The wrongful motive of the actor is theoretically more important to restitutionary relief than the actual guilt or innocence of the complainant. [**Bank of Tucson v. Adrian,** 245 F. Supp. 595 (D. Minn. 1965); **Gillikin v. Whitley,** 311 S.E.2d 677 (N.C. 1984)]

(2) Can plaintiff recover payments? [§948]

Courts are split as to whether the person making the payments under threat of criminal charge is entitled to restitutionary relief. [**Clifford v. Great Falls Gas Co.,** 216 P. 1114 (Mont. 1923)—allowing restitution; **Union Exchange National Bank v. Joseph,** 231 N.Y. 250 (1921)—denying relief]

(a) Arguments against [§949]

If the plaintiff (the duressed person) is actually *guilty*, the payment to the defendant is itself a crime (compounding; *see* Criminal Law Summary), and recovery of the payment would be contrary to public policy. Moreover, if parties are "in pari delicto," restitutionary relief is denied (*see infra,* §§1351-1356). If the plaintiff is actually *innocent*, then restitutionary relief should be denied because submission to the demand for payment is not the only alternative; *i.e.,* the plaintiff should have defended against the charge, particularly because the quantum of proof in a criminal proceeding favors the accused. If she lost the trial, she could have appealed the conviction. If she won, she could sue for damages for malicious prosecution.

d. Duress through civil proceedings or threat thereof [§950]

An example of this type of duress is when the defendant files a civil suit against the plaintiff (or threatens to do so), and refuses to dismiss the case unless the plaintiff makes some payment or other consideration demanded by the defendant.

(1) Generally no restitution for payments made [§951]

The mere filing of a civil suit—even with improper motives and without any belief in its merits—is not considered such an exercise of duress as to justify restitution of payments made by the plaintiff to get rid of the suit. [**Dickerman v. Lord & Smith,** 89 Am. Dec. 579 (Iowa 1866)]

(a) Note

Nor is the result changed by the fact that in connection with the lawsuit, the defendant obtained a writ of attachment against the plaintiff's property, or invoked any other ancillary remedy (*e.g.,* recording a lis pendens, tying up title to the plaintiff's land). [45 Mich. L. Rev. 571]

(b) Rationale

The reason for denying restitutionary relief is that submitting to the defendant's unlawful demand for money is ***not*** the only alternative open to the plaintiff. The plaintiff could have defended against the lawsuit right then and there; thus, she should not be permitted to raise the same issues at a later date (when the defendant's evidence may have vanished, etc.). [**Dickerman v. Lord & Smith,** *supra*] Moreover, many courts hold that a lawsuit (or an attachment, etc.) *filed for an improper purpose* is actionable per se as an *abuse of process*—itself a tort. Unlike malicious prosecution, a claim for damages for abuse of process *can be filed as a cross-demand in the main action;* the plaintiff does not have to wait until after she first wins the lawsuit. [**White Lighting Co. v. Wolfson,** 68 Cal. 2d 336 (1968)]

(2) Exceptions [§952]

However, there are cases in which the pendency of the civil action or the attachment, etc., threatens the plaintiff with such irreparable loss that there is no realistic alternative but to submit to the defendant's unlawful demand. In such cases, restitutionary relief is proper. [**Chandler v. Sanger,** 114 Mass. 364 (1874)—defendant attached plaintiff's ice wagons on a claim defendant knew was invalid; since the ice would have melted by the time plaintiff could obtain court order for release, plaintiff was permitted to recover payment made to defendant]

e. Oppressive refusal to perform a public duty without payment [§953]

Restitution of payments wrongfully extracted by bureaucrats has generally been allowed—despite the alternative remedy of mandamus.

Example: Restitution will be granted where there is a refusal of the grant of a liquor license, or refusal of a public utility to turn on water, except upon payment of money not owed. [**B & B Amusement Enterprises, Inc. v. City of Boston,** 8 N.E.2d 788 (Mass. 1937)]

f. **Business compulsion—"economic coercion" [§954]**
    The rather limited common law notion of "duress to property" (*see supra,* §936), when placed in the context of commercial transactions and coupled with equitable doctrines such as "undue influence" and the restriction on "inequitable exercise of legal rights," has produced the concept of "business compulsion."

    (1) "Inequitable exercise of legal rights" [§955]
        This includes:

        (i)   Threats to *exercise a reserved right to terminate* a contract;

        (ii)   Threats to *breach* contracts or leases [**Hochman v. Zigler's Inc.,** 50 A.2d 97 (N.J. 1946)]; and

        (iii) *Refusals to deal* at all or except on exorbitant terms.

        None of the above may be duress by itself, but several in combination may give rise to economic duress in single cases.

Example: Lawyer improperly claims Client owes him a fee and attaches Client's bank account, thereby preventing consummation of a land deal. To close the deal, Client agrees to pay Lawyer the fee. The agreement is coerced and voidable; Lawyer's conduct constitutes economic coercion and is also actionable as the tort of interference with contract. [**Fizzell v. Meeker,** 339 F. Supp. 624 (W.D. Mo. 1970)—punitive damages also awarded]

Example: A lumber wholesaler financing a sawmill operator breached the finance agreement as part of a pattern intending financially to ruin the borrower and thereby acquire his assets. The wholesaler was held liable in damages for the destruction of the business. [**Terrel v. Duke City Lumber Co.,** 524 P.2d 1021 (N.M. 1974)]

Example: Insurance companies doing business in Oklahoma required employers to sign "consent to rate" forms as condition to obtaining workers' compensation insurance at premiums in excess of rates approved by a state agency. Employers filed a class action to avoid the agreements and for punitive damages. Rescission was allowed but,

FORM OF DURESS	RESULT
FORCED PHYSICAL ACTS; INVOLUNTARY INTOXICATION; HYPNOSIS	Transaction generally is *void* and treated as if it had not taken place. An action for trespass to chattels, conversion, or the like will lie.
PHYSICAL DURESS	Transaction generally is *voidable*. An action for rescission will lie.
DURESS TO CHATTELS	Transaction generally is *voidable*. An action for replevin will lie. Restitution might be available if the plaintiff was damaged by loss of the chattel or had to pay an improper charge to get it back.
DURESS TO LAND	Transaction generally is *voidable*. An action for ejectment or to quiet title will usually lie. If the defendant obtained a deed by coercion, rescission and cancellation will lie. Restitution will lie in special circumstances as under duress to chattels.
DURESS THROUGH CRIMINAL PROCEEDING	Transaction *might be voidable,* but cases are split. (Some courts deny a remedy because if guilty, payment constitutes a crime and if innocent a remedy at law is available—defend against the charges and sue for malicious prosecution.) Where a remedy is available, rescission will be granted only if the defendant was acting in bad faith.
DURESS THROUGH CIVIL PROCEEDING	Transaction generally *not* voidable (remedy at law—defending against suit and bringing a counterclaim for abuse of process—is deemed sufficient).
OPPRESSIVE REFUSAL TO PERFORM PUBLIC DUTY	Transaction generally is *voidable*. Restitution is generally allowed despite the fact that the legal remedy (writ of mandamus) may be available.
BUSINESS COMPULSION	Transaction generally is *voidable*. Rescission may be available if the defendant took advantage of the plaintiff's situation by unconscionable conduct; punitive damages may also be available.

since "economic duress" is not an independent tort in Oklahoma, punitive damages were not. [**Cimarron Pipeline Construction, Inc. v. USF&G,** 848 P.2d 1161 (Okla. 1993)]

e.g. **Example:** Contractor agrees to pay higher than agreed prices demanded by supplier. Contractor could not obtain substitute supplies elsewhere in time to avoid penalty payments under his contract with the Navy. Contractor's agreement to pay the higher prices is voidable for economic duress. [**Austin Instrument Co. v. Loral Corp.,** 29 N.Y.2d 124 (1971); *and see* **Rich & Whillock, Inc. v. Ashton Development, Inc.,** 157 Cal. App. 3d 1154 (1984)—relief granted to subcontractor who was forced to settle for less than the contract price]

e.g. **Example:** Employer threatens to terminate employee unless a promissory note is signed involving a transaction personal to the parties. At the time, employee is faced with large hospital expenses for his daughter. *Held:* Note is voidable for duress. [**Shurtleff v. Giller,** 527 S.W.2d 214 (Tex. 1975)]

(a) Duress must result from defendant's acts [§956]
Duress must result from acts or conduct of the defendant. It is not enough to show that the victim was in a situation of financial embarrassment or economic necessity. [**USLife Title Co. v. Gutkin,** 732 P.2d 579 (Ariz. 1986)]

(2) Limitation—antitrust law [§957]
The conduct involved in these cases often borders on unfair trade practices. To the extent that the practice operates as a restraint on trade or to cause a monopoly, the conduct may violate the antitrust laws. In such event, the antitrust laws *supersede* any right to recovery under state laws of restitution.

B. Undue Influence

1. Definition and Substantive Nature [§958]
"Undue influence" is the equitable counterpart to common law duress and is derived from equitable jurisdiction over fiduciary and confidential relationships.

a. Restatement definition [§959]
Restatement of Contracts section 497 gives these elements:

(1) *Domination of one party* over the other or the existence of a relationship justifying the second party's assumption that the first party would not act in a way inconsistent with his welfare.

(2) *"Unfair persuasion"* by the dominant person.

b. Expanded definition [§960]

A broader definition is given in the Field Codes [*e.g.,* Cal. Civ. Code §1575; *see* **Odorizzi v. Bloomfield School District**, 246 Cal. App. 2d 123 (1966)], which adds: "The *wrongful taking advantage* of another's weakness of mind, or in taking grossly unfair advantage of another's necessities or distress."

(1) Note

Under this expansive definition, the parties do not necessarily have to be in a relationship of trust or confidence. Moreover, unlike duress, the defendant may be liable for unjust enrichment as the *recipient* of benefits, because of pressures created by some third party.

 Example: Testator is induced by Xavier's undue influence to bequeath money to Desi; even though Desi is innocent, Desi must disgorge.

---

(2) Distinguish—duress

The rule is contra as to benefits received as a result of common law *duress* by third persons; in such case no restitution is available (*see supra,* §930).

2. Remedies

a. Equitable relief [§961]

Historically, undue influence was cognizable only in equity. Therefore, the normal remedies for undue influence were equitable suits to *rescind*, the imposition of *constructive trusts* or liens on the property obtained, or the *cancellation* of deeds or instruments. [**Francois v. Francois**, 599 F.2d 1286 (3d Cir. 1979)—constructive trust employed to restore property wrongfully obtained]

(1) And note

The question of whether "undue influence" existed was determined solely by the judge; there was *no* right to a jury trial (again reflecting the equitable derivation of the concept).

b. Modern merger of duress, undue influence [§962]

Modern courts tend to *disregard* the historical background of "duress" as remediable at law, and "undue influence" as remediable only in equity. Rather, both are treated as a single concept—*coercion*. Consequently, the procedural distinctions between the two are blurred in many modern cases. The right to jury trial has been extended to all issues of fact; and the quasi-contract action, as well as equitable remedies, have been granted interchangeably.

C. Unconscionability

1. No Precise Definition [§963]

Unconscionability refers to the "conscience of the chancellor"—the essence of equitable jurisdiction—and escapes precise definition. Even where the concept is embodied by statute (*e.g.,* U.C.C. section 2-302), no attempt is made to define it.

2. Categories [§964]

For purposes of analyzing available remedies, *three categories* of unconscionability may be recognized:

a. Procedural unconscionability [§965]

The unconscionability doctrine may apply where unjust enrichment results from recognized *unfair methods of dealing*. This means nothing more than the use of methods of misrepresentation, nondisclosure, duress, undue influence, etc., resulting in unjust enrichment, that have already been elaborated in detail. [**World Enterprises v. Midcoast Aviation Services**, 713 S.W.2d 606 (Mo. 1986)—"Procedural unconscionability arises during the contracting process and involves fine print, misrepresentation and unequal bargaining positions"]

(1) Inequality in bargaining power alone [§966]

Mere inequality in bargaining power alone does not give rise to a claim of unconscionability.

> **Example:** Subcontractor agreed to perform additional work not within the original contract if Contractor would pay for the extra costs. After completing the work, Subcontractor demanded $120,000, but Contractor refused to pay more than $67,000. Subcontractor accepted the payment because it was in desperate financial straits. The court refused to set aside the settlement. [**Selmer Co. v. Blakeslee-Midwest Co.**, 704 F.2d 924 (7th Cir. 1983)]

(2) Remedies [§967]

Rescission and restitution of benefits are the available remedies.

b. Substantive unconscionability ("hardship") [§968]

Substantive unconscionability relates to *bad bargains* (*i.e.,* inadequate consideration or financial hardship to one party), but made in an arm's length transaction, and lacking any other element of duress, fraud, or undue influence.

(1) Restitution denied [§969]

Because the transactions are already executed, the claim of hardship is weaker than when executory. Therefore, most courts deny restitution in ordinary cases between individuals (although *inadequate consideration or hardship alone* may be a *defense to a specific performance* suit in equity; *see supra*, §§133-135). [*Compare* **Brower v. Gateway 2000, Inc.,** 246 A.D.2d 246 (1998)—arbitration clause in contract not enforced because of the exorbitant costs imposed on the buyer; *with* **Hill v. Gateway 2000, Inc.,** 105 F.3d 1147 (7th Cir. 1997)—same arbitration clause held enforceable]

(2) Unconscionable contracts unenforceable under the U.C.C. [§970]

U.C.C. section 2-302 states that unconscionable transactions are *unenforceable*. However, this falls short of providing affirmative restitutionary relief for executed transactions. [**Best v. United States National Bank,** 714 P.2d 1049 (Or. 1986)]

(a) Distinguish—reformation [§971]

Reformation to eliminate excessive interest or add-on charges in a boilerplate retail installment sales contract may be available. [**Jones v. Star Credit Corp.,** 59 Misc. 2d 189 (1969)]

(b) Distinguish—class actions [§972]

Consumer class or statutory actions may result in *restitution of overcharges*. Usually elements of "procedural" unconscionability (unfair trade practices) are also present. Recovery of excess charges, or even *rescission*, has been decreed in favor of the *entire* class—even though many individuals might be unable to show grounds other than the overcharge itself. [**Kugler v. Romain,** 279 A.2d 640 (N.J. 1971)] (*Injunctive* relief is also routine in such cases even if not specifically provided in statute.)

(c) Right to jury trial? [§973]

Because of the equitable nature of substantive unconscionability, there is *no* right to a jury trial on the issue of whether a contract or other transaction is voidable for "unconscionability." [**County Asphalt, Inc. v. Lewis Welding & Engineering Corp.,** 444 F.2d 372 (2d Cir. 1971)]

(3) Substantive unconscionability as basis for unilateral rescission (statutory) [§974]

To meet the problem of overcharging by hard sell techniques, particularly in door-to-door sales, many states have enacted statutes allowing the buyer a "cooling off" period (a few days or a week)—to *rescind or cancel without cause,* upon restoration of the goods. A slight fee may be charged. [*See, e.g.,* N.Y. Pers. Prop. Law §§427 *et seq.*] In some states, similar statutes apply as to purchase contracts in rural real estate subdivisions [Cal. Bus. & Prof. Code §11028—14 days]; and likewise as to avoidance of releases of liability on personal injury claims [Ind. Code

Ann. art. 79 §11—any release signed within five days of injury can be avoided within six months].

c. **Remedial unconscionability [§975]**

Remedial (or, as it is sometimes called, administrative) unconscionability refers to harsh contract provisions relating to the enforcement of bargains—particularly collection procedures that are legally sanctioned but subject to abuse.

Example: Person on welfare makes repeated installment purchases of luxury items much in excess of prospective income. Provision in sales contract calls for distribution of payments so that no single item is ever paid for and hence all remain subject to repossession. Assume that there is no "procedural" unconscionability (*i.e.,* no fraud, undue influence, etc.), or "substantive" unconscionability (*i.e.,* price not excessive). Even so, this unfairness has been denounced as unconscionable. [**Williams v. Walker-Thomas Furniture Co.,** 350 F.2d 445 (D.C. Cir. 1965)]

Example: Collection agency files small claims actions in inconvenient locations, making it impossible for impoverished debtors to defend. Such a practice may be found to be unconscionable.

(1) **Remedies [§976]**

Because it is technically lawful, "remedial" unconscionability must be met with equitable remedies. *Comment:* Actually, this type of case is among the most ancient examples of the exercise of equitable jurisdiction, dating back to injunctions against enforcing judgments of a law court obtained legally but inequitably. [**J.R. v. M.P.,** Y.B. 37 Hen. 6, fol. 13, pl. 3 (1459)]

(a) **Injunctions [§977]**

Thus, appropriate remedies include an *injunction against enforcement* or *reformation* to eliminate the unconscionable provisions. [*See* **Vockner v. Erickson,** 712 P.2d 379 (Alaska 1986)—reformation of unconscionable payment terms in sale of apartment building]

(b) **Generally defensive [§978]**

The buyer *cannot rescind* the entire contract because of harsh provisions therein. Remedial unconscionability gives rise to only *defensive* protection and not, in general, to affirmative relief.

Chapter Eleven:
Mistake

CONTENTS

Chapter Approach

Chapter Approach

Mistake in the formation or performance of a contract provides few remedial problems. Because a mistake is not a tort, the *only* remedy available necessarily is *restitutional.*

The tricky part of this topic is to determine which mistakes provide a basis for remedial action, because the tests formulated by the courts are virtually devoid of content. In considering the fact situation of your question, be sure you distinguish mistake from *assumption of risk.* If the latter is involved, relief is always *denied.*

If the mistake involves a writing, be sure to consider *reformation* as a remedy. The significant fact is the underlying agreement; the relevant mistake is the incorporation of that agreement into a document. The remedy then is to reform the writing to conform to that underlying agreement.

A. General Considerations

1. **Definition [§979]**

   Mistake is a belief that is not in accord with existing facts. [Rest. 2d Contracts §293] It may result from forgetfulness or unconscious ignorance. [Rest. Restitution §6]

2. **Remedies—In General [§980]**

   The *only* remedies are of the *restitutionary* variety based on the enrichment of the transferee. Obviously, there are no preventive remedies (the plaintiff does not know that he is going to make a mistake). And damages are not allowable because no "wrong" has been committed by the other party. [**Holm v. Shilensky,** 269 F. Supp. 359 (S.D.N.Y. 1967)—ex-wife received supposedly valuable works of art under marriage settlement agreement; money damages denied because no fraud shown (both parties mutually mistaken as to value of paintings)]

B. Mistake in Bargaining Transactions

1. **Overperformance of Contract [§981]**

   This refers to the situation where the parties are free from error in entering into the contract, but a mistake is made in performance. Typical examples arise from incorrect surveys of land, clerical errors in documents of title, mistaken endorsements on insurance policies, or payments based on faulty calculations. [**Wheadon v. Olds,**

20 Wend. 174 (N.Y. 1838)—sale of oats at 49¢ per bushel, but parties mistakenly used a half bushel basket to measure the grain] *Note:* Restitution in these cases does *not* depend on whether the mistake is mutual or unilateral. The defendant in a bargaining transaction can hardly claim that he was receiving an undeserved award.

a. Overpayment of money [§982]

The usual situation is when the purchaser has overpaid the seller and seeks restitution of the amount overpaid.

(1) Remedy [§983]

The appropriate remedy is a *quasi-contract* action at law.

Example: Broker overpays because of a mistake in identifying the corporation in which the stockholder owned stock. [**Ohio Co. v. Rosemeier,** 288 N.E.2d 326 (Ohio 1972)—two corporations with identical names; **Messersmith v. G.T. Murray & Co.,** 667 P.2d 655 (Wyo. 1983)—reverse stock split; **Monroe Financial Corp. v. DiSilvestro,** 529 N.E.2d 379 (Ind. 1988)]

Example: Bank erroneously paid out money on a check that was dishonored. *Held:* The bank had a common law right of restitution in addition to the remedies provided by the U.C.C. [**Great Western Bank & Trust v. Nahat,** 674 P.2d 323 (Ariz. 1983)]

(a) Note

No equitable remedy is allowed because the quasi-contract remedy is adequate. Moreover, an equitable lien or constructive trust as to money received by mistake is unnecessary as against a solvent defendant, and would be unfair as to other claimants against an insolvent defendant. [*In re* **Archer, Harvey & Co.,** 289 F. 267 (D. Md. 1923); *but see* **Cocke v. Pacific Gulf Development Corp.,** 594 S.W.2d 545 (Tex. 1980)—constructive trust may be imposed on funds paid by mistake]

b. Errors in conveyance of land

(1) Shortage of acreage—overpayment of money [§984]

If the contract for sale is *by the acre,* and the purchaser overpays because the acreage is mistakenly overestimated, the restitutionary remedy is clear. However, if the sale is *in gross,* a mistaken overestimation of the area *cannot* be made the subject of partial restitution of price advanced. *Rationale:* The seller agreed to the price as a unit, and not on the basis of so much per acre. [**Marcus v. Bathon,** 531 A.2d 690 (Md. 1987)—restitution denied for sale in gross; **Ewing v. Bissell,** 777 P.2d 1320 (Nev. 1989)—restitution granted where sale classified as by the acre]

(a) Rescission of contract [§985]

A contract may be rescinded for a deficiency of acreage only if it can be shown that the agreed acreage was material or basic to the contract. [*See* **Meas v. Young**, 405 N.W.2d 697 (Wis. 1987)—buyer denied rescission to correct deficiency in acreage because no special concern was shown for precise acreage agreed upon in contract]

(2) Conveyance of too much land [§986]

The most appropriate remedy would be an equitable decree to *compel a reconveyance or to reform the deed* to exclude overage. [**Findlay v. State**, 250 S.W. 651 (Tex. 1923)—nearly 60,000 acres of Texas public lands conveyed by mistake in payment for construction of state capitol] However, such a decree may be refused as *impracticable* if the particular area of overage is unidentifiable.

(a) Alternative remedy

Rescission would be possible if the mistake is basic.

(b) Another alternative remedy

Or the court may allow the defendant-buyer the *choice* of rescission or of paying extra compensation at the contract rate.

(c) But note

Just as in cases of shortages (*see supra*, §984), a court may find that the sale was in gross and deny any relief to the seller.

c. Overperformance of services [§987]

Overperformance of services refers to the situations such as where an employee works overtime without request to do so, or a housepainter paints the garage and house although the owner asked him to paint only the house. In these cases, no remedy is generally allowed (in restitution or otherwise), unless the recipient was *aware* of the extra work being performed and of plaintiff's mistake, and failed to advise plaintiff to stop. [Rest. Restitution §41]

EXAM TIP — gilbert

You might see an overperformance fact pattern on your exam. Painting more than was requested is a typical scenario. Resolution of the issue is fairly straightforward—ask yourself whether the defendant *was aware of and could have stopped* the overperformance. If so, restitution is allowed; if not, no restitution is allowed. Thus, if the defendant set up his lawn chair and watched the plaintiff paint each day, the defendant will be liable in restitution for the over-performance. But if the plaintiff hired the painter, told him to start painting, went on vacation, and on his return was surprised to find more painting done than he bargained for, the painter will not be allowed to recover in restitution.

d. Insurance policy endorsements [§988]

Overstatement of insurance benefits under a policy may be remedied by reformation of the policy endorsement to state the correct amount. However, no

REMEDIES IN TYPICAL OVERPERFORMANCE CASES   gilbert

SITUATION	EXAMPLE	REMEDY
OVERPAYMENT OF MONEY	Purchaser double pays seller of goods	*Quasi-contract* action seeking repayment of overpayment.
SHORTAGE OF ACREAGE	Purchaser receives less land than he paid for	If sale was by the acre, the remedy is a *quasi-contract* action to recover the overpaid sum. If sale was in gross, no *restitution* is allowed but the contract may be *rescinded* if the deficiency is material.
CONVEYANCE OF TOO MUCH LAND	Seller drafts deed including land not intended by the parties to be conveyed	*Equitable injunction* compelling reconveyance or *equitable decree reforming* the deed. *Rescission* is possible if mistake is basic, or court might allow buyer to retain extra land on payment of extra compensation.
OVERPERFORMANCE OF SERVICES	Painter paints garage in addition to house when contract called for only the house to be painted	Generally *no remedy* is allowed *unless* the recipient was aware of the extra work and could have stopped it, in which case, *quasi-contract* action for restitution of benefit is allowed.
INSURANCE POLICY ENDORSEMENTS	Insurance company sends an endorsement for $1,000,000 instead of $100,000	*Reformation* of the endorsement generally is available but not if there was a change of position that would make reformation harsh.

reformation will be allowed if there is a change of position such that imposition of reformation would be harsh.

---

e.g. **Example:** Suppose the insured, under a straight life policy, requests a statement from the insurance company as to available options if the policy is dropped. The insurance company sends an erroneous overstatement as to the amount of paid-up insurance available and an endorsement to that effect is supplied. *Reformation* is the appropriate remedy. [**New York Life Insurance Co. v. Gilbert,** 256 S.W. 148 (Mo. 1923)]

---

cf. **Compare:** If the insured elects to take term insurance as an option, and the company overstates the term (*e.g.,* three years instead of two) in the endorsement, and insured dies two and a half years later, there is *no* remedy for the mistake (*see* "change of position" defense, *infra*, §§1021-1022).

---

2. **Mistaken Performance in Reliance on a Nonexistent Contract [§989]**

Some of these cases are based on *misunderstandings* preventing a meeting of minds required by the subjective theory of contract (*e.g.,* third persons posing as "agents" frequently cause parties to believe they have entered into a "contract" although each has a different notion as to the terms). Others involve situations where no enforceable contract existed because of lack of authority by an agent or noncompliance with the Statute of Frauds. [*See* **Campbell v. Tennessee Valley Authority,** 421 F.2d 293 (5th Cir. 1969)]

a. **Remedy [§990]**

The normal remedy is *restitution* of any payments or value given. Possessory actions such as replevin, or occasionally equitable relief, may be appropriate if transfers or conveyances have been made.

(1) **Note**

Although many cases speak of rescission as a remedy, this is technically an unnecessary procedure because there is *no contract* to disaffirm. [*See, e.g.,* **Volpe v. Schlobohm,** 614 S.W.2d 615 (Tex. 1981)—"no meeting of minds" on material issue; rescission is proper remedy]

b. **Measure of recovery [§991]**

Suppose Placido by mistake ships to Domingo goods intended for Antonio. The goods are marked $100 per unit. Domingo receives them believing them to be from Bruno, his normal supplier, who gives Domingo a 10% discount because of his volume of purchases. The goods are used in Domingo's business. Placido is entitled to recover the "value" of the goods from Domingo. Should this be $100 (thereby fulfilling Placido's expectancy) or $90 (protecting Domingo's expectancy)?

(1) Comment

In principle Placido should recover $90, as otherwise Domingo is being held to a breach of contract measure of damages when he has broken no contract. However, the cases are not uniform.

Example: A misunderstanding arose between an owner and a contractor involving a contract to build a Turkish bathhouse. The misunderstanding was the fault of neither party (it was caused by the architect's machinations). The owner thought the price was $23,200, whereas the contractor thought it was $33,720. The market value of the labor and materials furnished (without charge for supervision) was $33,500, and the actual cost to the builder was $32,950. The enhanced market value of the premises was only $22,000 (owner's actual enrichment—but this was in part due to bad judgment of the owner). The court allowed the contractor to recover the market value of his labor and materials ($33,500). [**Vickery v. Ritchie**, 88 N.E. 835 (Mass. 1909)]

---

(2) Restatement view [§992]

In the *Vickery* case, Restatement of Restitution section 155 would limit the owner's liability to the value of what was received but not less than what the recipient expected to pay nor more than the claimant expected to receive.

(3) Alternative view—split the difference [§993]

Commentators have suggested that the difference between the owner's and contractor's expectancies be split.

c. Distinguish—mistake the fault of party performing [§994]

When the work is done by reason of the unilateral mistake of the plaintiff (that he was under a contractual duty to do so), and defendant *did not request* the work and *did not know* that it was being done, the restitutionary remedy is denied. [**Rohr v. Baker**, 10 P. 627 (Or. 1886)]

3. Mistake in Basic Assumptions [§995]

The phrase "mistake in basic assumptions" refers to cases where a contract exists, but one or both parties executed the contract under a mistake as to some basic fact or circumstance affecting the value of the contract.

a. Rescission as remedy [§996]

The normal remedy in such cases is *rescission*, following the procedures for avoidance outlined *supra*, §898.

b. Mistake must be "basic" [§997]

Commercial convenience dictates that executed transactions not be set aside because of mistaken evaluation of the facts underlying the bargain. Therefore, rescission will not be granted unless the mistake goes to the *very basis of the bargain*; mere "materiality" is not enough. [*See* **Reliance Finance Corp. v. Miller,** 557 F.2d 674 (9th Cir. 1977)—mistake must go to "very essence" of bargain]

(1) Sale of goods contracts [§998]

In contracts for the sale of goods, the idea of "basic" fact is expressed as "one going to the *nature or identity* of the subject matter." [*See* **Fernandez v. Western Railroad Builders,** 736 P.2d 1361 (Idaho 1987)—no rescission where mistake went to usefulness rather than identity of used railroad equipment]

(a) Suit by buyer [§999]

Where the plaintiff is the buyer who has received apples which both he and seller assumed to be oranges, the case is usually disposed of on a *breach of warranty* rather than mistake analysis. The buyer is favored because he did not get the thing bargained for. [*But see* **Smith v. Zimbalist,** 2 Cal. App. 2d 324 (1934)—parties assumed fiddle was a "Stradivarius"; both warranty (the seller referred to the fiddle as a "Strad") and mistake rationales were used]

(b) Suit by seller [§1000]

Where the plaintiff is the seller who has sold something more valuable than she realized, the mistake analysis must be used, but it is awkward.

Example: The leading case allowing rescission is **Sherwood v. Walker,** 33 N.W. 919 (Mich. 1887), where both parties thought the item sold was a barren cow (valuable only as beef); instead it was with calf. It was treated as a mistake as to the identity of the thing sold.

Compare: A contrary approach was taken by the court in **Wood v. Boynton,** 25 N.W. 42 (Wis. 1885), where the parties believed that an object offered for sale for $1 was a "stone" rather than a $700 diamond. The seller's suit for rescission was *denied. Rationale:* The seller got what he bargained for: From his standpoint, the basis of the bargain was the *money*—not the object for sale.

(c) Proposed Restatement test [§1001]

Noting the difficulty involved in attempting to apply this terminology, the tentative draft of the Restatement (Third) of Restitution, section 5, proposes a two-pronged test. To support a claim for rescission, it must be shown that (i) the contract would not have been entered into but for the mistake; and (ii) the risk of mistake has not been assigned to the transferor.

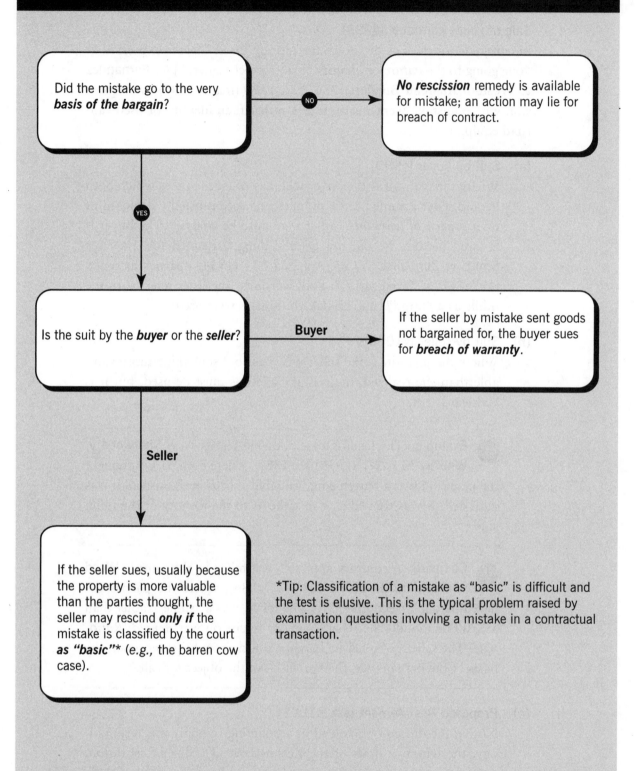

Did the mistake go to the very *basis of the bargain*?

NO → *No rescission* remedy is available for mistake; an action may lie for breach of contract.

YES ↓

Is the suit by the *buyer* or the *seller*?

Buyer → If the seller by mistake sent goods not bargained for, the buyer sues for *breach of warranty*.

Seller ↓

If the seller sues, usually because the property is more valuable than the parties thought, the seller may rescind *only if* the mistake is classified by the court *as "basic"** (e.g., the barren cow case).

*Tip: Classification of a mistake as "basic" is difficult and the test is elusive. This is the typical problem raised by examination questions involving a mistake in a contractual transaction.

(2) Conveyances of interests in land

(a) Mistake as defense [§1002]

As long as the transaction is *executory*, the element of mistake may be asserted as a *defense* to specific performance. A mistake as to a *material* fact will be a valid defense to specific performance—even though it falls short of the *basic* fact test required for rescission.

(b) Mistake as to quantity [§1003]

If the sale is *by acre*, the appropriate remedy for a deficiency is restitution for the overpayment (*see supra*, §984). If the sale is *in gross*, there is *no* remedy, unless it can be said that what remains is an essentially different piece of ground—*i.e.*, a "basic" mistake. (*Possible example:* The farm Blackacre is bargained for, but the conveyance is short to the extent that it cannot be operated as a *farm*.) [*See* **Dlug v. Woolridge**, 538 P.2d 883 (Colo. 1975)—rescission proper remedy where only 16.5 acres of 26.5 acres bargained for could be conveyed by seller]

(c) Mistake as to quality [§1004]

The term "mistake in quality" refers to the situation where, for example, both parties assume land sold contains iron ore, but subsequent tests show no ore.

1) General rule [§1005]

The general rule is that quality deficiencies (unless expressly made conditional) are *not* considered "basic," and hence *rescission* is not available.

2) Exception [§1006]

Where the *intended use* of land turns out to be impracticable for reasons unknown to parties at the time they contracted, rescission may be sought. [**Dover Pool & Racquet Club, Inc. v. Brooking**, 322 N.E.2d 168 (Mass. 1975)—rescission allowed for mutual mistake as to whether applicable zoning laws permitted use of land for tennis club; **Carey v. Wallner**, 725 P.2d 557 (Mont. 1986)—basic misconception that state license not needed to run adult foster care home]

a) Distinguish—where risk allocated to aggrieved party [§1007]

A court may, in these cases, find that there is a mutual mistake as to a basic fact but nevertheless bind the disadvantaged party to the contract because risk is allocated to that party by the agreement. Thus, the court held the buyer to a contract to buy an apartment building that was subsequently condemned as uninhabitable by finding that the risk of loss was allocated to the buyer by an "as is" clause in the contract. [**Lenawee County Board of Health v. Messerly,** 331 N.W.2d 203 (Mich. 1982); **Atkins v. Kirkpatrick,** 823 S.W.2d 547 (Tenn. 1991)]

b) Where title to land passes [§1008]

Where title to land has been transferred, courts *rarely* grant relief based on such disappointed expectations. [*But see* **Vermette v. Andersen,** 558 P.2d 258 (Wash. 1976)]

c) Lease of land cases [§1009]

But in the case of executed *leases*, such relief is more common. The terms of the lease generally set forth the tenant's intended use, from which it may be concluded that the use is "basic." (Whereas, deeds rarely reveal the buyer's intended use, and where they do, the fact that the use was not made a condition on the estate conveyed is another reason for denying relief.)

(3) Settlement of claims [§1010]

Ordinarily, compromises *cannot* be rescinded for "mistake," as the very possibility of mistake is an element of compromise. However, this is subject to the above principles as to errors concerning "basic" facts—*i.e.,* unknown conditions outside the area of compromise. Thus, the distinction is between an incorrect diagnosis, which may be a basis for rescission, and an incorrect prognosis, which is not. [**Quintana v. Motel 6, Inc.,** 693 P.2d 597 (N.M. 1984); **Gleason v. Guzman,** 623 P.2d 378 (Colo. 1981)]

(a) Typical illustration

A personal injury claim for a broken leg is settled. This does *not* preclude rescission of the compromise if, unknown to the parties, a broken back was also incurred. [*See* **McCamley v. Shockey,** 636 F.2d 256 (8th Cir. 1981)—rescission granted where release was executed for $700 based on diagnosis of cervical sprain, but subsequently fractured vertebra discovered; *compare* **La Fleur v. C.C. Pierce Co.,** 496 N.E.2d 827 (Mass. 1986)—rescission of a release for unknown injury, *with* **Bennett v. Shimoda Floral, Inc.,** 739 P.2d 648 (Wash. 1987)—rescission not allowed where mistake was as to extent of known injuries]

(b) Limitation by agreement [§1011]

The broader the language of the release (*e.g.,* to cover "all injuries unknown or unanticipated"), the less likelihood that the existence of uncontemplated "basic" facts not included in the settlement can be claimed. [**Mangini v. McClung,** 24 N.Y.2d 556 (1969)] But such broad language will not in itself bar relief for injuries unknown at the time the release was signed. [*See* **Bushkin, Gaims, Gaines, Jones & Stream v. Garber,** 677 F. Supp. 774 (S.D.N.Y. 1988); **Mangini v. McClung,** *supra*]

1) Limited exception

Some extreme cases intimate that the mere fact that a personal injury claim is settled for a sum which later developments show was far too little indicates a "basic" error.

(c) How issue raised [§1012]

Current practice does ***not*** require that a suit to rescind the release be brought before an action for personal injury damages can be maintained. Rather, the personal injury action can be filed, and the release asserted by way of ***defense*** can be challenged by the plaintiff for "mistake" in the personal injury action.

(4) Property settlement agreement [§1013]

Erroneously omitting an asset valued at $205,000 in negotiating a property settlement in a divorce action was held to be a mistake going to the essence of the transaction. [**Wallace v. Wallace,** 619 P.2d 511 (Haw. 1980)] Similarly, a mutual mistake about the profitability of a business (an accountant mistakenly omitted $48,000 in accounts payable) was grounds to rescind a contract to buy out one of the owners of the business. [**Simonson v. Fendell,** 675 P.2d 1218 (Wash. 1984)]

4. Unilateral Mistake

a. No relief for "purely" unilateral mistake [§1014]

It usually is said that there may be no rescission for a "purely unilateral" mistake not known to or taken advantage of by the other party. [**First Trust Co. v. Reinhardt,** 655 P.2d 891 (Haw. 1982)—applying Restatement of Contracts rules; **Hopper Furs, Inc. v. Emery Air Freight Corp.,** 749 F.2d 1261 (8th Cir. 1984)—no relief where shipper mistakenly placed value of lost shipment of furs in ZIP code box rather than "declared value" box]

b. Relief granted if coupled with other factor [§1015]

Notwithstanding the general rule above, such relief has been granted where: (i) the mistake is *"basic"* as defined above; ***and*** (ii) ***unconscionable hardship*** would follow if the bargain is allowed to stand. [**Home Savers v. United Security Co.,** 741 P.2d 1355 (Nev. 1987)—rescission allowed to buyer who purchased wrong tract because of seller's misleading information]

(1) Relief granted conditionally [§1016]

When restitution is allowed, the defendant is held entitled to compensation for any *reliance* losses sustained as a result of setting aside the bargain. (This in effect allows the plaintiff—who because of his own error would otherwise suffer serious financial loss if he were to perform, or heavy benefit-of-the-bargain damages if he were to default—to *rescind* on condition of making good the defendant's *out-of-pocket loss*.) [**Cummings v. Dusenbury,** 472 N.E.2d 575 (Ill. 1984)]

c. Errors in construction bids [§1017]

Suppose a contractor, through error in clerical addition, bids the wrong amount (*e.g.,* $70,000 instead of $100,000). If the contractor is held to benefit-of-the-bargain damages, it would cost him $30,000 (or more) for nonperformance. The actual cost to the owner of taking rebids, etc., may only be a few hundred dollars (and he may have insisted on bid bonds that cover even these reliance damages).

(1) What relief? [§1018]

The actual holdings in these cases are by no means uniform in outcome. At one extreme, no relief is afforded the mistaken bidder at all. At the other extreme, the entire contract has been thrown out (including liability on the posted bond accompanying the bid). [**M.F. Kemper Construction Co. v. Los Angeles,** 37 Cal. 2d 696 (1951)]

(a) *The "better" rule* is believed to be to *allow* rescission for such mistakes, conditional on paying reliance damages. This result is consistent with the rule allowing unconscionability as a defense to enforcement of a contract, and at the same time is consistent with contract rules calling for damages for breach. [**Department of Transportation v. Roulee, Inc.,** 518 So. 2d 1326 (Fla. 1988)—rescission, not reformation, is proper remedy for a mistaken bid]

(b) *A few cases* have denied rescission and reformed the bid to state the correct amount where both the mistaken and corrected bids were the lowest received by the builder. [**Dick Corp. v. Associated Electric Cooperative, Inc.,** 475 F. Supp. 15 (W.D. Mo. 1979)]

(2) Limitation [§1019]

Relief in these mistaken bid cases is generally limited to cases of *clerical error*. If the mistake was caused by faulty *judgment* of the contractor, *no* relief is generally allowed (even though the economic disaster to the contractor is just as great, or greater). [**Powder Horn Constructors v. City of Florence,** 754 P.2d 356 (Colo. 1988)—mistaken bid may be rescinded only if mistake is clerical or mathematical and made in good faith] In a few cases, this latter distinction has been repudiated. [**White v. Barrenda Mesa Water District,** 7 Cal. App. 3d 894 (1970)]

C. Defenses

1. In General [§1020]

Because the defendant is mistaken and therefore equally innocent, certain defenses are recognized to a claim for restitution for mistake. These defenses are not recognized when the enrichment results from the defendant's tort or breach of contract.

2. Change of Position [§1021]

If the defendant has *disposed* of the benefit received by mistake, without knowledge of the error, so that compelling restitution in money would be *harsh* (even though the defendant is solvent and could pay the judgment by liquidating other assets), restitution will be denied. [Rest. Restitution §142; **Bank Saderat Iran v. Amin Beydoun, Inc.,** 555 F. Supp. 770 (S.D.N.Y. 1983)—detrimental change of position in reliance on a mistaken down payment shown by loss of right of action against party principally liable on account; **Hilliard v. Fox,** 735 F. Supp. 674 (W.D. W. Va. 1990)—loss of value in investment made with money mistakenly paid to the defendant constitutes change of circumstances and thus a defense against restitution claim]

a. Application

The change-of-position defense *applies* where:

(1) The benefit received is disposed of *gratuitously*.

(2) An agent receiving money by mistake has already paid the money to the principal. (*Exception:* An *undisclosed* agent receiving a benefit by mistake under a *voidable* contract cannot assert the defense of payment over.) [Rest. Restitution §143]

(3) Overpayment was made by *welfare or pension authorities*. (As a practical matter, however, many administrative agencies of government simply offset the amount of overpayment against later payments due, but may adopt guidelines embodying the "equitable" essence of this defense.) [**Adams v. Secretary of Health & Human Services,** 653 F. Supp. 249 (C.D. Ill. 1986)—it is against equity and good conscience to require repayment of Social Security benefits where a mother would otherwise have received child support payments]

(4) The overpayment causes the defendant "*to change his lifestyle.*" (This is a rare case, because the size of a benefit having this effect would normally put the recipient on notice.) [**Woolsey v. Nationwide Insurance Co.**, 697 F. Supp. 1053 (Ark. 1988)—parents of decedent, who were destitute, spent money on medical bills and funeral of decedent]

b. Caveat [§1022]

The defense *does not apply* if the benefit has been used by the defendant to pay his bills or normal living expenses, or if used in business to produce *other* income. [**Westamerica Securities, Inc. v. Cornelius**, 520 P.2d 1262 (Kan. 1974); **Messersmith v. G.T. Murray & Co.**, *supra*, §983—money spent for down payment on the purchase of a home; **Monroe Financial Corp. v. DiSilvestro**, 529 N.E.2d 379 (Ind. 1988)—money spent on home improvements]

c. As partial defense [§1023]

If the defendant *consumes* a benefit received by mistake, he will be liable only to the extent of his *actual* enrichment. For example, a manufacturer of candy receives mistaken shipment of maple sugar and uses it; his liability is limited to the wholesale costs of purchase he would have otherwise incurred.

3. Discharge for Value [§1024]

If the defendant has *paid* for the benefit mistakenly conferred upon him, or accepted it in satisfaction of a debt owed to him by another, this is a valid defense (closely related to the change-of-position defense, above). Having paid for it, he is not unjustly enriched.

a. Money [§1025]

Suppose Alex owes money to Becky. Cindy mistakenly pays money to Becky, who equally mistakenly believes that the payment was coming from Alex, and therefore accepts it in satisfaction of Alex's debt. If the satisfaction of the debt cannot be recalled (as where a promissory note is stamped "paid" and returned to the debtor), Becky has a valid defense to any action by Cindy for restitution of the mistaken payment. [*See* **Equilease Corp. v. Hentz**, 634 F.2d 850 (5th Cir. 1981)—restitution denied where money paid to Defendant by mistake was used to satisfy valid obligation owed to Defendant because money received in good faith in satisfaction of valid claim is not recoverable from innocent payee; **St. Mary's Medical Center v. United Farm Bureau Family Life Insurance**, 624 N.E.2d 939 (Ind. 1993)—money mistakenly paid to satisfy medical claim not recoverable; *and see* **Banque Worms v. Bankamerica International**, 928 F.2d 538 (2d Cir. 1991)—rule applied to mistaken electronic fund transfers between banks]

b. Checks [§1026]

Suppose Becky fraudulently induces Alex to make out a check payable to Cindy; Cindy accepts the check in satisfaction of a debt owed by Becky, and cashes the check. Alex then discovers the fraud and seeks restitution. Under U.C.C. section 3-302(a), the payee (Cindy) may qualify as a "holder in due course"—one who pays "value" (discharging Becky's indebtedness), and takes without knowledge of any defense to the instrument (Becky's fraud). This is an application of the discharge-for-value defense, and operates to cut off any claim for restitution by Alex.

c. **Goods [§1027]**

Suppose Becky owes Cindy; Becky fraudulently persuades Cindy to accept coal as payment. Becky then tells Alex, a coal dealer, that Cindy desires to purchase a quantity of coal which Alex delivers; Cindy accepts the coal in satisfaction of her claim against Becky (*e.g.,* by returning Becky's note marked "paid"). Alex probably *cannot* get restitution of either the coal or its value from Cindy, because under the U.C.C. a preexisting debt is value. [*See* **Concord Coal Co. v. Ferrin,** 51 A. 283 (N.H. 1901)—a pre-U.C.C. case]

d. **Discharge of "nonexistent" claims [§1028]**

Suppose Becky forges Xavier's name on a mortgage and note in favor of Cindy who pays Becky for them. Cindy, of course, mistakenly believes that she has a "valid" claim against Xavier. Becky then forges another note and a mortgage on the same property in favor of Alex who pays off the prior "note and mortgage" held by Cindy. Later, Alex discovers the fraud and seeks restitution of his mistaken payment from Cindy. The cases are divided:

(i) *Some courts deny recovery* on the ground that the mistaken payment was accepted by Cindy as a discharge of a preexisting debt for value. [Rest. Restitution §14, Illus. 7]

(ii) *Others allow recovery* on the ground that Cindy *had no valid claim* to be discharged—*i.e.,* Cindy's actual claim was an unknown one in tort *against Xavier,* and the payment was not received in satisfaction of that claim. [**National Shawmut Bank v. Fidelity Mutual Life Insurance Co.,** 61 N.E.2d 18 (Mass. 1945)]

(1) Distinguish

Alex executes a personal note to Becky secured by a mortgage on stolen property (usually an automobile). Alex then sells the property to Cindy, using the purchase money to pay off the note to Becky. When the theft is discovered, Cindy seeks restitution of her money from Becky. Most courts deny recovery, ruling that Becky has a good defense of discharge for value because Becky did satisfy and discharge a valid (although worthless) note executed by Alex, the thief. [**Associate Discount Corp. v. Clements,** 321 P.2d 673 (Okla. 1958)]

4. **Compromise and Settlement [§1029]**

Rather than a defense to restitution, compromise and settlement is really an assertion that no mistake was actually made. The parties were conscious of the possibility that the benefit transferred may not have been due. Recovery of insurance payments is frequently barred for this reason because the insurance company assumed the risk of mistake. [**Terra Nova Insurance Co. v. Associates Commercial Corp.,** 697 F. Supp. 1048 (E.D. Wis. 1988)]

---

e.g. **Example:** Defendant, a jeweler, could not find plaintiff's ring which had been left with defendant for repairs. After a delay of weeks, defendant finally agreed to replace plaintiff's ring with a new ring. Six months later, defendant found plaintiff's original ring and requested plaintiff to exchange rings. Plaintiff refused. Defendant sought rescission on the basis of a mutual mistake. *Held:* Rescission is denied. Defendant entered into the agreement with a conscious uncertainty as to the facts and not under a mistaken belief as to the whereabouts of the ring. He assumed the risk that the ring would be found. [**Tarrant v. Monson,** 619 P.2d 1210 (Nev. 1980)]

EXAM TIP	gilbert

Compromise agreements occur often in commercial and private settings, and the courts would undermine such agreements if they were to set them aside for mistake. Don't forget this very important point on your exam. For example, suppose Seller finds a painting in his attic. He thinks it is by a local artist—Paul Picasto—and that it is worth $500. He takes the painting to Dealer. Dealer honestly advises Seller that he thinks the Picasto is worth $300, and the parties agree to a sale for $250. It turns out that the Picasto was actually worth $1,000. Seller probably cannot obtain rescission because the parties *assumed the risk that they were mistaken* as to value. However, if it turns out that the painting was actually an original *Picasso* worth $1 million, rescission may be granted if the court rules that this was a risk not assumed by the parties.

5. Mistake of Law [§1030]

It is usually said that there is no restitution for payments made under a mistake of law (*e.g.,* where a person pays a debt barred by the statute of limitations). [**Young v. Cities Service Oil Co.,** 364 A.2d 603 (Md. 1976); **Webb v. Webb,** 301 S.E.2d 570 (W. Va. 1983)—relief denied for mistake of law of intestate succession] However, numerous "exceptions" to this rule are recognized—*e.g.,* fiduciary relationship between the parties, superior knowledge by one party, etc. Actually, it is more helpful to reverse the rule and exceptions, and to state that restitution for payments made under a mistake of law *will* be granted *except* where the benefit is conferred in response to an *honest claim* made under mistake of law. This is the position taken by the tentative draft of the Restatement (Third) of Restitution, section 5, which makes no distinction between mistakes of fact or law.

a. Comment

Viewed from the Restatement Third tentative draft perspective, mistake of law is no more than a variation of the compromise-and-settlement defense already discussed. Honest compromises based on unsettled or uncertain points of law are thus upheld, whereas anything other than honest compromises are remediable by restitution. [**Kirk v. Allegheny Towing, Inc.,** 620 F. Supp. 458 (D. Pa. 1985)—"money voluntarily paid on a mistake of law cannot be recovered on the ground that the party supposed he was bound to pay it when in truth he was not"; **Guthrie v. Times-Mirror Co.,** 51 Cal. App. 3d 879 (1975)]

---

e.g. Example: Alice pays Boyd, relying on a line of Supreme Court opinions going back 50 years. The Supreme Court then overrules the precedents and *changes* the law. Alice cannot recover from Boyd; there was no mistake here.

---

e.g. Example: Buyer purchases a liquor store, believing that a liquor license could be obtained within 90 days. Unknown to either buyer or seller, a state law requires a two-year residency period. Buyer may rescind and recover her payment. [**Glasgow v. Greenfield,** 657 S.W.2d 578 (Ark. 1983)]

---

e.g. Example: Insurance company settled a claim for loss of cattle although an exclusionary clause relieved the company from liability for the loss. *Held:* This was a voluntary payment of an honest claim; hence, restitution should be denied. [**The Hartford v. Doubler,** 434 N.E.2d 1189 (Ill. 1982); *and see* **Jursich v. Arlington Heights Federal Savings & Loan,** 441 N.E.2d 864 (Ill. 1982)—recovery of charges for late payments based on interpretation of note denied]

---

6. Negligence of Plaintiff [§1031]

Failure to read documents or other carelessness on the part of the mistaken plaintiff is often asserted to bar a remedy.

a. Comment

Actually, negligence per se is *not* a defense because, by definition, all mistakes can be ascribed to a measure of carelessness. However, "negligence" is a factor that, when other defenses are present, may determine the outcome in close cases.

D. Mistake in Integration—Reformation as Remedy

1. Nature of Mistake [§1032]

Mistake in integration refers to the case where the parties made an oral agreement as to which there was *no* mistake, but a mistake has been made in putting the oral agreement into writing ("scrivener's mistakes"—*e.g.,* leaving out terms, or misstating any of the terms or conditions).

Example: Parties agreed on a note and mortgage at 8% interest, but interest payments were incorrectly calculated at 4%. Because both parties intended the instrument to reflect interest at 8%, reformation was granted. [**Yeargan v. Bank of Montgomery County**, 595 S.W.2d 704 (Ark. 1980); *and see* **Beynon Building Corp. v. National Guardian Life Insurance**, 455 N.E.2d 246 (Ill. 1983)—monthly mortgage payments reformed to reflect intention of parties]

a. Mutual or unilateral [§1033]

A mistake in integration may be either mutual (neither party discovered the deviation from the oral agreement when he signed the written contract) or unilateral (one party knew and the other did not—in which case it is in the nature of a fraud by the one who knew).

2. Nature of Relief [§1034]

Reformation is a decree granted by equity to *reform the writing*—i.e., to make the writing conform to the parties' original oral agreement or understanding. (This remedy is known in some jurisdictions as "rectification" or "revision.") The contract will be made to read as originally understood and agreed upon.

a. Original agreement ambiguous [§1035]

It follows that reformation is *not* a proper remedy where the original oral agreement was ambiguous or incomplete. Reformation cannot be used to "make" an agreement for the parties. (But if the ambiguity only appears in the writing, and the parties' oral agreement was clear, the writing can be reformed to conform to the unambiguous oral agreement.)

Example: Parties entered into an agreement for the sale of certain riverfront lots, but failed to specify the boundary lines of the lots. Reformation of contracts to include acreage bordering the river was denied. [**National Resort Communities v. Cain**, 526 S.W.2d 510 (Tex. 1975)]

b. Mistake as to meaning of words used [§1036]

Neither is reformation the proper remedy where the mistake relates to the *meaning of the words* used *both* in the oral agreement and in the written contract.

Example: Porter, a produce exporter, receives an order from a foreign customer for "feveroles." Not knowing what this means, he asks his own supplier, Supp. Supp makes an *honest misstatement* that they are "ordinary horsebeans." Porter then asks Supp to supply these beans (oral agreement) and later the parties sign a written contract whereby Supp sells Porter "horsebeans." When shipped abroad to the customer, it is learned that "feveroles" have a special meaning. Porter, being liable to the customer for breach of warranty, seeks to reform his purchase contract with Supp to make "horsebeans" read "feveroles" (which would cast the loss on Supp by making him automatically liable to Porter for breach of warranty). However, Supp never agreed to sell "feveroles"; the only agreement—oral or written—was for "horsebeans," and hence reformation was *not* allowed. [**Frederick Rose Ltd. v. William H. Pim Co.,** 2 C.B. 450 (1953)]

c. **Mistake as to legal effect of words used [§1037]**

If the parties have agreed on what they intend to accomplish, and the mistake consists of using words that do not accomplish that effect, reformation is the proper remedy, even though the words used in the written instrument conform to the words chosen by the parties. [**Haslem v. O'Hosen,** 689 P.2d 27 (Utah 1984)—failure of a warranty deed to reserve mineral rights because of mistake of law; reformation allowed]

Example: Aldous and Bertha want to purchase a house and to take title in a manner that will give either the right of survivorship. They mistakenly believe that taking title as "tenants in common" will accomplish this purpose, and the agreements are drawn and executed accordingly. Technically, they have written down their exact agreement. However, the words they used (orally or in writing) did not carry into effect the ultimate *legal result* intended, and reformation has been permitted. In reality, the written instrument and the mistaken oral agreement that preceded it are both reformed to accomplish the basic *result* intended by the parties. [Rest. Restitution §51, Illus. 3; **Rosenbaum v. Texas Energies,** 736 P.2d 888 (Kan. 1987)—reformation where parties chose legal terms that had different legal effect than agreed upon]

(1) **Statutes**

This principle is sometimes embodied in statute. For example, California Civil Code section 3401 states: "In revising a written instrument, a court may inquire as to what the instrument was intended to mean and what were its *intended legal consequences*, and is not confined to an inquiry as to what the language of the instrument was intended to be."

3. **Reformation and the Statute of Frauds**

a. **Statute of Frauds not a defense to reformation [§1038]**

In a suit seeking reformation of a writing, neither the parol evidence rule nor the Statute of Frauds applies to bar proof in the form of parol or extrinsic evidence of the underlying agreement. However, the proponent of reformation must meet a very high standard of proof. [**Chimart Associates v. Paul,** 66 N.Y.2d 570 (1986)]

b. Application

(1) To correct incorrect description of land [§1039]

The Statute of Frauds does not bar reformation of a deed or other conveyance to correct the description (change "Lot 376" to "Lot 375"), on the rationale that the document is merely being *revised*.

(2) To cut down amount of land conveyed [§1040]

Similarly, reformation of a deed or other conveyance is allowed to *reduce* the amount of land conveyed by the deed to that originally intended by the parties.

Example: Cleghorn owns three-fifths of Blackacre, but both Cleghorn and Zumwalt mistakenly believe that Cleghorn owns only an undivided one-fifth interest. Cleghorn orally and in writing agrees to convey "all my interest" in Blackacre to Zumwalt. The deed is drawn and executed accordingly. When Cleghorn later discovers that she owned more land, reformation will be allowed. The parties only intended to convey a one-fifth interest, and therefore the court will reform the deed to carry out the parties' intent—by *cutting down* the size of the conveyance (*e.g.*, by writing "one-fifth interest" into the deed). The analysis is that the deed incorrectly expresses the parties' agreement. [**Cleghorn v. Zumwalt,** 83 Cal. 155 (1890)]

---

(3) Reformation increasing amount of land conveyed [§1041]

In a few states, reformation to enlarge the area covered by a deed is not allowed because there is no memorandum in writing to cover the grant of the additional land. Most jurisdictions, however, *permit* the conveyance to be reformed either to enlarge or to decrease the size of the grant if there is clear and convincing evidence of the underlying agreement.

Example: Samantha orally agrees to convey 180 acres to Zack. The actual deed conveys only 140 acres. Reformation is granted in most jurisdictions.

Compare: The parties mistakenly believe Samantha owns a three-fourths interest in Blackacre, which she orally agrees to sell to Zack. The deed as drawn conveys "an undivided three-fourths interest." When it is discovered that Samantha actually owns more, Zack *cannot* get reformation to *increase* the land conveyed. *Rationale:* There is no agreement to cover the additional land; reformation cannot be granted where the instrument to be reformed accurately reflects the underlying agreement, even though that agreement is itself mistaken. [*See* **Metzler v. Bolen,** 137 F. Supp. 457 (D.N.D. 1956)]

---

c. Not allowed to supply missing terms [§1042]

Some courts refuse to grant reformation where essential terms required to satisfy the Statute of Frauds are omitted from the memorandum or written instrument. To rule otherwise would undermine the Statute of Frauds in every case. [**Brechman v. Adamar of New Jersey,** 440 A.2d 480 (N.J. 1981)—no reformation where duration of tenancy not specified]

(1) Note

Restatement (Second) of Contracts section 156 permits reformation where both parties agree upon the missing term but inadvertently fail to include it in the writing.

4. Multiple Successive Documents [§1043]

Frequently, a copyist's error in a document (such as a mortgage) may be carried through a series of transactions with the error mechanically repeated (*e.g.,* into foreclosure proceedings, judicial sales, and sheriff's deed). Strictly speaking, reformation as an equitable remedy should be granted only in personam—between the parties to the individual transactions. However, this is often impractical, and hence a decree in favor of the plaintiff (the party shortchanged in the last transaction) *will be held to reform all previous documents in the chain* (although the original parties are long gone). [**Stubbs v. Standard Life Association,** 242 P.2d 819 (Colo. 1952); **Johnston v. Sorrels,** 729 S.W.2d 21 (Ark. 1987)]

a. Effect

This amounts to a quiet title suit—in contravention of the general rule that an equitable title cannot be quieted as against the legal title; hence, the guise of reformation. (Of course, there must be *no BFP* of the parcels omitted by clerical error, or the equitable remedy is cut off.)

5. Reformation of Long-Term Executory Contracts [§1044]

Historically, periodic inflationary spirals have imposed unanticipated losses in the performance of many long-term contracts, particularly where one of the terms (usually the price) is tied to some economic indicator. Strictly speaking, reformation of the terms of these agreements would be improper because the writing accurately incorporates the intention of the parties. Some courts nevertheless modify contracts to reflect the new economic reality and enforce the contract as modified. [*See* **Aluminum Co. of America v. Essex Group, Inc.,** 499 F. Supp. 53 (W.D. Pa. 1980)—output contract in which court modified price charged for aluminum] Other courts refuse any remedy. [*See* **Woolridge v. Exxon Corp.,** 473 A.2d 1254 (Conn. 1984)—rescission denied regarding rental term in a long-term lease; **United States v. Southwestern Electric Cooperative, Inc.,** 869 F.2d 310 (7th Cir. 1989)—rescission denied in case involving long-term requirements contract for wholesale power]

6. Reformation as Alternative to Rescission [§1045]

In some cases, contracts have been rewritten by courts, rather than rescinded, because of the particular equities involved. [*See, e.g.,* **Vockner v. Erickson,** 712 P.2d

379 (Alaska 1986)—unconscionable contract signed by an elderly vendor reformed to bring it into conformity with minimal standards of fairness; **Justin Belt Co. v. Yost,** 502 S.W.2d 681 (Tex. 1973)—restrictive covenant reformed to make it reasonable as to time and place; **Turney v. Roberts,** 501 S.W.2d 601 (Ark. 1973)—usurious contract reformed to comply with usury law]

E. Mistake in Gratuitous Transactions

1. Gifts

a. Remedies of donor

(1) Mistake as to basic assumptions [§1046]

The term "mistake as to basic assumptions" here refers to gifts made by mistake as to the identity of a donee, or under a mistaken belief that other intended donees had died, or in forgetfulness of a previous gift made for the same purpose, or for tax savings that cannot be accomplished.

(a) Restitution granted for "basic" mistakes [§1047]

The mistake as to a "basic" assumption goes to the creation of a donative intent. Had the facts been known to the donor, she would not have made the gift at all; hence, it would be unjust enrichment to allow the donee to retain it. Where such a mistake is shown, the property given or its value is recoverable in restitution. [**Lady Hood of Avalon v. MacKinnon,** [1909] 1 Ch. 476]

1) May be unilateral [§1048]

The mistake here may be purely *unilateral*. It need *not* appear that the donee was also mistaken as to the facts inducing the gift (whereas, in the case of executed bargains, it usually must be shown that the mistake was mutual).

2) No relief where mistake not "basic" [§1049]

Restitution is not proper where the mistake is such that the donor would have probably made the gift anyhow (*e.g.,* a birthday present given early under mistake as to the date of the donee's birthday).

(b) Remedies [§1050]

If restitution of the gift is appropriate, the donor may be granted specific restoration of the property (replevin), rescission of deeds, or cancellation of documents, etc.

Is the *donor* or the *donee* seeking the remedy?

Donor

Donee

Was the mistake related to a *basic assumption*?

NO

YES

Restitution is *not* available because the donor probably would have made the gift anyway.

The donor can be granted *specific restoration* of the property, *rescission* of deeds, *cancellation* of documents, *reformation* of documents, etc., as long as the donor is alive, subject to any defense that the donee may assert.

If the donor is *alive*, the donee is *denied a remedy* because the donor can rectify her own mistake, but the donee might be granted a remedy for *detrimental reliance* based on promissory estoppel. If the donor is dead, many cases allow *"quasi-specific performance"* against the donor's estate.

(c) Defenses [§1051]

The same defenses apply as in bargaining transactions (*see supra*) except, of course, that the donee could not claim a discharge for value.

(2) Mistake as to size of gift [§1052]

The term "mistake as to size of gift" refers to the situation where, *e.g.,* a donor intended to give 10 acres to each of her two children, but by mistake gave 20 acres to one child and nothing to the other, or where the donor, intending to retain a life estate, mistakenly executes a fee simple conveyance. [*See* **Yano v. Yano**, 697 P.2d 1132 (Ariz. 1985)] Most courts allow the donor to obtain restitution (or reformation of documents) to recover the amount of the overage. (Some courts hold that the entire gift must be set aside, so that the donor can start over.)

(a) Limitation [§1053]

If the donor has *died* without availing herself of a *known* right of restitution, restitution will *not* be granted. The reason is that the delivery was complete during her lifetime, and having taken no action to set aside the gift or to recover the overage given, the requisite intent for a gift may now be inferred.

b. Remedies of donee [§1054]

These are cases in which the donee claims that the donor failed to make a gift she had intended to the donee; or that the *amount* actually given was less than that intended by the donor.

(1) During donor's lifetime [§1055]

As long as the donor is still alive, the donee is denied any relief. *Rationale:* Having wholly or partly failed to execute an intended transfer, the donor can always rectify her own mistake, and hence there is no basis for restitutionary relief.

(a) Note

Even so, if the donee has changed his position in detrimental reliance on the donor's gift promise, recovery on a *promissory estoppel* theory may be had. [Rest. Contracts 90; *and see* Contracts Summary]

(2) After donor's death [§1056]

If the donative intent is *clear*, many cases allow "quasi specific performance" of gift promises against the estate of the donor. These cases ascribe to the donor the intent to fulfill her promises. Neither the donor's estate nor her heirs are bona fide purchasers and hence the donee's claim is assertable in equity against them. [**Hazlett v. Bryant**, 241 S.W.2d 121 (Tenn. 1951)]

(a) Some cases contra

There is also authority contra on this, refusing relief to the intended donee on the rationale that "equity does not aid a volunteer" (meaning here, one who is no more than a prospective donee). [128 A.L.R. 1295]

2. Inter Vivos Trusts [§1057]

There is no problem as to reformation of mistakes in a trust document if the trust is revocable. However, if a trust is irrevocable, relief may be had only in accordance with the rule that the mistake must be "basic."

Example: Settlor sets up an irrevocable trust for beneficiary which results in an unexpectedly large gift tax to the settlor. If the primary purpose of the trust is to aid the beneficiary, the mistake would not be basic, and therefore, no relief would be granted. Perhaps there would be the opposite result if the primary purpose was tax saving. [*See* **Walton v. Bank of California,** 218 Cal. App. 2d 527 (1963); **duPont v. Southern National Bank,** 575 F. Supp. 549 (S.D. Tex. 1983)]

---

3. Wills

a. Reformation [§1058]

The doctrine of "probable intent of the testator" in will construction has been extended to allow reformation of probated wills embodying an elaborate estate plan to minimize taxes where, because of changes in tax law *after* the decedent's death, heavy unexpected taxes would be imposed unless the plan and documents were rewritten. [*In re* **Estate of Branigan,** 609 A.2d 431 (N.J. 1992)] Note that this markedly departs from the standard rules of reformation in that the mistake is (i) unilateral, and (ii) not the result of a scrivener's error.

b. Mistake in revoking a will—constructive trust [§1059]

If the testator makes a mistake in revoking his will, the court may use a constructive trust to effect the testator's intent. For example, if the testator, intending to revoke a codicil to his will, destroyed a photostatic copy, mistaking it for the original, the court held that the law of wills required that the codicil be probated, but at the same time decreed a constructive trust in favor of the original beneficiary named in the will itself. [*In re* **Estate of Tolin,** 622 So. 2d 988 (Fla. 1993)]

Chapter Twelve: Remedies for Breach of Contract

CONTENTS

Chapter Approach

Chapter Approach

Study this chapter carefully because breach of contract questions tend to predominate in Remedies exams. The following are useful guidelines for the various types of contract questions you might encounter on your exam:

1. In a *land sale contract* question:

   a. Make an initial classification of the contract as a *marketing* or *installment* type contract, because this has important remedial implications (*e.g.*, foreclosure by the seller is possible as a remedy for installment type contracts).

   b. Always determine whether some aspect of the *equitable conversion doctrine* is applicable.

   c. Last, examine whether the *party seeking relief is in default,* because this impacts on the remedial choices.

2. In a *sale of goods* problem, the measure of damages is, of course, important, but you need to consider as well the possibility of U.C.C. remedial innovations—specifically, *cover* by the buyer and *resale* by the seller.

3. Breach of *construction contracts* has long been a favorite exam topic because of the varying formulas for computing damages and the interesting problems raised when restitution is sought as an alternative remedy. In answering these questions:

   a. Again, determine initially whether the *party seeking relief is in default* on the contract.

   b. Mention the possibility of *equitable* relief, but keep in mind the historical reluctance of equity courts to enforce building contracts.

4. If the question involves an *employment contract*, your task is to consider whether *equitable* relief is available. While you can decide easily that affirmative promises to employ or work are not specifically enforceable, negative covenants enforceable by injunction may require a more extensive discussion. Be alert for an employer's breach of an "at will" employment contract, because recent decisions allow a tort remedy if the breach is in bad faith.

A. Special Conditions Applicable to Specific Performance

1. **Introduction [§1060]**

   The materials that follow state the remedies available to the parties for breach of contracts of various kinds: land sale contracts, contracts for the sale of chattels, construction contracts, employment contracts, and contracts with negative covenants. In each situation, the measure of damages, the availability of specific performance, and the various restitutionary remedies must be separately considered. There are, however, certain *conditions of general application* to the equitable remedy of specific performance that must be satisfied *regardless of the type of contract* being litigated. These conditions were previously set forth and include the requirements that:

   (i)   The remedy at law is *inadequate* (*see supra*, §122);

   (ii) The contract is *definite and certain* (*see supra*, §129);

   (iii) All *conditions precedent* are met (*see supra*, §130);

   (iv) Enforcement *operates equitably* (*see supra*, §133); and

   (v)   Enforcement is *feasible* (*see supra*, §136).

   Note finally that specific performance is an equitable remedy and neither party is entitled to a jury trial. [**State v. Attman/Glazer**, 594 A.2d 138 (Md. 1991); *and see supra*, §111]

2. **Mutuality of Remedy No Longer Required [§1061]**

   Specific performance will be granted in proper circumstances to an aggrieved party even though the remedy of specific performance is not mutual and would not be available to the other party to the contract were he to seek such relief.

   a. **Older view—"negative mutuality" [§1062]**

      At one time, equity courts applied the "negative mutuality" rule, denying specific performance to an injured party if, at the time the contract was executed, specific performance was not available to the other party. This rule is still followed in some jurisdictions. [*See* **Burger Chef Systems, Inc. v. Burger Chef of Florida, Inc.**, 317 So. 2d 795 (Fla. 1975)—franchisee cannot sue franchisor for specific performance because franchisor does not have same equitable remedy against franchisee; **Dixon v. City of Monticello**, 585 N.E.2d 609 (Ill. 1991)]

      (1) **Comment**

          Numerous exceptions to the negative mutuality doctrine developed over the years until the exceptions virtually swallowed up the rule.

   b. **Modern view—mutuality of performance [§1063]**

      Today, most states accept the rule stated in the Restatement of Contracts, which requires *mutuality of performance*, rather than mutuality of remedy—

i.e., under the Restatement approach, specific performance is denied to the injured party only in situations *where he has not performed* his part of the bargain or where *his performance cannot be secured* by the decree. [Rest. 2d Contracts §363] Simply stated, a court of equity will not compel a defendant to perform unless he can be assured of getting the performance promised by the plaintiff. [**Van Zandt v. Heilman,** 214 P.2d 864 (N.M. 1950); **Beecher v. Conte,** 29 Cal. 3d 345 (1981)—trial court adjusted "the equities" by decree to assure performance]

EXAM TIP   **gilbert**

The switch to requiring mutuality of performance instead of "negative mutuality" has important exam implications. Suppose Mitch, a 16-year-old minor, has always admired his neighbor Nate's classic 1967 Camaro convertible. One evening while discussing cars, Nate agrees to sell the Camaro to Mitch for $2,500. Mitch gives Nate a $250 deposit, and the two write up and sign a contract giving Mitch two months to come up with the rest of the money. A week later, Nate mentions the sale to his friend Fred. Fred tells Nate that he would have given Nate $5,000 for the car. Nate says, "sold" and tells Mitch the next day that the deal is off. Mitch, being the son of a lawyer, brings an action for specific performance. Under the old negative mutuality rule, specific performance would be denied because Nate could not enforce the contract against Mitch because he is a minor. Under the mutuality of performance rule, Mitch **can get specific performance** because the court can condition the decree on Mitch's tendering the remainder of the purchase price.

---

3. **Contractual Modification of Remedies [§1064]**

Section 2-719 of the U.C.C. specifically provides that remedies in sale of goods cases are subject to alteration, modification, or substitution by agreement of the parties. Liquidated damages provisions are an obvious example (*see infra*, §1095), but it has also been held that in a land sale contract, the parties may agree to exclude the remedy of specific performance where the provision is mutual and reasonable. [*See, e.g.,* **Greenstein v. Greenbrook, Ltd.,** 413 So. 842 (Fla. 1982)]

B. Land Sale Contracts

1. **Introduction [§1065]**

In analyzing the possible remedies for breach of a land sale contract, it is necessary to determine whether the breach of contract occurred *prior to or after* execution and delivery of the deed by the seller. It may also be necessary to determine whether the contract is a simple buy-sell agreement, calling for the payment of the price on a particular date, or whether the contract calls for periodic payments over an extended period of time (the installment land sale contract).

a. **Doctrine of equitable conversion [§1066]**

It is important to recognize that executory land sale contracts create *immediate equitable interests* in land as the result of a doctrine known as "equitable conversion." In equity, the buyer is regarded as the beneficial owner of the property *from the moment the contracts are executed*. This "equity" is based on the readiness of courts to enforce the contract specifically. [**Cain & Bultman, Inc. v. Miss Sam, Inc.,** 409 So. 2d 114 (Fla. 1982); **First Mustang State Bank v. Garland Bloodworth,** 825 P.2d 254 (Okla. 1991)] The interests of buyer and seller created by the application of this doctrine may be described as follows:

(1) Seller's interest—vendor's lien [§1067]

When a specifically enforceable land sale contract is executed, the seller retains legal title to the property subject to the contractual duty to convey. The seller also acquires a contractual right to payment of the price. This right to payment is secured by a "vendor's lien" on the property— *i.e., a charge on the buyer's equity in the land* arising by operation of law from the seller's retention of legal title. [**First National Bank v. S.O.Y. Investment Group,** 512 N.E.2d 121 (Ill. 1987)—seller becomes a "lienholder" when contract executed; **Askren v. 21st Street Inn,** 988 F.2d 38 (7th Cir. 1993)—vendor's lien is created whenever seller is not paid in full at the closing]

(a) Purpose of lien [§1068]

The function of the lien is to provide a device for *foreclosing the buyer's equity* as a method of compelling payment of the price. (It is to be distinguished from the grantor's lien, discussed *infra*, §1144.) [*See* **Estate of Somers v. Clearwater Power Co.,** 684 P.2d 1006 (Idaho 1984)]

(b) Assignability [§1069]

An assignment of the contract (purchase money) to a third party operates impliedly to transfer the vendor's lien to the assignee, on the rationale that the security follows the debt. It has also been held that if the seller conveys legal title to a third party, the transferee gets the contractual right to the purchase money as well.

1) Note

Because the separation of ownership of the debt from that of the legal title may cause complications, some jurisdictions prohibit transfer of legal title without a simultaneous assignment of the contract obligation.

(2) Seller's interest—devolution on death [§1070]

By the doctrine of equitable conversion, the seller's beneficial interest in an enforceable land sale contract is regarded as a right to the contract price. That right passes as part of the *personalty* to the seller's next of kin (if the seller dies intestate) or to her legatee (if there is a will). The heir or devisee of the seller takes bare legal title, subject to the duty to convey to the buyer. [*In re* **Estate of Sweet,** 254 So. 2d 562 (Fla. 1971); **Coe v. Hoys,** 614 A.2d 576 (Md. 1992)]

(a) Seller intestate [§1071]

Because in intestacy situations modern statutes make no distinction between the descent of realty and personalty (*i.e.*, the same persons inherit in both instances), the doctrine of equitable conversion has no practical effect in such cases.

(b) Seller testate [§1072]

If, however, a *will* is executed leaving realty to one person and personalty to another, the beneficiary receiving personalty is entitled to the proceeds of the sale and the beneficiary receiving realty merely holds legal title until a conveyance to the buyer is required. [*In re* **Estate of Krotzsch,** 326 N.E.2d 758 (Ill. 1975)]

EXAM TIP   **gilbert**

If you see an equitable conversion problem on your exam, it will likely involve a will that leaves testator's real property to one person and testator's personal property to another. For example, suppose Tesla's will leaves his $1 million bank account to his son and his Niagara Falls generating plant to his daughter. These are Tesla's main assets. Tesla enters into a contract to sell the plant for $1 million and doesn't give his will a second thought. After he enters into the contract but before the closing on the plant, Tesla is electrocuted in a freak accident at the plant. Who takes the plant? Tesla's daughter gets *bare legal title*, but under the doctrine of equitable conversion, Tesla's son will get *both* the $1 million proceeds from the sale of the plant, as well as the $1 million bank account. Hopefully, he is on good terms with his sister and willing to share!

(c) Option contract [§1073]

If the seller has entered into an option contract for the sale of the property and the option is not exercised prior to her death, the person who succeeds to the real estate is entitled to the proceeds of the sale. Simply put, this means that equitable conversion does not occur *before the option is exercised* by the buyer. [**Bauserman v. Dignilian,** 297 S.E.2d 671 (Va. 1982); *but see* **Shaffer v. Flick,** 520 A.2d 50 (Pa. 1987)—conversion related back to time option given]

(d) Enforcement by personal representative [§1074]

In any event, the proper party to enforce the contract is the executor or administrator of the seller's estate. Even where the contract rights and benefits are treated as personalty, they pass to the administrator of the estate *for the benefit of* the next of kin or legatees.

(3) Buyer's interest—equitable ownership [§1075]

The buyer has a contractual right to a conveyance conditioned on the performance of the buyer's contractual duty to pay the price stipulated in the agreement. The buyer's ability specifically to enforce the seller's correlative duty to convey creates the "equity" in the land previously mentioned. This "equity" is sufficient to allow the buyer to maintain a quiet title action. [**First National Bank v. McGinnis,** 810 P.2d 1080 (Colo. 1991)] The buyer is also regarded as the owner for purposes of tort liability in connection with injuries on the premises. [**Klebe v. Patel,** 616 N.E.2d 1018 (Ill. 1992)]

(a) "Vendee's lien" [§1076]

To the extent that the buyer has made a *partial payment* of the price, an equitable lien on the property (a "vendee's lien") is created *to secure restitution (including the price paid, improvements, etc.) in case the seller breaches* the contract by refusing to convey. [**Garcia v. Atmajian,** 113 Cal. App. 3d 516 (1980)]

(b) Cut off by sale to bona fide purchaser [§1077]

Because the buyer's interest and lien are both equitable in nature, transfer of title by the seller to a BFP cuts off the buyer's right to specific performance and limits the buyer to an action against the seller for breach of contract. [**Stanovsky v. Group Enterprise & Construction Co.,** 714 S.W.2d 836 (Mo. 1986)]

(c) Risk of loss on buyer [§1078]

By a rigid adherence to the logic of the equitable conversion doctrine, the traditional view is that the risk of loss from destruction of the subject matter of the contract is placed on the *buyer* from the moment the contract is executed. This follows from the premise that, as of that time, the buyer is the *beneficial owner* of the property. Thus, even though there is a partial or total destruction of the subject matter (by fire, wind, flood, etc.), the seller may still compel full payment of the price by the buyer.

1) Effect of insurance [§1079]

The rigors of this doctrine are mitigated by the rule applied in many jurisdictions that any insurance proceeds collected by the seller are held in a constructive trust for the benefit of the buyer to the extent of the unpaid contract price. [**Kindred v. Boalbey,** 391 N.E.2d 236 (Ill. 1979); **Patrick & Wilkins Co. v. Reliance Insurance Co.,** 456 A.2d 1348 (Pa. 1983)]

2) Modern trend contra [§1080]

The rule placing the risk of loss on the buyer has been changed in a number of jurisdictions by statute (Uniform Vendor and Purchaser Risk Act), or by judicial decisions, so that the risk of loss is shifted from the seller to the buyer only if the buyer has taken *possession* of the land or legal title to the land has actually been transferred to the buyer. [**Skelly Oil Co. v. Ashmore,** 365 S.W.2d 582 (Mo. 1963)]

3) Uniform Vendor and Purchaser Risk Act [§1081]

Under the Uniform Act, if the destruction is *not material*, either the seller or the buyer may specifically enforce the contract (regardless of the allocation of risk of loss) *with abatement* of the price as explained *infra*, §§1097-1103. If the risk of loss is on the seller and the destruction is *material*, the Uniform Act provides that the seller cannot enforce the contract and that the buyer is entitled to restitution of any portion of the price paid.

a)   The Act does not specifically address itself to the question of whether the buyer may, if he chooses, specifically enforce the contract *with abatement*. The courts in New York have allowed this to be done, but California has taken the opposite position. (*See infra*, §1102.)

EXAM TIP   **gilbert**

If you see a risk of loss issue arising in an *executory land sale contract* (*e.g.,* Alex agrees to sell Blackacre to Becky for $250,000, but before closing, the house on Blackacre is destroyed by a tornado), don't stop with the result that would be obtained under the doctrine of equitable conversion (*i.e.,* buyer Becky will bear the loss). Be sure to note that many jurisdictions will allow the buyer to recover *insurance payments* that the seller received as a result of the destruction, at least to the extent of the unpaid purchase price. Still other jurisdictions, through statute or judicial decision, *reverse the rule* and place the risk of loss on the seller *unless* the buyer has taken possession of the land or legal title has otherwise passed to the buyer.

---

(4) Buyer's interest—transferability [§1082]

The buyer's equitable interest in the property may be transferred or mortgaged [**Rush v. Anestos,** 661 P.2d 1229 (Idaho 1983)], and is considered real estate within the meaning of the judgment lien statute [**Cascade Security Bank v. Butler,** 567 P.2d 631 (Wash. 1977); **Bank of Santa Fe v. Garcia,** 698 P.2d 458 (N.M. 1985)—judgment lien attaches to buyer's (not seller's) interest in land]. An *assignment* of the buyer's interest is to be distinguished from a *subsale* by the buyer, which is not, in any event, a breach of a nonassignability agreement.

(a) Note

Assignments of the buyer's interest in violation of a *non-assignment clause* are generally held to be effective. The assignee may compel specific performance by fully performing the buyer's duties under the contract. [**Paperchase Partnership v. Bruckner**, 693 P.2d 587 (N.M. 1985); **Obermeier v. Bennett**, 430 N.W.2d 524 (Neb. 1988)]

(b) And note

There has been disagreement over whether the assignee of a buyer's equitable interest assumes the burdens as well as the benefits of the contract. Modern cases generally hold that the assignee does assume the burdens of the contract in the absence of express provisions to the contrary and hence is subject to the seller's action to enforce the contract. [**Kunzman v. Thorsen**, 740 P.2d 754 (Or. 1987); **Pelz v. Streator National Bank**, 496 N.E.2d 315 (Ill. 1986)]

(5) Buyer's interest—devolution on death [§1083]

By the doctrine of equitable conversion, the buyer's beneficial interest in an enforceable land sale contract is regarded as *realty* and that interest descends to the buyer's heir (if buyer dies intestate) or devisee (if there is a will). The duty to pay the purchase price is a contractual obligation which the buyer's administrator is required to pay out of the personal estate available for the payment of debts owed by the decedent. The effect of the doctrine is thus to deplete the personal estate of the buyer for the benefit of those parties inheriting the realty (this is known as the "right of exoneration"). [**Milner v. Mills,** 25 Eng. Rep. 307 (1729); **Panushka v. Panushka,** 349 P.2d 450 (Or. 1960)]

(a) Enforcement of contract [§1084]

If the buyer dies before the contract is performed, the proper party to enforce the contract is the buyer's heir or devisee, because the beneficial interest in the contract passes to the party inheriting the realty. [**Keirsey v. Hirsch**, 265 P.2d 346 (N.M. 1954)]

(b) Right of exoneration [§1085]

It has been held that the right to exoneration is available only if the debt is a personal obligation of the buyer. If, as is true in some jurisdictions, no personal liability is imposed on the buyer because the transaction is a purchase money mortgage or land sale contract, the heir's right of exoneration is lost. [*In re* **Estate of Brown**, 240 Cal. 2d 818 (1966)]

(6) Buyer's interest—change of ownership [§1086]

Because the buyer becomes the equitable owner of the property upon execution of a land sale contract, it has been held that this constitutes a "change of ownership" triggering the acceleration of payment clause in the seller's mortgage. [**Blue Ash Building & Loan Co. v. Hahn**, 484 N.E.2d 186 (Ohio 1984)]

EQUITABLE CONVERSION IN LAND SALE CONTRACTS—A SUMMARY

gilbert

	SELLER	BUYER
INTEREST	*Legal title* subject to the duty to convey to buyer.	The right to have the property conveyed (*equitable title*) conditioned on payment. This right is transferable and may be mortgaged. It may also trigger an acceleration clause in seller's mortgage (if seller's mortgage contains such a clause).
LIEN	After entering contract, seller has right to receive payment secured by *vendor's lien* that arises by operation of law and allows seller to foreclose on buyer's equitable interest in the property should buyer default.	If buyer has made part payment, buyer has an equitable *vendee's lien* on the property to secure restitution of the payment, improvements, etc., should seller refuse to convey title.
DEVOLUTION ON DEATH	After making contract, seller's right is to receive payment, which is treated as *personalty*. It passes to the person who takes seller's personal property if seller dies before the conveyance.	After making contract, buyer's right to have the property conveyed is treated as *realty*. It passes to the person who takes buyer's real property if buyer dies before the conveyance.

2. Buyer's Remedies for Seller's Breach of Executory Land Sale Contract

a. Damages

(1) Damages for refusal to convey [§1087]

In an action by the buyer against the seller for breach of contract to convey title, two rules have been adopted for measuring damages.

(a) Out-of-pocket loss [§1088]

Some jurisdictions apply an English common law rule limiting the buyer to a recovery of any payments made plus reimbursement of expenditures incurred in reliance on the contract (*e.g.*, title search, escrow expenses). [**Potts v. Moran's Executors**, 32 S.W.2d 534 (Ky. 1930); **Wolfsky v. Behrman**, 454 So. 2d 614 (Fla. 1984)]

1) Rationale

The common law rule was designed to protect the seller from liability for damages for a defective title at a time when title searches were difficult and uncertain. The limitation to out-of-pocket damages was justified by analogizing it to the measure of damages for breach of covenants in a deed. [**Beard v. S/E Joint Venture,** 531 A.2d 1275 (Md. 1990)—discussed the rule]

2) Statutory modifications

This rule has been modified in some jurisdictions to permit recovery of benefit-of-the-bargain damages (discussed below) if the seller's breach is in *bad faith*. The clearest case of a "bad faith" breach is where the seller conveys the property contracted for to a third person for a higher price.

(b) Benefit of the bargain [§1089]

Other jurisdictions apply the ordinary contract "benefit-of-the-bargain" rule and permit the buyer to recover the difference between the contract price and the market value of the land on the date set for performance, plus any partial payments that may have been made. [**Donovan v. Bachstadt,** 453 A.2d 160 (N.J. 1982); **Burges v. Arita,** 704 P.2d 930 (Haw. 1985)]

(c) Consequential damages [§1090]

If the rule of **Hadley v. Baxendale** (*supra*, §23) is satisfied, a few courts have permitted recovery of lost profits from a contemplated *resale* of the property by the buyer. [**Republic National Life Insurance v. Red Lion Homes,** 704 F.2d 484 (10th Cir. 1983)—lost profits awarded to tract home developer; 11 A.L.R.3d 719] Such cases are unusual because a seller who knows that a prospective buyer intends to resell at a profit is unlikely to enter into a contract at the lower price. Some courts have gone even further and permitted the buyer to recover for *emotional distress* resulting from the breach of contract. [61 A.L.R.3d 922]

(2) Damages for delay [§1091]

If the seller transfers title but delays beyond the date agreed upon in the contract for the conveyance, the buyer may recover damages for delay resulting from the breach, *if* such damages were within the *contemplation of the parties* at the time the contract was executed (rule of **Hadley v. Baxendale**). [**Christensen v. Slawter,** 173 Cal. App. 2d 325 (1959)]

b. Specific performance [§1092]

As an alternative to the remedy of damages for breach of a land sale contract, the buyer may seek specific performance and damages incident to the delay by the seller in performing the contract. [**Bacmo Associates v. Strange,** 388 A.2d 487 (D.C. 1978)]

(1) Equity jurisdiction [§1093]

Equity jurisdiction is based on the inadequacy of the remedy at law. "A compensation in damages will not afford adequate relief, because the peculiar locality, soil, advantages of market, and other conveniences of an estate contracted for cannot be replaced by other land of equal value"; *i.e.*, no two tracts of land are the same in the contemplation of the law. [**Losee v. Morey & Cramer,** 561 Barb. 56 (N.Y. 1865)]

(2) Any estate in land [§1094]

The uniqueness principle applies to contracts for the transfer of such lesser interests as tenancies for years or easements, because again, money cannot replace the interest bargained for in the contract. [**Hunt v. Shamblin,** 371 S.E.2d 591 (W. Va. 1988)—contract to sell equitable interest in land is specifically enforceable; *but see* **Van Wagner Advertising v. S & M Enterprises,** 67 N.Y.2d 177 (1986)—contract to lease exterior wall of building for advertising space not specifically performable because damages were adequate remedy]

(3) Effect of liquidated damages provision [§1095]

The presence of a liquidated damages clause in these contracts does *not* preclude the buyer from obtaining specific performance. Such clauses may be placed in the contract because of the difficulty of measuring damages due to the uncertain value of land. While these clauses (if valid and not a penalty) will control in an action at law for damages, money cannot replace the unique land bargained for and thus specific performance is decreed. [**Mahoney v. Tingley,** 529 P.2d 1068 (Wash. 1975)]

(a) Distinguish

If the liquidated damages clause is construed as an *option*—giving the seller the right either to perform *or* pay a stipulated amount—specific performance will be denied, because an election to pay damages is then not a breach of the contract.

EXAM TIP   **gilbert**

Carefully examine liquidated damages provisions in land sale contracts. Look at the language to determine whether the parties included a *true liquidated damages* provision that reasonably estimates the harm that would be caused in case of breach, an *unreasonable penalty* for breach, or an *optional performance*. If the language provides for a true liquidated damages provision, specific performance still is available; the clause does not make the legal remedy adequate. And, of course, if the language shows that the liquidated damages provision is a penalty, it will be unenforceable and will not affect the availability of specific performance. Only in cases where the language indicates that the clause was intended to provide an alternative performance will an action for specific performance be barred.

---

(4) Equitable compensation for delay [§1096]

Ancillary to a decree for specific performance, a court compensates the plaintiff for losses incurred as a result of the delay in performance. This award is not the same as legal damages limited by the requirement of **Hadley v. Baxendale,** but rather consists of a kind of accounting between the parties. [**Bravo v. Buelow,** 168 Cal. App. 3d 208 (1985); **Bohlin v. Jungbauer,** 615 N.E.2d 438 (Ind. 1993)—equities are adjusted by setting off against rental value of property the interest on purchase money retained by buyer]

Example: Seller's delay resulted in a higher rate of interest on buyer's loan. Compensation for this differential in interest rates was held appropriate in a suit for specific performance. [**Currington v. Johnson,** 685 P.2d 73 (Alaska 1984)]

---

c. Specific performance with abatement [§1097]

If the seller is unable to perform as promised because of some defect in title, either as to quantity or quality, the buyer may nevertheless insist on specific performance with an abatement of the purchase price to reflect the value of the defect. Thus, the buyer obtains both enforcement of the contract and compensation for the seller's breach in a single remedy.

(1) Defect as to quantity of land conveyed [§1098]

If the seller is unable to convey as much land as agreed, abatement generally is effected by a *pro rata* reduction in the price—without regard to the rule of damages prevailing in the jurisdiction for seller's breach of a land sale contract.

Example: The contract called for sale of 13 acres for $15,000 but the seller had title to only eight acres. Abatement was accomplished by subtracting the value of the buildings and other improvements (which the buyer got) from the total price. This balance was then reduced by a pro rata abatement in the price for the missing acreage. [**Flygare v. Brundage,** 302 P.2d 759 (Wyo. 1956); *and see* **Chastain v. Schomburg,** 367 S.E.2d 230 (Ga. 1988)—"Damages for breach of contract may be awarded in conjunction with specific performance if this is necessary to make a purchaser whole"]

---

(2) Defect as to quality of title conveyed [§1099]

If the defect is one as to the quality of the title (liens, easements, covenants, dower rights, etc.), the computation of the abatement is less easily accomplished:

(a) If defect can be reasonably valued [§1100]

If the defect can be valued with reasonable certainty, abatement to that extent is allowed. [**Wittick v. Miles,** 545 P.2d 121 (Or. 1976)—

abatement for the existence of a leasehold interest; **Carpenter v. Folkerts,** 627 P.2d 559 (Wash. 1981)—encumbrances to secure seller's personal loans]

---

e.g. **Example:** Where husband and wife own land as tenants in common and only the husband enters into a contract to sell the property, the buyer is entitled to specific performance of the contract with a proportionate abatement of the purchase price. [**Fleenor v. Church,** 681 P.2d 1351 (Alaska 1984); **Sanders v. Knapp,** 674 P.2d 385 (Colo. 1983); *but see* **Bass v. Smith,** 360 S.E.2d 162 (Va. 1987)—specific performance only if buyer pays full purchase price]

(b) If defect uncertain and difficult to value [§1101]

If the defect is uncertain and difficult to value, as in the case of dower rights, some courts refuse to permit any abatement at all if specific performance is sought. However, the buyer can still sue for damages. [**Sterling v. Wilson,** 621 N.E.2d 767 (Ohio 1993); *compare* **Box v. Dudeck,** 578 S.W.2d 567 (Ark. 1979)—abatement of purchase price after valuing the wife's dower interest]

(3) Destruction of premises where risk of loss on seller [§1102]

As previously discussed, the common law placed the risk of loss from fire, wind, etc., on the buyer from the moment the contract was executed. In such cases, the buyer may be compelled to pay the full purchase price with no reduction or abatement in the price for the value of that part of the subject matter destroyed. Under modern cases and statutes, however, the risk of loss may be placed on the *seller,* in which event, if the premises are destroyed, the buyer may seek specific performance with abatement of the price for the value of the building, etc., that was destroyed. [**Burack v. Chase Manhattan Bank,** 9 App. Div. 2d 914 (1959)—abatement accomplished by deducting value of destroyed house from contract price (rather than by compelling buyer to pay market value of remaining property as contended by seller); *but see* **Dixon v. Salvation Army,** 142 Cal. App. 3d 463 (1983)—where there has been a material destruction of the property, neither buyer nor seller may specifically enforce contract with abatement]

(4) Limitation—enforcement must not operate inequitably [§1103]

Specific performance with abatement is permitted only where not inequitable and where it will not result in undue hardship to the seller. [**Dlug v. Woolridge,** *supra,* §1003—abatement for deficiency in quantity denied because of gross inadequacy of price; **Ide v. Joe Miller & Co.,** 703 P.2d

590 (Colo. 1985)—abatement of 38% of price denied for deficiency in providing an adequate well]

---

e.g. **Example:** An abatement in the purchase price was refused where a $9,300 reduction was sought in a contract calling for a purchase price of $12,500, to compensate for construction of sewer connections *innocently* represented as being available. [**Merritz v. Circelli,** 64 A.2d 796 (Pa. 1949)—court also held there could be no abatement for collateral representations (affecting value of estate conveyed)]

---

e.g. **Example:** An abatement was refused where a reduction of £1,000 was sought from a purchase price of £3,500 because of the discovery of certain easements *unknown* to the seller at the time the contract was executed. [**Ruud v. Lascelles,** [1900] 1 Ch. 815]

---

d. Specific performance—in lieu of damages [§1104]

If the inability of the seller to convey as promised did not appear until trial, traditional equity doctrine allowed the court to award damages in lieu of specific performance. [*See* **Ross v. Eichman,** 529 A.2d 941 (N.H. 1987)] Some courts, however, do not allow damages in this situation, holding that the buyer had made an election of remedies precluding the damages remedy. [*See* **Canton v. Monaco Partnership,** 753 P.2d 158 (Ariz. 1988)] For the implications of this doctrine on the right to jury trial, *see supra,* §§111-114.

e. Rescission and restitution [§1105]

Instead of seeking damages or specific performance, the buyer may *rescind* the contract upon the seller's material breach (*e.g.,* refusal or inability to convey) and seek restitution of benefits conferred on the seller. [**Brown v. Yacht Club of Coeur D'Alene,** 722 P.2d 1062 (Idaho 1986)—buyer may recover reliance damages; **Racicky v. Simon,** 831 P.2d 241 (Wyo. 1992)]

(1) Accounting required [§1106]

The buyer is entitled to recover partial payments of the purchase price (with interest), the cost of improvements less depreciation, maintenance costs, and expenditures for taxes and insurance. In turn, the buyer must account to the seller for the *value of the use* of the property—which may be computed at the buyer's option either by fair rental value or the actual value of the benefit received.

(2) Vendee's lien on property [§1107]

A vendee's lien may also be imposed on the property which may be foreclosed to realize the money found due to the buyer under the accounting. [*See* **Hillblom v. Ivancsits,** 395 N.E.2d 119 (Ill. 1979); **Warner v. Peterson,** 762 P.2d 872 (Mont. 1988)]

CHECKLIST OF BUYER'S REMEDIES FOR SELLER'S BREACH OF EXECUTORY LAND SALE CONTRACT **gilbert**

IF A SELLER BREACHES AN EXECUTORY LAND SALE CONTRACT, THE BUYER MAY CHOOSE FROM AMONG THE FOLLOWING REMEDIES:

☑ *Damages* measured by:

- *Out-of-pocket loss* (payments made plus reliance expenditures, such as title search costs)

  OR

- *Benefit of the bargain* (the difference between the contract price and the market value of the land *on the date set for performance*)

  PLUS

- *Consequential damages* (in some jurisdictions) *if they were foreseeable*

☑ *Specific performance* (with abatement if seller cannot deliver the quantity or quality agreed to)

☑ *Restitution* (rescind the contract and seek restitution of the benefits conferred)

---

3. **Buyer's Remedies for Seller's Breach After Conveyance**

   a. **Damages for breach of covenant [§1108]**

   If the seller's breach is discovered after the buyer has accepted a deed, the buyer's remedy for failure of title or for some encumbrance or cloud on title is an action on the covenants in the deed. [**Bakken v. Price,** 613 P.2d 1222 (Wyo. 1980)] In general, an out-of-pocket measure of damages is employed, with the buyer awarded a part of the price proportionate to the value of the realty lost.

   b. **No remedy where quitclaim [§1109]**

   If the buyer accepted a quitclaim deed, she assumes the risk of a defective title and has no remedy for failure of the grantor's title.

   c. **Restitution for overpayment [§1110]**

   If the seller has transferred title as agreed in the contract, but, as a result of mistakes, *less land* was conveyed than the parties believed, the buyer may have a restitutionary action for overpayment. [**Cundiff v. Cline,** 752 S.W.2d 409 (Mo. 1988); *and see supra,* §984]

   d. **Warranty of habitability [§1111]**

   Today in many jurisdictions an implied warranty of habitability is applied to the sale of new homes. The warranty is breached by substandard construction and even by the failure to supply potable well water. Damages are measured by the normal warranty standard of diminution in value. [**McDonald v. Mianecki**, 398 A.2d 1283 (N.J. 1979); *and see* **Atlas Construction Co. v. Slater**, 746 P.2d 352 (Wyo. 1987)—besides diminution in value, rental expenditures made in another home after buyer's home became uninhabitable allowed]

4. Remedy of a Seller in Default

a. Immaterial default [§1112]

If the seller cannot convey in accordance with the contract, he may nevertheless be granted specific performance with an abatement in the price *if* the breach is *immaterial*. [*See* **Baugh v. Johnson**, 641 S.W.2d 730 (Ark. 1982)—defect of title "small and unimportant"]

> **Example:** Samantha and Becky agree to the sale of a city lot at $100 per foot, both believing that the lot has 100 feet of frontage. In fact, the lot has only 99 feet of frontage. Samantha is entitled to specific performance with a $100 abatement in the price.

EXAM TIP   gilbert

Note the very important difference between the buyer's and seller's rights to specific performance of a land sale contract in cases where the seller cannot deliver the quantity or quality promised: The *buyer can usually press for specific performance with abatement* in price for the defect even if the defect is quite large, but the *seller* can press for specific performance with abatement *only* if the breach is immaterial.

---

b. Material default [§1113]

If the breach is material, however, the seller will *not* be awarded specific performance against the buyer. The reason for limiting the seller's remedy in this manner is that courts are reluctant to force a buyer to accept property that is *substantially different* from that bargained for.

> **Example:** Seller sought specific performance of a contract to convey 160 acres with abatement for the value of 1.8 acres held in adverse possession by a third party. Relief was denied because, although the loss of acreage itself was immaterial, this particular land bordered a section of road and precluded access to the tract. Seller's breach was therefore material. [**Friede v. Pool**, 14 N.W.2d 454 (Minn. 1944)]

(1) Buyer's remedy [§1114]

Of course, if the *buyer* still wants the property, she can get specific performance with an abatement, whether the defect is *material or immaterial*.

(Note that this is a variation of the problem discussed *supra*, §1078, in connection with the risk of destruction of the premises.)

5. Seller's Remedies for Buyer's Breach of Executory Land Sale Contract [§1115]
The seller's remedies may depend on classification of the contract as a buy-sell agreement or an installment land sale contract.

a. Breach of a buy-sell or marketing contract [§1116]
These contracts call for payment of the price and delivery of the deed on a given date; *e.g.*, on April 1, Seller agrees to convey Blackacre to Buyer on June 1, upon concurrent payment of $10,000. Buyer breaches the contract by refusing to tender payment.

(1) Damages [§1117]
The seller's damages are the difference between the market value of the land and the contract price at the time of the breach *plus* consequential damages.

(a) "Market value" defined [§1118]
"Market value" means value in a cash sale (no mortgages, etc.). The actual resale price of the property is evidence of its value on the date of breach, but is not conclusive.

(b) Seller's expenses on resale [§1119]
The seller is also entitled to recover additional expenses incurred in the resale—*e.g.*, a second broker's commission or added closing costs. [**Conway v. Judd**, 723 S.W.2d 905 (Mo. 1987)—abstract expense, title opinion, appraisal, additional insurance expense]

 Example: The first sale called for a broker's commission of $1,200. When buyer defaulted, the deposit was forfeited, resulting in the broker receiving $400. Seller then resold the property for a lesser price, incurring a broker's commission of $1,100. Seller was entitled to recover $300 from the first purchaser as an added expense of resale ($1,100 plus $400 previously paid, minus the $1,200 that would have been paid if the first sale had gone through). [**Royer v. Carter**, 37 Cal. 2d 544 (1951)]

(c) Other consequential damages [§1120]
The seller may also recover consequential damages within the contemplation of the parties at the time of contracting—*e.g.*, loss of rent, additional insurance costs, taxes, and mortgage payments.

Example: Seller purchased a second home after execution of the contract and before buyer's breach. Following buyer's breach, seller continued to live in the first home until a resale of it was accomplished. Seller was *not* entitled to recover the expenses of living in the first home, but could recover expenses of the empty second home if that purchase was foreseeable and reasonable. [**Abrams v. Motter,** 3 Cal. App. 3d 828 (1970); *and see* **Turner v. Benson,** 672 S.W.2d 752 (Tenn. 1984)]

---

cf. **Compare:** On breach by the defendant buyer, seller resold the property in a cash sale for a higher price. The cash sale resulted in a higher tax liability which seller sought to recover as damages. The court held that this is not an item of compensable damages. [**Daly v. Kling,** 96 Cal. App. 3d 217 (1979)]

(d) Duty to mitigate [§1121]

Because a resale at a higher price following the buyer's breach would establish that there was no loss of bargain damages, the law imposes a duty on the seller to exercise diligence and to make the resale within the shortest time possible. [**Spurgeon v. Drumheller,** 174 Cal. App. 3d 659 (1985)—no recovery for failure to mitigate; **American Mechanical Corp. v. Union Machine Co.,** 485 N.E.2d 680 (Mass. 1985)]

(2) Specific performance [§1122]

The seller may specifically enforce the contract by seeking a decree ordering the buyer to pay the *full purchase price.* [**B.D. Inns v. Pooley,** 218 Cal. App. 3d 289 (1990)]

(a) Why remedy at law inadequate [§1123]

Several reasons are advanced as to why the damages remedy at law would be inadequate. First of all, damages would give the seller only the *difference* between the contract price and the fair market value of the land, and he was *bargaining for the full purchase price*; *i.e.,* he may need that sum to buy another house, etc. Other reasons advanced are that the seller was bargaining to rid himself of the burden of maintaining the property, and also that the contract itself clouds his ability to resell and hence, as a practical matter, damages may not be available. [*See* **Shuptrine v. Quinn,** 597 S.W.2d 728 (Tenn. 1979)]

1) Affirmative mutuality of remedy [§1124]

Another reason traditionally advanced is the "*affirmative* mutuality of remedy" rule; *i.e.,* because the *buyer* is entitled to specific performance of the contract, the same remedy should be available to the seller. [*See* Rest. Contracts §360]

2) **Liquidated damages clause [§1125]**

The seller's right to specific performance of a land sale contract is not foreclosed by the presence of a forfeiture or liquidated damages clause unless the agreement clearly indicates that the clause was intended to give an option to perform or pay damages. [**Kohrs v. Barth,** 570 N.E. 1273 (Ill. 1991); *but see* **Leeber v. Deltona Corp.,** 546 A.2d 452 (Me. 1988)—Florida law precludes specific performance of land sale contract containing liquidated damages clause]

3) **Condominiums [§1126]**

In **Centex Homes Corp. v. Boag,** 302 A.2d 194 (N.J. 1974), the court rejected these reasons in a suit to specifically enforce a contract for the sale of a single unit in a condominium building. The damages sustained by the seller from the buyer's breach were found to be "readily measurable" and therefore the damages remedy was "wholly adequate." [*But cf.* **Giannini v. First National Bank,** 483 N.E.2d 924 (Ill. 1985)—buyer may specifically enforce contract to buy condominium unit]

(b) **Consequential damages [§1127]**

In addition to specific performance, the seller is awarded lost interest on the unpaid balance of the purchase price because of the buyer's delay. Additional awards may be made to the seller in the accounting process if necessary to give full relief. [**Sandusky Properties v. Aveni,** 473 N.E.2d 798 (Ohio 1984)—vendor's mortgage costs recoverable]

(c) **Decree to pay purchase price not enforceable by contempt [§1128]**

As discussed earlier, money decrees generally are not enforceable by contempt. Hence, if the buyer fails to pay the purchase price as decreed, the seller's only remedy will be to execute on whatever other assets of the buyer he can find.

(3) **Rescission and restitution [§1129]**

Alternatively, the seller may rescind the contract for the buyer's material breach, restoring to the buyer any partial payment less any damages sustained by the seller. [**Earven v. Smith,** 621 P.2d 41 (Ariz. 1980)]

(a) **Note**

Election to pursue this remedy is usually *not* advantageous for the seller, but assumes importance in cases of installment land sale contracts discussed below.

(4) **Quiet title [§1130]**

The seller may, if he chooses, sue to quiet title and thus clear the title of the equity of the buyer arising from the contract. Because ordinarily the contract is wholly executory, no forfeiture is involved.

b.   Seller's remedies for buyer's breach of installment land sale contract [§1131]
Installment land sale contracts differ from those just considered in that they contemplate *periodic payments* for an extended period of time until the full contract price is paid. Such contracts provide an alternative to the mortgage as a method of financing the purchase of realty. Generally, they include a "time is of the essence" clause, plus a provision for forfeiture of the buyer's payments in case of default.

---

e.g. **Example:** Samantha agrees to sell Blackacre to Becky for $10,000—$1,000 down and $100 per month until the contract price is paid, at which time title is to be transferred. Becky makes payments for two years and then defaults and fails to pay any further installments. The contract provides that "time is of the essence" and for forfeiture of all payments in case of default.

---

(1)   Damages [§1132]
In many jurisdictions, the seller may sue the buyer for the installments due under the contract. If the contract includes an acceleration clause (*i.e.,* a clause providing that the full contract price is due upon failure to pay any installment on the due date), the seller may then sue the buyer for the unpaid balance of the purchase price. [*And see* **Aveco Properties v. E.J. Nicholson,** 747 P.2d 1358 (Mont. 1987)—specific performance of acceleration clause and sale of property allowed if decree not satisfied]

(a)   Minority view [§1133]
In *some* jurisdictions, the buyer is not personally liable for the payments due under an executory land sale contract of residential property. The contract is treated as a "purchase money security" obligation (one in which the seller is held by law to look solely to the *property sold* as security for the purchase price). [*See* Cal. Civ. Proc. Code §580(b); **Venable v. Harmon,** 233 Cal. App. 2d 297 (1965)]

(2)   Foreclosure of the vendor's lien [§1134]
Alternatively, the seller may foreclose his vendor's lien on the buyer's equity and seek a judicial sale of the property. Such a decree is frequently sought in conjunction with a cause of action for the balance of the price. The land is sold and a judgment is rendered for any balance that may still be owed by the buyer on the contract after crediting the proceeds of the sale. [**Sebastian v. Floyd,** 585 S.W.2d 381 (Ky. 1979); **Skendzel v. Marshall,** 301 N.E.2d 641 (Ind. 1973); **Looney v. Farmers Home Administration,** 749 F.2d 310 (7th Cir. 1986)—foreclosure rather than forfeiture is appropriate remedy for buyer's default]

(a) Limitation [§1135]

Where the seller's remedy is foreclosure of the vendor's lien, courts have held that no deficiency judgment may be entered without proof that the property's value was less than the balance owed on the debt. [**Arnold v. Hall,** 478 N.E.2d 696 (Ind.), *rehearing denied,* 481 N.E.2d 409 (Ind. 1985)]

(b) Minority view [§1136]

In jurisdictions in which there is no personal liability on the buyer (*see* above), the seller may retain the proceeds of the sale only up to the amount of the contract price and is *not* entitled to a personal judgment against the buyer for any deficiency.

(3) Strict foreclosure [§1137]

Alternatively, the seller may seek a decree of "strict foreclosure." Such a decree provides that any interest the buyer may have in the land arising from the contract is foreclosed unless the buyer pays the entire amount due on the contract by a date prescribed in the decree.

(a) Limitation

A decree of strict foreclosure results in a forfeiture of both the buyer's equity in the land and of any payments previously made. Because of the severe hardship that this may cause the buyer, present day courts seek to *limit or avoid the forfeiture.* [**Yu v. Paperchase Partnership,** 845 P.2d 158 (N.M. 1992); *and see infra,* §1152]

(b) Note

The amount of the payments made by the buyer may amount to no more than the seller's actual damages from the buyer's breach. In these cases, there is no inequitable forfeiture. [**Ryan v. Kolterman,** 338 N.W.2d 747 (Neb. 1983)—amount owed exceeded the value of the property; **Clampitt v. A.M.R. Corp.,** 706 P.2d 34 (Idaho 1985)—actual damages sustained by seller almost equaled amount forfeited by buyer, and hence no unconscionable forfeiture; **Dallam v. Hedrick,** 826 P.2d 511 (Kan. 1990)—payments made insubstantial (8% of purchase price)]

(4) Quiet title [§1138]

Alternatively, the seller may seek a decree quieting title thus foreclosing the buyer's equity. This has the same consequences for the buyer as a strict foreclosure, above (and is subject to the same limitation). [**Grombone v. Krekel,** 754 P.2d 777 (Colo. 1988)]

(5) Rescission and restitution [§1139]

The seller may, if he so elects, rescind the contract for the buyer's material breach. This requires the seller to account for the payments received from the buyer, but the buyer in turn must account for the value of the use of the land.

(6) Ejectment [§1140]

Once the equity of the buyer is terminated, the seller is entitled to immediate possession of the property. If the buyer refuses to surrender the property, ejectment is available to regain possession wrongfully withheld by the buyer. Forcible entry and detainer may be allowed by statute. [**Moreno v. Garcia,** 821 P.2d 247 (Ariz. 1991)]

(7) Statutory limitations on remedies—antideficiency statutes [§1141]

As stated above, in some jurisdictions the buyer is not personally liable for payments due under an executory land sale contract. [Cal. Civ. Proc. Code §580(b); **Venable v. Harmon,** *supra*, §1133] In other jurisdictions, a statutory period is provided for correcting the default. [N.D. Cent. Code §32-18-04; **Johnson v. Gray,** 265 N.W.2d 861 (N.D. 1978)] In still others, a statutory procedure limits the buyer's liability for a deficiency by providing for an "upset price." [**Kramer v. Davis,** 124 N.W.2d 292 (Mich. 1963)]

CHECKLIST OF SELLER'S REMEDIES FOR BREACH OF EXECUTORY LAND SALE CONTRACT	**gilbert**
BUY-SELL AGREEMENT	☑ *Benefit-of-the-bargain damages* (difference between contract price and market value of property *at time of breach*) plus consequential damages such as additional costs of resale ☑ *Specific performance* plus consequential damages ☑ *Rescission and restitution*
INSTALLMENT CONTRACT	☑ *Damages* equal to the installments due, which may include the remaining purchase price if the contract provided for acceleration of payments on default ☑ *Foreclosure* of the vendor's lien (have the property sold to pay off the debt; obtain a judgment for any balance remaining) ☑ *Strict foreclosure* (take the property in full satisfaction of the buyer's debt), retaining any payments made by the buyer ☑ *Quiet title action* (has the same effect as strict foreclosure) ☑ *Rescission and restitution*, but seller must pay back payments made by buyer less the value of the buyer's use of the land ☑ *Ejectment* if buyer refuses to vacate the property after his equity interest has terminated

(a) But note

The antideficiency statute does not apply when the vendor sues for damages based on fraudulent misrepresentations of the purchaser. [*See* **Manson v. Reed,** 186 Cal. App. 3d 1493 (1986); **Guild Mortgage Co. v. Heller,** 193 Cal. App. 3d 1485 (1987)]

6. Grantor's Remedies for Buyer's Breach After Conveyance of Title [§1142]

A buyer may breach after the conveyance of title when the seller conveys title before receiving the full purchase price from buyer. The seller becomes a grantor conveying legal title to the buyer-grantee.

a. Damages [§1143]

If the buyer fails to perform her promise to pay a certain sum of money after the seller has performed by executing a deed to the property, the seller has an action at law for the price. If the buyer's promised exchange is something other than money (*e.g.,* to provide support, or for the construction of a building), the seller has the burden of establishing the damages resulting from the buyer's breach as measured by the rules applicable to such contracts.

b. Foreclosure of the grantor's lien [§1144]

If a seller, pursuant to a land sale contract, conveys property to a buyer without obtaining a mortgage or other security to secure the payment of the price, equity *implies a lien* in favor of the seller called *a grantor's lien.* If the buyer defaults, that lien may be foreclosed against the property to realize the price. [**Sewer v. Martin,** 511 F.2d 1134 (3d Cir. 1975); **Whelan v. Midland Mortgage Co.,** 591 P.2d 287 (Okla. 1979)]

(1) Note

The grantor's lien is *nontransferable* (being only an equitable lien) and is cut off by sale of the property to a bona fide purchaser. [**Sewer v. Martin,** *supra*]

c. Specific performance [§1145]

The equitable remedy of specific performance is ordinarily *not* available. If the grantee's promise is to pay money, the remedy at law for breach of contract is adequate. If the promise is to provide personal services (support contracts), the contract is not specifically enforceable anyhow (*see infra*). If the promise is to build, the remedy of damages may be considered adequate.

d. Quasi-contract [§1146]

For historical reasons, the right to restitution is *not* available where the injured party has fully performed and is entitled to a *liquidated* sum of money. Modern courts retain this rule, and hence, where the buyer's promise is to pay a fixed amount, the quasi-contract remedy is not available to the seller.

e. Specific restitution [§1147]

The grantor is ordinarily *not* entitled to specific restitution of the property (*i.e.*, a decree rescinding the sale and ordering the grantee to reconvey the land to the seller). Courts are reluctant to undo such transactions in the absence of some showing that other remedies are inadequate.

(1) Cases where granted [§1148]

Specific restitution as a remedy *has* been granted in a *few* cases, usually where property is conveyed in exchange for a promise to support the grantors, usually for life. Upon repudiation of such a promise by the grantee, the injured party has no adequate remedy because damages, by necessity, are speculative and conjectural.

Example: Plaintiffs conveyed a home to defendant in exchange for a promise to support plaintiffs for the remainder of their lives. Upon repudiation by defendant, plaintiffs sought rescission and cancellation of the deed. Rescission was granted because damages would be speculative, and specific performance of personal service contracts is not allowed. Rescission and restitution should therefore be granted conditioned upon an accounting by plaintiffs of benefits received by way of support and by defendant of the value of the use of the property. [**Caramini v. Tegulias,** 186 A. 482 (Conn. 1936); *but see* **Robitaille v. Robitaille,** 613 N.E.2d 993 (Mass. 1993)—damages assessed on value of services for duration of parent's life]

CHECKLIST OF GRANTOR'S REMEDIES WHEN BUYER BREACHES AFTER CONVEYANCE OF TITLE **gilbert**

A GRANTOR MAY CHOOSE FROM AMONG THE FOLLOWING REMEDIES IF THE BUYER BREACHES AFTER THE GRANTOR HAS CONVEYED TITLE:

- ☑ *Damages*—the grantor may recover the price

- ☑ *Foreclosure of grantor's lien*—a grantor's lien is implied in equity if grantor conveyed title and did not retain a mortgage or other security interest

Note: Specific performance, quasi-contract, and specific restitution generally are *not available*

7. Remedies of Buyer in Default

a. Introductory note [§1149]

The problem raised here is whether a buyer who defaults after partially performing a land sale contract has any cause of action against the seller. Two examples will serve to illustrate the problem.

Example: Steve and Bob enter into a contract for the sale of Blackacre for $10,000 payable on June 1, with Bob immediately paying $1,000

down. On June 1, Bob is unable to raise the balance of the purchase money and defaults.

Example: Steve and Bob enter into an installment land sale contract in which Bob agrees to buy Blackacre for $10,000, paying $1,000 down and the balance in monthly installments of $100. After performing for two years, Bob defaults and makes no further payments.

---

b. Restitution [§1150]

If the buyer seeks restitution of the money paid to the seller, the court will face conflicting policies. On the one hand, there is a policy against forfeitures and unjust enrichment. On the other, there is a reluctance to permit a party who has breached the contract to take advantage of his own wrong. As a result, the cases are split:

(1) Traditional view denies recovery [§1151]

Courts emphasizing the policy against breachers taking advantage of their own breach deny restitution to the buyer. [**Maxton Builders v. Lo Galbo,** 68 N.Y.2d 373 (1986)]

(a) Note

In a number of these cases, however, the amount of money paid by the buyer is the equivalent of the seller's damages (*e.g.,* decline in property value and costs of resale), and hence there is in fact no forfeiture. This is particularly true in the buy-sell contracts discussed *supra*, §1116.

(b) But note

There are cases where the payments exceed damages and relief is nevertheless denied. These cases emphasize the provisions of the contract making "time of the essence" and expressly providing for forfeitures in case of default. "A bargain is a bargain."

(2) Modern trend allows recovery [§1152]

Other courts emphasize the policy against forfeitures and seek to avoid unjust enrichment of the seller. These courts permit the buyer to recover all payments made *in excess* of the loss that the buyer has caused by his own breach. [Rest. 2d Contracts §374; **Vines v. Orchard Hills, Inc.,** 435 A.2d 1022 (Conn. 1980); **Ben Lomond v. Allen,** 758 P.2d 92 (Alaska 1988)]

(a) Note

Some argument has been made that the buyer should be entitled to recover all of his payments in excess of the *rental* value of the property—the same as where the seller rescinds (*see supra*). However, courts have rejected this argument; the choice to elect rescission rests with the seller, not the defaulting buyer. [*See* **Honey v. Henry's Franchise & Leasing Corp.,** 64 Cal. 2d 801 (1966)]

(b) Resale expenses [§1153]

The seller's damages include expenses incurred in reselling the property—*e.g.,* the broker's commission, advertising costs, etc. Therefore, these items may be offset by the seller against the payments recoverable by the buyer.

(c) Maintenance expenses [§1154]

It is unclear whether courts will permit the seller to offset expenses for *ordinary maintenance and upkeep* on the property during the period the seller remained in possession pending resale. These may or may not be considered legal damages within the contemplation of the parties, but in any event, such costs may be regarded as "additional expenses" or losses caused by the buyer's breach, to be offset against any recovery for unjust enrichment by the defaulting buyer.

EXAM TIP **gilbert**

If you see a fact pattern in which a buyer has breached a land sale contract (*e.g.,* a long-term installment contract) and seeks to recover for improvements he made on the land or for payments he made in excess of the reasonable rental value of the land, be sure to discuss *both the traditional rule* (*i.e.,* no recovery for breaching buyer because the courts are reluctant to aid a breacher) *and the modern trend* (*i.e.,* recovery allowed because courts abhor forfeiture and unjust enrichment).

---

c. Specific performance [§1155]

A buyer in default *cannot* specifically enforce the contract, because the material breach excuses the seller from the duty of further performance. The policy against forfeitures (*see supra,* §1150) does *not* justify granting specific performance to a party in default. [**Flath v. Bauman,** 722 S.W.2d 125 (Mo. 1986); *but see* **Cimina v. Bronich,** 537 A.2d 1355 (Pa. 1988)—decreeing specific performance where buyer's breach was immaterial and only technical]

 Example: In **Ellis v. Butterfield,** 570 P.2d 1334 (Idaho 1977), the defaulting buyer was denied both specific performance and the right of redemption. The court held that unless the amounts paid by the buyer and retained by the seller constituted a penalty, the buyer was bound by the contract. The buyer has the burden of proving that the losses caused by the breach do not exceed the amount paid to the seller.

---

(1) Minority view [§1156]

Some courts do grant specific performance to a defaulting buyer, even if the default is willful. Relief is carefully circumscribed, however. The buyer must not be guilty of laches and is required to pay the full balance owed to the seller. The analogy relied on to justify this result is redemption by a defaulting mortgagor.

Example: Buyer *willfully* refused to make further payments on a land sale contract. Two years after serving notice of default, seller sued to quiet title, at which point buyer counterclaimed seeking specific performance. Specific performance was *granted* upon full payment of the balance owed and proof that buyer had not been guilty of unclean hands or laches. [**MacFadden v. Walker,** 5 Cal. 3d 809 (1971)] *Rationale:* Specific performance avoids proof of unjust enrichment and is in accord with the policy against penalties and forfeitures. Willfulness does not defeat redemption by a mortgagor, and the same result should apply in these cases. [**Bartley v. Karas,** 150 Cal. App. 3d 336 (1983)—buyer has one last chance to get title by paying full balance of purchase price plus damages resulting from the default]

(a) Latest decision

In its latest consideration of this problem, the California Supreme Court ruled as a "matter of sound policy" that a buyer who has made substantial payments on the contract or substantial improvements on the property, and who willfully defaults solely by failure to pay installments due on the contract, has an *unconditional right* to a reasonable opportunity to complete the purchase by paying the balance of the price due plus damages. [**Peterson v. Hartell,** 40 Cal. 3d 102 (1985)]

(2) Statutory remedy [§1157]

Some jurisdictions have enacted antiforfeiture legislation giving the defaulting buyer the right to redeem upon paying full compensation to the seller. [*See* **Sharp v. Holthusen,** 616 P.2d 384 (Mont. 1980)]

(3) Restatement solution [§1158]

The 1997 revision of the Restatement (Third) of Property sought to resolve the remedial quagmire set out above by adopting (in section 3.4(b)) a simple and unambiguous statement that an installment land sale contract creates a mortgage. Thus remedies for the breach of these contracts are those available under mortgage law and only those remedies. Whether this approach will finally resolve the varying state views remains to be seen.

C. Contracts for the Sale of Chattels

1. **Caveat [§1159]**

   In August 2001, a proposed revision of Article 2, Sales, of the U.C.C. was submitted to the Commission on Uniform State Laws. If approved by the Commissioners and adopted by the states, the sections of the outline below will require some modification. While most of the revisions affecting the remedial provisions are in matters of clarification, there are certain substantive changes as well, *e.g.,* the addition of consequential damages to the remedies given to the seller in sections 2-706 - 2-710.

2. **Buyer's Remedies Against Seller for Nondelivery**

   a. **Damages [§1160]**

      If the seller fails to make delivery or repudiates the contract, the buyer may recover damages measured by (i) the difference between the market price at the time the buyer learned of the breach and the contract price, (ii) together with any incidental and consequential damages, (iii) but less expenses saved by the breach. [U.C.C. §§2-711, 2-713]

      (1) **Market price [§1161]**

          Market price is determined at the place of tender as of the time the buyer learned of the breach. This is important in cases of anticipatory breach. [U.C.C. §2-713; *and see* **Cargill, Inc. v. Stafford,** 553 F.2d 1222 (10th Cir. 1977)]

      (2) **Lost profits [§1162]**

          The U.C.C. permits recovery of lost profits as consequential damages, as long as this is a foreseeable result of the breach. [*See* **Merion Spring Co. v. Muelles Hnos. Garcia Torres,** 462 A.2d 686 (Pa. 1983); *and see* **R.I. Lampus Co. v. Neville Cement Products Corp.,** 378 A.2d 288 (Pa. 1977)— consequential damages]

          (a) **Limitation**

              Such consequential damages are not recoverable if they could have been avoided by procuring replacement goods ("cover," *see* below), and the buyer failed to do so. [U.C.C. §2-715] This limitation is, in effect, an embodiment of the avoidable consequences doctrine.

          (b) **And note**

              If the buyer does not cover, and the market-contract price formula yields damages far in excess of the buyer's actual loss, the buyer may be limited to the amount it expected to make on the sale.

 Example: Seller breached a contract to sell raisins to buyer, which had a subcontract of sale at a price yielding a profit of $4,462. Seller breached the contract by not delivering the raisins at a time when heavy rain severely damaged the crop. The shortage caused a sharp increase in market price so that the market-contract price formula yielded damages in the amount of $150,000. In the absence of a bad faith breach, the court limited recovery to lost profits. [**Allied Canners & Packers v. Victor Packing Co.**, 162 Cal. App. 3d 905 (1984); *and see* **Sun Maid Raisin Growers v. Victor Packing Co.**, 146 Cal. App. 3d 787 (1983)]

b.   Cover [§1163]

As an alternative to compensatory damages, the buyer may "cover" by making a *substitute purchase* of the goods due from the seller, as long as this is reasonable and done without undue delay. The buyer may then recover the difference between the cost of cover and the contract price, together with any incidental or consequential damages; *i.e.*, by proper exercise of "cover," the buyer's damages are measured by *cost of replacement*, not necessarily market value. [U.C.C. §2-712; **Productora e Importadora de Papel v. Fleming**, 383 N.E.2d 1129 (Mass. 1978)]

(1)   Costs [§1164]

The cost of effecting cover (*e.g.*, transportation, advertising for goods, freight and delivery charges, etc.) may also be recovered as incidental damages. [U.C.C. §2-715]

(2)   Consequential damages [§1165]

Recovery of consequential economic damages, such as lost profits, increased production costs, etc., depends on satisfying the "contemplation of the parties" test of **Hadley v. Baxendale.** As stated in U.C.C. section 2-715(2)(a), the loss must be one "which the seller at the time of contracting had reason to know . . . ."

Example: Seller breached a contract to sell certain minerals. Buyer obtained substitute ores, but had to buy different processing equipment. *Held:* In procuring substitute ores, only reasonable diligence need be shown, but to recover for the purchase of the equipment, buyer had to satisfy the "contemplation of the parties" test. [**Apex Mining Co. v. Chicago Copper & Chemical Co.**, 306 F.2d 725 (8th Cir. 1962)]

Example: Seller breached a contract to sell a bar and bar equipment. Buyer did not cover but instead sued for general damages and lost profits. The court denied recovery of lost profits on two grounds: (i) having failed to cover, it was up to buyer to prove that the lost profits could not have been avoided by covering; and (ii) because this was a new business, the anticipated profits were speculative and the proof offered did not meet the required standard of certainty. [**Gerwin v. Southeastern California Association of Seventh Day Adventists,** 14 Cal. App. 3d 209 (1971)]

c. Replevin [§1166]

U.C.C. section 2-716(3) provides for replevin of goods identified to the contract if cover cannot be effected. "Identification to the contract" refers to the seller's segregating goods (*i.e.,* setting them aside or otherwise designating them) as those to which the contract refers. [U.C.C. §2-501]

d. Specific performance [§1167]

U.C.C. section 2-716(1) restates the common law rule that specific performance may be decreed where goods *"are unique or in other proper circumstances."*

(1) Unique chattels [§1168]

"Uniqueness" is defined in precisely the same terms as in the conversion cases previously considered (*see supra,* §337). Thus, chattels that cannot be replaced on the market (due to scarcity, etc.) satisfy the requirement. [*See* **Triple-A Baseball Club v. Northeastern Baseball,** 832 F.2d 214 (1st Cir. 1987)—baseball franchises are unique]

(2) Other proper circumstances [§1169]

Specific performance may also be decreed for contracts involving nonunique chattels if damages are difficult to estimate—*e.g.,* in the case of output contracts for a long term, or when an equivalent substitute performance is either unavailable or can be procured only with great inconvenience and hardship. [**Missouri Public Service Co. v. Peabody Coal Co.,** 583 S.W.2d 721 (Mo. 1979)—10-year coal supply agreement specifically enforced]

> **(e.g.) Example:** Specific performance of a contract to cut timber on defendant's land was granted on a showing that tracts of land available for logging were in short supply, and plaintiff would therefore be unable to procure a substitute; moreover, damages would be difficult to estimate in this situation. [**Paulus v. Yarbrough,** 347 P.2d 620 (Or. 1959)]

> **(e.g.) Example:** Buyer was awarded specific performance of contract to purchase two "quality aircraft, no damage." Buyer had arranged for resale at a profit of $165,000. The aircraft were characterized as possibly the best of their kind, but were not proven to be unique because others of the same make or model could be had. However, buyer could not effectuate cover under the U.C.C. because there was no possibility of finding craft of similar or better quality. [**King Aircraft Sales, Inc. v. Lane,** 846 P.2d 550 (Wash. 1993)]

e.g. **Example:** Specific performance of an option contract to purchase stock was granted on showing that the stock was not traded on the market and was seldom exchanged. [**Chadwell v. English,** 652 P.2d 310 (Okla. 1982); **Dominick v. Vassar,** 367 S.E.2d 487 (Va. 1988)—pecuniary value of stock was uncertain]

CHECKLIST OF BUYER'S REMEDIES FOR NONDELIVERY OF GOODS — **gilbert**

IF A SELLER FAILS TO DELIVER GOODS, THE BUYER MAY CHOOSE FROM AMONG THE FOLLOWING REMEDIES:

☑ *Damages* measured by:

- *Benefit of the bargain* (difference between market price and contract price) *plus* incidental and consequential damages

- Costs of *cover* (difference between cost of purchasing substitute goods and contract price) *plus* incidental and consequential damages

☑ *Replevin,* if goods have been "identified" to the contract

☑ *Specific performance* if goods are unique or in short supply, damages are hard to estimate, or the circumstances are otherwise proper

---

e. Rescission [§1170]

For the seller's material breach, the buyer could rescind, but in the case of a wholly executory contract as here, where the seller has not delivered, such remedy would be worthless to the buyer.

3. Buyer's Remedies Against Seller Following Delivery or Acceptance

a. Delay in delivery [§1171]

If the seller fails to deliver the goods on the agreed upon date, the buyer must first determine if the delay constitutes a material breach of the contract. If so, the buyer may be excused from further performance if she so elects (*i.e.,* she can reject the goods when tendered). If the breach is immaterial, on the other hand, the buyer must accept the goods but may recover the damages for the delay.

(1) Limitation on damages [§1172]

U.C.C. section 2-715 permits recovery of expenses due to delay and any consequential damages the seller had reason to know about. Thus, the limitation of **Hadley v. Baxendale** applies and recoverable damages are restricted to those losses caused by the delay that were within the contemplation of the parties.

> **e.g.** **Example:** Seller delayed delivery of "spacers" from July until September, causing buyer to extend construction time into the winter months. *Held:* Damages for delay were within the contemplation of the parties, but winter construction was not. Hence, buyer could recover for increased overhead caused by the delay and labor costs connected with loading of defective spacers, but not for the increased costs of winter construction. [**Oliver Electrical Manufacturing Co. v. I.O. Teigen Construction Co.,** 177 F. Supp. 572 (D. Minn. 1959)]

b. Delivery of nonconforming goods [§1173]

If the seller delivers goods that are defective or are otherwise not in conformity with the contract, the buyer has a choice of remedies: She may accept the goods and sue for breach of warranty, or she may reject the goods when tendered or revoke acceptance after delivery.

(1) Breach of warranty [§1174]

Buyer may accept delivery, but sue for breach of warranty. U.C.C. section 2-714 provides that for breach of warranty, the measure of damages is the difference at the time and place of acceptance between the value of the goods accepted and the *value they would have had if they had been as warranted*, unless "special circumstances" show proximate damages of a different amount. Incidental and consequential damages may also be recovered.

(a) Value as warranted defined [§1175]

In determining the value of the chattel as warranted, fair market value is generally thought to be the most appropriate measure. In most cases, fair market value and the contract price will be the same, but the buyer may produce evidence that market value exceeded the agreed upon price. [**Chatlos Systems Inc. v. National Cash Register Corp.,** 635 F.2d 1081 (3d Cir. 1980)]

(b) Incidental and consequential damages [§1176]

In addition to the above "benefit-of-the-bargain" damages, the buyer may recover incidental and consequential damages.

1) Incidental damages defined [§1177]

Incidental damages include expenses of inspection, receipt, transportation, and care and custody, etc., of the goods. [U.C.C. §2-715(b)]

2) Consequential damages defined [§1178]

Consequential damages include:

a) *Any loss resulting from general or particular requirements and needs* of which *seller at time of contracting had reason to know* and which could not reasonably be prevented by cover or otherwise. [**Carnation Co. v. Olivet Egg Ranch,** 189 Cal. App. 3d 809 (1986)] (*Note:* This is the contract damage limitation of **Hadley v. Baxendale.**)

---

e.g. **Example:** Seller delivered wine that was spoiled due to the presence of Fresno mold. The court allowed the wine merchant consequential damages for breach of warranty of merchantability, which included lost profits and lost good will. [**Delano Growers' Cooperative Winery v. Supreme Wine Co.,** 473 N.E.2d 1066 (Mass. 1985)]

---

b) *Any injury to person or property proximately resulting from any breach of warranty.* (*Note:* This subsection embodies the tort measure of damages proximately caused, *not* limited by **Hadley v. Baxendale.**)

---

e.g. **Example:** Damage for a breach of warranty as to a machine part that causes a shutdown of the buyer's plant is controlled by the *Hadley* doctrine, but the damages for loss of a leg caused by the same breach of warranty do not have to be foreseen.

(c) Limiting liability for breach of warranty [§1179]

The effect given to contractual disclaimers or limitations on liability varies. Limitations of liability to replacement or repair of defects have been upheld, at least if the seller has carried out his part of the bargain. [**Soo Line Railroad v. Fruehauf Corp.,** 547 F.2d 1365 (8th Cir. 1977); *and see* **Rubin v. Telemet America,** 698 F. Supp. 447 (S.D.N.Y. 1988)—limitation on consequential damages enforceable]

1) Limit cannot be unconscionable [§1180]

Such contractual limitations are subject to review for *unconscionability* under U.C.C. section 2-302 (*see supra,* §§963-976). [**Tuttle v. Kelly-Springfield Tire Co.,** 585 P.2d 1116 (Okla. 1978)—warranty limitation that excludes recovery for personal injuries is prima facie unconscionable; **Goddard v. General Motors Corp.,** 396 N.E.2d 761 (Ohio 1979)—damage action allowed where new car was so riddled with defects that limitation of buyer's remedy to repair failed in its essential purpose; **A&M Produce Co. v. FMC Corp.,** 135 Cal. App. 3d 473 (1982)—adhesion contract allocating risks in economically unreasonable manner]

2) Limitation strictly construed [§1181]

Disclaimers of liability are strictly construed and clauses that are intended to restrict the buyer's remedy for defects in the chattel are *not* applicable to a claim for losses arising from delay in delivering the chattel at the time set by the contract. [**Anderson & Nafziger v. G.T. Newcomb, Inc.,** 595 P.2d 709 (Idaho 1979)—crop failure resulting from delay in the delivery of sprinklers]

3) Distinguish—limitations of remedies [§1182]

A disclaimer of warranty is a means of controlling the seller's liability by limiting the number of situations in which a seller can be said to breach the contract. It is different from a *limitation of remedies* clause that restricts the remedies available to the injured party once a breach is established. [**Collins Radio Co. v. Bell,** 623 P.2d 1039 (Okla. 1981)]

(2) Revocation of acceptance [§1183]

Alternatively, when the buyer receives nonconforming goods, she may reject the merchandise when tendered, or even revoke acceptance after delivery. The U.C.C. does not use the term "rescission," but provides for revocation of acceptance of nonconforming goods. This must be done *promptly* after discovery of the defect by notification to the seller. [*See* U.C.C. §2-608; **Sobiech v. International Staple & Machine Co.,** 867 F.2d 778 (2d Cir. 1989)—failure to give notice for three years precludes right to revoke] The Code section does not supplant other common law theories (*e.g.,* misrepresentation) that may support an action based on rescission. [**H.B. Fuller Co. v. Kinetic Systems, Inc.,** 932 F.2d 681 (7th Cir. 1991)]

(a) Remedies [§1184]

The buyer may be granted:

1) Recovery of so much of the price as the buyer has paid; *and*

2) Damages for nondelivery, measured in the usual way; *and*

3) A security interest in the rejected goods in the buyer's possession for any payment on the price and for any incidental expenses incurred by the buyer in the transaction. The buyer is permitted to resell the goods to recover her losses, paying the surplus to the seller. [U.C.C. §§2-711, 2-706]

 Example: Plaintiff purchased an irrigation machine that proved defective after delivery. Plaintiff gave defendant notification of rescission (revocation of acceptance) and sought recovery of the purchase price and the loss of crops. *Held:* Plaintiff was entitled to recover the price paid and to have a lien on the machine to secure the judgment; *consequential* damages (loss of crop), however, were *denied*. [**Irrigation Motor & Pump Co. v. Belcher**, 483 P.2d 980 (Colo. 1971)]

e.g. **Example:** Buyer revoked acceptance of a "lemon," a defective new automobile, and recovered the price less a deduction for use plus cost of storage, insurance, rental of a substitute vehicle, and interest on the loan. [**McGinnis v. Wentworth Chevrolet Co.**, 645 P.2d 543 (Or. 1982); **Seaton v. Lawson Chevrolet-Mazda**, 821 S.W.2d 137 (Tenn. 1991)—allowing both rescission and punitive damages]

(b) Post-revocation use of chattel [§1185]

Use of the chattel by the buyer after giving notice of revocation does not negate revocation if the use is reasonable and minimizes economic waste. [**CPC International v. Techni-Chem**, 660 F. Supp. 1509 (N.D. Ill. 1987)] However, the seller may be entitled to a setoff for the value of the use. [**Johnson v. General Motors Corp.**, 668 P.2d 139 (Kan. 1983)]

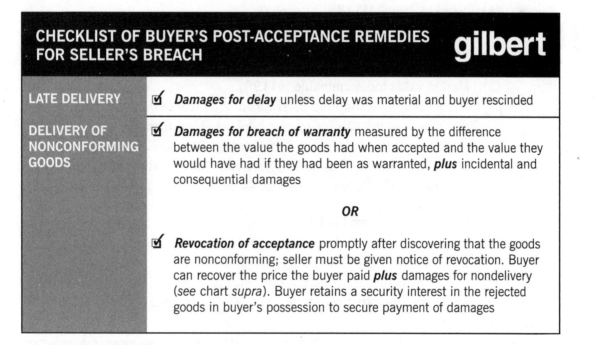

CHECKLIST OF BUYER'S POST-ACCEPTANCE REMEDIES FOR SELLER'S BREACH — **gilbert**

LATE DELIVERY	☑ *Damages for delay* unless delay was material and buyer rescinded
DELIVERY OF NONCONFORMING GOODS	☑ *Damages for breach of warranty* measured by the difference between the value the goods had when accepted and the value they would have had if they had been as warranted, *plus* incidental and consequential damages
	OR
	☑ *Revocation of acceptance* promptly after discovering that the goods are nonconforming; seller must be given notice of revocation. Buyer can recover the price the buyer paid *plus* damages for nondelivery (*see* chart *supra*). Buyer retains a security interest in the rejected goods in buyer's possession to secure payment of damages

4. Remedies of Buyer in Default [§1186]

Under the U.C.C., a buyer who is in default is entitled to restitution of any amount by which the sum of her payments *exceeds reasonable liquidated damages* as specified in the contract; or, in the absence of such specification, she can get 20% of the value of the total performance for which she is obligated under the contract or $500, whichever is smaller. [U.C.C. §2-718; **Stanturf v. Quality Dodge,** 596 P.2d 1247 (Kan. 1979)]

a. Former law [§1187]

Prior to the adoption of the U.C.C., a number of jurisdictions denied any recovery to a defaulting buyer. The U.C.C. now firmly establishes a *policy against forfeitures* by compelling the seller to pay back money received in excess of his damages. [*See* **Silverman v. Alcoa Plaza Associates,** 37 App. Div. 2d 166 (1971); *and see* **Amtorg Trading Corp. v. Miehle Printing Press & Manufacturing Co.,** 206 F.2d 103 (2d Cir. 1953)—discussion of pre-U.C.C. law]

5. Seller's Remedies for Buyer's Nonacceptance of Goods

a. Damages [§1188]

The measure of damages for nonacceptance or repudiation by the buyer is the difference between the *market price* (at the time and place for tender or in comparable markets) and the unpaid contract price, together with incidental damages. [U.C.C. §2-708(1); **Northwest Airlines v. Flight Trails,** 3 F.3d 292 (8th Cir. 1993)] *Rationale:* The basis for this rule is that the seller will be "made whole" because he can sell at market value and recover any loss on the contract from the buyer.

(1) "Market value" [§1189]

Market value in case of an anticipatory repudiation is determined *at the time the seller learns* of the breach. [U.C.C. §2-723]

(2) Market value indeterminable [§1190]

If market value cannot be determined (*e.g.*, where there is no market for the goods or the subject matter is perishable), then the cost of performance or manufacture is used. [*See* **Jagger Bros. Inc. v. Technical Textile Co.,** 198 A.2d 888 (Pa. 1964); **American Broadcasting Co. v. American Manufacturer's Mutual Insurance,** 48 Misc. 2d 397 (1965)]

(3) Incidental damages [§1191]

The seller's incidental damages are defined in section 2-710 to include expenses incurred in stopping delivery, in the care and custody of the goods, in connection with resale, and in refinancing. [*See* **Sprague v. Sumitomo Forestry Co.,** 709 P.2d 1200 (Wash. 1985)]

EXAM TIP **gilbert**

Note that while the U.C.C. provides that the injured seller may recover *incidental* damages, it treats injured sellers slightly differently than injured buyers in that it does not provide for recovery of *consequential* damages by injured sellers.

(4) Note

Where the buyer has notified the seller of the repudiation of the contract, the seller must stop further performance (*i.e.*, discontinue manufacturing). Again, the *avoidable consequences rule* applies and the seller must minimize the loss.

b. Alternative measure of damages [§1192]

The usual measure of damages does not give adequate compensation for the buyer's breach in situations where the seller has an *unlimited supply of the commodity* and the *demand* is limited (a "lost volume seller" situation). For example, if a buyer repudiates the contract to purchase a new car from a dealer with an unlimited supply of cars, the contract price-market value test (or resale price test) yields the seller no recovery. In this situation, U.C.C. section 2-708(2) provides that where the ordinary measure of damages is inadequate to put the seller in as good a position as performance would have done, then the measure of damages is the *profit* (including reasonable overhead) the seller would have made from full performance by the buyer. [*See* **Islamic Republic of Iran v. Boeing Co.**, 771 F.2d 1279 (9th Cir. 1985); **R.E. Davis Chemical Corp. v. Diasonics, Inc.**, 826 F.2d 678 (7th Cir. 1987)]

Example: Buyer repudiated a contract to buy a new boat, after having made a $4,250 down payment. Buyer sued for return of the deposit; seller counterclaimed for damages for breach of contract. *Held:* (i) Under U.C.C. section 2-718 (above), buyer is entitled to restitution of the down payment in *excess* of seller's damages. (ii) Seller's damages here are the *profit* he would have made (plus incidental damages) had buyer performed. The fact that seller was able to resell the particular boat to another buyer for the same price is immaterial, because seller had an unlimited supply of new boats to sell, and hence buyer's breach deprived him of the profit he would have made on one sale. [**Neri v. Retail Marine Corp.**, 30 N.Y.2d 393 (1972)]

Example: Buyer repudiated a contract to purchase 50,000 memorial coins after seller had completed manufacture of 29,000. Seller was held entitled to recovery of the lost profit on the 21,000 coins not manufactured at the time of repudiation because there was *no market* for such special order coins, and hence an award of profits was the only way to put seller in as good a position as he would have been had the contract been performed. [**Anchorage Centennial Development Co. v. Van Wormer & Rodrigues**, 443 P.2d 596 (Alaska 1968); **Tigg Corp. v. Dow Corning Corp.**, 962 F.2d 1119 (3d Cir. 1992)—stating lost profits also are recoverable where subject matter of contract is specialty goods with no resale market]

---

c. Resale [§1193]

The basic remedy provided for a seller upon breach of the contract by a buyer is the right to sell the goods and recover the difference between the resale price and the contract price, together with any incidental damages. [U.C.C. §2-706; **Allied Grape Growers v. Bronco Wine Co.**, 203 Cal. App. 3d 432 (1988)]

(1) Note

The resale price is an application of the avoidable consequences doctrine. As long as the sale is conducted in good faith and in a commercially reasonable manner, the price obtained is accepted as the basis for measuring damages. If the sale yields a profit, it may be retained by the seller. [U.C.C. §2-706]

Example: After breach by a buyer, seller sold the goods to an affiliated company. This was held not to be a commercially reasonable sale and could not be used to set the cover price. [**Afram Export Corp. v. Metallurgiki Halyps, S.A.**, 772 F.2d 1358 (7th Cir. 1985)]

d. Rescission [§1194]

If the buyer repudiates the contract, refuses to accept delivery, or revokes acceptance, the seller may "cancel" the contract. [U.C.C. §2-703(f)]

e. Specific performance [§1195]

Because ordinarily the only duty of the buyer in contracts for the sale of chattels is to pay money, the seller's remedy at law is usually adequate. But there may be unusual circumstances, such as an agreement to provide security, or where there is an independent basis of equitable jurisdiction, such as a trust or fiduciary relationship, in which equitable relief may be granted. [*See* **Carolinas Cotton Growers Association, Inc. v. Arnette**, 371 F. Supp. 65 (D.S.C. 1974)—cooperative marketing association contract—statutory provision]

f. Action for the full price [§1196]

If the buyer has repudiated the contract prior to delivery, the seller is generally restricted to an action for damages. He may recover the full price only if he is *unable after reasonable effort to resell* the goods at a reasonable price, or where the circumstances indicate that such an effort will be unavailing. [U.C.C. §2-709(1)(b)]

6. Seller's Remedies After Delivery and Acceptance of Goods

a. Action for full price [§1197]

If the seller has fully performed his part of the contract by the delivery of the goods and the only breach by the buyer is the failure to pay a liquidated sum of money, the seller may recover judgment for the price. [U.C.C. §2-709(1)(a)]

CHECKLIST OF SELLER'S REMEDIES WHERE BUYER WRONGFULLY REFUSES GOODS

gilbert

DAMAGES	☑ Measured by: • The difference between the ***market price and the contract price*** plus incidental damages *OR* • ***Lost profits*** (if the seller had an unlimited supply of the goods and demand for the goods is limited) *OR* • The difference between the ***resale price*** and the contract price, plus incidental damages
RESCISSION	☑ If the buyer repudiates, refuses to accept delivery, or revokes acceptance, the seller may cancel the contract
SPECIFIC PERFORMANCE	☑ Specific performance generally is ***not*** available because money damages generally are adequate, but in unusual circumstances, the remedy may be available
ACTION FOR PRICE	☑ If the seller cannot resell the goods after reasonable effort (such as where they are specially manufactured), an action for the full contract price is available

(1) Note

It is well settled that under these circumstances the seller is restricted to an action for the price. The seller may *not* rescind for the buyer's material breach and seek restitution of the reasonable value of the goods (in an effort to obtain priority over other creditors of the buyer). Where a debt is created, only an action on the debt will lie.

b. Reclaim goods when buyer becomes insolvent [§1198]

If the goods are sold on credit and the seller learns that the buyer has become insolvent at the time of delivery, the seller may reclaim the goods on demand made *within 10 days after delivery* (but if the buyer made a written representation of solvency to the seller within three months before delivery, the 10-day limitation does not apply). [U.C.C. §2-702(2); *In re* **Flagstaff Food Service Corp.**, 14 B.R. 462 (S.D.N.Y. 1981); *In re* **Pester Refining Co.**, 964 F.2d 842 (8th Cir. 1992)]

(1) Exclusive remedy [§1199]

The remedy thus provided is exclusive. No common law action for fraud is permitted.

(2) Limitation [§1200]

The seller's rights are subject to the rights of a *buyer in the ordinary course* of business or other *good faith purchaser.*

Example: Seller sells his car at auto auction to buyer, who pays for the car with a worthless check. Buyer immediately resells the car to BFP. Upon discovery that the check is worthless, seller *cannot* reclaim the car from BFP. (Seller would be entitled, however, to an "equitable lien" against any monies still owing from BFP to buyer.) [**Greater Louisville Auto Auction, Inc. v. Ogle Buick, Inc.**, 387 S.W.2d 17 (Ky. 1965); *but see* **Foley v. Production Credit Association**, 753 S.W.2d 876 (Ky. 1988)]

---

c. Restitution when buyer repudiates after part performance by seller [§1201]

If the buyer repudiates the contract after partial performance by the seller, the seller may treat this as a material breach which *excuses* further performance on his part. The seller may thereupon seek restitution for the reasonable value of any benefit already conferred on the buyer.

(1) Measure of recovery [§1202]

The seller is entitled to recover for the *reasonable value* of the goods in the buyer's hands and is not limited by the contract price. The contract price is merely evidence of value. [**Wellston Coal Co. v. Franklin Paper Co.**, 48 N.E. 888 (Ohio 1897)]

(2) Unique property [§1203]

The seller may even be entitled to specific restitution where the property transferred to the buyer was "unique." [**Alder v. Drudis,** 30 Cal. 2d 372 (1947)]

(3) Requirement of minimizing damages [§1204]

In cases of repudiation after partial performance, the seller must minimize damages. He is given the right at the time of breach to identify to the contract any conforming finished goods and to use reasonable judgment in completing unfinished goods. He then has the remedies previously mentioned of resale or an action for the price. [U.C.C. §2-704]

CHECKLIST OF SELLER'S REMEDIES AFTER DELIVERY AND ACCEPTANCE   **gilbert**

IF THE SELLER DELIVERED THE GOODS AND THE BUYER ACCEPTED BUT HAS NOT PAID, THE SELLER MAY CHOOSE FROM AMONG THE FOLLOWING REMEDIES:

☑ *Action for full price*

☑ *Reclaim* the goods if: (i) the goods were sold on credit, (ii) the buyer has become insolvent, and (iii) the seller makes demand within *10 days* after delivery (but no 10-day limit if buyer made a written representation of solvency to seller within three months before delivery)

☑ Action for *restitution* of the reasonable value of the goods in the buyer's hands if the buyer repudiates after partial performance (note that this is *not* limited to the contract price)

---

7. Remedy of Seller in Default

a. Common law rule [§1205]

At common law, and by specific provisions of the Uniform Sales Act, a seller who partially performed his contract, and then repudiated it, was nevertheless entitled to recover the reasonable value of the goods to the buyer less any damages sustained by the breach. [Uniform Sales Act §44]

(1) Note

The rule was based on the principle of avoiding unjust enrichment. The seller's recovery is limited to the benefit accruing to the buyer in excess of the injury resulting from the breach. [*See* **H.J. McGrath v. Wisner,** 55 A.2d 793 (Md. 1947)]

(2) Distinguish

The seller would recover the full contract price where the buyer accepted the goods *knowing* of the seller's repudiation.

b. U.C.C. [§1206]

The U.C.C. has *no* provision comparable to section 44 of the Uniform Sales Act and hence there is no apparent basis for any remedy to a seller in default for part performance. (Perhaps it can be argued that the same result can be reached by a proper interpretation of U.C.C. sections 2-106(2), 2-601, and 2-612; or by applying pre-code existing state law. [*See* **Page v. Dobbs Mobil Bay Co.,** 599 So. 2d 38 (Ala. 1992)—seller who breached contract for the sale of a vehicle is entitled to offset value of use against buyer's recovery])

(1) Cure

Where a seller offers nonconforming goods to a buyer who properly rejects them, the U.C.C. provides that the seller may avail itself of section 2-508(b) by offering to cure the defect within a reasonable period beyond the date set for performance. [*See* **T.W. Oil Inc. v. Consolidated Edison Co.,** 57 N.Y.2d 574 (1982)]

D. Construction Contracts

1. Builder's Remedy of Damages Against Owner

a. Before any performance by builder [§1207]

If the owner repudiates a contract to build prior to any performance by the builder, damages are the builder's *lost profit*. These are determined by deducting from the contract price the total cost of the contemplated performance.

b. After full performance [§1208]

If the builder completely performs his part of the contract, but the owner fails to pay the stipulated contract price, the builder's sole remedy is an action for the price.

c. After part performance

(1) Formulas for measuring damages [§1209]

If the owner repudiates the contract after partial performance by the builder, one of three possible formulas for measuring damages is used [*see* **Petropoulos v. Lubienski,** 152 A.2d 801 (Md. 1959)]:

(a) *The contract price minus the cost of completing* the contract and any salvage or partial payments by the buyer. For example, suppose the contract price is $10,000 and the builder has done $4,000 worth of work with an additional $4,000 worth of work needed to complete performance. No partial payments have been made and there is no salvage. Recovery is computed as follows:

$10,000	Contract price
- 4,000	Work to complete
$ 6,000	Damages

[**McGee Construction v. Neshobe Development**, 594 A.2d 415 (Vt. 1991)]

(b) *The contract price minus the total cost of performance* (which yields the profit) and the cost of partial performance minus salvage. Using the facts above, the computation is as follows:

$10,000	Contract price
- 8,000	Total cost of performing
$ 2,000	Expected profit
+ 4,000	Cost of partial performance
$ 6,000	Damages

(c) *Such proportion of the contract price as the fair cost of the work done bears to the fair cost of the whole work* required; and in respect to the work *not* done, only such profit (if any) as the builder would have made by doing it. [**Kehoe v. Borough of Rutherford**, 27 A. 912 (N.J. 1893)] Again, using the facts above, the computation is as follows:

$4,000 / $8,000 = 1/2		Ratio of cost of work done to cost of whole work
× $10,000		Contract price
	$ 5,000	Proportionate share of price

Plus:

1/2		Ratio (as above)
× ($10,000 - $8,000)		Total expected profit
	$ 1,000	Proportionate share of profit
	$ 6,000	Damages

(2) Profitable contracts [§1210]

The three formulas yield the same recovery under the facts above, where the builder is able to establish the total cost of the job and that the contract is a profitable one. However, if the builder is unable to prove construction costs, the first formula is unworkable, whereas the second will at least yield a recovery of the amount invested in the job.

(3) Losing contracts [§1211]

If the total construction costs *exceed* the contract price (and the contract is thus a losing one), the first formula may yield a recovery of less than the builder has invested, whereas the second formula will at least give the builder the amount of his expenditures, because the expected loss on the contract would not be deducted from the recovery of the amounts expended in performing the breached contract. The third formula gives a recovery somewhere between the other two. Using the same facts of a $10,000 contract with expenditures of $4,000 but a total construction cost of *$12,000*, the results of the three formulas are as follows:

(i)   *Contract price less cost of completion:* $10,000-$8,000 = $2,000.

(ii) *Contract price less cost of performance:* $10,000-$12,000 = 0 (profit) + $4,000 = $4,000.

(iii) *Proportional method:* $4,000/$12,000 × $10,000 = $3,333.33;

   ($10,000-$12,000) = 0;

   $3,333.33 + 0 = $3,333.33.

Situations such as the above suggest that where the builder is faced with a loss on the contract, his best bet is to seek a *restitutionary* remedy, considered below. [*See* **United States v. Algernon Blair, Inc.**, 479 F.2d 638 (4th Cir. 1973)]

d.   Mechanic's lien [§1212]

Frequently, the contractor's damages claim (or restitutionary claim) can be secured by a mechanic's lien against the owner's property, provided the proper statutory steps have been taken to perfect the lien claim (recording notice of intent to lien, etc.). In many states, mechanic's liens are limited to the value of the labor and materials expended *or* the contract price, whichever is *less*. [*See* Cal. Civ. Code §3123]

2.   Builder's Restitutionary Remedy Against Defaulting Owners [§1213]

If the owner repudiates the contract after partial performance, the builder may elect to *rescind* the contract and sue in quasi-contract for the value of the benefit conferred.

a.   Measure is cost of replacement by owner [§1214]

As long as the performance rendered is that bargained for by the owner, the builder is entitled to recover the *value* of his performance—which is measured by what it would cost the owner to purchase these services and materials elsewhere. Normally, this is equal to the amount of the builder's expenditures less any salvage value or partial payments by the owner. [**City of Portland v. Hoffman Construction Co.,** 596 P.2d 1305 (Or. 1979)]

(1)   Recovery

Under this approach, the recovery is *not limited by the contract price* (the contract has been rescinded). Hence, the builder may end up recovering far in excess of what he would have had to accept if the contract had been fully performed. [**Boomer v. Muir,** 24 P.2d 570 (Cal. 1933)—

builder allowed to recover $250,000 as value of part performed prior to owner's repudiation, even though total contract price had only been $20,000]

(2) Comment

To avoid such a result, the owner should simply perform the contract. Of course, problems arise if it is not clear which party is in breach—*e.g.*, if the builder encounters unforeseen delays or difficulties in construction and claims excuses that the owner does not accept. The owner who kicks the builder off the job faces the restitutionary liability above if the builder's excuses are valid.

b. Minority limits builder to contract price [§1215]

Some jurisdictions have limited the builder to a recovery of a proportionate part of the contract price, or deny recovery of any excess above the contract price. *Rationale:* If the owner had breached after full performance, the plaintiff would be limited to the contract price, and the same rule should apply in cases of partial performance. [**Kehoe v. Borough of Rutherford**, *supra*, §1209]

(1) Criticism

However, this ignores the fact that the contract *has been rescinded* and no longer exists, and that the remedy sought is restitutionary with the object of restoring the status quo.

3. Restitutionary Remedy for Builder in Default [§1216]

If the builder has committed some *material* breach of the construction contract, he is not entitled to enforce the contract and hence has no adequate remedy at law. There is general agreement that the builder should be entitled to restitution for the value of the work performed, to avoid unjust enrichment of the owner. However, there is wide disagreement as to the conditions under which such recovery can be had.

a. Willfulness of breach [§1217]

A number of authorities, supported by the Restatement, hold that the builder is entitled to *no recovery* whatsoever if his breach is "willful." [Rest. Contracts §357] However, determining whether a breach is "willful" is not always easy, and most courts today probably do *not* regard this as a controlling factor.

b. Measure of recovery [§1218]

Several formulas have been used in measuring the owner's unjust benefit in such cases:

(1) *Contract price less cost of completion, plus consequential damages for delay.* This is the usual method employed by the courts. Thus, if the contract price is $10,000, the builder has expended $8,000, the cost of

completion is $5,000, and the loss of rent from delay is $500, the unjust benefit to the owner is $5,500, and the builder recovers $4,500.

(2) *The amount the premises increased in value as a result of the builder's partial performance, less special damages.* The rationale for this view is that the owner (who is not in breach) should have to pay *only* for actual *economic* betterment received. [**Gillis v. Cobe,** 59 N.E. 455 (Mass. 1901)— court placed on the builder the burden of proving the added value]

    (a) *Comment:* The defect in this formula is that the builder may spend considerable sums in constructing a building desired by the owner but which adds very little to the value of the premises.

(3) *The Restatement* (Second) of Contracts limits recovery to the *excess of benefit* received over the *losses* suffered by the owner caused by the contractor's breach, in no case exceeding a *ratable* proportion of the contract price. [*See* **Beeman v. Worrell,** 612 S.W.2d 953 (Tex. 1981); Rest. 2d Contracts §374]

c. Limitations [§1219]

Whichever formula is used, the builder who is in material breach of the contract will *not* be permitted to recover more than the contract price; *i.e.,* he will not be permitted to profit from his own wrongdoing. Moreover, unlike prior situations where the owner is in breach, the measure of recovery is *not* the cost to the builder of the work done. In the present situation, the test of recovery is the *net value to the owner.*

d. Distinguish—immaterial breach [§1220]

If the builder's breach is immaterial and he has *substantially completed* the job, he may sue for the *contract price less damages* resulting from his immaterial breach, under the doctrine of "substantial performance." [*See* **Perryman v. Sims,** 506 S.W.2d 753 (Tex. 1974); *and see* Contracts Summary] (The owner's damages in such a case are discussed below.)

4. Owner's Remedy of Damages for Builder's Breach

a. After substantial performance by builder [§1221]

If the builder has substantially performed, but there are defects in the building, damages are measured by: (i) the *cost of repair or replacement* to bring the building up to contract specifications, if this can be done without undue expense; *or* (ii) if repair or restoration is not economically feasible (*e.g.,* where all the pipes in a home must be torn out and replaced), the *difference in the value* of the building as built and its value if it had been constructed in accordance with the specifications in the contract. [**Vezina v. Nautilus Pools,** 610 A.2d 1312 (Conn. 1992); *and see* **Grossman Holdings, Ltd. v. Hourihan,** 414 So.

2d 1037 (Fla. 1982)—in computing difference between value as built and value as contracted, value should be determined as of date of delivery; **Mayfield v. Swafford,** 435 N.E.2d 953 (Ill. 1982)—recovery is the lesser of cost of repair or diminution in value of property]

b. If builder abandons project after part performance [§1222]

If the builder abandons the contract and is in material breach, damages are measured by what the owner must pay to another to complete the construction, less anything still owing to the builder under the contract, plus special damages. [**Brewer v. Custom Builders Corp.,** 356 N.E.2d 565 (Ill. 1976)]

Example: If the contract price is $10,000, and the owner has made progress payments to the builder totaling $6,000, and completion costs are an additional $6,000, damages are $6,000 less $4,000, or $2,000.

---

(1) Special damages [§1223]

The owner can also recover any special damages resulting from delay (loss of rents, financing charges, etc.). If the builder's delay results in lost profits, the owner may recover this loss as consequential damages. [**Perini Corp. v. Greate Bay Hotel & Casino,** 610 A.2d 364 (N.J. 1992)—delay in completing renovation of a casino] Compensation for this loss may be governed by a valid liquidated damages clause. [**Orto v. Jackson,** 413 N.E.2d 273 (Ind. 1980)—$3,500 awarded for aggravation and inconvenience]

5. Owner's Restitutionary Remedy Against Builder [§1224]

Ordinarily, restitution is not available to the owner, because usually the owner has not made payments in excess of the benefit received by the builder's partial performance.

a. Exception

If the owner has paid the builder in advance for the job, rescission and restitution are advisable only in cases where the contract work can be completed at a cost *less than* the contract price. In such a case, the owner would obtain restitution from the builder for the price paid minus the reasonable value of the benefits received. A new contractor would then be retained to complete the job at a cost below the contract price.

6. Owner's Remedy of Specific Performance Against Builder [§1225]

As a general rule, specific performance of contracts to build or repair is denied. The reason for this rule is found partly in the belief that in most of these cases there is an adequate remedy at law, and partly in the historical reluctance of equity courts to enter mandatory injunctions involving difficult problems of supervision and enforcement. [**Northern Delaware Industrial Development Corp. v. E.W. Bliss Co.,** 245 A.2d 431 (Del. 1968)—plaintiff sought mandatory injunction ordering builder to employ 300 workers on a night shift; court refused, citing practical problems of enforcement; **Bisset v. Gooch,** 409 N.E.2d 515 (Ill. 1980)]

a. When specific performance appropriate [§1226]

Nonetheless, if it can be clearly shown that there is in fact *no* adequate remedy at law (*e.g.,* where the building is to be done by defendant on his own land), courts today balance the difficulty of supervision against the advantages of having the contract performed. [**Fran Realty v. Thomas,** 354 A.2d 196 (Md. 1976)] Where only minor problems of supervision are present, specific performance will be granted. [**Ammerman v. City Stores Co.,** 394 F.2d 950 (D.C. Cir. 1968)—specific performance granted of contract to construct building on Defendant's own land; damages inadequate because there was no way Plaintiff could do the work himself or hire anyone else to construct building on Defendant's land; **Becker v. Sunrise at Elkridge,** 543 A.2d 977 (N.J. 1988)—specific performance of contract to build condominium]

E. Service Contracts

1. Damages—Breach by Employee [§1227]

The measure of damages for breach of an employment contract by an employee is the *cost of obtaining services* equivalent to those promised, plus compensation for any consequential damages within the contemplation of the parties when the contract was made. (From this recovery, the employee may offset any unpaid wages due from the employer.)

e.g **Example:** Speck agreed to work for Roth as a hairdresser for one year at $75 per week. After six months had elapsed, Speck left his employment for a new position paying $100 per week. *Held:* Roth was entitled to recover the difference between $100 and the contract rate of $75 for six months. The new wage was *evidence* of the value of Speck's services and hence the cost of obtaining equivalent services. [**Roth v. Speck,** 126 A.2d 153 (D.C. 1956)]

a. Avoidable losses [§1228]

The avoidable consequences rule applies and the employer must make reasonable efforts to secure a replacement at the same rate.

2. Damages—Breach by Employer

a. Wages due [§1229]

If the employer's breach is simply a failure to pay wages due under the contract, the employee may sue for the amount due and continue the employment.

b. **Future wages [§1230]**

If the employer wrongfully discharges the employee contrary to the provisions of the contract, the employee may recover the *total* amount of earnings promised for *full performance* of the contract, less the amount that the employee *earned or could reasonably have earned* performing similar services with another employer during the period of the contract. [*See* **Fite v. First Tennessee Production Credit Association**, 861 F.2d 884 (6th Cir. 1988); *and see* **Diggs v. Pepsi-Cola Metropolitan Bottling Co.**, 861 F.2d 914 (6th Cir. 1988)—interesting discussion of prejudgment interest under Michigan law]

(1) **Recovery [§1231]**

Some jurisdictions restrict recovery to losses sustained by the employee to the date of trial [**Lewis v. Loyola University of Chicago**, 500 N.E.2d 47 (Ill. 1986)—damages beyond date of trial disallowed as speculative], but the majority rule regards wrongful discharge as a total breach and permits recovery of all losses, *past and prospective*. In applying this majority rule, the life expectancy of the employee must be considered and the total amount of wages must be *reduced to its present value*. [**Dixie Glass v. Pollack**, 341 S.W.2d 530 (Tex. 1960)]

c. **"Wages" include fringe benefits [§1232]**

Included in the computation of loss of income are such fringe benefits as pensions, bonuses, and insurance policies. [**Jeannont v. New Hampshire Personnel Commission**, 392 A.2d 1193 (N.H. 1978); **Rodgers v. Georgia Tech Athletic Association**, 303 S.E.2d 467 (Ga. 1983)—interesting discussion of fringe benefits and perquisites of a big time head football coach]

d. **Consequential damages [§1233]**

The employee may also recover for consequential damages (*e.g.*, not allowing performer to appear on nationwide television program may cause loss of exposure and foreclose other employment opportunities) and also for the expenses incurred in reasonable attempts to mitigate damages by *seeking other employment* (*e.g.*, employment agency fees). To be recoverable, consequential damages must have been reasonably contemplated or foreseen by the parties. [**Erickson v. Playgirl**, 73 Cal. App. 3d 850 (1977)—loss of general publicity for failure to place photograph on magazine cover held not compensable; **Redgrave v. Boston Symphony Orchestra**, 602 F. Supp. 1189 (D. Mass. 1985)—consequential damage for harm to Redgrave's career and reputation due to Orchestra's breach of contract was within parties' contemplation but disallowed when the message conveyed by the cancellation was no more than a statement of fact]

e. **Burden of proof on employer to show other employment available [§1234]**

While the rule of avoidable consequences applies in these cases, the burden of proof is placed on the *employer* to show what the employee *earned or could have earned* with reasonable diligence during the period of wrongful discharge. [**Sayre v. Musicland Group,** 850 F.2d 350 (8th Cir. 1988)—mitigation is an affirmative defense that must be pleaded by the employer]

(1) Note

In determining whether a reasonable effort to secure employment was made, most courts only require an employee to accept *similar* work in the *same locality*. [**Rabago-Alvarez v. Dart Industries,** 55 Cal. App. 3d 91 (1976)—improper to reduce recovery by the amount that could have been earned in "inferior" employment]

Example: While employed by City, plaintiff also worked in a liquor store. City wrongfully discharged plaintiff, and in an action brought by plaintiff for damages, City sought to deduct the wages earned by plaintiff in the liquor store during the period following his discharge. *Held:* There should be no deduction. City is only entitled to set off wages earned in *inconsistent* employment and here the liquor store job was compatible with his city employment. [**People *ex rel.* Bourne v. Johnson,** 205 N.E.2d 470 (Ill. 1965)]

---

f. Collateral sources rule [§1235]

There is a difference of opinion among courts as to whether money received by an employee as unemployment compensation is deductible from the damage award. Some courts disallow the deduction by applying the collateral sources rule, treating these payments as a benefit earned by the employee. [**Hayes v. Trulock,** 755 P.2d 830 (Wash. 1988); **Technical Computer Services v. Buckley,** 844 P.2d 1249 (Colo. 1992)—unemployment compensation benefits not deductible; *compare* **Seibel v. Liberty Homes,** 752 P.2d 291 (Or. 1988)—Social Security disability payment] Other courts allow the deduction, reasoning that the fund is created by the employer's payments. [**Mers v. Dispatch Printing Co.,** 529 N.E.2d 958 (Ohio 1988)]

g. Contracts terminable at will [§1236]

The traditional rule is that where a contract is for an indefinite term, the employer may discharge the employee for good cause, no cause, *or even a cause that is morally wrong.* [*See* **Brockmeyer v. Dun & Bradstreet,** 335 N.W.2d 834 (Wisc. 1983)] In recent years, a number of exceptions to this harsh doctrine have been developed by judicial decisions:

(1) Public policy exception [§1237]

Recent cases hold an employer liable in tort for the wrongful discharge of an employee who refused to perform services that violate public policy. Justification for this exception is based on the argument that otherwise the threat of discharge could be used to coerce employees to commit crimes. [**Potter v. Village Bank of New Jersey,** 543 A.2d 80 (1988)—

retaliatory discharge for reporting illegal laundering of drug money; **Southwest Forest Industries v. Sutton,** 868 F.2d 352 (10th Cir. 1989)—retaliatory discharge for filing workers' compensation claim; **Tameny v. Atlantic Richfield Co.,** 27 Cal. 3d 167 (1980)—retaliatory firing of employee who refused to participate in a price-fixing scheme; **Pierce v. Ortho Pharmaceutical Corp.,** 417 A.2d 505 (N.J. 1980)—employee has a cause of action where the discharge is contrary to a clear mandate of public policy]

(2) Breach of covenant of good faith and fair dealing [§1238]

Some courts imply a covenant of good faith and fair dealing in employment contracts and allow a tort action for damages (including punitive damages) for its breach. [*See* **Flanigan v. Prudential Federal Savings & Loan,** 720 P.2d 257 (Mont. 1986)] However, in one widely noted decision, **Foley v. Interactive Data Corp.,** 47 Cal. 3d 654 (1988), the California Supreme Court held that tort remedies are *not* available to employees who allege that they have been discharged in violation of the implied covenant. In a subsequent opinion **[Newman v. Emerson Radio Corp.,** 48 Cal. 3d 973 (1989)], the court further held that this restriction to contract damages applied retroactively to all cases not final on the date of the *Foley* decision.

(3) Exception for implied-in-fact contracts [§1239]

A number of courts have found that employment contracts originally at will have been modified by self-imposed termination guidelines or the employer's manual or handbook. As thus modified, the employer's right to terminate arbitrarily is limited, and a discharge without a showing of good cause gives the employee a cause of action for contract damages. [*See* **Foley v. Interactive Data Corp.,** *supra*]

h. Caveat [§1240]

The causes of action and remedies discussed here should not be confused with the civil rights actions considered *supra*, §735, which are provided for statutorily.

3. Restitution—Action by Employee for Employer's Breach

a. Employer repudiates after part performance by employee [§1241]

If the employer breaches a contract for specific services by a lawyer, architect, etc., after partial performance, the employee may elect a restitutionary remedy and sue in quantum meruit for the *reasonable value* of her services. [*See* **Fracasse v. Brent,** 6 Cal. 3d 784 (1972)—attorney wrongfully discharged required to sue in quantum meruit; *see* Annot., 92 A.L.R.3d 684]

(1) Recovery [§1242]

While some jurisdictions limit recovery to the contract rate, most jurisdictions permit the employee to recover for the value of her work even if it *exceeds* the contract price.

(2) Value of work [§1243]

The value of the employee's services is determined by what it would cost to contract for similar services and *not* whether the performance rendered resulted in any net benefit to the employer. For example, if architects' plans are prepared as required by contract, the employer must pay for the value of those services even though the project is abandoned and the plans therefore are useless.

b. No restitution after full performance [§1244]

If the contract calls for payment of a fixed sum of money for services and the employee *fully performs* before repudiation by the employer, no restitutionary action is permitted. The employee is restricted to a recovery of the amount due by the terms of the contract. [**Oliver v. Campbell,** 43 Cal. 2d 298 (1954)]

4. Restitution—Action by Employer for Employee's Breach [§1245]

If payment has been advanced to an employee who subsequently repudiates the contract, the employer may rescind and seek restitution of the money paid, but not in fact earned, because of the employee's premature termination of the contract.

a. Specific restitution when appropriate [§1246]

If the compensation advanced by the employer included stock in the employer-corporation, it has been held that the employer is entitled to rescission and *specific restitution* of the stock upon material breach of contract by the employee. [**Maytag Co. v. Alward,** 112 N.W.2d 654 (Iowa 1962)]

5. Restitution—Action by Employee in Default

a. Unintentional breach [§1247]

If the employee's failure to perform is due to circumstances beyond the employee's control (*e.g.,* illness or disability), all courts permit restitution for the reasonable value of the services rendered, not to exceed the contract rate.

(1) And note

The recovery is *not* subject to offset on account of the employer's costs in replacing the employee because the illness or disability constitutes sufficient *impossibility of performance* as to excuse the employee from further liability under the contract. (*See infra,* §1297.)

b. Intentional breach [§1248]

Whether an employee who *willfully* breaches the employment contract may recover the value of the benefit conferred on the employer is subject to conflicting views.

(1) Early view [§1249]

The early view denied any recovery to the employee. This result was viewed as necessary to deter contract breaking, and was justified by the argument that one who breaches a contract has no right to enforce any claim arising under the contract.

(2) Modern view [§1250]

The more modern view, first enunciated in **Britton v. Turner,** 26 Am. Dec. 713 (1834), permits the breaching employee to recover for the value of the benefit conferred, not exceeding the contract price, *less damages* incurred by the employer as a result of the breach.

Example: Plaintiff agreed to thresh wheat and flax but quit after threshing only the wheat. The flax was destroyed in the field by rain. Plaintiff was held entitled to recover for the value of his services, regardless of the breach. Interestingly, no setoff was allowed. The court held that the damage to the flax caused by rain was too remote. [**Lynn v. Seby,** 151 N.W. 31 (N.D. 1915)] *Note:* This result might be different under the Restatement (Second) of Contracts because the loss of the flax was clearly the result of defendant's breach even if not legal damages under **Hadley v. Baxendale.** [*See* Rest. 2d Contracts §374]

Example: A lawyer retained to represent a client prepared the case but withdrew without good cause. The case was settled favorably by another attorney. There being no prejudice to the client, the lawyer may recover compensation for the benefits that his work conferred on the client, but his compensation should be reduced by the reasonable amount needed to employ another lawyer to complete the work. [**May v. Siebert,** 264 S.E.2d 643 (W. Va. 1980)]

---

6. Injunctive Relief

a. No specific performance of employment [§1251]

Neither the employer nor the employee may specifically enforce an employment contract. The denial of affirmative relief is based partly on the difficulty of supervising enforcement of the decree and partly on the undesirability of imposing an employment relationship on persons who are in serious disagreement. [**Zannis v. Lake Shore Radiologists,** 392 N.E.2d 126 (Ill. 1979)—reinstatement of a radiologist denied; **Redgrave v. Boston Symphony Orchestra,** 557 F. Supp. 230 (D. Mass. 1983)—suit by performer-employee to enforce contract of employment denied because of difficulties cited in text above]

(1) Qualification [§1252]

Upon completion of the personal service part of the employment contract, it may be possible to specifically enforce the agreement as to compensation. Thus, a promise to fund a pension plan was specifically enforced. The remedy at law was ruled inadequate because the employee would be required to wait until he reached retirement age and then sue if the pension was not paid. This was found to be less efficient and practical than the equitable remedy. [**Munchak Corp. v. Caldwell,** 265 S.E.2d 654 (N.C. 1980)]

(2) Reinstatement view [§1253]

Note that in employment discrimination cases brought under the various civil rights statutes, reinstatement of an aggrieved employee is commonly provided for in the award. Some cases extend the remedy to include promotion to partnership status. [**Hopkins v. Price Waterhouse,** 920 F.2d 967 (D.C. Cir. 1991); *and see* **Brown v. Trustees of Boston University,** 891 F.2d 337 (1st Cir. 1989)—reinstated a professor with tenure; **Squires v. Bonser,** 54 F.3d 168 (3d Cir. 1995)—reinstated a township roadmaster]

b. Breach of negative covenants may be enjoined [§1254]

If an employment contract for a stated term expressly provides that the employee should work *exclusively* for the employer *and no one else* during the life of the contract, a breach of that negative covenant (the promise *not* to work for anyone else) will be enjoined, at least *where the services contracted for are unique and extraordinary.*

---

e.g. **Example:** Defendant had agreed to sing in plaintiff's theatre for three months and not to sing for anyone else during that period, but then quit her job with plaintiff to sing in a rival music hall. An injunction was granted to prohibit defendant's violation of the negative covenant. [**Lumley v. Wagner,** 42 Eng. Rep. 687 (1852); *and see* **MCA Records, Inc. v. Newton-John,** 90 Cal. App. 3d 18 (1979)—breach of an exclusive recording contract enjoined]

---

(1) "Uniqueness" [§1255]

A necessary prerequisite to equitable relief is that the employee's services be unique, because such proof establishes the inadequacy of the remedy at law—*i.e.*, no one else could be hired to do this job. [*See* **American Broadcasting Co. v. Wolf,** 52 N.Y.2d 394 (1981)]

(2) Effect of injunction [§1256]

If granted, the relief takes the form of a *prohibitory* injunction forbidding the employee from working for others. Such injunctions are enforceable without the difficulties referred to above (*see supra,* §1251). The fact that the injunction may have the *indirect* effect of coercing the employee to perform the contract does not prevent courts from granting such relief, because in these cases the employee always retains the option of not working for anyone, and affirmative relief would be granted but for enforcement and supervision difficulties.

(a) Note

Whether the other employer who induced the employee to breach the contract may be enjoined is subject to conflicting views. [*Compare* **Central New York Basketball v. Barnett,** 181 N.E.2d 506 (Ohio 1961)—yes; *with* **Beverly Glen Music v. Warner Communications,** 178 Cal. App. 3d 1142 (1986)—no, interpreting Cal. Civ. Code]

(3) Negative covenant may be implied [§1257]

Some jurisdictions enforce a negative covenant only if express and in writing, but others permit the covenant to be *implied* from provisions calling for "exclusive" services.

(4) Remedy conditioned on employer's performance [§1258]

Generally, courts condition the injunction on the continued willingness and ability of the employer to perform his promise. This is to assure *"mutuality of performance."* [**Lumley v. Wagner,** *supra; and see supra,* §1063]

Example: Barnett, a star basketball player, signed an exclusive player contract with plaintiff. Later, in breach of the contract, Barnett agreed to play for another team in a rival league. Because Barnett was an exceptional basketball player, damages were inadequate. An injunction therefore was granted for the remaining period of the contract prohibiting Barnett from playing for any other team, *upon condition* that plaintiff stand ready to perform the contract, so that there would be no problem with mutuality of performance. [**Central New York Basketball v. Barnett,** *supra*]

---

7. Covenants Not to Compete

a. In general [§1259]

Equity will enforce covenants not to compete after termination of an employment contract or in connection with the sale of a business, or the dissolution of a partnership, *provided* the restriction is *reasonable* as to *time* and *place* and *no broader than necessary* to protect the employer. [**James S. Kemper & Co. v. Cox & Associates, Inc.,** 434 So. 2d 1380 (Alaska 1983); **McCart v. H&R Block, Inc.,** 470 N.E.2d 756 (Ind. 1984)—covenant not to compete for two years within 50 miles of franchised territory held to be reasonable]

(1) "Reasonable" [§1260]

In determining whether a covenant not to compete is "reasonable," more flexibility is allowed in cases of a covenant barring an *employee* from competing while *still engaged* in the business or partnership (or in cases of covenants by a *seller* of a business and its goodwill to refrain from competing with the buyer) than is allowed where a covenant bars an employee from competing after the *termination* of the employment. [**Bradford v. New York Times,** 501 F.2d 51 (2d Cir. 1974)] A covenant that has no purpose other than to restrict an employee from competing with a former employer will not be enforced. [**Robbins v. Finlay,** 645 P.2d 623 (Utah 1982); **Hill v. Mobile Auto Trim,** 725 S.W.2d 168 (Tex. 1987)]

b. Adequacy of damages [§1261]

Injunctive relief is granted only if the remedy at law is not adequate. Such inadequacy is shown where the contract calls for unique services, or where the employee is carrying away *trade secrets or goodwill* belonging to the employer. [**Cherne Industrial v. Grounds & Associates,** 278 N.W.2d 81 (Minn. 1979)]

(1) Distinguish—"ordinary" workers [§1262]

However, in cases where covenants are exacted from ordinary workers (*e.g.,* salespeople, artisans, and the like), injunctive relief is often denied and the employer is restricted to an action at law for damages. [**Purchasing Associates, Inc. v. Weitz,** 13 N.Y.2d 267 (1963)—*public policy against* enforcement of such covenants except when necessary to protect trade secrets or when services bargained for are unique; *and see* **American Broadcasting Co. v. Wolf,** *supra,* §1255—no equitable relief enforcing a 90-day good faith negotiation clause after termination of employment contract]

> **EXAM TIP** **gilbert**
>
> In the late 1990s it was very common, especially in the computer industry, to have all employees sign a covenant not to compete, whether or not their services were unique. Courts routinely held such covenants to be unenforceable, but that did not deter many companies from continuing the practice because most employees simply just did not know that the covenants were not enforceable. Therefore, you should be wary of such covenants in exams and in practice. Remember that unless the employee's services are *rare or unique*, or the employee has *access to trade secrets*, enforcement of the covenant is *against public policy*.

(2) Liquidated damages [§1263]

The presence of a *liquidated damages* clause in the employment contract does *not* preclude injunctive relief. *Rationale:* Damages, whether liquidated or otherwise, are not adequate for loss of truly unique personal services. [**Karpinski v. Ingrasci,** 28 N.Y.2d 45 (1971); *but see* **Knight, Vale & Gregory v. McDaniel,** 680 P.2d 448 (Wash. 1984)—liquidated damage clause providing for 35% of any fee collected from former clients held to be reasonable]

(3) Profits [§1264]

In addition to injunctive relief, the violator of a covenant not to compete may be required to account for profits arising from the use of information

COMPARISON OF REMEDIES FOR BREACH OF EMPLOYMENT CONTRACT

gilbert

EMPLOYER'S REMEDIES	EMPLOYEE'S REMEDIES
DAMAGES	
Measured by cost of obtaining equivalent services **plus** consequential damages reasonably contemplated by parties at time of contracting	Measured by all wages due (past, present, and future), including costs of fringe benefits, **plus** consequential damages reasonably contemplated by parties at time of contracting, **minus** wages employee made or could have made by seeking similar employment in the same market
RESTITUTION	
If employee repudiates after employer pays in advance, employer may rescind and seek **restitution** of money paid but not earned	Quantum meruit for **reasonable value** of services performed. An employee who unintentionally fails to perform (*e.g.,* because of illness) can also recover the **reasonable value** of any services performed. The modern view even allows an employee who intentionally breaches to recover the reasonable value of performance minus the employer's damages
SPECIFIC PERFORMANCE	
Not available to enforce affirmative covenant to work, but may be available to enforce an employee's promise to **work exclusively** for the employer during the contract term if (i) the services are rare or unique (*e.g.,* a professional ball player, singer, artist) and (ii) the employer performs. Courts will also enforce a **covenant not to compete** if the restriction is reasonable as to time and place and no broader than necessary to protect the employer	Generally not available

wrongfully obtained from the employer. [**Cherne Industrial v. Grounds & Associates,** *supra*; *compare* **Robert S. Weiss & Associates v. Wiederlight,** 546 A.2d 216 (Conn. 1986)—loss sustained by Plaintiff from breach of covenant not to compete may be measured by nonbreaching party's lost profits]

c. "Blue pencil" rule [§1265]

If the restrictive covenant is overbroad, some courts hold it void and unenforceable. [**Smith, Batchelder & Rugg v. Foster,** 406 A.2d 1310 (N.H. 1979)—overbroad restriction in an accounting employment contract unreasonable and not reformable because of employer's bad faith; **Valley Medical Specialists v. Farber,** 982 P.2d 1277 (Ariz. 1999)—covenant held unreasonable as to area and duration] Other courts, applying the "blue pencil" doctrine, will enforce the covenant if the reasonable and unreasonable restraints are severable. [**BDO Seidman v. Hirshberg,** 93 N.Y.2d 382 (1999)]

(e.g.) **Example:** Defendant, a dentist, was employed by plaintiff, an oral surgeon, for three years with a covenant not to practice dentistry or oral surgery "forever" in certain named counties. Defendant breached the agreement. An injunction was granted to enforce the covenant, but only as to the practice of oral surgery in the county *where defendant was in competition with plaintiff.* [**Karpinski v. Ingrasci,** *supra*; **Westec Security Services v. Westinghouse Electric Corp.,** 538 F. Supp. 108 (E.D. Pa. 1982)—covenant modified from a 20-year to a 10-year period]

---

d. Feasibility as limitation [§1266]

If the covenant extends over a long period of time (*e.g.,* an exclusive agency contract), injunctive relief may be denied because of the continuous and protracted supervision that would be required. [*See* **Long Beach Drug Co. v. United Drug,** 13 Cal. 2d 158 (1939)—court refused to enjoin breach of exclusive agency contract that had been in effect for 30 years because it was too complex a relationship to supervise; injured party left to remedy at law]

8. Contracts to Lend Money [§1267]

The traditional measure of damages for breach of a contract to lend money is the additional interest required for a replacement loan. That rule has been broadened to permit recovery of compensation for resulting injuries that were within the contemplation of the parties at the time the contract was made. [**United California Bank v. Prudential Insurance Co.,** 681 P.2d 390 (Ariz. 1984)—borrower awarded $10,494,000, representing loss of equity in a hotel; **Native Alaskan Reclamation & Pest Control v. United Bank Alaska,** 685 P.2d 1211 (Alaska 1984)—reliance, expectancy, and mitigation damages in an aborted contract to purchase aircraft; **W-V Enterprises, Inc. v. Federal Savings & Loan,** 673 P.2d 1112 (Kan. 1983)—loss of future profits; *and see* **Weinberg v. Farmers State Bank of Worden,** 752 P.2d 719 (Mont. 1988)—excessive interest, crop and herd loss, plus punitive damages for breach of the covenant of good faith and fair dealing]

Chapter Thirteen: Remedies in Connection with Unenforceable Contracts

---

CONTENTS

Chapter Approach

Exam questions sometimes involve one of the four basic types of *"unenforceable contracts."* Keep an eye out for:

(i)   Contracts that *should be in writing* but are oral (*Statute of Frauds* problem);

(ii) Contracts that cannot be performed due to *impossibility or frustration of purpose;*

(iii) Contracts that involve a *minor* or a person lacking mental capacity to contract or, as you are more likely to see, a *municipal corporation acting beyond the scope of its powers;* and

(iv) Contracts that are *criminal, tortious,* or *against public policy.*

Whenever you see an oral contract, think of the *Statute of Frauds.* Ask yourself whether the Statute applies. If so, and the contract has not been reduced to a writing, remember that there are only two remedies worth serious consideration: *restitution* and *specific performance,* with the possibility of damages based on an estoppel principle. The principal problem you may have with the restitutionary award is the *computation* of the award; so study the section of this chapter on restitutionary remedies carefully. For specific performance, be sure you consider the equitable doctrines of *part performance* and *estoppel.*

For the other three types of unenforceable contracts (impossible to perform, ultra vires, or illegal contracts), the available remedy, if any, is *restitutionary.* Use the following two steps to analyze these questions:

1.   Determine whether the applicable law provides a *basis for relief* (there may be no remedy at all). (For illegality problems, be sure to consider the "in pari delicto" and "locus poenitentiae" doctrines.)

2.   If restitution is available, determine how that award will be measured.

A. Contracts Unenforceable Because Not in Writing

1.   In General [§1268]

For present purposes, it is assumed that an applicable variety of the Statute of Frauds (or Statute of Wills) bars any affirmative action relative to the contract in question. Under certain circumstances, the bar to enforcement may be removed by invoking the equitable doctrines of part performance or estoppel (below). Otherwise, the sole remedy is *restitution* (legal or equitable) for benefits conferred. Obviously, restitutionary relief is appropriate only when there is partial or full performance on the plaintiff's part.

2. **Types of Statutes—Remedial Effect [§1269]**

The language of the statutes varies from jurisdiction to jurisdiction. Under some statutes, the contract will be declared *"void"* as distinguished from *"unenforceable."* However, statutes making the contract "unenforceable" are much more common.

a. **Contract made "unenforceable" [§1270]**

Under the more common interpretation that the contract is simply "unenforceable," the remedial impact is that *restitution may be had only against a party who has repudiated* the oral contract; *i.e.,* as long as the defendant stands ready to perform, he is not liable to restore anything received under the oral contract. [**Hayes v. Hartelius,** 697 P.2d 1349 (Mont. 1985)]

b. **Contract declared "void" [§1271]**

But if the interpretation is that the oral contract is "void," the plaintiff may repudiate the contract and seek restitution. The defendant's willingness to perform is immaterial. [**Reedy v. Ebsen,** 242 N.W. 592 (S.D. 1932)]

c. **Distinguish—oral real estate contracts [§1272]**

One type of Statute of Frauds is given a literal reading to bar even restitutionary remedies. This is directed at *oral real estate brokerage* or similar contracts and is designed to prevent brokers from claiming commissions when the alleged engagement of their services has not been put down in writing. Such statutes usually read "no contract for the payment of a commission or reward for . . . procuring a purchase of real estate for another shall be valid (except if in writing)." If quantum meruit were allowed for such services, the policy of the statute (which goes beyond mere regulation of the quality of proof relating to civil remedies between parties) would be defeated. Hence *no remedies, including restitution,* are allowed. [**Hale v. Kriesal,** 215 N.W. 227 (Wis. 1927); **Buckingham v. Stille,** 379 N.W.2d 30 (Iowa 1988)] However, the broker may possibly recover by asserting that the client is estopped from asserting the statute. [**Tenzer v. Superscope, Inc.,** 39 Cal. 3d 18 (1985); *but see* **Phillippe v. Shapell Industries,** 43 Cal. 3d 1247 (1987)—restricting Tenzer doctrine to unlicensed finders and ruling that licensed broker could not avoid the requirements of the Statute of Frauds by asserting equitable estoppel]

3. **Restitutionary Remedies—Common Problems**

a. **Admissibility of evidence of "contract" rate or price [§1273]**

If the benefit conferred in reliance on an unenforceable contract is tangible (*e.g.*, money or goods that remain intact, or land), specific restitution can be granted and there are no valuation problems. If the benefit is goods that have been consumed, the market value controls; in the case of land, rental value controls. The problem, as usual, is the *valuation* of the services or materials rendered, or improvements to land—and the question arises whether the orally agreed rate or price is admissible.

(1) Contract price [§1274]

The argument *against* admissibility of the contract rate is that this defeats the purpose of the Statute of Frauds by indirectly enforcing the contract; the sole relevant issue should be the *benefit* to defendant. However, notwithstanding this argument, *most courts permit* introduction of the agreed rate of compensation *as evidence* of the monetary value of the benefit received by defendant, but it is *not conclusive*. [**Clark v. Coats & Suits Unlimited**, 352 N.W.2d 349 (Mich. 1984)—agreement admissible "if helpful" in estimating plaintiff's damages]

(2) Value of services rendered [§1275]

The ultimate measure of the "benefit" is the value of the services, etc., *rendered by the plaintiff* (rather than their usefulness to the defendant). Since the defendant has broken the contract (even though oral), the equities are in favor of measuring the value of services from the standpoint of the plaintiff—*i.e.*, the *detriment* to the plaintiff.

(a) Note

This is not really made clear by Restatement of Restitution section 155(1), which states that recovery is "the value of benefit in advancing the purposes of the contract."

b. "Contract" price not ceiling on restitutionary recovery [§1276]

This issue is related to that above. The majority of cases allow the plaintiff to recover *above* the contract price if "unjust enrichment" over that amount is proved.

Example: McGilchrist was hired under a "permanent" oral contract (unenforceable under Statute of Frauds because not performable in one year), at $25 per week for three years, after which he was to get permanent employment at $2,500 per annum. Woolworth, the employer, repudiated after McGilchrist performed for several years. McGilchrist was held entitled to a quantum meruit recovery in *excess* of the agreed salary. [**McGilchrist v. F.W. Woolworth Co.**, 7 P.2d 982 (Or. 1932)]

---

(1) Rationale

The oral contract is unenforceable, but it is not illegal. Therefore, the same measure of restitution should be applied as where written contracts are *broken* and the plaintiff elects the restitution remedy (*see supra*, §1241).

(2) Criticism

However, the rule is criticized as forcing the defendant to the choice of either asserting the Statute of Frauds as a defense and thereby risking recovery *above* the contract ceiling, or abandoning the protection of the Statute altogether.

c. Reliance damages excluded when restitution sought [§1277]

Although the defendant's liability in quantum meruit for part performance of an unenforceable contract may (as discussed above) *exceed* the contract price and rate, it is important to note that it is still theoretically "unjust enrichment," not damages.

(1) No recovery where no "unjust enrichment" [§1278]

Thus, there can be no recovery for reliance losses suffered by the plaintiff that have resulted in *no* "unjust enrichment" of the defendant.

---

e.g. **Example:** Defendant orally agreed to convey land to Plaintiff in exchange for a monument to be constructed by Plaintiff. Plaintiff built the monument and tendered it to Defendant, who rejected it (*i.e.*, no benefit) and then stood on the Statute of Frauds in refusing to convey the land. Restitution for the value of Plaintiff's services on the monument was *denied*—because Defendant had rejected the monument, no benefit had passed to him, and there was no basis for a quantum meruit recovery. [**Dowling v. McKenney,** 124 Mass. 478 (1878)]

(a) Consequential damages [§1279]

Likewise, consequential damages incurred in reliance on the unenforceable contract, and which have not resulted in any "unjust enrichment" to the defendant, are generally, but not invariably, *denied.* [**Boone v. Coe,** 154 S.W. 900 (Ky. 1913)—moving expenses in getting ready to perform oral contract not recoverable in restitution act]

1) But note

There is authority contra on this, allowing such recoveries. [*See* **Randolph v. Castle,** 228 S.W. 418 (Ky. 1921)—coal miners relying on unenforceable oral contracts moved to the mine and held themselves ready for work, which was not assigned to them; restitution allowed for recovery of their moving expense]

(2) Analysis [§1280]

To explain the seeming inconsistency in the quantum meruit cases, a distinction is sometimes attempted between oral contracts for services that are continuing, and those that are made to reach a *particular result—* *e.g.*, the building of a monument. In the latter case, the services represent only reliance damages and are not recoverable in a restitutionary action.

(a) Comment

The more likely explanation, however, is that damages for breach of an unenforceable oral contract are disguised as "unjust enrichment" in an unrecognized application of *estoppel* to assert the Statute of Frauds (*see* below).

4. Part Performance Doctrine—Remedy of Specific Performance in Equity [§1281]

Because the restitutionary remedy in many cases fails to compensate the plaintiff for part performance in reliance on an unenforceable contract (particularly because consequential damages are generally excluded), equity mitigated the harshness of the Statute of Frauds by the "part performance doctrine" applicable to *land sale contracts.* (*Note:* This is strictly a creature of equity and *not* a basis for any remedy at law.) [**Trollope v. Koerner,** 470 P.2d 91 (Ariz. 1970)]

a. Typical land sale case [§1282]

In the typical case, Seller makes an oral contract to sell land to Purchaser. Purchaser pays part of purchase price, takes possession, and makes improvements. Purchaser can compel a conveyance notwithstanding the Statute of Frauds. Purchaser's acts of part performance are said to take the contract out of the Statute.

b. Acts constituting part performance of land sale contracts

(1) Payment of purchase price insufficient [§1283]

Payment of all or part of the purchase price is *not* enough by itself to constitute "part performance" of a land sale contract. *Rationale:* Payment is equivocal (does not prove a contract), and quasi-contract is an adequate remedy for recovery of the payment. [*See* **Hoffman v. SV Co.,** 628 P.2d 218 (Idaho 1981); **Chomicky v. Buttolph,** 513 A.2d 1174 (Vt. 1986)]

(2) Taking possession insufficient [§1284]

The taking of possession is also *not enough by itself* to constitute part performance because it does not necessarily refer to a contract of sale and is not detrimental to the possessor. [**Kurland v. Stolker,** 533 A.2d 1370 (Pa. 1987)—failure to show exclusive possession]

(3) Payment plus possession [§1285]

Together these are generally regarded as sufficient. In combination, they satisfy either of the rationales discussed below.

(4) Improvement by buyer [§1286]

Improvements to the property by the buyer are themselves held sufficient in many courts because restitution may not fully restore the status quo or compensate buyer for the improvements. [**Green v. Gustafson,** 482 N.W.2d 842 (N.D. 1992)]

(5) Other acts [§1287]

Payment and possession *plus* other acts, such as improvements on the property are sufficient. [**Bradshaw v. McBride,** 649 P.2d 74 (Utah 1982); **Ben Holt Industries v. Milne,** 675 P.2d 1256 (Wash. 1984)—payment, possession, plus long acquiescence in the tenancy is a sufficient evidentiary basis]

c. Rationale for part performance doctrine

(1) Evidence [§1288]

One explanation for the doctrine is that the acts of part performance themselves are *evidence* of the existence of the oral contract. Following this rationale, several courts restrict evidence of part performance to acts "unequivocally referable" to the oral contract. [**Burns v. McCormack,** 233 N.Y. 230 (1922); **Anostario v. Vicinanzo,** 59 N.Y.2d 662 (1983)]

(a) Criticism

However, this is a weak argument because the contract must in any event have been proved by "clear and convincing evidence" *before* evidence of the part performance could properly be accepted.

(b) Comment

This approach excludes such matters as the plaintiff's giving up other property, changing jobs, moving to new locale, etc., because such acts are not exclusively "referable" to a contract. At the same time, the buyer's improvements to the property under an oral contract are universally considered acts of part performance (*see supra,* §1286); yet such improvements are not called for in the contract and may not be "unequivocally referable" thereto.

(2) Detrimental reliance [§1289]

The other rationale advanced for the part performance doctrine is that it justifies enforcement of the contract where one party has allowed the other to rely to his detriment on the former's apparent willingness to perform the contract. This comes close to the "estoppel" approach discussed below.

d. Part performance doctrine and sales of goods [§1290]

Under the U.C.C., the doctrine of part performance is given limited application. Section 2-201 provides that oral contracts for the sale of goods are enforceable only "with respect to goods for which *payment* has been made and accepted, or which have been *received* and accepted." [*See* **In re Augustin Bros.**, 460 F.2d 376 (8th Cir. 1972)]

---

cf. **Compare:** U.C.C. section 2-201(3)(b) states an exception to the Statute of Frauds, where the party against whom the contract is enforced admits in pleading, testimony, or otherwise in court that a contract of sale was made. [Annot., 88 A.L.R.3d 416]

---

5. Estoppel to Assert Statute of Frauds as a Defense [§1291]

A number of jurisdictions allow enforcement of oral contracts by invoking the doctrine of "estoppel to assert the Statute of Frauds" as a defense. Evidence of any acts by the plaintiff in reliance on the defendant's promise are admissible even though not "referable" to the contract. The important remedial effect is that because the defendant cannot assert the Statute as a defense, the plaintiff may recover *damages* as well as sue for specific performance (unlike the part performance doctrine, which is recognized only where equitable relief is sought; *see* above). [**Oxley v. Ralston Purina Co.**, 349 F.2d 328 (6th Cir. 1965); **Family Medical Building v. State**, 684 P.2d 77 (Wash. 1984)]

a. Restatement of Contracts position [§1292]

The Restatement (Second) of Contracts provides that a promise made with the reasonable expectation of inducing action by the plaintiff, and which does so, is enforceable notwithstanding the Statute of Frauds if injustice is otherwise unavoidable. The remedy granted for breach is to be framed *as justice requires*, taking into consideration the adequacy of other remedies such as cancellation or restitution. [Rest. 2d Contracts §139; **Bower v. AT&T Technologies**, 852 F.2d 361 (8th Cir. 1988)—damages awarded for breach of oral promise to employ]

(1) Note

Damages may be limited to reliance damages rather than full-scale enforcement of the promise relied on when this accomplishes a just result. [**Green v. Interstate United Management Services Corp.**, 748 F.2d 827 (3d Cir. 1984)]

(2) And note

Another section of the Restatement allows *specific performance* of such contracts when the plaintiff, in *reasonable reliance* on the continuing assent of the defendant, has so changed position that injustice can be avoided only by granting specific performance. [Rest. 2d Contracts §129]

6. Oral Agreements to Devise Realty in Exchange for Services [§1293]

Suppose Becky agrees to take care of Alex "for the rest of Alex's life," in consideration of Alex's oral promise to devise his home to Becky. Becky performs, but Alex leaves no will. Special considerations affect Becky's remedial possibilities against

Alex's estate including the *nature of Becky's services* and *how long Alex lived*. (Note that the remedies are based on equitable doctrines and hence are discretionary with the court.)

a. Quasi-contract [§1294]

If Becky's services are ordinary and Alex died soon after making the agreement, *quasi-contract* for the value of the services is appropriate. This is consistent with the rule (*see supra,* §1283) that payment of the purchase price is not sufficient part performance to take a land sale contract out of the Statute of Frauds. [**Kennedy v. Bank of America,** 237 Cal. App. 637 (1965); **Hastoupis v. Gargas,** 398 N.E.2d 745 (Mass. 1980)] Note also that recovery depends on a finding that the services were rendered *in reliance on a promise of compensation* and not gratuitously. [*See* **In re Estate of Boothby,** 532 A.2d 1007 (Me. 1987)—compensation denied; *and see supra,* §237]

b. Specific performance [§1295]

If Becky's services are unusual (*e.g.,* specialized nursing) and Alex lived a long time, *specific performance* would be the more appropriate remedy to prevent unjust enrichment. [*Compare* **Henderson v. Fisher,** 236 Cal. App. 2d 468 (1965)—agreement to convey in exchange for nursing care specifically enforced; *with* **Martin v. Scholl,** 678 P.2d 274 (Utah 1983)—employment as a ranch foreman for 30 years in reliance on oral promise to devise "the home place" not sufficient part performance to take case out of Statute because service performed was consonant with foreman's employment; *and see* **Shepherd v. Mazzetti,** 545 A.2d 621 (Del. 1988)—promise to convey family home in return for son's promise to manage the family business held enforceable]

(1) Note

When the oral agreement is enforced because of the nature of the services rendered, specific performance takes the form of a constructive trust imposed on the decedent's property for the benefit of the other party to the contract. [**Musselman v. Mitchell,** 611 P.2d 675 (Or. 1980)]

c. Damages [§1296]

If the doctrine of estoppel to assert the Statute of Frauds is recognized, Becky could sue for *damages*; *i.e.,* Becky is entitled to ordinary contract damages measured by the benefit-of-the-bargain rule.

B. Contracts Unenforceable Because of Impossibility or Frustration of Purpose

gilbert

Did the party who cannot perform **assume the risk of loss** or otherwise agree that full performance is a condition precedent to recovery?

YES → **That party cannot recover** and the other party has an action for breach of contract.

NO ↓

Was one party **at fault** for the impossibility or frustration?

YES → **That party cannot recover** and the other party has an action for breach of contract.

NO ↓

Neither party can profit, but each party must pay for what he received, generally measured by the detriment incurred by the party seeking recovery.

1. **Effect of Impossibility or Frustration [§1297]**

   If full performance by one party is expressly made a condition precedent to recovery on a contract, or one party *assumes* the risk of loss (or the risk is placed on that party by operation of law, *e.g.*, Uniform Vendor and Purchaser Risk Act), supervening impossibility simply results in breach of contract with the usual remedial alternatives. Otherwise, however, supervening impossibility or frustration of purpose *excuses both parties from further performance* and restitution (if anything) *is the only remedial possibility.*

   a. **Application**

      The rule as stated applies when (i) the plaintiff has partly performed and impossibility prevents completion; (ii) the plaintiff has performed completely and impossibility prevents the rendering of the agreed exchange ("failure of consideration"); or (iii) performance is possible but its commercial value has been destroyed by unforeseen events ("frustration of purpose").

2. **General Guidelines for Restitution**

   a. **English rule [§1298]**

      The earlier English decisions, particularly in the class of cases in which the plaintiff had performed in advance and his expectations were defeated by impossibility or frustration of purpose, tended to let the loss remain where it fell. Thus, for example, in the **Coronation Cases,** [1904] 1. K.B. 493, Plaintiff rented a room for $141 from which to view the coronation parade of Edward VII, and paid $ 100 in advance. The parade did not come off. Plaintiff sued for restitution of $100 and Defendant counterclaimed for $41. The court denied relief to both parties.

   b. **American rule [§1299]**

      The American rule is that where there is no fault on either side, neither party can be compelled to pay for the other's disappointed expectations. But on the other hand, neither can be allowed to profit by the situation; *each must pay for what he has received.* [Rest. Contracts §468(3)]

      (1) **Recovery [§1300]**

         The measure of recovery is generally the detriment to the plaintiff—the reasonable value of the services or goods supplied in performance of the contract, but not in excess of the contract price (or contract rate, if there is one); *i.e.*, plaintiff cannot recover on a more profitable basis than the contract affords. [Rest. Contracts §468(3)]

3. **Application of Guidelines Where Impossibility Intervenes After Partial Performance**

   a. **Employment cases [§1301]**

      If an employee fails fully to perform the contract because of death or disability, all courts allow a quantum meruit recovery for the employee's services up to the time of death or disability (*see supra*, §1247).

(1) Replacement costs [§1302]

A *few* courts have permitted the employer to offset any costs incurred in hiring a replacement. [**Patrick v. Putnam,** 27 Vt. 759 (1855)] However, this appears clearly wrong because the death or disability constitutes impossibility which *excuses* further performance by the employee, and hence there is no basis for awarding *damages* to the employer—by offset or otherwise.

(2) Contract rate [§1303]

On the other hand, the contract *rate is* generally held to be the upper limit on plaintiff's recovery for his services—*i.e.*, the employee cannot profit from the situation by recovering more than the contract rate, because after all the employer is not at fault either. [Rest. Contracts §468]

b. Remodeling and repair contracts [§1304]

Where an owner employs a contractor to remodel or repair her house, and after the remodeling is partly finished the house is destroyed by fire, restitution is generally allowed. (*Compare*: The rule is contra in ordinary *construction* contracts; the finished job is a condition precedent to the owner's duty to pay anything, and therefore no recovery in contract or quasi-contract is generally allowed.)

EXAM TIP | **gilbert**

Be sure to remember the important difference between a contract *to build* and a contract *to remodel*. If Alex hires Becky *to build* a house, and after Becky completes three-fourths of the construction, the house is destroyed by fire, Becky cannot recover because performance is not impossible—she can rebuild. On the other hand, if Alex hires Becky *to remodel* his house, and after Becky completes three-fourths of the remodeling, the house is destroyed by fire, Becky's performance is impossible—there is nothing to remodel—and she can recover as long as the fire was not her fault.

---

(1) Limitation—value of materials [§1305]

Many cases limit recovery to the value of the materials *"incorporated"* into or *"affixed"* to the building at the time it was destroyed, together with labor and supervisory costs related thereto. [**Carroll v. Bowerstock,** 164 P. 143 (Kan. 1917)]

(a) Note

Some courts expand this to include the value of materials at the *building site* if they also were destroyed by the fire, etc., even though not yet incorporated into the structure. [28 A.L.R.3d 788]

(2) Limitation—proportion of contract price [§1306]

Other courts allow recovery of a proportionate part of the total contract price—*i.e.*, plaintiff can recover the proportion that the value of the work finished bears to the value of the work if wholly completed, multiplied by the contract price. [**Anderson & Son v. Shattuck,** 81 A. 781 (N.H. 1911)]

(a) Comment
This may turn out to be a boon to the contractor if the contract was turning out to be a *losing* proposition.

Example: Phil contracted to remodel Davida's hotel for $12,000, and had performed two-thirds of the work at a cost of $10,000 when the building was destroyed by fire. It would have cost Phil an additional $5,000 to complete the job (*i.e.,* a loss on the job of $3,000). Under this approach, Phil recovers two-thirds of $12,000, or $8,000 (thus losing only $2,000). *Note*: This has been criticized because it saves the contractor from part of the loss he otherwise would have sustained on full performance, and hence may tempt destruction of the building.

---

4. Application in "Failure of Consideration" Cases [§1307]
If the plaintiff has fully performed his side of the bargain, but the counterperformance is prevented by supervening impossibility, restitutionary relief is also granted. (*Example:* Buyer pays $1,000 for racehorse, which seller is unable to deliver because it breaks its leg and has to be destroyed.)

a. Specific relief [§1308]
If practicable, specific restitution of benefits is the appropriate remedy; *i.e.,* whatever property has been paid over or transferred is ordered returned.

b. Value of performance rendered [§1309]
Alternatively, the plaintiff is entitled to the value of that which he has transferred to the defendant, less the value of any part performance rendered by the defendant. [**Louisville & Nashville Railroad v. Crowe,** 160 S.W. 759 (Ky. 1913)]

(1) Alternative—value of performance excused [§1310]
Sometimes courts have based restitutionary relief on the value of the performance *excused.*

Example: Where plaintiff leased land to defendant for one year in return for which defendant was to pay $1,000 and move a barn, but the barn was destroyed before it could be moved, plaintiff was held entitled to recover what it would have cost defendant to move the barn; the measure of restitution was the cost to defendant of the excused performance. [**Jones-Gray Construction Co. v. Stephens,** 181 S.W. 659 (Ky. 1916)]

---

5. **Remedies Where Impossibility Occurs After Breach [§1311]**

The right to a judicial remedy arises at the *time* of breach. Hence, if the party breaching has no excuse at that time, subsequent developments do not affect his liability.

---

e.g. **Example:** Employee wrongfully quits his job and later becomes too ill to work. Employee is liable for damages for breach of contract notwithstanding the subsequent illness (impossibility).

---

a. **Distinguish—anticipatory breach [§1312]**

The rule is different, however, when the breach consists solely of an *anticipatory repudiation*—e.g., Seller, whose performance is due on September 1, tells Buyer on August 1 that he will not deliver. In these cases, it is generally recognized that the repudiator could have *withdrawn* the repudiation (at least until the other party relied on it). Hence, the repudiator's liability for damages is cut off by some supervening impossibility—*i.e.*, if the goods are irreplaceable and are destroyed by fire on August 15, any liability for damages terminates as of that time. [**Model Vending, Inc. v. Stanisci,** 180 A.2d 393 (N.J. 1962)]

C. Contracts Unenforceable Because of Lack of Capacity to Contract

1. **Minors' Contracts [§1313]**

Contracts entered into by a person under the age of majority are generally unenforceable against him (with certain statutory exceptions).

a. **Disaffirmance by minor; necessity for restitution of benefits received [§1314]**

Most statutes provide that the minor has the right to disaffirm any such contract during minority or within a reasonable time after attaining the age of majority. However, the statutes vary as to whether the minor must *restore* whatever was received or obtained under the contract as a condition to disaffirming the obligations.

(1) **Restoration where possible [§1315]**

Some courts hold that the minor must make restoration if possible, but inability to restore because of destruction, consumption, or dissipation of whatever was received excuses this requirement. [**Halbman v. Lemke,** 298 N.W.2d 562 (Wis. 1980)—minor "may recover his purchase price without liability for use, depreciation, damage, or other diminution in value"]

(2) **Restoration or restitution [§1316]**

Other courts require the minor to restore or pay (as restitution) the value of anything obtained in *exchange* for the benefits received under the unenforceable contract. [**Merrick v. Stephens**, 337 S.W.2d 713 (Mo. 1960)]

(3) No restitution [§1317]

Still other jurisdictions permit the minor to disaffirm *without* restitution of the purchased items—*i.e.*, no accounting required for the property or any profits obtained from the property or other items obtained in exchange for the property. [*See* Cal. Family Code §6710]

b. Estoppel to disaffirm [§1318]

Because a minor is liable for his own torts, a misrepresentation as to age (if reasonably relied upon) has been held to be sufficient fraud to estop the minor from disaffirming liability under the contract. (But there is also authority contra on this.)

c. Transfers to bona fide purchaser [§1319]

Unlike the usual rule as to voidable contracts, a purchaser who acquires property previously sold by a minor takes *subject to the minor's power of disaffirmance* in most states.

(1) But note

A few states are contra by statute, protecting the BFP. [*See, e.g.,* Cal. Family Code §6713]

d. Exculpatory contracts [§1320]

A minor may avoid an otherwise valid agreement releasing another party from liability for prospective injuries to the minor, even if the agreement is also signed by a parent. [**Del Bosco v. United States Ski Association**, 829 F. Supp. 1470 (D. Colo. 1993)]

e. Quasi-contractual liability for necessities of life [§1321]

Quite apart from any contractual liability, a person is liable for the reasonable value of food, clothing, shelter, or other necessities of life furnished to him during his minority. [*See* Cal. Family Code §6712]

(1) Liability [§1322]

The liability here is quasi-contractual in nature; hence, reasonable value is the measure. However, most courts hold that the value *cannot exceed* the contract price, if there was one. [**Hyman v. Cain**, 48 N.C. 111 (1855)]

2. Contracts Voidable Because of Mental Incapacity

a. Quasi-contractual liability for necessities of life [§1323]

The liability is the same as with respect to minors, above.

b. Right to disaffirm contracts; necessity of restitution [§1324]

The rules here are also the same as in the case of minors, except that most courts *require full restitution* of any benefits obtained—*i.e.,* either the goods or property sold to the incompetent or their *value* if the goods have been wasted, consumed, or destroyed—as long as the party furnishing the goods was *unaware* of the incapacity.

c. No estoppel against disaffirmance [§1325]

Because mentally deficient persons are generally not capable of forming the requisite intent to deceive (as to their capacity), no estoppel can be created by their representations.

3. Contracts by a Corporation Unenforceable Because "Ultra Vires" [§1326]

The concept of "ultra vires" refers to contracts made by a *corporation* that are *beyond the powers* of the corporate entity.

a. Contracts by private corporation [§1327]

Basically, a private corporation has only the powers conferred upon it by its charter (articles of incorporation) or by statute. If it seeks to enter into a contract that is not within the powers so conferred, the contract can be challenged as "ultra vires." (*See* detailed discussion in Corporations Summary.)

(1) Common law [§1328]

At common law, unauthorized contracts were rendered null and void by the ultra vires doctrine.

(2) Modern law [§1329]

The common law doctrine has been abolished by modern statutes, which generally provide that lack of corporate powers is *no defense* as between the corporation and private parties dealing with the corporation.

(a) Quo warranto proceedings [§1330]

Acts in excess of corporate powers are remediable *by the state* in a proceeding to *revoke the charter* of the corporation—"quo warranto" proceedings ("by what warrant" is the corporation acting beyond its powers).

(b) Shareholder action [§1331]

Alternatively, shareholders of the corporation may *sue to enjoin* the corporation from entering into ultra vires transactions, or may bring a representative suit (on behalf of the corporation) against the officers or directors for any *damages* or losses caused to the corporation as a result of an ultra vires act that the officers or directors authorized.

b. Contracts made by municipal and public corporations [§1332]

Municipal and other public corporations (governmental entities) have only such powers as are conferred upon them by the sovereign power creating them (the state). Statutes specify in detail the type of contracts that the entity can make and the manner in which they must be approved and executed. The effect of violation of such statutes depends on the *legislative purpose* of the statute or regulation involved. [**Blue Ridge Sewer Improvement v. Lowry & Associates,** 718 P.2d 1026 (Ariz. 1986)—no recovery in quantum meruit for services rendered in performing unenforceable contract]

(1) Violation of administrative regulations [§1333]

In general, *restitution* is allowed for benefits conferred upon a governmental entity where there has been a violation of *administrative regulations* in making the contract but the governmental entity has been clearly benefited. Alternatively, an *estoppel* may be asserted to allow the person furnishing the benefit to recover on the contract. [**Advance Medical Diagnostic Laboratory v. County of Los Angeles,** 58 Cal. App. 3d 263 (1976)—estoppel against county to deny contracts; **Noel v. Cole,** 655 P.2d 245 (Wash. 1982)—ultra vires doctrine applies to governmental contracts, but the other party can recover for benefits conferred on an unjust enrichment basis; **Lanphier v. Omaha Public Power District,** 417 NW.2d 17 (Neb. 1987)—city failed to enact ordinance; recovery allowed for fair and reasonable value of services]

(2) Statutes prohibiting collusion

(a) No recovery by contractor [§1334]

If the violation is of legislation that expresses a clear public policy to prevent *collusive* action and to protect the public treasury (*e.g.*, requirements of open bidding and letting of contracts to lowest bidder), most cases have *denied quasi-contractual recovery* to the contractor. [**Edwards v. Renton,** 409 P.2d 153 (Wash. 1965)]

1) Minority view [§1335]

Some recent cases (a minority) permit quasi-contractual recovery if the party furnishing the benefit did so in *good faith*, and *no fraud or collusion* is involved. [33 A.L.R.3d 1154; **City of Damascus v. Bevins,** 726 S.W.2d 677 (Ark. 1987)—where there was a failure to publish notice of bids, contractor was allowed to recover based on unjust enrichment] The measure of quasi-contract recovery, where allowed, is frequently limited to the value of the benefit to the municipality, or in such a way as to exclude any profit to the contractor. [**Arnjo v. Cebolleta,** 732 P.2d 426 (N.M. 1987)]

(b) Recovery by municipality [§1336]

If there *is* collusion by the contractor to suppress competitive bidding required by statute, the municipality in a taxpayer's action may recover any money paid, possibly without setoff for the value of items installed by contractor. [**Gerzof v. Sweeney,** 22 N.Y.2d 297 (1968)—after being compelled to return full purchase price of generators, contractor was permitted to retake generators upon posting bond to secure city against damages stemming from removal and replacement]

4. Contracts by Unlicensed Building Contractors [§1337]

Many statutes preclude an unlicensed contractor from suing on a construction contract, and in most cases the contractor also is given no remedy in quasi-contract or to enforce a mechanic's lien.

a. Setoff [§1338]

However, if the owner asserts a claim on the contract, the unlicensed contractor may assert his claim by the way of a *setoff*. [**Summer Development Corp. v. Shivers,** 517 P.2d 757 (Alaska 1974)—note that the court treated this as an "illegal" bargain, *see infra,* §§1340-1344]

b. Quantum meruit [§1339]

Some courts suggest that the sanction in these cases should be to limit recovery to quantum meruit in an amount less than the contract price. [**Town Planning & Engineering Associates v. Amesbury Specialty Co.,** 342 N.E.2d 706 (Mass. 1976)]

D. Agreements Unenforceable Because of Illegality

1. In General

a. Illegal bargain defined [§1340]

An "illegal" contract is one that is criminal, tortious, or otherwise against *public policy*. [Rest. Contracts §512]

b. Policy considerations [§1341]

Claims arising from illegal contracts raise a conflict of policy between (i) preventing unjust enrichment, and (ii) rewarding illegal conduct.

c. General rule—no remedy [§1342]

The supposed "general rule" is that neither party to an illegal contract can enforce the contract or obtain any other judicial remedy. The law will leave the parties in the position they placed themselves. [**Holman v. Johnson,** Ch. 1775—opinion by Lord Mansfield; **Wal-Mart Stores v. Crist,** 855 F.2d 1326 (8th Cir. 1988)]

(1) Severability [§1343]

If the illegal provisions in an agreement can be severed from the lawful provisions, lawful promises *may* be enforced if supported by *independent consideration*.

Example: An agreement to provide sexual services in exchange for a financial consideration is illegal and unenforceable. But an agreement to perform services as a housekeeper, cook, and spouse in return for a promise to accumulate and share property may be partially enforceable. Thus, a homosexual partner who agreed to act as Defendant's chauffeur, bodyguard, secretary, and business associate has been held to state a cause of action for breach of a promise to share property and provide financial support. [**Whorton v. Dillingham,** 202 Cal. App. 3d 447 (1988)]

---

(2) Qualification [§1344]

As applied to executory transactions, the rule leaves the parties to stew in their own juices. However, as discussed below, courts have developed "exceptions" to the supposed general rule so as to allow restitutionary relief where the magnitude of the loss to the plaintiff is much more serious than the affront to public policy resulting from the "illegality" of the bargain. (*See infra,* §§1350-1359.) In such cases the policy against unjust enrichment of the defendant is deemed simply to *outweigh* the concern about rewarding illegal conduct.

d. "Illegality" compared to "unclean hands" doctrine [§1345]

The unclean hands doctrine bars *equitable* remedies (and possibly quasi-contractual relief that is equitable in nature) where the plaintiff has acted "inequitably." Illegality bars *legal or equitable* remedies where the plaintiff has acted illegally. In other words, the plaintiff may be deprived of equitable remedies because of "unclean hands" while still retaining *legal* remedies, as long as the plaintiff's conduct is merely inequitable rather than illegal. But, if the conduct is illegal, the plaintiff may be denied *any* remedy. [**Truitt v. Miller,** 407 A.2d 1073 (D.C. 1979); *and see* **Sparks v. Sparks,** 353 S.E.2d 508 (Ga. 1987)—unclean hands barred imposition of resulting trust on home, but did not preclude division as marital property in divorce proceeding]

2. Cases in Which Defense of Illegality Not Applied [§1346]

The defense of illegality applies only where the public interest would be directly offended by enforcement of the contract. Hence, where the claimed "illegality" is not directly involved in the performance or enforcement of the contract, the defense will be rejected. In these cases, the contract is enforceable, and appropriate contract remedies will be granted (damages, specific performance, etc.).

a. Failure of intended illegal purpose [§1347]

Where a seller conveys to a buyer in trust to defraud creditors, but no creditors are actually defrauded, most courts permit the seller to recover the property conveyed as against the defense of illegal purpose. [**Hanscom v. Hanscom,** 208 P.2d 330 (Or. 1949); **Bailey v. Banther,** 314 S.E.2d 176 (W. Va. 1983); *but see* **Senter v. Furman,** 265 S.E.2d 784 (Ga. 1980)—restitution denied where doctor conveyed property to nursing assistant when facing malpractice claim]

b. **Illegality "collateral" or "remote" [§1348]**

Similarly, where plaintiffs have sold goods knowing that the goods would be later smuggled, resold illegally, etc., plaintiffs are generally allowed to enforce the sale contract and recover the purchase price. Likewise, rent for premises known to be used for gambling or for prostitution is recoverable. The illegality is *collateral* to the sale or rental. [**Fuchs v. Goe,** 163 P.2d 783 (Wyo. 1945)]

Example: To comply with a statute, a father filed an affidavit stating he had no interest in a parcel of land placed in his son's name. In fact, there was an agreement by the son to hold the land for his father's benefit. After improvements had been completed by the father, the son refused to convey the land. *Held*: A constructive trust should be imposed for the benefit of the father. The misconduct was not directed against the son and did not affect the transaction between the parties. [**Hocken v. Hocken,** 650 P.2d 803 (Nev. 1982)]

---

(1) **Limitation**

If the intended use by the receiver of the goods above or the lessee above involves a *serious crime,* or the supplier or landlord in any other way *furthers the commission* of the crime, no recovery may be had. To illustrate, think of the difference between the sale of a shotgun to one who intends to shoot ducks out of season, and a sale to an angry person whose declared intention is to kill a business competitor of the seller. [Rest. Contracts §602(1)]

c. **Third party may not invoke [§1349]**

The defense of illegality is *not* available to third persons who are not parties to the illegal transaction. For example, absent a statute, a bank may not refuse to pay its depositor on the ground that depositor had obtained the deposited funds illegally.

3. **"Exceptions" to Defense of Illegality—Restitution Allowed [§1350]**

These are the cases where the performance of the contract or transaction involved *does* violate some statute or public policy, but the interest in punishing the violation is *outweighed* by the interest in preventing unjust enrichment. Accordingly, while the contract itself is not enforceable in most cases, restitutionary relief is allowed.

a. Plaintiff not "in pari delicto" [§1351]

If one party to the illegal contract or transaction is not "equally at fault" with the other, and *no serious crime* is involved, the relatively innocent party may be entitled to relief. The following cases illustrate application of this doctrine.

(1) Plaintiff member of statutorily protected class [§1352]

If the statute that has been violated is for the special *protection of the party seeking relief,* or for the public in general, recovery is permitted. [**Truitt v. Miller,** *supra,* §1345; **Capo v. Century Life Insurance Co.,** 610 P.2d 1202 (N.M. 1980)]

---

e.g. Example: Corporate securities acts ("blue sky" laws) are for the protection of the purchaser; "the sale only is penalized, not the purchaser." Hence, a sale made in violation of the disclosure or registration requirements is unenforceable *against* the purchaser, but she can obtain restitutionary relief for any monies paid over to the corporation-issuer.

(a) Other protective acts

Examples of the other protective acts include rent ceiling ordinances (tenant can recover excessive rent paid) and statutes prohibiting lotteries (ticket buyer can recover purchase price). In one case, the holder of the winning lottery ticket was allowed to collect the lottery prize (*i.e.,* to *enforce* the illegal contract). [**Hardy v. St. Mathew's Community Center,** 240 S.W.2d 95 (Ky. 1951)]

(2) Ignorance or mistake [§1353]

If the plaintiff's *justifiable* ignorance or mistake of the facts makes the bargain illegal, she can avoid the defense and enforce the contract, or at least claim restitution. For example, an actress may recover for her services if it is shown that she was unaware that the theater was unlicensed and hence that the performance was in violation of statute. [**Goldberg v. Sanglier,** 639 P.2d 1347 (Wash. 1982)—even an unreasonable belief in the legality of a transaction is sufficient to find a party not in pari delicto]

(3) Coercion [§1354]

Likewise, where the plaintiff was subjected to coercion, duress, or undue influence to secure participation in the illegal transaction, she is not in pari delicto and is entitled at least to restitutionary relief.

(a) Note

Restitution is generally permitted in favor of a person coerced into an illegal transaction by the other party—*e.g.,* a debtor enters into a composition agreement (a type of debt relief agreement) with creditors, but one creditor refuses to cooperate unless a secret payment is made to him in violation of bankruptcy laws. Because of the creditor's duress, the debtor may recover. [**Batchedler & Lincoln Co. v. Whitmore,** 122 F. 355 (1st Cir. 1903)]

(b) Distinguish

An illegal payment to stifle a threatened criminal prosecution is generally *not* recoverable as long as the accusation of crime was made in good faith. [**Ellis v. Peoples National Bank of Manassas,** 186 S.E. 9 (Va. 1936); *and see supra,* §§946-949]

1) Note

In theory, the guilt or innocence of the payor as to the alleged crime is irrelevant because the payment is illegal in either event; yet the point is important in determining whether the payee is a deliberate extortionist in making the accusation.

2) Exception

There may be exceptions.

> **Example:** Where imprisonment in a Mexican jail coerced the execution of a document admitting an embezzlement and promising restitution, the court held the contract was void and constituted the offense of compounding. [**Lewkowiez v. El Paso Apparel Corp.,** 625 S.W.2d 301 (Tex. 1982)]

(4) Fraud [§1355]

The plaintiff is not in pari delicto where she was induced by fraud to enter into the illegal transaction.

> **Example:** Restitution is allowed where the defendant misleads the plaintiff into believing the transaction is not illegal. [**American Mutual Life Insurance Co. v. Bertram,** 70 N.E. 258 (Ind. 1904)—insurer misrepresented that applicant had insurable interest]

> **Example:** Restitution is also usually allowed if the defendant induces the plaintiff to enter into an illegal transaction and then defrauds him. [**Grim v. Chestwood,** 257 P.2d 1049 (Okla. 1953)—marked cards in poker game; **Bradley v. Doherty,** 57 Cal. App. 3d 963 (1976)—gambling game controlled by defendants by means of hidden electronic, magnetic, and sonic devices]

> **Compare:** The cases are divided as to whether the plaintiff, who is misled into a con game believing he is cheating someone else and is

himself cheated, may have restitution. [**Steward v. Wright,** 147 F. 321 (8th Cir. 1906)—recovery allowed in case concerning notorious "Buckfoot Gang," who induced suckers to bet on fake foot races under carefully nurtured impression that they were in on a fraudulent scheme to win; *but see* **Abbe v. Marr,** 14 Cal. 210 (1859)—contra]

cf. **Compare—securities law:** Similar cases have arisen in the securities law field. For example, it is illegal for a "tippee" of inside information to profit from such information by buying or selling stock before the information is released to the public. It is also illegal to induce the sale or purchase of stock by giving out misleading information. The situation has frequently arisen where a "tippee" has been deliberately induced to buy stock by being fed false inside information. When the purchaser sues the seller for fraud, the defense is that the act of purchasing the stock was itself illegal. [**Bateman Eichler, Hill Richards, Inc. v. Berner,** 472 U.S. 299 (1985)—parties were not in pari delicto; "tippee" could recover against broker who misrepresented that information provided was material nonpublic information where denial of relief would frustrate the purpose of the Security Act, *and see* **Dahl v. Pinter,** 787 F.2d 985 (5th Cir. 1980)—buyer who knew the securities were unregistered could recover]

(5) Government "stings" [§1356]

If a government law enforcement agency stages a "sting" operation (*e.g.*, by furnishing money to agents to purchase drugs), the government agency is not precluded from recovering the money by the doctrine of in pari delicto. [*See* **Licking County v. Maharg,** 575 N.E.2d 529 (Ohio 1990)]

b. "Locus poenitentiae"—partially executed illegal transactions [§1357]

Even though parties are in pari delicto, restitution will be permitted if the plaintiff backs out of the bargain before the illegal part has been accomplished. *Rationale*: By encouraging early repentance, a socially damaging act may be prevented.

 Example: Aldous gives money to stakeholder pursuant to an illegal bet with Barrimore. Aldous may have restitution from the stakeholder *before* the outcome of the event. [**Cox v. Lee,** 530 S.W.2d 273 (Mo. 1976)]

(1) Note

Some cases hold that the bettor can recover even *after* the event. [**Lewy v. Crawford,** 23 S.W. 1041 (Tex. 1893)] However, where *stakeholding* of illegal wagers is *itself illegal,* the unlawful transaction is complete and the bettor cannot recover. [8 A.L.R.2d 307]

(2) Limitation—no serious crime [§1358]

Most cases limit the locus poenitentiae exception to cases where the illegality does *not* involve serious moral turpitude (or those that are merely malum prohibitum, rather than malum in se). [Rest. Contracts §605]

 Example: Anton pays Balzak to murder Cato and Donatello. Balzak murders Cato but Anton repents before Donatello is killed. Anton cannot obtain restitution of any part of the money. [*See* **Kearley v. Thompson,** [1890] 24 Q.B.D. 742]

 Example: Likewise, a bribe paid to a public official is *not* recoverable even prior to any illegal act by the public official.

---

c. Public policy exception [§1359]

An illegal bargain may be rescinded by either party if a condition contrary to public policy would otherwise *continue* to exist. *Rationale*: This exception has nothing to do with unjust enrichment, but is recognized solely to *implement* public policy.

 Example: Where a statute prohibits a corporation from an illegal diminution of outstanding capital stock by the purchase of its own shares, either the shareholder-seller *or* the corporation-buyer may set aside the transaction. [**Duddy-Robinson Co. v. Taylor,** 242 P. 21 (Wash. 1926)]

---

4. Restitution of Illegal Gains as Among Participants—"Dividing the Spoils"

a. As among partners in the illegal enterprise [§1360]

The general rule is that a court will *not* decree the division of spoils of an illegal joint venture among the parties thereto. [**Chateau v. Singla,** 114 Cal. 91 (1986); **Morelli v. Ehsan,** 756 P.2d 129 (Wash. 1988)—accounting denied even though neither party knew that agreement was illegal] Moreover, where a contract is unenforceable because it is illegal, the prevailing party (*i.e.,* the party successfully asserting the illegality defense) cannot recover attorneys' fees even though the illegal contract so provides. [**Bovard v. American Horse Enterprises,** 201 Cal. App. 3d 832 (1988)]

(1) Exception—regular business partners [§1361]

However, where there is a *regular business partnership* handling a variety of transactions, the defense of illegality is not available to prevent an accounting when the alleged illegal transaction is otherwise completed and the violation of the law only incidental (*e.g.,* lack of license). [**Norwood v. Judd,** 93 Cal. App. 2d 276 (1949)]

(2) Exception—no innocent victims [§1362]

And where there is no real "division of spoils" involved (no gains derived from innocent third parties), courts may fashion remedies to reach an equitable result, and at the same time not encourage violation of the law.

Example: Defendant is a veteran entitled to a federal housing loan; his brother-in-law, Plaintiff, is a nonveteran. To evade the law, a house is bought and the loan obtained in Defendant's name, but Plaintiff makes the payments and occupies the house for 12 years. Defendant then repudiates and claims title. Plaintiff sues for a declaration of a resulting trust, which would in effect consummate the illegal transaction. A lower court ruling against Plaintiff on ground of illegality was reversed on appeal, but Plaintiff's remedy was limited to an *equitable lien* against the property for all outlays, including interest, taxes, and insurance; at the same time, he was denied title to the property, which had increased in value. [*See* **Hainey v. Narigon,** 247 Cal. App. 2d 528 (1966)]

Example: Son negotiated a G.I. loan to purchase a home for his mother using her money. All payments on the loan were made by the mother, but the son refused to transfer title to her. *Held:* A resulting trust should be imposed in favor of the mother where the son is the guilty party with the greatest fault. [**Johnson v. Johnson,** 192 Cal. App. 3d 551 (1987)]

b. **As between principals and agents [§1363]**

The general rule is that an agent who merely receives proceeds from an illegal transaction on behalf of the principal must account to the principal. The principal's illegality is no defense to the agent's duty to account. *Rationale:* Fiduciary obligations outweigh policy reasons against remedies for illegal transactions; moreover, the agent is a third person who cannot assert illegality as a defense.

(1) **Limitation [§1364]**

If the agent *participates actively* in carrying on the illegal transaction, the principal and agent are treated as *coparticipants* and the principal *cannot* compel an accounting of proceeds.

Example: Lemon runs an illegal lottery and hires Grosskopf to sell tickets. Grosskopf sells tickets and receives the proceeds of ticket sales from other agents. Grosskopf can be compelled to account for the latter proceeds (Grosskopf is merely a conduit), but cannot be compelled to account for proceeds of tickets he himself sold (Grosskopf is an active participant). [**Lemon v. Grosskopf,** 99 Am. Dec. 58 (Wis. 1868)]

Review Questions
and Answers

Review Questions

1. Belinda, a swimsuit model, is advised by her long-time friend and physician, Doc, that she should undergo an operation for ulcers. Before she will consent to the operation, Belinda has Doc sign an agreement warranting that she will suffer no permanent scars from the surgery. Several months after the operation, Belinda consults two other doctors, who inform her that the scar on her stomach is permanent. Belinda loses her modeling job and brings an action against Doc for her lost wages.

    a. Assume that there is no evidence that Doc performed the operation negligently. Would Belinda nevertheless be better off suing Doc on a tort theory because of the rule of **Hadley v. Baxendale**? _____

    b. Assume Doc proves that Belinda could have retained her job if she had been willing to model one-piece swimsuits, but that she insisted on modeling only bikinis and so was discharged. If Belinda has been unable to find another job, may she recover the full amount of the wages she has lost as a result of being fired? _____

    c. Assume that Belinda sues on the basis that Doc breached his contractual warranty to her. If Belinda proves that Doc intentionally failed to take any precautions to avoid causing her a permanent scar, may she recover punitive damages? _____

2. Without permission, Dumper dumps several tons of garbage on Landowner's residential property.

    a. If Landowner brings an action against Dumper for trespass, must Landowner state in his complaint that he is seeking damages measured by the rental value of the property affected? _____

    b. Assume that the garbage dumped on the property immediately draws a pack of rats, and that one of the rats bites Landowner. If Landowner seeks to recover the cost of undergoing a series of rabies shots in his action against Dumper for trespass, must he state in his complaint that he is claiming such damages? _____

3. Ted, a thief, stole Ellen's car and fraudulently sold it to Una, an unknowing purchaser for value. Ellen found the car in Una's driveway and retook possession. Una then brought a suit against Ellen for possession, which suit Ellen successfully defended.

a. If Ellen now sues Ted for damages, may she recover the attorneys' fees she incurred in defending the suit brought by Una?   _____

b. In her action against Ted, must Ellen "specially plead" the attorneys' fees she paid in defending the suit brought by Una?   _____

4. While constructing a stone wall, Diego negligently piles large rocks at the top of a hill overlooking Pedro's property. The rocks break loose and roll down the hill, flattening a bed of Pedro's roses and two young maple trees before coming to rest in the living room of Pedro's residence. May Pedro sue in equity to compel Diego to repair the damage?   _____

5. Professor Whimsey tells her class, "As long as an equity court has jurisdiction over the subject matter and the person of defendant, the court's decree cannot be held void for lack of jurisdiction." Is she correct?   _____

6. Sue is indicted in State Silver on a charge of prostitution. She claims that key evidence was obtained against her in violation of her federal constitutional rights. Should a federal court enjoin Sue's trial to determine the validity of her claim?   _____

7. State Purple enacts a statute making certain business practices illegal. Businessman is fearful of being prosecuted by the state for violation of this new law because he regularly engages in the business practices now prohibited. If Businessman claims that the statute violates his constitutional rights, is any relief available to him in the federal courts?   _____

8. Joe constructed a shed, part of which extended onto the property of the adjacent landowner, Sam. Sam called Joe several times a week to ask Joe to remove the shed, but Sam did not file suit in hopes that he could settle the matter amicably. After a year, Sam gave up protesting and filed suit for removal of the encroaching shed. May Joe successfully block Sam's suit by asserting the defense of laches?   _____

9. Penny plans to have a large reception in her backyard following her daughter's wedding. Nancy, a neighbor who hates Penny intensely, calls Penny and threatens to crash the reception. Penny obtains a court decree enjoining Nancy from coming onto Penny's property on the day of the wedding.

a. If Nancy disobeys the court order and attends the reception, may she be imprisoned for contempt?   _____

b. Assume that shortly before the reception, Nancy tells her son, Stan, about the injunction, to which he replies, "Don't worry Mom, I'll take care of everything." If Stan thereafter "crashes" the reception, may he be held in contempt for disobeying the injunction against Nancy?   _____

10. Samuel, a resident of South Carolina, contracts with Peter, a resident of Pennsylvania, to sell Peter some land Samuel owns in Hawaii. The parties enter into the

contract in South Carolina. Before the time set for performance, Samuel backs out of the deal.

    a.   If Peter brings suit against Samuel in Hawaii, may Peter obtain specific performance of the land sale contract?   _____

    b.   If Peter brings suit against Samuel in South Carolina, may Peter obtain specific performance of the land sale contract?   _____

    c.   If Peter brings suit against Samuel in Pennsylvania, can Peter obtain specific performance of the land sale contract?   _____

    d.   Assuming that Peter brings suit in South Carolina for a decree of specific performance, would he be better off to get (A) a decree ordering Samuel to convey the land, or (B) a decree by which the court itself directly conveys the land to Peter?   _____

11.   Pia is the owner of an AKC registered champion dachshund, frequently named best in show. Daphne stole the dog from Pia's kennels, took it to Canada, and falsified the dog's papers. Daphne then entered it in a provincial championship contest where it won the first prize of $50,000. Daphne is now using the dog for breeding purposes. Upon Daphne's return to the United States to buy more dogs for her kennels, she is served with process in an action brought by Pia.

    a.   If the action is for a mandatory injunction ordering Daphne to return the dog, plus an accounting for the prize money and stud fees, may a court having equity powers properly enter such a decree?   _____

    b.   Assuming the court actually entered the foregoing decree, could it be enforced by contempt?   _____

    c.   Could the decree be enforced by the appointment of a receiver to go to Canada to return the animal?   _____

12.   Professor Whimsey tells her class, "Temporary restraining orders and interlocutory injunctions are intended to preserve the rights of the complainant and so may be issued *ex parte* in emergency situations." Is she correct?   _____

13.   Dean obtains a promissory note from Pam by fraudulent means. Dean refuses to return the note to Pam and she is afraid that if Dean negotiates the note to a holder in due course she might be held liable thereon. Can Pam obtain a decree requiring Dean to surrender the note for cancellation?   _____

14.   Tenant leases pastureland from Landlord for a five-year period. After four years, Tenant begins terracing the land in order to plant crops. The land is ideally suited for such use if graded and terraced, and will be much more valuable than if left as pastureland. Is Landlord liable to Tenant in a restitutionary action for the unjust enrichment resulting from the enhancement in the value of the land?   _____

15. Deanna, a claims agent for an insurance company, embezzles $5,000 from her employer, Paul, and uses it to pay her doctor bills. Which of the following remedies, if any, would Paul have against Deanna?

(A) Conversion.

(B) Money had and received.

(C) Constructive trust.

(D) Equitable lien.

16. Same facts as in the previous question. In a suit by Paul against the doctor to whom the money was paid, to which of the following remedies, if any, would Paul be entitled?

(A) Replevin.

(B) Money had and received.

(C) Some other remedy.

(D) No remedy at all.

17. Anna, a claims agent for an insurance company, embezzles $5,000 from her employer, Pablo, and uses it to pay all premiums on a $100,000 life insurance policy naming her son, age 10, as beneficiary. She dies the next day. Which, if any, of the following statements is true?

(A) Pablo may have a constructive trust on the entire proceeds ($100,000) from the policy.

(B) Pablo may sue in quasi-contract for the entire $100,000.

(C) Pablo may have an equitable lien imposed on the entire proceeds.

(D) Pablo has no remedy to recover any of the proceeds because the beneficiary of the policy is innocent of any wrongdoing.

18. Dawn embezzles $5,000 from her employer, Phipps, and uses it to add a front porch to her home. Which, if any, of the following statements is true?

(A) Phipps may recover $5,000 in a quasi-contract action.

(B) Phipps may have a constructive trust imposed on the house.

(C) Phipps may have an equitable lien imposed on the house for $5,000.

19. Enya embezzles $5,000 from her employer, Plebe, and deposits it in her personal account, which at that time has a balance of $10,000. Enya writes a check for

$7,500 on the account to pay off the mortgage on her house and another check for $5,000 for a trip to Europe, leaving $2,500 in the account. Which, if any, of the following statements is correct?

(A) Plebe is entitled to have a constructive trust imposed on the house.

(B) Plebe is entitled to subrogation of the mortgagee's claim against the house.

(C) Plebe can trace the money used to finance the trip to Europe and recover $5,000 in a quasi-contract action from the travel agent who handled the transaction.

(D) Plebe can have an equitable lien imposed on the balance in the account.

(E) Plebe can have a constructive trust imposed on the balance in the account.

20. Jeff stole an expensive sports car and forged the title papers. He then borrowed $5,000 from Mary, giving a lien on the car as security. Jeff then sold the car to Phil for $10,000. Phil paid $5,000 to Jeff and $5,000 to Mary to discharge the lien on the car.

a. May the owner replevy the car from Phil without compensation for the money expended by Phil?

b. If the owner recovers possession of the car, may Phil maintain a quasi-contractual action for $10,000 had and received against Jeff?

21. Pia is the owner of an AKC registered champion dachshund, frequently named best in show. Daphne stole the dog from Pia's kennels, took it to Canada and falsified the dog's papers. Daphne then entered it in a provincial championship contest where it won the first prize of $50,000. Daphne is now using the dog for breeding purposes. Upon Daphne's return to the United States to buy more dogs for her kennels, she is served with process in an action for conversion brought by Pia. Which of the following would be the proper measure of recovery?

(A) Value of the dog at the time of conversion plus interest.

(B) Value of the dog at the time of trial plus the prize money and stud fees.

22. While constructing a pipeline, Dent negligently piled pipes at the top of a hill overlooking Payton's farm. The pipes broke loose and rolled down the hill flattening a stand of sweet corn, 10 mature apple trees, and a hen house before coming to rest in the living room of Payton's farmhouse.

a. Can Payton recover damages measured by the diminution in the value of his farm?

b. Can Payton recover damages measured by cumulating the value of the destroyed items separately from the land itself?

c. Can Payton recover the cost of repairs to his home, plus the loss of use, even though these exceed the diminution in value of the farm? _____

d. If Payton values the destroyed hen house separately, which of the following is the common way of determining value? _____

    (A) Reproduction cost less physical depreciation.

    (B) Payton's prospective profits from the poultry business for the next 10 years, discounted to present value.

e. If Payton values the destroyed apple trees separately, is the common way of determining value loss of profits from the prospective yield of the trees for the rest of their effective productive life? _____

f. If Payton values the crops separately from the land, would he be denied damages because an immature crop has no value? _____

g. Can Payton sue in equity to compel Dent to repair the damage to the farm? _____

23. Tenant leases pastureland from Landlord for a five-year period. After four years, Tenant begins terracing the land in order to plant crops. The land is ideally suited for such use if graded and terraced, and will be much more valuable than if left as pastureland.

a. May Landlord recover damages from Tenant in an action for waste? _____

b. May Landlord obtain an injunction against further grading? _____

24. Phyllis and David are next door neighbors in State Terra. They also own adjacent beach property in State Aqua. David orders a contractor to put up a beach cabin on his property in State Aqua. David's instructions as to the location of his property are misinterpreted by the contractor and the contractor puts the cabin on Phyllis's lot by mistake. David occupies the cabin during vacations.

a. In an action filed in State Aqua, may Phyllis recover possession of the beach cabin? _____

b. May Phyllis bring a quasi-contract action in State Terra for the value of David's use of the land in State Aqua? _____

25. Same facts as in previous question. When Phyllis learns of the error regarding the beach cabin, she immediately orders a survey of the boundary between her house and that of David in State Terra. She discovers that for the past 15 years David's house has encroached five feet over the boundary line.

a. At common law, may David bring a restitutionary action to recover the value of the improvements mistakenly placed on Phyllis's land? _____

b.   Assume that Phyllis sues for damages for the encroachment of the house on her property in State Terra. Will Phyllis be denied damages if the statute of limitations has run on all Phyllis's causes of action? (For purposes of this question, no issue of adverse possession is considered to exist.)   _____

c.   Is Phyllis entitled to a mandatory injunction ordering David to remove the encroachment?   _____

26.   Aldo owns a large tract of desert land mainly valuable for its gypsum deposits. Dupert mistakenly claims title, enters onto the property, and commences mining operations. One hundred thousand tons of gypsum are removed prior to Aldo's discovery of the trespass. Seventy-five thousand tons have been sold, and the other 25,000 tons are piled up at the mine awaiting shipment.

a.   If Aldo seeks a preliminary injunction against further mining by Dubert, will a claim of title by Dubert result in a dismissal of the complaint?   _____

b.   Assuming that Aldo establishes title to the property, will a permanent injunction be issued prohibiting further mining by Dubert?   _____

c.   Assuming clear title in Aldo, will an injunction be issued against Dubert's shipping any of the 25,000 tons of gypsum already extracted?   _____

d.   Is Dubert liable in quasi-contract for the gypsum extracted even if he is not enriched?   _____

27.   Same facts as in previous question. Assume that Aldo brings an action for damages for the taking of the 75,000 tons of gypsum that were sold. It is proved that the 75,000 tons were sold for $8 per ton at the nearest market; the cost of transportation from the mine to the market was $4 per ton; the expenses of extraction were $3 per ton; and the going rate for permission or a license to mine gypsum is 50 cents per ton.

a.   Assuming that Dubert was innocent and Aldo was not able to exploit the gypsum deposit himself, how much (per ton) should Aldo recover?   _____

b.   Assuming that Dubert was innocent, but that Aldo was in the business of mining gypsum, how much should Dubert recover?   _____

c.   Assuming that Dubert acted willfully, and that Aldo is in the business of mining, how much should Aldo recover?   _____

28.   Tyson is a long-established slaughterhouse doing an annual business of $10 million net, employing 100 people, and providing the principal tax base of a sparsely settled rural county which has never had zoning controls. Purdue, finding the climate of this area ideal and the land prices low (for obvious reasons), constructed a convalescent home one-quarter mile to the east of Tyson. The home was soon fully occupied

by aged and infirm individuals, but it quickly became apparent that during warm days with westerly breezes, the place was virtually untenantable. Those patients who could afford to, moved, but others who were unable to move became nauseated or even more seriously ill on the intermittent occasions when such conditions occurred. Purdue loses money when occupancy of the home falls below 70% of capacity. Purdue brings an action for damages against Tyson.

a. May Purdue recover for lost profits and for the discomfort of the patients up to the time the action is filed?

b. May Purdue recover damages measured by the diminution in the value of the premises?

c. In his action for damages will Purdue's recovery be reduced if he fails to install air conditioning filtration equipment that would purify the air and eliminate the odors?

29. Same facts as in previous question. If Purdue sues for an injunction, which, if any, of the following statements is true?

(A) A judgment for damages entered in favor of Purdue in part b. of question 28., above, would bar a subsequent suit for an injunction by Purdue.

(B) Purdue cannot sue for an injunction because he has moved to the nuisance and is therefore guilty of unclean hands.

(C) In some jurisdictions, Purdue is entitled to a decree ordering the slaughterhouse to close if the offensive odors are not completely eliminated.

(D) In some jurisdictions, Purdue is entitled to a decree ordering the slaughterhouse to install the best anti-pollution devices available at reasonable cost, although this will not completely eliminate the nuisance.

(E) In some jurisdictions, Purdue is not entitled to a decree, but will be allowed permanent damages in lieu thereof, because of the economic hardship on Purdue and the difficulty the court would have in continuously supervising the decree.

(F) In some jurisdictions, Purdue is entitled to a decree, but only on condition that he pay the costs of removing the slaughterhouse to a new location.

30. A State Silver statute makes it a crime for anyone to practice law in State Silver without meeting certain minimum standards of education and training. The statute imposes a fine for violation of these requirements. Lucas, a lawyer licensed to practice in State Teal, but not in State Silver, sets up an office in State Silver and begins to practice law. May a State Silver court enjoin Lucas from practicing law in State Silver?

31. Cheryl, a chanteuse, is employed to perform nightly on stage at Pop's Bamboo Room on the Las Vegas strip. She immediately becomes the greatest show attraction on the strip. Her contract with Pop is for an exclusive engagement for six months at $5,000 per week. Don, the owner of a nearby nightclub whose star entertainer becomes ill, offers Cheryl $10,000 per week to perform at his nightclub under a one-year contract. Cheryl accepts. Almost at once, Don's profits double, while Pop's business declines drastically.

    a. In an action against Don, is Pop entitled to damages measured by the expense of hiring another chanteuse? _____

    b. May Pop obtain an injunction against Don's continuing to employ Cheryl? _____

    c. May Pop sue for the profits made by Don attributable to the employment of Cheryl by Don? _____

32. Testator is an elderly wealthy man whose sole heir is his nephew, Ned. Jack, an acquaintance of Testator, falsely tells him that Ned has been killed in an auto accident. Testator is then induced by Jack to make a will naming Jack as beneficiary. Testator dies soon thereafter. In a suit by Ned, will the court impose a constructive trust on the estate of Testator in favor of Ned? _____

33. An aircraft manufacturing corporation paid $250,000 to the purchasing agent of Skyway Airlines to secure a contract for the sale of an expensive cargo plane. However, the actual contract price obtained from Skyway was exactly the same as that which the corporation received from sales of the same plane to other airlines where no such payments were made. May Skyway recover the $250,000 from its agent even if it has sustained no pecuniary loss? _____

34. Proff is the chair of the research faculty of Xian Institute of Technology. As part of his research on pollution control, he discovers a chemical additive which, when added to gas, eliminates carbon monoxide emissions from auto engines. He discloses the formula in confidence to Dupont, an engine manufacturer, who is so impressed that he offers Proff $500,000 for use of the formula. Proff declines the offer, but Dupont nevertheless makes use of the formula and begins an advertising campaign using Proff's name and picture in connection with the sale of the additive. The use of Proff's name and picture in this way brings him into disrepute in the academic community, and causes Proff to disclose the formula and dedicate it to the public without charge. May Proff obtain an injunction against Dupont's further use of the additive in his business? _____

35. Dexta, a recording company, produced a series of CDs reproducing the music of the "swing" era of the 1940s. A modern orchestra was hired to burn CDs utilizing the same musical arrangements (uncopyrighted) made popular by the original bands. Tommy, one of the band leaders of great renown during the "swing" era, files suit claiming that Dexta has invaded his privacy, has made unauthorized use of his name, has damaged his reputation, and is guilty of unfair competition.

a. Can Tommy recover damages for injury to his professional reputation because of the copying of his arrangements? _____

b. May Tommy obtain an injunction against the use of his arrangements? _____

c. May Tommy obtain an injunction against the use of his name in conjunction with the sale of the records? _____

36. Proff is the chair of the research faculty of Xian Institute of Technology. As part of his research on pollution control, he discovered a chemical additive which, when added to gas, eliminates carbon monoxide emissions from auto engines. He disclosed the formula in confidence to Dupont, an engine manufacturer, who was so impressed that he offered Proff $500,000 for use of the formula. Proff declined the offer, but Dupont nevertheless made use of the formula and began an advertising campaign using Proff's name and picture in connection with the sale of the additive. A statute of the jurisdiction provides that the use of a name or picture of another for purposes of advertisement or trade without written authorization is a misdemeanor punishable by fine or imprisonment. The use of Proff's name and picture in this way has brought him into disrepute in the academic community because such conduct by a faculty member is contrary to the regulations of the Institute. The embarrassment has led Proff to disclose the formula and dedicate it to the public without charge.

a. Does Proff have the remedy of damages for libel as the result of Dupont's conduct? _____

b. May Proff obtain an injunction against Dupont's further use of his name and likeness in such a way as to defame him? _____

c. In an action at law, may Proff join a claim for defamation and invasion of privacy and recover damages for each? _____

d. May Proff recover damages in an action based on invasion of his privacy resulting from the commercial exploitation of his name and picture? _____

e. May Proff obtain an injunction against further use of his name or likeness for purposes of advertising or trade? _____

37. Neil, a partner in a successful photography studio, was severely hurt when the automobile in which he was riding was negligently struck by the defendant. Neil was hospitalized for six months with multiple head injuries which have resulted in an inability to focus his eyes; thus, he cannot continue as a photographer. Otherwise Neil has fully recovered physically, and his medical insurance has paid most of his medical and hospital expenses.

a. May Neil recover the cost of hiring someone to do his work in the photography business while he was in the hospital? _____

b. May Neil recover damages for his inability to earn his living as a photographer for the rest of his life? _____

c. Is Neil entitled to recover a lump sum for the future loss of enjoyment of life resulting from his impaired vision, discounted to its present value? _____

d. May Neil recover for his medical expenses even though they were mostly paid for by insurance? _____

38. April, a bright and lively six-year-old girl, was killed when the automobile in which she was riding was negligently struck by the defendant. A wrongful death action was filed by April's widowed mother in State Blue, where the wrongful death statute provides that damages are to be awarded in accordance with the pecuniary loss to the decedent's survivors.

a. May the mother recover damages even though the death of the child relieves her of an economic burden? _____

b. May the mother recover damages for the loss of the child's society, comfort, and protection? _____

c. May the mother recover for the loss of monetary support that the child would have furnished her during the child's minority and even afterward? _____

d. May the mother recover as an economic loss the "investment" the child represented, less the cost of rearing? _____

e. May the mother recover funeral expenses incurred? _____

f. May the mother recover punitive damages for the death of the child? _____

39. Pia purchased and received the deed to an inn at a ski resort area after receiving assurances from the seller (Darby) that the inn's septic tank had been approved by the local authorities. A local syndicate had attempted to buy the inn at the same price as Pia paid but had been turned down. Pia took possession during the summer season, added 10 rooms to the inn's capacity, and paid all taxes and insurance on the premises. Six months after the deed was delivered and just before the first snow, Pia was advised by the county health officer that the septic tank system was not in compliance with regulations and that Pia would not be permitted to operate until modifications were made. The cost of bringing the system up to standard would be $40,000, and could not be completed until the ground thawed in the spring. The local syndicate has again offered to buy the property from Pia "as is" at the original purchase price plus cost of improvements.

a. Assume that after discovering the deceit, Pia decides that the best solution is to resell the inn to the local syndicate and sue Darby for damages. Pia files the action for deceit, but the syndicate withdraws its offer. Can Pia now rescind the purchase? _____

b. Assume that after discovery of the deceit, Pia gives notice of rescission of the purchase which Darby rejects. Pia initiates a suit to rescind. Shortly thereafter, the local syndicate ups its offer. May Pia change plans and amend the complaint to state a cause of action for damages? _____

40. Same facts as in the previous question except assume that Darby was never notified that the septic system of the inn had not received local approval and that his representations to that effect were honest.

   a. Does Pia have a common law remedy of damages against Darby? _____

   b. Does Pia have the remedy of a suit to rescind the transaction? _____

41. Pia purchased and received the deed to an inn at a ski resort area. The purchase price was $175,000: $50,000 down and a note for the balance secured by a deed of trust. Payments of the principal and interest on the note were to be amortized over a 20-year period. At the time of purchase, the seller (Darby) represented that the septic system had been approved by the local authorities. Pia took possession during the summer season and added 10 rooms to the inn's capacity, at a cost of $60,000, in preparation for the ski season. Pia paid all taxes and insurance on the premises totaling $3,500. Six months after the deed was delivered and just before the first snow, Pia was advised by the county health officer that the septic tank system was not in compliance with regulations and that Pia would not be permitted to operate until modifications were made. The cost of bringing the system up to standard would be $40,000, and could not be completed until the ground thawed in the spring.

   a. In an action for damages for deceit, what would Pia's *general* damages be in a jurisdiction following the benefit-of-the-bargain rule? _____

   b. In addition to any general damages, may Pia recover as consequential damages the loss of profits from the business for the ski season? _____

   c. If Pia elects to rescind the conveyance, which, if any, of the following may Pia recover? _____

      (A) Payments on the purchase price with interest.

      (B) Cost of improvements.

      (C) Taxes and insurance.

      (D) Lost profits for the season.

   d. If Pia elects to rescind the sale because of Darby's deceit, would Darby be permitted to set off against any recovery by Pia the rental value of the premises during the time Pia occupied them? _____

42. Max ran a large motel in Vale City. Unknown to Max, Lou, a former owner of the motel, had often failed to pay the utility bills. Knowing that Max could not stay in business without utility service, the Vale City Utility Company threatened to cut off power to the motel unless Max paid Lou's bill. Can Max get restitution of the amounts paid to cover Lou's bills?   _____

43. Boyer agrees to purchase a topaz ring from Sharpie for $200. In paying Sharpie, Boyer counts out three bills which he believes are one $100 bill and two $50 bills. In fact, all three bills are $100s.

    a. Upon discovery of his mistake, can Boyer recover the amount by which he overpaid Sharpie?   _____

    b. If it later turns out that the ring Boyer purchased was a diamond worth $1,000, whereas both parties had believed it was a topaz ring at the time of the sale, can Sharpie rescind the contract and recover the ring?   _____

44. Builder suffered injuries resulting from the collapse of a defective scaffold manufactured by Manufacturer. Manufacturer conceded liability and offered settlement. Builder's doctor took X-rays that indicated no fractures and, thus, Builder and Manufacturer entered into a settlement for payment of medical bills plus $500. Builder signed a document releasing Manufacturer from further liability for damages, both known and unknown, arising out of the accident. Builder soon developed paralysis which was traced to a fracture of the spinal column. Further investigation showed that the X-ray plates that Builder's doctor used were defective and failed to show the fracture.

    a. Is Builder prevented from rescinding the release on the ground that he assumed the risk of unknown injuries?   _____

    b. Can Builder rescind the release on the ground of a basic mistake outside the area of compromise?   _____

    c. May Builder sue for reformation of the release to restate the amount of damages in line with those actually sustained?   _____

    d. May Builder not bother with rescission or reformation of the release but simply go ahead and bring an action for damages for personal injuries?   _____

45. Jeff stole an expensive sports car and forged the title papers. He then borrowed $5,000 from Mary, giving a lien on the car as security. Jeff then sold the car to Lori for $10,000. Lori paid $5,000 to Jeff and $5,000 to Mary to discharge the lien on the car. Upon discovery that the car was stolen, is Lori entitled to restitution from Mary for the $5,000 paid to discharge Mary's lien on the car because this is money paid under mistake?   _____

46. Alex owned two contiguous lots, #1 and #2. His residence is on lot #1. He orally agreed to sell the entire property to Betty for $50,000. The attorney who drew

up the deed mistakenly omitted lot #2 from the description. Both parties relied on the attorney's assurance that the deed was in proper form. Betty took possession of the entire property and completed extensive landscaping and improvements. When the next tax bills were delivered, Betty asked Alex to correct the deed to include lot #2, but Alex refused and insisted that the entire transaction be canceled. Alex took this position because land values had become greatly inflated during the previous year.

    a.   May Alex rescind the transaction because of the mutual mistake in the deed?   _____

    b.   In a suit for reformation of the deed, will Betty be denied relief because she negligently failed to read the deed in which she was grantee?   _____

    c.   In a suit by Betty for reformation of the deed, may Alex successfully defend by pleading the Statute of Frauds?   _____

47.   Donna orally promises Bert that she will give him $10,000 as a Christmas present. Later, Donna gives Bert a promissory note promising to pay him $5,000 on Christmas Day as his present. Can Bert get reformation of the promissory note to increase the amount to the $10,000 originally promised?   _____

48.   Vendor contracted to sell Blackacre to Purchaser, who planned to use it as an industrial plant. After the contract was signed, but prior to the date set for closing, the land was unforeseeably rezoned for residential use only.

    a.   May Vendor obtain a decree for specific performance of the land sale contract?   _____

    b.   May Vendor obtain damages in an action at law against Purchaser?   _____

49.   On January 1, Vendor and Purchaser agree that on June 1, Vendor shall convey 100 acres of land to Purchaser and Purchaser shall pay $10,000. On May 1, Vendor transfers title to BFP, a bona fide purchaser. If Purchaser tenders the $10,000 to BFP on June 1, but BFP refuses to convey title, may Purchaser obtain a decree of specific performance against BFP?   _____

50.   Vendor and Purchaser entered into a contract for the sale of Vendor's house and lot to Purchaser for $250,000. The contract was executed on March 1, 2003, and provided for a down payment of $10,000 (receipt of which was acknowledged by Vendor) and for closing upon payment of the balance and delivery of the deed on July 1, 2003. It was agreed that Vendor was to remain in possession of the house until the closing date. On May 22, 2003, an earthquake totally destroyed the house, which was uninsured against this risk. On June 25, 2003, Purchaser died, leaving a will designating Hubert as devisee of his realty, Lana as legatee of his personalty, and Xian as executor of his estate. On July 1, 2003, Vendor tendered a good deed to the property to Hubert, Lana, and Xian and demanded

payment of the balance of the purchase price. Hubert, Lana, and Xian not only refused to proceed with the contract, but also Xian demanded return of the $10,000 down payment. (Assume that the jurisdiction has adopted the Uniform Vendor and Purchaser Risk Act.)

a.   May Vendor sue for specific performance of the contract and obtain a decree compelling payment of the full purchase price? _____

b.   Assuming specific performance in favor of the vendor is permitted, is Hubert the proper party-defendant liable for the purchase price? _____

c.   May Xian recover the $10,000 down payment? _____

d.   May Hubert specifically enforce the contract against Vendor by tendering the value of the property subsequent to the earthquake? _____

51.   Val contracts to sell Purpleacre to Pam for $50,000. Val innocently represents to Pam that Purpleacre consists of 100 acres. Actually, it consists of only 90 acres.

a.   Can Pam obtain a decree compelling specific performance of the contract with an abatement in the purchase price? _____

b.   Assuming Pam can get specific performance with abatement, how much will she have to pay for Purpleacre? _____

c.   Can Val obtain a decree for specific performance against Pam with an abatement in the purchase price? _____

52.   Vernon contracts to sell Orangeacre to Paula for $10,000. At the date set for closing, Paula can only raise $9,500.

a.   Can Paula specifically enforce the contract against Vernon with an abatement in proportion to the money which Paula is short? _____

b.   Can Vernon obtain a decree ordering Paula to specifically perform the contract by paying the full purchase price? _____

53.   Pat entered into a written contract to buy a house and lot from Vic for $150,000—$15,000 down and $1,500 per month until the balance of $135,000 was paid, at which time Vic would convey the property by deed. The agreement recited that "time is of the essence," and that upon Pat's failure to pay any installment within 30 days of the due date, the contract would be terminated and all payments previously made would be retained by Vic as liquidated damages. In addition, there was an acceleration clause to the effect that upon default in the payment of any one installment, all subsequently scheduled payments would become immediately due and owing. Pat made the down payment and paid 24 monthly installments. He also made improvements worth $15,000. At this point, a business recession

occurred and property values declined so that the current market value of the property, even with the improvements, is now approximately only equal to the unpaid balance of the purchase price. Uncertain as to his economic prospects, Pat has hesitated and missed payments on the last two installments.

a.   May Vic sue Pat for specific performance and foreclosure of the vendor's lien?   _____

b.   May Vic bring an action against Pat for past due installments?   _____

c.   May Vic bring an action against Pat for the unpaid balance of the purchase price?   _____

d.   May Vic sue for strict foreclosure terminating the contract and forfeiting the payments made?   _____

e.   May Vic sue to rescind the contract and seek recovery of possession of the property?   _____

54.   Same facts as in previous question.

a.   May Pat repudiate the contract and seek restitution of his payments?   _____

b.   Assuming a sudden upsurge in property values, can Pat sue for specific performance upon tendering the overdue installments?   _____

55.   Al contracts to sell his next year's tomato crop to Bill, a commercial tomato canner. When the crop ripens, Al decides to sell it to Chip, who offers a better price than Bill contracted to pay. Tomatoes are in very short supply, and without that crop Bill will have to close his cannery. Can Bill secure specific performance of the contract with Al?   _____

56.   Builder entered into a contract to construct a small building on Owner's land according to certain terms and specifications. The contract price was $25,000. After Builder expended $15,000 on labor and materials, Owner, without justification, ordered the work stopped.

a.   If it would cost $5,000 to complete construction of the building, may Builder recover from Owner the $15,000 expended plus $5,000 for damages in an action for breach of contract?   _____

b.   If it would cost $12,000 to complete construction of the building, would Builder recover less than the actual costs in an action for damages for breach of contract?   _____

c.   If Builder expended $27,000 in completing the construction of the building, is the recovery against Owner nevertheless limited to $25,000?   _____

d.   If Builder completed the building but failed to comply with the specifications in certain minor details, may Builder nevertheless sue on the contract and recover $25,000 less Owner's damages?   _____

57.   Same facts as in previous question except assume that instead of Owner breaching the contract, Builder wrongfully stopped performance after expending $15,000 on labor and materials. If Owner employed Thirdy to complete the construction for $18,000, may Builder recover $15,000 from Owner?   _____

58.   Jake owns a lot which is entirely surrounded by land owned by Kate. Kate enters into a contract with Jake promising to build a road across her land to Jake's lot. If Kate later refuses to build the road, can Jake sue for specific performance of the contract?   _____

59.   Cheryl, a chanteuse, is employed to perform nightly on stage at Pop's Bamboo Room on the Las Vegas strip. She immediately becomes the greatest show attraction on the strip. Her contract with Pop is for an exclusive engagement for six months at $5,000 per week. Don, the owner of a nearby nightclub whose star entertainer becomes ill, offers Cheryl $10,000 per week to perform at his nightclub under a one-year contract. Cheryl accepts. Almost at once Don's profits double, while Pop's business declines drastically.

a.   May Pop recover damages from Cheryl for breach of contract measured by the cost of obtaining equivalent services?   _____

b.   Can Pop compel Cheryl to perform her original contract?   _____

c.   Can Pop obtain an injunction prohibiting Cheryl from working for Don?   _____

60.   Alex owned two contiguous lots, #1 and #2. His residence is on lot #1. He orally agreed to sell the entire property to Betty for $50,000. The attorney who drew up the deed mistakenly omitted lot #2 from the description. Both parties relied on the attorney's assurance that the deed was in proper form. Betty took possession of the entire property and completed extensive landscaping and improvements. When the next tax bills were delivered, Betty asked Alex to correct the deed to include lot #2, but Alex refused and insisted that the entire transaction be canceled. Alex took this position because land values had become greatly inflated during the previous year.

a.   May Betty sue in restitution for recovery of the portion of the purchase price she paid for lot #2?   _____

b.   May Betty sue Alex for specific performance of Alex's contract to convey lot #2 despite the Statute of Frauds?   _____

c.   May Betty sue for damages for Alex's breach of the oral agreement to convey lot #2?   _____

61. Aged, an old man and widower, lived alone in his house. He told Bob and Carol (husband and wife) who lived in an adjacent county, that if they gave up their home and business and cared for him during the remainder of his life, he would give them his house and lot upon his death. Bob and Carol agreed, moved in with Aged, and cared for him until he died about 18 months after their arrival. The original agreement was oral and Aged died intestate with title to the property still in his name.

    a.   May Bob and Carol recover for the reasonable value of their services even though the contract was oral?   _____

    b.   May Bob and Carol sue for specific performance of Aged's promise to devise the property to them?   _____

62. An aircraft manufacturing corporation paid $250,000 to the purchasing agent of Skyway Airlines to secure a contract for the sale of an expensive cargo plane. However, the sale of the aircraft was never consummated because Skyway canceled the contract upon discovery of the bribe. May the aircraft manufacturer obtain restitution of the $250,000 on the ground that the agent would otherwise be unjustly enriched?   _____

63. Gert, a professional gambler, agreed to pay Alex, a professional baseball player, $10,000 to "throw" a game on which Gert had bet heavily on the opposing team. To assure Alex's nonperformance, Gert required Alex to deposit $1,000 with him as security. Alex regretted his action and played the game to win. He not only played without error but also hit a home run each time at bat. Nevertheless, his team lost 15-14 and Gert won $50,000 on the outcome.

    a.   If Gert refuses to pay as promised, can Alex recover $10,000 plus his deposit from Gert for breach of contract?   _____

    b.   Does Alex have a restitutionary remedy to recover the $1,000 deposit because he repented his agreement and Gert would otherwise be unjustly enriched?   _____

Answers to Review Questions

1.a. NO Here the contract action would be the equivalent of strict liability because of Doc's failure to fulfill his contractual promise, whereas the tort action would require proof of negligence or other wrongful conduct. The rule of **Hadley v. Baxendale** would not limit Belinda's damages here because both parties knew of the particular facts which made Belinda's special damages (loss of wages) expectable. [§§23-24]

b. NO A party must take reasonable steps to avoid unnecessary losses. Although this does not require accepting employment that differs in kind, the jobs of modeling bikinis and one-piece swimsuits seem alike enough that Belinda was probably not justified in refusing to continue her employment. [§47]

c. NO Punitive damages are not awarded in contract cases, regardless of how intentional the breach. [§61]

2.a. NO Such damages are "general damages"—*i.e.*, ones that would be expected to flow from the type of substantive wrong inflicted by the defendant. [§41]

b. YES The cost of the shots is an item that is peculiar to Landowner, and so must be specially pleaded. Such damages would not be expected to occur regularly to other plaintiffs in Landowner's situation. [§§40, 42]

3.a. YES Attorneys' fees may be recovered as an item of *damages* where the defendant's tort or breach of contract forces the plaintiff to incur those attorneys' fees in litigation with a third party. [§72]

b. YES A claim for attorneys' fees incurred in other litigation is a claim for special damages and is subject to the rules requiring that the claim be "foreseeable" and specially pleaded. [§§40, 42]

4. NO The legal remedy of damages is adequate. [§122] Besides, such a decree would be a mandatory injunction to construct or repair, which equity is reluctant to grant because it is not feasible to enforce. [*cf.* §1225]

5. YES However, if the court lacks *equitable* jurisdiction (*e.g.*, there was an adequate remedy at law, etc.), the decree may be subject to reversal on appeal as an abuse of the court's discretion. [§§117, 124]

6. NO Proceedings in state courts may not be enjoined by federal courts except where specifically authorized by statute, or in cases of proven harassment, bad faith, or other "extraordinary circumstances" (which do not appear here). [§§145-147]

7.	**YES**	As long as no criminal prosecution is yet pending, federal declaratory relief is available to test the constitutionality of a state criminal statute. [§149]
8.	**NO**	Sam's continuous protests would negate this defense. Moreover, delay alone is not sufficient for laches. Joe would have to show that the delay was unreasonable (*i.e.*, caused him prejudice) and nothing in the question so indicates. [§164]
9.a.	**YES**	However, the contempt sentence here would be of the criminal type (since the court can no longer coerce Nancy's compliance with the original order). Therefore, Nancy must be afforded all of the safeguards required in criminal proceedings. [§172]
b.	**YES**	Although nonparties are generally not bound by an equitable decree, there is an exception where the nonparty had knowledge of the decree and was acting to aid the enjoined party in violating the injunction. [§§184-185]
10.a.	**YES**	Since Samuel owns land in Hawaii, Peter could obtain quasi in rem jurisdiction by attaching the land and notifying the defendant. The equity court in Hawaii could itself transfer title to the land within its borders. [§189]
b.	**YES**	Peter could obtain specific performance based on personal service of Samuel in South Carolina. [§191]
c.	**NO**	There does not appear to be any basis for jurisdiction in Pennsylvania. [§191]
d.	**(A)**	The South Carolina court can validly issue an in personam order, but it has no power to affect title to land in other states directly. [§190]
11.a.	**YES**	Theoretically it is a proper decree. [§194] The court has personal jurisdiction over Daphne, and the animal could be considered unique for purposes of "equitable replevin." [§§336-339] Given equitable jurisdiction, an accounting for profits may be considered proper.
b.	**MAYBE**	It could be said that enforcement by contempt is impractical because Daphne would have to leave the jurisdiction in order to comply. [§194] Indeed, this consideration may affect the exercise of equitable jurisdiction in the first place (*see* previous question). If Daphne has assets in the United States, they may be reached to satisfy the monetary portions of the decree. [§§187-188]
c.	**NO**	A receiver has no authority outside the jurisdiction where appointed. However, if the appointment were made, it might possibly work—*i.e.*, Daphne might be compelled through threat of contempt to give the receiver a power of attorney. [§§194, 217]
12.	**NO**	A t.r.o. may be granted *ex parte*, but a preliminary injunction requires notice to the defendant and a hearing on the motion. [§§203, 207]

13.	**YES**	A bill quia timet (or its statutory equivalent) is appropriate to prevent the type of loss Pam fears. [§§227, 229]
14.	**NO**	Tenant comes within the category of an officious intermeddler. [§§237-238]
15.	**(B)**	(A) is possible but very unlikely because Paul would have to identify the specific sums taken. [§§266-267] (B) is correct because for quasi-contract Paul need only show that Deanna is unjustly enriched. [§268] (C) is wrong because here there is no trust res. [§272] (D) is wrong because there is also no property upon which to impose a lien. [§§254, 279]
16.	**(D)**	Paul is not entitled to any remedy in the absence of any knowing participation by the doctor. [§270]
17.	**(A)**	Constructive trust is closest to being correct because the policy itself was acquired with the embezzled funds—as contrasted with payment of subsequent premiums on an already-owned policy. [§§249-252] (However, some courts would limit recovery to the amount of the embezzled funds, leaving the balance of the proceeds to the beneficiary who was innocent of wrongdoing.) (B) is wrong because quasi-contractual recovery would be limited to $5,000. [§§268-269]
18.	**(A) and (C)**	(A) is correct because otherwise Dawn is unjustly enriched. [§268] (B) is incorrect because title to property was not acquired with the misappropriated funds. [§§256, 272, 274] (C) is correct and the advantage of the equitable lien is apparent; the quasi-contract claim is unsecured. [§§254-256, 279]
19.	**(B) (with qualifications), (D), and (E)**	(A) is not correct because the money was not used to *acquire* title to the house. [§§256, 272] Subrogation to the claims of a secured creditor is the appropriate equitable remedy where misappropriated funds have been used to pay off such claims. [§259] However, whether subrogation for the *full* amount of the $5,000 misappropriated may be claimed depends on the rules of tracing accepted by the particular jurisdiction (*e.g.*, the *Oatway* presumption would support full subrogation). [§§259-263] (C) is wrong because the agent was not unjustly enriched. [§245] Using the approach of section 211 of the Restatement of Restitution, the lien would be proper for the balance up to the amount of the claim not otherwise satisfied by subrogation. The constructive trust could properly be claimed only up to one-third of the balance in the account because this represents the proportionate *ownership* of the commingled account. [§§286-291]
20.a.	**YES**	Title cannot be acquired from a thief. [§§315, 357]
b.	**YES**	A quasi-contractual action covers money expended to discharge the obligation of a wrongdoer—in addition to any direct enrichment. [§§245-246, 268]

21. **(A)**   It should be kept in mind that the fact the animal won the prize is relevant to the determination of its value at the time of conversion. [§331]

22.a. **YES**   This is one of several measures of damage. [§358]

b. **YES**   A common but not invariably accepted approach. [§§359-364]

c. **PROBABLY NOT**   Under the rule as generally stated. [§§360-361]

d. **(A)**   (A) is the most common method. [§359] The prospective profits are from the poultry business rather than from the building as such, and are therefore too speculative. [§§32-34, 359]

e. **SPLIT**   The cases are divided between this and the diminution in value rule. Fruit trees have a productive value per se. [§364]

f. **NO**   The loss is computed by considering probable income from the ultimate yield less cost of production and marketing. [§363]

g. **NO**   *See* answer to question 4., *supra*.

23.a. **MAYBE**   There is, of course, no diminution in value, but because of the short time remaining on the lease, resort to the cost of a restitutionary measure could be justified. [§§374-376]

b. **YES**   Equity will enjoin ameliorating waste where the landlord is reasonably entitled to return of the land in its condition at the time of leasing. The lease is 80% expired, and an inference that Tenant may now change the character of the use is no longer justified. [§376]

24.a. **YES**   Phyllis has been wrongfully ousted from her property and may recover possession in an action of ejectment. [§385]

b. **NO**   For historical reasons. [§397]

25.a. **NO**   However, this rule may be modified by present statutory enactments permitting equitable adjustments between the parties. [§§387-391]

b. **DEPENDS**   On whether the encroachment is classified as "permanent" or "continuing." A classification as "permanent" in some states would mean that Phyllis has no remedy in damages. A classification as "continuing" would at least allow damages for loss of use—measured by rental value of the area encroached upon for the period corresponding to the local statute of limitations governing trespass actions. [§398]

c. **MAYBE**   Equitable jurisdiction exists because the remedy at law for ejectment is inadequate, on the theory that there is no practical way to enforce the judgment of ouster. [§§399-401] However, it must be assumed that Phyllis is not barred by the equitable doctrine of laches. [§§164-167, 405] The court will also balance the hardships—*i.e.*, whether the cost of removing the encroachment together with the economic injury to the rest of David's house outweighs the hardship on Phyllis of being deprived of the use of a substantial amount of her property. Such injunction, if denied, should be conditioned on David's payment of the value of the property. [§§402, 404]

26.a. **NO**   This was historically true. But under a merged system of law and equity the title issue will be severed for trial by jury if demanded. [§418]

b. **YES**   The legal remedy is considered inadequate because of the continuous nature of the trespass and the unique value of land. [§§416-417]

c. **NO**   After severance, the gypsum may be regarded as an ordinary chattel, the conversion of which will not be enjoined, as the remedy of damages would be adequate. [§417]

d. **YES**   Dubert is liable to the same extent in quasi-contract as in tort. [§411]

27.a. **50¢/ton**   Since Dubert was innocent and Aldo was unable to exploit the minerals himself. [§414]

b. **$1/ton**   Value of product after mined less the reasonable cost of mining it. [§414]

c. **$8/ton**   Value of product with no deduction for cost of mining. [§415]

28.a. **YES**   Assuming liability, this is an acceptable measure of damages. The patients would have individual personal injury actions if their physical harm rose to that level. [§448]

b. **DEPENDS**   If considered a permanent nuisance, this is an appropriate measure of damages. [§§449-450]

c. **NO**   This is not, strictly speaking, a matter of "avoidable consequences." This doctrine applies to the minimization of damages *after* a tort has occurred, not to measures taken to *prevent* the tort itself. [§47] On the contrary, if Purdue does purchase the equipment, he probably could recover the money spent as a cost of abatement. [§448]

29. **(A), (C), (D), and (E)**   (A) is true; where a nuisance is permanent, judgment in a prior action is res judicata. [§450] (B) is wrong because moving to the nuisance is not a defense to an equity suit for an injunction, nor is it "unclean hands." [§§157, 461] (C) is correct in a jurisdiction that declines to balance the hardships. [§456] (D) is true, with qualifications, in jurisdictions applying the relative hardship principle. [§§457-458] However, the usual application of the doctrine would also allow Purdue diminution in value damages to the extent Tyson's operations

still constitute a nuisance. (E) is true in jurisdictions adopting the rule of **Boomer v. Atlantic Cement Co.** [§459] (F) is wrong because although there is some authority for such a decree, it would obviously be unrealistic on these facts. [§461]

30. **YES**   Although equity generally will not enjoin a crime, an exception is made for activities that also constitute a public nuisance. Since legislative standards of professional training are enacted for the protection of the public, the court would probably grant the injunction on grounds that an incompetent lawyer should not be permitted to practice simply because he can pay any fines assessed. [§§466-474]

31.a. **MAYBE**   Because of the unique qualifications of the employee, such a measure of damages is not usually susceptible of satisfactory proof. A more common measure is simply the general tort rule of damages, but even these are speculative in this situation. [§§497-499]

b. **YES**   But query as to whether the injunction could be made to run beyond the term of Cheryl's original employment contract with Pop. [§§504-506]

c. **MAYBE**   Such a remedy (if sanctioned) would be granted only where an injunction is also sought. [§§507-511]

32. **YES**   Ned's interest was a mere expectancy, but clearly Ned would have received the estate had Jack not intervened to divert it. [§516]

33. **YES**   Fiduciaries are accountable for all secret profits made regardless of whether pecuniary loss is sustained by the one to whom the fiduciary obligation is owed. [§§524-526]

34. **MAYBE**   Where a trade secret is acquired by breach of confidence, some cases have held that the wrongdoer should be permanently barred from profiting from the wrong. However, after full disclosure, the protectability of the trade secret ends. To deprive Dupont of the competitive advantages gained by the misappropriation while a protectable interest in the trade secret existed, a "lead time" injunction might be issued. [§573]

35.a. **NO**   Unless there is palming off or confusion and the copies are inferior. [§§591, 594]

b. **NO**   The arrangements (*i.e.*, "style") are in the public domain and Dexta is free to copy them. [§§615-616] This is to be distinguished from an actual misappropriation of Tommy's "performance," which might be enjoined in some states. [§619]

c. **YES**   If there is actual "palming off." A limited injunction might be issued to insure against listener confusion—*i.e.*, truthful references to Tommy may be made as long as the impression that he is connected with Dexta's recording is avoided. [§§593-594, 596, 618]

36.a. **YES** This is personal defamation rather than injury to a trade or business. There is no loss of customers. [§§657, 667-670]

b. **NO** Not on such express grounds. [§§673-680] Equity will not enjoin personal defamation. An anomaly exists here because equitable jurisdiction has been invoked to enjoin publications invading the right to be left alone where no defamation exists—subject to constitutional limitations suggested in §§688-691. [§§696-700]

c. **NO** In both types of cases, a plaintiff seeks recovery for mental anguish and humiliation. In this case, the mental anguish and humiliation result from the same wrongful act. Thus, only one recovery should be allowed. [§686]

d. **YES** Although the amount recoverable is discretionary with the trier of fact. [§§693-695]

e. **DEPENDS** In the absence of statute the answer would be yes because this is a continuing invasion of privacy and no adequate legal remedy exists. [§§696-700] However, the criminal statute affects the answer, because equity will not ordinarily enjoin a crime unless it is also a public nuisance. [§§138-139] The continued existence of a *private* remedy might well be implied, unless the statute is specifically made exclusive.

37.a. **NOT EXACTLY** The proper measure would be loss of compensation from the partnership attributable to the injury. Additional business costs involved (hiring a substitute) enter into the overall calculation. [§§747-753]

b. **NOT EXACTLY** He is entitled to recover for the *impairment* of his earning capacity. The possibility of earnings in other employment should be considered. [§§754-763]

c. **NO** Neil may recover in many jurisdictions for loss of enjoyment of life's amenities, but future *noneconomic* damages are granted in a lump sum, *not* discounted to present value. [§§739, 776] Economic losses that will accrue in the future may be discounted—*i.e.*, Neil will receive a lump sum which, if presently invested at a judicially or legislatively determined rate, would yield the total award approved by the court. [§§84-88]

d. **YES** This is the ordinary application of the collateral sources rule. [§§75, 793-796] The medical insurers may or may not seek subrogation, depending on the contract. [§79]

38.a. **YES** A primitive approach to the theory of wrongful death recovery would suggest the opposite to be true in purely economic terms. However, a *monetary* valuation—even though rather minimal in some states—is given to certain noneconomic losses. *See* next question and answer. [§835]

b. **YES**   Though noneconomic, such losses are usually construed as other than merely sentimental. [§830]

c. **YES (in principle)**   But such claims may not satisfy the rule of certainty of damages. [§§32-33] This claim requires proof as to the earning ability of the child during minority (a movie star?). Even more uncertain is the claim that the child would have continued to contribute to the mother's support after majority when any legal claim to the child's earnings or service would likely cease. In view of the child's age, lack of prior earnings record, or example of contribution to parents, it is very doubtful that such a claim is supportable.

d. **POSSIBLY**   A minority approach. [§835]

e. **YES**   In most jurisdictions. This is a distinct economic cost. [§827]

f. **NO**   Even assuming the defendant's conduct warrants it. [§841] Had the child not died immediately, a cause of action for punitive damages may have accrued in her behalf which could be pursued by her personal representative under some survival statutes. [§§804-807]

39.a. **NO**   Beginning an action for damages for deceit is an election of substantive rights under the general rule. [§858]

b. **YES**   As long as no prejudice to Darby can be shown. [§860]

40.a. **NO**   The common law action of deceit requires scienter. Some jurisdictions allow damages for innocent misrepresentation restricted to the difference between the value of what the other has parted with and the value of what was received. [§§870-872]

b. **YES**   The suit to rescind is equitable and rescission may be had for an innocent misrepresentation. [§890]

41.a. **$0**   In jurisdictions following the benefit-of-the-bargain rule, Pia could recover the difference between the actual value of what is received and the value it would have had as represented—the question does not give this latter figure, however. [§878] A variation of the benefit-of-the-bargain rule is the "make good rule" which would allow Pia $40,000. [§880]

b. **YES**   Again within the limitations of the rule of certainty in damages. A track record of past profits can probably be established here. [§882]

c. **(A), (B), and (C)**   (A) is correct because consideration paid plus interest is recoverable. [§914] (B) is correct, and cost rather than enhanced market value is allowed because this "benefit" results from Darby's wrongdoing. [§914] (C) is true although a question might be raised as to whether Darby should be charged with the insurance premiums which may not be of benefit to him even indirectly. Moreover, had the premises burned, Pia probably would have collected the insurance. [§914] (D) is wrong. Lost profits are recoverable as consequential damages when the sale of a business is rescinded, but *only* up to the time that notice of rescission is given.

d. **YES**   Note, however, that the rental value has been increased as the result of Pia's improvements. If Pia is charged with rent on her own improvements then Darby should not be permitted to claim depreciation on the *cost* of improvements with which he is charged. [§§914, 918]

42. **YES**   The Utility Company's refusal to provide service except upon Max's payment of money he did not owe constitutes duress. Max can therefore get restitution of the payments wrongfully obtained. [§953]

43.a. **YES**   In a quasi-contract action at law. [§§982-983]

b. **NO**   The mistake here is as to a *collateral* fact, and most courts deny rescission on the ground that the mistake affected only the motive for entering the transaction and not the transaction itself. [§§998, 1000]

44.a. **NO**   Although "unknown" injuries are covered by the release, the court will generally interpret this as a reference to unknown injuries that the parties realize might exist. Here there was justifiable reliance on X-rays so that the parties did not actually consider the possibility of unknown injuries. [§§1010-1012]

b. **YES**   This is an exception to the general principle that a compromise cannot be rescinded for mistake. [§1010]

c. **NO**   Reformation is not appropriate. The error was not in the integration of the release because there was no prior agreement that the release incorrectly incorporated. [§§1032-1033]

d. **DEPENDS**   Upon procedural rules of the particular jurisdiction. The release would be pleaded as a defense, thereby raising the issue of mistake. The elements necessary for relief, however, remain the same. [§1012]

45. **NO**   The money was paid under mistake, but Mary has the defense of discharge for value. The lien may be invalid because the security for it was stolen, but Mary's claim against Jeff was a valid preexisting legal claim that was given up for value. [§1024]

46.a. **NO**   Rescission would be a proper remedy for mistake in the underlying agreement. There was none here. [§§995-996]

b. **NO**   Failure to read a document is not a bar to a remedy for mistake. [§1031]

c.	**NO**	Reformation is an appropriate remedy in most jurisdictions. [§§1032-1033] A minority would not grant reformation of a deed so as to increase size of the grant in absence of a prior memo to satisfy the Statute of Frauds. [§1041]
47.	**NO**	Absent any detrimental reliance by the donee, relief is denied. [§1055]
48.a.	**NO**	Because enforcement of the contract would now work unanticipated hardships on Purchaser, the change in the law would probably be a valid defense to Vendor's suit for specific performance. [§133]
b.	**YES**	Unless the doctrine of frustration of purpose could be applied. [§§1117, 1297]
49.	**NO**	BFP is under no duty to convey title to Purchaser. Transfer of title to a bona fide purchaser cuts off all hidden equitable claims and rights, including the interest of a first purchaser. [§1077]
50.a.	**NO**	The traditional equity rule places the risk of loss on the buyer from the time the contract is executed. Under this rule, the answer to the question would be yes. [§1078] But the equity rule has been modified in many jurisdictions to shift the risk of loss to the buyer only upon transfer of possession or the execution of a conveyance. The Uniform Vendor and Purchaser Risk Act incorporates this modification, so that under this latter rule the answer to the question is no. [§1080]
b.	**NO**	The purchase price is a contract debt payable by the estate. [§1083]
c.	**YES**	Restitution is allowed where the seller bears the risk of loss and there is material destruction. [§1081]
d.	**NOT CLEAR**	From language of the Act itself, but courts have allowed specific performance in cases involving a material destruction. [§1081]
51.a.	**YES**	As long as this remedy would not result in undue hardship to the seller, a buyer can get specific performance with abatement, regardless of whether the defect is material or immaterial. [§§1097-1098, 1103]
b.	**$45,000**	Abatement is generally a pro rata reduction in the purchase price. [§1098]
c.	**DEPENDS**	On whether Val's breach is considered material. If it is, Val could not get specific performance, because such a decree would force Pam to accept a substantially different parcel than that bargained for. [§§1112-1113]
52.a.	**NO**	Courts never allow a purchaser who is in default (by being unable to tender the full purchase price) to specifically enforce the contract against the seller. To do so might result in the seller holding one small piece of land that would be valueless to him. [§1155]

b. **YES**   However, because money decrees are not enforceable by contempt, Vernon's remedy would be limited to executing on other assets belonging to Paula. [§1128]

53.a. **YES**   In lieu of suing for damages. [§1134]

b. **YES**   Unless the action is brought in a jurisdiction that regards the land sale contract as a purchase money security obligation. [§§1132-1133]

c. **YES**   By virtue of the effect given to the acceleration clause at common law. (Note, however, a growing hostility toward such clauses, particularly in boilerplate contracts.) [§1132]

d. **YES (but caution)**   This was long a standard remedy in conformity with the agreed terms of the bargain. However, the attitude of equity toward forfeitures and statutory provisions aimed at "unconscionable bargains" may bar this remedy in many, perhaps most, jurisdictions. [§1137]

e. **YES**   Assuming a decree can be framed adjusting the equities of the parties with regard to payments, interest, value of improvements, and value of use. (This remedy might not be appealing in a business sense.) [§1139]

54.a. **NO**   Because he is in willful default and, in this instance, Vic is apparently willing to perform the contract. In some jurisdictions, a restitutionary action might be permitted in this situation, but even in such event there may be no enrichment to recover because of declining land values. [§§1149-1152]

b. **NO**   In most jurisdictions. [§1155] A minority of jurisdictions would permit this remedy as being no more than the equivalent of the "equity of redemption" allowed in the law of mortgages. [§1156]

55. **YES**   Damages here are inadequate because equivalent substitute performance is unavailable. Moreover, Bill wants to be a canner, and only the tomatoes, not damages, will enable him to remain in the canning business. [§§1167-1169]

56.a. **YES**   *See* the various computations in §1209.

b. **MAYBE**   This statement is true according to the first and third but not the second formula set out in §1209. Under these circumstances, where the owner breaches a losing contract, the appropriate remedy for the builder is in quasi-contract for the value of the benefit conferred rather than for damages. [§§1213-1215]

c. **YES**   Builder's remedy after completion of full performance is for the contract price. [§1208]

d. **YES**   Where there has been substantial performance of a construction contract, the contractor is permitted an action on the contract less damages resulting from the breach. [§1220]

57. **NO**   Builder is entitled to restitution because Owner accepted the part performance by having Thirdy complete the building. The value of that part performance is measured in various ways. A common formula is to allow Builder to recover the contract price ($25,000) less the cost of completion ($18,000) or $7,000 in this case, plus any consequential damages. [§§1216-1218]

58. **YES**   Damages would not be adequate here. Jake could not hire anyone else to go onto Kate's land and build the road because Kate could have them thrown off her land. [§1226]

59.a. **YES**   But this answer is open to the same practical objections as the tort action against Don in question 31, part a., *supra*. [§1227]

b. **NO**   Personal service contracts are not specifically enforceable. [§1251]

c. **YES**   Cheryl's services are unique and there are no difficult problems of supervision. The remedy is particularly appropriate because the contract calls for exclusive rights to the services. [§§1254-1258]

60.a. **YES**   She is entitled to the overpayment made in reliance on a contract under the Statute of Frauds. [§1268] The amount recoverable might be an allocable portion of the purchase price or, under another line of authorities, the value of lot #2 as determined separately. [§§1273-1274]

b. **YES**   The equitable doctrine of "part performance" would take the contract out of the Statute of Frauds. (Note that this approach obtains the same result as reformation.) [§§1281-1289]

c. **MAYBE**   Depending on whether the jurisdiction accepts the doctrine of estoppel to assert the Statute of Frauds. [§§1291-1292]

61.a. **YES**   While the Statute of Frauds may bar an action on the contract because it is for the sale of land, recovery in quasi-contract is allowed. [§§1268, 1293-1294] (*Compare:* In those jurisdictions following the "estoppel" doctrine, recovery on the contract may be available.) [§§1291-1292]

b. **PROBABLY NOT**   Recall that the equitable remedy of specific performance is discretionary. [§1293] The factors weighing against specific performance here include: (1) adequacy of the legal remedy—*i.e.*, quasi-contractual recovery for value of services which do not appear to be unique; (2) short duration of the services (had Bob and Carol taken care of Aged for a long period of time, such as 20 years, without other consideration than the promise, the matter might be weighed differently); and (3) insufficient part performance. The price (services) has been paid by the plaintiffs, but they did not receive exclusive possession of the premises, since Aged continued to live in the home. Giving up the business and moving to the property by Bob and Carol is not sufficiently referable to the contract so as to constitute part performance. [§1284] Note, however, that these actions may constitute a basis for estoppel to assert the Statute of Frauds in some jurisdictions. [§§1291-1292]

62. **NO**   The payment itself is contrary to public policy and the parties are in pari delicto—although some courts might consider that the intended purpose failed and therefore no public policy was violated. [§§1342, 1347]

63.a. **NO**   Even assuming (from Gert's standpoint at least) that Alex was not himself in default, the bargain was illegal and no action may be brought by either party to enforce the contract. [§1342]

b. **NO**   Restitution may be permitted if a participant in an illegal transaction repents before the socially damaging act is performed. [§1357] However, the deposit of $1,000 as security for throwing a professional baseball game is in itself the performance of an illegal bargain involving moral turpitude. [§1358]

Exam Questions
and Answers

Some law professors today favor objective questions or problems requiring relatively short answers, while others still use traditional essay questions. Part I, below, provides questions that require only a few sentences to answer. Part II provides a number of traditional essay questions.

PART I—SHORT ANSWER PROBLEMS

SHORT ANSWER PROBLEM SET A

The cases summarized below involve the application of familiar rules governing the measurement of legal damages. Identify by a phrase or sentence the doctrine involved in each case:

1. In **Boryla v. Pash**, 937 P.2d 813 (Colo. 1996), defendant negligently diagnosed a malignant lump in plaintiff's breast, resulting in a 92-day delay in detecting breast cancer. After later obtaining a correct diagnosis, plaintiff received medical treatment and is now cancer free. She sued defendant for malpractice, alleging that the delay in diagnosis exposed her to an increased risk of a recurrence of the cancer. She sought damages arising from her fear of a recurrence of the cancer. In resisting the claim, defendant should rely on:

    _____

    _____

2. Torrington Construction Company entered into a supply contract for structural steel with Fort Pitt Company, a steel fabricator. The contract includes a schedule for the place and date of delivery. The date of delivery was important to Torrington because the actual construction was to take place in northern Wisconsin where completion before the first freeze was imperative. Fort Pitt delivered the steel three weeks later than the date set out in the contract. As a result, Torrington incurred added expense because it was forced to adopt an expedited schedule of concrete pouring to beat the freeze. The added expense amounted to $7,653, and Torrington filed an action to recover this amount from Fort Pitt. In resisting this claim, Fort Pitt should rely on:

    _____

    _____

3. Defendant, a broker, misappropriated stock belonging to plaintiff and sold the stock for $10,000 to meet personal margin calls. Plaintiff was unaware of the misappropriation until sometime later when he directed defendant to sell the stock.

The broker then disclosed the theft. The stock was worth $15,000 at the time of plaintiff's demand, although it increased in value to $18,000 within the next 30 days. Plaintiff filed an action to recover $18,000 in damages for conversion. In demanding judgment for this amount, plaintiff relies on the rule:

_____

_____

4.   Defendant took logs belonging to plaintiff. When plaintiff discovered the theft sometime later, he demanded the return of the logs. Defendant refused to return them, claiming ownership. Shortly thereafter, defendant sold the logs to the operator of a sawmill. The logs had a market value of $10,000 at the time of the theft, $15,000 at the time of plaintiff's demand, and $12,000 at the time of defendant's sale. Plaintiff filed an action for conversion of the logs, asking for a judgment in the amount of $15,000. In demanding a judgment for $15,000, plaintiff relies on the rule:

_____

_____

5.   Briggs Plumbing manufactured inexpensive bathroom sinks, hundreds of which Fieldstone Home installed in a residential development. Fieldstone purchased the sinks by means of a subcontract with a plumbing supply company. The sinks deteriorated within one to five years requiring Fieldstone to spend $250,000 replacing 1,900 sinks. Fieldstone filed a lawsuit against Briggs Plumbing to recover for this expenditure. No other losses were shown. The alleged basis of liability was negligent manufacture. Defendant moved for summary judgment. What argument would you expect Briggs to make in support of its motion for summary judgment?

_____

_____

6.   Plaintiff bought a large water tank for $1,000 for use at his mountain home. He hired a moving company to transport the tank up to his cabin for a $100 fee. A winter storm delayed his installation plans and he was forced to leave the tank near the entrance to his property. A neighboring rancher saw the tank alongside the road. Assuming it was abandoned, he loaded the tank on his truck, transported it back down the mountain, and sold it for $1,000. Plaintiff filed an action against the rancher seeking damages for conversion rather than an action in quasi-contract for restitution. Plaintiff's reason for electing a conversion rather than a waiver of tort and quasi-contract theory is:

_____

_____

SHORT ANSWER PROBLEM SET B

The bifurcated remedial system we inherited has caused many problems. In particular, courts and scholars have trouble understanding the history and scope of restitutionary remedies. In the cases below, briefly identify the flaw in the court's pronouncements.

1. In **Perez v. Boatmen's National Bank**, 788 S.W.2d 296 (Mo. 1990), the court made the following statement: "In general, where a plaintiff can choose to proceed in tort [for conversion] or quasi-contract on a course of conduct involving two possible defendants and he chooses to proceed to final judgment against the defendant on a quasi-contract claim, he may not later attempt to pursue a tort action against the second defendant; the initial waiver of tort waived tort for all purposes."

    _____

    _____

2. In **Doherty v. Retirement Board**, 680 N.E.2d 45 (Mass. 1997), the appellate court noted that the constitutional right to jury trial did not apply "to cases which traditionally would have fallen within the jurisdiction of a court of equity. As the remedy of restitution is equitable in nature, [the constitution] does not require a jury trial."

    _____

    _____

3. In **Terra Nova Insurance Co. v. Associates Commercial Corp.**, 697 F. Supp. 1048 (E.D. Wis. 1988), the federal district court in Wisconsin discussed the following theories of the litigants: "The plaintiffs argue that Associates should make restitution under a theory of unjust enrichment. Associates [defendant] counters that plaintiffs are really asserting a claim that payment was made under a mistake of fact."

    _____

    _____

4. In **Elliott v. Elliott**, 231 Cal. App. 2d 205 (1964), plaintiff sought to make defendant a constructive trustee of a jointly owned promissory note. The note was uncollectible because of defendant's lack of diligence in commencing an action to enforce it. In imposing a constructive trust, the California Court of Appeals stated the following: "To charge a constructive trustee with an unconscionable loss he has caused the beneficiary is simply the converse of charging him with profits rightfully belonging to the beneficiary . . . . To apply the constructive trust doctrine in both instances lends congruity to the law."

    _____

    _____

5. In **Season Comfort Corp. v. Ben A. Borenstein Co.,** 655 N.E.2d 1065 (Ill. 1995), the court stated: "It is axiomatic that an unjust enrichment claim is viable only when there is no adequate remedy at law."

_____

_____

SHORT ANSWER PROBLEM SET C

The following three cases involve equitable remedies and some of the problems arising from the merger of law and equity. What flaws do you detect in these judicial pronouncements?

1. In **Floyd v. Floyd,** 412 S.E.2d 397 (S.C. 1991), the South Carolina Supreme Court expressed concern that courts were denying jury trial in cases where the complaint asked for both legal and equitable relief. It therefore decided to state the following new rule for making this classification: "Where legal and equitable issues or rights are asserted in the same complaint, the legal issues are for determination by the jury and the equitable issues are to be decided by the court."

_____

_____

2. In **Phelps v. Kozakar,** 146 Cal. App. 3d 1078 (1983), a California superior court ordered a defendant, over whom it had obtained personal jurisdiction, to execute a deed to land situated in Nevada, and upon his failure to do so, directed a clerk of the court to execute the deed. On appeal, the judgment was affirmed. The court of appeals offered the following explanation: "If the court had power to order a party to convey land outside the state, it follows that upon his failure to do so the court has power to enforce the order by directing the clerk to execute the conveyance."

_____

_____

3. In **Crawford v. Weisman,** 938 P.2d 540 (Colo. 1997), plaintiff filed an action for damages for wrongful termination of an employment contract at will. At trial, evidence was presented showing that plaintiff had made false statements on her employment application. In denying relief, the court stated the following: "An employee who engages in resumé fraud does not have 'clean hands' and is not entitled to hold an employer liable on a contract theory."

_____

_____

SHORT ANSWER PROBLEM SET D

In answering the following problems, apply the tracing principles of the Restatement of Restitution.

1. Wrongdoer deposits $2,000 of Victim's money with $1,000 of her own money. Wrongdoer then invests $1,500 of the commingled fund in Intel stock. Wrongdoer then dissipates all of the money in the account.

   Victim is entitled to an equitable lien in the amount of $ _____.

   Reason: _____

   _____

   Victim is entitled to a constructive trust in the amount of $ _____.

   Reason: _____

   _____

2. Wrongdoer deposits $2,000 of Victim's money with $1,000 of her own money. Wrongdoer invests $1,500 of the commingled fund in IBM stock and $1,500 in General Motors stock. The IBM stock declines in value to $1,000 and the General Motors stock declines to $500.

   On these facts, Victim's preferred remedy is:

   (1) Equitable lien or
   (2) Constructive trust?

   Answer: _____

   Reason: _____

   _____

3. Wrongdoer misappropriates $2,000 belonging to A and commingles it with $2,000 of Wrongdoer's own money. Wrongdoer withdraws and dissipates $3,000. Wrongdoer then deposits in the account $2,000 of her own money, and invests the $3,000 in Ford Motor Company stock.

   Victim is entitled to an equitable lien in the amount of $_____.

   Reason: _____

   _____

Victim is entitled to a constructive trust in the amount of $_____.

Reason: _____

_____

_____

SHORT ANSWER PROBLEM SET E

1. A state statute provides: "Any person operating a pet animal facility shall possess a valid pet facility license issued by the commissioner in accordance with the provisions of this article . . . ." The statute further authorizes the commissioner to enjoin the operation of an unlicensed facility "without proof of the inadequacy of the remedy at law." The commissioner sought an injunction against defendant for operating an animal shelter without first obtaining a license. The district court denied the injunction, although it found defendant had operated the facility without a license. The district judge reasoned that defendant had made good faith efforts toward compliance with the statute and would likely in the near future bring the facility into compliance.

    The commissioner appealed. What argument would you make for the commissioner to obtain a reversal of the district court's order?

    _____

    _____

    _____

2. The city of San Jose filed a civil public nuisance action in the superior court seeking an injunction against the activities of the members of the VST gang. After a hearing, a preliminary injunction was entered against five defendants who appeared and 33 who did not appear. Among other provisions, the injunction prohibited gang members from "standing, sitting, walking, driving, or appearing in public view with any other known VST member." Defendant was arrested and charged with criminal contempt for violating this injunction. Defendant moved for a dismissal of the contempt proceeding and for a writ of habeas corpus, arguing that the injunction was unconstitutional. The superior court summarily denied the motion. Defendant appeals from the contempt conviction and from the denial of habeas corpus.

    What argument would you make for the city to uphold the conviction?

    _____

    _____

    _____

3.   Defendant, after obtaining all the necessary permits, operated facilities for the deep well disposal of wastes. By the use of this process, waste was inserted more than 2,600 feet below the surface of the earth. It is uncontested that some of the injected substances were carcinogenic. Plaintiff claimed that the injectate migrated below the surface of her property in the natural brine flowing through existing geological formations. She therefore filed an action seeking compensation for the trespass. No proof was produced to show any physical damage to plaintiff's property, nor could she show a drop in market value. She nevertheless asserted that she was entitled to a substantial monetary award. In making this argument, plaintiff relies on:

_____

_____

_____

PART II—TRADITIONAL ESSAY QUESTIONS

EXAM QUESTION I

On November 1, Sue, a resident of the state of Black, made a written offer to Bob, a resident of the state of White, to sell her champion Welsh terrier for $5,000. Bob, the owner of a Welsh terrier kennel in White, desired to purchase the dog for breeding purposes.

On November 20, Bob mailed a written acceptance to Sue. Subsequently, Sue changed her mind and wrote to Bob stating that she could not part with the dog. Bob thereupon brought suit in White, seeking specific performance of the promise made by Sue to sell the dog. The White court obtained personal jurisdiction over Sue by means of personal service. The court granted Bob the remedy of specific performance, issued a mandatory injunction ordering Sue to deliver the dog (which remained in Black) to Bob within 10 days, and enjoined other disposition of the animal by Sue.

Sue returned to Black and refused to deliver the dog to Bob. Two weeks later, Sue reentered White where, after she was again properly brought under the personal jurisdiction of the White court, she was adjudged to be in contempt.

Discuss the propriety of the White court's contempt proceedings.

EXAM QUESTION II

Railroad, at a total cost of $1 million, built a spur line through farm and timberlands to a sawmill town. Although it had power by its charter to condemn land for its right of way, Railroad did not use this power; it merely took the land it needed. It built the spur line, without permission, across fields and through woods. It destroyed crops in its path and cut down trees in orchards as well as ornamental trees. Large piles of earth and stone were left on the lands, also without permission. The public authorities refused to interfere.

While this was going on, 80 separate suits were started by the injured landowners against Railroad. Some of the suits were at law for damages for completed trespasses and some in ejectment to recover lands of which plaintiffs were dispossessed by Railroad. Other suits were in equity to enjoin defendant's unlawful entries and destruction of crops or trees, or to require defendant to remove the piles of earth and stone.

What decision in the suits in equity? Discuss.

EXAM QUESTION III

As a favor to Alan, Barnes, a neighboring farmer, permitted Alan to store 200 bushels of soybeans worth $1,000 in an unused barn on Barnes's premises. Pressed for funds to pay her debts, Barnes wrongfully sold Alan's soybeans to Cooper, a mill owner, for $1,200 (although the market value of the beans on that date was $1,400). Cooper processed the soybeans, turning them into oil and meal worth $3,000. When the market value of soybeans rose to $8 a bushel, Alan demanded their return from Barnes, at which time he learned of the sale to Cooper. He also learned that Barnes is insolvent except for shares of stock that she purchased with the $1,200 realized from the sale of the beans to Cooper. That stock is now worth $3,000. What are Alan's remedies against Barnes and Cooper? Discuss.

EXAM QUESTION IV

Platt, a research engineer at Knox University in State Red, discovered a process for greatly delaying the failure of metals under stress. Platt freely offered her new process to the public.

Devore, a manufacturer of internal combustion engines, adopted Platt's process. He offered to pay Platt $300,000 for the exclusive right to use Platt's name and picture in advertising the fact that he used Platt's process, but Platt declined the offer. Devore nevertheless began an advertising campaign in which he used Platt's name and picture, the latter bought from a press photographer who had taken it with Platt's consent.

A statute of State Red provides that the commercial use of the name or picture of another without consent is a misdemeanor, punishable by fine and imprisonment.

The use of Platt's name and picture is also contrary to the policy of Knox University and has brought Platt into disrepute among her professional colleagues.

Can Platt have Devore restrained from continuing the publication of his advertisements? Discuss.

EXAM QUESTION V

Seller and Buyer entered into a contract for the sale of Seller's home for $300,000. The agreement provided for a down payment of $25,000, and monthly installments of $2,000 until the balance of the principal and interest is paid. As part of the inducement for the sale, Seller expressly represented that the house was constructed on natural soil. In fact, as Seller knew, there was as much as 15 feet of fill on some parts of the lot.

Buyer made the down payment and entered into possession of the property. Buyer spent $40,000 modernizing the kitchen and bathroom, and $4,000 for taxes and insurance. During the 11th month of occupancy, Buyer discovered cracks in the walls and foundation of the house. Further investigation revealed that the house was built on insufficiently compacted soil. There is no doubt that this seriously affects the value of the property.

What are Buyer's remedies against Seller? Discuss.

EXAM QUESTION VI

Alex owned two farms, Greenacre and Blackacre, each worth $100,000. Alex orally agreed to sell Becky both farms for $200,000. Alex prepared and executed a deed to Becky conveying Greenacre only, and deliberately omitted Blackacre. Alex took the deed to Becky's house to close the deal. Becky asked for some extra time because she had lost her spectacles and could not read without them. Alex replied that Becky would have to take the deed then or never. At Becky's request, Alex read the deed aloud to Becky, but Alex falsely recited a description of Blackacre that was not actually included in the deed. Relying upon Alex's general reputation for honesty, Becky paid Alex $200,000 cash and accepted the deed. Becky then recorded the deed and filed it with her property papers.

Alex immediately put Becky in possession of Greenacre, but Alex retained possession of Blackacre, giving Becky one excuse after another for three years. Alex then sold Blackacre for $100,000 cash to Xavier, who bought in good faith, and without notice of any claim by Becky. Xavier immediately took possession of Blackacre and made improvements on it.

When Becky learned of Xavier's possession, Becky complained to Alex, who told her that she had gotten just what she bargained for and what was described in the deed—namely, Greenacre only. Becky now sues Alex and Xavier in equity (1) to reform Becky's deed to include Blackacre; (2) to impress an equitable lien upon Blackacre for Becky's damages;

and (3) to rescind Becky's purchase contract and recover back the $200,000 paid, on receipt of which Becky would reconvey Greenacre to Alex.

What results? Discuss.

EXAM QUESTION VII

On August 1, 2002, Alice entered into a written contract with Benny whereby Alice agreed to convey Blackacre to Benny on December 1, 2002. In consideration of Alice's transfer, Benny agreed to convey his interest in Whiteacre to Alice on November 15, 2002, and also to personally supervise Alice's dairy business from August 1, 2002, to January 1, 2003. At the time of the contract both Alice and Benny assumed Blackacre's chief value was as agricultural land. They also understood that Benny had only an undivided one-fifth interest in Whiteacre.

On November 10, 2002, Alice learned that Benny had three-fifths interest in Whiteacre. She refrained from advising Benny of this, and on November 16, 2002, Benny conveyed to Alice all his right, title, and interest in Whiteacre. On November 20, 2002, oil was discovered on Blackacre and its market value soared.

On December 1, 2002, Benny demanded a deed to Blackacre and Alice refused to convey. Benny continued to supervise the dairy to the best of his ability until January 1, 2003. On that date, Benny learned that he had in fact owned a three-fifths interest in Whiteacre.

On January 5, 2003, Alice agreed for value to convey an undivided three-fifths interest in Whiteacre to Carlo, a bona fide purchaser, deed to be delivered on January 10. On January 8, 2003, Benny informed Carlo of his interest and advised Carlo that he intended to bring suit for reformation against Alice. On January 10, 2003, Alice gave Carlo her deed as agreed.

On January 15, 2003, Benny brought suit against Alice and Carlo in which he prayed (1) for reformation of his deed to Alice of Whiteacre so that the deed would convey only an undivided one-fifth interest, and (2) for specific performance of Alice's agreement to convey Blackacre. What results? Discuss.

EXAM QUESTION VIII

Lew leased Blackacre to Tess in 2000 for 10 years. The lease agreement, for which separate consideration was given, contained an option to purchase, exercisable in writing by the lessee at any time during that 10-year period. On exercise of the option, Tess was to pay $10,000 and execute a first mortgage on the premises in favor of the lessor to secure payment of her promissory note for the balance of $100,000.

In 2001, Tess, for sufficient consideration, assigned to Alvin "all rights" she acquired under the lease agreement with Lew. Lew died on January 2, 2002, leaving a will in which he devised all of his real property to his son Rudolph and all of his personalty to his son Pat.

In May 2003, Alvin notified both Rudolph and Pat in writing that he was exercising the option to purchase contained in the original lease. Alvin tendered $100,000 in cash to the sons, together with a promissory note for the balance and a first mortgage on the premises, and simultaneously Alvin demanded a deed. Both sons insisted that Alvin's interest was only to the use of the property and refused to execute the conveyance that Alvin demanded. When they refused to comply, Alvin initiated a specific performance suit.

Is Alvin entitled to any relief? If so, against whom should the suit be filed? Is Rudolph or Pat entitled to the purchase price tendered by Alvin?

EXAM QUESTION IX

Smith owned a tract of land on which there was a deposit of fine clay having special qualities that adapted it to the making of fine pottery. Brown desired to establish a plant to make pottery in a neighboring city. He made a contract in writing with Smith whereby Smith agreed to deliver to Brown's plant 300 tons of clay each month for 10 years, and Brown agreed to pay $10 on the first day of each month for each ton of clay delivered during the preceding month.

Brown completed the plant and took delivery from Smith of 300 tons for each of the first three months of the plant's operation. Brown made payment for the clay as required by the contract. On the second day of the fourth month, Brown received a letter from one Thomas, stating that Smith held title to an undivided one-half interest in the land as trustee to pay to Thomas one-half of the proceeds from the sale of any products of the land. Thomas further stated that Smith had repudiated the trust and refused to account to Thomas for any portion of the payments already received from Brown.

Brown was unable to determine the truth or falsity of Thomas's claim and, on the 10th of the month, Brown notified Smith that he would thereafter deposit one-half of each payment due under the contract in escrow to be paid to whoever established his right to it. Smith immediately refused to make any more deliveries under the contract but continued to remove clay and sell it to others. Brown can get similar clay only from land 1,000 miles away and would have to pay $15 a ton, plus freight.

What remedy, if any, is available to Brown? Discuss.

EXAM QUESTION X

Builder and Owner enter into a contract for the construction of a building on Owner's lot for a total contract price of $25,000. After expending $10,000 on labor and materials, Builder repudiates the contract after discovering that it will cost an additional $20,000 to complete the project. Progress payments in the amount of $7,500 have been made to Builder.

1.   What are the remedies of Owner and Builder?

2.   Suppose instead that Owner repudiates the contract. What are Builder's remedies?

PART I—ANSWERS TO SHORT ANSWER PROBLEMS

ANSWERS TO PROBLEM SET A

1. The rule of certainty—speculative damages are not recoverable.

2. The rule of **Hadley v. Baxendale**—damages not within the contemplation of the parties when the conduct was entered into are not recoverable.

3. That when the commodity converted has a fluctuating value, plaintiff may set damages as the highest value reached within a reasonable time after notice of the conversion.

4. That damages for conversion may be set as the value of the chattel at the time of seizure, demand, and refusal to return, or disposition.

5. An economic loss (as distinguished from personal injury or property damage) negligently caused by breach of a sales contract is not recoverable.

6. The conversion theory allows a recovery of plaintiff's loss which is the market value at the place of conversion ($1,000) plus $100 freight. The restitution (quasi-contract) claim would be for the rancher's gain or $900.

ANSWERS TO PROBLEM SET B

1. The court mistakenly treats the fictional waiver of tort implicit in the election to sue for restitution as if it were an actual waiver. If there had been a valid real waiver, there would be no tort basis for claiming defendant's enrichment unjust.

2. Restitution is both a legal and an equitable remedy. If the basis of the restitutionary claim is quasi-contract, the remedy is legal and there is a constitutional right to jury trial.

3. The court assumes that there are two theories whereas in both situations, money is unjustly retained because it was transferred as the result of a mistake of fact.

4. To impose a constructive trust, there must be a trust res. You cannot impose a trust on nothing and that is the situation in *Elliott* where defendant sustained a loss and had no money on which the trust could be imposed.

5. This is clearly wrong since the entire law of quasi-contract is legal and provides an alternative legal remedy to compel disgorgement of unjust enrichment.

ANSWERS TO PROBLEM SET C

1. The test proposed by the court is unworkable because issues by themselves are neither legal nor equitable. The determination must be made with reference to the remedy sought.

2. The court's power to order defendant to execute a deed rests on its power (jurisdiction) over the defendant, and it is the defendant's act in executing the deed in compliance with the court order that effectuates the actual transfer of title. The court itself, lacking (in rem) jurisdiction, cannot by its own decree transfer an interest in land in another state.

3. The traditional view is that unclean hands is a defense only where equitable remedies are sought. It is not a defense to an action brought to recover damages for breach of contract, absent special circumstances.

ANSWERS TO PROBLEM SET D

1. Equitable lien in the amount of $1,500.
   Victim may trace the money to the stock and claim a lien on the stock to the full extent of the claim.
   Constructive trust in the amount of $1,000.
   Since Victim had $2,000 and Wrongdoer $1,000 in the commingled $3,000, Victim may claim a proportionate share of anything traced from the commingled fund. Since Victim had a 2/3 share, Victim can claim 2/3 of the $1,500 stock or $1,000.

2. Equitable lien.
   If Victim asserts a lien against the stock, Victim has a claim for $2,000 secured by a lien on $1,500 worth of stock to which her money can be traced. A constructive trust based on Victim's 2/3 proportionate share of any assets traced from the commingled fund would yield $1,000 (2/3 of IBM stock = $666.66; 2/3 of General Motors Stock = $333.33).

3. Equitable lien—$1,000.
   The $1,000 amount is the lowest balance of the commingled account, and Victim can claim a lien on the account and on anything traced from it to that extent. Victim has no claim on the later deposit.
   Constructive trust—$500.
   On a constructive trust theory, Victim is only entitled to a proportionate share of the commingled account, which was dissipated to $1,000. This was only 1/3 ($1,000) of the money invested in the Ford Stock. Victim's proportionate share of the original commingled account is 1/2, and hence Victim is entitled to claim 1/2 of 1/3 of the amount invested in the Ford stock. Hence 1/2 of 1/3 = 1/6 × $3,000 = $500.

ANSWERS TO PROBLEM SET E

1. The commissioner would argue that the legislature in adopting this statute has determined what conditions must be established to justify the issuance of an injunction. Thus once those conditions are established, the court has no discretion to balance the equities and deny relief. The remedy is mandatory.

2. The collateral bar rule. The defendant may not attack the decree for error collaterally; it may be attacked only by appealing directly from the injunction itself.

3. The restitutionary doctrine that where a defendant obtains a benefit from the tortious use of plaintiff's property, plaintiff is entitled to recover the value gained from that unauthorized use.

PART II—ANSWERS TO TRADITIONAL ESSAY QUESTIONS

ANSWER TO EXAM QUESTION I

The propriety of the contempt proceedings depends on whether the initial White decree was jurisdictionally valid.

The court in White had obtained personal jurisdiction over Sue by personal service in White and therefore had power to enter a valid in personam judgment. The White court entered such a decree by ordering specific performance by Sue of her promise to deliver the dog to Bob. The correctness of that judgment is open to question, however, for the following two reasons:

First, no decree specifically enforcing a contract should be entered if there is an *adequate remedy at law* by way of damages. Here, the adequacy of the remedy at law depends on the uniqueness of the dog. If it was established that this particular champion Welsh terrier was in a class by itself, and hence was not replaceable on the market, the decree for specific performance was correct. Otherwise, the decree was an improper exercise of equitable jurisdiction.

Second, the decree required Sue to go into another jurisdiction (Black) to obtain the dog and deliver it to Bob in White. Courts are reluctant to enter such a decree because of the potential *difficulty in enforcing* it (because compliance with the decree requires the defendant to leave the forum state), and because performance of the required acts may conflict with the laws of the other state (thus placing the defendant in an untenable position). In the instant case, there is little chance that the decree of specific performance would result in any conflict with the laws of Black. There is, however, a serious question of enforceability if Sue chooses to remain in Black. Nevertheless, a court may decide to issue the decree, hoping either that the defendant will comply, or that the decree can be made effective by contempt—as in fact happened in the instant case.

Even if the court was in error in deciding that the remedy at law was inadequate and in ordering an act to be done in a foreign state, however, these considerations affect only the *propriety* of the court's action and *not its validity*. (In traditional terminology, these considerations affect the exercise of equity jurisdiction.) When a court acts in excess of equity jurisdiction, its decree is erroneous but not void. Hence, the decree must be obeyed until it is reversed for error, and failure to comply subjects the recalcitrant party to contempt proceedings. Attack on the decree must be made directly by appeal; it cannot be made collaterally in habeas corpus proceedings attacking the validity of the imprisonment for contempt.

In the instant case, the White court had personal jurisdiction over Sue and could therefore validly enter its decree. If that decree is erroneous, Sue must nevertheless obey it until it is reversed. Thus, Sue must either purge herself of contempt by delivering the dog or stay enforcement (by filing a supersedeas bond, if that is necessary) pending review for error on appeal. Sue cannot successfully attack the contempt proceedings collaterally by habeas corpus.

ANSWER TO EXAM QUESTION II

Injunctive relief to prevent the construction of the spur line should be denied, but a mandatory injunction compelling the removal of the piles of earth and stone may be granted.

Railroad invaded the property rights of the landowners in three distinct ways: (i) by destroying trees and crops, (ii) by constructing a railroad across their land, and (iii) by dumping and leaving piles of earth and stone on their land adjacent to the right of way.

Destruction of trees and crops: As to this first wrong, no injunctive relief is possible. The destruction of the trees and crops constitutes a *completed trespass*, and for such a wrong, Railroad can only be compelled to pay damages. The measure of damages for crop destruction is the value of the crops, and for the destruction of the trees, the measure is either the value of the trees or the diminution in the value of the land.

Construction of railroad right of way: This second wrong is an intentional trespass resulting in occupation by Railroad of the landowners' property. Clearly the remedy of *damages would not be adequate*, because plaintiffs are permanently deprived of their realty. *Ejectment is impracticable* because the sheriff or other official could not possibly remove Railroad from the land. Consequently, this appears to be a proper case for a mandatory injunction compelling the removal of the encroachment. There would be no balancing of hardships because the trespass was willful.

However, one additional fact defeats the injunctive remedy. Here it is stated that Railroad has condemnation powers, and courts are unwilling to enter an order that can be *rendered ineffective* by the defendant's own action in exercising its right of condemnation.

Thus, the court would deny the injunction, grant damages measured by the value of the property taken, and treat the action as one for inverse condemnation (*i.e.*, a case where the landowner rather than the condemning party sues).

Piling dirt and stone on adjacent land: For this third wrong, injunctive relief should be granted (assuming that these piles are not on property that could be properly seized in eminent domain proceedings for the construction of the railroad). The remedy of damages for trespass is available, but it is not considered adequate. In some jurisdictions damages are inadequate because they are measured by rental value, and their recovery thus results in a *multiplicity of actions*. In other jurisdictions the cost of removal is the measure, but this imposes on the landowner the *burden of removing the encroachment*. Consequently, under such circumstances, a mandatory injunction is granted ordering the defendant wrongdoer to remove the encroachment.

ANSWER TO EXAM QUESTION III

1. **Alan v. Barnes**

    Alan may recover a money judgment against Barnes for either damages or restitution, or a constructive trust may be imposed on the stock.

    The selling of the soybeans by Barnes constituted a *conversion*. The measure of damages for this tort is the value of the property on the date of the conversion plus interest. Value ordinarily means market value, thus permitting judgment for the $1,400 value of the soybeans rather than Barnes's $1,200 selling price.

    As an alternative remedy, Alan may seek *restitution* of the benefit gained by Barnes from the tort (waiver of tort and suit in assumpsit). If Alan elects to sue on a common count for money had and received, his recovery is limited to $1,200, but if he elects to sue on a common count for goods sold and delivered, the benefit to Alan is measured by the market value of the beans ($1,400).

    Both the damages and restitutionary remedies result in a money judgment, which is of questionable value because of Barnes's insolvency. The most effective remedy for Alan is to find property upon which a *constructive trust* can be imposed. Here, Alan can trace the $1,200 Barnes realized from the wrongful sale of the soybeans to the acquisition of the shares of stock. Since Barnes obtained title to the stock with Alan's money, a court may impose a constructive trust on the stock to avoid an unjust gain by Barnes. The constructive trust takes the form of a decree declaring Barnes to be a constructive trustee of the stock and ordering her to transfer it to Alan. Because the theory of tracing permits a party to pursue his property into whatever form it takes, Alan would claim the stock as his own property, and thus gain a preference over the other creditors of Barnes.

    Since Barnes has disposed of the soybeans, remedies for specific restitution of the property (such as replevin) are not available.

2. Alan v. Cooper

Alan may recover a money judgment against Cooper either for damages or for restitution. Alan may also seek replevin if title to the beans has not shifted to Cooper by accession.

Since Cooper bought the soybeans from Barnes, a thief, Cooper never acquired legal title to them. Thus, even though he paid value for the beans, Cooper is a *converter*. An innocent converter is liable for the value of the property on the date of the conversion, but not for the enhanced value resulting from improvements made to the chattel. Thus, Cooper is liable for conversion in the amount of $1,400, but not for the $3,000 value of the beans after processing.

As an alternative remedy, Alan may seek *restitution*—again on the theory that Cooper gained a benefit as a result of the conversion and hence wrongfully. The benefit is measured by the value of the soybeans on the date of acquisition and not by the enhanced value resulting from Cooper's processing. The same distinction drawn between innocent and willful converters in measuring damages in conversion cases is applicable where the alternative restitutionary remedy is sought.

Finally, Alan may seek to *replevy* the soybeans. Alan has title and right to possession, and the conversion resulted in a wrongful detention of the soybeans. Cooper has the beans (as processed), which could be seized by the sheriff in executing the writ of replevin. The only issue remaining is whether title to the soybeans shifted to Cooper by accession. Because Cooper was an innocent converter, he could have gained title if the processing resulted in a substantial change in value of the converted property. If Cooper has gained title by accession, replevin is denied. If not, the remedy is available, and Alan may recapture the personalty without paying for the improvements made by Cooper.

There appears to be no basis for an equitable remedy. Soybeans are not unique chattels, and Cooper did not obtain title to anything that could be the subject matter of a constructive trust, or upon which an equitable lien could be imposed.

ANSWER TO EXAM QUESTION IV

Platt may get a decree enjoining the use of her name and picture for advertising purposes.

Theories of liability: In seeking a remedy against Devore, Platt might consider three theories of liability: breach of contract, defamation, and invasion of privacy. The first, *breach of contract*, is not available because Platt in fact never entered into any contract with Devore.

The second, *defamation*, does provide a possible basis for liability. The publication of the advertisement holds Platt up to the ridicule and contempt of her colleagues and thus is defamatory. Furthermore, since this is written defamation, damages may be recovered without proof of special damages. This is not an adequate remedy, however, because damages in cases of injury to reputation are speculative and conjectural, and would not necessarily result in a termination of the advertising. Nonetheless, injunctive relief against a defamatory publication is denied, generally on the rationale that constitutional guarantees of freedom of speech do not permit prior restraints on publication.

The third possible theory available to Platt is the invasion of her common law *right of privacy*. In those jurisdictions recognizing this right, a person is granted protection against the commercial exploitation of her name and picture. Invasion of this right of privacy gives rise to an action for damages. However, in the instant case, damages are an inadequate remedy in that there is no precise measure of the value of Platt's name and picture (she is not a public figure or performer), and because the damages remedy would not preclude further publications of the advertisement. Thus, in jurisdictions where a common law right of privacy is recognized, an injunction would be granted prohibiting further publication of the advertisement.

Effect of statute: The final issue in this case is whether Platt's right to such injunctive relief is affected by the criminal statute making Devore's conduct a misdemeanor. Clearly this statute creates a specific right to be free from commercial exploitation of one's name and picture. The statute also provides a criminal sanction. This creates a problem because the usual rule is that an injunction will not be granted to enjoin an act which is already declared to be a crime. There are, however, two possible answers to this objection.

First, equity has always made an exception where the criminal law remedy is inadequate and the wrong is classified as a public nuisance. In jurisdictions where public nuisance is given an expansive definition, it could be argued that false advertising, as in the instant case, falls within the exception.

Second, statutes such as the one considered in this case have been construed to permit the implication of civil remedies in cases where the criminal law sanctions are ineffective. It could be argued that the possibility of prosecution by public officials of a misdemeanor such as this does not provide an effective remedy for an injured party. Moreover, the use of an injunction would seem to further the legislative policy of protecting a person's right to be free from commercial exploitation of her name and picture. On this reasoning, Platt could be granted injunctive relief prohibiting further publication of the advertisement.

ANSWER TO EXAM QUESTION V

Buyer may recover compensatory damages for fraud, or in the alternative may rescind the contract and seek restitution.

Because the statement by Seller that there was no fill was an intentional misrepresentation of a material fact causing pecuniary loss, Buyer has a claim for compensatory damages against Seller. There are two standards for measuring damages for fraud: the out-of-pocket rule and the benefit-of-the-bargain rule.

The out-of-pocket (or tort) rule measures damages by the difference between the contract price and the actual value of the property received by the buyer. In this case, Buyer would have to establish that a house constructed on fill has a value less than the contract price. Buyer could then recover the difference, plus any consequential damages (none indicated here); and, if the representation was willful and malicious, there is the additional possibility of punitive damages.

The benefit-of-the-bargain (or contract) rule of damages states that recovery is measured by the difference between the value of the property as represented and the actual value received. Because in this case the value represented probably was the contract price, this formula yields the same result as the out-of-pocket rule.

As an alternative to the damages remedy, Buyer may rescind the contract and seek restitution. The basis of rescission is the intentional misrepresentation of a material fact relied on by Buyer to his detriment. To effect the rescission, Buyer must promptly give notice of his election to rescind after discovering the fraud and must offer to restore the property to Seller. Because Buyer has had the use of the property for 11 months, he must also compensate Seller for the value of the use—which may be computed at fair rental value or by the actual benefit to Buyer if that is less. After effecting the rescission, Buyer is entitled to restitution from Seller of the $25,000 down payment plus interest; any monthly installments paid plus interest; the expenditure of $40,000 for improvements less depreciation; the $4,000 for taxes and insurance; and any incidental expenses incurred in the transaction.

ANSWER TO EXAM QUESTION VI

Becky can probably rescind the contract, but she is not entitled to reformation or the imposition of an equitable lien.

1. **Reformation**

   In this case there was a prior oral agreement between Alex and Becky for the sale of *both* Greenacre and Blackacre. This agreement was not incorporated in the deed as a result of Alex's fraud and Becky's mistake. Thus, there is a proper basis for the remedy of reformation—which is in the form of an equitable decree conforming the deed to the parties' original oral agreement.

   Reformation is not defeated by Becky's failure to read the deed. Even if this failure were conceded to be negligent, courts invariably rule that a plaintiff's carelessness does not constitute a defense to this action.

Because the underlying agreement was oral, another possible defense is the Statute of Frauds. Reformation in the instant case would have the effect of enlarging the conveyance on the basis of proof of an oral agreement. Despite this fact, most courts permit a conveyance to be enlarged where there is clear and convincing evidence of the prior agreement.

Since a three-year period elapsed between the execution of the deed and the discovery of the mistake, laches is a third possible defense. Here, Becky knew that she was not in possession of Blackacre, but she did not know of the mistake in the deed. Because she took action promptly after Alex informed her of the terms of the deed, there was no unreasonable delay after discovery of the fraud and hence no defense of laches.

Thus, Becky would be entitled to reformation on these facts were it not for the sale of Blackacre to Xavier, who purchased for $100,000 and without notice of Becky's claim. Since Becky's right to reform is an equitable remedy, it is cut off by sale of the property to a bona fide purchaser. Hence, Becky is not entitled to reformation against Xavier, who takes free of the equity, or against Alex, who no longer has any title to Blackacre that could be transferred to Becky.

2. **Equitable Lien**

To impress an equitable lien on Blackacre, Becky must trace the funds that she paid to Alex ($200,000) to the acquisition or improvement of Blackacre. In addition, she must show that retention of the property so acquired results in the unjust enrichment of Alex. Here, no tracing can be established since Alex already owned Blackacre and there is no proof that any of Becky's $200,000 was used to improve it. Moreover, any equitable lien would be cut off by the sale of the property to Xavier, a bona fide purchaser. Xavier, having paid value for the property, is not unfairly enriched at Becky's expense.

3. **Rescission**

The basis of Becky's action for rescission is the intentional misrepresentation by Alex of the size of the conveyance. This was certainly a material misrepresentation of fact which was relied on by Becky and caused her pecuniary loss. However, to avail herself of the remedy of rescission, Becky must have given prompt notice of her election to rescind after discovering the fraud and must have offered to restore anything of value received in the transaction. Here, Becky gave notice of rescission by filing suit immediately after she was told by Alex of the provisions of the deed, and she has offered to reconvey Greenacre. (She will also have to account for the use value of the property during the three-year period of her occupancy.) There is no showing that during the three-year period that Becky had any actual knowledge of the error in the deed and, in any case, there is no showing that a delay was prejudicial to Alex, who at all times knew the facts. Hence, rescission would appear to be a remedy available to Becky and would permit recovery of the $200,000 plus interest.

4. Damages

Becky has an alternative to rescission: an action at law for damages for fraud. Again, the basis of the action is an intentional misrepresentation of a material fact—the size of the conveyance. If Becky elects this remedy, she affirms the contract and seeks compensation for her loss. If damages are measured by the out-of-pocket rule, Becky would recover the difference between the contract price ($200,000) and the actual value of what she received (Greenacre). If the benefit-of-the-bargain rule is applied, Becky recovers the difference between the value as represented (*i.e.,* both Greenacre and Blackacre) and the actual value received (Greenacre). Since the value as represented may be the same as the contract price, the two measures may yield the same dollar result.

ANSWER TO EXAM QUESTION VII

Benny is entitled to both reformation of the deed to Whiteacre and to specific performance of the contract to convey Blackacre.

1. Reformation

The deed to Whiteacre should be reformed to reduce the size of the conveyance to a one-fifth interest. Both parties to the contract understood that the agreement was to convey an undivided one-fifth interest, and the deed—by the use of the words, "all my interest" failed to correctly incorporate that understanding. The error in integration was the result of Benny's mistake, which Alice knew about at the time the deed was executed. Because the underlying agreement was fair and understood by both parties, the deed should be reformed to correctly carry it out.

There are two possible defenses to Benny's suit for reformation. The first is the Statute of Frauds. If the original written contract stated that Benny was to convey a one-fifth interest, the statutory requirement of a memorandum might be met. But if it did not, oral evidence must be introduced to establish the underlying agreement, and, because transfer of an interest in land is involved, the Statute of Frauds would be violated. Nevertheless, American courts unanimously agree that a deed can be reformed to reduce the size of a conveyance when the underlying agreement is established by clear and convincing evidence.

The second defense is the conveyance of Whiteacre by Alice to Carlo. If Carlo were a bona fide purchaser of Whiteacre, Benny's equity would be cut off. On the facts given, however, Carlo had notice of Benny's interest at the time the *deed* was executed. While he had no notice of Benny's interest at the time the *contract* with Alice was executed, that contract merely created an equity in Carlo. Because Benny also had an equity, the applicable rule states that where equities are equal, the first in time prevails. Thus, Carlo could not defeat the suit for reformation, but he would have an action against Alice for restitution of the price he paid, based on the material breach of contract by Alice.

2. **Specific Performance**

Because the contract called for the conveyance of land (Blackacre) in exchange for Benny's personal services and Whiteacre, specific performance is a proper remedy. The purchaser's remedy at law for breach of a land sale contract is considered inadequate because of the uniqueness of land. Thus, unless Alice has some defense to the suit, the equitable remedy should be granted.

Three possible defenses could be asserted by Alice. The first is negative mutuality, because part of the consideration for the conveyance was the performance of personal services by Benny, and personal services cannot be judicially compelled. The argument would be that a court should not order the defendant, Alice, to perform her promise where it cannot assure her of getting what was promised in exchange (here, the personal services). The argument fails in this case, however, because Benny completed the personal service part of the contract before filing the suit for specific performance. Hence, there will in fact be mutuality of performance, and, under modern interpretations of the negative mutuality doctrine, that is all that is required today.

The second possible defense available to Alice is hardship. The argument would be that the consideration for Blackacre is grossly inadequate because the discovery of oil makes Blackacre much more valuable. Specific performance should therefore be denied because it imposes an undue hardship on Alice. There are two responses to this argument. First, courts have traditionally been unwilling to deny specific performance for mere inadequacy of consideration where not accompanied by sharp practice, mistake, fraud, or some other form of misconduct. Moreover, adequacy of consideration is always measured at the time the contract is *executed*, and there is no showing that in August of 2002 this bargain was not a fair exchange.

The third and final argument would be that the parties were mutually mistaken as to a basic fact (the nature and condition of Blackacre), that this mistake provides a basis for rescission, and that *a fortiori* it is a defense to specific performance. However, mistake as to the *nature and value* of land is always regarded as extrinsic and collateral. In other words, courts generally require the parties to assume the risk that the land that is the subject matter of the contract may turn out to be more or less valuable than was originally thought. The disadvantaged party is not permitted to escape by tearing up the contract. Hence, the mistake here provides no basis for rescission and no defense to Benny's suit for specific performance.

ANSWER TO EXAM QUESTION VIII

Alvin may be entitled to specific performance and should sue Rudolph, who is entitled to the proceeds (the contract price) upon transfer of the title.

The first issue in the case is whether a valid contract for the sale of the land was executed. Here, the decedent leased the property and gave an option to purchase, supported by separate consideration, to Tess. Because there was no restriction in the lease prohibiting assignment, Tess could validly assign the lease to Alvin. The option ran with the land and hence to Alvin. Because the option was supported by consideration, it was not terminated by Lew's death and was a valid contract claim against his estate. Hence, when Alvin exercised the option within the 10-year time period, a valid contract was formed.

The second issue in the case is whether that contract is specifically enforceable. In a suit for specific performance of a land sale contract by a buyer against a seller, the remedy at law is considered inadequate because of the uniqueness of land. Because Alvin, the party seeking specific enforcement in this case, is an assignee of the original party, he stands in the shoes of the assignor and must meet all of the conditions of the contract. That contract calls for a down payment, and a note and mortgage for the balance. In agreeing to these terms, the seller bargained for both the personal credit of the original buyer and the security of the land. Hence, under the majority rule, Alvin can meet the terms of the contract only by tendering a note executed by Tess (the assignor). In the minority of jurisdictions, which have a rule disallowing personal liability in purchase money mortgage situations, it is sufficient for the assignee, Alvin, to tender his own note.

Assuming that there is a valid contract that is specifically enforceable by Alvin, the final issue in the case is the effect of the death of Lew on the determination of the proper parties to the suit. This calls for an analysis of the application of the doctrine of equitable conversion.

The doctrine of equitable conversion recognizes that certain equitable interests are created immediately upon the execution of a specifically enforceable land sale contract. In equity, the buyer is regarded as the beneficial owner of the realty and the seller, who has legal title, is regarded as having a beneficial interest in personalty (the right to the contract price). Thus, on the death of the seller, the right to the contract price (the seller's beneficial interest) passes as personalty whereas the heir or devisee takes legal title subject to a duty to convey it to the buyer. In the instant case, had Lew died after the exercise of the option, Pat would get the contract price as part of Lew's personalty and Rudolph would inherit the title subject to the duty to convey it to Alvin.

However, here the option was not exercised (*i.e.*, the contract was not formed) until after the death of Lew. Under such circumstances, no conversion occurs until the option is exercised. Rudolph, who inherits the property subject to the option, is regarded as the seller. Thus, in a suit for specific performance, Alvin need only join Rudolph as defendant. Rudolph will be ordered to convey title to the property to Alvin, and Rudolph has the right to the proceeds of the sale.

In this situation, a minority of courts apply a "relation back" doctrine. Once the option is exercised, the resulting contract "relates back" to the time the option was given.

Thus, the decedent is regarded as dying with a land sale contract in effect, and the ordinary rule of equitable conversion is applied. Under this rule, Alvin would join Rudolph and Pat as defendants, with Pat getting the money as part of the decedent's personal estate, and Rudolph, who inherits legal title, being ordered to convey it to Alvin.

ANSWER TO EXAM QUESTION IX

Brown should interplead Thomas and Smith, pay the contract price into court, and seek specific performance.

The agreement between Brown and Smith is a contract for the sale of goods, because it is the seller's obligation to sever or remove the clay from the realty. For breach of a contract for the sale of goods by the seller, the buyer has alternative remedies. Brown may recover damages measured by the difference between the market price and the contract price at the time of the breach, together with any incidental and consequential damages. Or, as an alternative, Brown may seek to "cover" by procuring a substitute supply, and then recover the difference between the cost of cover and the contract price plus any incidental or consequential damages. If Brown elected to cover here, he would recover the difference between the contract price of $10 per ton and the substitute price of $15 per ton plus the additional freight charges.

In the instant case, however, Brown's best remedy is specific performance. The damages remedies above are considered inadequate because of the difficulty of computing the loss where the contract is for a long term and market prices can be expected to fluctuate. "Cover" is not considered adequate because of the great inconvenience and hardship of forcing Brown to procure supplies at a distance of 1,000 miles from his factory. Thus, specific performance of this contract by Smith would be granted even though the contract is for the sale of non-unique goods.

To enforce the contract specifically, Brown must comply with its conditions, and the contract requires Brown to pay $10 for each ton of clay delivered on the first day of each month. But Brown now has notice that Smith may be trustee for Thomas of a one-half interest in the property. If Brown pays Smith the full contract price, knowing that Smith has violated his fiduciary obligation to Thomas, Brown may be liable to Thomas.

To enforce the contract, and at the same time protect his interests, Brown obviously needs to join Thomas and Smith and obtain a judicial determination of the proper interest of each party in the contract price. The appropriate procedure for this purpose is interpleader. Brown owes one debt for the purchase of the clay and there are overlapping and conflicting claims. Brown should therefore interplead Thomas and Smith and pay the contract price into court. Under modern codes, interpleader is permitted as long as the claims of the interpleaded parties (Thomas and Smith) are mutually exclusive. The additional requirements of privity, identity, disinterest, and indifference found in chancery practice have largely been abandoned. Once the interpleader is successfully accomplished, Brown may enforce the contract because the payment stipulated in the contract has been made. The actual disposition of these funds will depend on the outcome of the dispute between Smith and Thomas as to the validity of the trust.

ANSWER TO EXAM QUESTION X

1. Owner may recover damages in the amount of $2,500. Builder has no remedy against Owner.

    Owner v. Builder: Owner has an action for damages for Builder's material breach of the contract. Because there has been part performance by Builder, the damages are measured by what Owner must pay to have another builder complete the construction, less anything owing to Builder under the contract, plus special damages. Here it would cost an additional $20,000 to complete the construction. Because $7,500 has been paid to Builder, Owner owes an additional $17,500 on the original contract. Owner's damages are $2,500 ($20,000 less $17,500).

    The remedy of specific performance is ordinarily not available because of the adequacy of the remedy at law and the unwillingness of courts to supervise construction contracts. Because Owner has paid less than the benefit received from Builder, restitution is not an appropriate remedy.

    Builder v. Owner: If Builder sought a remedy, it would have to be restitutionary and based on a claim of unjust enrichment of Owner. Builder cannot enforce the contract itself because of his material breach. In the instant case, some courts would deny even a restitutionary remedy because Builder's breach was willful. Other courts do not regard the nature of the builder's conduct as controlling and allow restitution.

    If relief is allowed, the method of measuring the recovery must take into account that it is the plaintiff, Builder, who has breached the contract. Thus, the usual formula is contract price less cost of completion plus consequential damages for delay. In the instant case, this formula yields $5,000 ($25,000 less $20,000). Because Owner already made progress payments of $7,500, Builder would not be entitled to any award. An alternative formula, proposed by the Restatement of Contracts, measures restitution by the excess of benefit received over harm suffered by the owner, in no case to exceed the ratable proportion of the contract price. Because Owner has paid $7,500 and is damaged in the amount of $5,000, the benefit he received ($10,000) does not exceed the harm suffered. Thus, this formula yields an identical result of no recovery.

2. Builder's best remedy is restitution, but damages may be recoverable in some jurisdictions.

Where the owner repudiates the contract after partial performance by the builder, there are several formulas for measuring damages. The usual measure is contract price, less cost of completion and any partial payments made by the owner. Application of this formula in the instant case would result in a denial of any recovery to Builder—$25,000 (contract price) less $20,000 (cost of completion) = $5,000 less $7,500 (partial payment) yields zero. A second measure is contract price less total cost of performance plus any partial payments made. In the instant case, the computation is $25,000 less $30,000 (total cost of performance) = $0 (profit), plus $10,000 (cost of partial performance). Deducting the $7,500 partial payment yields a recovery of $2,500. A third formula measures damages by such proportion of the contract price as the fair cost of the work completed bears to the fair cost of the whole work required; and in respect to the work not done, only such profit as the builder would have made by doing it. In this case, the computation is as follows: $10,000/$30,000 x $25,000 = $8,333.33. $25,000 - $30,000 = $0 (profit). $8,333.33 + $0 = $8,333.33. Since $7,500 has been paid to Builder, that amount is deducted from $8,333.33, yielding a result of $833.33.

The above calculations indicate that where the contract is a losing one, the damages remedy for Builder may not be a particularly useful or desirable one. Builder's best remedy under such circumstances is restitution. This permits Builder to recover the value of the benefit conferred on Owner. Normally this would be measured by Builder's expenditures and would not be limited by the contract price (although there is a minority rule imposing such a limitation). In this case, Builder has expended $10,000 and has received progress payments of $7,500 from Owner. Thus, Builder would recover an additional $2,500.

Table of Cases

Archer v. Stone - **§895**

Archer, Harvey & Co., *In re* - **§983**

Arians v. Larkin Bank - **§946**

Armory Park Neighborhood Association v. Episcopal
Community Services - **§446**

Arnjo v. Cebolleta - **§1335**

Arnold v. Hall - **§1135**

Askren v. 21st Street Inn - **§1067**

Associate Discount Corp. v. Clements - **§1028**

Atkins v. Kirkpatrick - **§1007**

Atlas Construction Co. v. Slater - **§1111**

Atlas Powder Co. v. Ireco Chemicals - **§534**

Attman/Glazer, State v. - **§1060**

Augustin Bros., *In re* - **§1290**

Austin Instrument Co. v. Loral Corp. - **§955**

Autocephalous Greek Orthodox Church v. Goldberg &
Fineman Fine Arts - **§318**

Aveco Properties v. E.J. Nicholson - **§1132**

B

B & B Amusement Enterprises, Inc. v. City of Boston -
§953

B.D. Inns v. Pooley - **§1122**

BDO Seidman v. Hirshberg - **§1265**

B.M.W. v. Gore - **§§58, 59**

Bachowski v. Salamone - **§§698, 700**

Bachynsky v. State - **§§179, 181**

Bacmo Associates v. Strange - **§1092**

Bailey v. Banther - **§1347**

Bailey v. West - **§237**

Baker v. Carr - **§731**

Baker v. General Motors - **§199**

Baker v. Libbie - **§587**

Bakken v. Price - **§1108**

Ball v. Joy Technologies - **§745**

Baltimore Orioles v. Major League Baseball Players -
§636

Banco Cafetero Panama, United States v. - **§282**

Bancorp Leasing v. Stadeli Pump - **§347**

Bancroft v. Woodward - **§863**

Bandel v. Friedrich - **§77**

Bank of Nova Scotia v. Bloch - **§237**

Bank of Santa Fe v. Garcia - **§1082**

Bank of Tucson v. Adrian - **§947**

Bank Saderat Iran v. Amin Beydoun, Inc. - **§1021**

Banque Worms v. Bankamerica International - **§1025**

Banton v. Hackney - **§262**

Baram v. Farugia - **§349**

Bartley v. Karas - **§1156**

Bashir v. Bache - **§194**

Bass v. Smith - **§1100**

Batchedler & Lincoln Co. v. Whitmore - **§1354**

Bateman Eichler, Hill Richards, Inc. v. Berner - **§1355**

Bauer v. P.A. Cutri Co. - **§167**

Baugh v. Johnson - **§1112**

Bausch & Lomb, Inc. v. Dressler - **§22**

Bauserman v. Dignilian - **§1073**

Bay Mills Indian Community, United States v. - **§138**

Bay Springs Forest Products, Inc. v. Wade - **§349**

Beard v. S/E Joint Venture - **§1088**

Beatty v. Washington Metro Area Transit Authority -
§451

Beaulieu v. Elliott - **§93**

Becker v. Sunrise at Elkridge - **§1226**

Beecher v. Conte - **§1063**

Beeman v. Manville Corp. - **§761**

Beeman v. Worrell - **§1218**

Belinsky v. Belinsky - **§426**

Bell v. Smith - **§529**

Belmont International v. American International Shoe -
§246

Ben Holt Industries v. Milne - **§1287**

Ben Lomond v. Allen - **§1152**

Ben Lomond, Inc. v. Campbell - **§324**

Bennett v. Haley - **§796**

Bennett v. Lembo - **§781**

Bennett v. Shimoda Floral, Inc. - **§1010**

Benyon Building Corp. v. National Guardian Life
Insurance - **§1032**

Berrien v. Pollitzer - **§716**

Berry, *In re* - **§181**

Berry v. Donovan - **§503**

Best v. United States National Bank - **§970**

Beverly Glen Music v. Warner Communications - **§1256**

Beynon Building Corp. v. National Guardian Life
Insurance - **§1032**

Biechele v. Norfolk & Western Railway - **§460**

Bingham v. Struve - **§676**

Bi-Rite Enterprises v. Button Master - **§636**

Birnbaum v. United States - **§694**

Bisset v. Gooch - **§1225**

Bistricher v. Bistricher - **§158**

Bivens v. Six Unknown Named Agents - **§156**

Blackwelder Furniture Co. v. Seilig Manufacturing Co. -
§208

Blain v. The Doctor's Co. - **§163**

Blakely v. Gorin - **§445**

Blasingame, *Ex parte* - **§168**

Blatt v. University of Southern California - **§714**

Blue Ash Building & Loan Co. v. Hahn - **§1086**

Blue Ridge Sewer Improvement v. Lowry & Associates -
§1332

Board of Curators of the University of Missouri v.
Horowitz - **§721**

Board of Directors v. Western National Bank - **§237**

Board of Education v. A, C and S, Inc. - **§31**

Board of Education v. Rettaliata - **§245**

Bocker Co. v. Eagle Bank of Madison City - **§255**

Boeing Co. v. Aetna Casualty & Surety Co. - **§18**

Boeing Co. v. Sierracin Corp. - **§568**

Bohlin v. Jungbauer - **§1096**

Dandoy v. Oswald - **§422**

DaSilva v. Musso - **§134**

Daugherty v. Young - **§916**

Davenport v. Vlach - **§899**

Davis v. Gage - **§61**

Davis v. Schuchat - **§672**

Davis, Estate of v. Johnson - **§832**

Dawson v. Hill & Hill Truck Lines - **§835**

Day v. Wiswall - **§197**

Deakyne v. Lewes Anglers, Inc. - **§385**

Dean v. Dean - **§26**

De Arellano v. Weinberger - **§194**

De Castris v. Gutta - **§81**

DeChico v. Metro-North Commuter Railroad - **§85**

Degroen v. Mark Toyota-Volvo - **§649**

Delano Growers' Cooperative Winery v. Supreme Wine Co. - **§1178**

Del Bosco v. United States Ski Association - **§1320**

Dellums v. Bush - **§732**

Dennis v. Ford Motor Co. - **§294**

Denver Milk Bottle Case & Can Exchange v. McKinzie - **§219**

Department of Human Services, State *ex rel.* v. Rael - **§177**

Department of Transportation v. Roulee - **§1018**

Desny v. Wilder - **§584**

De Spirito v. Bristol County Water Co. - **§302**

Developers Three v. Nationwide Insurance Co. - **§510**

Devlin v. Kearney Mesa - **§64**

De Weerth v. Baldinger- **§318**

Diamond v. Oreamuno - **§527**

Dick Corp. v. Associated Electric Cooperative, Inc. - **§1018**

Dickerman v. Lord & Smith - **§951**

Diggs v. Pepsi-Cola Metropolitan Bottling Co. - **§1230**

Dior v. Milton - **§615**

Di Salle v. P.G. Publishing Co. - **§672**

Dixie Glass v. Pollack - **§ 1231**

Dixon v. City of Monticello - **§1062**

Dixon v. Salvation Army - **§1102**

Dlug v. Woolridge - **§§1003, 1103**

Doherty v. Allman - **§376**

Dombrowski v. Pfister - **§147**

Dominick v. Vassar - **§1169**

Don v. Trojan Construction Co. - **§421**

Donnel v. Lara - **§695**

Donovan v. Bachstadt - **§1089**

Doran v. Salem Inn, Inc. - **§147**

Dorey v. Dorey - **§196**

Dorsett Carpet Mills v. Whitt Tile & Marble - **§499**

Dorsey v. Speelman - **§367**

Douglass v. Hustler Magazine - **§691**

Douthit v. Swift - **§177**

Dover Pool & Racquet Club, Inc. v. Brooking - **§1006**

Dowling v. McKenney - **§1278**

Duddy-Robinson Co. v. Taylor - **§1359**

Dumas v. Ropp - **§386**

Dun & Bradstreet, Inc. v. Greenmoss Builders, Inc. - **§§657, 667, 668, 669, 670, 671**

Dunfee v. Baskin-Robbins - **§97**

Dunkin' Donuts of America v. Middletown Donut - **§135**

Dunn v. Hovic - **§66**

Dunwoody v. Trapnell - **§807**

duPont v. Southern National Bank - **§1057**

Dura Corp. v. Harned - **§783**

Dworkin v. Hustler Magazine - **§637**

E

EEOC v. Dresser Industries, Inc. - **§164**

E.L. Husting Co. v. Coca-Cola - **§505**

Earhart v. William Low Co. - **§239**

Earl v. Bouchard Transportation Co. - **§756**

Earl v. Saks & Co. - **§895**

Earl v. Times-Mirror Co. - **§789**

Earven v. Smith - **§1129**

Eaton v. Engelcke Manufacturing, Inc. - **§242**

Edwards v. Lee's Administrators - **§§438, 496**

Edwards v. Renton - **§1334**

Eggert v. Weisz - **§267**

Elden v. Sheldon - **§844**

El Greco Leather Products Co. v. Shoe World - **§644**

Ellis v. Butterfield - **§1155**

Ellis v. Peoples National Bank of Manassas - **§1354**

Elvis Presley International Memorial Foundation v. Crowell - **§635**

Empire Fire & Marine Insurance Co. v. Fremont Indemnity Co. - **§528**

Environmental Defense Fund Inc. v. Alexander - **§164**

Equilease Corp. v. Hentz - **§1025**

Erick Bowman Remedy Co. v. Jensen-Salsberg Laboratories - **§644**

Erickson v. Playgirl - **§1233**

Erlich v. Menzes - **§26**

Escobar v. Continental Baking Co. - **§462**

Escrow Agents' Fidelity v. Superior Court - **§227**

Esparza v. Specht - **§885**

Estate Counseling Service v. Merrill Lynch, Pierce, Fenner & Smith, Inc. - **§860**

Estate of - *see name of party*

Evra Corp. v. Swiss Bank Corp. - **§29**

Ewing v. Bissell - **§984**

Ex parte - *see name of party*

Executive Jet Aviation v. United States - **§293**

Exxon Corp. v. Brecheen - **§825**

Exxon Valdez, *In re* - **§67**

Eyoma v. Falco - **§782**

F

F.E.L. Publications v. Catholic Archbishop of Chicago - **§163**

Glasgow v. Greenfield - §1030
Gleason v. Guzman - §1010
Glover v. Santangelo - §445
Goddard v. General Motors Corp. - §1180
Goff, State ex rel. v. O'Neil - §469
Goldberg v. Sanglier - §1353
Golden Cone Concepts v. Villa Linda Mall - §921
Gooch v. Lake - §763
Goodrich, United States v. - §524
Gorder v. Sims - §705
Gordon v. Schumacher- §132
Goshgarion v. George - §64
Goss v. Lopez - §722
Gould v. Taco Bell - §60
Goulding v. Cook - §404
Gow, People ex rel. v. Mitchell Brothers Santa Ana
    Theater - §472
Great Western Bank & Trust v. Nahat - §983
Greater Louisville Auto Auction, Inc. v. Ogle Buick, Inc. -
    §1200
Green v. Franklin - §842
Green v. General Petroleum Corp. - §§423, 424
Green v. Gustafson - §1286
Green v. Higgins - §157
Green v. Interstate United Management Services Corp. -
    §1292
Greenstein v. Greenbrook, Ltd. - §1064
Griffin v. Axsom - §857
Grim v. Chestwood - §1355
Grimes, In re - §713
Grombone v. Krekel - §1138
Grossinger Motorcorp v. American National Bank & Trust
    - §53
Grossman Holdings, Ltd. v. Hourihan - §1221
Gruenberg v. Aetna Insurance Co. - §95
Guerrero v. Hagco Building Systems - §898
Guild Mortgage Co. v. Heller - §1141
Guthrie v. Times-Mirror Co. - §1030

H

H.B. Fuller v. National Starch & Chemical Corp. - §540
H.B. Fuller Co. v. Kinetic Systems, Inc. - §1183
H.J. McGrath v. Wisner - §1205
H.K. Porter Co. v. National Friction Products - §168
H. Russell Taylor's Fire Prevention Service, Inc. v. Coca-
    Cola Bottling - §247
Haber Oil Co., In re - §275
Hackethal v. California Medical Association - §717
Haddigan v. Harkins - §826
Hadley v. Baxendale - §§23, 24, 25, 29, 46, 95, 498,
    850, 919, 1090, 1091, 1096, 1165, 1172,
    1178, 1250
Hainey v. Narigon - §1362
Hajek v. Bill Mowbray Motors - §649
Halbman v. Lemke - §1315

Hale v. Allinson - §222
Hale v. Kriesal - §1272
Hallett's Estate, Re - §283
Hamilton v. Nakai - §186
Hammond v. North American Asbestos Corp. - §845
Hanscom v. Hanscom - §1347
Hansen v. Mountain Fuel Supply Co. - §§744, 745, 746
Hanson v. Ford Motor Co. - §883
Hardin, State ex rel. v. Sanders - §838
Hardy v. St. Mathew's Community Center - §1352
Harford Penn-Cann Service v. Zymblosky - §458
Harker Heights v. Sun Meadows Land - §244
Harmon v. Harmon - §250
Harmon Motors v. Farmers Union Grain Terminal - §461
Harper v. Adametz - §530
Harris v. Atlantic Richfield Co. - §97
Hart v. E.P. Dutton & Co. - §683
Hartford, The v. Doubler - §1030
Hartigan, People ex rel. v. Candy Club - §272
Haslem v. O'Hosen - §1037
Hastings v. Matlock - §906
Hastoupis v. Gargas - §1294
Hatzlachh Supply Co. v. United States - §247
Haumont v. Security State Bank - §905
Hawks v. Yancy - §697
Hayes v. Hartelius - §1270
Hayes v. Trulock - §1235
Hayes-Albion v. Kuberski - §574
Hazelwood Water District v. First Union Management -
    §238
Hazlett v. Bryant - §1056
Head & Seeman v. Greg - §917
Health Maintenance Network v. Blue Cross - §161
Heaton v. Imus - §242
Hebron Public School District v. United States Gypsum -
    §238
Hector Martinez & Co. v. Southern Pacific Transportation
    Co. - §24
Helix Land Co. v. City of San Diego - §228
Hellwig v. Hellwig - §188
Helton v. City of St. Joseph - §369
Henderson v. Fisher - §1295
Hendricksen v. California Newspapers Inc. - §§690, 692
Henry Hope X-Ray Products v. Marron Carrel, Inc. -
    §572
Hernandez v. Atlantic Finance Co. - §924
Herrin v. Opatut - §463
Hewlett v. Barge Bertie - §307
Hickman v. Mulder - §380
Hicks v. Miranda - §147
Hicks Corp. v. National Training Association - §646
Hicks ex rel. Feiock v. Feiock - §174
High v. Howard - §847
Highland Construction Co. v. Union Pacific Railroad -
    §32
Hiland Apartments v. City of Hillsboro - §238

Hill v. Gateway 2000, Inc. - **§969**
Hill v. Mobile Auto Trim - **§1260**
Hillblom v. Ivancsits - **§1107**
Hiller v. Manufacturers Product Research Group of North America, Inc. - **§34**
Hilliard v. Fox - **§1021**
Hinville v. Wilson - **§112**
Hirko v. Hirko - **§187**
Hitaffer v. Argonne Co. - **§844**
Hoagburg v. Harrah's Marina Hotel - **§653**
Hoaglin v. Decker - **§429**
Hobbs v. Smith - **§465**
Hochman v. Zigler's Inc. - **§955**
Hocken v. Hocken - **§1348**
Hodnett v. Harmon - **§267**
Hofer v. Lavendar - **§807**
Hoffman v. SV Co. - **§1283**
Hogan v. New York Times Co. - **§659**
Holm v. Shilensky - **§980**
Holman v. Johnson - **§1342**
Homart Development Co. v. Sigman - **§129**
Home Box Office v. Showtime/The Movie Channel - **§608**
Home Savers v. United Security Co. - **§1015**
Honda Motor Co. v. Oberg - **§57**
Honey v. Henry's Franchise Leasing Corp. - **§1152**
Hooker Chemicals v. Attorney General - **§220**
Hopkins v. Price Waterhouse - **§1253**
Hopper Furs, Inc. v. Emery Air Freight Corp. - **§1014**
Hopwood v. State of Texas - **§720**
Horn v. Seth - **§501**
Horseshoe Estates v. 2M Co. - **§235**
Hoxworth v. Blinder, Robinson & Co. - **§213**
Hudson v. Lazarus - **§77**
Huff v. Tracy - **§780**
Huffman v. Pursue Ltd. - **§148**
Hull v. United States - **§739**
Humble Oil & Refinery Co. v. Kishi - **§427**
Hunt v. Hunt - **§702**
Hunt v. Liberty Lobby - **§656**
Hunt v. Shamblin - **§1094**
Huntworth v. Tanner - **§143**
Hurd v. Nelson - **§78**
Hyman v. Cain - **§1322**

I

Ide v. Joe Miller & Co. - **§1103**
Illinois v. City of Milwaukee - **§470**
Imperial Ice v. Rossiter - **§505**
In re - *see* name of party
Indiana & Michigan Electric Co. v. Harlan - **§922**
Intermarkets U.S.A. v. C-E Natco - **§267**
International Harvester Credit Corp. v. Hellend - **§326**
International Industries, Inc. v. Warren Petroleum Corp. - **§562**
International News Service v. Associated Press - **§§613, 619**

International Union, United Mine Workers v. Bagwell - **§174**
Iota Management v. Boulevard Insurance Co. - **§§914, 915**
Irrigation Motor & Pump Co. v. Belcher - **§1184**
Isabell v. Brighton Area Schools - **§157**
Islamic Republic of Iran v. Boeing Co. - **§1192**
Island Creek Coal Co. v. Lake Shore, Inc. - **§62**
Ives Laboratories, Inc. v. Darby Drug Co. - **§§616, 618**

J

J.A. Sullivan Corp. v. Commonwealth - **§244**
J. Abrams & Co. v. Clark - **§939**
J & K Computer Systems v. Parrish - **§556**
J.R. v. M.P., Y.B. - **§976**
Jackson v. Johns-Manville Products Corp. - **§66**
Jacque v. Steenberg Homes - **§431**
Jaffe-Spindler Co. v. Genesco, Inc. - **§381**
Jagger Bros. Inc. v. Technical Textile Co. - **§1190**
J'Aire Corp. v. Gregory - **§30**
James v. Public Finance Corp. - **§62**
James S. Kemper & Co. v. Cox & Associates, Inc. - **§1259**
Janigan v. Taylor - **§886**
Jankowski v. Preiser Animal Hospital - **§304**
Jeannont v. New Hampshire Personnel Commission - **§1232**
Jensen v. Torr - **§215**
Jim Walter Homes v. Reed - **§30**
Jim's Hot Shot Service v. Continental West Insurance Co. - **§482**
Joannin v. Ogilvie - **§930**
Johnson v. Baker - **§75**
Johnson v. General Motors Corp. - **§1185**
Johnson v. Gray - **§1141**
Johnson v. Healy - **§§871, 872**
Johnson v. Jensen - **§409**
Johnson v. Johnson - **§1362**
Johnson v. Jones - **§547**
Johnson v. Kelly - **§148**
Johnson Building Co. v. River Bluff Development - **§886**
Johnston v. Sorrels - **§1043**
Jones v. Consolidated Rail Corp. - **§47**
Jones v. Hoar - **§352**
Jones v. Star Credit Corp. - **§971**
Jones v. Wagner - **§400**
Jones & Laughlin Steel Co. v. Pfeiffer - **§94**
Jones-Gray Construction Co. v. Stephens - **§1309**
Jordan v. Long Beach Community Hospital - **§738**
Journigan v. Eastover Bank for Savings - **§114**
Juidice v. Vail - **§148**
Julian v. Ralph - **§§307, 308**
Julius Hyman & Co. v. Velsicol Corp. - **§§564, 572**
Jursich v. Arlington Heights Federal Savings & Loan - **§1030**
Justin Belt Co. v. Yost - **§1045**

Los Angeles Memorial Coliseum Commission v. National Football League - **§208**

Losee v. Morey & Cramer - **§1093**

Lothschuetz v. Carpenter- **§679**

Loughry v. Lincoln First Bank - **§60**

Louisville & Nashville Railroad v. Crowe - **§1309**

Lovelace Medical Center v. Mendez - **§850**

Loveridge v. Pendleton Woolen Mills - **§209**

Lowder v. Missouri Baptist College - **§34**

Lowe v. Foundation Northern Trust Co. - **§516**

Loy v. Bunderson - **§232**

Lucky Auto Supply v. Turner - **§440**

Lugosi v. Universal Pictures - **§635**

Lumley v. Wagner - **§§1254, 1258**

Lynch v. Uhlenkopp - **§713**

Lynn v. Seby - **§1250**

Lyon v. Izen - **§712**

M

M & M Pipe & Pressure Vessel Fabricators, Inc. v. Roberts - **§834**

MCA Records, Inc. v. Newton-John - **§1254**

M.F. Kemper Construction Co. v. Los Angeles - **§1018**

MacFadden v. Walker - **§1156**

MacLean & Associates v. American Guaranty Life Insurance Co. - **§34**

McAlister v. Carl - **§781**

McAnarney v. Newark Fire Insurance Co. - **§359**

McCamley v. Shockey - **§1010**

McCart v. H&R Block, Inc. - **§1259**

McCoy v. West - **§918**

McCramm v. United States Lines - **§71**

McCullough v. Bill Swad Chrysler-Plymouth - **§856**

McDermott v. Kansas Public Service Co. - **§66**

McDonald v. Mianecki - **§1111**

McDougald v. Garber - **§780**

McFaddin v. H.S. Crocker Co. - **§322**

McGee Construction v. Neshobe Development - **§1209**

McGilchrist v. F.W. Woolworth Co. - **§1276**

McGinnis v. Wentworth Chevrolet Co. - **§1184**

McGlothlin v. Kilebert - **§392**

McGregor v. Mommer - **§§855, 899**

McKay v. Palmer - **§197**

McKee v. Colt Electronics Co. - **§§819, 831**

McKee v. Neilson - **§846**

McKinley v. Weidner - **§163**

McKinney v. Christiana Community Builders - **§361**

McMerty v. Herzog - **§277**

McPherson v. Schlemmer - **§294**

McQuady v. McQuady - **§171**

Macon-Bibb County Water & Sewer Authority v. Tuttle/ White Constructors - **§82**

Madore v. Ingram Tank Ships - **§89**

Mahen & Rowsey, *In re* - **§288**

Maheu v. C.B.S. - **§588**

Maheu v. Hughes Tool Co. - **§672**

Mahoney v. Tingley - **§1095**

Maier Brewing Co. v. Fleischmann Distilling Corp. - **§609**

Malacynski v. McDonnell Douglas Corp. - **§834**

Malzof v. United States - **§782**

Mangini v. McClung - **§1011**

Manko v. United States - **§796**

Manown v. Adams - **§163**

Manson v. Reed - **§1141**

Marcus v. Bathon - **§984**

Marcus v. Otis - **§274**

Maritote v. Desilu Productions - **§635**

Mark v. State Department of Fish and Wildlife - **§473**

Marks v. Gates - **§135**

Marshak v. Green - **§609**

Martin v. Reynolds Metals Co. - **§648**

Martin v. Scholl - **§1295**

Martin v. U-Haul Co. of Fresno - **§97**

Martin v. United States - **§759**

Maryland Casualty v. ARMCO - **§18**

Mash v. C.B.S., Inc. - **§616**

Masinter v. Tenneco Oil Co. - **§757**

Mass Transit Administration v. Granite Construction Co. - **§247**

Massachusetts Society of Optometrists v. Waddick - **§473**

Matanuska Electric Association v. Weissler - **§69**

Matarese v. Moore-McCormack Lines, Inc. - **§585**

Mathews v. DeSoto - **§69**

Mattingly, Inc. v. Beatrice Foods Co. - **§483**

Mattson v. Commercial Credit Business Loans - **§§352, 357**

Matuz v. Gerardin Corp. - **§820**

Maumelle Co. v. Escola - **§898**

Maurer v. United States - **§741**

Maxton Builders v. Lo Galbo - **§1151**

May v. Bell - **§450**

May v. Siebert - **§1250**

Mayfield v. Swafford - **§1221**

Maytag Co. v. Alward - **§1246**

Mead Data Central v. Toyota Motor Sales - **§602**

Meas v. Young - **§985**

Medafrica Line S.P.A. v. American West African Freight Conference - **§213**

Meisner v. Patton Electric Co. - **§302**

Mel Foster Co. Properties v. American Oil Co. - **§450**

Memphis Community School District v. Stachura - **§735**

Memphis Development Foundation v. Factors, etc. Inc. - **§635**

Menominee Indian Tribe, United States v. - **§138**

Merion Spring Co. v. Muelles Hnos. Garcia Torres - **§1162**

Merrick v. Stephens - **§1316**

Merritz v. Circelli - **§1103**

Mers v. Dispatch Printing Co. - **§1235**

Messersmith v. G.T. Murray & Co. - **§§983, 1022**

Odorizzi v. Bloomfield School District - **§960**
Ohio Co. v. Rosemeier - **§983**
Ohio Power Co. v. Huff - **§307**
O'Keefe v. Snyder - **§318**
Okuda v. Superior Court - **§391**
Okun v. Morton - **§§129, 136**
Oliver v. Campbell - **§1244**
Oliver Electrical Manufacturing Co. v. I.O. Teigen
    Construction Co. - **§1172**
Oliveri v. Delta Steamship Lines - **§85**
Ollerman v. O'Rourke Co. - **§869**
Olson, United States v. - **§225**
Olwell v. Nye & Nissen Co. - **§356**
Omaha Indemnity Co. v. Wining - **§217**
Omegas Group, Inc., *In re* - **§275**
Oneida Indian Nation v. Oneida County - **§388**
O'Neil v. Shuckardt - **§702**
Orgel v. Clark Boardman - **§549**
Orloff v. Los Angeles Turf Club Inc. - **§734**
Orndorff v. Christiana Community Builders - **§361**
Ortega v. Plaxco - **§840**
Ortiz v. Fireboard Corp. - **§67**
Orto v. Jackson - **§1223**
Osage Corp. v. Simon - **§946**
Osbourne v. Capital City Mortgage Corp. - **§882**
Oscar v. University Students Co-op Association - **§474**
O'Shea v. Hatch - **§856**
O'Shea v. Littleton - **§150**
Ostano Commerzanstalt v. Telewide Systems - **§885**
Osterberger v. Hites Construction Co. - **§892**
Otto v. Jackson - **§1223**
Overton v. United States - **§796**
Owens-Corning Fiberglass Corp. v. Malone - **§66**
Oxley v. Ralston Purina Co. - **§1291**

P

Pacific Mutual Life Insurance Co. v. Haslip - **§56**
Padilla v. Lawrence - **§457**
Page v. Dobbs Mobil Bay Co. - **§1206**
Palmer v. Schornhorn Enterprises, Inc. - **§634**
Palmland Villas I Condominium Association v. Taylor -
    §251
Palmyra Board of Education, Borough of v. F.C. - **§214**
Panushka v. Panushka - **§1083**
Paperchase Partnership v. Bruckner - **§1082**
Papish v. Board of Curators of the University of Missouri
    - **§722**
Parish of the Advent v. Protestant Episcopal Diocese -
    §727
Pasulka v. Koob - **§446**
Patrick v. Putnam - **§1302**
Patrick & Wilkins Co. v. Reliance Insurance Co. - **§1079**
Paularena v. Superior Court - **§862**
Pauley Petroleum, Inc. v. United States - **§116**
Paulus v. Yarbrough - **§1169**

Paulsen v. Golden Gate University - **§721**
Payne v. Snyder - **§381**
Pearce v. G.R. Kirk Co. - **§409**
Pease v. Beech Aircraft Corp. - **§841**
Pedini v. Bowles - **§180**
Pelz v. Streator National Bank - **§1082**
Pena v. Toney - **§274**
Pennzoil Co. v. Texaco, Inc. - **§148**
People *ex rel.* - *see* name of party
Pepitone v. Russo - **§881**
Perez v. Las Vegas Medical Center - **§39**
Perfect Fit Industries v. Acme Quilting Co. - **§173**
Perini Corp. v. Greate Bay Hotel & Casino - **§1223**
Perry v. Larson - **§75**
Perry v. Sindermann - **§725**
Perryman v . Sims - **§1220**
Persinger v. Lucas - **§310**
Pester Refining Co., *In re* - **§1198**
Peter Saltpeter Energy Co. v. Crystal Oil Co. - **§345**
Peters v. Archambault - **§404**
Peterson v. Hartell - **§1156**
Petropoulos v. Lubienski - **§1209**
Petty v. Darin - **§861**
Pfaff v. Chrysler Corp. - **§199**
Pfeifer v. Christian Science Committee - **§727**
Philadelphia, City of v. Pierre Uniforms - **§373**
Philadelphia Newspapers, Inc. v. Hepps - **§669**
Phillippe v. Shapell Industries - **§1272**
Phillips v. Western Co. - **§75**
Phipps v. Robinson - **§167**
Pierce v. Ortho Pharmaceutical Corp. - **§1237**
Pinsker v. Pacific Coast Society of Orthodontists - **§715**
Pittsburgh Athletic Co. v. KQV Broadcasting Co. - **§613**
Pizza v. Sunset Fireworks Co. - **§472**
Playboy Enterprises, Inc. v. Baccarat Clothing Co. - **§609**
Playboy Enterprises, Inc. v. P.K. Sorren Export Co. -
    §609
Pliske v. Yuskis - **§432**
Plymouth Fertilizer Co. v. Balmer - **§350**
Pollock v. Johns-Manville Sales Corp. - **§35**
Poltrock v. Chicago & North Western Transportation Co. -
    §76
Porras v. Bass - **§855**
Porter County Democratic Precinct Review Committee v.
    Spinks - **§731**
Portland, City of v. Hoffman Construction Co. - **§1214**
Posner v. Davis - **§§868, 880**
Potter v. Firestone Tire & Rubber Co. - **§36**
Potter v. Village Bank of New Jersey - **§1237**
Potts v. Moran's Executors - **§1088**
Pottstown Daily News Publishing Co. v. Pottstown
    Broadcasting Co. - **§619**
Powder Horn Constructors v. City of Florence - **§1019**
Powell v. Kansas Yellow Cab - **§753**
Poyzer v. McGraw - **§780**
Prah v. Maretti - **§444**

Pratt v . Blunt - **§159**

Precision Plating & Metals v. Martin-Marietta Corp. - **§555**

Premier Wine & Spirits v. E. & J. Gallo Winery - **§97**

Prentice Medical Corp. v. Todd - **§209**

Presbyterian Church v. Mary Elizabeth Blue Hull
    Presbyterian Church - **§728**

Presley, Estate of v. Russen - **§§208, 635**

Price, United States v. (1982) - **§212**

Price, United States v. (1961) - **§792**

Procunier v. Martinez - **§154**

Productora e Importadora de Papel v. Fleming - **§1163**

Proimos v. Fair Automotive Repair - **§159**

Provencher v. Berman - **§256**

Providence, City of v. Kalian - **§175**

Providence Journal Co., *In re* - **§183**

Prudential Insurance v. Spencer's Kenosha Bowl - **§380**

Pullem v. Evanston Y.M.C.A. - **§396**

Purchasing Associates, Inc. v. Weitz - **§1262**

Purvis, *Ex parte* - **§180**

Pyrodyne Corp. v. Pyrotronics Corp. - **§610**

Q

Quintana v. Motel 6, Inc. - **§1010**

R

RCA Manufacturing Co. v. Whiteman - **§615**

R.E. Davis Chemical Corp. v. Diasonics, Inc. - **§1192**

R.I. Lampus Co. v. Neville Cement Products Corp. -
    §1162

RSO Records, Inc. v. Peri - **§546**

Rabago-Alvarez v. Dart Industries - **§1234**

Raben-Pastal v. City of Coconut Creek - **§252**

Racicky v. Simon - **§1105**

Radio Steel & Manufacturing Co. v. MTD Products, Inc. -
    §539

Rambaum v. Swisher - **§86**

Ramirez v. Veeley - **§81**

Ramona Manor Convalescent Hospital v. Care Enterprises
    - **§499**

Ramsey v. Ellis - **§244**

Randall v. Loftsgaarden - **§911**

Randolph v. Castle - **§1279**

Rannels v. S.E. Nichols, Inc. - **§654**

Rauser v. LTV Electrosystems, Inc. - **§344**

Raven Red Ash Coal Co. v. Ball - **§437**

Raven's Cove Townhomes, Inc. v. Knuppe Development
    Co. - **§360**

Re - *see name of party*

Reading v. Attorney General - **§525**

Redgrave v. Boston Symphony Orchestra - **§§1233,
    1251**

Reebok International v. Marinatech Enterprises - **§217**

Reed v. Alvey - **§129**

Reedy v. Ebsen - **§1271**

Regent International Hotels v. Las Colinas Hotels - **§167**

Regents of the University of California v. Bakke - **§720**

Reliance Finance Corp. v. Miller - **§997**

Renner v. Kahl - **§920**

Rensch v. Riddles Diamonds - **§300**

Republic National Life Insurance v. Red Lion Homes -
    §1090

Republic Supply Co. v. Richfield Oil Co. - **§289**

Rich & Whillock, Inc. v. Ashton Development, Inc. -
    §955

Richmond v. General Engineering Enterprises - **§426**

Right to Life Advocates, Inc. v. Aaron Women's Clinic -
    §158

Riley v. Koneru - **§838**

Rizzo v. Goode - **§150**

Roam v. Koop - **§860**

Robbins v. Finlay - **§1260**

Robert R. Jones Associates v. Nine Homes - **§547**

Robert S. Weiss & Associates v. Wiederlight - **§1264**

Roberts v. Fuhr - **§216**

Roberts v. Sears, Roebuck & Co. - **§913**

Robertson v. Granite City Community Unit School District
    - **§211**

Robichaud v. Theis - **§801**

Robinson v. Katz - **§903**

Robitaille v. Robitaille - **§1148**

Roche v. Barbaro - **§329**

Rodgers v. Georgia Tech Athletic Association - **§1232**

Rodriguez v. Bethlehem Steel Corp. - **§844**

Rodriguez v. United States - **§831**

Roe v. Operation Rescue - **§433**

Roesch v. Wachter - **§388**

Rohr v. Baker - **§994**

Roland Machinery Co. v. Dresser Industries - **§122**

Rosebud Sioux Tribe v. Strain - **§252**

Rosenbaum v. Texas Energies - **§1037**

Rosenberg v. Lee's Carpet & Furniture Warehouse Outlet,
    Inc. - **§630**

Rosenfield v. Choberka - **§307**

Ross v. Bernhard - **§114**

Ross v. Eichman - **§1104**

Ross v. Forest Lawn Memorial Park - **§26**

Roth v. Speck - **§1227**

Rova Farms Resort, Inc. v. Investors Insurance Co. - **§95**

Royer v. Carter - **§1119**

Rubin v. Telemet America - **§1179**

Ruderer v. United States - **§220**

Rufo v. Inmates of Suffolk County Jail - **§155**

Ruiz v. Ruiz - **§111**

Runyon v. Pacific Air Industries - **§919**

Rush v. Anestos - **§1082**

Rushia v. Town of Ashburnham - **§147**

Russell Box Co. v. Grant Paper Box Co. - **§539**

Ruud v. Lascelles - **§1103**

Ryan v. Kolterman - **§1137**

University Computing Co. v. Lykes-Youngstown Corp. - **§567**

University of Pittsburgh v. Champion Products, Inc. - **§164**

University of Texas Medical School v. Than - **§722**

Uptown Enterprises v. Strand - **§153**

Utemark v. Samuel - **§915**

V

Valencia v. Shell Oil Co. - **§310**

Valenzuela v. Aquino - **§698**

Valley Medical Specialists v. Farber - **§1265**

Van Bibber v. Norris - **§§303, 304**

Van De Kamp, People *ex rel.* v. American Art Enterprises - **§471**

Van Wagner Advertising v. S & M Enterprises - **§1094**

Van Zandt v. Heilman - **§1063**

Velvel v. Nixon - **§732**

Venable v. Harmon - **§§1133, 1141**

Venegas v. United Farm Workers - **§215**

Vermette v. Andersen - **§1008**

Vezina v. Nautilus Pools - **§1221**

Vickery v. Ritchie - **§§991, 992**

Village of - *see* name of village

Vines v. Orchard Hills, Inc. - **§1152**

Vockner v. Erickson - **§§977, 1045**

Volpe v. Schlobohm - **§990**

Vuitton et Fils S.A. v. Carousel Handbags - **§184**

WX

W.E. Bassett Co. v. Revlon, Inc. - **§561**

W-V Enterprises, Inc. v. Federal Savings & Loan - **§1267**

Wade v. Brooks - **§237**

Waffenschmidt v. Mackay - **§185**

Waits v. Frito Lay - **§637**

Waldorf v. Shuta - **§§758, 771**

Walker v. City of Birmingham (1967) - **§183**

Walker v. City of Birmingham (1966) - **§203**

Walker v. Columbia Broadcasting System, Inc. - **§§72, 73**

Wallace v. Miller - **§215**

Wallace v. Wallace - **§1013**

Wal-Mart Stores v. Crist - **§1342**

Walraven v. Martin - **§863**

Walt Disney Co. v. Powell - **§550**

Walter Implement v. Focht - **§50**

Walter J. Schmidt Co., *In re* - **§291**

Walton v. Bank of California - **§1057**

Ward v. Taggart - **§530**

Waring v. WDAS Broadcasting Station, Inc. - **§615**

Warlier v. Williams - **§396**

Warner v. Peterson - **§1107**

Wartzman v. Hightower Productions, Ltd. - **§22**

Washington Capitols Basketball Club, Inc. v. Barry - **§162**

Washington University Medical Center Redevelopment Corp. v. Wolfgren - **§112**

Watkins v. FMC Corp. - **§364**

Webb v. Webb - **§1030**

Wedgwood Diner v. Good - **§858**

Weichert Co. Realtors v. Ryan - **§244**

Weida v. Ferry - **§461**

Weinberg v. Farmers State Bank of Worden - **§1267**

Weinburger v. Romero-Barcelo - **§123**

Weiss v. Marcus - **§§265, 272**

Weitzenkorn v. Lesser - **§585**

Welch v. Mr. Christmas Inc. - **§625**

Weld County Board v. Slovek - **§358**

Wellston Coal Co. v. Franklin Paper Co. - **§1202**

Wenzler & Ward Plumbing & Heating Co. v. Sellen - **§33**

West Hartford, Town of v. Operation Rescue - **§433**

West Haven Sound Development v. City of West Haven - **§487**

Westamerica Securities, Inc. v. Cornelius - **§1022**

Westec Security Services v. Westinghouse Electric Corp. - **§1265**

Whalen v. Union Bag & Paper Co. - **§456**

Wheadon v. Olds - **§981**

Wheat v. United States - **§738**

Wheatly Grading Contractors Inc. v. DFT Investments - **§211**

Wheelock v. Noonan - **§§421, 425, 426**

Whelan v. Midland Mortgage Co. - **§1144**

White v. Barrenda Mesa Water District - **§1019**

White v. Valenta - **§§653, 654**

White Lighting Co. v. Wolfson - **§951**

Whorton v. Dillingham - **§1343**

Widdon v. Malone - **§794**

Widmer v. Leffelman - **§918**

Wiggins v. Shewmake - **§129**

Wilkinson v. Smith - **§921**

Williams v. Bright - **§787**

Williams v. O'Neal Ford - **§300**

Williams v. South & South Rentals - **§§398, 401**

Williams v. Tritt - **§113**

Williams v. Walker-Thomas Furniture Co. - **§975**

Williams v. Weisser - **§578**

Williamson v. Waldman - **§744**

Willing v. Mazzocone - **§676**

Wilson v. B.F. Goodrich Co. - **§760**

Wilson v. Great American Industries - **§870**

Wilson v. Klein - **§130**

Wilson v. Superior Court - **§676**

Wilson v. Wylie - **§835**

Wilsonville, Village of v. SCA Services Inc. - **§470**

Winant v. Bostic - **§17**

Wisconsin Gas Co. v. Federal Energy Regulatory Commission - **§122**

Wittick v. Miles - **§1100**

Wolfsky v. Behrman - **§1088**

Wong v. Paine, Webber, Jackson & Curtis - **§344**

Wood v. Boynton - **§1000**

Wood v. Strickland - **§723**

Woolridge v. Exxon Corp. - **§1044**

Woolsey v. Nationwide Insurance Co. - **§1021**

World Enterprises v. Midcoast Aviation Services - **§965**

Wycko v. Gnodtke - **§835**

Wyle v. Alioto - **§113**

Wyman v. Wallace - **§704**

Y

Yackey v. Pacifica Development Co. - **§135**

Yano v. Yano - **§1052**

Yeargan v. Bank of Montgomery County - **§1032**

Yonkers, City of, United States v. - **§155**

Young v. Cities Service Oil Co. - **§1030**

Young, State *ex rel.* v. Crookham - **§66**

Young Electric Sign v. United Standard West - **§51**

Younge, Estate of v. Huysmans - **§167**

Younger v. Harris - **§§147, 148, 220**

Yowell v. Piper Aircraft - **§828**

Yu v. Paperchase Partnership - **§1137**

Z

Zahn v. International Paper Co. - **§460**

Zannis v. Lake Shore Radiologists - **§1251**

Zauner v. Brewer - **§371**

Zegers v. Zegers, Inc. - **§536**

Index

hedonic, §§779-782, 840

inducing breach of contract, §§497-504. *See also* Inducing breach of contract

interest, §§68-70, 87-90

land sale contracts. *See* Breach of contract

limitations

    certainty requirement, §§32-39

    contracts cases, §§23-26

    torts cases, §§27-31

liquidated damages, §§50-53

mental anguish, §26

mesne damages, §386

misappropriation of money, §§265-270

mitigation

    compensation paid for defendant, §§790-792

    credit for benefit, §82

    provocation, §789

    repudiation, §1204

nominal defined, §4

nuisance, §§444-452, 464

oil drilling, §427

oral agreement (realty for services), §1296

patent infringement, §§535-540

personal injury. *See* Personal injury

police acts, §156

product disparagement, §§641-645

punitive damages

    conduct required for, §54

    constitutionality, §§55-59

    contract cases, §61

    defamation, §§671-672

    defined, §5

    excessive damages, §§55-59

    fraud, §§885, 922

    insurance for, §65

    loss of consortium, §845

    measure of, §§63-64

    misappropriation of money, §269

    multiple plaintiffs, §§66-67

    partial destruction of business, §492

    survival actions, §807

    vicarious liability, §60

reliance damages, §§22, 1277-1280

right of privacy, §§693-695

right of publicity, §§629-630

seduction, §710

special damages, §§40, 42-44

tortious damage to chattels, §§305-307

tortious destruction of chattels, §§292-304

tortious destruction or injury to real property, §§358-365

trade secrets, §§555-566

trademarks, §609

trees, §364

trespass, §§429-431

waste, §§367-370, 372

wrongful death. *See* Wrongful death

DECLARATORY JUDGMENTS

See Declaratory relief

DECLARATORY RELIEF

bills quia timet, §§227-232

criminal statutes, §144

defamation, §680

defined, §11

unconstitutional state statutes, §149

DEFAMATION, §§652-683, 686

actionable per se, §§653-654

    defamatory per se distinguished, §654

constitutional limitations, §§655-657, 661-670

    news media, §§661-670

        private citizens, §§657, 663-670

        public figures—malice, §§656, 662

damages, §§658-672

    news media, §§661-670

        constitutional limitations, §§661-670

        private citizens, §§663-670

        public officials, §662

    punitive damages, §§671-672

declaratory relief, §680

injunctions, §§673-680

mitigation, §681

repetition, §§679-680

restitution, §§682-683

right of privacy compared, §686

when general damages presumed, §§658-660, 665-666

DETENTION DAMAGES, §§322-328

DETINUE, §316

See also Replevin

DISCLOSURES MADE IN CONFIDENCE, §§582-586

DIVERSION OF BENEFITS, §§519-530

fiduciaries, §§519-527

    breach of duty, §§519-520

    bribes, §§525-526

        treble awards, §526

    corporate opportunities, §§522-523

    inside information, §527

nonfiduciaries, §§528-530

    brokers, §530

    impostors, §529

DOCTRINAL DISPUTES, §727

DUMPING DEBRIS, §§419-426

See also Trespass

damages, §§420-424

injunctions, §§425-426

DURESS, §§925-957

See also Undue influence

bribery, §953

business compulsion, §§954-957

    antitrust aspects, §957

    inequitable exercise of legal rights, §§955-956

civil proceedings
  as duress, §§950-952
  chattels, §940
  land, §945
  restitution, §§948-949
criminal proceedings, §§946-949
  bad faith requirement, §947
  plaintiff recovery, §§948-949
  restitution, §§948-949
defined, §927
  fraud compared, §928
  person of average firmness, §929
  source of duress, §930
  subjective test, §929
  submission, §931
economic coercion, §§954-957
merger with undue influence, §962. *See also* Undue
                influence
oppressive refusal to perform public duty, §953
restitution, §§926, 939, 944, 948-949, 952
tort law aspects, §925
void transactions, §§932-933
voidable transactions, §§934-945
  duress to property, §§936-945
    chattels, §§937-940
      civil proceedings, §940
      replevin usual remedy, §938
      restitution, §939
    land, §§941-945
      civil proceedings, §945
      legal remedies, §942
      rescission and cancellation, §943
      restitution, §944
  physical duress, §935

E

EASEMENTS, INTERFERENCE WITH, §§439-445
damages, §§439-441
injunctions, §§442-445
  restrictive covenants, §445

ECCLESIASTICAL DISPUTES, §727

ECONOMIC COERCION, §§954-957
See also Duress

EJECTMENT
breach of contract, §1140
encroachment, §399
improvements by trespasser, §§387-391
mesne damages (profits), §386
setoffs, §388

ELECTION OF REMEDIES
See Fraud

EMPLOYMENT CONTRACTS
breach of, §§1227-1267. *See also* Breach of contract
impossibility or frustration, §§1301-1303

ENCROACHMENT, §§398-407
damages, §398
ejectment, §399
injunctions, §§401-407
  balance of hardships, §§402-406
  inadvertent encroachment, §404
  laches, §405
self-help, §400

ENFORCEMENT OF EQUITY DECREES, §§168-188
contempt, §§168-185
  affirmative or mandatory, §§170-172
  civil vs. criminal, §§169, 174-177
  negative or prohibitory, §173
  parties bound, §§184-185
  specificity required, §168
  valid but erroneous order, §§179-180
    collateral bar rule, §180
  void orders, §§181-183
    First Amendment rights, §183
out-of-state decrees, §§190-199
writ of assistance, §186
writ of sequestration, §§187-188

EQUITABLE CONVERSION, §§1065-1086
See also Breach of contract

EQUITABLE DEFENSES
laches, §§164, 404, 610
  and statute of limitations, §§165-167
  defined, §164
  encroachment, §404
  Lanham Act, §610
unclean hands, §§157-163, 610, 1345
  defined, §157
  discretionary, §161
  illegality compared, §1345
  Lanham Act, §610
  no injury required, §158
  public frauds exception, §160
  recovery at law, §163

EQUITABLE LIEN
bona fide purchaser, §257
commingled funds, §§286-291
constructive trust compared, §256
defined, §254
enforcement, §258
foreclosure and sale, §258
in general, §§254-258
misappropriation, §§279, 286, 288-291. *See also*
                Misappropriation of money
requirements for, §255

EQUITABLE REMEDIES, §§99-232
ancillary remedies, §§200-215
  bills of peace. §§218-223. *See also* Bills of peace
  bills quia timet, §§227-232. *See also* Bills quia timet
  civil arrest, §216

elements required, §§866-877
materiality, §874
measure of compensatory damages, §§878-881
misrepresentation of fact, §§867-869
reliance, §§873, 875
scienter, §§870-872
consequential damages, §§882-887
buyer's fraud, §886
damages collateral to purchase, §883
fraud not involving property sale, §887
punitive, §885
sale of goods, §884
consumer protection statutes, §924
duress compared, §928
election of remedies, §§853-865
affirmance of contract, §§854-858
accepting benefits, §§855-856
delay in disaffirming, §857
suit for damages, §858
damages vs. restitution, §853
rescission and restitution, §§859-861
filing suit not election, §860
judgment, effect of, §861
offer and acceptance, §862
suing in the alternative, §§863-864
U.C.C. rule distinguished, §§856, 865
rescission, §§888-895
elements required, §§888-895
injury, §895
materiality, §§891-893
innocent misrepresentation, §892
intentional misrepresentation, §893
misrepresentation of fact, §889
reliance, §894
equitable remedies, §§912-918
jurisdiction, §912
land sale contracts, §§914-917
buyer's fraud, §917
seller's fraud, §§914-916
restitution in equity, §913
sale of business, §918
legal remedies after, §§907-911
conversion, §909
quasi-contract, §910
replevin, §908
securities fraud damages, §911
mechanics of, §§896-906
at law, §§897-903
notice and offer, §§898-899
tender excused, §§900-903
declaratory judgment as alternative, §896
in equity, §§904-906
notice and tender back, §905
procedural distinctions, §906
punitive damages, §§885, 922, 924
securities fraud distinguished, §877

special damages, §§919-921
U.C.C.—solvency misrepresentation, §923

FREE RIDE CASES, §613
See also Unfair competition

FRUSTRATION OF PURPOSE
See Impossibility or frustration

FULL PRICE, ACTION FOR THE, §§1196-1197

FUNERAL EXPENSES, §827
See also Wrongful death

G

GIFTS, §§1046-1059
See also Mistake, gratuitous transactions

"GOLDEN RULE" ARGUMENT, §770

GOOD FAITH AND FAIR DEALING, BREACH OF, §§95-97
insurance cases, §95
special relationship contracts, §97
tort action, §§95-97
wrongful discharge, §96

GOODWILL
covenants not to compete, §1261
unfair competition, §611

H

HABITABILITY, WARRANTY OF, §1111

HADLEY V. BAXENDALE, RULE OF
See Damages

HEDONIC DAMAGES
See Damages

HISTORICAL ORIGINS
classifications of remedies, §§12-15
equitable distinct from law, §§105-109
ne exeat writ, §216
ouster, §397
procedural merger of law and equity, §§110-116
quantum counts, §§243-244
quasi-contracts, §246
replevin, §316
unconscionability, §976
wrongful death, §812

I

ILLEGAL CONTRACTS, §§1340-1364
defined, §1340
failure of illegal purpose, §1347
general rule—no remedy, §§1342-1345
illegality inapplicable, §§1346-1349
collateral or remedy, §1348
failure of purpose, §1347
no third parties, §1349

466 | REMEDIES

restitution, §1324

minors, §§1313-1322. *See also* Minors' contracts

ultra vires, §§1326-1336. *See also* Ultra vires contracts

unlicensed contractors, §§1337-1339

LAND SALE CONTRACTS

See Breach of contract; Statute of Frauds

LANHAM ACT, §§605-609, 625, 651

See also Trademarks

LEGAL REMEDIES, §12

LENDING CONTRACTS, §1267

LETTERS, PRIVATE, §§587-589

LIBEL

See Defamation

LOCUS POENITENTIAE, §§1357-1358

See also Illegal contracts

LORD CAMPBELL'S ACT, §812

See also Wrongful death

M

MALICE

See Defamation

MECHANIC'S LIEN, §§1212, 1337

MENTAL INCAPACITY, §§1223-1225

See also Lack of capacity

MENTAL SUFFERING

See Defamation; Personal injury

trespass, §365

MESNE DAMAGES, §363

MESNE PROFITS, §386

MIMICRY, §637

MINERALS, §§413-415

MINORS' CONTRACTS, §§1313-1322

bona fide purchaser, §1319

estoppel to disaffirm, §1318

exculpatory contracts, §1320

necessaries, §1321

quasi-contract, §1321

restitution, §§1316-1317

restoration, §§1315-1316

MISAPPROPRIATION OF CREATIVE WORK, §§575-589

See also Copyright infringement

accounting, §580

common law copyright, §575

damages, §§577, 580

disclosures made in confidence, §§582-586

   quasi-contract, §585

injunctions, §§579, 586

private correspondence, §§587-589

quasi-contract, §585

restitution, §§579, 580

state protection, §§576, 581

MISAPPROPRIATION OF MONEY, §§265-291

equitable remedies, §271

  commingled funds, §§280-291

    common law, §§281-285

    constructive trust, §287

    equitable lien, §§279, 286, 288-291

  constructive trust, §§272-278, 291

    bona fide purchaser, §277

    commingled funds, §291

    defined, §272

    insolvent wrongdoer, §275

    other assets, §278

    tracing, §§274-277

      insurance proceeds, §276

  equitable lien, §§279, 286-291

legal remedies, §§265-270

  bona fide purchaser, §270

  conversion, §§266-267

  punitive damages for tort, §269

  quasi-contract, §268

MISREPRESENTATION

See Fraud

MISTAKE, §§979-1059

bargaining transactions, §§134, 981-1019

  mistake in basic assumptions, §§995-1013

    conveyances of land, §§1002-1009

    property settlements, §1013

    rescission, §996

    sale of goods, §§998-1001

    settlement of claims, §§1010-1012

  overperformance, §§981-988

    conveyancing mistakes, §§984-986

    insurance indorsements, §988

    overpayment, §§982-983

    quasi-contract, §983

    reformation, §§986, 988

    rescission, §§984-986

    services, §987

  reliance upon nonexistent contract, §§989-994

    restitution, §990

  unilateral mistake, §§134, 1014-1019

    and specific performance, §134

    construction bids, §§1017-1019

    relief granted, §§1015-1016

defenses, §§1020-1031

  change of position, §§1021-1023

  compromise and settlement, §1029

  discharge for value, §§1024-1028

    of nonexistent claim, §1028

  in general, §1020

  mistake of law, §1030

  negligence of plaintiff, §1031

defined, §979

gratuitous transactions, §§1046-1059

donee's remedies, §§1054-1056
    deceased donor, §1056
    living donor, §1055
donor's remedies, §§1046-1053
    basic assumptions, §§1046-1051
    restitution, §§1047-1048, 1052
    size of gift, §§1052-1053
inter vivos trusts, §1057
wills, §§1058-1059
    constructive trust, §1059
    reformation, §1058
in general, §§979-980
mistakes in integration, §§1032-1045
    ambiguity, §1035
    legal effect of words, §1037
    long-term executory contracts, reformation of, §1044
    meaning of words, §1036
    multiple successive documents, §1043
    nature of mistake, §§1032-1033
    reformation, §§1044-1045
        alternative to rescission, §1045
    Statute of Frauds, §§1038-1042. *See also* Statute of
        Frauds
        amount of land, §§1040-1041
        land description, §1039
        missing terms, §1042
        no defense to reformation, §1038
    reformation, §§1034, 1038, 1042, 1044-1045. *See
        also* Reformation
restitution, §980
wills, §§1058-1059

MUNICIPAL CORPORATIONS, §§1332-1336

MURDER, BENEFITS OBTAINED BY, §§517-518
See also Expectancies, interference with

N

NATIONAL POLICY, §732

NECESSARIES, §§1321, 1323

NEGATIVE COVENANTS
See Covenants not to compete

NEGATIVE MUTUALITY, §1062

NEWS MEDIA
See Defamation

NO-FAULT INSURANCE, §§784, 797

NUISANCE, §§446-474
permanent, §§449-450
    election doctrine, §451
private, §§446-465
    damages, §§447-452, 464
        avoidable consequences, §452
        common law, §448
        election doctrine, §451
        permanent nuisance doctrine, §§449-450

injunctions, §§453-460
    balance of hardships, §§455-459
    class actions, §460
    coming to the nuisance, §§461-462
    right to farm statutes, §463
    zoning, effect of, §465
public, §§466-474
    bawdy houses, §468
    environmental laws, §470
    injurious activities, §§469-471
    private suits to enjoin, §§473-474
    purprestures, §467
    remedy, §470
    RICO actions, §474
    saloons, §468

O

OIL DRILLING, §§427-428

**OPPRESSIVE REFUSAL TO PERFORM PUBLIC DUTY,
    §953**

ORAL REAL ESTATE CONTRACTS, §1272
See also Statute of Frauds

OUSTER, §§385-397
See also Trespass

OVERPAYMENT
See Mistake

OVERPERFORMANCE
See Mistake

P

PAIN AND SUFFERING
See Personal injury

PALMING OFF, §§591-592

PART PERFORMANCE DOCTRINE, §§1283-1290
See also Statute of Frauds

PASSING OFF, §618

PATENT INFRINGEMENT, §§531-541
attorneys' fees, §541
damages, §§535-540
federal preemption, §§531-532
injunctions, §534
reasonable royalty, §§537-540

PERFORMERS' REMEDIES
See Right of publicity

PERMANENT NUISANCE DOCTRINE, §§449-450

PERMISSIVE WASTE, §§371-373, 382
See also Waste

PERSONAL INJURY, §§83-94, 736-852
avoidable consequences, §§785-787
collateral sources rule, §§793-797

in general, §§233-239

inducing breach of contract, §§507-511

land sale contracts. *See* Breach of contract

legal restitution, §§240-247. *See also* Quasi-contract

minors' contracts, §§1314-1317

misappropriation of creative work, §577

mistake, §980. *See also* Mistake

nature and purpose of, §§233-264

    accounting for gains, §264

    constructive trust, §§249-253

    equitable lien, §§254-258

    purpose, §239

    quasi-contract. *See* Quasi-contract

    subrogation, §§259-263

    unjust enrichment, §§233-238

personal injury, §849

procedural unconscionability, §§965-966

purpose, §239

quasi-contract, §§240-247. *See also* Quasi-contract

reliance on nonexistent contract, §990

service contracts, §§1241-1250

severance of timber, §§408-412

specific remedies, §8. *See also* Breach of contract; Specific relief

Statute of Frauds, §§1268-1280. *See also* Statute of Frauds

subrogation, §§259-263

    defined, §§259, 261

    secured creditor, §262

    unjust enrichment required, §260

    unsecured creditor, §263

substantive basis, §§233-238

    "benefit" explained, §§234-235

    unjust retention, §236

    voluntary benefits, §§237-238

substitutionary, §7

tortious taking and retention of chattels, §§312-357

tracing, §263

trespass, §§435-438

unenforceable contracts. *See also* Unenforceable contracts

    illegal contracts, §§1350-1364. *See also* Illegal contracts

    impossibility or frustration, §§1297-1300

    mental incapacity, §1324

    minors' contracts, §§1314-1317

    not in writing, §§1268-1280. *See also* Statute of Frauds

    ultra vires contracts, §§1333-1337

RIGHT OF PRIVACY, §§621-623, 684-701

damages, §§693-695

    punitive, §695

elements of, §§684-692

    constitutional limitations, §§688-691, 698

    defamation distinguished, §686

    false light cases, §691

    right of publicity distinguished, §§621-623, 687

    survival of actions, §692

injunctions, §§696-700

    harassment, §700

restitution, §701

RIGHT OF PUBLICITY, §§620-640

nonstatutory protection, §§632-637

    mimicry and imitation distinguished, §637

    survival of celebrity's death, §635

property right, §§620-623

    celebrities vs. noncelebrities, §§622-623

    right of privacy distinguished, §621

statutory protection, §§624-631, 636

    advertising or trade purposes, §625

    criminal sanctions, §626

    damages, §§629-630

    injunctions, §628

    no preemption, §636

works of art, §§638-640

ROBINSON-PATMAN ACT, §526

S

SALES

See Breach of contract; Statute of Frauds

SCRIVENER'S MISTAKES, §§1032-1045

See also Mistake

SEDUCTION, §§702, 710

SELF-HELP

tortious taking and retention of chattels, §§313-314

SEQUESTRATION OF PROPERTY, §187

SEVERANCE, §§408-418

injunctions, §§416-418

minerals, §§413-414

timber, §§408-412

SICK PAY, §§75, 749

See also Personal injury

SLANDER

See Defamation

SOCIAL CLUBS, §714

SOUND RECORDINGS, §553

SPECIFIC PERFORMANCE

See Breach of contract; Specific relief

SPECIFIC RELIEF

breach of contract, §§128-135, 1060. *See also* Breach of contract

defined, §9

oral agreement (realty for services), §1295

Statute of Frauds, §§1281-1290

STATUS

academic, §§719-726

associational, §§714-718

Notes

Notes

Notes

Notes

Notes

Notes